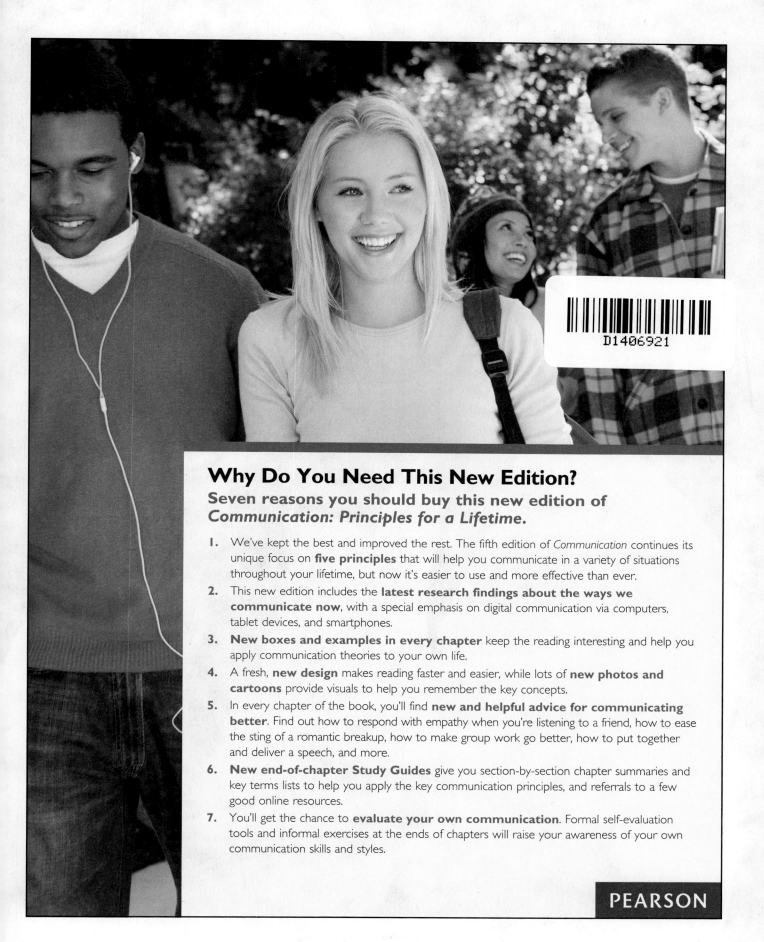

# Why Do You Need This New Edition?

**Seven reasons you should buy this new edition of**
*Communication: Principles for a Lifetime.*

1. We've kept the best and improved the rest. The fifth edition of *Communication* continues its unique focus on **five principles** that will help you communicate in a variety of situations throughout your lifetime, but now it's easier to use and more effective than ever.

2. This new edition includes the **latest research findings about the ways we communicate now**, with a special emphasis on digital communication via computers, tablet devices, and smartphones.

3. **New boxes and examples in every chapter** keep the reading interesting and help you apply communication theories to your own life.

4. A fresh, **new design** makes reading faster and easier, while lots of **new photos and cartoons** provide visuals to help you remember the key concepts.

5. In every chapter of the book, you'll find **new and helpful advice for communicating better**. Find out how to respond with empathy when you're listening to a friend, how to ease the sting of a romantic breakup, how to make group work go better, how to put together and deliver a speech, and more.

6. **New end-of-chapter Study Guides** give you section-by-section chapter summaries and key terms lists to help you apply the key communication principles, and referrals to a few good online resources.

7. You'll get the chance to **evaluate your own communication**. Formal self-evaluation tools and informal exercises at the ends of chapters will raise your awareness of your own communication skills and styles.

**PEARSON**

FIFTH EDITION

# Communication

## PRINCIPLES FOR A LIFETIME

### Steven A. **BEEBE**

Texas State University–San Marcos

### Susan J. **BEEBE**

Texas State University–San Marcos

### Diana K. **IVY**

Texas A&M University–Corpus Christi

## PEARSON

Boston  Columbus  Indianapolis  New York  San Francisco  Upper Saddle River  Amsterdam  Cape Town  Dubai
London  Madrid  Milan  Munich  Paris  Montreal  Toronto  Delhi  Mexico City  São Paulo  Sydney
Hong Kong  Seoul  Singapore  Taipei  Tokyo

Editor-in-Chief, Communication: Karon Bowers
Senior Acquisitions Editor: Melissa Mashburn
Director of Development: Eileen Calabro
Development Editor: Sheralee Connors
Editorial Assistant: Megan Hermida
Marketing Manager: Blair Zoe Tuckman
Associate Development Editor: Angela Mallowes
Senior Digital Editor: Paul DeLuca
Digital Editor: Lisa Dotson
Project Manager: Anne Ricigliano
Project Coordination, Text Design, and Electronic
   Page Makeup: Cenveo Publisher Services

Cover Design Manager: Nancy Danahy
Cover Designer: Nancy Sacks
Cover Image: © Sean2008/iStock
Text Permissions: Karen Black/A Critical Eye
Photo Research: Stefanie Ramsay/Bill Smith Group
Procurement Specialist: Mary Ann Gloriande
Printer/Binder: Quad/Graphics Dubuque
Cover Printer: Lehigh-Phoenix Color/Hagerstown

Frontispiece photo credit: Photodisc /Getty Images

Credits and acknowledgments borrowed from other sources and reproduced, with permission, in this textbook appear on the appropriate page within text or on pages 435–462.

**Library of Congress Cataloging-in-Publication Data**

Beebe, Steven A.
  Communication: principles for a lifetime/Steven A. Beebe, Susan J. Beebe, Diana K. Ivy.—5th ed.
     p. cm.
  ISBN-13: 978-0-205-02943-3
  ISBN-10: 0-205-02943-4
  1.  Communication.  I. Beebe, Susan J. II. Ivy, Diana K. III. Title.
  HM1206.B44 2012
  302.2—dc23

                2012000854

10 9 8 7 6 5 4 3 2 1—QDB—15 14 13 12

Student Edition:
ISBN 10: 978-0-205-02943-3
ISBN 10: 0-205-02943-4

À la carte:
ISBN 13: 978-0-205-24872-8
ISBN 10: 0-205-24872-1

www.pearsonhighered.com

*For our teachers . . . and our students*

# Brief Contents

vi

# Detailed Contents

## UNIT II   INTERPERSONAL COMMUNICATION

B  **Sample Speeches for Discussion and Evaluation**    **430**

# Boxed Features

## Communication & DIVERSITY

## Communication & TECHNOLOGY

# Communication&ETHICS

# DEVELOPING YOUR PRESENTATION
## stepbystep

# Preface

Communication is essential for life. The purpose of this book is to document this claim by presenting fundamental principles of human communication that enhance the quality of our communication with others as well as the quality of our own lives. Most students who read this book will take only one course in communication during their entire college career. We want students to view this course on communication as a vital, life-enriching one that will help them enhance their communication with others—not just as another course in a string of curricular requirements. Because communication is an essential element of living, we want students to remember essential communication principles and skills for the rest of their lives. To remember and apply these essential communication principles, we believe students need a digest of classic and contemporary research and practice that will help them with both the mundane and the magnificent, the everyday and the ever-important communication experiences that constitute the fabric of their lives.

In this edition, as in the four that preceded it, we strive to create a highly appealing, easy-to-use text that is more effective than ever in helping students understand and use five vital principles of communication.

## What's New to the Fifth Edition?

Reviewers, instructors, and our students have given us feedback about the four previous editions. This feedback has helped us make this new edition the best possible teaching and learning resource. We listened and responded (Principle Four) to their suggestions. Our commitment to providing a digest of essentials that does not overwhelm students has also led us to make some changes. One immediate change you'll see in this edition is a fresh new design with an almost entirely new set of photos and cartoons to help draw today's visually-oriented learners into the text.

We have also included the following new features in *every* chapter:

- A new chapter-end Study Guide helps students master chapter content and prepare for exams by providing a concise summary of the chapter and its key terms.
- Three end-of-chapter application features help students apply chapter concepts to their own lives: "Applying Principles for a Lifetime" is a bulleted listing of ways that the principles can be used in students' real-life communication. "Assessing Your Skill," offers self-tests and skill assessment tools, many of which can be used either for individual analysis or for collaborative learning class activities. "Web Resources" let students explore online resources to expand their understanding.
- Significantly updated and expanded research incorporates the latest research findings about human communication principles and skills.

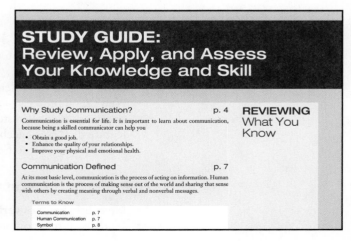

**STUDY GUIDE:**
Review, Apply, and Assess
Your Knowledge and Skill

Why Study Communication?                                p. 4       REVIEWING
Communication is essential for life. It is important to learn about communication,          What You
because being a skilled communicator can help you                                   Know

- Obtain a good job.
- Enhance the quality of your relationships.
- Improve your physical and emotional health.

Communication Defined                                    p. 7
At its most basic level, communication is the process of acting on information. Human
communication is the process of making sense out of the world and sharing that sense
with others by creating meaning through verbal and nonverbal messages.

Terms to Know

Communication          p. 7
Human Communication    p. 7
Symbol                 p. 8

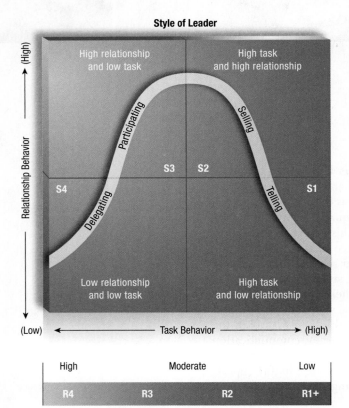

**Style of Leader**

High relationship and low task

High task and high relationship

Participating

Selling

S3    S2

S4                    S1

Delegating

Telling

Low relationship and low task

High task and low relationship

(High) Relationship Behavior

(Low) ◄—— Task Behavior ——► (High)

| High | Moderate | | Low |
|------|----------|---|-----|
| R4 | R3 | R2 | R1+ |

**Readiness of Follower(s)**

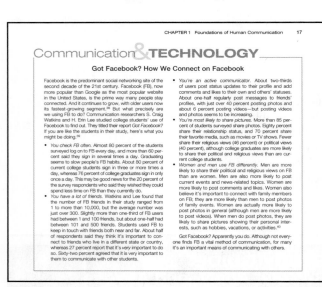

- Fresh, contemporary examples and illustrations to which students can relate.
- New cartoons and other illustrations to amplify the content of our message.

We've also updated popular continuing features that appear throughout the book, including these:

- Revised "Communication & Diversity" features complement and expand discussions of new applications of research about diversity throughout the book.
- Revised "Communication & Technology" features include an expanded discussion of the role of online communication in relationships.
- Revised "Communication & Ethics" features reinforce the importance of being an ethical communicator and may spark discussion of ethical questions.
- Revised "Developing Your Speech Step by Step" features in the presentational speaking chapters walk students through the process of designing and delivering a speech.
- Two new speeches in Appendix B model best practices in presentational speaking.

We've made many other specific changes to chapter content throughout the book. Here's a brief list of selected major revisions, changes, and additions that we've made to specific chapters:

## Chapter 1: Foundations of Human Communication

- Expanded discussion highlights the value of communication skills.
- Updated coverage summarizes recent research on mediated communication and how the Internet, text messages, and e-mail continue to change the way we interact with others.
- New "Communication & Technology" box summarizes research on the habits of college Facebook users.

## Chapter 2: Self-Awareness and Communication

- Revised "Communication & Diversity" feature contrasts self-concept in Eastern and Western cultures.
- Expanded discussion of identity formation helps students examine factors contributing to their own identities.
- New "Communication & Technology" feature explores the relationship between Facebook and self-esteem, and new research in the "Communication & Ethics" feature discusses Facebook and narcissism.
- New research on self-esteem across the lifespan increases readers' self-awareness.

## Chapter 3: Understanding Verbal Messages

- New discussion of verbal bullying increases awareness.
- Updated discussion points out the benefits of using inclusive language.

## Chapter 4: Understanding Nonverbal Messages

- Updated coverage summarizes recent research on nonverbal online communication, nonverbal communication and relationships, functions of movement, the role of the voice in nonverbal communication, and improving nonverbal communication.
- New discussion shows the nonverbal communication role the environment plays for people with disabilities.
- New examples throughout the chapter enhance students' understanding.

## Chapter 5: Listening and Responding

- Updated discussions summarize new research on the importance of listening, listening styles, emotional intelligence, meta-messages, and gender differences in listening.
- Updated advice for improving listening skills is based on the most recent research.
- New "Communication & Ethics" box explores the ethics of paraphrasing others' words.

## Chapter 6: Adapting to Others: Diversity and Communication

- New and expanded discussion points out the importance of establishing an accepting communication climate for GLBT people.
- Expanded discussion of age diversity includes the post-millennial generation, to which many readers belong.
- New and expanded section on adapting to others suggests ethical adaptations be based on communication goals.

## Chapter 7: Understanding Interpersonal Communication

- New emphasis throughout the chapter helps students compare and contrast mediated and in-person interpersonal communication.
- New discussion explores how online and other mediated communications have changed the role of physical proximity in relationships.
- New discussion reveals a new pattern in pairs socializing, known as "frugaling."
- Expanded discussion summarizes recent research on the success of using pick-up lines to attract romantic partners.
- New discussion summarizes the health benefits of interpersonal relationships.
- Updated "Communication & Technology" feature explores the advantages and pitfalls of online self-disclosure.
- New "Assessing Your Skill" activity "Too Private to Talk About, Unless It's on Facebook?" encourages students to evaluate their levels of online disclosure.

## Chapter 8: Enhancing Relationships

- New "Communication & Ethics" feature offers research-based advice for easing the pain of romantic breakups.
- New discussion introduces an emerging trend in romantic relationships, the post-dissolutional relationship.
- Updated "Communication & Technology" box summarizes recent research on attitudes toward cyberinfidelity.
- New "Assessing Your Skill" activity helps students to determine their style of responding to conflict.

## Chapter 9: Understanding Group and Team Performance

- Updated coverage summarizes recent research on group goals, virtual groups, social ostracism in groups, communication networks in groups, stages of group development, and conflict in groups.

- Revised "Communication & Technology" box summarizes the "Virtues (and Vices) of Virtual Groups."
- New discussion of monochronic and polychronic time orientations reveals a source of diversity that can affect group norms.

### Chapter 10: Enhancing Group and Team Performance

- New discussion and figure explore the relationship of group readiness and effective leadership styles.
- New "Communication & Diversity" feature contrasts deep-level and surface-level diversity, and offers advice on enhancing the outcomes of diverse groups.
- Updated coverage summarizes recent research on sharing information in groups, group decision making, and group problem solving.

### Chapter 11: Developing Your Presentation

- Updated coverage summarizes recent research on public speaking anxiety.
- Updated examples throughout the chapter help students relate to chapter material.
- A new student speech for the "Developing Your Presentation Step by Step" feature focuses on Facebook addiction, a topic of current interest.
- New "Communication & Technology" feature stresses the importance of checking facts found on the Internet.
- New examples throughout the supporting materials section model exemplary presentations.

### Chapter 12: Organizing and Outlining Your Presentation

- New sample preparation and delivery outlines provide continuity by showing the development of the same speech in the "Developing Your Presentation Step by Step" feature.
- Updated examples from both student presentations and some of the most acclaimed presentations of the day model techniques students can apply in their own presentations.

### Chapter 13: Delivering Your Presentation

- Many new examples throughout the chapter model techniques used by exemplary speechmakers.
- New "Communication & Technology" feature introduces a mobile phone app to help students speak more smoothly.
- New figure in "Assessing Your Skill" section at the end of the chapter visually reinforces advice from Chapters 11 through 13.

### Chapter 14: Speaking to Inform

- Techniques of informative speaking are modeled in the chapter construction and via many well-chosen new examples.
- A new sample informative presentation is annotated to model for students how one student speaker effectively used techniques discussed in the chapter.

### Chapter 15: Speaking to Persuade

- Carefully chosen new examples throughout the chapter model techniques of persuasive speaking.
- A new sample persuasive presentation is annotated to model for students how one student speaker effectively used techniques discussed in the chapter.

### Appendix A: Interviewing

- New material on developing a personal brand reflects current interviewing research and practice.

### Appendix B: Sample Speeches for Discussion and Evaluation

- New sample informative and persuasive speeches showcase presentation techniques discussed in Chapters 11–15.

# What Stays the Same in This Edition?

In our fifth edition of *Communication: Principles for a Lifetime*, our goal remains the same as in the first edition: to provide a cogent presentation of what is essential about human communication by organizing the study of communication around five fundamental communication principles that are inherent in the process of communicating with others.

## Our Integrated Approach Remains Unchanged

To help students remember and integrate essential communication principles, we've organized the study of human communication around five fundamental communication principles:

Principle One: Be aware of your communication with yourself and others.
Principle Two: Effectively use and interpret verbal messages.
Principle Three: Effectively use and interpret nonverbal messages.
Principle Four: Listen and respond thoughtfully to others.
Principle Five: Appropriately adapt messages to others.

We don't claim that everything you need to know about communication is embedded in our five communication principles. These principles do, however, synthesize essential research and wisdom about communication. They are designed to help students in an introductory communication course see the "big picture" of the role and importance of communication, both as they sit in the classroom and as they live their lives.

The problem with many introduction to communication courses is there is often too much of a good thing. An introductory course covers a vast terrain of communication concepts, principles, and skills. Besides learning about several theories of communication, students are also presented with what may appear to them to be miniature courses in interpersonal communication, group communication, and public speaking. At the end of a typical hybrid or introductory communication fundamentals course, both students and instructors have made a breathless dash through an astounding amount of information and number of skills. The barrage of ideas, contexts, and theories can leave students and instructors feeling overwhelmed by a seemingly unrelated hodgepodge of information. Students may end up viewing communication as a fragmented area of study that includes a bushel basket full of concepts and applications, but have little understanding of what is truly fundamental about how we make sense out of the world and share that sense with others. Rather than seeing communication as a crazy quilt of unrelated ideas and skills, we want students to see a unified fabric of common principles that they will remember long after the course is over. The five fundamental principles provide a framework for understanding the importance of communication in our lives.

Our pentagon model illustrates the relationships among the five communication principles that are the overarching structure of the book. As a principle is being introduced or discussed, the appropriate part of the model is highlighted. In most texts, communication principles are typically presented in the first third of the book and then abandoned, as material about interpersonal, group, and public communication is presented. We don't use a "hit-and-run" approach. Instead, using examples and illustrations to which students can relate, we carefully discuss each principle early in the book. Throughout the latter two-thirds of the book we gently remind students of how these principles relate to interpersonal relationships, group and team discussions, and public presentations.

We link the five communication principles with specific content by using a margin icon to indicate that a discussion in the text of a skill, concept, or idea is related to one or more of the five communication principles. The icons, described in Chapter 1 and illustrated here, first appear in the margin in Chapter 7, "Understanding Interpersonal Communication," which is the first context chapter of the book. The icons help students see the many applications our five communication principles have to their lives as they read about interpersonal communication, group and team communication, and presentational speaking.

A subtext for these five principles is the importance of communicating ethically with others. Throughout the book we invite students to consider the ethical implications of how they communicate with others, through the use of probes and questions. As we discuss in Chapter 1, we believe that in order to be effective, a communication message must achieve three goals: (1) it must be understood; (2) it must achieve its intended effect; and (3) it must be ethical. Our five Communication Principles for a Lifetime are designed to help students achieve these three goals.

## The Successful Structure of the Book Stays the Same

This fifth edition retains the overall structure of the four previous editions and is organized into four units. Unit I introduces the five principles (Chapter 1), and then each principle is explained in a separate chapter (Chapters 2 through 6). Each communication principle is discussed and illustrated to help students see its value and centrality in their lives. Chapter 2 discusses the principle of being self-aware. Chapter 3 focuses on using and interpreting verbal messages, and Chapter 4 focuses on using and interpreting nonverbal messages. Chapter 5 includes a discussion of the interrelated processes of listening and responding, giving special attention to the importance of being other-oriented and empathic. The final principle, appropriately adapting to others, is presented in Chapter 6; we use this principle to illustrate the importance of adapting one's behavior to culture and gender differences among people.

Unit II applies the five communication principles to interpersonal relationships. Unlike many treatments of interpersonal communication, our discussion links the concepts and strategies for understanding interpersonal communication with our five Communication Principles for a Lifetime. Chapter 7 presents information to help students better understand the nature and function of communication in relationships. Chapter 8 identifies strategies that can enhance the quality of interpersonal relationships with others.

Unit III discusses how the five communication principles can help students understand and enhance communication in small groups and teams. Chapter 9 explains how groups and teams work. We offer practical strategies for collaboratively solving problems, leading groups and teams, and running and participating in meetings in Chapter 10.

Finally, Unit IV presents classic content to help students design and deliver a speech, referring to contemporary research and using the latest tools of technology. Based on our popular audience-centered approach to developing a presentation, we emphasize the importance of adapting to listeners while also being an ethically vigilant communicator. Chapters 11 through 15 offer information and tips for developing presentation ideas, organizing and outlining presentations, delivering a presentation (including using presentational and multimedia aids), crafting effective informative presentations, and developing ethical persuasive messages.

We conclude the book with two appendixes designed to supplement our instruction about communication fundamentals. Appendix A includes practical strategies for being interviewed and for interviewing others. We relate our discussion of interviewing to the five Communication Principles for a Lifetime. Appendix B includes examples of recent presentations to illustrate what effective, well-planned presentations look like.

## Our Partnership with Students to Help Them Learn Stays the Same

A textbook is essentially a "distance learning" tool. As we write the book, we are separated from the learner by both time and space. To help lessen the distance between author and reader, we've incorporated a variety of learning resources and pedagogical features to engage students in the learning process. As we note in the text, information alone is not communication. Communication occurs when the receiver of information responds to it. Our special features help turn information into a responsive communication message that has an effect on students' lives.

**Principles Model and Icons**  Our pentagon model and margin icons help students see connections between the various communication concepts and skills we present. Throughout the book we provide an integrated framework to reinforce what's fundamental about human communication. Long after students may have forgotten the lists they memorized for an exam, we want them to remember the five fundamental principles we highlight throughout the book. Remembering these principles can also help them remember strategies and concepts to enhance their interpersonal relationships, improve group and team meetings, and design and deliver effective presentations.

**Chapter-End Summary of Communication Principles for a Lifetime**  In addition to using the margin icons to highlight material in the text related to one or more communication principles, we conclude each chapter with a summary of the chapter content organized around the communication principles. Our chapter summaries at the ends of the first six chapters distill essential information about the specific communication principle presented in the chapter. Starting in Chapter 7, we review and summarize the chapter content using all five Communication Principles for a Lifetime as a framework. Miniature versions of our principles icons appear with headings to highlight the five fundamental principles. The purpose of this chapter-end feature is to help students synthesize the material related to the context discussed (e.g., interpersonal communication) and the five principles that undergird the descriptive and prescriptive information presented in the chapter. This feature will help students connect the variety of ideas and skills with the five communication principles.

**Communication and Ethics**  To help students consider the ethical dimensions of human communication, in each chapter we provide a special boxed feature called "Communication & Ethics." Students are asked to consider a case study or to ponder their responses to questions of ethics. The cases and questions we pose are designed to be thought-provoking, to spark insightful class discussion, or to

## Communication&ETHICS

### What Are the Sources of Your Ethical Views?

Many people think that success means achieving what they want to achieve. Success is often equated with acquiring money, power, position, and influence. But when communicating with others, we've suggested, we achieve success if the communication message is understood as intended, achieves its intended effect, and satisfies a third criterion: It is ethical. Success is based not only on the communication outcome, but also on the methods and approaches used to communicate. If you lie, knowingly withhold key information, or use force to achieve your communication goals, then your message has not been successful, even if you are understood perfectly and you

_____ The Internet
_____ Government officials and public figures
_____ Laws and the legal system
_____ Music
_____ Works of art
_____ Sacred and inspired writing (e.g., the Bible)
_____ Religious beliefs
_____ Clergy and religious leaders
_____ Fiction and poetry
_____ TV and radio
_____ Newspapers and magazines
_____ Teachers

be used in combination with a journal assignment or other learning method to help students see connections between ethics and communication.

## Communication & TECHNOLOGY

### Got Low Self-Esteem? Get Facebook!

Facebook statistics are staggering: The popular social networking site now boasts more than 750 million active users, half of whom log on in any given day. People spend more than 700 billion minutes *per month* on Facebook. More than 250 million users access Facebook through their mobile devices (such as cell phones and iPads), and mobile users are twice as active on Facebook as nonmobile users. Do you think Facebook is fun and exciting, or do you think it is an "awful waste of time," as Betty White called it, when she was hosting *Saturday Night Live*? What relationships exist between Facebook usage and some of the topics we discuss in this chapter?

Research has examined a connection between Facebook use and self-esteem. One study found that receiving positive feedback from Facebook "friends" enhanced people's views of themselves in terms of their physical at-

Cornell University scholars Amy Gonzales and Jeffrey Hancock studied these two self-esteem possibilities for college students who use Facebook.[40] The researchers wondered if comparing one's hobbies, likes and dislikes, "wall posts," and "status updates" to others' would make people aware of their limitations and shortcomings, thus diminishing their self-esteem, or if the sharing of select information (meaning a profile that emphasizes one's best features while filtering negative qualities) would have the opposite effect, thus increasing self-esteem. Their results favored the second possibility. According to Gonzales and Hancock, "exposure to information presented on one's Facebook profile enhances self-esteem, especially when a person edits information about the self or *selectively self-presents*."[41] They concluded that Facebook offers a unique opportunity for self-awareness enhancement, be-

**Communication and Technology**    Because of the importance of technology in our lives, in each chapter we include special material about technology and communication to help students become sensitive to the sometimes mindboggling impact of new technology on our communication with others. We also discuss the importance and role of technology in several chapters throughout the book. The prevalence of technology in students' lives offers powerful teachable moments to help students learn and apply communication principles.

## Communication & DIVERSITY

### How to Adapt to Your Diverse Audience

One of the principles we've stressed throughout this book is the importance of adapting your message to others. Many, if not most, of the presentations you give will be to audiences that represent a mix of cultures and backgrounds rather than a single cultural tradition. In this speaking situation, it is important to realize that not all audience members expect information to be presented as *you* prefer. Here are some ideas to help you adapt when you speak to an audience of people who have cultural backgrounds different from your own.[35]

• *Adapt your supporting materials.* Telling a good story to illustrate your ideas is an especially effective strategy to appeal to a wide range of audience preferences. Most audiences value a good story with a point or moral that is relevant to the point you want to make.

• *Adapt your visual support.* You might want to use

a structured presentation that follows an outlined pattern; they also prefer an introduction that previews the ideas you'll present and a conclusion that crisply summarizes the essential points you've made. A Russian or Eastern European audience would expect a less tightly structured presentation, however. When you're in doubt about listener preferences, we recommend being structured and organized.

• *Adapt your delivery style.* One study found that members of some cultures prefer a more formal oratorical style of delivery than the conversational, extemporaneous style that is usually taught in American presentational speaking classes.[36] For example, Japanese speakers addressing a predominantly Japanese audience begin a presentation by making respectful references to their audience.

**Communication and Diversity**    Each chapter includes a "Communication & Diversity" feature designed to help students see the importance of diversity in their lives. Yet we don't relegate discussions of diversity only to a boxed feature. Because we believe diversity is such an important communication topic in contemporary society, we discuss diversity in the text, not only in relation to our fifth principle of communication (appropriately adapt messages to others) in Chapter 6, but throughout the book.

**Comprehensive Pedagogical Learning Tools**    To help students master the material, we've built in a wealth of study aids:

• Learning objectives provide a compass to help students know where they are headed.
• Chapter outlines preview key concepts.
• Concise and highly praised Recap boxes distill essential content.
• Key terms in boldface with marginal glossary help students master essential terms.
• Chapter-end Study Guides offer narrative summaries and key terms lists.
• Chapter-end summaries of the five Communication Principles recap applications of the principles to students' real-life communication.
• Many chapter-end skills assessment and collaborative learning activities have been revised and updated for this edition.
• Chapter-end website information gives students a wealth of ideas and applications available on the Internet.

# Our Partnership with Instructors Stays Strong

As authors, we view our job as providing resources that instructors can use to bring communication principles and skills to life. A textbook is only one tool to help teachers teach and learners learn. As part of our partnership with instructors to facilitate learning, we offer an array of print and electronic resources to help teachers do what they do best: teach. In addition to the vast array of learning resources we've built into the text, we offer a dazzling package of additional resources to help instructors generate both intellectual and emotional connections with their students.

# Resources in Print and Online

| NAME OF SUPPLEMENT | AVAILABLE | INSTRUCTOR OR STUDENT SUPPLEMENT | DESCRIPTION |
|---|---|---|---|
| Instructor's Manual | In Print Online | Instructor Supplement | Prepared by Leonard M. Edmonds, Arizona State University, the Instructor's Manual includes a wealth of resources for each chapter. There is an instructional outline that can be used for planning, developing, and delivering lectures. Each chapter also features discussion/journal questions, which are designed to increase student engagement and can also be used for assignments, essay questions, or as review questions for an exam. In addition, there are classroom activities, sample assignments, and suggestions for outside resources. Available at www.pearsonhighered.com/irc (access code required). |
| Test Bank | In Print Online | Instructor Supplement | The Test Bank, also prepared by Leonard M. Edmonds, Arizona State University, contains more than 1200 fully reviewed multiple-choice, true/false, and essay questions organized by chapter. Each question is referenced by topic and page. Available at www.pearsonhighered.com/irc (access code required). |
| MyTest | Online | Instructor Supplement | This flexible online test-generating software includes all questions found in the printed Test Bank, allowing instructors to create their own personalized exams. Instructors can also edit any of the existing test questions and even add new questions. Other special features of this program include random generation of test questions, creation of alternate versions of the same test, scrambling of question sequence, and test preview before printing. Available at www.pearsonmytest.com (access code required). |
| PowerPoint™ Presentation Package | Online | Instructor Supplement | Prepared by Amy M. Wisner, Michigan State University, this text-specific package provides a basis for your lectures with PowerPoint™ slides for each chapter of the book. Available at www.pearsonhighered.com/irc (access code required). |
| Pearson's Introduction to Communication Video Library | VHS/DVD | Instructor Supplement | Pearson's Introduction to Communication Video Library contains a range of videos from which adopters can choose. The videos feature a variety of topics and scenarios for communication foundations, interpersonal communication, small group communication, and public speaking. Please contact your Pearson representative for details and a complete list of videos and their contents to choose which would be most useful to your course. Some restrictions apply. |
| Lecture Questions for Clickers for Introduction to Communication | Online | Instructor Supplement | Prepared by Keri Moe, El Paso Community College, this is an assortment of questions and activities covering culture, listening, interviewing, public speaking, interpersonal conflict and more, presented in PowerPoint. These slides will help liven up your lectures and can be used along with the Personal Response System to get students more involved in the material. Available at www.pearsonhighered.com/irc (access code required). |
| *A Guide for New Teachers of Introduction to Communication, Fourth Edition* | In Print Online | Instructor Supplement | Updated by Christine North, Ohio Northern University, this guide is designed to help new teachers effectively teach the introductory communication course. It is full of basics for course planning and management, first day of class tips, great teaching ideas for both traditional and hybrid/online courses, a guide to Pearson resources including MyCommunicationLab, and sample activities, handouts, and assignments. Available at www.pearsonhighered.com/irc (access code required). |

*(continued)*

# Resources in Print and Online *(continued)*

| NAME OF SUPPLEMENT | AVAILABLE | INSTRUCTOR OR STUDENT SUPPLEMENT | DESCRIPTION |
|---|---|---|---|
| *Preparing Visual Aids for Presentations,* Fifth Edition (ISBN: 020561115X) | In Print | Student Supplement | Prepared by Dan Cavanaugh, this 32-page visual booklet provides a host of ideas for using today's multimedia tools to improve presentations, including suggestions for planning a presentation, guidelines for designing visual aids and storyboarding, and a walkthrough that shows how to prepare a visual display using PowerPoint™ (available for purchase). |
| Pearson's Introduction to Communication Study Site (Open access) | Online | Student Supplement | This open-access, student resource features practice tests, learning objectives, and Web links organized around the major topics typically covered in the Introduction to Communication course. Available at www.pearsonintrocommunication.com. |
| *Public Speaking in the Multicultural Environment,* Second Edition (ISBN: 0205265111) | In Print | Student Supplement | Prepared by Devorah A. Lieberman, Portland State University, this booklet helps students learn to analyze cultural diversity within their audiences and adapt their presentations accordingly (available for purchase). |
| *The Speech Outline* (ISBN: 032108702X) | In Print | Student Supplement | Prepared by Reeze L. Hanson and Sharon Condon of Haskell Indian Nations University, this workbook includes activities, exercises, and answers to help students develop and master the critical skill of outlining (available for purchase). |
| *Multicultural Activities Workbook* (ISBN: 0205546528) | In Print | Student Supplement | Prepared by Marlene C. Cohen and Susan L. Richardson of Prince George's Community College, Maryland, this workbook is filled with hands-on activities that help broaden the content of speech classes to reflect diverse cultural backgrounds. The checklists, surveys, and writing assignments all help students succeed in speech communication by offering experiences that address a variety of learning styles (available for purchase). |
| *Speech Preparation Workbook* (ISBN: 013559569X) | In Print | Student Supplement | Prepared by Jennifer Dreyer and Gregory H. Patton of San Diego State University, this workbook takes students through the stages of speech creation—from audience analysis to writing the speech—and includes guidelines, tips, and easy-to-fill-in pages (available for purchase). |
| Study Card for Introduction to Speech Communication (ISBN: 0205474381) | In Print | Student Supplement | Colorful, affordable, and packed with useful information, the Pearson Study Cards make studying easier, more efficient, and more enjoyable. Course information is distilled down to the basics, helping students quickly master the fundamentals, review a subject for understanding, or prepare for an exam. Because they're laminated for durability, they can be kept for years to come and pulled out whenever students need a quick review (available for purchase). |
| MyCommunicationLab | Online | Instructor & Student Supplement | MyCommunicationLab is a state-of-the-art, interactive, and instructive solution for communication courses. Designed to be used as a supplement to a traditional lecture course or to completely administer an online course, MyCommunicationLab combines a Pearson eText, MySearchLab™, MediaShare, Pearson's class preparation tool, multimedia, video clips, activities, research support, tests, and quizzes to completely engage students. See next page for more details. |

# MyCommunicationLab®

## The moment you know.

Educators know it. Students know it. It's that inspired moment when something that was difficult to understand suddenly makes perfect sense. Our MyLab products have been designed and refined with a single purpose in mind—to help educators create that moment of understanding with their students.

MyCommunicationLab can be used by itself or linked to any learning management system. To learn more about how the new MyCommunicationLab combines proven learning applications with powerful assessment, read on!

MyCommunicationLab delivers **proven results** in helping individual students succeed. Pearson MyLabs are currently in use by millions of students each year across a variety of disciplines. MyCommunicationLab works—but don't take our word for it. Visit our MyLab/Mastering site (www.pearsonhighered.com/mylabmastering) to read white papers, case studies, and testimonials from instructors and students that consistently demonstrate the success of our MyLabs.

MyCommunicationLab provides **engaging experiences** that personalize, stimulate, and measure learning for each student. MyCommunicationLab is available for Introduction to Communication, Interpersonal Communication, Mass Communication, and Public Relations courses.

- **The Pearson eText:** Identical in content and design to the printed text, the Pearson eText lets students access their textbook anytime, anywhere, and any way they want—including downloading to an iPad. Students can take notes and highlight, just like in a traditional book.

- **Assessments:** Pre- and Post-Tests for each chapter enable students and instructors to track progress and get immediate feedback. Results from the Pre- and Post-Tests generate a personalized study plan that helps students master course content. Chapter Exams allow instructors to easily assign exams online. Results feed into the MyLab grade book.

- **MediaShare:** This comprehensive file upload tool allows students to post speeches, outlines, visual aids, video assignments, role plays, group projects, and more in a variety of formats including video, Word documents, PowerPoint™, and Excel. Structured much like a social networking site, MediaShare can help promote a sense of community among students. Uploaded files are available for viewing, commenting, and grading by instructors and class members in face-to-face and online course settings. Integrated video capture functionality allows students to record video directly from a webcam to their assignments, and allows instructors to record videos via webcam in class or in a lab and attach them directly to a specific student and/or assignment. Instructors also can upload files as assignments for students to view and respond to directly in MediaShare. Grades can be imported into most learning management systems, and robust privacy settings allow instructors and students to ensure a secure learning environment.

- **Videos and Video Quizzes:** Interactive videos provide students with the opportunity to watch and evaluate multimedia pertaining to chapter content. Many videos are annotated with critical thinking questions or include short, assignable quizzes that report to the instructor's grade book.

- **Class Preparation Tool:** Pearson's class preparation tool is designed to make lecture preparation simpler and less time-consuming. This searchable database collects the very best class presentation resources—art and figures from our texts, videos, lecture activities, audio clips, classroom activities, demonstrations—in one convenient online destination.

- **MyOutline:** This valuable tool provides step-by-step guidance and structure for writing an effective outline, along with a detailed help section to assist students in understanding the elements of an outline and how all the pieces fit together. Students can download and e-mail completed outlines to instructors, save their outlines for future editing, and even print them as notecards. Instructors can choose from existing templates or create their own structure for use.
- **Topic Selector:** This interactive tool helps students get started generating ideas and then narrowing down topics. Our Topic Selector is question-based, rather than drill-down or simply a list of ideas, in order to help students really learn the process of selecting their topic. Once they have determined their topic, students are directed to credible online sources for guidance with the research process.
- **MyPersonalityProfile:** Online resources that provide students with opportunities to learn about the various communication styles of themselves and others are housed in MyPersonalityProfile, Pearson's online library for self-assessment and analysis. Instructors can use these tools to show learning and growth over the duration of the course.
- **MySearchLab:** Pearson's MySearchLab™ is the easiest way for students to start a research assignment or paper. Complete with extensive help on the research process and four databases of credible and reliable source material, MySearchLab™ helps students quickly and efficiently make the most of their research time.
- **Audio Chapter Summaries:** Every chapter includes an audio chapter summary, formatted as an MP3, perfect for students reviewing material before a test or instructors reviewing material before class.

MyCommunicationLab comes from a **trusted partner** with educational expertise and a deep commitment to helping students, instructors, and departments achieve their goals.

- Pearson supports instructors with workshops, training, and assistance from Pearson Faculty Advisors—so you get the help you need to make MyCommunicationLab work for your course.
- Pearson gathers feedback from instructors and students during the development of content and the feature enhancement of each release to ensure that our products meet your needs.

No matter what course management system you use—or if you do not use one at all, but still wish to easily capture your students' grades and track their performance—Pearson has a MyCommunicationLab option to suit your needs. A MyCommunicationLab access code is available at no additional cost when packaged with print versions of select Pearson Communication texts. To get started, contact your local Pearson Publisher's Representative at www.pearsonhighered.com/replocator.

# Acknowledgments

Although our three names appear on the cover as authors of the book you are holding in your hands, in reality hundreds of people have been instrumental in making this book possible. Communication scholars who have dedicated their lives to researching the importance of communication principles, theories, and skills provide the fuel for this book. We thank each author we reference in our voluminous endnotes for the research conclusions that bring us to our contemporary understanding of communication principles. We thank our students who have trusted us to be their guides in a study of human communication. They continue to enrich our lives with their enthusiasm and curiosity. They have inspired us to be more creative by their honest quizzical looks and challenged us to go beyond "textbook" answers with their thought-provoking questions.

We are most appreciative of the outstanding editorial support we continue to receive from our colleagues and friends at Pearson. We thank Joe Opiela for helping us keep this project moving forward when we wondered if the world needed another communication book. Karon Bowers, Pearson Editor-in-Chief, has continued to provide valued support and encouragement. Our new editor, Melissa Mashburn, has quickly become another valued supporter. Our exceptionally thoughtful and talented development editor, Sheralee Connors, helped us polish and prune our words and gave us a wealth of ideas and suggestions. Karen Black, Diana Ivy's sister, who conducted permissions research, was again a true blessing to us in providing skilled assistance with important details and administrative support. We acknowledge and appreciate the ideas and suggestions from Mark Redmond, a valued friend, gifted teacher, and skilled writer at Iowa State University. His coauthorship with us on *Interpersonal Communication: Relating to Others* significantly influenced our ideas about communication, especially interpersonal communication.

We are grateful to the many educators who read the manuscript and both encouraged and challenged us. We thank the following people for drawing on their teaching skill, expertise, and vast experience to make this a much better book:

**Reviewers of the First Edition:** Michael Bruner, University of North Texas; Diana O. Cassagrande, West Chester University; Dan B. Curtis, Central Missouri State University; Terrence A. Doyle, Northern Virginia Community College; Julia F. Fennell, Community College of Allegheny County, South Campus; Phil Hoke, The University of Texas at San Antonio; Stephen Hunt, Illinois State University; Carol L. Hunter, Brookdale Community College; Dorothy W. Ige, Indiana University Northwest; A. Elizabeth Lindsey, The New Mexico State University; Robert E. Mild, Jr., Fairmont State College; Timothy P. Mottet, Texas State University–San Marcos; Alfred G. Mueller II, Pennsylvania State University, Mont Alto Campus; Kay Neal, University of Wisconsin–Oshkosh; Kathleen Perri, Valencia Community College; Beth M. Waggenspack, Virginia Tech University; Gretchen Aggert Weber, Horry-Georgetown Technical College; Kathy Werking, Eastern Kentucky University; Andrew F. Wood, San Jose State University

**Reviewers of the Second Edition:** Lawrence Albert, Morehead State University; Leonard Assante, Volunteer State Community College; Dennis Dufer, St. Louis Community College; Annette Folwell, University of Idaho; Mike Hemphill, University of Arkansas at Little Rock; Teri Higginbotham, University of Central Arkansas; Lawrence Hugenberg, Youngstown State University; Timothy P. Mottet, Texas State University–San Marcos; Penny O'Connor, University of Northern Iowa; Evelyn Plummer, Seton Hall University; Charlotte C. Toguchi, Kapi'olani Community College; Debra Sue Wyatt, South Texas Community College

**Reviewers of the Third Edition:** Dom Bongiorni, Kingwood College; Jo Anne Bryant, Troy University; Cherie Cannon, Miami–Dade College; Thomas Green, Cape Fear Community College; Gretchen Harries, Austin Community College; Xin-An Lu, Shippensburg University of Pennsylvania; Sara L. Nalley, Columbia College; Kristi Schaller, University of Hawaii; David Shuhy, Salisbury University; John Tapia, Missouri Western State College

**Reviewers of the Fourth Edition:** Ellen B. Bremen, Highline Community College; Patricia A. Cutspec, East Tennessee State University; Edgar D. Johnson III, Augusta State University; Peter S. Lee, California State University, Fullerton; Kelly Aikin Petcus, Austin Community College; Natalia Rybas, Bowling Green State University; Sarah Stout, Kellogg Community College

**Reviewers of the Fifth Edition:** Leonard Assante, Volunteer State Community College; Sandra Bein, South Suburban College; Robert Dixon, St. Louis Community College; Glynis Holm Strause, Coastal Bend College; Linda Kalfayan, Westchester Community College; Barbara Maxwell, Linn State Technical College; Kay Neal, University of Wisconsin Oshkosh; Jeff Pomeroy, Southwest Texas Junior College

We have each been influenced by colleagues, friends, and teachers who have offered support and inspiration for this project. Happily, colleagues, friends, and teachers are virtually indistinguishable for us. We are each blessed with people with whom we work who offer strong support.

Steve and Sue thank their colleagues at Texas State University–San Marcos for their insights and ideas that helped shape key concepts in this book. Cathy Fleuriet and Tom Burkholder, who served as basic course directors at Texas State, influenced our work. Tim Mottet, also a former basic course director at Texas State and now Dean of the College of Fine Arts and Communication, is a valued, inspirational friend and colleague who is always there to listen and freely share his ideas and experience. Marian Houser, the current basic course director at Texas State, is a wonderful friend and provides important insight and support. Richard Cheatham continues to provide enthusiastic encouragement for this project. Kosta Tovstiadi, University of Kentucky, provided skilled research assistance to help us draw upon the most contemporary interpersonal communication research. Michael Hennessy, Patricia Margerison, and Daniel Lochman are Texas State English faculty who have been especially supportive of Sue's work. Finally, Steve thanks his skilled and dedicated administrative support team at Texas State. Administrative assistant Sue Hall, who continues to be Steve's right hand, is a cherished friend and colleague. Graphic designer Malinda Murray and technical support expert Bob Hanna are two additional staff members who provide exceptional support and assistance for this project and many others. Meredith Williams offered tremendous support and assistance in manuscript preparation.

Ivy is grateful to her students, colleagues, and friends at Texas A&M University–Corpus Christi, for their patience and unwavering support for her continued involvement in this book project. In particular, Dean Kelly Quintanilla and Chair Don Luna constantly reaffirm the value of a well-written, carefully crafted book—one that speaks to students' lives. Their support of Ivy's research efforts, along with constant fueling from her wonderful students, always make this project a joy. Special thanks go to research assistant Jason Escamilla, for his help with the fifth edition. Ivy's deepest thanks also go to Steve and Sue Beebe for their generosity in bringing her into this project, and for their extraordinary friendship.

Finally we express our appreciation to our families. Ivy thanks her ever-supportive mother Carol Ivy, sister Karen Black, and nephew, niece, and grandnieces Brian, Sumitra, Mackenzie, and Sidney Black. They have been constant and generous with their praise for her writing accomplishments. Ivy will always be especially grateful to her late father, Herschel Ivy, for lovingly offering many lessons about living the highly ethical life.

Sue and Steve especially thank their parents, Herb and Jane Dye and Russell and Muriel Beebe, who taught them much about communication and ethics that truly are principles for a lifetime. They also thank their sons, Mark and Matthew Beebe, and their daughter-in-law, Brittany Beebe, for teaching them life lessons about giving and receiving love that will remain with them forever.

Steven A. Beebe and Susan J. Beebe
Diana K. Ivy

# Communication

## PRINCIPLES FOR A LIFETIME

Good communication is as stimulating as black coffee and just as hard to sleep after.

ANNE MORROW LINDBERGH

## **Chapter** OUTLINE

- Why Study Communication?
- Communication Defined
- Communication Competence
- Communication Models
- Communication in the 21st Century
- Communication Characteristics
- Communication Principles for a Lifetime
- Communicating with Others: Interpersonal, Group, and Presentational Communication
- Study Guide: Review, Apply, and Assess Your Knowledge and Skill

## **Chapter** OBJECTIVES

After studying this chapter, you should be able to

1. Define communication and explain why it is an important course of study.
2. Describe three criteria that can be used to determine whether communication is competent.
3. Compare and contrast communication as action, interaction, and transaction.
4. Identify five characteristics of communication.
5. List and explain five fundamental principles of communication.
6. Define and describe communication in interpersonal, group, and presentational communication contexts.

Jack Hollingsworth/Thinkstock

# 1 | Foundations of Human Communication

Communication is essential for life. It is a fundamental aspect of being human. Even if you live in isolation from other people, you talk to yourself through your thoughts. Like life-sustaining breath, communication is ever-present in our lives. Understanding and improving how we communicate with others is a basic life skill.

Human communication is inescapable. Consider the number of times you have purposefully communicated with someone today, as you worked, ate, studied, shopped, or went about your daily duties. Most people spend between 80 and 90 percent of their waking hours communicating with others.[1] It is through the process of communication that we convey who we are, both to ourselves and to others; it is our primary tool for making our way in the world.

This book presents fundamental principles that undergird all aspects of communicating with others. In the course of our study of human communication, we will discuss myriad skills, ideas, concepts, and contexts. To help you stitch together the barrage of ideas and information, we will organize our study around five fundamental communication principles. Together, these five Communication Principles for a Lifetime will provide a framework for our discussion of the importance and pervasiveness of human communication.

| | |
|---|---|
| Principle One: | Be aware of your communication with yourself and others. |
| Principle Two: | Effectively use and interpret verbal messages. |
| Principle Three: | Effectively use and interpret nonverbal messages. |
| Principle Four: | Listen and respond thoughtfully to others. |
| Principle Five: | Appropriately adapt messages to others. |

These five principles distill decades of research as well as the wisdom of those who have taught communication over the years. We don't claim that everything you need to know about communication is covered by these five principles. They do, however, summarize considerable knowledge about the communication process and what constitutes effective and ethical communication.

Before we elaborate on the five fundamental communication principles, it is important to provide some background for our study of communication. The purpose of this first chapter is to provide that background. We will discuss why it is important to study communication, define communication, examine various models of or perspectives on communication, and identify characteristics of human communication. Having offered this prelude, we then discuss the five foundational principles of human communication that we will use throughout the book to help you organize the concepts, skills, and ideas we present in our discussion of interpersonal, group, and presentational speaking situations.

# Why Study Communication?

Why are you here? No, we don't mean "Why do you exist?" or "Why do you live where you do?" What we mean is "Why are you taking a college course about communication?" Perhaps the short answer is "It's required." Or maybe your advisor, parent, or friend encouraged you to take the course. If it is a required course, what's the rationale for that requirement? And required or not, what can a systematic study of human communication do for you?

Communication touches every aspect of our lives. To be able to express yourself to other people is a basic requirement for living in a modern society. From a practical standpoint, it's very likely that you will make your living with your mind rather than your hands.[2] Even if you do physical labor, you will need communication skills to work with others. When you study communication, you are developing leadership skills. "The art of communication," says author James Humes, "is the language of leadership."[3]

Although the value of being a competent communicator is virtually undisputed, there is evidence that many people struggle to express themselves clearly or to accurately understand messages from others. One study estimated that one-fifth of the students in the United States were not successful with even elementary communication tasks; in addition, more than 60 percent of the students could not give clear oral directions for someone else to follow.[4] When leaders in major corporations were asked to specify the most important skills for workers to have, 80 percent said listening was the most important work skill; 78 percent identified interpersonal communication skill as the next most important. However, the same leaders said only 28 percent of their employees had good listening skills and only 27 percent possessed effective interpersonal communication skills.[5] In support of these leaders' observations, another national study found that adults listen with 25 percent accuracy.[6] In addition to lacking communication skills, there is also evidence that the majority of adults are fearful of speaking in public; about 20 percent of the population is acutely apprehensive of presentational speaking.[7]

Aren't some people just born to be better communicators than others? If so, why should you work to develop your communication skill? Just as some people have more innate musical talent than others, there is evidence that some people may have an inborn biological ability to communicate with others.[8] This does not mean you should not work to develop your communication ability. Throughout the book, we will offer ample evidence that if you work to improve your skill, you will be rewarded by enjoying the benefits of enhanced communication competence. What are these benefits? Read on.

## To Improve Your Employability

Regardless of your specific job description, the essence of what you do when working at any job is to communicate; you talk, listen, relate, read, and write, whatever your job title. People who can communicate effectively with others are in high demand. As noted by John H. McConnell, CEO of Worthington Industries, "Take all the speech and communication courses you can because the world turns on communication."[9] McConnell's advice is supported by research as well as by personal observations. Another well-known leader, Warren Buffett, one of the richest people on the planet, is a major advocate of communication skill training and has noted that taking a communication training course was one of the best investments he ever made. Buffet once announced to M.B.A. students at his alma mater, Columbia University, that he would offer $100,000 to any student in the audience in return for 10 percent of future earnings. Recognizing the value of communication skills, Buffet then added that he would increase his offer to $150,000 if the student would take a communication skill development course that included public speaking training, one focus of this book![10]

Based on a survey of personnel managers—those people who are in charge of hiring you for a job—here's a ranking of the top factors in obtaining employment immediately after college:[11]

1. Oral communication (speaking) skills
2. Written communication skills
3. Listening ability
4. Enthusiasm
5. Technical competence
6. Work experience
7. Appearance
8. Poise
9. Resumé
10. Part-time or summer work experience

We're sure you know why we cited this survey. Communication skills were the number one factor; note that listening ability was also highly valued. And this survey isn't the only one that reaches the same conclusion; several other research studies have shown that communication skills are the most sought-after skills in the workplace.[12]

The better your communication skills, the more employable you are. Can you think of any job that would not require communication?

Jaimie Duplass/Shutterstock.com

## To Improve Your Relationships

We don't choose our biological families, but we do choose our friends. For unmarried people, developing friendships and falling in love are the top-rated sources of satisfaction and happiness in life.[13] Conversely, losing a relationship is among life's most stressful events. Most people between the ages of 19 and 24 report that they have had from five to six romantic relationships and have been "in love" once or twice.[14] Understanding the role and function of communication can help unravel some of the mysteries of human relationships. At the heart of a good relationship is good communication.[15]

Virginia Satir, a pioneer in family enrichment, described family communication as "the largest single factor determining the kinds of relationships [we make] with others."[16] Learning principles and skills of communication can give us insight into why we relate to other family members as we do. Our early communication with our parents had a profound effect on our self-concept and self-worth. According to Satir, people are "made" in families. Our communication with family members has shaped how we interact with others today.

Many of us will spend as much or more time interacting with people in our places of work as we do at home. And although we choose our friends and lovers, we don't always have the same flexibility in choosing those with whom or for whom we work. Increasing our understanding of the role and importance of human communication with our colleagues can help us better manage stress on the job as well as enhance our work success.

## To Improve Your Health

Life is stressful. Research has clearly documented that the lack or loss of close relationships can lead to ill health and even death. Having a social support system—good friends and supportive family members—seems to make a difference in our overall health and quality of life. Good friends and intimate relationships with others help us manage stress and contribute to both physical and emotional health. For example, physicians have noted that patients who are widowed or divorced experience more medical problems, such as heart disease, cancer, pneumonia, and diabetes, than do married people.[17] Grief-stricken spouses are more likely than others to die prematurely, especially around the time of the departed spouse's birthday or near their wedding anniversary.[18] Terminally ill patients with a limited number of friends or social support die sooner than those with stronger ties.[19] Without companions and close friends, our opportunities for intimacy and stress-managing communication are diminished. Studying how to enrich the quality of our communication with others can make life more enjoyable and enhance our overall well-being. Because of Facebook and other social networking software, we are increasingly involved in relationships with others even when we are not interacting face to face. Relating to others, whether online or in person, occurs through communication.[20]

So again, we ask the question: Why are you here? We think the evidence is clear: People who are effective communicators are more likely to get the jobs they want; have better quality relationships with friends, family, and colleagues; and even enjoy a healthier quality of life.

# Communication Defined

*Communication* is one of those words that seem so basic you may wonder why they need to be formally defined. Yet scholars who devote their lives to studying communication don't always agree on its definition. One research team counted more than 126 published definitions.[21]

In its broadest sense, **communication** is the process of acting on information.[22] Someone does or says something, and others think or do something in response to the action or the words as they understand them.

Communication is not unique to humans. It is possible, for example, for you to act on information from your dog Martin. Martin barks; you feed him. Your canine friend can also act on information from you. If you say to Martin, "Do you want a treat?" and he enthusiastically barks in response, there's no doubt that you and your pet have communicated with each other. Although researchers study communication between species as well as communication systems used by particular animal species, these fields of study are beyond the scope of this book. The focus of our study is human communication: people communicating with other people.

To refine our definition of communication, we can say that **human communication** *is the process of making sense out of the world and sharing that sense with others by creating meaning through the use of verbal and nonverbal messages.*[23] Let's look at the key components of this definition.

## Communication Is About Making Sense

We make sense out of what we experience when we begin to interpret what we see, hear, touch, smell, and taste with sensations, feelings, thoughts, and words. Identifying patterns and structure in what we experience is key to making sense out of what happens to us. Although we often think that "making sense out of something" means rationally and logically interpreting what we experience, we also make sense through intuition, feelings, and emotions.[24]

## Communication Is About Sharing Sense

We share what we experience by expressing to others and to ourselves what we experience. We typically use words to express our thoughts, but we also use music, art, clothing, and a host of other means to convey what we are thinking and feeling to others.

## Communication Is About Creating Meaning

It's more appropriate to say that meaning is *created* through communication rather than sent or transmitted. To say that we send or transmit messages is to imply that what we send is what is received. In human communication, however, what is expressed by one person is rarely interpreted by another person precisely as intended.

**communication**
The process of acting on information.

**human communication**
The process of making sense out of the world and sharing that sense with others by creating meaning through verbal and nonverbal messages.

Presenting information to others does not mean communication has occurred: *Information is not communication.* "But I told you what to do!" "It's there in the memo. Why didn't you do what I asked?" "It's in the syllabus." These exasperated communicators assumed that if they sent a message, someone would receive it. However, communication does not operate in a simple, linear, what-you-send-is-what-is-received process.

In reality, meaning is *co-created* by both the speaker and the listener. All individuals who are involved in the communication process shape how a message is understood by drawing on their own experiences while attempting to make sense of the message. Meaning is created in the hearts and minds of both the message source and the message receiver, based on such things as the characteristics of the message, the situation, and the perceptions and background of the communicators.

## Communication Is About Verbal and Nonverbal Messages

One way we communicate is by using words that trigger meaning in others symbolically. **Symbols** are words, sounds, gestures, or visual images that represent thoughts, concepts, objects, or experiences. The words on this page are symbols you use to derive meaning that makes sense to you.

**symbol**
A word, sound, gesture, or visual image that represents a thought, concept, object, or experience.

Not all symbols are verbal; some are nonverbal. You use gestures, posture, facial expression, tone of voice, clothing, and jewelry to express ideas, attitudes, and feelings. Nonverbal messages primarily communicate emotions, such as our likes and dislikes, whether we're interested or uninterested, and our feelings of power or lack of power.

Some scholars assert that *all* human behavior is really communication. When you cross your arms while listening to your friend describe her day, she may conclude that you're not interested in what she's talking about. But it could just be that you're chilly. While all human expression has the potential to communicate a message (someone may act or respond to the information they receive from you), it does not mean that you *intentionally* are expressing an idea or emotion. People don't always accurately interpret the messages we express—and this unprofound observation has profound implications.

Because of the ever-present potential for misunderstanding, communication should be *other-oriented*—it should acknowledge the perspective of others, not just the creator of the message. Communication that does not consider the needs, background, and culture of the receiver is more likely to be misunderstood than other-oriented communication. We'll emphasize the importance of considering others or considering your audience throughout the book. Knowing something about the experiences of the person or persons you're speaking to can help you communicate more effectively and appropriately.

Signs are usually carefully crafted examples of symbolic communication. What are the creators of this sign trying to communicate?
© Patrick Strattner/AGEfotostock.com

# Communication Competence

What does it mean to communicate competently? Does it mean that you are able to present a well-delivered speech? Or does it mean that you are able to carry on a brilliant conversation with someone? Is it evidence of communication competence if you often are asked to chair committee meetings because you are so organized? Being a competent communicator is more than just being well liked, glib, able to give polished presentations, or able to interact smoothly with individual people or in groups and teams. Although it is difficult to identify core criteria that define competent communication in all situations, we believe that certain goals of communication serve as measures of competence regardless of the setting. We suggest the following three criteria:[25]

- The message should be understood as the communicator intended it to be understood.
- The message should achieve the communicator's intended effect.
- The message should be ethical.

## The Message Should Be Understood

A primary goal of any effective communication transaction is to develop a common understanding of the message from both the sender's and the receiver's perspectives. You'll note how the words *common* and *communication* resemble each other. We acknowledge the challenge of communicating with others; differences in culture, language, experience, gender, education, and background all are sources of misunderstanding. One of the aims of the principles we discuss in this book is to create clarity of expression and a common understanding.

Message clarity is missing in the following headlines, which have appeared in local U.S. newspapers:

**Panda Mating Fails: Veterinarian Takes Over**

**Drunks Get Nine Months in Violin Case**

**Include Your Children When Baking Cookies**

**Police Begin Campaign to Run Down Jaywalkers**

**Local High School Dropouts Cut in Half**

Meanings are fragile, and messages can be misunderstood. An effective message is one that the receiver understands.

## The Message Should Achieve Its Intended Effect

Another criterion for judging the effectiveness of communication is whether the intent of the message is achieved. When you communicate intentionally with others, you do so for a specific purpose: to achieve a goal or to accomplish something. Because different purposes require different strategies for success, being aware of your purpose can enhance your probability of achieving it.

We often use specific types of communication to achieve typical goals:

- The goal of *public speaking* may be to inform, to persuade, or to entertain.
- In *small groups*, our goals are often to solve problems and make decisions.
- In our *interpersonal relationships*, our goals may be to build trust, develop intimacy, or just enjoy someone's company.

## The Message Should Be Ethical

Communication can be used to achieve good or bad objectives. A message that is understood and achieves its intended effect but that manipulates listeners, unfairly restricts their choices, or uses false information may be effective, but it is not appropriate or ethical. **Ethics** are the beliefs, values, and moral principles by which we determine what is right or wrong. Ethics and ethical behavior have long been considered critical components of human behavior in a given culture.

Philosophers have debated for centuries whether there is such a thing as a universal moral and ethical code.[26] British author and scholar C. S. Lewis suggested that there is a universal ethical code that serves as the basis for interpreting the "goodness" or

**ethics**
The beliefs, values, and moral principles by which we determine what is right or wrong.

# Communication&ETHICS

## What Are the Sources of Your Ethical Views?

Many people think that success means achieving what they want to achieve. Success is often equated with acquiring money, power, position, and influence. But when communicating with others, we've suggested, we achieve success if the communication message is understood as intended, achieves its intended effect, and satisfies a third criterion: It is ethical. Success is based not only on the communication outcome, but also on the methods and approaches used to communicate. If you lie, knowingly withhold key information, or use force to achieve your communication goals, then your message has not been successful, even if you are understood perfectly and you get what you want.

The question of who gets to decide what constitutes ethical behavior is one that arises often. Ethics are the beliefs, values, and moral principles by which we determine what is right or wrong. But where do your ethical beliefs, values, and principles come from? What are the sources of your sense of what is right and wrong?

Use the checklist below to identify the key sources of your ethical views.

INSTRUCTIONS: First, rate the influence of each factor listed below on a scale from 1 (a minor influence on your ethical beliefs and practices) to 5 (a major influence on your ethical beliefs and practices).

_____ Grandparents
_____ Parents
_____ Other family members (e.g., brothers, sisters, aunts, uncles)
_____ Friends

_____ The Internet
_____ Government officials and public figures
_____ Laws and the legal system
_____ Music
_____ Works of art
_____ Sacred and inspired writing (e.g., the Bible)
_____ Religious beliefs
_____ Clergy and religious leaders
_____ Fiction and poetry
_____ TV and radio
_____ Newspapers and magazines
_____ Teachers
_____ Other sources

After you have rated the sources of influence, circle the sources of ethical influence that you rated the highest. (Perhaps you rated several sources a 5.) Of those items you circled, rank-order the top three. Assign a rank of 1 to the most important ethical influence, 2 to the second most important, and 3 to the third most important.

• What connection can you make between the top sources of ethical influence in your life and the way you communicate with others?
• Can you think of specific ways in which the sources of your ethical beliefs and practices have directly influenced your communication with others?

Often we are unaware of the underpinnings of our ethical beliefs. This activity invites you to consciously examine the link between the sources of your perceptions of what is right and wrong and your communication behavior toward others.

"badness" of human behavior; evidence for such a code can be found, said Lewis, in the teachings of cultures throughout the world and through time.[27] In their book *Communication Ethics and Universal Values*, communication scholars Clifford Christians and Michael Traber make the following claim: "Every culture depends for its existence on norms that order human relationships and social institutions."[28] What are these universal norms—these beliefs and behaviors that describe what is normal, appropriate, or inappropriate? Christians and Traber suggest there are three universal cultural norms: (1) the value of truth, (2) respect for another person's dignity, and (3) the expectation that innocent people should not suffer harm.[29]

Scholars and philosophers who suggest that a universal code of ethics exists do not claim that people in all cultures always behave in ways that are true to universal standards. Proponents of a universal ethical code do suggest that a universal moral code is the ideal basis for evaluating right and wrong behavior, including communication behavior.

All religions of the world have a moral code that provides guidance for how people should treat others.[30] For example:

• The Ten Commandments serve as ethical guidelines for those who adhere to Judeo-Christian ethical principles.

- In Christianity, the Golden Rule—"Do unto others what you would have others do unto you"—is a fundamental value.
- Scholars point to Confucius (551–479 BCE) as the first to suggest, "Never do to others what you would not like them to do to you."[31]
- Buddhism teaches a similar value: "One should seek for others the happiness one desires for oneself."
- Hinduism asks adherents to live by the precept, "Do nothing to others which would cause pain if done to you."
- Judaism teaches, "What is hateful to you, do not do to others."
- Islam suggests, "No one of you is a believer until he desires for his brother that which he desires for himself."

The underlying ethic of how to treat others can clearly be seen across most of the world's religions.[32]

Our purpose is not to prescribe a specific religious or philosophical ethical code, but rather to suggest that humans from a variety of cultures and traditions have sought to develop ethical principles that guide their interactions with others.

Philosophy and religion are not the only realms that focus on ethical behavior. Most professions, such as medicine, law, and journalism, have explicit codes of ethics that identify appropriate and inappropriate behavior. The National Communication Association has developed a Credo for Communication Ethics to emphasize the importance of being an ethical communicator:

> Ethical communication is fundamental to responsible thinking, decision making, and the development of relationships and communities within and across contexts, cultures, channels, and media. Moreover, ethical communication enhances human worth and dignity by fostering truthfulness, fairness, responsibility, personal integrity, and respect for self and others.[33]

Echoing the wisdom offered by others, we suggest that competent communication is grounded in an other-oriented ethical perspective that is fundamental to all human interactions.

For most people, being ethical means being sensitive to others' needs, giving people choices rather than forcing them to behave in a certain way, respecting others' privacy, not intentionally decreasing others' feelings of self-worth, and being honest in presenting information. Unethical communication does just the opposite: It forces views on others and demeans their integrity.

Throughout this book, we will offer opportunities for you to examine ethical issues in a feature called Communication & Ethics.

# Communication Models

Communication researchers have spent considerable time trying to understand precisely how communication takes place. In the course of their study, they have developed visual models that graphically illustrate the communication process.

By reviewing the development of communication models, you can see how our understanding of communication has evolved over the past century. Early models viewed communication as a transfer or exchange of information, but this view evolved to include a more interactive, give-and-take approach. Researchers' understanding then progressed even further to today's view that communication is a process in which meaning is co-created simultaneously among people. The three models of the communication process that we show here begin with the simplest and oldest perspective and then move to more contemporary models.

## Communication as Action: Message Transfer

"Did you get my message?" This simple question summarizes the communication-as-action approach to human communication. In this model, communication takes

## Figure 1.1 A Model of Communication as Action

Source: From *The Mathematical Theory of Communication.* Copyright 1949, 1998 by the Board of Trustees of the University of Illinois. Used with permission of the authors and University of Illinois Press.

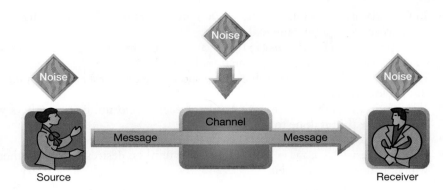

place when a message is sent and received. Period. Communication is a way of transferring meaning from sender to receiver. In 1948, Harold Lasswell described the process as follows:

> Who (sender)
> Says what (message)
> In what channel
> To whom (receiver)
> With what effect[34]

Figure 1.1 shows a simplified representation of the communication process developed by communication pioneers Claude Shannon and Warren Weaver, who viewed communication as a linear input/output process consisting of a source, a message, a channel, a receiver, and noise. Today, although researchers view the process as more complex, they still define most of the key components in this model in basically the same way that Shannon and Weaver did.

**Source**   The **source** of communication is the originator of a thought or an emotion. As the developer of that thought or emotion, the source puts a message into a code that can be understood by a receiver.

- **Encoding** is the process of translating ideas, feelings, and thoughts into a code. Vocalizing a word, gesturing, and establishing eye contact are means of encoding our thoughts into a message that can be decoded by someone.

- **Decoding**, the process that is the opposite of encoding, occurs when the words or unspoken signals are interpreted by the receiver.

**Receiver**   The **receiver** is the person who decodes the signal and attempts to make sense of what the source encoded. Think of a TV station as a source broadcasting to a receiver (your TV) that picks up the station's signal. In human communication, however, there is something between the source and the receiver: We filter messages through past experiences, attitudes, beliefs, values, prejudices, and biases.

**Message**   **Messages** are the written, spoken, and unspoken elements of communication to which we assign meaning. You can send a message intentionally (talking to a friend before class) or unintentionally (falling asleep during class); verbally ("Hi. What's up?"), nonverbally (a smile and a handshake), or in written form (this book); or through any number of electronic channels.

**Channel**   A message is communicated from sender to receiver via some pathway called a **channel**. With today's technological advances, we receive messages from a variety of channels. With your landline phone, the Internet, or a fax transmission, the communication channel may be a telephone line. Cell phones and iPads use a wireless channel. Ultimately, communication channels correspond to your senses. When you

**source**
The originator of a thought or emotion who puts it into a code that can be understood by a receiver.

**encoding**
The process of translating ideas, feelings, and thoughts into a code.

**decoding**
The process of interpreting ideas, feelings, and thoughts that have been translated into a code.

**receiver**
The person who decodes a message and attempts to make sense of what the source has encoded.

**message**
Written, spoken, and unspoken elements of communication to which people assign meaning.

**channel**
The pathway through which messages are sent.

call your mother on the telephone, the message is conveyed via an electronic channel that activates auditory cues. When you talk with your mother face to face, the channels are many. You see her: the visual channel. You hear her: the auditory channel. You may smell her perfume: the olfactory channel. You may hug her: the tactile channel.

**Noise** **Noise** is interference. Noise keeps a message from being understood and achieving its intended effect. Without noise, all our messages would be communicated with considerable accuracy. But noise is always present. It can be literal—the obnoxious roar of a power lawn mower—or it can be psychological, such as competing thoughts, worries, and feelings that capture our attention. Instead of concentrating on your teacher's lecture, you may start thinking about the chores you need to finish before the end of the day. Whichever kind it is, noise gets in the way of the message and may even distort it. Communicating accurate messages involves minimizing both literal and psychological noise.

It may appear that scholars have neatly identified the components of communication, such as source, message, channel, receiver, and noise, and can prescribe precisely what is needed to make communication effective. While the communication-as-action approach is simple and straightforward, it has a key flaw: Human communication rarely, if ever, is as simple a matter as "what we put in is what we get out." Others cannot automatically know what you mean, even if your meaning seems very clear to *you*.

## Communication as Interaction: Message Exchange

The communication-as-interaction perspective uses the same elements as the action model but adds two new ones: feedback and context.

**Feedback** is the response to a message. Without feedback, communication is less likely to be effective. When you order your pepperoni pizza and the server asks in response, "That's a pepperoni pizza, right?" he has provided feedback to ensure that he decoded the message correctly.

Think of a Ping-Pong game. Like Ping-Pong balls, messages bounce back and forth. We talk; someone listens and responds; we respond to this response. This perspective can be summarized using a physical principle: For every action, there is a reaction.

Feedback can be intentional (applause at the conclusion of a symphony) or unintentional (a yawn as you listen to your uncle tell his story about bears again); or it can be verbal ("That's two burgers and fries, right?") or nonverbal (blushing after being asked for a date).

**Context**—the physical, historical, and psychological communication environment— is a second component recognized by the interaction perspective. All communication takes place in some context. As the cliché goes, "Everyone has to be somewhere." The literal or psychological "somewhere" of communication is the context. A conversation with your good friend on the beach would likely differ from one the two of you might have in a funeral home. Context encompasses not only the physical environment but also the number of people present, their past relationship with the communicators, the communication goal, and the culture in which the communicators are steeped. The psychological context includes the effect of what is going on in the minds of the communicators; the speaker's and listener's personalities and styles of interacting with others influence how messages are understood.

The communication-as-interaction model, as shown in Figure 1.2 on page 14, is more realistic than the communication-as-action model, but it still has limitations. Although it emphasizes feedback and context, it does not quite capture the complexity of the communication process if the communication takes place *simultaneously*. The interaction model of communication still views communication as

**noise**
Interference, either literal or psychological, that hinders the accurate encoding or decoding of a message.

**feedback**
The response to a message.

**context**
The physical, historical, and psychological communication environment.

## Figure 1.2
## A Model of Communication as Interaction

Interaction models of communication include feedback as a response to a message sent by a communication source and place the process in a context.

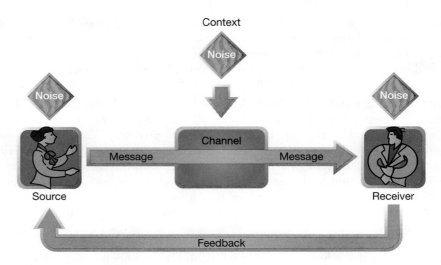

# RECAP

## COMPONENTS OF THE HUMAN COMMUNICATION PROCESS

| Term | Definition |
| --- | --- |
| Source | Originator of an idea or emotion |
| Receiver | Person or group toward whom a source directs messages and who decodes the message |
| Message | Written, spoken, and unspoken elements of communication to which we assign meaning |
| Channel | Pathway through which messages pass between source and receiver |
| Noise | Any literal or psychological interference with the clear encoding or decoding of a message |
| Encoding | Translation of ideas, feelings, and thoughts into a code |
| Decoding | Interpretation of ideas, feelings, and thoughts that have been translated into a code |
| Context | Physical, historical, and psychological communication environment |
| Feedback | Verbal and nonverbal responses to a message |

a linear, step-by-step process. But in many communication situations, both the source and the receiver send and receive messages at the same time.

## Communication as Transaction: Message Creation

The communication-as-transaction perspective, which evolved in the 1960s, acknowledges that when we communicate with another, we are constantly reacting to what our partner is saying and expressing. Most scholars today view this perspective as the most realistic model of communication. Although this model uses such concepts as action and interaction to describe communication, all the interaction is simultaneous. As Figure 1.3 indicates, we send and receive messages concurrently. Even as we talk, we are also interpreting our partner's nonverbal and verbal responses. Transactive communication also occurs within a context, and noise can interfere with the quality and accuracy of our encoding and decoding of messages.

As we send a message, we simultaneously monitor the degree to which the other person understands the message. For example, if you ask your friend out for coffee but you're not sure she'd like to go with you, even as you're talking to her you carefully observe her reactions to determine if she's really interested in your invitation. If you'd really like her company and you sense she'd rather not go with you, you may try harder, using your best persuasive pitch to get your friend to join you. During each communication transaction you have with another person, you look for information about how your message is being received even before you finish talking.

One research team says that communication is "the coordinated management of meaning" through episodes during which the message of one person influences the message of another.[35] Technically, only the sender and receiver of those messages

Context

Noise | Noise | Noise

Message/Feedback

Source/
Receiver

Source/
Receiver

**Figure 1.3**
**A Model of**
**Communication**
**as Transaction**
The source and the receiver
of a message experience
communication simultane-
ously.

can determine where one episode ends and another begins. We make sense out of our world
in ways that are unique to each of us.

# Communication in the 21st Century

When you use media such as a cell phone or
the Internet to carry your message, you are using **mediated communication**.

Although Facebook and other contemporary methods of communicating with others
are relatively recent inventions, people have
been communicating with others without
being face to face for centuries; sending letters and other written messages to others is a
long-standing human practice. The book you
are currently reading provides a form of mediated "distance learning" in that the words were
written some time ago and you are just now
reading them. What's new today is that there
are so many different ways of *immediately* connecting with someone.

## Mediated and Face-to-Face Communication

How is mediated communication different
from live, face-to-face conversation? We provide four key differences:

- *Anonymity.* You may not always know precisely with whom you are communicating when you receive an electronically mediated message. Some methods
  of communicating allow you to make comments and provide feedback without
  revealing who is sending the message.
- *Personal appearance.* We typically place *less* emphasis on a person's physical appearance in mediated communication. Whether you are using a phone, are sending an
  e-mail, are tapping out a text, or are one of over 750 million people connecting
  with others via Facebook, you undoubtedly establish and maintain communication with people you may never meet in person. Yes, we may be curious about

**RE**CAP

## AN EVOLVING MODEL OF HUMAN COMMUNICATION

**Human Communication as Action**
Human communication is linear, with
meaning sent or transferred from
source to receiver.

Human Communication as Action

**Human Communication
as Interaction**
Human communication occurs as the
receiver of the message responds to
the source through feedback. This
interactive model views communication
as a linear sequence of actions
and reactions.

Human Communication as Interaction

**Human Communication
as Transaction**
Human communication is simultaneously interactive. Meaning is created
based on mutual, concurrent sharing
of ideas and feelings. This transactive
model most accurately describes
human communication.

Human Communication as Transaction

**mediated communication**
Any communication that is carried
out using some channel other
than those used in face-to-face
communication.

ZITS © Zits Partnership, King Features Syndicate

**asynchronous communication**
Communication in which timing is out of sync; there is a time delay between when you send a message and when it is received.

**synchronous communication**
Communication in which messages occur in real time—when you speak or write, someone immediately responds to your message.

what our online partner looks like—and webcams and Facebook photos let us see the person with whom we're communicating—but much mediated communication occurs with people we don't see.

- *Distance.* Although we certainly can and do send e-messages to people who live and work in close proximity to us, there is typically greater physical distance between people who are communicating online. Via the Internet, we can just as easily send a message to someone on the other side of the globe as we can to someone who is on the other side of town.
- *Time.* With mediated communication, you have greater control over the timing and pacing of the messages you send and receive than with face-to-face communication. You can decide, for example, when to read posts from your Facebook friends, when to retrieve e-mail and text messages, and when to respond to them. Your interaction with others can be **asynchronous communication**, or out of sync; that is, there may be a time delay between when you send a message and when it is received. With **synchronous communication**, you communicate in real time; when you speak, someone immediately responds to your message.

Switching between face-to-face and mediated communication is a normal, seamless way of communicating with others, especially if you are using computers, mobile phones, iPads, iPods, BlackBerrys, and other technological tools that have always seemed to be part of your life. If you're under age 25, you are much more likely to text friends than to phone them, for example.[36] But, can you really communicate *interpersonally* with someone on the Internet? Yes, of course. You probably do so every day.

We use the Internet to share both dramatic and routine information, as well as to enrich relationships. Research has found, for example, that immediately after the terrorist attacks on September 11, 2001, both the telephone and the Internet were prime means of spreading news of the attacks. People used e-mail not only to share the shocking news, but also to seek interpersonal support and reassurance from friends that their loved ones were safe. We increasingly rely on the Internet to help us form and maintain interpersonal relationships.

Artist Cristin Norine, left, created the Public Isolation Project to demonstrate how we can be simultaneously alone, yet connected to others via mediated communication. She spent one month living alone, but on display in a glass-windowed gallery. Although she was unable to talk with friends and visitors, people such as the guest on the right still found ways to communicate. In what ways do you feel isolated or connected by today's media?

Michael Lloyd/The Oregonian

If you are attending a college or university away from family, friends, and loved ones, you may have found that sending text messages or connecting on Facebook can help you stay in touch with others who are important to you. The evidence summarized in the Communication & Technology box suggests that Facebook is especially helpful in maintaining relationships.[37] College freshmen and their parents also report that e-mail connections reduce homesickness and the sadness parents often feel when their son or daughter leaves home.

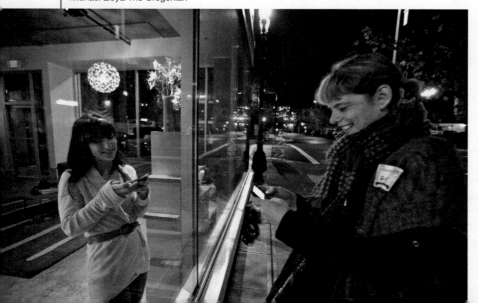

# Communication&TECHNOLOGY

## Got Facebook? How We Connect on Facebook

Facebook is the predominant social networking site of the second decade of the 21st century. Facebook (FB), now more popular than Google as the most popular website in the United States, is the prime way many people stay connected. And it continues to grow, with older users now its fastest-growing segment.[38] But what precisely are we using FB to do? Communication researchers S. Craig Watkins and H. Erin Lee studied college students' use of Facebook to find out. They titled their report *Got Facebook?* If you are like the students in their study, here's what you might be doing.[39]

- *You check FB often.* Almost 80 percent of the students surveyed log on to FB every day, and more than 60 percent said they sign in several times a day. Graduating seems to slow people's FB habits. About 80 percent of current college students sign in three or more times a day, whereas 76 percent of college graduates sign in only once a day. This may be good news for the 20 percent of the survey respondents who said they wished they could spend less time on FB than they currently do.
- *You have a lot of friends.* Watkins and Lee found that the number of FB friends in their study ranged from 1 to more than 10,000, but the average number was just over 300. Slightly more than one-third of FB users had between 1 and 100 friends, but about one-half had between 101 and 500 friends. Students used FB to keep in touch with friends both near and far. About half of respondents said they think it's important to connect to friends who live in a different state or country, whereas 27 percent report that it's *very* important to do so. Sixty-two percent agreed that it is very important to them to communicate with other students.

- *You're an active communicator.* About two-thirds of users post status updates to their profile and add comments and likes to their own and others' statuses. About one-half regularly post messages to friends' profiles, with just over 40 percent posting photos and about 6 percent posting videos—but posting videos and photos seems to be increasing.
- *You're most likely to share pictures.* More than 85 percent of students surveyed share photos. Eighty percent share their relationship status, and 70 percent share their favorite media, such as movies or TV shows. Fewer share their religious views (46 percent) or political views (40 percent), although college graduates are more likely to share their political and religious views than are current college students.
- *Women and men use FB differently.* Men are more likely to share their political and religious views on FB than are women. Men are also more likely to post current events and news-related topics. Women are more likely to post comments and likes. Women also believe it's important to connect with family members on FB; they are more likely than men to post photos of family events. Women are actually more likely to post photos in general (although men are more likely to post videos). When men do post photos, they are likely to share pictures showing their personal interests, such as hobbies, vacations, or activities.[40]

Got Facebook? Apparently you do. Although not everyone finds FB a vital method of communication, for many it's an important means of communicating with others.

## Concerns About Mediated Communication

Although some research has found that mediated communication can be as satisfying as face-to-face conversation,[41] the title of communication researcher Sherry Turkle's book *Alone Together* suggests that even though we may be "connected" electronically, we are nonetheless literally alone, separated from others. As Turkle notes, "Our networked life allows us to hide from each other, even as we are tethered to each other. We'd rather text than talk."[42]

Other researchers have also wondered whether spending a lot of time online reduces people's face-to-face interactions. A team of researchers led by Robert Kraut and Sara Kiesler made headlines when they published the results of their study, which concluded that the more people use the Internet, the less they interact with people in person.[43] These researchers also found a relationship between people who said they were lonely and those who used the Internet. Yet three follow-up studies found that people who use the Internet are *more* likely to have a large number of friends; they are more involved with community activities and overall have greater levels of trust in other people.[44]

The follow-up research suggests that for some people—those who are already prone to being shy or introverted—there may be a link between Internet use and loneliness or feelings of social isolation. This link might exist, however, because shy and introverted people are simply less likely to make contact with others in any way, not because they use the Internet a lot. For people who are generally outgoing and who like to interact with others, in contrast, the Internet is another tool with which to reach out to others. An ever-increasing number of people are meeting in Internet chat rooms or on Facebook or Twitter and eventually developing in-person relationships.

So what do researchers *really* believe about the relationship between Internet use and loneliness? Although a difference of opinion remains about the role of the Internet and its effect on social relationships and loneliness, those people who spend much time online may not be more lonely; rather, they may just feel more comfortable having the ability to control the timing of how they interact with others.

A link may also exist between general apprehension about communicating with others face to face and using the Internet. Cyberspace can be a more comfortable place to communicate with others if you are apprehensive about talking in face-to-face situations or even on the phone. One study found that you are more likely to call a romantic partner on your cell phone when the relationship is going well than when the relationship isn't as positive.[45] When you may be feeling some apprehension or relationship uncertainty, you may prefer to use a less immediate communication channel.

Our recommendation? Your method of communication should fit well with your communication goal. Even though connecting to others via the Internet seems to be a normal way to communicate for a significant and growing percentage of the world's population, at times, relating to someone live and in person is best—especially for expressing feelings and emotions. In other situations, the ease and speed of mediated communication make it preferable to face-to-face communication.

# Communication Characteristics

Now that we have defined communication, noted its importance, and seen how our understanding of communication in general—and the pervasive influence of mediated communication in particular—evolved over the last half of the 20th century, we turn our attention to describing how it works by examining its characteristics. The following characteristics are evident when communication occurs: Communication is inescapable, irreversible, and complicated; it emphasizes content and relationships; and it is governed by rules.

## Communication Is Inescapable

Opportunities to communicate are ubiquitous—they are everywhere. Even before we are born, we respond to movement and sound. With our first cry, we begin the process of announcing to others that we are here. And once we make contact with other humans, we communicate and continue to do so until death. Even though many of our messages are not verbalized, we nonetheless intentionally, and very often unintentionally, send them to others. As noted earlier, some communication scholars question whether it is possible to communicate with someone unintentionally. What experts do agree on is that communication with others plays an ever-present role in our lives. We spend most of our waking hours sending messages to or interpreting messages from others.[46] Even as you silently stand in line at a supermarket checkout line, your lack of eye contact with others waiting in line suggests you're not interested in striking up a conversation. Your unspoken messages may provide cues to which others respond. Even when you don't intend to express a particular idea or feeling, others may try to make sense out of what you are doing—or not doing. Remember: People judge you by your behavior, not your intent.

## Figure 1.4
## A Helical Model of Communication

Interpersonal communication is irreversible. This helical model shows that communication never loops back on itself. Once it begins, it expands infinitely as the communication partners contribute their thoughts and experiences to the exchange.

Source: Copyright © F. E. X. Dance in *Human Communication Theory* (Holt, Rinehart and Winston, 1967), 294. Reprinted with permission.

## Communication Is Irreversible

"Disregard that last statement made by the witness," instructs the judge. Yet the clever lawyer knows that once her client has told the jury that her husband gave her a black eye during an argument, the client cannot really "take back" the message. In conversation, we may try to modify the meaning of a spoken message by saying something like "Oh, I really didn't mean it." But in most cases, the damage has been done. Once created, communication has the physical property of matter; it can't be uncreated. As the helical model in Figure 1.4 suggests, once communication begins, it never loops back on itself. Instead, it continues to be shaped by the events, experiences, and thoughts of the communication partners. A Russian proverb nicely summarizes the point: "Once a word goes out of your mouth, you can never swallow it again."

## Communication Is Complicated

Check out any news source and you will see that there is conflict brewing or erupting in some part of the world. Perhaps you experience conflict and disagreement in your own home or in a relationship with someone you care about. Communicating with others is not simple. If it were, we would know how to reduce dramatically the number of misunderstandings and conflicts in our world. This book could also offer you a list of simple techniques and strategies for blissful management of your communication hassles. You won't find that list in this book or any other credible book. Human communication is complicated because of the number of variables and unknown factors involved when people interact. To illustrate the complexity of the process, communication scholar Dean Barnlund has suggested that whenever we communicate with another person, at least six "people" are really involved:

1. Who you think you are
2. Who you think the other person is
3. Who you think the other person thinks you are
4. Who the other person thinks he or she is
5. Who the other person thinks you are
6. Who the other person thinks you think he or she is.[47]

Whew! And when you add more people to the conversation, it becomes even more complicated.

Life is not only complicated, but also uncertain. There are many things we do not know. We seek information about such everyday things as the weather or about such questions as what others think about us. Several communication theorists suggest that we attempt to manage our uncertainty through communication.[48] In times of high uncertainty (when there are many things we do not know), we will communicate more actively and purposefully so as to manage our uncertainty. For example, we are likely to ask more questions, seek information, and listen intently when we are uncertain.

Adding to the complexity of communication and the problem of our own uncertainty is that messages are not always interpreted as we intend them. Osmo Wiio, a Scandinavian communication scholar, points out the challenges of communicating with others when he suggests the following maxims:

1. If communication can fail, it will.
2. If a message can be understood in different ways, it will be understood in just the way that does the most harm.
3. There is always somebody who knows better than you what you meant by your message.
4. The more communication there is, the more difficult it is for communication to succeed.[49]

Although we are not as pessimistic as Wiio, we do suggest that the task of understanding each other is challenging.

## Communication Emphasizes Content and Relationships

What you say—your words—and how you say it—your tone of voice, amount of eye contact, facial expression, and posture—can reveal much about the true meaning of your message. If one of your roommates loudly and abruptly bellows, "HEY, DORK! CLEAN THIS ROOM!" and another roommate uses the same verbal message but more

What are the informal rules for riding in a crowded elevator?

George Doyle/Thinkstock

gently and playfully suggests, with a smile, "Hey, dork. Clean this room," both are communicating a message aimed at achieving the same outcome. But the two messages have different relationship cues. The first shouted message suggests that your roommate may be grumpy and frustrated that the room still harbors the remains of last night's pizza party, while roommate number two's more calmly expressed request suggests that he or she may be less frustrated and simply wants the room tidied up a bit.

The **content dimension** of communication messages refers to the new information, ideas, or suggested actions the speaker wishes to express. When you tell your roommate you want the room cleaned, you convey an intentional message that you want a tidier room. The **relationship dimension** of a communication message is usually less explicit; it offers cues about the emotions, attitudes, and amount of power and control the speaker directs toward others.[50]

Another way to distinguish between the content and relationship dimensions of communication is to consider that the content of a message refers to *what* is said. The relationship cues are provided in *how* the message is communicated. For example, when you read a transcript of what someone says, you can get a different meaning than you would if you actually heard the person's words.

## Communication Is Governed by Rules

When you play Monopoly, you know there are explicit rules about how to get out of jail, buy Boardwalk, or pass "Go" and get $200. The rules are written down. When you play a game with others, there may even be some unwritten rules, such as "When you play Monopoly with Grandpa, always let him buy Boardwalk. He gets grumpy as a bear before breakfast if he doesn't get to buy it." Rules also govern how we communicate with others. Most of the rules are imbedded in our culture or discussed verbally rather than written in a rulebook.

According to communication researcher Susan Shimanoff, a **rule** is a "followable prescription that indicates what behavior is obligated, preferred, or prohibited in certain contexts."[51] The rules that help define appropriate and inappropriate communication in any given situation may be explicit or implicit. For a class, explicit rules are probably spelled out in your syllabus. But your instructor has other rules that are more implicit. They are not written or verbalized because you learned them long ago: Only one person speaks at a time; you raise your hand to be called on; you do not send text messages.

Communication rules are developed by those involved in the interaction and by the culture in which the individuals are communicating. Most people learn communication rules from experience, by observing and interacting with others.

# Communication Principles for a Lifetime

As you saw on page 4, underlying our description of human communication are five principles that provide the foundation for all effective communication, whether we are communicating with others one on one, in groups or teams, or by presenting a public speech to an audience. Throughout this book, we will emphasize how these principles are woven into the fabric of each communication context. We will expand on the discussion here with a brief introduction and then provide a more comprehensive discussion in the following five chapters to describe and illustrate the scope and power of these principles. Recall the five Communication Principles for a Lifetime that we presented at the beginning of this chapter:

Principle One:      Be aware of your communication with yourself and others.
Principle Two:      Effectively use and interpret verbal messages.
Principle Three:    Effectively use and interpret nonverbal messages.
Principle Four:     Listen and respond thoughtfully to others.
Principle Five:     Appropriately adapt messages to others.

**content dimension**
The new information, ideas, or suggested actions that a communicator wishes to express; *what* is said.

**relationship dimension**
The aspect of a communication message that offers cues about the emotions, attitudes, and amount of power and control the speaker directs toward others; *how* something is said.

**rule**
A followable prescription that indicates what behavior is required or preferred and what behavior is prohibited in a specific situation.

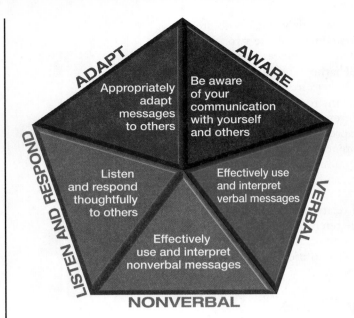

**Figure 1.5**
**Communication Principles for a Lifetime**

These five principles operate together rather than independently to form the basis of the fundamental processes that enhance communication effectiveness. The model in Figure 1.5 illustrates how the principles interrelate. Moving around the model clockwise, the first principle, being aware of your communication with yourself and others, is followed by the two principles that focus on communication messages, verbal messages (Principle Two) and nonverbal messages (Principle Three). The fourth principle, listening and responding, is followed by appropriately adapting messages to others (Principle Five). Together, these five principles can help explain why communication can be either effective or ineffective. A violation of any one principle can result in inappropriate or poor communication.

Throughout this book, we will remind you of how these principles can be used to organize the theory, concepts, and skills we offer as fundamental to human communication. Chapters 2 through 6 will each be devoted to a single principle. Chapters 7 through 15 will apply these principles to the most prevalent communication situations we experience each day—communicating with others interpersonally, in groups and teams, and when giving a talk or presentation.

*To help you see relationships among the five communication principles and the various skills and content we will present in Chapters 7 through 15, we will place in the margin a small version of the model presented in Figure 1.5, like the one that appears in the margin here.* We will also label which principle or principles we are discussing. Refer to the principles pentagon in Figure 1.5 as we introduce the principles.

## Principle One: Be Aware of Your Communication with Yourself and Others

The first foundation principle is to be aware of your communication with yourself and others. Effective communicators are conscious, or "present," when communicating. Ineffective communicators mindlessly or thoughtlessly say and do things that they may later regret. Being aware of your communication includes being conscious not only of the present moment, but also of who you are, your self-concept, your self-worth, and your perceptions of yourself and others. Being aware of your typical communication style is also part of this foundation principle. For example, some people realize that their communication style is to be emotional when interacting with others. Others may be shy.

As noted, self-awareness includes being conscious of your intrapersonal communication messages. By **intrapersonal communication**, we mean the communication that occurs within yourself, including your thoughts, your emotions, and your perceptions of yourself and others. Talking to yourself is an example of intrapersonal communication. Although our intrapersonal communication is often the focus of psychologists, our intrapersonal messages also form the basis of our communication with others.[52]

Competent communicators are aware of the choices they make when they communicate both intrapersonally and with others; incompetent communicators react to others' messages with thoughtless, quick, knee-jerk responses. Because they do not mindfully censor themselves, they may blurt out obscene, offensive, or profane words. Ineffective communicators operate in an unthinking "default" mode. Being aware of our communication is a foundation principle because all the choices we

**intrapersonal communication**
Communication that occurs within yourself, including your thoughts and emotions.

make when communicating rest on our ability to make conscious choices when we respond to others.

Earlier in this chapter, we noted that human communication is the process of making sense out of the world and sharing that sense with others. Being aware of who we are and how we perceive, or "make sense of," what we observe is a fundamental principle that helps explain both effective and ineffective communication. In the next chapter, we develop this principle and foreshadow how it relates to a variety of communication situations.

## Principle Two: Effectively Use and Interpret Verbal Messages

The second principle we introduce here and elaborate on in Chapter 3 is to use and interpret verbal messages effectively. Verbal messages are created with language. A **language** consists of symbols and a system of rules (grammar) that make it possible for people to understand one another.

As noted earlier, a symbol is a word, sound, gesture, or other visual signal that represents a thought, concept, object, or experience. When you read the words on this page, you are looking at symbols that trigger meaning. The word is not the thing it represents; it simply symbolizes the thing or idea.

Your reading skill permits you to make sense out of symbols. The word *tree*, for example, may trigger a thought of the tree you may be reading under now, a tree in your own yard or a nearby park, or a great sequoia you saw on your family vacation in Yosemite National Park. Effective communicators use appropriate symbols to create accurate meaning. Author Daniel Quinn once commented, "No story is devoid of meaning, if you know how to look for it. This is as true of nursery rhymes and daydreams as it is of epic poems."[53] Meaning is created when people have a common or shared understanding.

The effective communicator both encodes and decodes messages accurately; he or she selects appropriate symbols to form a message and interprets carefully the messages of others. The process of using and interpreting symbols is the essence of how we make sense out of the world and share that sense with others. Some fear that greater use of texting would lead to lower skills in language use and overall literacy. Research doesn't support that supposition, however: People who send and receive numerous text messages show no deterioration of language and literacy skills.[54]

Words have power. The words we use to describe ourselves and our world have considerable influence on how we perceive what we experience. Any good advertising copywriter knows how to use words to create a need or desire for a product. Political consultants tell politicians how to craft sound bites that will create just the right audience response. And words can hurt us. As Robert Fulghum wisely noted, "Sticks and stones may break our bones, but words break our hearts."[55] Words have the ability to offend and create stress. For example, derogatory words about someone's gender or ethnicity can do considerable harm. Throughout this book, we will present strategies and suggestions for selecting the best word or symbol to enhance your listeners' understanding.

## Principle Three: Effectively Use and Interpret Nonverbal Messages

Messages are also nonverbal. **Nonverbal communication** is communication by means other than written or spoken language that creates meaning for someone. Nonverbal messages can communicate powerful ideas or express emotions with greater impact than mere words alone. An optimistic hitchhiker's extended thumb and an irate driver's extended finger are nonverbal symbols with clear and intentional meaning. But not all nonverbal symbols are clearly interpreted or even consciously expressed. You may not be aware of your frown when someone asks if he or she may sit next to you in a

**language**
The system of symbols (words or vocabulary) structured by rules (grammar) that makes it possible for people to understand one another.

**nonverbal communication**
Communication by means other than written or spoken language that creates meaning for someone.

vacant seat in a restaurant. Or your son may excitedly be telling you about his field trip to the fire station while you stare into the screen of your computer. You have no intention of telling your son he is not important, but your lack of nonverbal responsiveness speaks volumes. Our nonverbal messages communicate how we feel toward others.

When there is a contradiction between what you say and what you do, your nonverbal message is more believable than your verbal message. When asked how your meal is, you may tell your server that the meal is "great," but your nonverbal message—facial expression and flat tone of voice—clearly communicates your unhappiness with the cuisine. As noted when we discussed the concept of content and relationship messages, our nonverbal cues often tell people how to interpret what we are saying.

Effective communicators develop skill in interpreting nonverbal messages of others. They also monitor their own messages to avoid unintentionally sending contradictory verbal and nonverbal messages. It's sometimes hard to interpret nonverbal messages because they don't have a neat beginning and ending point—the flow of information is continuous. It may not be clear where one gesture stops and another begins. Cultural differences, combined with the fact that so many different nonverbal channels (such as eye contact, facial expression, gestures, posture) can be used at the same time, make it tricky to "read" someone's nonverbal message accurately. We amplify our discussion of the power of nonverbal messages in Chapter 4.

## Principle Four: Listen and Respond Thoughtfully to Others

So far, our list of principles may appear to place much of the burden of achieving communication success on the person sending the message. But effective communication with others also places considerable responsibility on the listener. As explained earlier in the chapter, because communication is a transactional process—both senders and receivers are mutually and usually simultaneously expressing and responding to symbols—listening to words with sensitivity and "listening between the lines" to nonverbal messages join our list of fundamental principles.

Listening can be hard because it looks easy. You spend more time listening than performing any other communication activity—probably more than any other thing you do except sleep.[56] Despite spending the greatest portion of our communication time listening, research suggests that many if not most of us do not always listen effectively. What's tricky about listening? Both psychological, or internal, noise (our own thoughts, needs, and emotions) and external distractions (noise in the surroundings in which we listen) can create barriers to effective listening. That it is perceived to be a passive rather than an active task makes listening and accurately interpreting information a challenge. Effective listening is *not* a passive task at all; the effective and sensitive listener works hard to stay on task and focus mindfully on a sender's message.

At the heart of this principle is developing sensitivity to others. We are not talking about the touchy-feely-emotional-what-I-hear-you-saying approach to interpersonal relationships. We are, however, suggesting that you develop an orientation or sensitivity to others when you listen and respond. When you are **other-oriented**, you consider the needs, motives, desires, and goals of your communication partners while still maintaining your own integrity. The choices you make in both forming the message and selecting when to share it should take into consideration your partner's thoughts and feelings.

Most of us are egocentric—self-focused. We are born with an innate desire to meet our own needs. As we grow and mature, we develop a consciousness of more than our own needs. Scholars of evolution might argue that it is good that we are self-focused; looking out for number one is what perpetuates the human race. Yet an *exclusive* focus on ourselves inhibits effective communication. Do you know anyone who is self-absorbed? Most of us find such a person tedious and uncomfortable to be around. People who are skilled communicators both listen and respond with sensitivity; they are other-oriented.

**other-oriented**
Being focused on the needs and concerns of others while maintaining one's personal integrity.

# Principle Five: Appropriately Adapt Messages to Others

It is not enough to be sensitive and to accurately understand others; you must use the information you gather to modify the messages you construct. It is important to **adapt** your response appropriately to your listener. When you adapt a message, you make choices about how best to formulate it and respond to someone to achieve your communication goals. Adapting to a listener does not mean that you tell a listener only what he or she wants to hear. That would be unethical. Adapting involves appropriately editing and shaping your responses so that others accurately understand your messages and so that you achieve your goal without coercing or using false information or other unethical methods. To adapt a message is to make choices about all aspects of message content and delivery.

Regardless of whether you are giving a presentation, talking with a friend, or participating in a small-group meeting, as an effective communicator you consider who the listeners are when deciding what to say and how best to say it. One of the elements of a message that you adapt when communicating with others is the structure or organization of what you say. Informal interpersonal conversations typically do not follow a rigid, outlined structure. Our conversation freely bounces from one topic to another.

**adapt**
To adjust both what is communicated and how a message is communicated; to make choices about how best to formulate a message and respond to others to achieve your communication goals.

# Communication & DIVERSITY

## Communication Principles for a Lifetime: Principles for All Cultures?

We've suggested that our five Principles for a Lifetime constitute a framework for all human communication. Again, let's review the five principles:

| | |
|---|---|
| Principle One: | Be aware of your communication with yourself and others. |
| Principle Two: | Effectively use and interpret verbal messages. |
| Principle Three: | Effectively use and interpret nonverbal messages. |
| Principle Four: | Listen and respond thoughtfully to others. |
| Principle Five: | Appropriately adapt messages to others. |

The question is "How applicable are these five Principles for a Lifetime to communication in a variety of cultures?" Culture is the learned system of knowledge, behavior, attitudes, beliefs, values, and norms that is shared by a group of people. People who were born and raised in Asian countries, for example, have different cultural expectations than do people who were born and raised in North America. But do these five communication principles apply to *all* people everywhere, despite cultural differences and the wide variety of cultural traditions and backgrounds in the world? Is it true that all people should be aware of their communication, use and interpret verbal and nonverbal messages, listen and respond thoughtfully, and appropriately adapt their messages to others?

We're not suggesting that all cultures use and interpret verbal or nonverbal messages the same way (Principles

Two and Three); there are obvious differences from one culture to another in language and use of nonverbal cues. But we are suggesting that in all cultures, the use and interpretation of verbal and nonverbal messages is important in determining whether communication is effective. We are also not saying that people from all cultures adapt messages in the same way (Principle Five). There are clear cultural differences in the way people choose to adapt messages to others. But do people in all cultures adapt messages to others in some way, even though the interpretation of the adapted message varies from culture to culture? We suggest that these five fundamental principles may provide a common framework for talking about communication in a variety of cultures. Do you agree or disagree with this statement?

In your communication class, there are undoubtedly people from a variety of cultural backgrounds. Perhaps some of your classmates grew up in countries other than your own. Respond to the following questions, and then compare your answers with those of your fellow students.

1. How applicable are the five communication principles to your cultural experience?
2. Do any of the communication principles *not* apply in your culture?
3. Can you think of another fundamental communication principle that is not included in our list of five? If so, what is it?
4. Do you agree that these communication principles apply to all people?

Formal presentations delivered in North America, however, are usually expected to have a more explicit structure—an introduction, a body, and a conclusion. The major ideas of a formal presentation are expected to be clearly identified. North American audiences also seem to prefer a presentation that could be easily outlined. Other cultures, such as those in the Middle East, expect a greater use of stories, examples, and illustrations, rather than a clearly structured, outlined presentation. Knowing your audience's expectations can help you adapt your message so that it will be listened to and understood.

Our point is that effective communicators not only listen and respond with sensitivity; they use the information they gather to shape the message and delivery of their responses to others. In Chapter 6, we will discuss this principle in greater detail by discussing the diverse nature of potential listeners and how to adapt to them. Adapting to differences in culture and gender, for example, may mean the difference between a message that is well received and one that creates hostility.

**interpersonal communication**
Communication that occurs simultaneously between two people who attempt to mutually influence each other, usually for the purpose of managing relationships.

**impersonal communication**
Communication that treats people as objects or that responds only to their roles rather than to who they are as unique people.

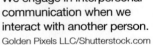

We engage in interpersonal communication when we interact with another person.
Golden Pixels LLC/Shutterstock.com

# Communicating with Others: Interpersonal, Group, and Presentational Communication

The five communication principles that we unveiled in this chapter operate whenever people communicate, regardless of the number of people present or the content of their messages. The three classic contexts to which communication researchers apply these principles are interpersonal communication, group communication, and presentational communication.

Each of the next five chapters is devoted to one of the five principles we've identified and relates these principles to the three most typical communication situations you will experience. As noted, a growing collection of research findings helps us understand how the Internet and other technological tools are affecting our communication. When appropriate, we'll offer some ideas and suggestions for interacting with others via mediated settings.

We now turn our attention to introducing these three contexts of communication: interpersonal, group, and presentational communication.

## Interpersonal Communication

**Interpersonal communication** is a special form of human communication that occurs when we interact simultaneously with another person and attempt to mutually influence each other, usually for the purpose of managing relationships. At the heart of this definition is the role of communication in developing unique relationships with other people.[57]

For many years, communication scholars considered any two-person interaction interpersonal communication. Today interpersonal communication is defined not by the number of people who communicate but by the quality of communication that occurs when we express and interpret verbal and nonverbal messages. Interpersonal communication occurs not just when we interact with someone, but when we treat the other person as a one-of-a-kind human being.

**Impersonal communication** occurs when we treat people as objects, or when we respond to their roles rather than to who they are as unique people. Based on this definition, asking a server for a glass of water at a restaurant is impersonal rather than interpersonal communication. If you strike up a conversation with the server—say you discover it's her birthday or that you both know the same people—your conversation moves from impersonal to interpersonal. We're not suggesting that impersonal communication is unimportant or necessarily inferior or bad. Competent communicators are able to interact with others in a variety of situations.

Interpersonal communication is not a one-sided monologue; it's a dialogue in the sense that all communicators are influenced and meaning is created simultaneously.[58] Interpersonal communication reflects the characteristics of the transactional model of communication discussed earlier.

A final attribute, and among the most important, is that interpersonal communication is the fundamental means we use to manage our relationships. A relationship is an ongoing connection we make with others through interpersonal communication. To relate to someone is to give and take, listen and respond, act and react. When we talk about a good or positive relationship with someone, we often mean that we are "together" or "in sync." In an effective relationship, the individuals involved believe that their verbal and nonverbal messages are understood and that there is a relational harmony based on a common understanding between the communicators. We will apply the five principles of human communication to interpersonal communication in Chapters 7 and 8.

## Group Communication

Human beings are social, collaborative creatures. We do most of our work and play in groups. One focus of this book is the communication that occurs in groups—how we make sense of our participation in groups and share that sense with others. We define **small group communication** as the verbal and nonverbal message transactions that occur among three to about fifteen people who share a common goal, who feel a sense of belonging to the group, and who exert influence on one another.[59] Let's examine some elements of our definition.

- *A number of people.* A **group** must have at least three people; two interacting people are usually referred to as a **dyad**. What is the upper limit on the number of people for meaningful group discussion? Some scholars say fifteen; others say more.[60] The bigger the group, the less influence each person has on the group and the greater the chance that subgroups or splinter factions will emerge.
- *A common goal.* Our definition of group communication includes the notion that to be considered a group, people need a common goal—a mutually acknowledged reason for the group's existence.
- *A sense of belonging.* Members of a small group need to have a sense of identity with the group; they should sense that it is their group. A group of travelers waiting for the subway may have a common goal of catching the train, but they probably don't see themselves as belonging to a group with a single goal of going to the same place.

Note that we do not mention a common location as part of this definition. Today's globe-shrinking technology makes it possible for people to be linked with others in virtual groups even when they are in different physical locations.[61] A common goal and sense of belonging become even more important in virtual groups. Some research suggests, for example, that technology can prolong disagreements, making virtual groups and teams lose steam and become less effective than other groups. In Chapters 9 and 10, we will discuss more thoroughly the five Communication Principles for a Lifetime as they apply to groups and teams.

## Presentational Communication

For many people, speaking in public is a major source of anxiety. **Presentational communication** occurs when a speaker addresses a gathering of people to inform, persuade, or entertain. In this book, we will focus on applying the principles of

**small group communication**
The transactive process of creating meaning among three to about fifteen people who share a common purpose, feel a sense of belonging to the group, and exert influence on one another.

**group**
A collection of people who have a common goal, feel a sense of belonging to the group, and influence one another.

**dyad**
Two interacting people.

**presentational communication**
Communication that occurs when a speaker addresses a gathering of people to inform, persuade, or entertain them.

communication when informing and persuading listeners. Effective presentational speakers are aware of their communication and how they interact with their audience. They also effectively use, interpret, and understand verbal and nonverbal messages; listen and respond to their audience; and adapt their message to their listeners.

Of the three contexts in which the principles we present in this book are applied, this context has the distinction of being the one that has been formally studied the longest. In 333 BCE, Aristotle wrote his famous *Rhetoric*, the first fully developed treatment of the study of speech to convince an audience. He defined **rhetoric** as the process of discovering the available means of persuasion in a given situation. In essence, persuasion is the process of using symbols to persuade others. Today many communication departments have several courses that focus exclusively on how to persuade others, design and deliver both informative and persuasive messages, and evaluate the messages of others. Although we have certainly advanced in our understanding of informing and persuading others in the past two millennia, much of what Aristotle taught has withstood the tests of both time and scholarly research.

Our focus in Chapters 11 through 15 is on basic strategies for designing and delivering a speech to others. As with interpersonal and group communication, we will discuss presentational communication through the perspective of the five principles that anchor our study.

Are interpersonal, group, and presentational communication the only contexts in which communication takes place? The answer is no—communication takes place in a variety of situations. One of the most prominent forms of communication in our lives involves the media.

As noted earlier, mediated communication is any communication expressed via some channel other than those used when we communicate in person. Some physical medium, such as a wire, a cable, a phone line, a cell phone, a TV set, a computer, or some other technology, carries the messages between sender and receiver. The channel of communication is not only physical but also electronic, in the form of the signal coming into your TV set, your phone, or your computer.

**Mass communication** occurs when a mediated message is sent to many people at the same time. A TV or radio broadcast is an example of mass communication. As noted earlier in this chapter, our focus in this book is on unmediated communication. This is not meant to suggest that mass communication is not important, only that it is beyond the scope of this book. At some colleges and universities, mass communication is a focus of study in a separate department; at other colleges and universities, the study of mass communication is included in the same department that studies all human communication.

Many researchers study the communication that occurs in organizations such as businesses, government agencies, and nonprofits such as the Red Cross and other charities. **Organizational communication** is the study of human communication as it occurs within organizations. Although organizational communication includes applications of interpersonal, group, and presentational communication, there are unique ways in which communication functions in contemporary organizations.

**Health communication**, a growing area of communication study, examines the role and importance of communication that has an effect on our health. Health communication researchers study the interaction between health care workers (such as physicians, physician's assistants, and nurses) and patients. They also study how to best design campaigns to encourage healthy habits (messages about getting fit, losing weight, avoiding sexually transmitted diseases, or quitting smoking).

In the chapters ahead, we will analyze the five Communication Principles for a Lifetime as they apply to the three typical unmediated communication situations—interpersonal, group, and presentational communication. Our primary goals are to help you better understand your communication and to help you improve your ability to communicate with others for the rest of your life.

**rhetoric**
The process of using symbols to influence or persuade others.

**mass communication**
Communication accomplished through a mediated message that is sent to many people at the same time.

**organizational communication**
The study of human communication as it occurs within organizations.

**health communication**
The study of communication that has an effect on human health.

# STUDY GUIDE:
## Review, Apply, and Assess Your Knowledge and Skill

## Why Study Communication? p. 4

Communication is essential for life. It is important to learn about communication, because being a skilled communicator can help you

- Obtain a good job.
- Enhance the quality of your relationships.
- Improve your physical and emotional health.

## Communication Defined p. 7

At its most basic level, communication is the process of acting on information. Human communication is the process of making sense out of the world and sharing that sense with others by creating meaning through verbal and nonverbal messages.

### Terms to Know

| | |
|---|---|
| Communication | p. 7 |
| Human Communication | p. 7 |
| Symbol | p. 8 |

## Communication Competence p. 8

To be both effective and appropriate, a communication message should

- Be understood as the communicator intended it to be understood.
- Achieve the communicator's intended effect.
- Be ethical.

### Terms to Know

| | |
|---|---|
| Ethics | p. 9 |

## Communication Models p. 11

Early models viewed human communication as a simple message-transfer process. Later models evolved to view communication as interaction and then as simultaneous transaction. Key components of communication include source, receiver, message, channel, noise, context, and feedback.

### Terms to Know

| | | | |
|---|---|---|---|
| Source | p. 12 | Channel | p. 12 |
| Encoding | p. 12 | Noise | p. 13 |
| Decoding | p. 12 | Feedback | p. 13 |
| Receiver | p. 12 | Context | p. 13 |
| Message | p. 12 | | |

# REVIEWING
## What You Know

## Communication in the 21st Century                 p. 15

Today, we commonly use various forms of media to communicate, either asynchronously or synchronously. Mediated communication is usually more anonymous than in-person communication and places less emphasis on a person's physical appearance. Shy or introverted people may prefer online to in-person communication, as do people who are feeling temporary uncertainty about their relationships.

### Terms to Know

| | | | |
|---|---|---|---|
| Mediated Communication | p. 15 | Synchronous Communication | p. 16 |
| Asynchronous Communication | p. 16 | | |

## Communication Characteristics                 p. 18

Communication has five characteristics: It is inescapable, it is irreversible, it is complicated, it emphasizes content and relationships, and it is governed by rules.

### Terms to Know

| | |
|---|---|
| Content Dimension | p. 21 |
| Relationship Dimension | p. 21 |
| Rule | p. 21 |

## Communication Principles for a Lifetime                 p. 21

Five principles are fundamental to good communication.

1. Be aware of your communication with yourself and others. Being mindful of your communication is important to help you improve your communication.
2. Effectively use and interpret verbal messages. Words are powerful and influence our thoughts, actions, and relationships with others.
3. Effectively use and interpret nonverbal messages. Unspoken cues provide important information about our emotions, feelings, and attitudes.
4. Listen and respond thoughtfully to others. Being able to interpret the messages of others accurately enhances comprehension and relational empathy.
5. Appropriately adapt messages to others. It is important to adapt messages to others to enhance both understanding and empathy.

### Terms to Know

| | | | |
|---|---|---|---|
| Intrapersonal Communication | p. 22 | Other-Oriented | p. 24 |
| Language | p. 23 | Adapt | p. 25 |
| Nonverbal Communication | p. 23 | | |

## Communicating with Others: Interpersonal, Group, and Presentational Communication                 p. 26

The five principles presented in this chapter are applicable to the most common communication contexts: interpersonal, group, and presentational communication.

- Interpersonal communication is a special form of communication that occurs when two people interact simultaneously and mutually influence each other, usually for the purpose of managing relationships.
- Small group communication is interaction among a small group of people who share a common purpose or goal, who feel a sense of belonging to the group, and who exert influence on the others in the group.

- Presentational communication occurs when a speaker addresses an audience for the purpose of informing, persuading, or entertaining.

### Terms to Know

| | | | |
|---|---|---|---|
| Interpersonal Communication | p. 26 | Presentational Communication | p. 27 |
| Impersonal Communication | p. 26 | Rhetoric | p. 28 |
| Small Group Communication | p. 27 | Mass Communication | p. 28 |
| Group | p. 27 | Organizational Communication | p. 28 |
| Dyad | p. 27 | Health Communication | p. 28 |

### Principle One:
### Be aware of your communication with yourself and others.

- Be aware of your intrapersonal communication.
- Be conscious of how your own "self-talk" has an effect on your communication with others and your overall communication behavior.
- Be aware of the communication behavior of others.

### Principle Two:
### Effectively use and interpret verbal messages.

- Use clear and precise words to explain ideas and concepts to others.
- Make a concerted effort to accurately interpret the words of others.

### Principle Three:
### Effectively use and interpret nonverbal messages.

- Use nonverbal, unspoken cues to express feelings and emotions to others or to modify the explicit verbal message you are communicating to others.
- Make a conscious effort to accurately decode the nonverbal messages of others.

### Principle Four:
### Listen and respond thoughtfully to others.

- Be other-oriented by taking special care to listen to both the verbal and the nonverbal messages of others.
- Be deliberate in how you provide feedback to those to whom you are listening.

### Principle Five:
### Appropriately adapt messages to others.

- Use your listening and nonverbal communication skills to help you appropriately adjust both your message and how you communicate it to others.
- Make ethical choices about how to best formulate a message and respond to others to achieve your communication goals.

# APPLYING
# Principles
# for a
# Lifetime

# ASSESSING Your Skill

## Assessing Your Willingness to Communicate (WTC)

As you begin your study of communication, complete the following assessment measure to determine your willingness to communicate in several communication situations.

*Directions:* Below are twenty situations in which a person might choose to communicate or not to communicate. Presume you have *completely free choice*. Indicate in the space at the left what percent of the time you would choose to communicate in each situation (0 = *never*, 100 = *always*).

1. ____ Talk with a service station attendant.

2. ____ Talk with a physician.

3. ____ Present a talk to a group of strangers.

4. ____ Talk with an acquaintance while standing in line.

5. ____ Talk with a salesperson in a store.

6. ____ Talk in a large meeting of friends.

7. ____ Talk with a police officer.

8. ____ Talk in a small group of strangers.

9. ____ Talk with a friend while standing in line.

10. ____ Talk with a waiter/waitress in a restaurant.

11. ____ Talk in a large meeting of acquaintances.

12. ____ Talk with a stranger while standing in line.

13. ____ Talk with a secretary.

14. ____ Present a talk to a group of friends.

15. ____ Talk in a small group of acquaintances.

16. ____ Talk with a garbage collector.

17. ____ Talk in a large meeting of strangers.

18. ____ Talk with a spouse (or girlfriend/boyfriend).

19. ____ Talk in a small group of friends.

20. ____ Present a talk to a group of acquaintances.

## Scoring Instructions

The WTC score is designed to indicate how willing you are to communicate in a variety of contexts with different types of receivers. The higher your overall WTC score, the more willing you are to communicate in general. Similarly, the higher your subscore for a type of context or audience, the more willing you are to communicate in that type of context or with that type of audience.

The WTC assessment permits computation of one total score and seven subscores. The subscores relate to willingness to communicate in four common communication contexts and with three types of audiences.

| *Subscore for Communication Context* | *Scoring Formula* |
| --- | --- |
| Group discussions | Add scores for items 8, 15, 19; then divide by 3. |
| Meetings | Add scores for items 6, 11, 17; then divide by 3. |
| Interpersonal conversations | Add scores for items 4, 9, 12; then divide by 3. |
| Public speaking | Add scores for items 3, 14, 20; then divide by 3. |
| *Subscore for Audience Type* | |
| Stranger | Add scores for items 3, 8, 12, 17; then divide by 4. |
| Acquaintance | Add scores for items 4, 11, 15, 20; then divide by 4. |
| Friend | Add scores for items 6, 9, 14, 19; then divide by 4. |

To compute your total WTC score, add the subscores for Stranger, Acquaintance, and Friend. Then divide by 3.

*Norms for WTC scores*

| | |
|---|---|
| Group discussions | > 89, high WTC; < 57, low WTC |
| Meetings | > 80, high WTC; < 39, low WTC |
| Interpersonal conversations | > 94, high WTC; < 64, low WTC |
| Public speaking | > 78, high WTC; < 33, low WTC |
| Stranger | > 63, high WTC; < 18, low WTC |
| Acquaintance | > 92, high WTC; < 57, low WTC |
| Friend | > 99, high WTC; < 71, low WTC |
| *Total WTC* | > 82, high overall WTC; < 52, low overall WTC |

Source: Richmond, Virginia P.; McCroskey, James C., *Communication: Apprehension, Avoidance, and Effectiveness* 5th Ed., © 1998. Reprinted and Electronically reproduced by permission of Pearson Education, Inc., Upper Saddle River, New Jersey.

Most colleges and universities offer courses in communication and allow students to major or minor in communication, speech communication, or communication studies. The study of human communication may also be among the offerings of a department that focuses on mass communication or theater. Students who select communication as a major or a minor pursue a variety of careers and professions, including business, law, government, education, and social services.

Several academic communication organizations offer a wealth of resources, information, and ideas about human communication. Chances are that the instructor for your communication course is a member of one or more of these organizations. The following websites offer a panoramic view of the communication discipline from an academic perspective.

- **The National Communication Organization** <www.natcom.org>
- **World Communication Organization** <http://wcaweb.org>
- **International Communication Association** <www.icahdq.org>

# WEB RESOURCES for More Review, Application, and Assessment

A person who buries his head in the sand offers
an engaging target.

MABEL A. KEENAN

# Chapter OUTLINE

- Self-Awareness: How Well Do You Know Yourself?
- Self-Concept: Who Are You?
- Self-Esteem: What Is Your Value?
- Communication and the Enhancement of Self-Esteem
- The Perception Process
- Communicate to Enhance Your Powers of Perception
- Study Guide: Review, Apply, and Assess Your Knowledge and Skill

# Chapter OBJECTIVES

After studying this chapter, you should be able to

1. Discuss the importance of self-awareness in the process of improving one's communication skills.
2. Define attitudes, beliefs, and values as they relate to self-concept development.
3. Describe the four factors and four characteristics of identity that affect the development of self-concept.
4. Describe how gender, social comparisons, self-expectations, and self-fulfilling prophecies affect one's self-esteem.
5. Explain the three stages of perception and why people differ in their perceptions of people and events.

Patricia Malina /Shutterstock.com

# 2 | Self-Awareness and Communication

**Figure 2.1**
**Communication Principles for a Lifetime**

Do you have your own personal web page? How about a Facebook page, where you can personalize your profile to let people know more about you? If you answered yes to either or both questions, how do you make decisions about what to include in your profile or website? What photos are on your website or Facebook wall? The Facebook photo that accompanies your profile—is it of you, other people, pets, or a media character such as Curly from *The Three Stooges*? How much information about yourself do you choose to reveal on your Facebook profile—physical characteristics, intellectual pursuits, personality traits, relationship status, hobbies and interests? Is your profile or website an accurate representation of who you are as a person, or does it just reflect a part of who you perceive yourself to be? Developing a personal website or Facebook profile is an activity that relies on a central, important element: awareness.

Stephen Covey, author of the best-selling book *The Seven Habits of Highly Effective People*, describes self-awareness as a characteristic that "enables us to stand apart and examine even the way we 'see' ourselves."[1] Interpersonal communication scholar David Johnson points out the importance of self-awareness: "Self-awareness is the key to self-knowledge, self-understanding, and self-disclosure. Being open with another person begins with being aware of who you are and what you are like. To disclose your feelings and reactions, you must be aware of them.[2]

Figure 2.1 presents the Communication Principles for a Lifetime model introduced in Chapter 1; the five principles provide the foundation for effective communication in various contexts you may encounter throughout your life. In this chapter, we explore the first principle: *Be aware of your communication with yourself and others.* Developing self-awareness involves being conscious not only of the present moment, but also of who you are, your values, and your perception of yourself and others.

# Self-Awareness: How Well Do You Know Yourself?

Many of us experience moments in our lives when we're acutely aware that we're learning something important—something that will change us in some profound way. (College years are typically full of these moments.) While a great deal of self-awareness comes gradually and simply, some is thrust upon us in dramatic fashion, and we take leaps in our maturity and understanding of ourselves. In this chapter, we deal with all forms of awareness—the simple and the profound, the casual and the dramatic—because any kind of awareness influence how we communicate and respond to communication from others. Becoming more self-aware is a never-ending process in life. You don't reach a point where you've maxed out your self-awareness.

By one definition, **self-awareness** is "the capacity to observe and reflect upon one's own mental states."[3] A related view holds that self-awareness, sometimes referred to as **symbolic self-awareness**, is the unique human ability to develop a representation of oneself and communicate that representation to others through language.[4]

Sociologist Derek Layder outlines five properties of the self; our challenge is to come to a greater understanding of each property within ourselves:[5]

- The self is psychological, but operates within a social context.
- An emotional aspect to the self—our inner mental existence—fuels our behavior.

**self-awareness**
The capacity to observe and reflect on one's own mental states.

**symbolic self-awareness**
A unique human ability to develop and communicate a representation of oneself to others through language.

- The self is a focal point of action and control.
- The self is flexible and pliable, in that we are complex and sometimes contradictory, communicating various sides of our personalities to reflect a multifaceted self.
- An important component of the self is a spiritual or "higher" self, which some people ignore or resist and which is often overlooked in research.

The better we understand the complex, multilayered nature of the self, the more aware we will become of our own being; and this awareness, we believe, is critical in becoming an effective communicator. A framework attributed to Abraham Maslow helps explain the process of becoming self-aware; it has also been used to explain the attainment of communication skill. The framework suggests that people operate at one of four levels:

1. *Unconscious incompetence.* We are unaware of our own incompetence. We don't know what we don't know.
2. *Conscious incompetence.* At this level, we become aware or conscious that we are not competent; we know what we don't know.
3. *Conscious competence.* We are aware that we know or can do something, but it has not yet become an integrated skill or habit.
4. *Unconscious competence.* At this level, skills become second nature. We know or can do something but don't have to concentrate to be able to act on that knowledge or draw on that skill.

To illustrate this framework, let's look at an example. Your coworker Stella sometimes says inappropriate things; she just doesn't seem to know how to talk to people in a way that doesn't make her come across like she was raised by wolves. Stella is at Maslow's level 1 when it comes to communication: She doesn't know that she communicates poorly. Eventually, customers and coworkers complain to Stella's supervisor. The supervisor calls Stella into the office, reprimands her for her poor communication skills, and requires her to enroll in communication training so that she can improve. Now Stella's at level 2 because she has become conscious of her own incompetence as a communicator. Stella embraces her communication training and, once back on the job, actively works to improve how she relates to coworkers, bosses, and customers. Her hard work pays off when her colleagues notice the changes she's making and provide positive feedback. Stella achieves level 3, in which she is conscious of her own competence as a communicator. If Stella continues to progress over time, at some point she may reach level 4, in which communication effectiveness is incorporated into her style and self-concept and is no longer something she must make a conscious effort to achieve.

Almost any communication skill can be described in terms of these four levels. It's also possible to be at one level with one skill and at another level with another skill. For instance, you may skillfully meet new people but poorly manage conflict with a close personal friend. Someone may be very engaging when conversing with friends, but she or he would rather have surgery than give a presentation.

Reading a book like this one and taking a communication course like the one you're enrolled in can spark moments of heightened self-awareness. You'll no doubt be challenged to think long and hard about who you are, inventorying what you believe about yourself and how such aspects of identity as gender, ethnicity, nationality, sexual orientation, and social class contribute to your view of self. You'll be encouraged to go a step further and to consider how you communicate that view of self to others. But the key beginning point is awareness. As Phil McGraw (a.k.a. Dr. Phil) says, "Can't fix what you don't acknowledge."

# Self-Concept: Who Are You?

If someone were to ask you "Who are you?" how would you respond? You might start with basic demographic information like your age and where you're from; perhaps you would describe yourself in relation to groups and organizations to which you belong.

Or you might talk about yourself according to various roles you assume, like "I'm a student at State" or "I'm so-and-so's daughter (or son)." Whatever answer you give will be incomplete because you can't really convey the totality of who you are to others.

Psychologist Karen Horney defines **self** as "that central inner force, common to all human beings and yet unique in each which is the deep source of growth."[6] Your "Who are you?" responses are also part of your **self-concept**—your interior identity or subjective description of who you think you are, which remains relatively stable despite the changing world in which you live.[7] Some people use the term *self-image* synonymously with self-concept, but we want to avoid confusion over these terms. We subscribe to a narrower meaning for the term self-image, in that **self-image** is your view of yourself *in a particular situation*.[8] That view changes from situation to situation. For example, you may be extroverted in chemistry class but not at a party where you don't know too many people. You may become very nervous when talking to an authority figure but be quite comfortable communicating with people your own age. You have several self-images, because they change as the situation changes, but they are part of the larger component we call self-concept. The self-concept is the way we *consistently* describe ourselves to others; it is deeply rooted and slow to change.

## Self-Concept Components

Three components are present within one's self-concept: **attitude**, **belief**, and **value**. Table 2.1 describes each in more detail. Of the three elements, attitudes are the most superficial and likely to change; values are more at the core of a person and least likely to change.

## One or Many Selves?

"I'm just not myself this morning," sighs Sandy, as she drags herself out the door to head to class. If she is not herself, *who is she?* Do each of us have just one self? Or is there a more "real self" buried somewhere within?

One of the most enduring and widely accepted frameworks for understanding the self was developed by philosopher William James. He identified three components of the self: the material self, the social self, and the spiritual self.[9]

**The Material Self**   Perhaps you've heard the statement "You are what you eat." The material self goes a step further by suggesting "You are what you have." The **material self** is a total of all the tangible things you own: your body, your possessions, your home.

**self**
The sum of who you are as a person; your central inner force.

**self-concept**
Your interior identity or subjective description of who you think you are.

**self-image**
Your view of yourself in a particular situation or circumstance.

**attitude**
A learned predisposition to respond to a person, object, or idea in a favorable or unfavorable way.

**belief**
The way in which you structure your understanding of reality—what is true and what is false.

**value**
An enduring concept of good and bad or right and wrong.

**material self**
The element of the self reflected in all the tangible things you own.

## Table 2.1
## Self-Concept Components

| COMPONENT | DEFINITION | DIMENSIONS | EXAMPLE |
| --- | --- | --- | --- |
| Attitude | Learned predisposition to respond favorably or unfavorably toward something | Likes–Dislikes | You like ice cream, video games, and free music downloads. |
| Belief | Way in which you structure reality | True–False | You believe your parents love you. |
| Value | Enduring concept of right and wrong | Good–Bad | You value honesty and truth. |

# Communication&**DIVERSITY**

## Self-Concept from East and West

The definition of self-concept in this chapter emphasizes that your self-concept stays relatively stable despite changes in your life and in the world around you. This view of self-concept is culturally rooted in a Western perspective, however. Communication scholar Gabriel Bukobza has found that people from Eastern cultures tend to view one's self-concept as "malleable, contextual, inconsistent, relational, interdependent, and oriented to group hierarchy."[10] According to this view, your self-concept could be quite open to change.

Perhaps one reason culture affects our ideas about the permanence of self-concept is that different cultures have different views of the *sources* from which we get our self-concepts. Studies suggest that in Asian countries, the self-concept is constructed around significant social groups—such as one's immediate family, extended family, groups—such as one's immediate family, extended family, or community—with each member wanting to fit in and feeling a strong commitment to group identity. In contrast, Westerners first use personal reflection and investigation to form the self-concept and then pursue feedback from others to validate the view of self.[11] We like it when others' views correspond with our own view of self, and we tend to reject messages (and people) who negate our self-concept.

In this global village in which we live, where access to members of other cultural groups is only a mouse click away, it's important to remember that even the most basic element—the self-concept—can vary interculturally. Americans tend to hold independence and individuality as core positive qualities within our self-concepts but let's refrain from judging someone from another culture whose self-concept stems from strong ties to others and an emphasis on community over individual.[12]

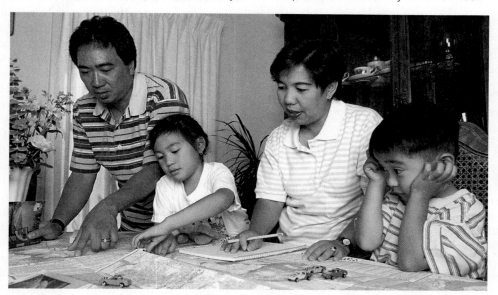

The self-concept that we develop through communication with our family stays with us throughout our life.
© Michael Newman/PhotoEdit

One element of the material self receives considerable attention in our culture: the body. Do you like the way you look? Most of us would like to change something about our appearance. Research has determined that in the United States, women experience more negative feelings about their bodies than men, which affects how they view themselves.[13] Many women hold images of very thin women, such as supermodels and other media personalities, as ideals and develop dissatisfaction with their own bodies in comparison. Women's dissatisfaction with their bodies has markedly increased over recent decades. A study conducted in 2010 by the National Institute on Media and the Family found that, by age 13, 53 percent of American girls report being unhappy with their bodies. That statistic grows to 78 percent by the time girls reach age 17.[14] However, research also shows that men are not immune to body dissatisfaction, in that they compare their own bodies with ideal muscular male bodies displayed in the media and are concerned about what others want and expect them to look like.[15] When there is a discrepancy between our desired material self and our self-concept, we may respond to eliminate the discrepancy. We may try to lose weight, have a nose job, or get another tattoo.

We also attempt to keep up with the proverbial Joneses by wanting more expensive clothes, cars, and homes. By extension, what we own becomes who we are. The bigger, better, more "high-tech," and more luxurious our possessions, we may subconsciously conclude, the better *we* are.

**The Social Self**   Your **social self** is that part of you that interacts with others. William James believed that you have as many social selves as you have people who recognize you and that you change who you are depending on the friend, family member, colleague, or acquaintance with whom you are interacting. For example, when you talk to your best friend, you're willing to "let your hair down" and reveal more thoughts and feelings than you might in a conversation with a professor, your parents, or your boss. Each relationship that you have with another person is unique because you bring to it a unique social self. This means that you are multifaceted, not false with people, because you have different selves in relation to different people.

**The Spiritual Self**   Your **spiritual self** is a mixture of your beliefs and your sense of who you are in relationship to other forces in the universe. Notice that this aspect of the self is termed "spiritual," not "religious." The term *religious* implies adherence to a specific religion or faith, typically accompanied by a belief in a supreme being or creator. However, people who see themselves as spiritual often do not subscribe to any one religion, preferring to develop their views from an array of philosophies and belief systems. From William James's perspective, the spiritual self contains all your internal thoughts and introspections about your values and moral standards. It is not dependent on what you own or with whom you talk; it is the essence of who you *think* you are and how you *feel* about yourself. It is your attempt to understand your inner essence, whether you view that essence as consciousness, spirit, or soul. Your spiritual self is the part of you that attempts to answer the question "Why am I here?"

# RECAP

## WILLIAM JAMES'S DIMENSIONS OF SELF

| Dimension | Definition | Examples |
|---|---|---|
| Material Self | The component of self derived from physical elements that reflect who you are | The self you reveal through your body, clothes, car, phone |
| Social Self | The variety of selves that appear in different situations and roles, reflected in interactions with others | Your informal self interacting with friends; your formal self interacting with your professors |
| Spiritual Self | The component of self based on introspection about values, morals, and beliefs | Belief or disbelief in a supreme being or force; regard for life in all its forms |

## How the Self-Concept Develops

Research suggests we address the question "Who am I?" through four basic means: (1) our communication with other individuals, (2) our association with groups, (3) roles we assume, and (4) our self-labels.

**social self**
Your concept of self as developed through your personal, social interactions with others.

**spiritual self**
Your concept of self based on your beliefs and your sense of who you are in relationship to other forces in the universe; also includes your thoughts and introspections about your values and moral standards.

**Communication with Others**   A valued colleague of ours often says, when he teaches communication courses, that every time you lose a relationship you lose an opportunity to see yourself. What he means is that we don't come to know and understand ourselves in a vacuum. We learn who we are by communicating with others, receiving their feedback, making sense out of it, and internalizing or rejecting all or part of it, such that we are altered by the experience. For example, let's say you like to think of yourself as a real comedian. Now think about it for a moment: How would you know you were funny if not for others' laughing at humorous things you say or do? Sure, you can crack yourself up, but the real test of whether you're funny or not is how others react to you.

In 1902, scholar Charles Horton Cooley first advanced the notion that we form our self-concepts by seeing ourselves in a figurative looking glass: We learn who we are by interacting with others, much as we look into a mirror and see our reflection.[16] Like Cooley, George Herbert Mead, author of *Mind, Self, and Society* and creator of symbolic interactionism theory, also believed that our sense of who we are is a consequence of our relationships with others.[17] Recent research confirms this idea. Results from a study of self-concept development in adolescents reinforced the important role parents play in developing a strong sense of self in their children. When a parent, both generally and through daily conversations, confirmed their adolescents' sense of self and challenged them to realize their greater potential, this form of communication had a powerful effect on the adolescents' self-concept development.[18]

Interpersonal communication scholar John Stewart and colleagues describe four characteristics of the self-concept, or one's identity, that reinforce the importance of our interactions with other people:[19]

- Identity is multidimensional and changing. Some aspects of identity are stable, such as genetic profile or ethnicity, but most aspects of the self are constructed and, therefore, fluid, meaning your identity may change because of circumstances and relationships with others.
- Identity involves responsiveness to others, meaning that the self isn't formed in a vacuum, but is negotiated, co-created, reinforced, and challenged through communication with others.[20]
- Identity develops through both past and present relationships. Who you are today is greatly a function of your family background and relationships. Early messages you received, nicknames you were given, and the ways family members related to you significantly influenced your view of self. Current relationships with family, friends, romantic partners, and coworkers continue to shape your self-concept and identity.
- We each have two components of our identity: Your **avowed identity** is one you personally assign to yourself and portray, such as student, athlete, or friend. Your **ascribed identity** involves characteristics others attribute or assign to you, and you may or may not agree with the assignment. For example, you think you have a great sense of humor (avowed self-concept), but others perceive your humor to be corny (ascribed identity). When contradictions emerge, you could simply dismiss others' views, but you'll enhance your self-awareness if you instead process the ascribed identity. Take it in, contemplate why people see you the way they do, and consider whether any changes are necessary in the way you relate to others. Avowed and ascribed identities aren't static; they shift and are negotiated through interactions with others.[21]

**avowed identity**
An identity you assign to yourself and portray.

**ascribed identity**
An identity assigned to you by others.

Although identities change along with our circumstances and relationships, messages we receive early on in life can have a long-lasting influence on our identities. How might an experience like this one shape these girls' later views of themselves?

Jupiterimages/Thinkstock

## Association with Groups
I'm a native New Yorker. I'm a soccer player. I'm a rabbi. I'm a real estate agent. I'm a member of the Tea Party. Each of these self-descriptive statements answers the "Who am I?" question by citing identification with a group or organization. Our awareness of who we are is often linked to those with whom we associate. Some groups we are born into; others we choose on our own. Either way, group associations are significant parts of our identities.

## Assumed Roles
A large part of most people's answers to the "Who am I?" question reflects roles they assume in their lives. Mother, aunt, brother, uncle, manager, salesperson, teacher, spouse, and student are labels that imply certain expectations for behavior, and they are important in shaping the self-concept.

Gender asserts a powerful influence on the self-concept from birth on. As soon as they know the sex of their child, many parents begin associating their child with a gender group by adhering to cultural roles. They give the child sex-stereotypical toys, such as catcher's mitts, train sets, or

# **RE**CAP

## HOW THE SELF-CONCEPT DEVELOPS

| | |
|---|---|
| Communication with Others | The self-concept develops as we communicate with others, receive their feedback, make sense out of it, and internalize or reject all or part of it. |
| Association with Groups | We develop our self-concept partly because of and through our identification with groups or organizations. |
| Assumed Roles | The self-concept is affected by roles we assume, such as son or daughter, employee, parent, spouse, or student. |
| Self-Labels | The terms we use to describe our attitudes, beliefs, values, and actions play a role in shaping the self-concept. |

guns for boys, and dolls, tea sets, and "dress-up" kits for girls. These cultural expectations play a major role in shaping our self-concept and our behavior.[22] By the time we reach adulthood, our self-concepts are quite distinguishable by sex, with men describing themselves more in terms of giftedness, power, and invulnerability and women viewing themselves in terms of likability and morality.[23]

**Self-Labels**   Although our self-concept is deeply affected by others, we are not blank slates for them to write on. The labels we use to describe our own attitudes, beliefs, values, and actions also play a role in shaping our self-concept.[24] Where do our labels come from? We interpret what we experience; we are self-reflexive. **Self-reflexiveness** is the human ability to think about what we're doing while we're doing it. We talk to ourselves about ourselves. We are both participants and observers in all that we do. This dual role encourages us to use labels to describe who we are.

**self-reflexiveness**
The human ability to think about what you are doing while you are doing it.

**self-esteem**
Your assessment of your worth or value as reflected in your perception of such things as your skills, abilities, talents, and appearance.

**self-concept clarity**
The extent to which beliefs about oneself are clearly and confidently identified and stable over time.

# Self-Esteem: What Is Your Value?

It may sound crass to consider our *value*, but we do this every day. Our assessment of our value as persons is termed **self-esteem**. Closely related to your self-concept, or your *description* of who you are, is your self-esteem, your *evaluation* of who you are. As feminist author Gloria Steinem described it in her book *Revolution from Within: A Book of Self-Esteem*, "It's a feeling of 'clicking in' when that self is recognized, valued, discovered, *esteemed*—as if we literally plug into an inner energy that is ours alone, yet connects us to everything else."[25]

While the self-concept pertains to one's enduring identity, self-esteem pertains more to one's current state of mind or view of self. But are the two aspects of the self related? Research continues to explore that very question, focusing on the notion of **self-concept clarity**, which Canadian psychologist Jennifer Campbell defines as the extent to which beliefs about oneself are clearly and confidently identified and stable over time.[26] It doesn't mean that you don't change as a person or that your view of yourself doesn't change; we know that people evolve as they mature and experience new things. But self-concept clarity relates to the stability associated with having a clear sense of who you are and being confident in your identity. One of the things Campbell and various colleagues have determined is that people who suffer from low self-esteem also tend to have a less clearly defined sense of self—in other words, they tend to have more questions about their identity.[27]

Self-esteem can fluctuate because of relatively minor events, such as getting a high grade on a paper, or major upheavals, such as the breakup of an important relationship.[28] Self-esteem can rise or fall within the course of a day; sometimes just a look from someone (or someone's failure to notice you) can send you into a tailspin and make you feel devalued. Or a certain level of self-esteem can last for a while—you may have a series of months or even years that you look back on thinking "I felt pretty lousy

WARNING OBJECTS IN MIRROR MAY BEAR // NO // RELATION TO REALITY

Theresa McCracken/CartoonStock

about myself in those days. Glad that period is over." Researchers have identified four factors that provide clues about the nature of self-esteem: gender, social comparisons, self-expectations, and the self-fulfilling prophecy.

## Gender

Your **gender** is a complex cultural construction that includes your biological sex (male or female); psychological and emotional characteristics that cause you to be masculine, feminine, or androgynous (a combination of feminine and masculine traits); your attitudes about appropriate roles and behavior for the sexes in society; and your sexual orientation (to whom you are sexually attracted).[29] All these elements play a role in how you feel about yourself, or your self-esteem.

Research that has primarily focused on the development of self-esteem in childhood and adolescence documents ways that boys' self-esteem develops differently from girls'. In a patriarchal (or male-dominated) culture, such as that of the United States, women and girls suffer loss of self-esteem to a much greater degree than men and boys.[30] A survey of 3,000 schoolchildren, conducted by the American Association of University Women, showed that self-esteem decreases between elementary grades and high school, but this decrease is significantly more pronounced in girls.[31] Myra Sadker and David Sadker, authors of the book *Failing at Fairness: How America's Schools Cheat Girls*, explain how boys experience a "self-esteem slide," while girls' self-esteem loss is a "free fall."[32]

The difference in self-esteem levels seems to pertain to such factors as boys feeling better able to do things than girls such as playing sports. This trend continues to change, as participation in and appreciation for women's athletics steadily increases.[33]

## Social Comparisons

One way we become more aware of ourselves and derive our sense of self-worth is by measuring ourselves against others, a process called **social comparison**.[34] I'm good at playing basketball (because I'm part of a winning team); I can't cook (because others cook better than I do); I'm good at meeting people (whereas most people seem to be uncomfortable interacting with new people); I'm not handy (but my dad can fix anything). Each of these statements implies a judgment about how well or badly you can perform certain tasks, with implied references to how well others perform the same tasks.

One powerful social comparison that contributes to self-esteem loss in girls and women is fueled by images of physical attractiveness in the media. Mass media create and reinforce for consumers notions of what is physically attractive, and achieving that media-driven standard is next to impossible for most people.[35] One line of research has found that females of a wide range of ages—from preadolescents through college students—compare their own physical attractiveness to that of models in ads. When they perceive that they don't measure up, they often experience the "model trap." This trap is a continual cycle of viewing physically "perfect" models, hating them, then growing to like them, and loving them, followed by efforts to emulate them, failing in those efforts, resenting them again, and repeating the cycle.[36]

It can be self-defeating to take social comparisons too far, to cause your self-esteem to suffer because you compare yourself unfairly or unrealistically to others. The wiser approach is to compare yourself to your friends and neighbors, people you know and who are similar to you in many ways, rather than to people who are obviously not like you.

## Self-Expectations

Another factor that affects your self-esteem is an estimation of how well you accomplish your goals. **Self-expectations** are goals we set for ourselves, such as losing weight, developing a "buff" body, making better grades, being appointed or elected to an important office in an

**gender**
A cultural construction that includes one's biological sex (male or female), psychological characteristics (femininity, masculinity, androgyny), attitudes about the sexes, and sexual orientation.

**social comparison**
Process of comparing oneself to others to measure one's worth.

**self-expectations**
Goals you set for yourself; how you believe you ought to behave and what you ought to accomplish.

High-school student Galia Slayen built this life-size Barbie doll to show how unrealistic standards for physical attractiveness can damage the self-esteem of girls and women. According to Slayen, if Barbie were a real woman, she would stand six feet tall and have an 18-inch waist.
CB2/ZOB/WENN.com/Newscom

# Communication&**TECHNOLOGY**

## Got Low Self-Esteem? Get Facebook!

Facebook statistics are staggering: The popular social networking site now boasts more than 750 million active users, half of whom log on in any given day. People spend more than 700 billion minutes *per month* on Facebook. More than 250 million users access Facebook through their mobile devices (such as cell phones and iPads), and mobile users are twice as active on Facebook as nonmobile users. Do you think Facebook is fun and exciting, or do you think it is an "awful waste of time," as Betty White called it, when she was hosting *Saturday Night Live*? What relationships exist between Facebook usage and some of the topics we discuss in this chapter?

Research has examined a connection between Facebook use and self-esteem. One study found that receiving positive feedback from Facebook "friends" enhanced people's views of themselves in terms of their physical attractiveness, romantic appeal, and success in maintaining close relationships.[37] Other research suggests that people who suffer from low self-esteem may benefit from the social opportunities an online outlet such as Facebook can provide.[38]

Of course, there's a downside: Research has also found that online social comparisons can hurt your self-esteem. For example, comparing your physical attractiveness to profile pictures of beautiful people can lower your self-esteem. Some research has shown that men who viewed profiles of highly successful men saw themselves and their current career status in a more negative light as a result.[39]

Cornell University scholars Amy Gonzales and Jeffrey Hancock studied these two self-esteem possibilities for college students who use Facebook.[40] The researchers wondered if comparing one's hobbies, likes and dislikes, "wall posts," and "status updates" to others' would make people aware of their limitations and shortcomings, thus diminishing their self-esteem, or if the sharing of select information (meaning a profile that emphasizes one's best features while filtering negative qualities) would have the opposite effect, thus increasing self-esteem. Their results favored the second possibility. According to Gonzales and Hancock, "exposure to information presented on one's Facebook profile enhances self-esteem, especially when a person edits information about the self or *selectively self-presents*."[41] They concluded that Facebook offers a unique opportunity for self-awareness enhancement, because users can reflect on the self as they update and refine their profiles and when they receive feedback and comments from their "friends." This kind of reflection can lead to a greater understanding of ourselves.

Because online activities take up an increasing part of our daily lives, it's important to consider the effect they have on our view of self and how we communicate that self-view to others. If you use social networking sites like Facebook, Twitter, or LinkedIn, think about what your use of these sites reveals about how you feel about yourself. Is your offline self-esteem different than the self-esteem level you project online? Does social media usage make you feel better about yourself or worse?

organization, graduating by a certain time, or acquiring wealth by a certain age. Self-esteem is affected when you evaluate how well you measure up to your own expectations. For instance, if you expect to receive all A's this semester and you don't, it's likely your self-esteem will be affected negatively. You may have to readjust your goals and expectations, or just become more determined to achieve the straight-A goal next semester.

Some people place enormous expectations on themselves, probably because their parents had enormous expectations for them when they were growing up. We wish people who are stressed out all the time could give themselves a break, because they place such unrealistic, high demands on themselves. The popular achievement gurus will tell you that you won't accomplish much if you set easily attainable goals. But we're suspicious of that advice; we see too many people whose self-esteem is low because they place such pressure and unrealistic demands on themselves. When they can't live up to those demands, they feel guilty and begin to see themselves as failures. A downward trend involving expectation, failure, guilt, and low self-esteem takes a lot of work to reverse.

## Self-Fulfilling Prophecy

**self-fulfilling prophecy**
The notion that predictions about one's future are likely to come true because one believes that they will come true.

A concept related to the creation of self-expectations is the **self-fulfilling prophecy**, the idea that what you believe about yourself often comes true because you expect it to come true.[42] If you think you'll fail a math quiz because you have labeled yourself inept at math, then you must overcome not only your math deficiency but also your low expectations of yourself. If you hold the self-perception that you're pretty good at conversation, then you're likely to act on that assumption when you approach a conversation with someone. Your conversations, true to form, go well, thus reinforcing your belief in yourself as a good conversationalist.

Your level of self-esteem also affects the kinds of prophecies you make about yourself and colors your interpretation of events. For example, one study found that college students who anticipated an intense conflict with a friend described that conflict as upsetting emotionally, involving personal attacks, and interfering with everyday life.[43] The expectation corresponded with the outcome. People with high self-esteem tend to anticipate or predict successes for themselves; they are then reinforced when they experience those suc-

## RECAP

### FACTORS AFFECTING SELF-ESTEEM

| | |
|---|---|
| Gender | In male-dominated cultures, girls and women suffer self-esteem loss to a much greater degree than boys and men, primarily as a result of males' feeling better able to do things than females. |
| Social Comparisons | Judgments about how well or poorly you can perform certain tasks compared to others can be self-defeating and can cause self-esteem to suffer. |
| Self-Expectations | Your estimation of how well you perform in comparison to your own goals or self-expectations has a profound effect on self-esteem. |
| Self-Fulfilling Prophecies | What you believe about yourself often comes true because you expect it to come true. |

cesses. Conversely, people with low self-esteem tend to interpret their successes as flukes; they attribute an achievement to luck rather than to their own efforts. Successes can enhance your self-esteem, but if you're in a downward spiral of low self-esteem, you may not recognize your own achievements to let them have a positive effect.

# Communication and the Enhancement of Self-Esteem

We know the damage low self-esteem can do to us—it can limit our ability to develop and maintain satisfying relationships, to experience career successes and advancement, and to create a generally happy and contented life. Teachers, psychologists, self-help gurus, clergy members, social workers, and even politicians suggest that many of our societal problems stem from our collective feelings of low self-esteem. Our feelings of low self-worth may contribute to our choosing the wrong partners; becoming addicted to drugs, alcohol, sex, online activities, or gambling; experiencing problems with eating and other vital activities; and opting, in too many cases, for death over life. So we owe it to society, as well as ourselves, to develop and work to maintain a healthy sense of self-esteem, as an integral part of the process of becoming more self-aware.

One team of researchers followed a group of approximately 4,000 Americans for sixteen years, assessing changes in these people's self-esteem during that time. During the study, participants ranged from 25 years old to 104 years old, allowing the researchers to describe a common trajectory of self-esteem as we age. The results suggest that self-esteem increases during young and middle adulthood, peaks around age 60, and then declines in old age.[44] This research doesn't seal one's fate. Your own self-esteem trajectory may differ from the results of the study for many reasons. But if there's one take-home message from this study, it's this: Now is *prime time* to develop a healthy self-esteem! Although no simple list of tricks can easily transform low self-esteem into feelings of being valued and appreciated, you can improve how you think about yourself. One thing is clear from research about self-esteem: Communication is essential in the process of building and maintaining self-esteem.[45]

# Communication & ETHICS

## Can You Have TOO Much Self-Esteem?

For decades, scholars, teachers, counselors, and others in helping roles in American culture have agreed that many people suffer from debilitatingly low levels of self-esteem. However, growing evidence suggests that the efforts of self-help gurus, psychologists, and parents to build children's self-confidence may have paid off in a big way, perhaps too big of a way. Now some are wondering, "How much self-esteem is too much?"

While every day in our classes we still witness countless numbers of students whose self-esteem could use a shot of caffeine, we are also beginning to see the fruits of a "be all that you can be" generation. Some children have now grown into adults whose self-esteem is so healthy that, in some instances, it has led to self-centeredness.

Jean Twenge, author of *Generation Me: Why Today's Young Americans Are More Confident, Assertive, Entitled—and More Miserable Than Ever Before*, contends:

> Today's young people . . . speak the language of the self as their native tongue. The individual has always come first, and feeling good about yourself has always been a primary virtue. . . . This is a time of soaring expectations and crushing realities.[46]

Twenge is the lead investigator on research into college students and **narcissism**, a personality attribute that carries as its primary characteristic a positive but inflated view of self, especially regarding areas of one's own power, importance, and physical attractiveness. In a study of more than 16,000 college students, Twenge and colleagues found that student narcissism had sharply risen since the 1980s.[47]

Interestingly, some of today's most popular ways of communicating also seem to lend themselves well to use by narcissistic people. People who score high on narcissism scales tend to check Facebook multiple times a day and spend more time in Facebook sessions than those who are low or moderate in narcissism, for example.[48] Narcissists are also drawn to social networking sites that allow them to self-select information for their profiles (possibly inflating their positive qualities), post photos that reveal their lives to the public, update their status to show others what they're doing or thinking about, and provide positive self-descriptions.[49]

While some positive correlates of narcissism exist, such as enhanced self-esteem, extroversion, and levels of life satisfaction, the downsides include distorted judgment of one's abilities, risky decision making, and potential addictive disorders and compulsions (e.g., alcohol abuse, compulsive shopping, and gambling).[50]

## Engage in Positive Self-Talk

**Intrapersonal communication** refers to how you take in information or stimuli in your environment and make sense of it.[51] It also involves communication within yourself—**self-talk**, or what some scholars term "inner speech."[52] Your self-concept and level of self-esteem influence the way you talk to yourself about your abilities and skills. The reverse is also true, in that your inner dialogue has an effect on both your self-concept and your level of self-esteem. Athletes use positive self-talk to motivate themselves to play better, especially if they're struggling on the court or field of play. Some also talk to themselves negatively when they perform poorly. Research shows, however, that athletes who engage in negative inner dialogue usually do nothing to improve their performance.[53]

Although becoming your own cheerleader may not enable you to win championships, there is evidence that self-talk, both positive and negative, is related to the building and maintaining of one's self-concept.[54] Realistic, positive self-talk can have a reassuring effect on your level of self-worth and therefore your interactions with others. Conversely, repeating negative messages about your lack of skill and ability can keep you from trying and achieving.

## Visualize

**Visualization**—imagining oneself behaving in a certain way—takes the notion of self-talk one step further. Besides just telling yourself that you can achieve your goal, you can actually try to "see" yourself conversing effectively with others, performing well

**narcissism**
An inflated view of self, especially about one's own power and importance.

**intrapersonal communication**
How you take in stimuli in the environment or information and make sense of it; also, thoughts and ideas that you say to yourself.

**self-talk**
Inner speech; communication with the self.

**visualization**
The technique of imagining that you are performing a particular task in a certain way; a method of enhancing self-esteem.

on a project, or exhibiting some other desirable behavior. Because the United States is such a visual culture, most of us have no trouble visualizing elaborate scenarios in our heads.

Research suggests that an apprehensive public speaker can manage her or his fears by visualizing positive results.[55] In fact, visualization reduces anxiety as well as negative self-talk or the number of debilitating thoughts that enter a speaker's consciousness.[56] If you are one of the many people who fear making presentations, try visualizing yourself walking to the front of the room, taking out your well-prepared notes, delivering a well-rehearsed and interesting presentation, and returning to your seat to the sound of applause from your audience. This visualization of positive results enhances confidence and speaking skill. The same technique can be used to boost your sense of self-worth about other tasks or skills. If you're nervous about a date, for example, visualize each step of the date (as realistically as you can). Think through what you might talk about on the date and how the night will progress. This mental rehearsal will help reduce your anxiety. In addition, visualizing yourself interacting or performing well can help you change long-standing feelings of inadequacy.

## Reframe

The process of redefining events and experiences, of looking at something from a different point of view, is termed **reframing**. When a movie director gets different "takes" or shots of the same scene, she or he is striving to get the best work possible. The director alters small details, like camera angles or actor movements, to get yet another look or vision for a scene. Just like that movie director, you can reframe your "take" on events or circumstances that cause you to lose self-esteem.

Here's an example. You get a report from your supervisor that says you should improve one area of your performance, but instead of engaging in self-talk that says you're terrible at your job, you reframe the event within a larger context. Tell yourself that one negative comment doesn't mean you are a bad employee.

Of course, you shouldn't leave negative experiences unexamined, because you can learn and profit from your mistakes. But it's important to remember that our worth as human beings is not contingent on a single *anything*—a single grade, a single failed relationship, a single response from a prospective employer, or a single play in a football game. Looking at the big picture—at the effect this one event will have on your whole life, on society, on history—places negative experiences we all have in realistic contexts.

Positive self-talk can motivate us to do our best in challenging situations. Are there situations in which you could make your own self-talk more encouraging?

Vitalii Nesterchuk/Shutterstock.com

## Develop Honest Relationships

The suggestion that you develop honest relationships may sound like the latest advice from some talk show, but it is actually harder to accomplish than it sounds. Think about it: How many people are in your life who really give you the straight scoop about yourself? How many people are so solid in their relationship with you that they can tell you the things that are the hardest to hear, things that no one else would dare tell you? Most of us can count the number of those people on one hand. That doesn't mean we aren't honest with the many friends and acquaintances we have in our lives, but most of us really trust only a select few enough to deal with the tough stuff.

Having at least one other person who will give you honest feedback and help you objectively reflect on your virtues and vices can be extremely beneficial in fostering healthy, positive self-esteem. As noted earlier, other people play a major role in shaping our self-concept and self-esteem. You don't want to find yourself at a point where you're oblivious to the feedback of others. That kind of attitude can make you

**reframing**
The process of redefining events and experiences from a different point of view.

narcissistic, unrealistic, and rigid, unable to adjust to life's changing circumstances. Most people who reject or overlook significant others' feedback end up isolated and with low self-esteem.

## Surround Yourself with Positive People

Related to the development of honest relationships is a suggestion about the people you choose to associate with the most in your life. If you want to improve your self-esteem and to develop a more positive outlook, it's better to surround yourself with people who tend to have higher levels of self-esteem than with people who are "Debbie Downers." Granted, sometimes you don't have a choice; you get assigned a roommate in college, you end up with an instructor's choice of lab or study partner, and you rarely get to choose the people you work with. So we're not suggesting that you disassociate yourself from people who have low self-esteem, because that's unrealistic. Plus, we all suffer from bouts of low self-esteem at some time or another. People with low self-esteem need to be around uplifting people—those whose positive self-regard will rub off on them.

As an example, we know an elderly woman, Hazel, who was in good enough health to be able to help the Meals on Wheels organization deliver food to shut-ins in her town. Hazel often talked about how sour many of the people on her route were, how their attitudes had "gone south" because of poor health, limited options, and fading hope. She believed that her main purpose wasn't to deliver a hot meal but to extend the gift of her positive outlook. She often told us about how many complaints she heard in the course of one day, but she was determined to stay optimistic and to offer hope to those she visited. One time Hazel described what she viewed as a personal triumph. The most sour person on her route—a woman with very low self-esteem and a cranky disposition, one who never did anything but gripe to Hazel when she visited—began to "thaw." One day when Hazel delivered her meal, the woman actually greeted her at the front door and seemed genuinely glad to see Hazel. She complained less often as she slowly began to enjoy the warm glow of Hazel's sunny disposition and empathic responses. Hazel felt that the woman's self-esteem had begun to improve, that her outlook on life had begun to change.

## Lose Your Baggage

Not making the team. Getting passed over for a key promotion at work. Seeing a long-term relationship end. Feeling like a failure. We've all had experiences we would like to undo or get a second chance at, so that we could do it differently or so that we would *be* different. We all carry around experiential or psychological "baggage," but the key question is, how much space does that baggage take up within your self-concept? To phrase this another way, how negatively is your self-esteem affected by your baggage?

# **RE**CAP

## STRATEGIES FOR ENHANCING SELF-ESTEEM

| | |
|---|---|
| Engage in Positive Self-Talk | If you want positive results, talk positively to yourself. If you are self-critical and negative, you may set yourself up for failure. Rephrase doubts and negative thoughts into positive, uplifting encouragement. |
| Visualize | In anticipation of a significant event, picture how you want the event to go, as a mental rehearsal. If you feel anxious or nervous, visualize success instead of failure. |
| Reframe | Try to look at experiences and events, especially those that can cause you to lose self-esteem, from a different point of view. Keep the larger picture in mind, rather than focusing on one isolated, negative incident. |
| Develop Honest Relationships | Cultivate friends you can confide in and who will give you honest feedback for improving your skills and abilities. Accept that feedback in the spirit of enhancing your self-esteem and making yourself a wiser, better person. |
| Surround Yourself with Positive People | Associating with people with high self-esteem can help you enhance your own self-esteem and develop a more positive outlook. |
| Lose Your Baggage | Dump your psychological and experiential baggage: Work to move beyond the negatives of your past so that you focus on the present and relieve your self-esteem of the burden of things you cannot change. |

Individuals with low self-esteem tend to lock on to events and experiences that happened years ago and tenaciously refuse to let go of or move past them. Looking back at what we can't change only reinforces a sense of helplessness. Constantly replaying negative experiences only serves to make our sense of self-worth more difficult to repair. A traumatic or defining experience in the past has a serious effect on your self-concept; it will probably always remain a part of you. But it doesn't have to affect your current level of self-esteem. It's important to take mental inventory of experiences in your past and then decide to let go of and move past those experiences that cause your present-day self-esteem to suffer.

LISTEN, I CAN CARRY 20 TIMES MY OWN WEIGHT, BUT NOT 20 TIMES YOUR EMOTIONAL BAGGAGE.

Dave Coverly/The Cartoonist Group

# The Perception Process

This chapter focuses on Principle One of our Communication Principles for a Lifetime: Be aware of your communication with yourself and others. Awareness involves developing greater understanding and skill by becoming more cognizant of yourself, others, and communication. Awareness includes exploring how we perceive ourselves and our communication with others, as well as the many ways in which we perceive other people and their communication. But just what is perception?

On the most basic level, **perception** is the arousal of any of our senses. A sound travels through the air, vibrates in the eardrum, activates the nerves, and sends a signal to the brain. A similar sequence of events takes place when we see, smell, feel, or taste something. So perception begins with the process of attending to stimuli in the environment. The process of perception also includes structuring and making sense of information provided by the senses. You come out of a building and see wet pavement and puddles of water, hear thunder, smell a fresh odor in the air, and feel a few drops of water on your head. You integrate all those bits of information and conclude that it's raining and has been for a while.

Perceiving people, however, goes beyond the simple processing of sensory information. We try to decide what people are like, making judgments about their personalities, and we give meaning to their actions by drawing inferences from what we observe.[57] When you meet someone new, you notice certain basic attributes, like the person's sex, general aspects of physical appearance, the sound of her or his voice, and whether or not he or she smiles, uses a friendly tone of voice, has an accent, and so forth. You also attend to specific details that the person communicates, verbally and nonverbally. Once you've chosen these stimuli to pay attention to, you then categorize the information into some sort of structure that works for you. Finally, you attempt to make sense of your structured perceptions; you assign meaning to what you have perceived. Let's examine each of these three stages in the perception process.

**perception**
The arousal of any of your senses.

Because we cannot process every stimulus in our environment, we need to select which ones will get our attention. When you communicate in a noisy, distracting setting, how can you focus your attention to improve your powers of perception?

Image Source/Getty Images

## Stage One: Attention and Selection

You're watching a group of parents at a playground with their children. The kids are playing, running around, laughing, and squealing, as children will do. You view the activity, hear the noise, feel the heat of the day on your skin, and smell hot dogs cooking on a grill. They smell so good you can almost taste them. After a moment, a parent jumps up and runs over to comfort a child who has fallen down and is crying. You were watching the action but didn't see the particular incident and didn't register the child's cry amidst all the noise. But the child's parent did. How did this happen?

The ability of parents to discern their own child's voice from a chorus of voices is one of the mysteries of human nature, but it also exemplifies the first stage of perception. Our human senses simply cannot process all the stimuli that are available at any given moment, so we select which sensations make it through to the level of awareness and ignore or filter out the rest. The activities of **attention** and **selection** constitute the first stage of the perception process. Have you ever listened to music in the dark so that you could eliminate visual sensations and focus only on what you were hearing? Have you ever watched TV with the sound turned off, just so you could enjoy the visual images without the "static" of sound? What we're doing in these instances is selecting what we will and will not attend to.

Selectivity can also cause us to fail to perceive information that is important.[58] Jack and Jill are having an argument; Jack is so absorbed in making his points that he fails to see that Jill is crying. By selecting certain stimuli, we sometimes miss other clues that might be important, that might help us better understand what is happening and how to respond.

## Stage Two: Organization

After we select stimuli to attend to and process, we start to convert the information into convenient, understandable, and efficient patterns that allow us to make sense of what we have observed. This activity, termed **organization**, makes it easier for us to process complex information because it allows us to impose the familiar onto the unfamiliar and because we can easily store and recall simple patterns.

Look at the three items in Figure 2.2. What does each of them mean to you? If you are like most people, you will perceive item A as a horseshoe, item B as the word *communication*, and item C as a circle. Strictly speaking, none of those perceptions is correct. For item A, you see a pattern of dots that you label a horseshoe because a horseshoe is a concept you know and to which you attach various meanings. The item really isn't a horseshoe; it could be an inverted U. It's actually a set of dots. But rather than processing a set of dots, it's much easier to organize the dots in a way that refers to something familiar. For similar reasons, we organize patterns of stars in the sky into various constellations with shapes, like the Big and Little Dippers.

In Figure 2.2, items B and C reveal our inclination to superimpose structure and consistency on what we observe. This tendency leads us to create a familiar word from the meaningless assemblage of letters in item B and to label the figure in item C a circle, even though a circle is a continuous line without any gaps. The process of filling in missing information is called **closure**, and it applies to our perceptions of people as well. When we have an incomplete picture of another human being, we impose a pattern or structure, classify the person on the basis of the information we do have, and fill in the gaps.

**attention**
The act of perceiving stimuli in your environment.

**selection**
The act of choosing specific stimuli in your environment to focus on.

**organization**
Converting information into convenient, understandable, and efficient patterns that allow us to make sense of what we have observed.

**closure**
The perceptual process of filling in missing information.

## Figure 2.2
## What Do You See?

Item A          Item B          Item C

OMMUNICATION

Perhaps you've sat in an airport or busy shopping mall watching people and tried to guess what they did for a living, what their personalities were like, or what their backgrounds were. Maybe you saw people you guessed were wealthy, hotheads, teachers, losers, athletes, loners, or surfer dudes. As you looked at people's clothing and saw how they walked or behaved, you made inferences about them. You superimposed some structure by using a general label and filling in the gaps in your information. This activity can get you into trouble, of course, but we'll save that discussion until the end of the chapter, when we focus on the problem of stereotyping.

## Stage Three: Interpretation

Once we have organized stimuli, we're ready to assign meaning, a process termed **interpretation**. We attach meaning to all that we observe. In some cases, the meanings are fairly standardized, as they are for language, for example. But others are much more personalized. If you meet someone whose cologne is too heavy and in a scent you don't like, what's your impression of that person? How do you make sense of the fact that the person is wearing enough cologne to flood a whole building with fragrance? What if the person also has a great handshake and warm smile? Does that change your interpretation of events and your impression of the person? This example illustrates how we impose meaning on what we observe to complete the perceptual process.

Of course, our interpretations can be inaccurate or off-base; we may perceive a situation one way when in fact something entirely different is occurring.[59] For example, the final scene in the movie *Swingers* is hilarious because it illustrates the faulty nature of human interpretation. The two leading male characters are sitting in a booth at a diner. One of them thinks that a woman several booths away is making eyes at him. She appears to be making flirtatious facial expressions and mouthing something which he interprets as a come-on. He's just about to make his move when he realizes that the woman is looking across her table at a baby in a portable carrier, positioned in the opposite side of the booth, and she's cooing and making faces at the child.

## When Perceptions Vary

George and Martha have been married for, well, forever; they know each other very well, and each knows how the other thinks. So you'd think their perceptions of things, events, and people would line up, right? Wrong. George and Martha are driving home from a party, chatting about what happened at the event. George believes that everyone had a good time; that the house was filled with interesting, pleasant, relatively good-looking people; and that he received positive responses from everyone he talked to. Martha saw the party differently. She tells George that the reason people looked good was that most of them either had had plastic surgery to "hold back Father Time"; were Botoxed beyond all recognition; or were younger, "replacement" partners for all the divorcees who attended the party. Some of the women brought younger men as their dates (a process known as "cougaring"), and many people at the party disliked each other so intensely that they stayed on opposite sides of the room all night. Martha's interpretation of events isn't based on prior or external knowledge, but on her perceptions

## RECAP

### THE PERCEPTION PROCESS

| Term | Explanation | Example |
|------|-------------|---------|
| Perception | The arousal of any of our senses | Hearing the sound of laughter |
| Attention and Selection | The first stage in the perception process, in which we perceive stimuli and choose which ones to focus our awareness on | Watching TV in your room while hearing giggling and laughter, and ignoring the TV show to eavesdrop on the giggler |
| Organization | The second stage in the perception process, in which we structure stimuli into convenient and efficient patterns | Realizing that the laughter is coming from your younger sister, who's on the phone |
| Interpretation | The final stage in the perception process, in which we assign meaning to what we have perceived | Deciding that your sister is talking on the phone to her boyfriend, because she only laughs like that when she talks to him |

**interpretation**
Attaching meaning to what is attended to, selected, and organized.

from observing and interacting with people at the party. And about George's perception that everyone at the party liked him? Martha says, "Think again." She tells George that as soon as he left one group of men in a conversation and walked away, they signaled to one another with their "body language" that they thought George was a doofus. What's going on here? Who's right, George or Martha?

In actuality, no one's right or both people are right, because what this example illustrates are differing perceptions of the same reality. There's no "truth" to be found, only different "takes" on the same people and set of events. Both sets of perceptions are correct and valid, even though they differ, because varying perceptions are the norm in life. You know this to be true in your own life experience—even people you're very similar to and know quite well can differ from you dramatically in their perceptions of people and events. Your life experiences, how you were raised, and how you developed contribute a great deal to how you perceive things, events, and people in your life. These elements create a filter through which you observe and process the world around you.

For example, let's say that you grew up with a loving grandmother whose house you always looked forward to visiting, mainly because of the wonderful aromas of grandma's cooking. Now, as an adult, when you walk into any bakery, those wonderful smells trigger fond memories of your grandmother, so the smells are positive stimuli for you. But for someone who had a stern, abusive grandmother who also had great smells in her house, those smells might trigger a different response when she or he encounters them later in life. You may be drawn to bakeries not just for the sweets, but because the stimulus evokes memories of your grandmother; for someone else, the memories of grandmother associated with the smells might trigger negative feelings of fear, possibly even anger. That person would likely want to go nowhere near a bakery. Similar experiences can trigger different meanings in people, so we shouldn't be surprised when different reactions occur.

# Communicate to Enhance Your Powers of Perception

Has anyone ever told you they formed a misperception about you when they first met you, but you proved them wrong over time? On occasion, people who are shy, serious, or simply more quiet in their communication style than others are misperceived as being conceited, aloof, or cocky. Outgoing, extroverted people may be viewed as overbearing, when really they just enjoy the company of others.

Sometimes our powers of perception are sharp, but other times we miss the mark.[60] Because our communication is affected by our perceptions of others, it's important to work toward forming the most accurate perceptions you can, because then you have better, more reliable information on which to act. How can you improve your ability to form accurate perceptions? Here are three suggestions: increase your awareness, avoid stereotypes, and check your perceptions against others' perceptions.

## Increase Your Awareness

We've made this topic—awareness—our first of five Communication Principles for a Lifetime for a reason. As we discuss in the next two chapters, developing your skills in perceiving and then decoding others' verbal and nonverbal communication is critical as you strengthen existing relationships and establish new ones.

Exercise your senses, especially your sense of hearing. Work at really listening to people—fully listening, without interrupting them to put in your two cents' worth. Try to be more verbally and nonverbally aware, meaning monitor how you communicate with others and how people respond to you. If you don't like the responses you're getting from people, it may be time for a change in *your* behavior, not theirs. You also want to monitor the verbal and nonverbal cues others exhibit. Pay attention to contextual cues, such as where an interaction is taking place, the time of day, the perceived moods of those interacting, and any physical or psychological barriers that impede the communication exchange. Learn from your mistakes, rather than repeating them.

## Avoid Stereotypes

"She's a snob." "He's a nerd." "They're a bunch of dumb jocks." All these statements reflect **stereotypes**, or generalizations we apply to persons because we perceive them to have attributes common to a particular group.[61] Social psychologist Douglas Kenrick and his colleagues suggest, "Stereotyping is a cognitively inexpensive way of understanding others: By presuming that people are like other members of their groups, we avoid the effortful process of learning about them as individuals."[62]

What comes to mind when you hear the term *homeless*? Do you associate the word with someone begging on the street, families living in shelters or their cars, or "bums" or "bag ladies" in parks, alleys, or subway stops? If these images came to mind, you've just invoked a stereotype. What may not have come to mind are the many families in the United States now who are homeless because of an economic recession that includes high rates of unemployment and home foreclosures. Research shows that many of us hold unfortunate stereotypes about homeless people and homelessness in general.[63]

Some positive or functional aspects of stereotypes emerge from our human nature to simplify and categorize stimuli in our environment, which we described as components of the perception process. Stereotypes serve as a baseline of information. If you know nothing else about a person other than she or he is a "northerner," for instance, then you can think about commonly held characteristics of other persons you've met from the northern part of the United States and go from there. But obviously, there's a serious downside.

Have you ever taken a class and, from day one, felt that the teacher pegged you a certain way? The teacher perceived you to be a slacker or uninterested in the course topic (on the negative side) or a straight-A student or future Ph.D. (on the positive side). The bottom line is that no one likes to be treated as a stereotype because it's limiting and impersonal. You can also feel pressure to try to live up to a stereotype, such as "all Asian students are exceptionally bright." Stereotypes are often degrading, as in age-old references to dumb blondes, bad women drivers, and dirty old men. Many of the worst stereotypes are related to gender, race/ethnicity, age, and physical appearance.[64]

Research has explored the ways we try to inhibit stereotypical thoughts before they have a chance to affect our behavior.[65] For example, if you grew up hearing family members invoke stereotypes about different ethnic groups, you may decide as an adult that you will not follow suit—that assigning ethnic stereotypes is inappropriate. However, because it's part of your upbringing and ingrained in you, your first thoughts may be stereotypical when you encounter someone from an ethnic group other than your own. You have to assert mental control to suppress the stereotypical thoughts. Remember that there's nothing inherently wrong with a stereotype, as a baseline of information. But the rigid way we enforce a stereotype, the expectations we form based on the stereotype, and our ensuing communication toward the stereotyped person are problematic.

## Check Your Perceptions

You can check the accuracy of your perceptions and attributions indirectly and directly so that you increase your ability to perceive things and people and respond to them effectively. **Indirect perception checking** involves an intensification of your own perceptual powers. You seek additional information to either confirm or refute your

**stereotype**
A generalization applied to persons perceived to have attributes common to a particular group.

**indirect perception checking**
Using your own perceptual abilities to seek additional information to confirm or refute your interpretations of someone's behavior.

interpretations of someone's behavior. If you suspect that your romantic partner wants to end your relationship, for instance, you are likely to look for cues in his or her tone of voice, eye contact, and body movements to confirm your suspicion. You will probably also listen more intently and pay attention to the language your partner chooses to use. The information you gain is "checked" against your original perceptions.

**Direct perception checking** involves asking straight out whether your interpretations of a perception are correct. You can accomplish this in two ways: asking people directly for their interpretations of their own actions or asking other observers for their take on a situation (going to a third or outside party). Asking people directly is often more difficult than asking a third party for an interpretation. For one thing, we don't like to admit uncertainty or suspicions to others; we might not trust that they will respond honestly. And if our interpretations are wrong, we might suffer embarrassment or anger. But asking someone to confirm a perception shows that you are committed to understanding his or her behavior.

Perception checking with colleagues, as well as with family members and trusted friends, is an invaluable tool, particularly when emotions are involved. It can be very helpful to discuss situations with other people and get their input as to what happened, why it happened, how they would feel about it if it happened to them, and what you might do about it. This is especially advisable in work settings, when the wisdom of someone else's perceptions can save you professional embarrassment or prevent you from losing your job. The "Can I run something by you?" strategy gives you a broader perspective and a basis of comparison.[66]

**direct perception checking**
Asking someone else whether your interpretations of what you perceive are correct.

# STUDY GUIDE:
## Review, Apply, and Assess Your Knowledge and Skill

## Self-Awareness: How Well Do You Know Yourself?    p. 36

Self-awareness is the ability to develop and communicate a representation of yourself to others. According to Layder, self-awareness includes five properties. The self is: psychological, operating within a social context; emotional, which fuels our behavior; a focal point of action and control; flexible and multifaceted; and spiritual.

### Terms to Know

| | | | |
|---|---|---|---|
| Self-Awareness | p. 36 | Symbolic Self-Awareness | p. 36 |

## Self-Concept: Who Are You?    p. 37

The self-concept is your interior identity or subjective description of who you think you are. Your self-image is your view of yourself in a particular situation. The self-concept contains three components: attitudes, beliefs, and values. Philosopher William James believed that three "selves" exist in each of us:

- Material self: the tangible things you own, such as your body, possessions, home, and so forth;
- Social self: that part of you that interacts with others; and
- Spiritual self: a mixture of your beliefs and your sense of who you are in relationship to other forces in the universe.

Our self-concept develops through our communication with others, our association with various groups, the roles we assume in our lives, and the labels we use to describe ourselves. Our avowed identity is assigned by ourselves, whereas our ascribed identity involves characteristics other people assign or attribute to us.

### Terms to Know

| | | | |
|---|---|---|---|
| Self | p. 38 | Material Self | p. 38 |
| Self-Concept | p. 38 | Social Self | p. 40 |
| Self-Image | p. 38 | Spiritual Self | p. 40 |
| Attitude | p. 38 | Avowed Identity | p. 41 |
| Belief | p. 38 | Ascribed Identity | p. 41 |
| Value | p. 38 | Self-Reflexiveness | p. 42 |

## Self-Esteem: What Is Your Value?    p. 42

Your assessment of your worth as a person in terms of skills, abilities, talents, and appearance constitutes your level of self-esteem. Self-esteem is affected by many things, but primary among them are your gender, your comparisons of yourself to others, the expectations you hold for yourself, and your self-fulfilling prophecies.

### Terms to Know

| | | | |
|---|---|---|---|
| Self-Esteem | p. 42 | Social Comparison | p. 43 |
| Self-Concept Clarity | p. 42 | Self-Expectations | p. 43 |
| Gender | p. 43 | Self-Fulfilling Prophecy | p. 44 |

## Communication and the Enhancement of Self-Esteem                              p. 45

Because enhanced self-esteem is a goal for most of us, we provide six means of improving the way you feel about yourself:

- Engage in positive self-talk;
- Visualize the behavior you want to enact or the attributes you wish to acquire;
- Reframe, meaning redefine events and experiences from a different point of view;
- Develop honest relationships, ones in which people tell you the truth about yourself so you can get some growth from the feedback;
- Surround yourself with positive people, not "Debbie Downers"; and
- Lose your baggage, meaning let go of the past and those experiences that can cause your self-esteem to suffer.

### Terms to Know

| | | | |
|---|---|---|---|
| Narcissism | p. 46 | Visualization | p. 46 |
| Intrapersonal Communication | p. 46 | Reframing | p. 47 |
| Self-Talk | p. 46 | | |

## The Perception Process                                                         p. 49

Perception, the process of receiving information from your senses, involves three stages:

1. Attention and selection, when you notice and choose stimuli in your environment on which to focus

2. Organization, when you convert stimuli into understandable information

3. Interpretation, when you attach meaning to what you have attended to, selected, and organized

People often differ in their perceptions of things, events, and other people. Your life experiences, how you were raised, and how you developed contribute a great deal to how you perceive the world around you.

### Terms to Know

| | | | |
|---|---|---|---|
| Perception | p. 49 | Organization | p. 50 |
| Attention | p. 50 | Closure | p. 50 |
| Selection | p. 50 | Interpretation | p. 51 |

## Communicate to Enhance Your Powers of Perception                               p. 52

If you want to enhance your perceptual accuracy, we recommend the following:

- Increase your awareness by fully listening, observing, and paying attention to your surroundings and other people.

- Avoid stereotypes or generalizations about people.

- Check your perceptions—indirectly and directly—to confirm or refute your interpretations of events or someone's behavior.

### Terms to Know

| | | | |
|---|---|---|---|
| Stereotype | p. 53 | Direct Perception Checking | p. 54 |
| Indirect Perception Checking | p. 53 | | |

### Principle One:
### Be aware of your communication with yourself and others.

- Becoming aware of yourself, as you develop your self-concept, involves communicating with others, associating with groups with whom you identify, assuming social roles, and selecting self-labels that describe who you are.

- Inventory yourself for any negative self-fulfilling prophecies that can be detrimental to your self-esteem.

- Engage in positive intrapersonal communication, or self-talk, because a heightened awareness of how you talk to yourself can help enhance self-esteem.

- Develop your perceptual abilities by becoming more aware of yourself and others.

- Use direct and indirect perception checks to sharpen your perceptual accuracy.

# APPLYING Principles for a Lifetime

## Rosenberg Self-Esteem Scale

One of the most widely used scales to measure a person's self-esteem is the Rosenberg Self-Esteem Scale, developed in the 1960s by Dr. Morris Rosenberg, a sociologist. Respond to items on the scale using the following system: SA = Strongly Agree, A = Agree, D = Disagree, and SD = Strongly Disagree. Scoring information follows the scale.

# ASSESSING Your Skill

| | | | | |
|---|---|---|---|---|
| 1. I feel that I'm a person of worth, at least on an equal plane with others. | SA | A | D | SD |
| 2. I feel that I have a number of good qualities. | SA | A | D | SD |
| 3. All in all, I am inclined to feel that I am a failure. | SA | A | D | SD |
| 4. I am able to do things as well as most other people. | SA | A | D | SD |
| 5. I feel I do not have much to be proud of. | SA | A | D | SD |
| 6. I take a positive attitude toward myself. | SA | A | D | SD |
| 7. On the whole, I am satisfied with myself. | SA | A | D | SD |
| 8. I wish I could have more respect for myself. | SA | A | D | SD |
| 9. I certainly feel useless at times. | SA | A | D | SD |
| 10. At times, I think I am no good at all. | SA | A | D | SD |

### Scoring Instructions

To score the scale, assign a value to each of the ten items as follows and total the values:

For items 1, 2, 4, 6, and 7: Strongly Agree = 3, Agree = 2, Disagree = 1, Strongly Disagree = 0.

For items 3, 5, 8, 9, and 10: Strongly Agree = 0, Agree = 1, Disagree = 2, Strongly Disagree = 3.

Scores on the scale range from 0 to 30, with 30 indicating the highest score possible, or the highest level of self-esteem the scale can measure.

Source: M. Rosenberg, *Society and the Adolescent Self-Image* rev. ed. (Middletown, CT: Wesleyan University Press, 1989). Reprinted with permission; retrieved from <http: www.bsos.umd.edu>.

## Inventory Your Self-Esteem

One way to begin to improve your self-esteem is to take an honest measure of how you feel about yourself *right at this very point in time*. Take a few (or many) minutes to think about yourself—who you used to be, who you were only a short time ago, and who you have developed into at this moment in time. Ponder those relationships that had the greatest effect on your development and maturation, and think about the events that caused you to change in some profound way. Then use the columns below to inventory where you stand and to reveal where you may need to put some energy into making change happen for yourself.

| Things I Like About Myself | Things I Don't Like About Myself | How to Make Some Changes |
| --- | --- | --- |
| | | |

## Assessing Some Everyday Stereotypes

Generate statements that reveal common stereotypes about people in the following groups. Try to generate stereotypes that reflect positive as well as negative perceptions. We provide a couple of examples to get you started. Then focus on the damage that stereotypes can do to someone's self-esteem. Also, think about how your communication with someone from each group might be affected by stereotypes.

| Group | Positive Stereotype | Negative Stereotype |
| --- | --- | --- |
| elderly | Old people are wise. | Old people can't fend for themselves. |
| women | Women are naturally more loving and nurturing than men. | Women are terrible drivers. |
| men | | |
| straight-A students | | |
| blondes | | |
| fundamentalist Christians | | |
| bodybuilders | | |
| southerners | | |
| overweight people | | |
| athletes | | |
| rednecks | | |
| video gamers | | |

- **MyCommunicationLab** Raise your awareness of how different people's perceptions of the same event can vary with the Perception video exercise in this chapter of MyCommunicationLab. <www.mycommunicationlab.com> (Access code required.)

- **The National Association for Self-Esteem (NASE)** The mission of NASE as described on its website is "to fully integrate self-esteem into the fabric of American society so that every individual, no matter what their age or background, experiences personal worth and happiness." Let NASE help you take a guided tour of your own self-esteem at <www.self-esteem-nase.org>.

- **Wilderdom** Wilderdom describes itself as "a project in natural living and transformation." As part of that project, the website offers a set of Psychological Exercises for Insight & Self-Awareness Groups. Try some to see if they add to your own self-awareness at <http://wilderdom.com/games/PsychologicalExercises.html>.

**WEB RESOURCES** for More Review, Application, and Assessment

Death and life are in the power of the tongue, and those who love it will eat its fruits.

PROVERBS 18:21

ampyang/Shutterstock.com

## Chapter OUTLINE

- Why Focus on Language?
- The Nature of Language
- The Power of Words
- Confronting Bias in Language
- Using Words to Establish Supportive Relationships
- Study Guide: Review, Apply, and Assess Your Knowledge and Skill

## Chapter OBJECTIVES

After studying this chapter, you should be able to

1. Describe the relationship between words (symbols) and meaning.
2. Explain denotative, connotative, concrete, and abstract meanings people develop for words.
3. Describe how words are both culture bound and context bound.
4. Identify five primary ways in which words have power.
5. Describe the major ways in which language reveals bias about race, ethnicity, nationality, religion, gender, sexual orientation, age, class, and ability.
6. Explain how language helps create supportive or defensive communication climates.

# 3 | Understanding Verbal Messages

"in da beginnin God cre8d da heaven & da earth."
"God luvd da ppl of dis wrld so much dat he gave his only son."

No, this isn't a Bible lesson, but many of you will know how to decipher the above lines and will quickly recognize them as variations on Bible verses—specifically, Genesis 1:1 and John 3:16. A *New York Times* article reported on a religious charity in Australia, known as the Bible Society, that translated the *Contemporary English Version Bible* into the abbreviated language of text messaging.[1] The group offers free software and a search engine so that people can download Bible verses and text them to their friends. (If you're interested, check out <www.biblesociety.com.au>.) A spokesperson for the group believes that sending the entire Bible via texting would require more than 30,000 messages.

Many students are familiar with and comfortable using this form of shorthand, which makes texting, instant messaging, and even e-mailing faster. These adaptations of the English language are becoming more popular in everyday communication.[2] A persistent use of slang may be fine when instant messaging with friends, but when it becomes such a habit that it slips into other written or oral communication—especially at inappropriate moments (like calling a potential boss at a job interview "dude")—you've got a problem. When it comes to different uses of language, the key is to be able to develop "code-switching" abilities, meaning that you use more standard or formal language when appropriate (as in college papers, professional resumés, and job interviews) and relegate the shortcuts and "slanguage" to informal texting, online chats, e-mail, and conversations with friends who translate.[3]

Figure 3.1 depicts our five core principles of communication. In Chapter 2, where we discussed the first of our five Communication Principles for a Lifetime, we explored ways to become more aware of yourself and your perceptions of things and people with whom you come into contact. An important step in this process of coming to know and understand yourself better is an honest, insightful examination of how you talk. How do you come across when meeting someone new? When talking with your best friends? What kind of communicator do your closest friends and family members think you are?

Consider this: *What you say is who you are*. That may sound like a strong statement, but it's true that the words you use reveal who you are. Granted, you communicate with more than your words. Your background, culture, values, experiences, and the way you express yourself nonverbally reveal who you are as well. But as we explore the power of words, we challenge you to think about the incredible tool you have at your disposal: verbal communication. Take an inventory of your use of language as you read this chapter. Do you use language that accurately and effectively represents to other people who you are? Do some areas need improvement? Because of the tremendous potential of verbal communication—its power to reveal the self, to make and break relationships and careers, and to shape cultures—we've chosen to make this one of our five key Communication Principles for a Lifetime.

**Figure 3.1**
**Communication Principles for a Lifetime**

# Why Focus on Language?

On occasion, we do stop to consider the effects of our language on others—usually when we're attempting to persuade or we've said something that has injured or angered someone else. We've all been in situations that made us wish we could get a conversational second chance. But it's a provocative notion that every time we speak, every time we use language, we reveal our thoughts, our very selves to others—no matter how inane, superficial, or emotion-laden the conversation.

One of our main messages in this chapter is this: *Words are powerful.* They affect your emotions, thoughts, actions, and relationships. They affect how you are perceived by others. In fact, interviews with employers reveal their concern about college graduates' lack of language skills, attributed to growing up in a culture that is more visual than oral, stressing nonverbal cues over language.[4] The concern is that students' verbal skills, including both speaking and writing, are underdeveloped. This is clearly a negative trend, in light of other research that has determined that one's ability to use words to effectively participate in conversation with others is a key component in judgments about one's competence as a communicator. In this study, people who talked less in conversation were perceived by others as being less interpersonally skilled than people who comfortably and actively engaged in conversation.[5] If you better understand the nature and power of language, if you attend to your use of language and work to use words with forethought and skill, you can exert great influence and enhance your relationships.

Leo Cullum/Cartoon Bank

Our second main theme in this chapter is this: *You choose language.* You don't use language involuntarily, in the way that your knee might jerk when rapped with a doctor's mallet as an involuntary reflex to a stimulus. You choose the language you use—even if you make that choice in the split second it takes your brain to select a symbol (word) to communicate your thought or impulse. At times we go into "default mode," choosing language we've chosen before. We're prone to patterns in our language because, as humans, we prefer regularity. We also choose particular words because we like them, they've worked well for us in the past, or we grew up with those words and have used them for many years. But pattern and history can breed too much comfort, preventing you from asking yourself, "Is this the best way to say this? Should I say this another way?" You have an incredible wealth of words from which to choose and the power to make choices that allow you to communicate who you are to others in the most effective way possible.

# The Nature of Language

A **language** is a system of symbols (words or vocabulary) structured by grammar (rules and standards) and syntax (patterns in the arrangement of words) common to a community of people. Two language researchers, Edward Sapir and Benjamin Lee Whorf, developed what has come to be known as the Sapir–Whorf Hypothesis.[6] This hypothesis suggests that human language and thought are so interrelated that thought is actually rooted in and controlled by language. One implication of the supposition is that you cannot conceive of something for which you have no word. As a quick illustration of what we mean by this, think about colors. A woman describes her new dress to her friend using the term *puce*, but if the friend does not have the term *puce* in her frame of reference as a color term, she will be unable to conceive of the color her friend mentions. (For those of you with a possibly underdeveloped color-term repertoire, puce is a brilliant purplish-red color.)

**language**
A system of symbols (words or vocabulary) structured by rules (grammar) and patterns (syntax) common to a community of people.

To extend this notion further, one could argue that the quality of one's language reflects the quality of one's thought. Your verbal communication reveals how you think and what you think about. This is only one supposition about how language and thought operate, but it's a provocative notion to consider that language has such a powerful influence on our everyday thinking processes.

## People Use Words as Symbols

As we noted in Chapter 1, words are **symbols** that represent something else. Just as a flag is a symbol of a country, words are symbols that trigger thoughts, concepts, or feelings. For instance, what comes to mind when you see or hear the word *freedom*? Perhaps you think historically, remembering what you studied in grade school about Abraham Lincoln's freeing the slaves, or perhaps you picture U.S. armed forces defending our national freedom. Or maybe you envision something a bit closer to home, like the feeling of freedom you get during a break between semesters at college.

## People Attach Meanings to Words

Now imagine that you use the word *freedom* in a conversation, in an effort to convey to the other person the concept or image in your mind. You know what you're thinking when you say the word; the challenge is for the other person to understand your thoughts behind your choice of word. In communication terms, this is the process of creating **meaning**. The meaning of a word is a person's interpretation of that symbol—it's how the person makes sense of the symbol. Meanings don't reside in the words themselves but in the ways in which communicators use the words. You attach a meaning to the word *freedom*, the symbol you choose in conversation; your listener creates meaning for the word when he or she attempts to interpret what you've said. Words aren't the culprits in communication problems; the meanings people create for words lead to successful or problematic communication.

Sometimes a speaker's and a receiver's meanings don't correspond because the same words mean different things to different people; the term for this communication problem is **bypassing**. Using the *freedom* example, think about a couple in a long-term romantic relationship. If one partner said to the other, "I need more

**symbol**
A word, sound, gesture, or visual image that represents a thought, concept, object, or experience.

**meaning**
A person's interpretation of a symbol.

**bypassing**
A communication problem that arises when the same words mean different things to different people.

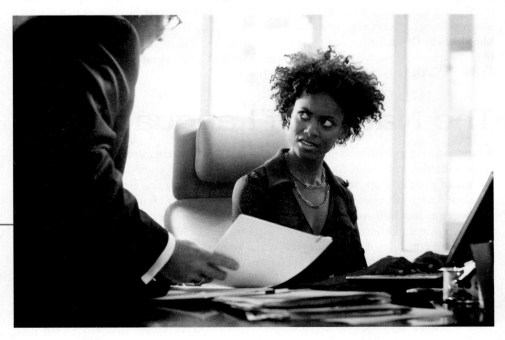

Because different people can attach different meanings to the same word, it's easy to get confused. What can you do to help clarify your own meaning so that others understand you?

Christopher Robbins/Thinkstock

freedom in this relationship," what might that mean? It might mean that the relationship is over because one partner wants out completely, to be *free* to explore other relationships. But it might also mean that the partner is suffocating or feeling a lack of *freedom* to do as she or he pleases in the relationship. If the partner is using *freedom* in this latter sense, the relationship might stay intact. The couple might need only to make some changes in the amount of time they spent together. Some conflicts in relationships can be boiled down to a simple difference in the meaning of the words that get exchanged.

## People Create Denotative and Connotative Meanings for Words

Symbol sharing through language isn't just a simple process of uttering a word and having its meaning clearly understood by another. People create meanings for language on two levels: the denotative and the connotative.[7]

The **denotative meaning** of a word conveys content. Denotation is the restrictive, or literal, meaning of a word. For example, one dictionary defines *apartment* as "a room or suite of rooms used as a residence."[8] This definition is a literal, or denotative, definition of the word *apartment*; it describes what the word means in American culture.

By contrast, the **connotative meaning** of a word conveys feelings; people create personal and subjective meanings for words. To you, the word *apartment* might mean a comfortable place to relax at the end of the day or a setting in which to entertain friends. To others, though, the word *apartment* might engender feelings of guilt (if the apartment hasn't been cleaned in a while) or feelings of dread (if apartment rent is draining the wallet or relationships with roommates leave something to be desired). Clearly, the connotative level of language is more individual. While the denotative or objective meaning of the word *apartment* can be found in any dictionary, your subjective response to the word is probably not contained there.

## People Convey Concrete and Abstract Meanings Through Words

Meanings for words can be placed along a continuum from concrete to abstract.[9] A word's meaning is **concrete** if we can experience what the word refers to (the referent) with one of our senses; if we can see it, touch it, smell it, taste it, or hear it, it's concrete. If we cannot do these things with the referent, the word's meaning is **abstract**. In general, the more concrete the language, the easier it is for others to understand and retain. The more abstract a word, the more difficult it is to understand or agree on a meaning. For example, the word *patriotism* is abstract because we cannot hear or taste patriotism. But a word that suggests a demonstration of patriotism, such as *voting*, is more concrete, because we can physically perform the act of voting. It's wise to minimize the use of abstract words when you're trying to clarify a message. Concrete terms help make a message more clear and memorable.[10]

## Meanings Are Culture Bound

**Culture** is a learned system of knowledge, behavior, attitudes, beliefs, values, rules, and norms that is shared by a group of people and shaped from one generation to the next.[11] The meaning of a word, just like the meaning of any symbol, can change from culture to culture and across co-cultures (cultural groups within a larger culture). To a European, for example, a *Yankee* is someone from the United States; to a player on the Boston Red Sox baseball team, a *Yankee* is an opponent; and to an American from the South, a *Yankee* is someone from the North. Some years ago, General Motors sold a car called a *Nova*. In English, *nova* means "bright star," and in Latin, *nova* means

**denotative meaning**
The restrictive, or literal, meaning of a word.

**connotative meaning**
The personal and subjective meaning of a word.

**concrete meaning**
Meaning that refers to something that can be perceived with one of the senses.

**abstract meaning**
Meaning that refers to something that cannot be perceived or experienced with one of the senses.

**culture**
A learned system of knowledge, behavior, attitudes, beliefs, values, rules, and norms that is shared by a group of people and shaped from one generation to the next.

# Communication&TECHNOLOGY

## Real or Virtual Desktop? Denotation, Connotation, and Computer Terms

What do you do when you "save" a "file" to a "folder"? Do you insert a piece of paper into a manila container with a label at the top? Or do you save a document you've been drafting on your computer into the computer's memory? Is what you're working on really a "document," or is a document a piece of paper with words on it? Does your computer really have "memory," or is that a metaphor for the way we store computer work for safekeeping?

Think about how many metaphors emerge in simple, everyday computer use. What about the "mouse"? Do these important hardware devices look like scurrying mice? You can save documents, files, folders, and so forth to your "desktop," which isn't a literal desktop at all, but rather a means of organizing your computer information.

Many of us enjoy Microsoft Office, which isn't a physical office at all but software—a means of organizing and accomplishing our computer work. The "office" metaphor helps us understand something new by relating it to something familiar, something we can understand. Had Microsoft called the software Microsoft Frzshmez, we wouldn't relate so easily to this **neologism** (a new term introduced into a language); we would have trouble pronouncing and remembering it, so we would be less likely to buy it.

Computer language is full of denotative and connotative meanings for terms that are largely metaphors, and using such language can get quite complicated. Metaphors are a bridge from the known and familiar to the new and different; they are commonly used in computing because so many novel concepts and mechanisms emerge that require terminology. Because metaphors are central to our language as well as our thought processes, they serve a useful communicative function.

Using metaphors also poses a challenge, because they add to the number of denotative definitions that people need to know for specific words. One team of British information scientists, for example, found significant variation among managers and employees regarding the denotations of the computer terms *save as* and *file*.[12] In another example, suppose you were in a meeting and someone asked you where to find a document that was needed. If you told that person to go into your office and get it from your desktop, would your coworker look on your physical desktop or on your computer?

The British researchers concluded that some terms are too embedded in computer usage to be changed. To communicate better, you may need to clarify which definition you mean when you use certain words. Other new words have yet to be invented. What term could best be applied to the process of hurling one's computer out of a window after it freezes or crashes?

---

**neologism**
A new term introduced into a language.

"new"—both appropriate connotations for a car. In Spanish, however, the spoken word *nova* sounds like the words *no va*, which translates to "It does not go." As you can imagine, this name was not a great sales tool for the Spanish-speaking market.

# RECAP

## THE NATURE OF LANGUAGE

- People use words as *symbols:* Symbols represent something else.
- People create *meanings* for words: Meaning is a person's interpretation of a symbol.
- Words have both *denotative* and *connotative* meanings: The denotative meaning is a restrictive, or literal, meaning; the connotation is a personal and subjective meaning.
- People convey *concrete* and *abstract* meanings through words: A word's meaning is concrete if we can experience what the word refers to with one of our senses; if not, the meaning is abstract.
- Meanings are *culture bound:* The meaning of a word can change from culture to culture.
- Meanings are *context bound:* The situation or context for communication aids people as they attach meanings to symbols.

## Meanings Are Context Bound

When Republican presidential nominee Senator John McCain quipped in 2008 that U.S. armed forces might be in Iraq as long as a hundred years, he was roundly criticized. But McCain explained that those words were taken out of the context of an exchange he was having with a reporter at a press conference, and thus his meaning was distorted. Likewise, McCain's opponent Barack Obama took heat for saying that, in tough times, people cling to their guns and religion. Focusing on that soundbite took the comment out of the context of the answer Obama was giving to a question about the declining American economy. The context of verbal messages plays a central role in how accurately they are interpreted by

# Communication & DIVERSITY

### "She Think She All That": Code Switching

At the beginning of this chapter, we mentioned the term **code switching**, which refers to the practice of using one form of language and then switching to another form, usually seamlessly. Here's an example from a recent conversation.

Two African American college students were talking in an elevator, recapping a class that had just let out. One said to the other, in regard to a classmate's behavior, "Can you believe she turn in she paper two weeks early?" The other replied, "She think she grades is above it all. She think she all that."

One of your textbook authors, a nerdy professor, overheard the exchange and politely asked the women if they wouldn't mind explaining their choice of that form of language versus more standard English. The women explained that they would never say "She think she grades is above it all" to a professor, other authority figure, or someone outside their peer group, because they realize that their slang is perceived as nonstandard English and that its use would make them appear uneducated or inappropriate. However, within the social context of their friendship, to

use standard English would be weird, as though they had something to prove or saw themselves as "uppity."

These women clearly demonstrated the effectiveness of code switching in language, something many of us perform in our own way at some point or another. Code switching can be an expression of ethnic or co-cultural identification.[13] At other times, it's a habit that develops when people feel a part of two or more worlds, adapting their language to the situation and people in it. In Texas, it's quite common to hear people who are bilingual switch in and out of Spanish and English, as one woman in a grocery store did when she asked a clerk, "Donde esta la ice cream?" Researchers suggest that bilingual code switching indicates linguistic flexibility—the ability to choose the best word to convey meaning, regardless of one's primary or secondary language.[14]

Do you ever code switch in interactions with people? If so, do you code switch as a communication adaptation strategy, a form of identity expression, or just a habit you've developed with certain friends? How should people who don't know the "code" react to code switching?

receivers. The context includes all of our words, plus the nonverbal elements ever present in communication, like the environment or setting in which the communication occurs as well as the facial expressions, tone of voice, and other nonverbal cues that surround and accompany a verbal message and help us decode it. Removing words from their context distorts the meaning. No matter their political persuasion, just about every day in the heated political arenas of our country, some politician's words are likely to be taken out of context. Placing one's words back into context is next to impossible, once they've been extracted and scrutinized.

# The Power of Words

No doubt you've heard the old schoolyard chant "Sticks and stones may break my bones, but words can never hurt me." We don't know who first came up with that statement, but we imagine it to be someone who never experienced the sting of name calling, the harmful effects of being labeled a "slow reader," or the legacy of an unfortunate family nickname. Words *do* hurt. With all the national headlines about tragic stories of the consequences of bullying, teasing, and harassment, it's important to consider the damage language can do. California educator Jane Close Conoley addressed this subject in her article "Sticks and Stones Can Break My Bones and Words Can Really Hurt Me." She encourages university students training to be schoolteachers to pay attention to the language that surrounds bullying, because violence usually begins with a verbal assault.[15]

Words have the power to evoke a wide range of emotions in listeners. But words can also heal and inspire and transform the human spirit, which is another reason for making the effective use and interpretation of verbal messages one of our five Communication Principles for a Lifetime. Let's explore five attributes of words.

- *The Power to Create and Label Experience.* Alzheimer's, Parkinson's, Tourette syndrome—these diseases are named after the person who discovered the

**code switching**
Practice of using one form of language and then switching to another form, usually seamlessly.

This woman's delight at reading a special e-mail shows the power of words to convey our emotions and to affect other people's thoughts and feelings. What steps help you to consider others' feelings when choosing your words?

Deborah Jaffe/Getty Images

condition, so the name of a phenomenon has the power to label the experience and make it more real.[16] The English language is always evolving; for example, the term *sexual harassment* didn't emerge until the 1970s when feminists generated the term to describe a very real behavior many experienced in the workplace.[17]

- *The Power to Communicate Feelings.* Words help communicate our moods and emotional states, giving labels to feelings that otherwise would be hard to convey.[18] If you get fired from a job, you might say you feel angry and helpless or liberated and relieved. The first response might lead to depression, the second to happiness. One study conducted over a thirty-five-year period found that people who described the world in pessimistic terms when they were younger experienced poorer health in middle age than those who had been optimistic.[19] Your words and corresponding outlook have the power to affect your emotional, mental, and physical health.

- *The Power to Affect Thoughts and Actions.* A few decades ago, a weight-loss product called Ayds came on the market. Ayds were small, brown, chewy squares that manufacturers claimed would help reduce appetite. You can guess why this product disappeared in the 1980s. Given what we now know about the disease AIDS, who today would willingly ingest a product called Ayds? Advertisers have long known that the way a product is labeled greatly affects the likelihood that consumers will buy it, because words affect the way we think about things and react to them.

- *The Power to Shape and Reflect Culture.* International students often puzzle over English slang and ask such questions as "What does it mean to 'cowboy up'?" or "When someone is called 'all that and a bag of chips,' is that a good or a bad thing? Does it mean you're fat?" Cultures and co-cultural groups within them develop unique languages of their own as a way of forging connections and enhancing solidarity, so the language you use both shapes and reflects your culture.

- *The Power to Make and Break Relationships.* Probably we have all had the experience of saying something to another person that we regret. But if you've ever said something so inappropriate that it cost you a romantic relationship or friendship, you know firsthand the power of words to make and break relationships. Granted, some people believe "actions speak louder than words," but both verbal and nonverbal communication are crucial to getting relationships going in the first place and then making them work.

# RECAP

## THE POWER OF WORDS TO . . .

- *Create and Label Experience.* New experiences may lead to new words. For example, *global weirding* is a newly coined term for strange or not-the-norm weather.

- *Affect Thoughts and Actions.* Words influence how we think. For instance, product names are critical to audience response and sales success. The critically acclaimed film *The Shawshank Redemption* was a box-office failure, which some attributed to the film's obtuse title.

- *Communicate Feelings.* Words help create and communicate our moods and emotional states. Think of how many terms exist for sadness: *blue, down, depressed, in the depths, mopey, bummed, down in the dumps, out of sorts, feeling punk.*

- *Shape and Reflect Culture.* Cultures change; language both creates and reflects the changing nature of culture.

- *Make and Break Relationships.* Verbal communication creates opportunities for us to know and be known by others. It's an important tool for establishing relationships and deepening them; it can also be a catalyst for a relationship to end.

# Confronting Bias in Language

We don't want to sound like the "language police"—that is, we don't want to dictate how you ought to talk. But we have found that oftentimes insensitive or stereotypical language usage arises out of ignorance or a lack of education. Even well-meaning, educated people can communicate bias through the language they choose to use. Words that reflect bias toward members of other cultures or groups can create barriers for listeners. In addition, such language ignores the fact that the world is constantly changing. In the following pages, we explore a few categories of language that illustrate the constant evolution of verbal communication and represent areas in which we can all heighten our sensitivity.

## Biased Language: Race, Ethnicity, Nationality, and Religion

Think about whether you have ever said or overheard someone say the following:

> "I got a great deal on a car; the sticker price was a lot higher, but I jewed the dealer way down."
> "You can't have that back, you Indian giver!"
> "She's a real Bible banger."
> "He doesn't have a Chinaman's chance to make the team."
> "That divorce settlement gypped me out of what's rightfully mine!"

That last statement tends to puzzle people more than the others. It includes the term *gypped*, which is derived from the word for the nomadic cultural group known throughout the world as gypsies. The stereotype relates to being suckered or cheated out of what one is due.

The language used in each of these examples demonstrates an insensitivity to members of cultural groups and a word barrier known as **allness**, which occurs when words reflect unqualified, often untrue generalizations that deny individual differences or variations. In this chapter, where we examine our day-to-day language, it's important to think about how language reflects your attitudes and reveals how you think.

You may remember that in 2007 shock jock Don Imus was fired from his radio program for using racially charged, derogatory language to describe the Rutgers women's basketball team, which the night before had clinched their division. While opinions varied about whether Imus's punishment fit his "crime," few disputed the egregious nature of the offense.[20]

Many of us try to stay current with our language, exhibiting sensitivity as we try to use appropriate terminology when referring to members of our own race and ethnicity, as well as members of other groups. But we're likely to hear—both off campus and on—racial language that is a throwback to an earlier time in our country's evolution; hearing or even hearing *about* that kind of language is jolting.

Terms pertaining to certain racial and ethnic groups have certainly changed over time. Check out Table 3.1 on page 70, which provides racial categories that appeared as options in the U.S. censuses of 1970, 1980, 1990, 2000, and 2010, and you'll see how much more specific our language has become in an attempt to better communicate racial and ethnic identity in this country. Sometimes it's a challenge to get your language to keep pace with the changing times, but try not to get lazy with language. It's important to inventory and revolutionize your language with regard to the racial, ethnic, national, and religious affiliations of people, because the language you choose to use is your primary tool for creating the reality of your existence, for revealing how you think, for being known by others, and for knowing them as well.[21]

## Biased Language: Gender and Sexual Orientation

Language that reveals bias in favor of one sex and against another, termed **sexist** or exclusive language, is more prevalent than you'd think. Decades of effort, spurred by the women's liberation movement in the 1960s, have raised the consciousness of American culture regarding exclusive language. But many people still do not alter their language to reflect and include both sexes. In addition, insensitivity or intolerance toward persons who are gay, lesbian, bisexual, or transgender is often reflected in what is termed **heterosexist** or **homophobic language**. A person who uses heterosexist

**allness**
A word barrier created through the use of language that reflects unqualified, often untrue generalizations that deny individual differences or variations.

**sexist (exclusive) language**
Language that reveals bias in favor of one sex and against another.

**heterosexist language**
Language that reveals an assumption that the world is heterosexual, as if homosexuality or bisexuality did not exist.

**homophobic language**
Language that overtly denigrates persons of nonheterosexual orientations, usually arising out of a fear of being labeled gay or lesbian.

## Table 3.1
## U.S. Census Racial Categories

| 1970 | 1980 | 1990 | 2000 | 2010 |
|------|------|------|------|------|
| White | White | White | White | White |
| Negro or Black | Negro | Black | Black or African American | Black, African American, or Negro |
| Indian (American) | Indian (American) | Indian (American) | American Indian or Alaska Native (specify tribe) | American Indian or Alaska Native |
| Japanese | Japanese | Japanese | Japanese | Japanese |
| Chinese | Chinese | Chinese | Chinese | Chinese |
| Filipino | Filipino | Filipino | Filipino | Filipino |
| Hawaiian | Hawaiian | Hawaiian | Hawaiian | Native Hawaiian |
| Korean | Korean | Korean | Korean | Korean |
| | Eskimo | Eskimo | | |
| | Aleut | Aleut | | |
| | Vietnamese | Vietnamese | Vietnamese | Vietnamese |
| | Asian Indian | Asian Indian | Asian Indian | Asian Indian |
| | Guamanian | Guamanian | Guamanian or Chamorro | Guamanian or Chamorro |
| | Samoan | Samoan | Samoan | Samoan |
| | | Other Asian Pacific Islander | Other Asian (print race) | Other Asian |
| | | | Other Pacific Islander (print race) | Other Pacific Islander |
| Other (print race) | Other (specify) | Other Race | Some Other Race | Some Other Race |
| | | | (Individuals who consider themselves multiracial can choose two or more races.) | (People who are of two or more races may choose to provide two or more races either by checking two or more race response check boxes, by providing multiple responses, or by some combination of check boxes and other responses.) |

*Source:* Table based on information from M. Anderson and S. Feinberg, 2000, "Race and Ethnicity and the Controversy over the U.S. Census," *Current Sociology* 48.3: 87–110; National Research Council, *Measuring Racial Discrimination* (Washington, DC: National Academies Press, 2004); U.S. Census Bureau, 2001, "Population by Race and Hispanic or Latino Origin for All Ages and for 18 Years and Over for the United States: 2000," <http://www.census.gov/PressRelease/www/2001/tables/st00_1.pdf>; U.S. Census Bureau, 2010, *Questionnaire Reference Book* (Washington, DC: U.S. Department of Commerce, Bureau of the Census, Washington D.C.), retrieved from <http://2010census.gov>.

language speaks from an assumption that the world is heterosexual, as if romantic and sexual attraction to those of the same sex or to both sexes simply were not possible. Homophobic language more overtly denigrates persons of nonheterosexual orientations and usually arises out of a fear of being labeled gay or lesbian. We consider sexist and heterosexist forms of biased language below.

**Language and the Sexes**    Even though women now constitute 50 percent of the U.S. population, to listen to the language of some people, you'd think it was still a man's world. Sexist language can reflect stereotypical attitudes or describe roles in exclusively male or female terms.[22] Research indicates that exclusive language usage does the following: (1) maintains sex-biased perceptions, (2) shapes people's attitudes about careers that are appropriate for one sex but not the other, (3) causes some women to believe that certain jobs and roles aren't attainable, (4) contributes to the belief that men deserve more status in society than women do, and (5) mutes the voices of many women, because the words and norms formed by the dominant group don't allow for the articulation of women's experiences.[23]

Even dictionaries fall into patterns of describing women and men with discriminatory language.[24] Included in the *Oxford English Dictionary* definition for *woman* are (1) an adult female being, (2) female servant, (3) a lady-love or mistress, and (4) a wife. Men are described in more positive and distinguished terms: (1) a human being, (2) the human creation regarded abstractly, (3) an adult male endowed with many qualities, and (4) a person of importance of position.

The most common form of sexism in language is the use of **generic language**, using a masculine term as though it were a term to describe all people. There are two primary ways in which masculine-as-generic language typically appears in written and oral communication: in pronoun usage and in man-linked terminology.

Consistent evidence from research on sexist language shows that people—particularly in American culture—simply do not tend to think in neuter; we think in male or female. We don't tend to think of living entities as *it*, and we rarely use that pronoun to refer to them. When most people read or hear the word *he*, they think of a masculine person, not a sexless person.[25] Using generic masculine language, in essence, turns all persons into male persons. For example, a student giving a speech on how to project a winning, confident style in a job interview said, "When you greet the boss for the first time, be sure to look him straight in the eye, give him a firm handshake, and let him know you're interested in the job." The student's exclusive language choice only allowed for the possibility of a male boss, not a female boss.

**generic language**
General terms that stand for all persons or things within a given category.

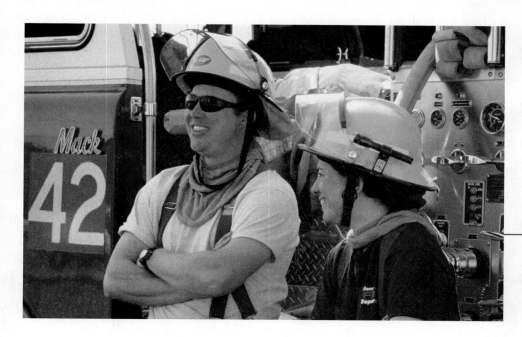

The gender-neutral term *firefighter* describes both of these people, whereas the sexist term *fireman* excludes the person on the right.
©/PhotoEdit

We don't know what you were taught in high school or in other college classes about generic language, but publishing standards today require the use of nonsexist language, which allows no masculine terms to stand for all persons.[26] You'll notice that we use inclusive language in this text—because it reflects our value system and because our publisher requires it.

The solution to the problem of sexist language is not to replace each *he* with *she*, but to use terms that include both sexes so that your language reflects the contemporary world. If you want to refer to one person—any person of either sex—the most clear, grammatical, nonsexist way to do that is to use either *she or he*, *he/she*, or *s/he*.[27] Other options include (1) omitting a pronoun altogether, either by rewording a message or by substituting an article (*a*, *an*, or *the*) for the pronoun; (2) using *you* or variations of the indefinite pronoun *one*; or (3) using the plural pronoun *they*.[28]

Consciously remembering to use nonsexist, inclusive language brings the following benefits.[29]

- Gender-inclusive language reflects inclusive attitudes. Monitoring your verbal communication for sexist remarks will make you aware of any sexist attitudes or assumptions you may hold.
- Using inclusive language helps you become more other oriented, which will have a positive effect on your relationships. Consciously ridding your language of sexist remarks reflects your awareness of others and their sensitivities.
- Inclusive language makes your communication more contemporary and unambiguous. If you say *he*, for example, how is a listener to know whether you're referring to a male person or to just any person in general?
- Nonsexist language strengthens your style and demonstrates sensitivity that can empower others. By eliminating sexist bias from your communication, you affirm the value of all individuals with whom you interact.[30]

**Language and Sexual Orientation**    We realize that sexual orientation is one of the more difficult topics to discuss, mainly because people tend to hold strong opinions about it. But no matter your views about sexuality, it's vital to use sensitive, appropriate communication with whomever you encounter.

Just as you have learned to avoid racially charged terms that degrade and draw attention to someone's ethnicity, it's important to learn to avoid language that denigrates a person's sexual orientation and draws undue attention to this element of cultural diversity. One of your authors was quite taken aback a few years ago when she received a paper from a first-year student in which the derogatory term *fag* frequently appeared. You've no doubt heard this term, probably bantered about in high school, but its use can be a signal of homophobia—the fear of being labeled or viewed as gay or lesbian. Heterosexist language is more subtle; it often emerges through omission, meaning what *is not* said, rather than by commission, or what *is* said. For example, in class, how many of your instructors give dating examples using two people of the same sex? Most examples about relationships that you read or hear about in courses such as Interpersonal Communication or Introduction to Psychology reflect heterosexual romantic relationships. As another example, how often do you hear or use the term *partner* instead of *husband* or *wife*? The first term, *partner*, is inclusive of all forms of couples, while the latter terms, at least in most states, refer only to heterosexual marriage. These forms of language usage can communicate a heterosexist bias and suggest that other sexual orientations are inappropriate or nonexistent.[31]

## Biased Language: Age, Class, and Ability

"Just turn the car, grandpa!" Ever heard a driver say this in irritation or said it yourself? Ever call an elderly person a "geezer" or an "old-timer"?

People sometimes use the word *retarded* in casual conversation to refer to occasions when someone does something foolish or incorrectly. The cast members of the hit TV series *Glee* who play Coach Sue Sylvester and her assistant, Becky (who has Down syndrome), have joined a campaign to stop this biased use of language.

Michael Yarish/© Fox/courtesy Everett Collection

# Communication&ETHICS

## "That's So Gay!"

We've said in this chapter that the primary definition of the term *homophobia* is a fear of being labeled or viewed as homosexual. However, a secondary meaning of *homophobia* is a discriminatory attitude toward or hatred of people who are homosexual, and some forms of language certainly reflect this negativity.[32]

A few years ago, a language usage surfaced that can still be heard, albeit to a much lesser extent than when it first became popular: saying "That's so gay" in response to someone's choice of clothing, accessories, or furnishings (typically things not expected to be owned or used by members of one sex or the other) or in response to someone's communication or actions. The language was made popular by the then-hit TV show *Friends*, whose characters Chandler and Joey could often be heard

criticizing something by saying "That's so gay." College students picked up this language, using the term *gay* to refer to anything disagreeable and often justifying its use by saying that it was just a funny thing to say, not meant to refer to homosexuals or to be discriminatory or inappropriate. Many communication professors, as well as gay rights activists and educators, across the country took a stand to curb the use of this form of language contending that it was indeed homophobic and discriminatory.[33] You may not hear this language much anymore; if so, we're glad that it's on its well-deserved way out of the lexicon, because here's the problem: Substitute any word for the term *gay* and see if it sounds derogatory. Would someone say "That's so Jew" or "That's so black" and dare to think that these phrases weren't racial/ethnic slurs?

Just as some people contend that Americans are hung up on gender and racial diversity, many believe that Americans are hung up on age. We live in a culture that glorifies youth and tends to put its elders "out to pasture."[34] Age discrimination is a very real problem in the workforce—so much so that laws have been enacted to guard against someone's being denied professional opportunities because of age. Likewise, some older people may hold stereotypes of young people and may speak to them as though their youth exempts them from intelligence or responsible action. We recommend that you inventory your language for any terms that either show disrespect for elders or are patronizing or condescending to younger people.

Another factor influencing language that has received research attention is socioeconomic class.[35] Class distinctions typically are revealed in derogatory references to "blue-collar workers," "manual laborers," or "welfare recipients." Another class slur is "white trash." In the late 1990s, when Paula Jones filed a sexual harassment lawsuit against then-president Bill Clinton, she was called "white trash" and "trailer trash" as she was ridiculed in the press and in living rooms across the country. Avoid references that reveal a condescending or disrespectful attitude toward someone's education (or lack of it) and socioeconomic status.

Finally, an area of bias in language that most people became conscious of by the turn of the 21st century relates to ability. Some years ago, Helen Keller was described as "deaf, dumb, and blind." Nowadays, the appropriate term for her inability to communicate vocally would be *mute*. Be careful that

## RECAP

### CONFRONTING BIAS IN LANGUAGE

Inventory your language for subtle and not-so-subtle indications of bias in several areas:

- *Race, Ethnicity, and Nationality.* Avoid language that denigrates members of a racial or ethnic group; be careful not to overemphasize race or ethnicity or "mark" a person by using adjectives referring to national origin, as in "that Oriental student in my class."

- *Religion.* Watch stereotypical language pertaining to religious affiliation, such as derogatory references to Jews, Muslims, or fundamentalist Christians, for example.

- *Gender.* Include both sexes in your language, especially in your use of pronouns; avoid masculine generic pronouns and male-linked terms that exclude women.

- *Sexual Orientation.* Be alert to the potential for heterosexism in your language—the assumption that everyone is heterosexual or that heterosexuality is the only possible orientation. Eliminate homophobic language that degrades and stereotypes gays, lesbians, bisexuals, and transgender individuals.

- *Age.* Avoid calling too much attention to a person's age in your verbal communication. Be especially vigilant not to label or stereotype the elderly or to condescend to or glorify youth.

- *Class.* Monitor references to socioeconomic differences, such as distinctions between blue-collar and white-collar workers.

- *Ability.* Avoid verbal communication that draws attention to a person's physical, mental, or learning ability.

your language doesn't make fun of or draw attention to someone's physical, mental, or learning disability, such as calling someone a "cripple," "retard," or "slow reader." Research has found that when people with disabilities are called demeaning names, they're perceived as less trustworthy, competent, persuasive, and sociable than when they're described in positive terms.[36]

# Using Words to Establish Supportive Relationships

For more than five decades, communication scholar Jack Gibb's research has been used as a framework for both describing and prescribing verbal behaviors that contribute to feelings of either supportiveness or defensiveness.[37] Gibb spent several years listening to and observing groups of individuals in meetings and conversations, noting that some exchanges seemed to create a supportive climate whereas others created a defensive one. Words and actions, he concluded, are tools we use to let someone know whether we support them or not. Thus, Gibb defined **supportive communication** as communication that uses language to create a climate of trust, caring, and acceptance. The language used in **defensive communication**, in contrast, creates a climate of hostility and mistrust. When someone gets defensive, communication is seriously impeded.

Two specific uses of language tend to engender negative reactions and defensiveness in most of us; thus, we view them as word barriers that can damage even the most secure of relationships.

- **Polarization** occurs when we describe things in extremes or opposites without any middle ground. One romantic partner might say to the other, "You either love me or you don't." Pronouncements of this kind can be interpreted as ultimatums, as though there were only two options and no compromise position. Former President George W. Bush was both praised and criticized for stating in his post–September 11, 2001, speech to Congress, "You're either with us or you're with the terrorists." It's wise to avoid language that creates a false or forced choice for people, making them feel controlled, hemmed in, or manipulated.
- **Trigger words** arouse our emotions. Travis, a former student, described in class a word his wife used during arguments that really sparked his anger more than anything else. When Travis would make a point that would frustrate his wife— one for which she had no comeback—she would look at him, toss her hand in the air, and say, "Whatever." Perhaps this word triggers you too, because it punctuates a conversation; it dismisses the other person and her or his point. Do you know what words trigger your emotions, both in positive and negative directions? Certain uses of language can make us feel accepted and appreciated or disrespected and hostile.[38]

Think about times when your words made someone defensive and how hard you had to work to get the person to let the defenses down. In the following section, we suggest ways to use verbal communication to create a supportive rather than an antagonistic climate.

## Describe Your Own Feelings Rather Than Evaluate Others

Most of us don't like to be judged or evaluated. One way to avoid evaluating others is to attempt to use "I" statements instead of accusatory "you" statements. Statements such as "You always say you'll call, but you never do" or "You need to pick up the dirty clothes in your room" attack a person's sense of self-worth and usually result in a defensive reaction. Instead, use the word *I* to describe your own feelings and thoughts

**supportive communication**
Language that creates a climate of trust, caring, and acceptance.

**defensive communication**
Language that creates a climate of hostility and mistrust.

**polarization**
The tendency to describe things in extremes, as though no middle ground existed.

**trigger words**
Forms of language that arouse strong emotions in listeners.

about a situation or event: "I find it hard to believe you when you say you'll call" or "I don't enjoy the extra work of picking up your dirty clothes." When you describe your own feelings instead of berating the receiver of the message, you take ownership of the problem. This approach leads to greater openness and trust because your listener is less likely to feel rejected or as if you are trying to control him or her.

## Solve Problems Rather Than Control Others

When you were younger, your parents gave you rules to keep you safe. Even though you may have resented their control, you needed to know that the stovetop was hot, when not to cross the street, and how dangerous it was to stick your finger in a light socket. Now that you're an adult, when people treat you like a child, it often means they're trying to control your behavior, to take away your options.

Most of us don't like to be controlled. Someone who presumes to tell us what's good for us instead of helping us puzzle through issues and problems to arrive at our own solutions or higher understanding is likely to engender defensiveness. In truth, we have little or no control over others. Open-ended questions such as "What seems to be the problem?" or "How can we deal with this issue?" create a more supportive climate than critical comments such as "Here's where you are wrong" and "You know what your problem is?" or commands like "Don't do that!"

## Be Genuine Rather Than Manipulative

To be genuine means honestly being yourself rather than attempting to be someone you are not. It also means taking a sincere interest in others, considering the uniqueness of each individual and situation, and avoiding generalizations or strategies that focus on your own needs and desires. A manipulative person has hidden agendas and her or his own concerns and interests most at heart. A genuine person has the other person's interests at heart and uses language to facilitate an open and honest discussion of issues and problems.

## Empathize Rather Than Remain Detached from Others

**empathy**
The ability to understand and feel what another person is feeling.

**Empathy**, one of the hallmarks of supportive relationships, is the ability to understand and actually feel or approximate the feelings of others and then to predict the emotional responses they will have to different situations.[39] You work to put yourself in the other person's shoes, to experience as closely as you can what she or he is experiencing. The opposite of empathy is neutrality. To be neutral is to be indifferent or apathetic toward others. (Even when you express anger or irritation toward another, you are investing some energy in the relationship.) A statement that epitomizes this concept of neutrality is "I don't love you or hate you; I just *don't* you."

Remaining detached from someone when empathy is obviously called for can generate great defensiveness and damage a relationship. Here's an example: You're upset about an argument you just had with someone you're dating, so you seek the support and listening ear of a good friend. But that friend is in "party mode" or such a good mood that he or she chooses not to concentrate and listen to what's going on with you. Rather than engage in your situation, your friend remains detached and blows off your concerns. In situations like this, most of us become defensive and frustrated, and the quality of our friendship may suffer. Empathy is a building block of a supportive relationship; it may come naturally to some people, but most of us have to work at it, just like many other skills we can develop with a bit of effort.[40]

Being genuine and showing empathy for others' feelings are two ways to help establish supportive relationships. What words can help convey your empathy when a friend is troubled?

Piotr Marcinski/Shutterstock.com

## Be Flexible Rather Than Rigid Toward Others

Some people are just *always* right, aren't they? (These people spend a lot of time alone, too.) Most people don't like someone who always seems certain that she or he is right. A "You're wrong, I'm right" attitude creates a defensive climate. This doesn't mean that you should have no opinions and go through life passively agreeing to everything. And it doesn't mean that there isn't a clear-cut right and wrong in a given situation. But instead of making rigid pronouncements, at times you may want to qualify your language by using phrases such as "I may be wrong, but it seems to me . . ." or "Here's something you might want to consider." Conditional language gives your opinions a softer edge that allows room for others to express a point of view; it opens the door for alternatives. Declarations tend to shut the door. Again, there are times when equivocation is not an appropriate or advisable way to communicate. But in those cases when you want to induce supportiveness and reduce the potential for defensiveness, conditional, flexible language works best.

## Present Yourself as Equal Rather Than Superior

You can antagonize others by letting them know that you view yourself as better or brighter than they are. You may be gifted and extraordinarily intelligent, but it's not necessary to announce or publicize it. And although some people have the responsibility and authority to manage others, "pulling rank" doesn't usually produce a supportive climate. With phrases such as "Let's work on this together" or "We each have a valid perspective," you can avoid erecting walls of resentment and defensiveness. "We" language can be preferable to "you" language; it builds a sense of camaraderie and shared experience, and by using it you avoid setting yourself apart from listeners.

Avoid using "high-falutin'" (unnecessarily complicated) words just to posture, impress others, or project some image. Sometimes referred to as "bafflegab," this kind of language can come in the form of words, phrases, or verbal shorthand that people use but no one understands. People with particular expertise may use abbreviated terms or acronyms (words derived from the first letters of several words in a phrase). The military is notorious for its use of language that doesn't easily translate outside of military circles. It's better to use informal language appropriate to the situation and your listeners than to attempt to talk over the heads of everyone in the room.

You can also create defensiveness by using language that is too simplistic for your listeners. Granted, when you communicate with someone from another culture or even from another U.S. co-cultural group, you may need to alter your message to get your meaning across. But this means that your verbal communication should be explicit, not condescending. For example, some people use oversimplified words when communicating with elderly people. It's inappropriate to assume that aging diminishes one's capacity to understand. Try to use language to present yourself on equal ground with your listeners and establish a supportive, open climate for communication.

## Avoid Gunny-Sacking

In one of his hit songs, Garth Brooks sings, "We buried the hatchet; we left the handle sticking out." Brooks makes mild reference

# RECAP

## USING WORDS TO CREATE A SUPPORTIVE CLIMATE

- Describe your own feelings instead of evaluating the point of view or behavior of others.
- Keep the focus on problem solving rather than controlling others.
- Be genuine rather than manipulative in your communication.
- Instead of ignoring someone's feelings, try to empathize.
- Use conditional language and demonstrate flexibility rather than rigidity in your communication.
- Present yourself as an equal rather than as a superior. Avoid acting like a know-it-all. Don't attempt to talk over the heads of listeners or condescend to them, because either approach can breed defensiveness.
- Avoid gunny-sacking, or reminding someone of past mistakes or issues.

here to a process known as "gunny-sacking," which can be like an ax handle sticking out within easy reach; when grasped, it serves to remind you of a past conflict or wound. Gunny-sacking involves dredging up someone's past mistakes or problems and linking them to a current situation. Suppose your best male friend has just been dumped by his "one true love," but you—being the good friend that you are—remind him that the last three people he dated were also his "one true love," at least at the time. Your friend wants empathy, but you respond by highlighting his tendency to turn "Ms. Right" into "Ms. Right Now." Such an approach will likely make him feel criticized and engender defensive reactions in him. This kind of scenario rarely deepens a relationship.

# STUDY GUIDE:
# Review, Apply, and Assess Your Knowledge and Skill

## REVIEWING What You Know

### Why Focus on Language?　　　　　　　　　　　p. 62

Words are powerful; they affect your emotions, thoughts, actions, and relationships, as well as how you're perceived by others. The better your choices of language, the better your overall communication skill and your relationships.

### The Nature of Language　　　　　　　　　　　p. 63

Language is a system of symbols (words or vocabulary) structured by grammar (rules and standards) and syntax (patterns in the arrangement of words) common to a community of people. The Sapir–Whorf Hypothesis suggests that language and thought are so interrelated that thought is rooted in and controlled by language. The limits of your language may be the limits of your thought.

Six important aspects of language are (1) people use words as symbols (something that represents something else); (2) people attach meanings to words, and sometimes meanings differ (bypassing); (3) people use denotative and connotative meanings for words; (4) people convey concrete and abstract meanings through words; (5) meanings are culture bound; and (6) meanings are context bound.

#### Terms to Know

| | | | |
|---|---|---|---|
| Language | p. 63 | Concrete Meaning | p. 65 |
| Symbol | p. 64 | Abstract Meaning | p. 65 |
| Meaning | p. 64 | Culture | p. 65 |
| Bypassing | p. 64 | Neologism | p. 66 |
| Denotative Meaning | p. 65 | Code Switching | p. 67 |
| Connotative Meaning | p. 65 | | |

### The Power of Words　　　　　　　　　　　p. 67

Words are extremely powerful. They can create and label our experiences, communicate our feelings, affect our thoughts and actions, shape and reflect our culture, and make and break our relationships.

### Confronting Bias in Language　　　　　　　　　　　p. 68

Our language often reveals our biases. Monitor your language to avoid bias in these categories: (1) race, ethnicity, nationality, and religion; (2) gender and sexual orientation; and (3) age, class, and ability.

#### Terms to Know

| | | | |
|---|---|---|---|
| Allness | p. 69 | Homophobic Language | p. 69 |
| Sexist (Exclusive) Language | p. 69 | Generic Language | p. 71 |
| Heterosexist Language | p. 69 | | |

## Using Words to Establish Supportive Relationships                        p. 74

Supportive communication creates a climate of trust, caring, and acceptance; defensive communication creates a climate of hostility and mistrust. Two uses of language that breed hostility and mistrust are: (1) polarization, which occurs when people describe things in extremes or opposites, as though there were no middle ground; and (2) trigger words, which are forms of language that trigger our emotions, both in positive and negative directions.

Here are seven tips for developing a supportive communication climate:

- Describe your own feelings rather than evaluate others;
- Solve problems rather than control others;
- Be genuine rather than manipulative;
- Empathize rather than remain detached from others;
- Be flexible rather than rigid toward others;
- Present yourself as equal rather than superior; and
- Stick to the present situation and avoid gunny-sacking (dredging up past mistakes, problems, and issues).

### Terms to Know

| | | | |
|---|---|---|---|
| Supportive Communication | p. 74 | Trigger Words | p. 74 |
| Defensive Communication | p. 74 | Empathy | p. 75 |
| Polarization | p. 74 | | |

### Principle Two:
### Effectively use and interpret verbal messages.

- Realize that communication problems may not have to do with the words used, but rather with the meanings people attach to the words.
- Recognize the difference between denotative and connotative language.
- Use concrete terms whenever appropriate, because abstract language is harder to understand and remember than concrete language.
- Understand that words are affected by the culture within which the language is used.
- Pay attention to the words communicators choose to use and attempt to interpret those words in the spirit and context in which they were intended.
- Avoid biased language when speaking about race, ethnicity, nationality, religion, gender, sexual orientation, age, class, and ability.
- Use words to engender supportiveness, rather than defensiveness.

# APPLYING Principles for a Lifetime

# ASSESSING
## Your Skill

## Practicing Denotation and Connotation

Below we review the differences between denotative and connotative meanings of words and provide examples.

| Level | Definition | Example |
|---|---|---|
| Denotative | Literal, restrictive definition of a word | *Teacher:* the person primarily responsible for providing your education |
| Connotative | Personal, subjective reaction to a word | *Teacher:* the warm, supportive person who fostered a climate in which you could learn, or the cold taskmaster who drilled lessons into you and made you feel inferior |

For each of the following terms, provide a denotative, or dictionary-type, definition; then generate connotative meanings of your own.

| Term | Denotative Definition | Connotative Meanings |
|---|---|---|
| work | | |
| parent | | |
| infidelity | | |
| professionalism | | |
| loyalty | | |

## Your Bias Is Showing

Here's an activity to illustrate how people reveal their biases through their use of language. Generate a list of stereotypical terms, both positive and negative, often associated with each word below. For example, for the word *Democrat*, you might think of positive and negative terms like "liberal," "tax and spend," "big government," "antiwar," "environmentalist," and "populist."

| Term | Positive Stereotypical Language | Negative Stereotypical Language |
|---|---|---|
| conservatives | | |
| foreign students | | |
| homeless people | | |
| churchgoers | | |
| movie stars | | |

# WEB RESOURCES
## for More Review, Application, and Assessment

- **MyCommunicationLab**  Think more about the power of words as you watch the video *Words That Wound* at while reviewing this chapter. <www.mycommunicationlab.com> (Access code required.)

- **Wordplay sites**  Visit Puzzability to expand your capacity for English through its creative plays on words, visual puzzles, and innovative approaches to crosswords and word search puzzles at <www.puzzability.com>. Try Wordsmith at <http://wordsmith.org> if you enjoy anagrams and such services as Word-A-Day e-mails.

- **Dictionaries** If a common dictionary doesn't help you decipher the meaning of a word you encounter, you can try the Extelligence Archaic and Creative Word Dictionary at <www.extelligence.co.uk>. The Urban Dictionary is popular for getting the meanings of the latest slang terms; see <www.urbandictionary.com>.

- **National Forum on People's Differences** This forum challenges users to "dare to ask"—either as postings or in a real-time chat format—questions that might be impolite or too embarrassing to ask in a face-to-face or even telephone format. You'll be amazed at the kinds of questions people ask about other people. Just a few examples include "What do retired people do all day?"; "Is it disrespectful for a straight person to go to a gay or lesbian bar?"; "Why do Muslim women cover their heads?; and "Is it considered offensive if a white person calls a black person 'black'"? See <www.yforum.com>.

We respond to gestures with an extreme alertness and, one might say, in accordance with an elaborate and secret code that is written nowhere, known by none, and understood by all.

EDWARD SAPIR

# Chapter OUTLINE

- Why Focus on Nonverbal Communication?
- The Nature of Nonverbal Communication
- Codes of Nonverbal Communication
- How to Interpret Nonverbal Cues More Accurately
- Study Guide: Review, Apply, and Assess Your Knowledge and Skill

# Chapter OBJECTIVES

After studying this chapter, you should be able to

1. Provide four reasons for studying nonverbal communication.
2. Describe the six ways in which nonverbal communication functions with verbal communication.
3. Discuss six elements that reveal the nature of nonverbal communication.
4. Identify and explain the seven nonverbal communication codes.
5. Explain Mehrabian's three-part framework for interpreting nonverbal cues.

anna karwowska/Shutterstock.com

# 4 | Understanding Nonverbal Messages

"Don't use that tone of voice with me, mister; I don't need your sarcasm right now."

"Why are you looking at me like that? Did something happen?"

"I knew it was you coming down the hall; your footsteps are a dead giveaway."

"I'm sure I'll get over the argument, but right now I just need some space."

What do these statements have in common? They all have to do with a form of human communication that occurs without words—what we term *nonverbal communication*. As we explained in Chapter 1, **nonverbal communication** is communication other than written or spoken language that creates meaning for someone. The one exception to this definition is that to hearing people, sign language appears to be nonverbal communication. However, to people who are deaf, sign language is verbal communication, with certain movements, signs, and facial expressions conveying words, phrases, and emphasis.[1]

We know you're becoming familiar with our five-sided model of Communication Principles for a Lifetime, but let's do a quick recap (see Figure 4.1). In Chapter 2, we explored ways to become more aware of yourself and your perceptions of things and people with whom you come into contact. An important step in this process of coming to know and understand yourself better is an honest, insightful examination of how you talk. In Chapter 3, we challenged you to consider the power of words, to take inventory of your use of language, and to think about ways to improve your verbal communication so that you extend yourself to others and respond to them in an appropriate, effective manner.

Now we get to what most people consider an even greater challenge—understanding and evaluating your nonverbal communication and improving your ability to interpret the nonverbal behavior of others. Nonverbal communication is of great importance; a person who can read others' nonverbal communication with sensitivity and skill makes a memorable impression on other people. Because of the power of nonverbal communication to complement verbal communication, to further reveal the self—particularly in those situations when talking is inappropriate, impossible, or inadequate—and to affect how you connect with others as you initiate and build relationships, we've chosen to make this the third of our five key Communication Principles for a Lifetime.

We have two primary goals in this chapter:

**nonverbal communication**
Communication other than written or spoken language that creates meaning for someone.

- To help you become more aware of your own nonverbal communication; and
- To enhance your nonverbal receiving skills, or your ability to detect and interpret the nonverbal cues of others more accurately.

You first have to become more aware of your own nonverbal behavior; such awareness helps you understand yourself—how and why you behave as you do. Because much nonverbal communication behavior is subconscious, most people have limited awareness or understanding of it. Your heightened awareness will lead to a more skillful use of nonverbal communication, as well as greater accuracy in interpreting others' nonverbal cues, so that you interact more effectively with other people.

**Figure 4.1**
**Communication Principles for a Lifetime**

ADAPT

AWARE

Appropriately adapt messages to others

Be aware of your communication with yourself and others

LISTEN AND RESPOND

Listen and respond thoughtfully to others

Effectively use and interpret verbal messages

VERBAL

Effectively use and interpret nonverbal messages

NONVERBAL

# Why Focus on Nonverbal Communication?

Have you ever watched someone interact with someone else and thought, "That person just doesn't have a clue"? We've all seen or met people who appear not to pick up on the communication clues of others. For example, have you ever tried to end a conversation because you were late or needed to be somewhere else, and the person you were talking to just wouldn't let you out of the conversation? The person didn't seem to notice you looking at your watch, angling your body away, taking a few steps back, and making minimal vocal responses to what was being said. Now, we all have times when we can't "catch a clue," even if we consider ourselves to be fairly sensitive, perceptive people. Certain people, places, moods, or topics of conversation may impede our ability to give and receive nonverbal communication effectively. But we don't want to be clueless. We want to be able to exhibit effective nonverbal communication and to read and interpret the clues others give us more sensitively and accurately.

However, no one can become a perfect interpreter of the nonverbal communication of others, because human beings are unique, complicated, and ever-changing creatures. Although we encourage you to deepen your understanding of nonverbal communication, sharpen your powers of observation, and develop greater skill in interpreting the meanings behind others' nonverbal actions, we also suggest that you remain keenly aware of the idiosyncratic and complex nature of nonverbal communication. To begin to explore this topic, let's look at four reasons for studying nonverbal communication.

## Nonverbal Messages Communicate Feelings and Attitudes

Nonverbal communication is a primary tool for conveying our feelings and attitudes and for detecting the emotional states of others. In the study of nonverbal communication, Albert Mehrabian is an expert. He concluded from his research that the most significant source of emotional information is the face, which can channel as much as 55 percent of our meaning. Vocal cues such as volume, pitch, and intensity convey another 38 percent of our emotional meaning. In all, we communicate approximately 93 percent of the emotional meaning of our messages nonverbally; as little as 7 percent of the emotional meaning is communicated through explicit verbal channels.[2] Although these percentages do not apply to every communication situation, Mehrabian's research illustrates the potential power of nonverbal cues to communicate emotion and attitude.

How aware are you of the power of your nonverbal communication with others? Think about confrontations you've had in the past. In your opinion, which communicates emotions most effectively: the volume, pitch, and intensity of the voice; nonverbal gestures, facial expressions, and body positions; or the meaning of the actual words spoken?

Ghislain & Marie David de Lossy/Getty Images

# Communication&TECHNOLOGY

## Texting and E-Mailing Your Emotions

Without the usual nonverbal mechanisms that allow us to reveal our emotions to others in face-to-face communication, how do we let others at a distance know what we're feeling? Text messaging, instant messaging, and e-mailing are so commonplace now that most people have learned the shorthand that allows us to send quick messages through our cell phone or computer. Acronyms and abbreviations such as "lol," "omg," and "bff" are speedy ways to get a message across. The sideways images made from punctuation marks, commonly referred to as emoticons, serve as nonverbal cues that help convey the meaning or emotion behind our messages, with the most common being the happy face, or "smiley." Here are some commonly used emoticons derived from various sources:[3]

| | |
|---|---|
| :-( | Depressed or upset by a remark |
| :-I | Indifferent |
| :-\| | Straight face |
| :-o | Surprise |
| ;-) | Winking at a suggestive or flirtatious remark |
| :-/ | Skeptical |
| :-P | Sticking your tongue out |
| :-D | Laughing |
| :-@ | Screaming |
| 8-) | Wearing sunglasses |
| ::-) | Wearing regular glasses |
| (-: | Left-handed |
| ((((BoB)))) | Hug |

Formatting options add nonverbal elements to our communication as well. For example, putting words in all caps, a technique known as shouting, typically reveals emphasis, frustration, or even anger. Another nonverbal element is the general look of the message itself; this applies more to e-mail and other computer-based exchanges than to text messages, since formatting options for texting are somewhat limited. While some reformatting occurs in the transmission of e-mail messages from computer to computer, most elements don't reformat. Research shows that styles of fonts (typefaces) convey different nonverbal cues that accompany our verbal messages.[4]

If someone sent you the following e-mail message, what would you guess the person was feeling, based on nonverbal cues conveyed through the choice of font and use of boldface?

**I'VE HAD AN INTERESTING DAY, BUT WOULD LIKE TO HEAR ABOUT YOURS FIRST.**

Might your sense of the message change if you received it in the font below?

*I'VE HAD AN INTERESTING DAY, BUT WOULD LIKE TO HEAR ABOUT YOURS FIRST.*

It's wise to consider the important but often-overlooked nonverbal signals embedded in our communication when it is mediated by technology.[5]

## Nonverbal Messages Are More Believable Than Verbal Ones

"Hey—are you mad or something?" asks Jonas.
(Big sigh.) "Oh, no. I'm not mad," responds Danita (in a subdued tone of voice and without making eye contact).
"You sure? Because you're acting funny, like you're ticked off." (One more try and then Jonas will likely give up.)
"I SAID I'M NOT MAD, OKAY? WILL YOU LEAVE IT ALONE PLEASE?"

Despite Danita's claim to the contrary, the real story is—she's mad. "Actions speak louder than words." This cliché became a cliché because nonverbal communication is more believable than verbal communication. Verbal communication is a conscious activity; it involves the translation of thoughts and impulses into symbols. Some nonverbal communication is conscious, but a great deal of it is generated subconsciously as we act and react to stimuli in our environment. It's easier to control your words than to control a quiver in your voice when you're angry, the heat and flush in your face when you talk to someone you're attracted to, or shaky knees when you're nervous.

When a person's verbal and nonverbal communication contradict, as in Danita's case, which should an astute observer believe? The nonverbal actions carry the truer message most of the time.

## Nonverbal Messages Are Critical to Successful Relationships

One researcher suggests that as much as 65 percent of the way we convey meaning in our messages is through nonverbal channels.[6] Of course, the meaning others interpret from our behavior may not be the one we intended. But we begin making judgments about people just a fraction of a second after meeting them, based on nonverbal information. We may decide whether a date is going to be pleasant or dull during the first thirty seconds of meeting the person, before he or she has had time to utter more than "Hello."[7]

Consider the handshake, a simple ritualistic greeting between two people used in many cultures. Have you ever considered the power of a handshake to communicate? If you get a half-handed, limp handshake from someone, what are you likely to conclude about that person? William Chaplin and his colleagues examined the judgments Americans make about someone's personality based on a handshake and determined that the most positive handshake was strong (but not as strong as to cut off the blood supply), vigorous, not too brief or too long, and complete (meaning that the people gripped each other's hands fully, with palms touching).[8] Participants in the study formed more favorable first impressions of those people with good handshakes than those with lousy ones, so even a simple nonverbal ritual like a handshake can have a definite and long-lasting impact on how others perceive you.[9]

Nonverbal cues are important not only in the early stages of relationships, but also as we maintain, deepen, and sometimes terminate those relationships. In fact, the more intimate the relationship, the more we use and understand the nonverbal cues of our partners. We also use nonverbal cues to signal changes in the level of satisfaction with a relationship. When we want to cool things off, we may start using a less vibrant tone of voice and cut back on eye contact and physical contact with our partner.

## Nonverbal Messages Serve Multiple Functions

Nonverbal messages function in a variety of ways:

- Nonverbal cues can *substitute for* verbal messages. Raising your index and middle fingers in the air can mean "peace" or "V" for victory, or it can simply be someone's way of ordering two of something in a noisy, crowded environment where it's hard to be heard.
- Nonverbal cues delivered simultaneously with verbal messages *complement*, clarify, or extend the meaning of the verbal cues, conveying more information and allowing for a more accurate interpretation. When someone waves, makes eye contact, and says "Hello," the gesture and eye contact are nonverbal complements to the verbal greeting, providing context and revealing emotions and attitudes.
- Sometimes our nonverbal cues *contradict* our verbal cues, like in the case of Danita in our earlier example, whose words said she wasn't mad but whose nonverbal cues showed her true emotional state. In most instances when verbal and nonverbal cues contradict, the nonverbal message is the one we should believe.
- We use nonverbal messages to *repeat* our verbal messages. You and a friend head in different directions after class. You yell, "See you at the dorm at 4," but your friend can't hear you over the hall noise, so he makes a face like he's confused.

What is this person trying to communicate? Nonverbal cues, such as this small gesture, can aid communication when they substitute for or complement our words.

Thomas Northcut/Thinkstock

# RECAP

You point in the direction of the dorm and then raise four fingers in the air, to which your friend nods his head up and down, signaling that he understands your message. In such a situation, the verbal message comes first, but the nonverbal cues repeat the message to create greater understanding.

- Nonverbal cues *regulate* our participation in conversation. When talking with people, we rely on such nonverbal cues as eye contact, facial expressions, audible intakes of breath, vocalizations like "um," shifts in posture or seating position, and movements closer to or farther away from others.

- We may use nonverbal cues to *accent* or reinforce a verbal message. "We simply must do something about this problem or we will all bear the blame," bellows the mayor. When the mayor says the word *must*, she pounds the podium and increases her volume for emphasis. Such a vocalization and gesture serve to accent or add intensity to the verbal message.

# The Nature of Nonverbal Communication

While the benefits of studying and improving one's facility with nonverbal communication are clear, deciphering unspoken messages is a tricky activity. Dictionaries help us interpret words, but no handy reference book exists to help decode nonverbal cues. Below are some of the challenges inherent in the interpretation of nonverbal communication.

## The Culture-Bound Nature of Nonverbal Communication

Some evidence suggests that humans from every culture smile when they are happy and frown when they are unhappy.[10] They also all tend to raise or flash their eyebrows when meeting or greeting others, and young children in many cultures wave to signal they want their parents, raise their arms to be picked up, and suck their thumbs for comfort. This evidence suggests that there is some underlying commonality in human emotion. Yet each culture tends to develop unique rules for displaying and interpreting the expression of emotion.[11]

Nonverbal behavior is culture bound. You will make critical errors in communicating nonverbally, as well as in attempting to interpret the nonverbal behavior of others, if you don't situate nonverbal actions within a cultural context. Intercultural communication scholars suggest that one culture's friendly or polite action may be another culture's obscene gesture.[12] During his second inaugural parade, President George W. Bush displayed the two-finger "hook 'em horns" gesture to salute members of the University of Texas marching band as they passed by his stand. According to the Associated Press, a Norwegian newspaper expressed outrage over the gesture, since it is considered an insult or a sign of the devil in Norse culture. In sign language used by and for deaf persons, the gesture translates into "bull_____." In Mediterranean countries, the gesture implies that a husband is the victim of an unfaithful wife. In Russia, it is considered a symbol for newly rich, arrogant, and poorly educated Russians; in many European countries, it serves to ward off the "evil eye"; and in some African nations, it's used to put a hex or curse on another person.[13]

# The Rule-Governed Nature of Nonverbal Communication

You operate according to many rules in your nonverbal communication. You may be unaware that you function according to these rules, but when your rules are violated, you definitely know it. For example, have you ever been in a conversation with someone who got too close, like all up in your face? For some reason, the other person's rule about appropriate distance differs from yours.

Communication scholar Judee Burgoon developed a theory for how nonverbal communication functions, termed the **expectancy violations model**.[14] The model suggests that we develop expectations for appropriate nonverbal behavior in ourselves and others, based on our cultural backgrounds, personal experiences, and knowledge of those with whom we interact. When those expectations (or rules) are violated, we experience heightened arousal (we become more interested or engaged in what's happening), and the nature of our interpersonal relationship with the other person becomes a critical factor as we attempt to interpret and respond to the situation.

When someone stands too close to you in conversation, expectancy violations theory claims that you will react to the nonverbal rule infraction according to the credibility, status, and attractiveness of the person who's violating your space. If the person isn't attractive (physically or personally) or of respectable status and credibility, you will likely compensate for the space invasion nonverbally, usually by stepping back or moving away from the person. Only rarely do most of us resort to a verbal response such as, "Please back up; you're violating my personal space." We all violate nonverbal rules from time to time, and at those moments we become acutely aware that rules or expectations of appropriateness have a powerful influence on nonverbal communication.

## The Ambiguous Nature of Nonverbal Communication

Most words are given meaning by people within a culture who speak the same language. But the exact meaning of a nonverbal message is known only to the person displaying it; the person may not intend for the behavior to have any meaning at all. Some people have difficulty expressing their emotions nonverbally. They may have frozen facial expressions or monotone voices. They may be teasing you, but their deadpan expressions lead you to believe that their negative comments are heartfelt. Often it's a challenge to draw meaningful conclusions about other people's behavior, even if we know them quite well. One strategy that helps us interpret others' nonverbal cues is called **perception checking**, a strategy we mentioned in Chapter 2 in our discussion of self-awareness. Jonas, whom we saw earlier in this chapter, was trying to check Danita's perceptions when he asked her if she was mad. To check your own perceptions, observe in detail the nonverbal cues, make your own interpretation, and then do one of two things (or both): (1) Ask the people you're observing how they feel or what's going on, and/or (2) run your interpretation by another observer to get a second opinion or more input before you draw a conclusion. Remember our earlier warning about not assuming that your interpretation is necessarily the right one; perception checking can enhance the likelihood that your interpretation will be accurate.

## The Continuous Nature of Nonverbal Communication

Words are discrete entities; they have a beginning and an end. You can point to the first word in this sentence and underline the last one. Our nonverbal behaviors are not as easily dissected. Like the sweep of a second hand on a watch, nonverbal

**expectancy violations model**
A model that suggests that we develop rules or expectations for appropriate nonverbal behavior and react when those expectations are violated.

**perception checking**
The skill of asking other observers or the person being observed whether your interpretation of his or her nonverbal behavior is accurate.

We're usually uncomfortable when someone breaks our unwritten rules for nonverbal communication. President Lyndon Johnson, for example, was known for standing too close when he talked to people, giving listeners what came to be called "the Johnson treatment." In this 1966 conversation, civil rights leader Whitney Young seemed to be so uncomfortable with President Johnson's space invasion that he closed his eyes. How do you typically respond when someone violates your nonverbal communication expectations?
LBJ Library photo by Yoichi Okamoto

behaviors are continuous. Imagine you're standing in the hallway after class, talking to a classmate. You both give eye contact as you talk and make facial expressions that coordinate with what you're saying. You stand a certain distance apart, move and change your posture as the conversation flows, add a hand gesture or two to emphasize what you're saying, and change your pitch, volume, and rate of speaking to further make yourself understood. Your classmate's cell phone rings; the person apologizes, looks down into his or her book bag to fish out the phone, and makes eye contact with you once again, along with a facial expression of apology. The person then signals to you with a hand gesture, while talking into the phone, that she or he has to go, and you understand that your conversation is over. You wave goodbye, break eye contact, and go your separate ways, and your nonverbal behaviors go with you. In this simple example, the nonverbal cues are flying faster than the verbal ones, but they're essential in getting the message across. The sheer volume and continuous flow of nonverbal cues—not to mention complications such as culture and emotion—make accurate interpretation a challenge.

## The Nonlinguistic Nature of Nonverbal Communication

Even though some writers in the 1960s and 70s tried to make readers think otherwise, there is no "language of the body." Julius Fast, author of the 1970 book *Body Language*, believed that nonverbal communication was a language with pattern and grammar, just like verbal communication.[15] He suggested that if you were savvy and observant enough, you could quickly and easily interpret certain nonverbal behaviors to mean certain things—in any case, at any time. For example, Fast contended that if a woman sat cross-legged and pumped her foot up and down while talking to a man, that was a clear-cut sign of her romantic interest in him. If someone didn't make eye contact, she or he was automatically dishonest and untrustworthy. If people crossed their arms in front of them, that indicated hostility.

The problem with this approach is that it didn't take into account the complexities of individual, contextual, and cultural differences. Pumping the foot might be an indication of nervousness, not attraction. Some people are shy; others come from a culture in which making direct eye contact is considered rude. It's important to remember that nonverbal communication doesn't conform to the patterns of a language.

## The Multichanneled Nature of Nonverbal Communication

Have you ever tried to watch two or more TV programs at once? Some TV sets let you see as many as eight programs simultaneously so that you can keep up with three ball games, two soap operas, the latest news, and your favorite sitcom. Like programs on a multichannel TV, nonverbal cues register on our senses from a variety of sources simultaneously. Just as you can pay close attention to only one program at a time on your multichannel TV, you actually attend to only one nonverbal cue at a time, although you can switch your attention very rapidly. Before you try to interpret the meaning of a single nonverbal behavior, look for clusters of corroborating nonverbal cues, in conjunction with verbal behavior, to get the most complete picture possible.

# Codes of Nonverbal Communication

Many individuals have long been fascinated with nonverbal communication, but those who have made perhaps the greatest contributions to our understanding are Paul Ekman and Wallace Friesen, sometimes referred to as the "great classifiers" of nonverbal behavior.[16] Although the primary categories or codes of nonverbal information researchers have studied stem from mainstream Western culture, realize that these behaviors are evidenced differently in other cultures. Below we introduce and explain each code, and then we provide a few research findings to illustrate how we can apply knowledge of nonverbal communication to further our understanding of human behavior.

## Appearance

Many cultures around the world place a high value on appearance—body size and shape, skin color and texture, hairstyle, and clothing. We realize that we're writing from an American perspective, but it seems as though

When your clothing functions as an artifact rather than simply a way to cover your body, it conveys some sense of your culture.
©Bill Bachmann/The Image Works

Americans place an undue emphasis on looks. For example, our views of and preferences for government leaders, especially presidents, are affected by their height.[17] College students perceive physically attractive teachers to be more approachable than other teachers and give them higher evaluation scores.[18] We put such pressure on ourselves and others to be physically attractive that our self-esteem may decline when we realize we cannot match up with some perceived "ideal."[19] Americans elevate onto a pedestal people who are perceived to be highly physically attractive, whether or not they actually deserve this kind of accolade. We also attach all sorts of desirable qualities to highly attractive people. Research shows that we tend to think physically attractive people are more credible, happy, popular, socially skilled, prosperous, employable, persuasive, honest, poised, strong, kind, outgoing, and sexually warm than other people.[20]

Clothing functions primarily to keep us warm and within society's bounds of decency. Another important function is to convey a sense of one's culture. Baseball caps, baggy pants, and distinctive T-shirts, as well as other appearance aspects, termed **artifacts** (jewelry, tattoos, piercings, makeup, cologne, eyeglasses, and so on), are displays of culture. Clothing and artifacts affect how we feel about ourselves and how we are perceived by others.[21]

## Body Movement, Gestures, and Posture

Have you ever traveled in a country where you couldn't speak the language? Or have you ever tried to have a conversation locally with a person who didn't speak English or who was deaf and didn't read lips? What do you do in these situations? Chances are that you risk looking extremely foolish by using overexaggerated gestures or slowly and deliberately shouting words the listener cannot understand. These responses are nonverbal attempts to compensate for a lack of verbal understanding. Even when we do speak the same language as others, we often use gestures to help us make our point.

**Kinesics** is a general term for human movements, gestures, and posture. Posture and movement are greatly affected by self-esteem and emotional state. For example, when you're feeling upbeat and good about yourself, you're likely to carry yourself more upright and possibly exhibit a "spring in your step." Conversely, if you're having a bad day, your posture might be more slumped over or stooped, because some days it's just hard to hold your head and shoulders up.

As we've said earlier in this chapter, gestures are culture bound, context bound, and rule governed. Nancy Armstrong and Melissa Wagner are the authors of a book entitled *Field Guide to Gestures*, in which they describe and interpret a wide variety of gestures, particularly as used in U.S. culture.[22] They organize gestures into such categories as Arrival and Departure, Approval and Disapproval, Mating, and Offensive and Profane. Among the gestures in the Arrival and Departure category are the Bow, the Blown Kiss, the Fist-Chest Pound, and the Live Long and Prosper gesture (which needs no interpretation for *Star Trek* fans).

In one of their most comprehensive contributions to nonverbal research, Ekman and Friesen classified movement and gestures according to their function. They identified five kinesic categories: emblems, illustrators, affect displays, regulators, and adaptors.[23]

**artifact**
Clothing or another element of appearance (e.g., jewelry, tattoos, piercings, makeup, cologne).

**kinesics**
Human movements, gestures, and posture.

**emblem**
A nonverbal cue that has a specific, generally understood meaning in a given culture and may substitute for a word or phrase.

**illustrator**
A nonverbal behavior that accompanies a verbal message and complements, contradicts, or accents it.

- **Emblems** are nonverbal cues that have specific, widely understood meanings and that may substitute for words or phrases. A librarian who wants people to stop talking puts an index finger up to pursed lips; someone who wants to direct our attention to something will point in the desired direction. Emblems emerge or are negotiated within cultures, so it's important to interpret the meaning of a gesture within its cultural context.[24]

- **Illustrators** are general nonverbal cues that accompany verbal messages; they can contradict, accent, or complement the message.[25] If you yawn while proclaiming you're not tired, your nonverbal illustrator contradicts your words. Slamming a book closed while announcing, "I just can't read this anymore" is a nonverbal accent to a verbal message. We often use complementary illustrators when giving people directions to a location—even when we're on the phone and can't be seen.[26]

- **Affect displays** are nonverbal cues that communicate our emotions and attitudes. As early as 1872, when Charles Darwin systematically studied the expression of emotion in both humans and animals, scientists realized that nonverbal cues are the primary ways humans communicate emotion.[27] Facial expressions, posture, gestures, and body movements (like how we walk) reveal our feelings.[28] Your face tends to express which *kind* of emotion you're feeling, whereas your body reveals the intensity or how *much* emotion you're feeling.
- **Regulators** control the interaction or flow of communication between people. When we're eager to respond to a message, we're likely to make eye contact, raise our eyebrows, open our mouth, take in a breath, and lean forward slightly. When we don't want to engage in conversation, we tend to do the opposite: avert our eyes, close our mouth, cross our arms, and lean back in our seats or away from the verbal action.
- **Adaptors** are nonverbal behaviors that help us satisfy a personal need or adapt to the immediate situation. When students take exams, nonverbal adaptors are in full swing, with students shifting frequently in their seats, tapping pencils or pens on their desktops, running their hands through their hair or twisting strands of hair, and adjusting their clothing.

Here's an interesting application of the research on kinesics. Some researchers have explored verbal and nonverbal indications of attraction.[29] One study found 52 gestures and nonverbal behaviors that women use to signal their interest in men. Among the top nonverbal flirting cues were smiling, surveying a crowded room with the eyes, and moving closer to the object of one's affection.[30] However, other studies have found that men tend to view flirting as more sexual than women do, and men often misinterpret women's friendly behaviors as signs of sexual attraction and interest.[31] Studies have found that the likelihood for this kind of misinterpretation greatly increases as alcohol consumption increases.[32]

## Eye Contact

Do you agree that the eyes are the "windows to the soul"? What can people tell about you by looking into your eyes? Are you comfortable making eye contact with most people or only with people you know well? Eye contact is extremely important in American culture, as well as in many other cultures around the world. Americans, in particular, make all kinds of judgments about others—particularly about their trustworthiness, truthfulness, and sincerity—on the basis of whether they make or avoid eye contact.[33] Table 4.1 on page 94 summarizes circumstances under which we are more or less likely to make eye contact with a conversational partner.[34]

Research shows that eye contact plays a significant role in judgments of a public speaker's credibility.[35] In the first televised presidential debate, John F. Kennedy appeared comfortable and confident as he made eye contact with television cameras. It seemed as though he was making eye contact directly with the American public. In contrast, Richard Nixon darted his eyes nervously from side to side at times and generally made less eye contact with the camera and the viewing audience. This created a perception that Nixon was shifty, untrustworthy, and lacking credibility.

## Facial Expressions

Actor/comedian Steve Carell has a very expressive face. Researchers suggest that the human face is capable of producing 250,000 different facial expressions.[36] Steve Carell can probably make them all.

The face is the exhibit gallery for our emotional displays.[37] Suppose you buy an expensive new gadget and show it to your romantic partner or a friend. Or as an

**affect display**
A nonverbal behavior that communicates emotions.

**regulator**
A nonverbal behavior that helps control the interaction or level of communication between people.

**adaptor**
A nonverbal behavior that helps satisfy a personal need and allows a person to adapt or respond to the immediate situation.

## Table 4.1
## When Do We Make Eye Contact?

| YOU ARE MORE LIKELY TO LOOK AT YOUR CONVERSATIONAL PARTNER WHEN YOU . . . | YOU ARE LESS LIKELY TO LOOK AT YOUR CONVERSATIONAL PARTNER WHEN YOU . . . |
| --- | --- |
| • are physically distant from the person.<br>• are discussing impersonal topics.<br>• have nothing else to look at.<br>• are interested in your partner's reactions.<br>• are romantically interested in or like your partner.<br>• wish to dominate or influence your partner.<br>• come from a culture that emphasizes visual contact in interaction.<br>• are an extrovert.<br>• are listening, rather than talking.<br>• are female. | • are physically close to the person.<br>• are discussing intimate topics.<br>• have other objects, people, or backgrounds to look at.<br>• aren't romantically interested in or dislike your partner.<br>• come from a culture that doesn't value visual contact in interaction.<br>• are an introvert.<br>• are embarrassed, ashamed, sorrowful, sad, or submissive.<br>• are trying to hide something.<br>• are male. |

interviewer reads your resumé you sit in silence across the desk. In both of these situations, you scan the other person's face, eagerly awaiting some reaction. To interpret someone's facial expressions accurately, you need to focus on what the other person may be thinking or feeling. It helps if you know the person well, can see her or his whole face, have plenty of time to observe, and understand the situation that prompted the reaction.[38]

How accurately do we interpret emotions expressed on the face? Researchers who have attempted to measure subjects' skill in identifying the emotional expressions of others have found it a tricky business. According to Ekman and Friesen, the human face universally exhibits six primary emotions: happiness, sadness, surprise, fear, anger, and disgust or contempt. But these researchers note that even though our faces provide a great deal of information about emotions, we quickly learn to control our facial

# Communication&DIVERSITY

## When Is Silence Really "Golden"?

Members of different cultures can have different expectations about when silence is appropriate. In his essay "Cultural Uses and Interpretations of Silence," communication scholar Charles Braithwaite explored the functions of silence "beyond one's own speech community" in an effort to discover cross-cultural generalizations.[39] He examined descriptions of the use of silence within many cultural groups and found two common themes:

• When people don't know each other very well or circumstances between them create a degree of uncertainty, silence may increase, but it is seen as expected and appropriate. This tendency emerged within cultural groups as diverse as some American Indian tribes, Japanese Americans in Hawaii, Americans in rural Appalachia, and native Japanese.

• Recognized status differences are associated with silence. When a difference in power level or status is detected, lower-status persons are expected to be silent and monitor when it is appropriate to engage in conversation. This tendency was particularly distinct within parent–child relationships, evidenced in such diverse peoples as the Anang of southwestern Nigeria, the Wolof of Senegal, some urban African American women, the residents of the LaHave Islands (off the coast of Nova Scotia), and some Indian tribes.

How do members of your cultural group use silence to communicate? Is silence among those in your social circles perceived as awkward, or is it a sign of the level of comfort people feel with each other?

expressions.[40] One fascinating study examined children's facial expressions when they received either wonderful, new toys or broken, disappointing toys.[41] When they received the disappointing toys, the children showed a flash of disappointment on their faces, but then very quickly they masked their disappointment and changed their facial expressions to reveal a more positive, socially appropriate reaction. Even very young children learn to control the way an emotion registers on their face.

## Touch

Touch is the most powerful form of nonverbal communication; it is also the most misunderstood and carries the potential for the most problems if ill used. Consider some moments involving accidental touch. Standing elbow to elbow in an elevator or sitting next to someone in a crowded airplane, you may find yourself in physical contact with total strangers. As you stiffen your body and avert your eyes, a baffling sense of shame and discomfort floods over you. Why do we react this way to accidental touching? Normally, we touch to express affection and intimacy. When affection or intimacy is not our intended message, we instinctively react to modify the impression our touch has created.

Countless studies on touch, termed **haptics** in research, have shown that intimate human contact is vital to our personal development, well-being, and physical health.[42] Think about your role models and the lessons you learned about touch while growing up. If you grew up in a two-parent family, did your parents display affection in front of you? If not, you may have grown up believing that affectionate touching should not be done in front of others. As an adult, you may be uncomfortable with public displays of affection. If you grew up with parents or family members who were affectionate with each other and their children, your **touch ethic**—what you consider appropriate touching—as an adult is influenced by that experience.[43] We don't mean to insinuate that a touch ethic that accepts public affection is somehow more psychologically healthy than one that reserves touching for private moments. But what if you date or partner with someone whose experiences while growing up led to a very different touch ethic than yours? You may be headed for some conflict, but ideally some compromise as well.

The amount of touch we need, initiate, tolerate, and receive depends also on our cultural background.[44] Certain cultures are high contact—meaning that touching is quite commonplace—such as some European and Middle Eastern cultures in which men kiss each other on the cheek as a greeting. Other cultures are low contact, like some Asian cultures in which demonstrations of affection are rare and considered inappropriate.[45]

## The Voice

"We have nothing to fear but fear itself."
"Ask not what your country can do for you—ask what you can do for your country."
"I have a dream . . . I have a dream today."
"I am not a crook."
"Mr. Gorbachev, tear down this wall."

If you read these statements and recognize them as having been made by American leaders, you are likely to read them using the same pauses and changes in pitch, volume, and emphasis as did the famous speaker. John F. Kennedy greatly emphasized the word *not*, as in "Ask NOT what your country. . . ." Martin Luther King Jr. used rising pitch and increased volume as he uttered the word *dream* over and over again in his speech. These leaders learned to use the tremendous capacity and versatility of the voice to create memorable moments.

Like your face, your voice is a major vehicle for communicating your thoughts and emotions. The pitch, rate, and volume at which you speak and your use of silence—elements termed **paralanguage** or **vocalics**—all provide important clues. The voice

**haptics**
The study of human touch.

**touch ethic**
A person's own guidelines or standards as to appropriate and inappropriate touch.

**paralanguage (vocalics)**
Nonverbal aspects of voice (e.g., pitch, rate, volume, use of silence).

# Communication&ETHICS

## Don't Lie to Me!

We have good information now as to how most people behave when they are being untruthful. Unless we have ice in our veins, most of us register some kind of higher activation in our bodies when we attempt to deceive, such as increased heart rate and elevated skin temperature. Lie detector machines track just such physiological changes as indications of deception.[46] Other instruments track patterns in the voice, such as vocal emphasis and rising intonation. Research has shown that most people's voices have a tendency to get higher in pitch when they try to deceive.[47] What lie detector professionals look for is a change in a person's normal behavior, any change from the baseline that is typically taken at the beginning of a lie detector session.

Do you think modern lie detectors are sophisticated enough that the results of lie detector tests should be allowed as evidence in court trials? Is is ethical to "wire up" a suspect to track bodily and vocal changes that might indicate deception?

reveals our thoughts, emotions, and the nature of our relationships with others; it also provides information about our self-confidence and influences how we are perceived by others.[48] Most of us would conclude, as has research, that a speaker who mumbles, speaks very slowly and softly, continually mispronounces words, and uses "uh" and "um" is less credible and persuasive than one who speaks clearly, rapidly, fluently, and with appropriate volume.[49] Sometimes it's jarring when a person's physical appearance doesn't seem to match her or his voice.[50] A famous example is former boxing champ Mike Tyson, whose high-pitched voice isn't what we tend to expect out of someone with such a muscular physique.

Sometimes it's not what we say or even how we say it that communicates our feelings. Pausing and being silent communicate volumes.[51] You may be at a loss for words or need time to think about what you want to contribute to a conversation, so pausing or being silent may be better than fumbling about for the right way to express yourself. Silence can be a sign of respect, but it can also be an indication of anger (as when you give someone "the silent treatment") or discomfort (as in "an awkward silence"). At other times, you may feel so comfortable with someone that words aren't necessary; psychologist Sidney Baker calls these moments "positive silence."[52]

## Physical Environment, Space, and Territory

Close your eyes and picture your bedroom as it is right now—whether it's a dorm room you share with someone, the room you've had since you were a child, or a bedroom shared with a spouse or partner. Try to get a clear, detailed mental image of how that room looks right now. Then think about this: If one of your professors were to walk into your bedroom right now, what would she or he think about you? What impressions about you would he or she form, given the physical setup of that room? Does the room reveal your need for privacy?

These questions all have to do with your interaction with the physical environment and the space around you. You may be unused to looking at the environment as a form of nonverbal communication, but the miniworld you create for yourself reveals a good deal about you. Also, your preferred amount of space, the level of ownership you attach to that space, and your behavior as you delineate and protect that space are fascinating nonverbal elements that researchers continue to study.[53]

**The Physical Environment**    What's so great about a corner office with wall-to-wall windows? It's one of many indications in American culture of high status. In a working world increasingly structured into cubicles, an employee's desk location serves as a symbol of importance.[54] The environment is important to the study of nonverbal communication in two ways:

- The choices we make about the environments in which we live and operate reveal a good deal about who we are; physical environments are extensions of our personalities.[55] We tend to put our "signature" on our environments by adorning the settings in which we work, study, and reside to make them unique and personal.
- Nonverbal behavior is altered by the various environments in which we communicate.[56] Formal settings may make our movements more restrained, our body posture more rigid, and our speech limited and whispered; informal settings tend to cause us to expand and relax our nonverbal behaviors.

One of the more cutting-edge and interesting lines of research into the environment as a form of nonverbal communication surrounds designing spaces for people with disabilities.[57] Although college students without physical disabilities might think this area pertains to building ramps and installing elevators in older campus buildings, design for disability means much more. Some examples include placing extensive Braille signage on campuses (not just in elevators), retrofitting computer labs to offer people with disabilities better access to technology, and providing furniture design in classrooms that assimilates into the environment and accommodates learners of all physical types.[58]

**Space**   Imagine that you're sitting alone at a long, rectangular table in your campus library. As you sit dutifully with your head in a textbook, you're startled when a complete stranger sits directly across from you at the table. Since there are several empty chairs at the other end of the table, you may feel uncomfortable that this unknown individual has invaded *your* area.

Every culture has well-established ways of regulating spatial relations. How physically close we are willing to get to others relates to how well we know them, to considerations of power and status, and to our cultural background.

A pioneer in helping us understand personal space was Edward T. Hall, who studied **proxemics**, or the distances that people allow between themselves and objects or other people. Hall identified four spatial zones (diagrammed in Figure 4.2):[59]

- *Intimate space.* The most personal communication occurs when people are from 0 to 1½ feet apart. Unless we're forced to stand in a crowded space, intimate space is only open to those with whom we are well acquainted.
- *Personal space.* Most of our conversations with family and friends occur when we are 1½ to 4 feet apart. We find it uncomfortable if someone we don't know well enters our personal space zone on purpose.
- *Social space.* The majority of formal group interactions and many of our professional relationships take place in the social space zone, which ranges from 4 to 12 feet.
- *Public space.* Many presentational speakers position themselves at least 12 feet away from their audiences, but interpersonal communication doesn't usually occur in the public space zone.

**Figure 4.2**
**Edward T. Hall's Four Zones of Space**

Labels in figure: Intimate Space 0 to 1½ feet; Social Space 4 to 12 feet; Self; Personal Space 1½ to 4 feet; Public Space 12 feet and beyond

**proxemics**
The study of how close or far away from people and objects we position ourselves.

The specific space that you and others choose depends on several variables, most specifically your cultural background.[60] Generally, however, the more you like people, the closer you tend to stand to them. Higher-status and larger people are afforded more space than lower-status and smaller people.[61] We also tend to stand closer to others in a large room than we do in a small room. In general, women tend to stand closer to others than men do.[62]

**Territory**   The study of how people use space and objects to communicate occupancy or ownership of space is termed **territoriality**.[63] You assumed ownership of that table in the library and the right to determine who sat with you. You may have reacted negatively not only because your sense of personal space was invaded, but also because the intrusive stranger broke a cultural rule governing territoriality.

You announce your ownership of space with **territorial markers**—things and actions that signify that an area has been claimed. When you arrive at class, for example, you may put your book bag on a chair while you get up and go out into the hall to make a call on your cell phone. That book bag signifies temporary ownership of your seat. If you returned to find that someone had moved your stuff and was sitting in your seat, you would probably become indignant. The most common form of territorial marker is a lock. We lock our doors and windows, cars, offices, briefcases, TVs (using V-chips), and computers to keep out intruders.

While we traditionally think of space as a physical dimension, with increased accessibility and use of technology that links us with cyberspace we have recently begun to think of space differently.[64] What if someone hacked into your e-mail account or stole your phone and read your messages or texts? You'd probably be very upset and view this as a territorial violation.

## RECAP

### CODES OF NONVERBAL COMMUNICATION

| | |
|---|---|
| Appearance | Influences perceptions of credibility and attractiveness |
| Body Movement, Gestures, and Posture | Communicate information, status, warmth, credibility, interest in others, attitudes, and liking |
| Eye Contact | Conveys trustworthiness, sincerity, honesty, and interest |
| Facial Expressions | Reveal thoughts and express emotions and attitudes |
| Touch | Communicates intimacy, affection, and rejection |
| Voice | Communicates emotion and clarifies the meaning of messages through pitch, rate, and volume |
| Environment | Communicates information about the person who functions in that environment; provides context that alters behavior |
| Space | Provides information about status, power, and intimacy |
| Territory | Provides cues as to use, ownership, and occupancy of space |

# How to Interpret Nonverbal Cues More Accurately

How do we make sense of all the nonverbal cues we receive from others? If you earnestly want to accurately interpret and sensitively respond to someone's nonverbal communication, you must be willing to spend time and effort to develop this skill. Enhancing your interpretive skills requires, first, an awareness of the importance of nonverbal elements in the communication process. A second requirement is the willingness and emotional maturity to make your own behavior secondary to that of someone else. In other words, if you're so wrapped up in yourself that you can only think about and deal with how *you're* feeling, what *you're* thinking, and what *you* want at a given moment, you can't possibly hope to take in others' nonverbal cues, interpret them accurately, and respond appropriately.

Beyond these suggestions, we recommend that you keep in mind a three-part framework developed by Albert Mehrabian to help you improve your nonverbal

**territoriality**
The study of how humans use space and objects to communicate occupancy or ownership of space.

**territorial marker**
A thing or action that signifies that an area has been claimed.

interpretive skills. Mehrabian found that we synthesize and interpret nonverbal cues along three primary dimensions: immediacy, arousal, and dominance.[65]

- *Immediacy.* Mehrabian contends that **immediacy**—nonverbal cues that communicate liking and engender feelings of pleasure and closeness—explains why we are drawn to some people, but not others.[66] In a social setting, to find out if someone likes us or views us favorably, we should watch for eye contact, smiling and other pleasant facial expressions, head nods, an open and relaxed posture, a body orientation toward us rather than away from us, close proximity, a rising intonation in the voice, and culture- and context-appropriate touch.[67]

- *Arousal.* Nonverbal cues of **arousal** communicate feelings of interest and excitement. As nonverbal scholar Peter Andersen puts it, arousal is "the degree to which a person is stimulated or activated."[68] Primary arousal cues include increased eye contact, closer conversational distances, increased touch, animated vocal expressions (like laughing), more direct body orientation, smiling and active facial expressions, and synchronized movements (mimicry or rhythmic responses between people).[69]

- *Dominance.* The third dimension of Mehrabian's framework communicates the balance of power in a relationship. **Dominance** cues indicate status, position, and importance. People high in status tend to have a relaxed body posture; less direct body orientation toward lower-status people; a downward head tilt; less direct eye contact; and less smiling, head nodding, and facial animation than lower-status people.[70] "Power people" usually have more space around them; they have bigger offices and more barriers (human and nonhuman) protecting them. They may communicate their sense of power through clothing, possessions, and their use of time.

When you attempt to interpret someone's nonverbal communication, realize that there is a good deal of room for error. Humans are complex, and they don't always send clear signals. But the more you learn about nonverbal communication and the more you become aware of your own communication and the communication of others, the greater your chances of accurately perceiving and interpreting someone's nonverbal message.

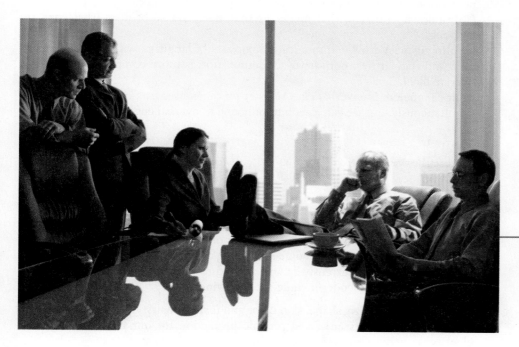

**immediacy**
Nonverbal behaviors that communicate feelings of liking, pleasure, and closeness.

**arousal**
Nonverbal behaviors that communicate feelings of interest and excitement.

**dominance**
Nonverbal behaviors that communicate power, status, and control.

Who is the most powerful person in this room? What nonverbal cues indicate that person's dominance?
Chabruken/Taxi/Getty Images

# STUDY GUIDE:
# Review, Apply, and Assess Your Knowledge and Skill

## REVIEWING
## What You Know

## Why Focus on Nonverbal Communication?    p. 84

Nonverbal communication is communication other than written or spoken language that occurs without words. It's important to become more aware of your own nonverbal communication and to enhance your ability to detect and interpret others' nonverbal cues more accurately. Nonverbal messages communicate our feelings and attitudes and are critical to successful relationships. They can substitute for, complement, contradict, repeat, regulate, and accent verbal messages. Nonverbal messages are also more believable than verbal messages.

### Terms to Know

Nonverbal Communication    p. 84

## The Nature of Nonverbal Communication    p. 88

Nonverbal communication is

- Culture bound: Interpret nonverbal cues within a cultural context.
- Rule governed: Expectancy violations theory suggests that you may not know that you have rules or expectations governing appropriate nonverbal communication until those expectations are violated.
- Ambiguous: Exact meanings for nonverbal cues are difficult to determine, but perception checking can help decipher the meaning of a nonverbal message.
- Continuous: Unlike verbal messages that start and stop, nonverbal cues are ongoing.
- Nonlinguistic: Verbal communication consists of language with patterns, grammar, and regularities; nonverbal communication is more complex and does not operate like language.
- Multichanneled: Nonverbal cues register on our senses from a variety of sources simultaneously, but we can attend to only one nonverbal cue at a time.

### Terms to Know

Expectancy Violations Model    p. 89          Perception Checking    p. 89

## Codes of Nonverbal Communication    p. 91

Ekman and Friesen provided the primary codes or categories of nonverbal behavior, which are enacted differently by people depending on their cultural background. Each code has been researched extensively and applied to different contexts and relationships. The seven primary codes include the following:

- Appearance: Body size, shape, skin color and texture, hairstyle, clothing, and other appearance aspects (artifacts) provide protection for our bodies, convey our identity, and communicate our culture.

- Kinesics includes human movements, gestures, and posture.
- Eye contact conveys interest and credibility and is an important nonverbal cue within most cultures.
- Facial expressions reveal our emotions.
- Touch (haptics) is the most powerful nonverbal cue, but also the most complex because of the potential for misunderstanding.
- The voice (paralanguage or vocalics) communicates our thoughts, emotions, and the nature of our relationships.
- The physical environment, space (proxemics), and how we delineate and protect that space (territoriality) are important nonverbal cues.

### Terms to Know

| | | | |
|---|---|---|---|
| Artifact | p. 92 | Haptics | p. 95 |
| Kinesics | p. 92 | Touch Ethic | p. 95 |
| Emblem | p. 92 | Paralanguage (Vocalics) | p. 95 |
| Illustrator | p. 92 | Proxemics | p. 97 |
| Affect Display | p. 93 | Territoriality | p. 98 |
| Regulator | p. 93 | Territorial Marker | p. 98 |
| Adaptor | p. 93 | | |

## How to Interpret Nonverbal Cues More Accurately  p. 98

It takes time and effort to develop our skills of detecting and accurately interpreting others' nonverbal communication. Albert Mehrabian suggested that nonverbal cues can communicate *immediacy*, or liking; *arousal*, or excitement and interest; and *dominance*, or status, position, and importance.

### Terms to Know

| | | | |
|---|---|---|---|
| Immediacy | p. 99 | Dominance | p. 99 |
| Arousal | p. 99 | | |

**Principle Three:**
### Effectively use and interpret nonverbal messages.

- Realize the importance of physical appearance and attractiveness in American culture.
- Use culturally appropriate body movement, including posture and gestures, to convey messages.
- Work on making appropriate eye contact with others, given that eye contact is the key nonverbal behavior linked with credibility and trustworthiness.
- Become more aware of your and others' facial expressions, because this nonverbal channel is a primary one for conveying emotions.
- Use touch appropriately, given the cultural context within which you communicate.
- Become more aware of the potential you have for vocal expression and how others use their vocal capacities to communicate emotions and ideas.
- Become more aware of your rules regarding space and territoriality so that you may better understand and enact appropriate, effective proxemic nonverbal behaviors when interacting with others.
- Recognize that body movement, eye contact, facial expressions, touch, vocal behaviors, and use of space and territory communicate liking, interest, and dominance.

**APPLYING**
Principles
for a
Lifetime

# ASSESSING
## Your Skill

## Body Movement and Emotion

Suggest examples of body movement that reveal each of the six primary emotions listed below. Then generate possible alternative meanings for the same movement. For example, arms crossed across your chest might reveal anger or that you're closed off and not open to conversation; it might also be that you're just chilly. We've provided an example to get you started.

| Emotion | Body Movements | Alternative Meanings |
| --- | --- | --- |
| Embarrassment | Covering your face with your hands | Could also indicate deception |
| Happiness | | |
| Anger | | |
| Surprise | | |
| Fear | | |
| Disgust | | |
| Sadness | | |

## Is This Space Invasion?

We've explore the nonverbal codes of space and territory, and you should now have a better understanding of the range of people's reactions to perceived invasions of their space. Read each situation below, decide if a proxemic or territorial violation has occurred, and then describe two tactics you might use in response to each situation. (Try to think of things you realistically *would* do in each situation, not just what you *might* do.)

a. You're at a bar or club, sitting alone, waiting for a friend to join you. A stranger sits down beside you and starts a conversation.
b. You're a business executive. You enter your office after lunch and find your administrative assistant sitting in your chair with her or his feet up on the desk, talking on the phone.
c. You're taking racquetball lessons, and it's your turn on the court. A group of people gather to watch your lesson.
d. You're interviewing for a part-time job. As the interview nears a close, the interviewer moves from behind the desk toward you and touches you on the knee.
e. You want to wear your favorite sweater but can't find it. You discover it wadded up in the bottom of the laundry hamper, reeking of cigarette smoke, and you realize your roommate or a family member wore it without your permission.

# WEB RESOURCES
for More Review, Application, and Assessment

- **MyCommunicationLab**  Test your skill at recognizing facial expressions of basic emotions and practice matching nonverbal cues to people's message with the activities in this chapter of MyCommunicationLab. <www.mycommunicationlab.com> (Access code required.)

- **Data Face**  Find a guide to how to "read" a face and much, much more at this website entirely devoted to the study of the human face. <www.face-and-emotion.com/dataface>

- **Truth About Deception**  Wonder if someone's lying to you? Here's an interesting website that summarizes nonverbal cues of deception: <www.truthaboutdeception.com>

Listening, not imitation, may be the sincerest form of flattery.

DR. JOYCE BROTHERS

# Chapter OUTLINE

# Chapter OBJECTIVES

After studying this chapter, you should be able to

1. Explain the principle of listening and responding thoughtfully to others.
2. Identify the elements of the listening process.
4. Describe four listening styles.
3. Identify and describe barriers that keep people from listening well.
5. Identify and use strategies that can improve your listening skills.
6. Identify and use appropriate responding skills.

Ilya Andriyanov/Shutterstock.com

# 5 | Listening and Responding

**Figure 5.1**
**What You Do with Your Communication Time**

It shows up on every list of what effective communicators do: They listen. You spend more time listening to others than doing almost anything else you do. Americans spend up to 90 percent of a typical day communicating with people, and they spend 55 percent of that communication time listening to others.[1] As shown in Figure 5.1, if you're typical, you spend the *least* amount of your communication time writing, yet you receive more training in writing than in any other communication skill.[2] One of the hallmarks of an effective leader is being a good listener.[3] To be sensitive is to be aware of others and to be concerned about others. Increasing your skill in listening to others is one of the most productive ways to increase your communication sensitivity.

Most people have not had formal training in listening or responding.[4] In this chapter, we focus on the principle of increasing your sensitivity to others by listening. Becoming sensitive to others includes more than just understanding and interpreting their words, thoughts, and ideas—sensitivity also involves understanding the emotions underlying the words and unspoken messages of others.

As shown in our familiar model of the Communication Principles for a Lifetime in Figure 5.2, effective communicators do more than absorb a message; they also provide an appropriate response to the speaker. We'll address both listening and responding to others in this chapter.

# The Importance of Listening and Responding Skills

Listening and responding skills are important for several reasons. Some researchers suggest that because listening is the first communication skill we learn (we respond to sounds even while in our mother's womb), it's also the most important skill.[5] Listening plays a key role in helping us learn to speak. Listening skills are vital as we develop relationships with others, collaborate, and listen to lectures and speeches.

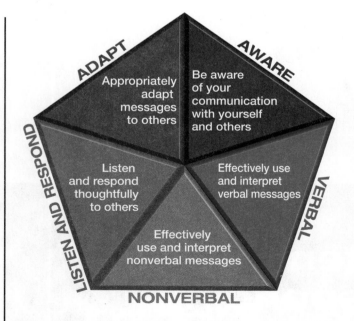

**Figure 5.2**
**Communication Principles for a Lifetime**

## Listening Enhances Our Relationships with Others

Your skill as a listener has important implications for the relationships you establish with others. In interpersonal communication situations, the essence of being a good conversationalist is being a good listener. Rather than focusing only on what to say, a person skilled in the art of conversation listens and picks up on interests and themes of others. Listening well can also earn you some tangible benefits. One research study found that a key difference between couples who remain married and those who divorce is the ability to listen to each other.[6] Partners in marriages that endure report that being a good listener is key to a satisfying marital relationship. People who are perceived to be good listeners enjoy greater success in their jobs than those who are perceived as poor listeners.[7] Physicians, nurses, and others who work in the health professions who are good listeners are perceived to be more competent and skilled.[8]

## Listening Helps Us Collaborate with Others

Being a good listener is also essential when communicating in small groups. Whether you are the appointed or emerging leader of a group or are a group or team member, your ability to listen and connect to others will affect your value to other group members.[9] One study found that being a good listener was the most important skill to have when working with others in groups and teams.[10] Group members afflicted with *baffle-gab*—those who verbally dominate group meetings—are not usually held in high esteem. Groups need people who can listen and connect conversational threads that often become tangled or dropped during group dialogue.

Research shows that listening is crucial to starting and maintaining your relationships. What areas of your listening skills do you think you could improve?

Polka Dot/Thinkstock

## Listening Links Speaker and Audience

Without effective listening skills, you'll likely miss some messages in public speaking situations. Listening skills are especially important when you need to understand and retain spoken information. There is evidence, for example, that listening skills correlate with academic ability. One study found that almost half of college students who had low scores on a listening test were on academic probation at the end of their first years in college. In comparison, just over 4 percent of the students who had high scores on the same listening test were on academic probation.[11] Improving your listening skill can improve your grade-point average.[12]

Listening is not just for audience members; it is also important for speakers. Good speakers are audience-centered. They consider the needs of their listeners first. They understand what will hold listeners' attention. Many effective speakers acquire this knowledge by listening to audience members one on one before a talk or lecture. Effective speakers also listen to the feedback from their audiences and to adjust their speeches while giving them.[13]

# How We Listen

Do you know someone who is interpersonally inert? Interpersonally inert people are those who just don't "get it." You can drop hints that it's late and you'd rather they head home instead of playing another hand of cards, but they don't pick up on your verbal and nonverbal cues. They may *hear* you, but they certainly aren't listening; they are not making sense out of your symbols.

**Hearing** is the physiological process of decoding sounds. You hear when the sound waves reach your eardrum and cause the bones of the middle ear (the hammer, anvil, and stirrup) to vibrate. Eventually, the sound vibrations are translated into electrical impulses that reach your brain. To listen to something, you must first select that sound from competing sounds.

**Listening,** defined succinctly, is the process we use to make sense out of what we hear; it is a complex process of receiving, constructing meaning from, and responding to verbal and nonverbal messages.[14] Listening involves five activities: (1) selecting, (2) attending, (3) understanding, (4) remembering, and—to confirm that listening has occurred—(5) responding.

Understanding these five elements in the listening process can help you diagnose where you sometimes get off track when listening. Having a framework to better describe the listening process can help you figure out how to get back on track and increase your listening skill.[15]

**hearing**
The physiological process of decoding sounds.

**listening**
A complex process of receiving, constructing meaning from, and responding to verbal and nonverbal messages, which involves selecting, attending, understanding, remembering, and responding.

"Love, honor & cherish" being too lofty a goal, do you promise to "look up, nod, & pretend to be listening"?

Huh? Oh, yeah. Sure.

BIZARRO.COM
Dist. by King Features 4·10·06

Dan Piraro/King Features Syndicate

## Selecting

To **select** a sound is to focus on one sound as you sort through the myriad noises competing for your attention. Even now, as you are reading this book, there are probably countless sounds within earshot. Stop reading for a moment. What sounds surround you? Do you hear music? Is a TV on? Maybe there is the tick of a clock, a whir of a computer, or a whoosh of a furnace or an air conditioner. To listen—to be sensitive to another person—you must first select the sound or nonverbal behavior that symbolizes meaning. The interpersonally inert person does not pick up on the clues because he or she is oblivious to the information.

## Attending

After selecting a sound, you attend to it. To **attend** is to maintain a *sustained* focus on a particular message. When you change channels on your TV, you first select the channel and then attend to the program you've selected. You may attend to the program or commercial for a moment and then move on or return to other thoughts or other sounds. Just as you tune in to TV programs that reflect your taste in information while you channel surf, you attend to messages of others that satisfy your needs or whims. Attending to a message is vital to being a good listener. There is clear evidence that a person who is skilled in maintaining sustained attention to a message (not interrupting and just listening) is perceived as a better listener than is someone with a "restless mind."[16]

What holds our attention? Typically, conflict, new ideas, humor, or something that we can see or that is concrete holds our attention more easily than abstract ideas that don't relate to us. If you're having difficulty sustaining attention to a message, it may be because what you're listening to does not immediately seem to relate to you. You may need to work a bit harder, either to concentrate on the message or to consider ways in which the message is relevant or important to you.

## Understanding

It's been estimated that we hear more than one billion words each year, but we understand a mere fraction of that number. To **understand** is to assign meaning to messages—to interpret a message by making sense out of what you hear. You can select and attend to sounds and nonverbal cues but not interpret what you see and hear. Hearing and seeing are physiological processes. Understanding occurs when you relate what you hear and see to your experiences or knowledge.[17] Perhaps you have heard the Montessori school philosophy: I hear, I forget; I see, I remember; I experience, I understand. It is when we can relate our experiences to what we hear and see that we achieve understanding.

## Remembering

Remembering information is considered part of the listening process because it's the primary way we determine whether a message was understood. To **remember** is to recall information. But you cannot retrieve or remember all the bits of information. Sometimes, even though you were present, you have no recollection of what occurred in a particular situation. You can't consciously remember everything; your eye is not a camera; your ear is not a microphone; your mind is not a hard drive.

**select**
To focus on one sound as you sort through various sounds competing for your attention.

**attend**
To maintain a sustained focus on a particular message.

**understand**
To assign meaning to messages.

**remember**
To recall information.

# Communication&TECHNOLOGY

## The Art of Listening to Voice Messages

Today's technological tools make it possible for us to listen to others anytime and anywhere, including listening to vast numbers of recorded messages.[18]

There has been a huge increase in **asynchronous listening,** which is what you do when you listen to someone's recorded message on an answering machine, to voice mail, or to messages retrieved from your cell phone. You listen, yet no person is available to respond to your feedback. The inability to ask for clarification increases the potential for the message to be misunderstood. How can you improve your skills in listening to and transmitting recorded messages?

When listening to a recorded message,

- *Focus.* Before playing the recorded message, stop what you are doing so that you can focus on the message; while driving, scurrying around the room, or coming in the door after a busy day may not be the best time to listen carefully to recorded messages.

- *Mentally summarize.* If you are listening to several recorded messages, mentally summarize the essence of the message you've just heard before playing the next one.
- *Increase redundancy.* If need be, replay the recorded message to ensure that you've absorbed the details.

When recording a message,

- *Slow down.* When you're leaving a recorded message for someone, speak slowly, clearly, and distinctly.
- *Keep it short.* Most people, when checking their messages, don't want to hear a lengthy story or detailed chronology of events. Make your message brief and to the point.
- *Leave follow-up information.* Do more than leave a phone number or e-mail address. Indicate when you're most likely to be available to receive a message in person, rather than encouraging a game of phone tag.

The first communication principle we presented in this book is to become self-aware. When we are not self-aware of our actions, thoughts, or what we are perceiving—when we are mindless—our ability to remember what occurs plummets. We increase our ability to remember what we hear by being not only physically present, but also mentally present.

You tend to remember what is important to you or something you try to remember or have practiced to remember (like the information in this book for your next communication test). You tend to remember dramatic information (such as where you were when you heard about the September 11, 2001, terrorist attacks) or vital information (such as your phone number or your mother's birthday).

## Responding

As you learned in Chapter 1, communication is a transactive process—not a one-way, linear one. Communication involves responding to others as well as simply articulating messages. You **respond** to people to let them know that you understand their message. Your lack of response may signal that you didn't understand the message. Your predominant response is often unspoken; direct eye contact and head nods let your partner know you're tuned in. An unmoving, glassy-eyed, frozen stupor may tell your communication partner that you are physically present, yet mentally a thousand miles away.[19] As you'll discover in the next section, most people have a certain style of listening and responding to others.

# Listening Styles

Although we've described the typical elements in the listening process, not everyone has the same style or approach to listening. Your **listening style** is your preferred way of making sense out of the messages you hear and see. Some people, for example,

**asynchronous listening**
Listening to recorded messages, such as those on an answering machine or voice mail, which do not allow an opportunity for you to get a response to your feedback.

**respond**
To confirm your understanding of a message.

**listening style**
A person's preferred way of making sense out of messages.

prefer to focus on facts and analyze the information they hear. Others seem more interested in focusing on the feelings and emotions expressed.

What's your listening style? Knowing your style can help you adapt and adjust it when listening to others. Listening researchers Debra Worthington, Graham Bodie, and Christopher Gearhart, building on the extensive work of other listening researchers,[20] have found that people tend to listen using one or more of four listening styles: relational, analytic, critical, and task oriented.[21]

## Relational Listening Style

**Relational listeners** tend to prefer listening to people's emotions and feelings. They are quite interested in hearing personal information from others. A person with a relational listening style searches for common interests and seeks to empathize with the feelings of others—she or he connects emotionally with the sentiments and passions others express.[22] There is some evidence that relational-oriented listeners are less apprehensive than people with other listening styles when communicating with others in small groups and interpersonal situations[23] and especially when listening to just one other person.[24]

Research shows that relational listeners have a greater tendency than those with other listening styles to be sympathetic to the person they are listening to.[25] A sympathetic listener is more likely to voice concern for the other person's welfare when that person is sharing personal information or news about a stressful situation. A sympathetic listener says, for instance, "Oh, Pat, I'm so sorry to hear about your loss. You must feel so lonely and sad." There is evidence that relational listeners may be more empathic than other listeners; they seem to have greater skill in understanding the thoughts and feelings of others.[26] One study found that jurors who are relational listeners (originally described as people oriented) are less likely to find a plaintiff at fault in a civil court trial, perhaps because of their tendency to empathize with others.[27]

## Analytical Listening Style

**Analytical listeners** listen for facts and tend to withhold judgment before reaching a specific conclusion. Analytical listeners would make good judges; they generally consider all sides of an issue before making a decision or reaching a conclusion. Analytical listeners tend to listen to an entire message before assessing the validity of the information they hear. To help them analyze information, they take the perspective of the person to whom they are listening, which helps them suspend judgment when listening to others. They also like information they hear to be well organized so that they can clearly and easily analyze it. While listening to a rambling personal story, the analytic listener focuses on the facts and details of the story, rather than on the emotions being expressed. Analytical listeners prefer listening to rich message content and then finding ways of organizing or making sense out of the information.

**relational listeners**
Those who prefer to focus on the emotions and feelings communicated by others verbally and nonverbally.

**analytical listeners**
Those who withhold judgment, listen to all sides of an issue, and wait until they hear the facts before reaching a conclusion.

# Critical Listening Style

**Critical listeners** are good at evaluating information that they hear. They are able to hone in on inconsistencies in what someone says. They are comfortable listening to detailed, complex information and focusing on the facts, yet they are especially adept in noting contradictions in the facts presented. Critical listeners are also likely to catch errors in the overall logic and reasoning being used to reach a conclusion.

Critical listeners tend to be a bit more skeptical and critical than relationship listeners of the information they hear. Researchers call this skepticism **second guessing**—questioning the assumptions underlying a message.[28] It's called second guessing because critical listeners don't always assume that what they hear is accurate or relevant; they make a second guess about the accuracy of the information they are listening to. Accuracy of information is especially important to critical listeners, because if they are going to use the information in some way, they want the information to be valid.

A task-oriented listener is interested in achieving a specific outcome. What is your usual listening style? How do you adapt your style when situations call for a different one?
CandyBox Images/Shutterstock.com

# Task-Oriented Listening Style

**Task-oriented listeners** are more interested in focusing on a specific outcome or task than on the communication relationship when listening to others. They emphasize completing a specific transaction such as solving a problem, taking action, or making a purchase. Task-oriented listeners focus on verbs—what needs to be done. Consequently, they don't like to listen to rambling, descriptive messages that don't seem to have a point. They appreciate efficient communicators who organize messages so that their listeners can focus on the outcomes—the "bottom line."

# Using Listening Styles

How does knowing that most people have preferences for particular types of messages benefit you? There are at least three reasons to think about your listening style and those of others: (1) to enhance your self-awareness, (2) to adapt your own listening style to different situations, and (3) to communicate more effectively.

**Enhance Your Self-Awareness**    Understanding your preferred listening style can help you become more aware of how you behave in communication situations. Your background may influence your listening style. Some research suggests that women are more likely to be relational listeners, whereas men have a tendency to assume one of the other listening styles.[29] Your listening style, however, may be less influenced by your gender than by the overall approach you take to interpreting and remembering the information you hear. Your cultural traditions, suggests one research team, may have a major influence on your particular listening style. People from a more individualistic, self-focused cultural perspective (such as people from the United States) tend to be more action-oriented listeners than people from other places. Relational listeners, according to research, are more likely to have collectivistic values, are group-oriented, or were raised in a collaborative cultural tradition (such as some Asian cultures).[30] We'll talk more about how communication is influenced by culture—specifically, individualistic and collectivistic cultural values—in the next chapter.

You may wonder, "Do I have just one listening style, or do I have more than one?" According to listening researchers Larry Barker and Kitty Watson, who have done extensive research about listening styles (although using different labels than the styles we've described), about 40 percent of all listeners have one primary listening style that they use, especially if they are under stress. Another 40 percent of listeners use more than one style—for example, they may prefer to listen to evaluate (critical listening style) and also want the information delivered in a short amount of time and focused

**critical listeners**
Those who prefer to listen for the facts and evidence to support key ideas and an underlying logic; they also listen for errors, inconsistencies, and discrepancies.

**second guessing**
Questioning the assumptions underlying a message.

**task-oriented listeners**
Those who look at the overall structure of the message to see what action needs to be taken; they also like efficient, clear, and briefer messages.

# RECAP

## LISTENING STYLES

| | |
|---|---|
| Relational-oriented listening style | Listeners prefer to attend to feelings and emotions and to search for common areas of interest when listening to others. |
| Analytical-oriented listening style | Listeners prefer to withhold judgment, listen to all sides of an issue, and wait until they hear the facts before reaching a conclusion. |
| Critical listening style | Listeners are likely to listen for the facts and evidence to support key ideas and an underlying logic; they also listen for errors, inconsistencies, and discrepancies when listening. |
| Task-oriented listening style | Listeners are focused on accomplishing something and look at the overall structure of the message to see what action needs to be taken; they also like efficient, clear, and briefer messages. |

on the task to be accomplished (task-oriented listening style). About 20 percent of people do not have a specific listening style preference; these individuals may want to avoid listening altogether because they are shy and don't like to be around others in social situations, they may have receiver apprehension, or they may just have listener burnout—they are weary of listening to other people.[31] Evidence suggests that the situation, time, and place all have an effect on the listening style or styles people adopt.[32]

**Adapt to Different Listening Situations**   Knowing your own listening style can help you adapt and adjust your listening style to fit the listening situation. If, for example, you are a relational-oriented listener and you're listening to a message that has little information about people but lots of technical details, you will have to work harder than other types of listeners to stay tuned in to the message.

**Adapt Your Own Messages**   It can be useful to be aware of others' listening style so that you can communicate messages that others are more likely to listen to. If you know that your spouse is an analytical listener, you should communicate a message that is rich in information because that's what your spouse prefers. Tell the analytical-oriented listener, "Here are three things I have to tell you," and then say those three things. The information preview tells your analytical-oriented listener that you are about to convey three pieces of information. Of course, it may be difficult to determine someone's listening style, especially if you don't know the person very well. But it is worth the time, as well as easier, to consider the listening styles of people you *do* know well (your family members, your coworkers, your boss).

# Listening Barriers

Although we spend almost half of our communication time listening, some say that we don't use that time well. One day after hearing something, most people remember only about half of what was said. It gets worse. Two days later, our listening comprehension drops by another 50 percent. The result: Two days after hearing a lecture or speech, most of us remember only about 25 percent of what we heard.

Our listening deteriorates not only when we listen to speeches or lectures, but also when we interact interpersonally. Even in the most intimate relationships (or perhaps we should say *especially* in the most intimate relationships), we tune out what others are saying. One study reported that we sometimes pay more attention to strangers than to our close friends or spouses. Married couples tend to interrupt each other more often than nonmarried couples and are usually less polite to each other than are strangers involved in a simple decision-making task.[33]

What keeps us from listening well? The most critical elements are (1) self barriers—personal habits that work against listening well, (2) information-processing barriers—the way we mentally manage information, and (3) context barriers—the surroundings in which we listen.

# Self Barriers

"We have met the enemy and he is us" is the oft-quoted line from the Vintage comic strip *Pogo*. Evidence suggests that we are our own worst enemy when it comes to listening to others—whether it's listening to enjoy, learn, evaluate, or empathize. We mentally comment on the words we hear and the behavior we observe. Our internal thoughts are like a play-by-play sports commentator's description of the action in a sports contest. If our internal narration is focused on the message, it may be useful. But we often attend to our own internal dialogues and diatribes instead of to others' message, and when we do, our listening effectiveness plummets.

**Self-Focus**     That personal play-by-play commentary we may be carrying on in our minds is typically about us. "How long will I have to be here for this lecture?" "Wonder what's for dinner tonight?" "I've got to get that report finished." "She's still talking—will we be out of here in ten minutes?" "Do I have a school meeting tonight, or is that tomorrow night?" Focusing on an internal message often keeps us from selecting and attending to the other person's message.

What can you do to regain your listening focus if you are focused on yourself rather than on the other person's message? Consider these suggestions:

- *Become aware of the problem.* Become consciously competent. Notice when you find yourself drifting off rather than concentrating on the speaker.
- *Concentrate.* If your internal "announcer" is telling you that the message is boring, useless, or stupid, make sure you don't mindlessly tune the message out. Yes, some messages are boring, useless, and stupid. But the habit of quickly dismissing ideas and messages without making an effort to stay focused on them will keep you from being nominated for the Listening Hall of Fame.
- *Be active rather than passive.* The key to concentration is finding ways to be involved in the communication process. Taking notes when appropriate and providing nonverbal and even sometimes verbal feedback to the speaker can help keep your focus on the speaker rather than on you. If you don't understand something the speaker says, ask for clarification. Don't just sit there and "take it"; if you find your concentration waning, you'll more than likely "leave it."

**Emotional Noise**     Emotions are powerful. What we see and hear affects our emotions. **Emotional noise** occurs when our emotional arousal interferes with communication effectiveness. Certain words or phrases can arouse emotions very quickly, and, of course, the same word may arouse different emotions in different people. You respond emotionally because of your cultural background, religious convictions, or political philosophy. Words that reflect negatively on your nationality, ethnic origin, or religion can trigger strong emotional reactions. Cursing and obscene language may also reduce your listening efficiency. If you grew up in a home in which R-rated language was never used, four-letter words may distract you.

Sometimes it's not just a word but a concept or idea that causes an emotional eruption. Third-trimester abortion and public school prayer, for example, are topics guaranteed to get radio talk show hosts' audiences involved in lively discussion. Whether you love him or hate him, TV talk show host Jerry Springer is a master at pushing emotional hot buttons for his talk show guests, and when emotions become heated, thoughtful listening is rare.

The emotional state of the speaker may also affect your ability to understand and evaluate what you hear. Research has shown that if you are listening to someone who is emotionally distraught, you will be more likely to focus on his or her emotions than on the content of the message.[34] Another researcher advises that when you are communicating with someone who is emotionally excited, you should remain calm and focused and try simply to communicate your interest in the other person.[35]

What are other strategies to keep your emotions from getting the best of you? Daniel Goleman offers several research-based strategies in his best-selling book

**emotional noise**
A form of communication noise caused by emotional arousal.

*Emotional Intelligence.*[36] To be emotionally intelligent is to have the ability to understand, manage, and appropriately express emotions. There is evidence that people who are emotionally intelligent—because of their skill in recognizing, expressing, and managing their emotions—are better listeners than others.[37] Being attuned to the emotions of your listening partner helps you discern the underlying, sometimes not explicitly expressed meaning of a message.[38] For example, one simple yet powerful strategy to manage emotions when you find you may be ready to lose control is to take a deep breath. Yes, just breathe. Taking a deep, slow breath is a way of regaining control by calming down. It helps make you more conscious of your anger or frustration, much like the old technique of counting to ten.

Another strategy for managing emotions is to use the power of self-talk, a concept we discussed in Chapter 2. Tell yourself you won't get angry. Early detection of the emotions bubbling inside you can help you assess and then manage emotions before your nonrational, emotional impulses take control.

Sometimes, of course, expressing your frustration is appropriate. We do suggest that you become aware of the effect that emotions have on your listening ability; it is a constructive first step to avoid being ruled by unchecked emotions. The principle of self-awareness gives you *choice* and control. Your listening challenge is to avoid emotional sidetracks and keep your attention focused on the message. When emotionally charged words or actions kick your internal dialogue into high gear, make an effort to quiet it down and steer back to the subject at hand. Becoming consciously aware of our emotions and then talking to ourselves about our feelings is a way of not letting emotions get out of hand.

**Criticism**    We usually associate the word *criticism* with negative judgments and attitudes. Although critiquing a message can provide positive as well as negative insights, most of us don't like to be criticized. Mother Teresa once said, "If you judge people, you have no time to love them."[39] Being inappropriately critical of the speaker may distract us from focusing on the message.

A person's appearance and speech characteristics can affect your ability to listen to him or her. Many a speaker's droning monotone, lack of eye contact, and distracting mannerisms have contributed to his or her ideas not being well received—even if the ideas are potentially life-changing for the listener. The goal of a sensitive communicator is to be conscious of when the delivery or other distracting features of the message or messenger are interfering with the ability simply to listen. In fact, now that you are studying principles of communication, you may find that this problem looms even larger, because you now pay more attention to nonverbal cues.

It would be unrealistic to suggest that you refrain from criticizing speakers and their messages. It is realistic, however, to monitor your internal critiques of speakers to make sure you are aware of your biases. Good listeners say to themselves, "Although this speaker may be distracting, I am simply not going to let appearance or mannerisms keep my attention from the message." For example, Stephen

Hawking is a prize-winning physicist at Cambridge University in England; because of a disability, he is able to speak only with the aid of computer-synthesized sounds. He is unquestionably brilliant. If you let his speaking delivery overpower you, you'd miss his marvelous message. The same could be said when listening to Roger Ebert, long-time film critic for the *Chicago Sun-Times* and featured film critic on *Ebert Presents at the Movies*. Cancer surgery left him facially disfigured and unable to speak. Like Hawking, he uses a computer to be his "voice."[40] His film reviews are as sharp and clever as they've always been, but if you were distracted by his appearance and voice, you'd miss his insightful commentary. Avoid using your mental energy to criticize a speaker unnecessarily; the longer your mental critique, the less you'll remember.

## Information-Processing Barriers

In addition to self barriers that contribute to our loss of focus on messages, the way in which we process the information we hear may keep us from being good listeners. Four information-processing listening barriers are (1) processing rate, (2) information overload, (3) receiver apprehension, and (4) shifting attention.

If an emotional response to Roger Ebert's computerized "voice" distracts you from paying attention to his message, you could miss the insights he shares in his movie reviews. What would help you to overcome such a barrier?

AP Photo/Charles Rex Arbogast, File

**Processing Rate**   One barrier to listening that has long been documented is the difference between our ability to process information and the rate at which information comes to us. The barrier boils down to this: You can think faster than people speak. Most people speak 125 words per minute, give or take a few words. You have the tremendous ability, however, to process four to ten times that amount of information. Some people can listen to 600 to 800 words a minute and still make sense out of what the speaker is saying; another estimate puts the processing rate up to 1,200 words per minute. Yet another estimate claims that we think not just in words but also in images and sounds: We can process 2,000 bits of information a minute for short periods of time. This difference between average speaking rate and your capacity to make sense out of words as they register in your cortical centers can cause trouble. You have extra time on your hands to tune in to your own thoughts, rather than focus on the speaker.[41]

You can use your information-processing rate to your advantage if you use the extra time to summarize mentally what a speaker is saying. By periodically sprinkling in mental summaries during a conversation, you can dramatically increase your listening ability and make the speech-rate/thought-rate difference work to your advantage.

**Information Overload**   Information abounds. Incoming messages and information on computers, fax machines, e-mail, cell phones, beepers, and other devices can interrupt conversations and distract us from listening to others. The amount of information coming at us on any given day also wears us out. The one word to describe many a poor listener is "weary." We spend 55 percent of our communication time listening, and the pace at which the information zips toward us exhausts us. The billion words that we hear each year contribute to our fatigue.

Again we recommend self-awareness. Be on the alert for drifting attention because of information overload. And when the encroaching information dulls your attentiveness, either take a break or consider conducting some *communication triage*—determining what's urgent and what's not urgent—so that you can focus on the information that is most important.

**Receiver Apprehension**   Just as some people are fearful of presenting a speech or speaking up during a meeting, research suggests that some people are fearful of receiving information. **Receiver apprehension** is fear of misunderstanding or misinterpreting the messages spoken by others or of not being able to adjust psychologically

**receiver apprehension**
The fear of misunderstanding or misinterpreting the messages spoken by others or of not being able to adjust psychologically to messages expressed by others.

to messages expressed by others.[42] Some people may just be fearful of receiving new information because they worry about being able to understand it. Or apprehension may just be a characteristic of the way some people respond psychologically to information; they may not be able to make sense out of some of what they hear, which causes them to be anxious or fearful of listening to others.[43] If you are fearful of receiving information, you'll remember less information.

What are the implications for you of research on receiver apprehension? If you know that you are fearful of listening to new information, you'll have to work harder than others to understand the information presented. Using an audio recorder to record a lecture may help you feel more comfortable and less anxious about trying to remember every point. Becoming actively involved in the listening experience by taking notes or mentally repeating information to yourself may also help.

**Shifting Attention**   Can you multitask? Some people can easily do two things at once; some people can't. Emerging research evidence suggests that men are more likely to have difficulty attending to multiple messages: When they are focused on a message, they may have more difficulty than women in carrying on a conversation with another person.[44] Men have a tendency to lock on to a message, whereas women seem more adept at shifting between two or more simultaneous messages. When many men watch a TV program, they seem lost in thought—oblivious to other voices around them. Women, on the other hand, are more likely to be carrying on a conversation with one person and also focusing on a message they hear nearby. No, this difference doesn't mean that women are more likely to eavesdrop intentionally, but it does mean that some women have greater potential to listen to two things at once. What are the implications? It may be especially important for women to stop and focus on the messages of others, rather than on either internal or external competing messages. And men may need to be sensitive to others who may want to speak to them, rather than becoming fixated on their own internal message or on a single external message such as a program on TV.

**Cultural Differences**   Different cultures place different emphases on the importance of listening; some cultures are more source- or speaker-oriented, whereas others are more receiver- or listener-oriented. North American communication, for example, often centers on the sender. Much emphasis is placed on how senders can formulate better messages, improve credibility, and polish their delivery skills. Most U.S. colleges and universities offer courses in *speaking*, but few provide courses in *listening*. In contrast, the emphasis in East Asia has typically been on listening and interpretation. A cultural focus on the sender rather than the receiver may result in a listening barrier.

The Chinese culture, for example, places considerable emphasis on the listener. Communication researcher C. Y. Cheng identified *infinite interpretation* as one of the main principles of Chinese communication.[45] It's understood by both speaker and listener that the listener can make infinite interpretations of what has been said. According to another researcher, a related process called **anticipatory communication** is common in Japan. Instead of the speaker having to tell or ask explicitly for what he or she wants, others guess and accommodate his or her needs, sparing him or her the embarrassment that could arise if the verbally expressed request could not be met.[46] Thus, foreign students from East Asia may be puzzled about why they are constantly being asked what they want when they are visiting in American homes. In their home countries, a good communicator should anticipate what others want and act accordingly, so the host or hostess should not have to ask what is needed.

With the emphasis on indirect communication in East Asian cultures, the receiver's sensitivity and ability to capture the under-the-surface meaning and to understand implicit meaning become critical. In North America, an effort has been made to improve the effectiveness of message senders through such formal training as debate and public speaking, whereas in East Asia, receivers work to be more sensitive to others

---

**anticipatory communication**
A listening process in which the listener guesses the speaker's needs and accommodates them so that the speaker does not have to say what he or she wants.

When a phone call comes at a time when you're busy with other things, it may be tempting to try to do two things at once. We have all tried to get away with a few "uh-huhs" and "mm-hmms" to indicate that we're listening to everything that's being said on the other end of the line. In this kind of situation, should you be honest and disclose that you're busy and would rather chat (and listen) when you can be more attentive? What sort of verbal strategies might you use?

© Michael Newman/PhotoEdit

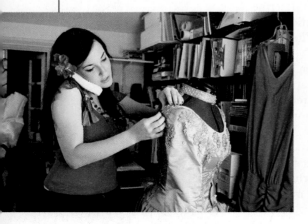

by emptying their minds of preconceptions and making them as clear as a mirror.[47]

Recently, there has been increased interest in listening in the United States. Communication scholars and practitioners recognize that listening is necessary not only to aid comprehension but also, and more importantly, to provide the speaker the satisfaction of being listened to.[48] The emphasis on listening is a cultural factor that can be a barrier to effective communication unless the communicators understand the importance of listening in the communication process.

## Context Barriers

In addition to the barriers that relate to how you process information and those that occur when your emotions and thoughts crowd out a message, listening barriers can arise from the communication context or situation. **Noise** is anything that interferes with your ability to listen to a message. Although you may think of it as sounds you hear, noise can be processed by any one of your five senses. Not only sounds, but also sights, the feeling of something touching you, and even tastes and smells can affect your listening ability. Two factors that can increase interfering noise are *when* you listen and *where* you listen.[49]

**Barriers of Time**  The time of day can interfere with your listening acuity. Are you a morning person or an evening person? Morning people are cheerfully and chirpily at their mental peak before lunch. Evening people prefer to tackle major projects after dark; they are at their worst when they arise in the morning.

If you know you are sharper in the morning, schedule your key listening times then whenever possible. Evening listeners should try to shift heavy listening to the evening hours. Of course, that's not always practical. If you can't change the time of listening, you can increase your awareness of when you will need to listen with greater concentration.

Respect the effect of timing on other people, too. Don't assume that because you are ready to talk, the other person is ready to listen. If your message is particularly sensitive or important, you may want to ask your listening partner, "Is this a good time to talk?" Even if he or she says yes, look for eye contact and a responsive facial expression to make sure the positive response is genuine.

**Barriers of Place**  Listening takes all the powers of concentration you can muster. A good listener seeks a quiet time and place to maximize listening comprehension. For most people, the best listening environment is one that offers as few distractions as possible.

When *you* want to talk to someone, pick a quiet time and place, especially if you know that you will be discussing a potentially difficult topic. Even in your own home, it may be a challenge to find a quiet time to talk. Closing a door or window, turning off the TV or radio, asking noisy or offensive talkers or texters to converse more quietly or not at all, and simply moving to a less distracting location are steps you may need to pursue to manage the noise barrier.

## RECAP

### MANAGING LISTENING BARRIERS

| Listening Barriers | What to Do |
|---|---|
| **Self Barriers** | |
| Self-Focus | • Shift attention back to the speaker. |
| | • Become actively involved in the message. |
| | • Take meaningful notes. |
| Emotional Noise | • Act calm to remain calm. |
| | • Use self-talk to stay focused on the message. |
| | • Take a deep breath if you start to lose control. |
| Criticism | • Focus on the message, not on the messenger. |
| **Information— Processing Barriers** | |
| Processing Rate | • Use the difference between speech rate and thought rate to mentally summarize the message. |
| Information Overload | • Realize when you or your partner is tired or distracted and not ready to listen. |
| | • Assess what is urgent and not urgent when listening. |
| Receiver Apprehension | • Record the message to be sure you capture it; review the audio later. |
| | • Take notes. |
| | • Make mental summaries of the information you hear. |
| Shifting Attention | • Make a conscious effort to remain focused on one message. |
| Cultural Differences | • Acknowledge that some cultures place greater emphasis on the listener than on the speaker. |
| **Context Barriers** | |
| Barriers of Time | • If possible, schedule difficult listening situations for when you're at your best. |
| Barriers of Place | • Eliminate distracting noise. |

**noise**
Anything that interferes with your ability to listen to a message.

# Improving Your Listening Skills

At the heart of listening is developing sensitivity to focus on the messages of others rather than on your own thoughts. Improving your listening involves a set of skills that can increase your sensitivity toward others. At first glance, these skills may look deceptively simple—as simple as the advice given to most elementary students about crossing the street: (1) stop, (2) look, and (3) listen. Despite the appearance of simplicity, these three words summarize decades of research and insight about how to avoid being labeled "interpersonally inert." Those steps may seem like common sense, but they are not common practice. Let's consider each separately.

## Stop: Turn Off Competing Messages

Many of the barriers to improved listening skill arise because we focus on ourselves and our own messages, rather than focusing on others. As noted earlier, while you are "listening," you may also be "talking" to yourself—providing a commentary about the messages you hear. These internal, self-generated messages may distract you from giving your undivided attention to what others are saying. To stop and focus on a message, you need to: (1) be aware of the competing messages, (2) stop the internal competing "chatter" and attend to the message, and (3) socially decenter—focus on the thoughts of others.

**Be Aware of Competing Messages**    To select and attend to the messages of others, we need to become aware of our internal dialogue and stop our own running commentary about issues and ideas that are self-focused rather than other-focused.[50] If you aren't aware that you're "talking" to yourself, you'll likely continue your internal monologue and miss a portion of the message from your listening and speaking partner. To be aware of what you are doing is to be consciously mindful of what you are attending to. At any given moment, you are either "on task" or "off task" when listening. Periodically ask yourself, "Am I on task? Am I focused on the speaker or my own 'conversation'? Am I aware of what I'm doing?"

**Stop Internal Noise**    Two listening researchers conducted a study to identify the specific behaviors that good listeners perform when listening.[51] What they discovered supports our admonition that after being aware of whether you're on task, the next step is to stop focusing on your own mental messages. Specifically, you should be other-oriented by taking the following actions during what the researchers called the *preinteraction phase* of listening:

- Put your own thoughts aside.
- Be there mentally, not just physically.
- Make a conscious, mindful effort to listen.
- Take adequate time to listen; don't rush the speaker; be patient.
- Be open-minded.

Members of some religious groups take a vow to be silent and not talk to anyone else. They literally stop talking. Does that make them better listeners than those who do not talk? One research team wanted to know the effect of various types of listening training, including being silent for twelve hours.[52] One group heard a lecture about how to be better listeners—probably like the lectures you hear in this course—and then took a test to assess their overall listening skill. A second group promised not to talk to anyone for twelve hours—they literally gave others the "silent treatment." Then they, too, took a test to assess their listening ability. A third group both heard a listening lecture and were silent for twelve hours; then they also took the listening test. The results: There were no differences in listening test scores among the groups. All groups seemed to listen equally well, according to test results—but those who kept silent for twelve hours reported thinking that they were more attentive to others and more conscious of being good listeners. The researchers concluded that literally stopping to listen more and talk less can increase awareness of listening. Their research supports the maxim, "You have been given two ears and one mouth so that you will listen more and talk less." We're not suggesting that you stop talking, but rather that you increase your awareness of how your own thoughts and talk can interfere with being a good listener. Stop—do your best to eliminate mental messages that keep you from listening well.

**Socially Decenter**  After being aware of competing messages and stopping your internal chatter, try a process called social decentering. **Social decentering** involves stepping away from your own thoughts and attempting to experience the thoughts of another. Instead of making yourself the center of your focus, you *decenter*—you place your focus on the other person. In essence, you're asking yourself, "If I were the other person, what would I be thinking?" Decentering actually requires you to practice the first principle of communication—self-awareness. You first need to become aware that your own thoughts are keeping you from focusing on another's message. Then you can focus on the other person.[53] Of course, we are not suggesting that your own ideas and internal dialogue should be forever repressed; that would be both impossible and inappropriate. We are suggesting, however, that to connect to another, you must focus on the other person rather than on yourself and, while doing so, consider what the other person may be thinking as he or she is communicating with you.

## Look: Listen with Your Eyes

As we discussed in Chapter 4, nonverbal messages are powerful, especially in communicating feelings, attitudes, and emotions.[54] A person's facial expression, level of eye contact, posture, and gestures speak volumes, even when no word is uttered. When words are spoken, the added meaning that comes from vocal cues provides yet another dimension to the emotion and nature of the relationship.

Sensitive listeners are aware of nonverbal as well as verbal messages; they listen with their eyes as well as their ears. A person's body movement and posture, for example, communicate the intensity of his or her feelings, whereas facial expression and vocal cues provide clues about the specific emotion being expressed. A competent listener notices these cues; an incompetent listener attempts to decode a message based only on what is said rather than "listening between the lines." When there is a contradiction between the verbal and the nonverbal message, we will almost always believe the unspoken message; nonverbal cues are more difficult to fake. How do you focus on nonverbal messages? We suggest two strategies: (1) attend to the meta-message, and (2) nonverbally communicate *your* interest in the other person.

**Attend to the Meta-Message**  *Meta-communication* is communication about communication. By attending to your interpersonal partner's unspoken message, you are looking for the **meta-message**—the message about the message. The nonverbal meta-message provides information about the emotional and relational effect of what a speaker is expressing with the verbal message. Accurately decoding unspoken meta-messages helps you understand what people really mean.

Often, a person will express a positive feeling nonverbally, such as by smiling, and also verbally, such as by saying "I'm happy to be here." Sometimes, though, the nonverbal communication contradicts the verbal message. Your buddy may say, "Oh, that's just great," but may use an exaggerated, sarcastic tone of voice and a facial expression

Some people find that yoga or quiet meditation helps dissolve the internal barriers that prevent effective listening. What strategies have you used to become more aware of your intrapersonal communication and any internal barriers to listening you may have experienced? What methods have you found helpful for making you conscious of the way your own "self-talk" affects your ability to listen to and communicate with others?

Chris Collins/Shutterstock.com

**social decentering**
Stepping away from your own thoughts and attempting to experience the thoughts of another.

**meta-message**
The message about the message.

that expresses just the opposite of the content of the verbal message. The sarcasm communicated by the tone of voice and facial expression (relationship cues) modifies the meaning of the verbal message (the actual content of the message).[55] The tone of voice and facial expression are a meta-message about what your friend really means. Your friend may not explicitly say that he or she is angry, upset, or irritated, but the nonverbal cues let you know that he or she is not happy.

How can you clarify the meaning of a nonverbal meta-message? Ask. For example, when you detect a smirk or a grimace from your listening partner, you can seek information about the communication: by asking "Is what I'm saying bothering you?"

**Nonverbally Communicate Your Interest in the Other Person**   A key aspect of the "look" step of good listening is to actually look at the person you are listening to—establish eye contact, which signals that you are focusing your attention on your partner. Even though mutual eye contact typically lasts only one to seven seconds, when you carry on an interpersonal conversation, establishing and reestablishing eye contact signal that you are on task and are listening. If you look as if you are listening, you will also be more likely to listen. We usually have more eye contact with someone when we are listening than when we are talking.[56]

In addition to eye contact, other nonverbal cues signal whether you are on task and responsive to the messages of others. Remaining focused, keeping your hands and feet still, and even leaning forward slightly communicate to someone that you are listening. Appropriate head nods and verbal responses also signal that you are attending to your partner's message.[57]

## Listen: Understand Both Details and Major Ideas

How do you improve your listening skill? Now that you've stopped your own internal dialogue and looked for nonverbal cues, it's time to listen. Here are six additional strategies for improving your listening skill.[58]

**Identify Your Listening Goal**   You listen to other people for a variety of reasons. Knowing your listening goal can increase your self-awareness of the listening process and increase your skill. If you're listening to Aunt Deonna talk about her recent trip to northern Minnesota for the annual bear hunt, you need not worry about taking extensive notes and trying to remember all the details of her expedition. But when your sociology professor tells a story to illustrate a sociological theory, you should be more attuned to the point he or she is making; the theory may be on a test. At other times, you need to be on your guard to evaluate the message of a politician or salesperson. There are four primary listening goals: to enjoy, to learn, to evaluate, and to empathize.

- *Listening to enjoy.* Sometimes we listen just because it's fun. You might listen to music, watch TV, go to a movie, or visit with a friend. Because you know you won't be tested on Jay Leno's monologue, you can relax and just enjoy the humor; you don't have to worry about passing a test to remember each punch line.
- *Listening to learn.* Nothing snaps a class to attention more quickly than a professor's proclamation such as "This next point will be covered on the test." Another key reason we listen is to learn. But you don't have to be a college student to listen to learn. Phone calls and conversations with family and friends contain information that we want to remember.
- *Listening to evaluate.* When you listen to evaluate, you try to determine whether the information you hear is valid, reliable, believable, or useful. One problem you may have when you listen to evaluate is that you may become so preoccupied with your criticism that you may not completely understand the message.
- *Listening to empathize.* The word *empathy*, which we introduced in Chapter 3 and will discuss in more detail later in this chapter, comes from a Greek word for

"passion" and the German word *Einfühlung*, meaning "to feel with." To empathize with someone is to try to feel what he or she is feeling rather than just think about or acknowledge the feelings.[59] In effect, you act as a sounding board for the other person. Empathic listening serves an important therapeutic function. Just having an empathic listener may help someone out. No, we are not empowering you to be a therapist, but we are suggesting that simply listening and feeling with someone can help your communication partner sort things out.

If you were listening to someone give you directions to Centennial Hall, one of the oldest buildings on campus, you would listen differently than if your sister were telling you about her fears that her marriage was on the rocks. In the case of your sister, your job is to listen patiently and provide emotional support. In trying to get to Centennial Hall, you would be focusing on the specific details and making either mental or written notes.

# Communication & DIVERSITY

## Does Gender Influence Listening Skill?

There is evidence that men and women can be equally good listeners, but research suggests that they sometimes (although not always) have different approaches to listening. They also have different approaches to interrupting others when listening, and the interruption patterns provide clues as to differences in listening styles. According to one study that reviewed a number of research investigations, men interrupt others more than women do. Specifically, men were sometimes perceived as interrupting to control the conversation. When women interrupted they were more likely either to express agreement or to add something to the conversation.[60]

Listening differences can be characterized as a feminine style (a more relational approach) or a masculine style (more task oriented). The following chart summarizes research conclusions from several studies about feminine and masculine listening styles.[61]

| | Feminine Listening Style | Masculine Listening Style |
|---|---|---|
| **Different Listening Focus** | • Tends to search for existing relationships among separate pieces of information<br>• Tends to identify individual facts and other isolated pieces of information<br>• Tends to shift from one idea to another or shift from listening to more than one person who may be speaking at the same time | • Tends to look for a new structure or organizational pattern when listening<br>• Tends to listen for the "big picture" and seek the major points being communicated<br>• Tends to lock on to a specific message without shifting between two or more conversations that he or she may be overhearing |
| **Different Listening Goals** | • More likely to listen to new information to gain new understanding and new insights<br>• Tends to use information to develop relationships with listening partners<br>• Tends to have a greater ability and motivation to listen when providing supportive and positive feedback[62] | • More likely to listen to new information to solve a problem<br>• Tends to listen to reach a conclusion; shows less concern about relationship cues and more concern about using the information gained<br>• Tends to have less ability and motivation to listen in situations that call for providing supportive feedback |
| **Different Application of Nonverbal Messages** | • Tends to emphasize meaning communicated through nonverbal cues<br>• Typically uses more eye contact with the other person when listening | • Tends to emphasize the meaning of the words and information exchanged<br>• Typically uses less eye contact with the other person when listening |

*(continued on next page)*

What does all this information mean? How is knowing differences in feminine and masculine listening styles useful to us? Although not all men and women fit into these categories of listening behavior, there are several good reasons to be mindful of gender-based differences in listening.[63]

### BE AWARE OF LISTENING DIFFERENCES

Being aware of listening differences can help us be less critical and more accepting of others if communication differences arise. Conflicts may arise simply because you and your listening partner are focusing on different parts of the message expressed.

### APPROPRIATELY ADAPT TO LISTENING DIFFERENCES

By being aware of whether you fit the general profile of a masculine or a feminine listener, you can determine whether you need to adapt your listening style. If, for example, you know that you have a tendency to be less interested in relational information and that you listen to get to the "bottom line" or solve a problem, being aware that your listening partner is not as focused on those objectives when listening can be helpful.

The best listener may be one who is the most flexible and doesn't always default to his or her typical pattern or preferred listening approach, but rather combines listening approaches.[64] Make an effort to listen for both individual facts and the overall ideas. Listening for both relational and emotional meaning as well as for explicit content can also enhance listening skill. Be more aware of the way you tend to listen to others, and expand your listening repertoire to increase your ability to be other oriented.

### DON'T STEREOTYPE OTHERS BASED ONLY ON PERCEIVED SEX OR GENDER

Although we've noted differences in the way some men and women listen, we repeat our caution: Don't assume that all men or all women have typical masculine or feminine listening styles. By noting some perceived differences in listening style, we don't want to be guilty of promoting gender- or sex-based stereotypes. Listening experts Stephanie Sargent and James Weaver suggest that studies of listening style differences between men and women may simply be measuring listening stereotypes.[65] What may be occurring is a self-fulfilling prophecy: Men and women assume that they *are* listening the way they think that they *should* listen.[66] Although there are some discernible patterns in masculine and feminine listening styles, the differences may not be as consistently pronounced as was once thought. And, listening differences are only a few of the many factors that explain why men and women sometimes have difficulty reaching a common understanding.

**Mentally Summarize the Details of the Message**  You can process words more quickly than a person speaks, so you can use the extra time to your advantage by periodically summarizing the names, dates, and facts embedded in the message. If the speaker is disorganized and rambling, use your tremendous mental ability to reorganize the speaker's information into categories or try to place events in chronological order. This suggestion may seem to contradict the suggestion to avoid focusing *only* on facts, but it is important to have a grasp of the details your partner presents. Yet to listen is to do more than focus on facts. Research suggests that poor listeners are more likely to focus on *only* facts and data, rather than the overall point of the message, than good listeners.[67] To listen is to connect the details of the message with the major points. If you miss the details, you will likely miss the main point.

**Link Message Details with the Major Idea of the Message**  As just pointed out, facts and data make the most sense when we can use them to support an idea or point. Mentally weave your summaries of the details into a focused major point or series of major ideas. So, as you summarize, link the facts you have organized in your mind with key ideas and principles. Use facts to enhance your critical thinking as you analyze, synthesize, evaluate, and finally summarize the key points or ideas your partner makes.

**Practice by Listening to Difficult or Challenging Material**  You learn any skill with practice. Listening experts suggest that our listening skills deteriorate if we listen only to easy and entertaining material. Make an effort to listen to news or documentary programs. As you listen to a lecture that seems full of content, make a conscious effort to stay focused, concentrate, and summarize facts and major ideas.

**Work to Overcome Listening Barriers**  If you can avoid the listening barriers presented earlier, you will be well on your way to improving your listening skill. Avoid being self-focused, letting emotional noise distract you, or criticizing a message before you've understood it. Watch out for information overload. And, when possible, take steps to minimize external noise and provide an environment more conducive to listening.

**Don't Interrupt**   One of the best things you can do to be perceived as a good listener is to not interrupt a speaker when he or she is talking. When we interrupt someone, we are saying, "What I have to say is more important than what you have to say." This translates to the other person as "I'm more important than you are." Interrupting others when listening is more than just rude; it decreases your credibility and lowers your ability to understand the other person. Do you want to make sure you *don't* get hired based on the impression you make during a job interview? Interrupt your interviewer and you're less likely to get the job, according to one research study.[68] To listen without interrupting seems simple, but because thoughts are bouncing around in our heads, we sometimes blurt them out,[69] or we think that we know what the other person is going to say, so we talk over her or him. Resist these temptations.

**Listen Actively**   Our suggestion that you listen actively is a distillation of the other recommendations we've offered. Active listeners are engaged listeners who listen with both their minds and their hearts. They are engaged physically and mentally in the listening process.[70] They are aware of what they are doing; they stop thinking about things that might take them off track.[71] They also have good eye contact with the speaker and communicate their interest with an intent facial expression and slight forward lean. By contrast, passive listeners are not involved listeners; they are detached and may fake attention with a frozen, nonexpressive facial expression. One listening research team noted that a passive listener receives information by being talked *to* rather than as an equal partner in the speaking-listening exchange.[72]

This same team described active listeners as people who do the following:

- Give full attention to others.
- Focus on what is being said.
- Expend considerable energy participating in the listening process.
- Have an alert posture.
- Maintain much direct eye contact.

Another research study found that listeners who offered person-centered comments (comments that acknowledge the feelings of others) as well as provided immediate nonverbal responses (eye contact, natural forward lean, appropriate head nods) were judged to be better listeners than those who did not use those skills.[73]

It seems that the best listeners are mentally alert, physically focused on the other person, and actively involved in seeking understanding. In short, they stop, they look, and they listen.

# **RE**CAP

## HOW TO LISTEN WELL

| What to Do | How to Do It |
|---|---|
| Identify your listening goal. | Decide whether you are listening to enjoy, to learn, to evaluate, or to empathize. Your listening goal should determine the strategies you use to achieve it. |
| Mentally summarize the details of the message. | Every few minutes, take time to create your own mental recap of the key information presented. In just a few seconds, you can summarize much information. |
| Link message details with the major ideas of the message. | Consciously relate the bits of information you hear to the key points the speaker is developing, rather than focusing only on facts and details or only on major points. |
| Practice by listening to difficult or challenging material. | Periodically make an effort to listen to material that is complex and richer in detail and information than what you typically listen to; while listening to this more complex material, make a conscious effort to stop, look, and listen. |
| Work to overcome listening barriers. | Identify the key obstacles that keep you from listening at peak effectiveness (self barriers, information-processing barriers, or context barriers); make conscious efforts to overcome their underlying causes. |
| Don't interrupt. | Increase your awareness of whether you interrupt others. Wait until the other person has finished speaking before you speak. |
| Listen actively. | Be engaged in the listening process by maintaining good eye contact with the speaker and an alert posture (slight forward lean; sitting up rather than slouching). |

# Responding Skills

To respond is to provide feedback to another about his or her behavior or communication. Your response can be verbal or nonverbal, intentional or unintentional.

Your thoughtful response serves several purposes. First, it tells a speaker how well you have understood his or her message. Second, your response lets a speaker know how the message affects you. It indicates whether you agree or disagree. Third, it provides feedback about statements or assumptions that you find vague, confusing, or wrong. It helps an individual keep the communication on target and purposeful. Finally, your response signals to the speaker that you are still "with" him or her—that you are still ready to receive messages. There is evidence that our ability to listen influences how we respond to others; when we are in the presence of someone whom we perceive to be a good listener, we're likely to respond with greater empathy and interest.[74] To respond appropriately and effectively, consider the following strategies.

## Be Descriptive

"I see that from a different point of view" sounds better than "You're wrong, I'm right." Effective feedback describes rather than evaluates what you hear. Although one listening goal is to evaluate and make critical judgments about messages, don't evaluate until you're sure you understand the speaker. We're not suggesting that it's easy to listen from a nonevaluative perspective or that you should refrain from ever evaluating messages and providing praise or negative comments. Remember: Feedback that first acts like a mirror to help the speaker understand what he or she has said is more useful than a barrage of critical comments. Describing your own reactions to what your partner has said rather than pronouncing a quick judgment on his or her message is also more likely to keep communication flowing. If your partner thinks that your prime purpose in listening is to take potshots at the message or the messenger, the communication climate will cool quickly. Listening researcher Eve-Anne Doohan not surprisingly found that when wives expressed negative emotions and critical evaluative comments to their listening husbands, the husbands were less satisfied with the overall quality of their relationships with their wives.[75] Being descriptive rather than evaluative encourages positive communication and has an effect on the overall quality of the relationship you have with another person.

## Be Timely

Feedback is usually most effective at the earliest opportunity after the behavior or message is presented, especially if the purpose is to teach. Waiting to provide a response after much time has elapsed invites confusion.

Now let us contradict our advice. Sometimes, especially if a person is already sensitive and upset about something, delaying feedback can be wise. Use your critical-thinking skills to analyze when feedback will do the most good. Rather than automatically offering immediate correction, use the just-in-time approach. Provide feedback just before the person might make another mistake, just in time for the feedback to have the most benefit.

## Be Brief

Less information can be more. Cutting down on the amount of your feedback can highlight the importance of what you do share. Don't overwhelm your listener with details that obscure the key point of your feedback. Brief is usually best.

## Be Useful

Perhaps you've heard this advice: "Never try to teach a pig to sing. It wastes your time, it doesn't sound pretty, and it annoys the pig." When you provide feedback to someone, be certain it is useful and relevant. Ask yourself, "If I were this person, how would I respond to this information? Is it information I can act on?" Immersing your partner in information that is irrelevant or that may be damaging to the relationship may make you feel better, but it may not enhance the quality of your relationship or improve understanding.

# Responding with Empathy

Empathy, as noted earlier in this chapter, is the process of feeling what another person is feeling. To empathize is more than to acknowledge that another person feels a particular emotion. Being empathic involves making an effort to feel the emotion yourself.[76]

Central to being empathic is being emotionally intelligent—having the ability to understand and express emotion, interpret emotions in yourself and others, and regulate or manage emotions.[77] Goleman suggests that people who are emotionally intelligent—sensitive to others, empathic, and other oriented—have better relationships with others than those who are not. He summarizes the importance of emotions in developing empathy by quoting Antoine De Saint-Exupery: "It is with the heart that one sees rightly; what is essential is invisible to the eye."[78] Researchers have found evidence supporting Goleman's ideas. Studies suggest that empathic listeners make better salespersons, teachers, counselors, and therapists and develop better relationships with others overall than nonempathic listeners.[79]

At the heart of empathic listening is the ability not only to know when to speak, but also to know when to be silent. Henri Nouwen eloquently expressed both the challenge and the rewards of empathic listening:

> To listen is very hard, because it asks of us so much interior stability that we no longer need to prove ourselves by speeches, arguments, statements, or declarations. True listeners no longer have an inner need to make their presence known. They are free to receive, to welcome, to accept. . . . Listening is a form of spiritual hospitality by which you invite strangers to become friends, to get to know their inner selves more fully, and even to dare to be silent with you.[80]

Psychologist Carl Rogers suggests that empathic listening is more than a technique; it's a "way of being."[81] Effective empathic listeners make empathy a natural and normal way of interacting with others. Some people are simply better at being empathic than others. Just as you inherit physical qualities from your parents, there is also evidence that you inherit communication traits as well.[82] This does not mean that if you are not naturally empathic, you can never develop empathic skills, but it does mean that you may have to work a bit harder than others to enhance these skills. Can people be taught to be more empathic? Research suggests that the answer is a clear "yes." One goal of this book is to enhance your skill in appropriately adapting to others; empathy is at the heart of focusing on the needs and emotions of others.[83]

## How to Respond with Empathy

Being empathic is not a single skill but several related skills that help you predict how others will respond.[84] Four strategies to help you respond empathically when you listen are understanding your partner's feelings, asking appropriate questions, paraphrasing message content, and paraphrasing emotions.

**Understand Your Partner's Feelings**    If your goal is to empathize, or "feel with," your partner, you might begin by imagining how you would feel under the same circumstances. If your roommate comes home from a hassle-filled day at work or school, try to imagine what you might be thinking or feeling if you had had a stressful day. If a friend calls to tell you his mother died, consider how you would feel were the situation reversed. Even if you've not yet experienced the loss of your mother, you can identify with what it would be like to suffer such a loss. Of course, your reaction to life events is unlikely to be exactly like someone else's response. Empathy is not telepathically trying to become your communication partner.[85] But you do attempt to decenter—to consider what someone may be thinking—by first projecting how you might feel and then asking appropriate questions and offering paraphrases to confirm the accuracy of your assumptions. Considering how others might feel has been called the Platinum Rule—even more valuable than the Golden Rule ("Do unto others as you would have others do unto you"). The Platinum Rule invites you to treat others as *they* would like to be treated—not just as *you* would like to be treated.

**Ask Appropriate Questions**    As you listen for information and attempt to understand how another person is feeling, you may need to ask questions to help clarify your conclusions. Most of your questions will serve one of four purposes: (1) to obtain additional information ("How long have you been living in Buckner?"), (2) to check how the person feels ("Are you frustrated because you didn't get your project finished?"), (3) to ask for clarification ("What do you mean when you say you want to telecommute?"), or (4) to verify that you have reached an accurate conclusion about your partner's intent or feeling ("So are you saying you'd rather work at home than at the office?").

Another way to sort out details and get to the emotional heart of a dialogue is to ask questions to help you (and your partner) identify the sequence of events. "What happened first?" and "Then what did he do?" can help both you and your partner clarify a confusing event.

Your ability to ask appropriate questions will demonstrate your supportiveness of your partner and signal that you are interested in what he or she is sharing. Of course, if you are trying to understand another's feelings, you can just ask how he or she is feeling in a straightforward way—don't ask questions just for the sake of asking questions. Also, monitor how you ask your questions. Your own verbal and nonverbal responses will contribute to the emotional climate of your interaction.

**Paraphrase Message Content**    After you have listened and asked questions, check whether your interpretations are accurate by paraphrasing the content you have heard. **Paraphrasing** is restating in your own words what you think a person is saying. Paraphrasing is different from repeating something exactly as it was spoken; that would be parroting, not paraphrasing. Your paraphrase can summarize the essential events, uncover a detail that was quickly glossed over, or highlight a key point. Typical lead-ins to a paraphrase include statements such as

"So here is what seems to have happened. . . ."
"Here's what I understand you to mean. . . ."
"So the point you seem to be making is. . . ."
"You seem to be saying. . . ."
"Are you saying . . . ?"

We are not suggesting that you paraphrase when clarification is not needed or appropriate; paraphrase only when you need to confirm your understanding of a murky message or to help the speaker sort out a jumbled or confusing situation. When a listener paraphrases the content and feelings of a speaker's message, the speaker is not only more likely to know that the message is understood but also more likely to trust and value the listener.

Does paraphrasing a speaker's message really enhance the overall quality and accuracy of communication? Yes. Several researchers have found considerable support for the value of paraphrasing the messages of others in enhancing communication.[86] Listening researcher Harry Weger and his colleagues found that people who skillfully used paraphrasing were perceived as more "socially attractive" by the listener than other people. That is, the listener liked the person who paraphrased more than a person who didn't use the paraphrasing skill. The researchers found that people liked skillful paraphrasers better even when listeners didn't feel well understood or satisfied with the conversation.[87]

**Paraphrase Emotions**   The bottom line in empathic responding is to make certain that you understand your communication partner's emotional state. You can paraphrase his or her feelings using common lead-in phrases, such as "So you feel . . . ," "So now you feel . . . , " and "Emotionally, you are feeling. . . ."

Using these or other ways of paraphrasing feeling (as well as content) can be especially useful in situations in which messages could escalate emotions or produce conflict, such as the following:

Before you take an important action
Before you argue or criticize
When your partner has strong feelings
When your partner just wants to talk
When your partner is speaking "in code"—using unclear jargon or unclear abbreviations
When your partner wants to understand your feelings and thoughts
When you are talking to yourself (you can question and check your own emotional temperature)
When you encounter new ideas[88]

As a final word on responding with empathy, realize that although we have discussed empathic responses and the active listening process using a tidy, step-by-step textbook approach, in practice the process won't be as neat and tidy. You may have to back up and clarify content, ask more questions, and rethink how you would feel before you summarize how your partner feels. Or you may be able to summarize feelings without asking questions or summarizing the content of the message. Be sure to adapt the skills appropriately, and ethically, to each specific communication situation. The Communication & Ethics box offers more advice for when and how to paraphrase.

**paraphrasing**
Checking the accuracy of your understanding by restating your partner's message in your own words.

# Communication&ETHICS

## Paraphrase Properly

If used with wisdom, paraphrasing can help both you and your partner clarify messages accuracy. The most essential guideline is to use your paraphrasing skills *only* if you are able to be open and accepting. If you try to color your paraphrased comments to achieve your own agenda, you aren't being ethical.

Also avoid the overuse of paraphrasing. Too much of it can slow down a conversation and make the other person uncomfortable or irritated. A sensitive communicator tries not to let his or her technique show.

Other guidelines to keep in mind when you ask questions and paraphrase content and feelings are the following:

- Use your own words—don't just repeat exactly what the other person says.
- Don't add to the information presented when paraphrasing.
- Be brief.
- Be specific.
- Be accurate.

## How to Provide Social Support

Responding with empathy is especially important if you are listening to provide social support or encouragement to someone. You provide **social support** to someone when you sensitively and empathically listen to him or her and then offer messages of comfort or confirmation that let the person know that he or she is both understood and valued. Providing social support does *not* mean trying to solve the issue or problem your communication partner has. Instead, it means communicating genuine concern, rather than just going through the motions of pretending to listen.

How much social support should you offer? One research study suggests that when we are experiencing sadness, disappointment, or trauma, most of us prefer a "midlevel" amount of social support—a moderate level of positive, genuine, supportive communication.[89] Although the women in the study preferred a bit higher level of comforting than did the men, most people studied didn't want over-the-top, dramatic expressions of support. Neither did they like mild or timid expressions of support.

What's the best way to express your support? There are no magic words or phrases that will always ease someone's stress or anxiety. However, research does suggest that following these guidelines as appropriate to the person's situation can help you develop positive, empathic, comforting messages that are likely to be appreciated by others.[90]

- Clearly express that you want to provide support. ("I would really like to help you.")
- Appropriately communicate that you have positive feelings for the other person; explicitly tell the other person that you are her or his friend, that you care about her or him, or that you love her or him. ("You mean a lot to me." "I really care about you.")
- Express your concern about the situation the other person is in right now. ("I'm worried about you right now, because I know you're feeling _____ [stressed, overwhelmed, sad, etc.].")
- Indicate that you are available to help, that you have time to support the person. ("I can be here for you when you need me.")
- Let the other person know how much you support him or her. ("I'm completely with you on this." "I'm here for you, and I'll always be here for you because I care about you.")
- Acknowledge that the other person is in a difficult situation. ("This must be very difficult for you.")
- Paraphrase what the other person has told you about the issue or problem that is causing stress. ("So you became upset when she told you that she didn't want to see you again.")
- Consider asking open-ended questions to see if the other person wants to talk. ("How are you doing now?")

**social support**
Sensitive and empathic listening, followed by messages of comfort or confirmation, that lets a person know that he or she is understood and valued.

- Let the other person know that you are listening and supportive by providing conversational continuers. ("Yes—then what happened?," "Oh, I see," or "Uh-huh.")
- After expressing your compassion, empathy, and concern, just listen.

Communication researchers have also determined that some types of responses are *less* helpful in conveying social support. Here are a few things *not* to do.

- Don't tell the other person that you know exactly how he or she feels.
- Don't criticize or negatively evaluate the other person; she or he needs support and validation, not judgmental comments.
- Don't tell the other person to stop feeling what he or she is feeling.
- Don't immediately offer advice. First, just listen.
- Don't tell the other person that "It's going to get better from here" or that "The worst is over."
- Don't tell the other person that she or he really has nothing to worry about or that "It's no big deal."
- Don't tell the other person that the problem can be solved easily. ("Oh, you can always find another girlfriend.")
- Don't blame the other person for his or her problems. ("Well, if you didn't always drive so fast, you wouldn't have had the accident.")
- Don't tell the other person that her or his expression of feelings and emotion is wrong. ("Oh, you're just making yourself sick. Stop crying.")

Don't be discouraged if your initial attempts to use these skills seem awkward and uncomfortable. Learning to use any new set of skills well takes time. The instructions and samples you have seen here should serve as a guide rather than as hard-and-fast prescriptions to follow every time. Being an empathic listener can be rewarding in both your personal and your professional life.[91] And here's some encouraging news about listening and responding skills: These skills can be improved. People who have received listening training show overall improvement in their ability to listen to others.[92] Reading this chapter, listening to your instructor give you tips on enhancing your skills, and participating in skill-building activities are well worth your time.

The following poem "Listen," by an unknown author, summarizes the essential ideas of how to listen and respond with empathy.

### Listen

When I ask you to listen to me and you start giving advice, you have not done what I asked.

When I ask you to listen to me and you begin to tell me why I shouldn't feel that way, you are trampling on my feelings.

When I ask you to listen to me and you feel you have to do something to solve my problems, you have failed me, strange as that may seem.

Listen! All I asked was that you listen. Not talk or do—just hear me.

Advice is cheap: 50 cents will get you both Dear Abby and Billy Graham in the same newspaper.

And I can do for myself; I'm not helpless. Maybe discouraged and faltering, but not helpless.

When you do something for me that I can and need to do for myself, you contribute to my fear and weakness.

But when you accept as a simple fact that I do feel what I feel, no matter how irrational, then I quit trying to convince you and can get about the business of understanding what's behind this irrational feeling.

And when that's clear, the answers are obvious and I don't need advice.

Irrational feelings make sense when we understand what's behind them.

Perhaps that's why prayer works, sometimes, for some people, because God is mute, and doesn't give advice or try to fix things,

God just listens and lets you work it out for yourself.

So, please listen and just hear me, and, if you want to talk, wait a minute for your turn; and I'll listen to you.

*—Anonymous*

# **RE**CAP

## HOW TO RESPOND WITH EMPATHY

| Strategy | Action |
|---|---|
| Understand Your Partner's Feelings | Ask yourself how you would feel if you had experienced a similar situation or recall how you *did* feel under similar circumstances. Or recall how your *partner* felt under similar circumstances. |
| Ask Questions | Seek additional information to better understand your partner's message. |
| Reflect Content by Paraphrasing | Summarize for your partner the essence of the information, as you understand it. |
| Reflect Feelings by Paraphrasing | When appropriate, try to summarize what you think your partner may be feeling. |

# STUDY GUIDE:
## Review, Apply, and Assess Your Knowledge and Skill

### The Importance of Listening and Responding Skills
p. 106

You spend more time listening than doing any other communication activity. Being a good listener and responding thoughtfully to others helps you

- Enhance the quality of your interpersonal relationships.
- Develop good collaboration skills.
- Forge a stronger link between speaker and audience.

### How We Listen
p. 107

Listening is a complex process of receiving, constructing meaning from, and responding to verbal and nonverbal messages. The five activities of listening are (1) selecting, (2) attending, (3) understanding, (4) remembering, and (5) responding.

#### Terms to Know

| | | | |
|---|---|---|---|
| Hearing | p. 107 | Understand | p. 108 |
| Listening | p. 107 | Remember | p. 108 |
| Select | p. 108 | Asynchronous Listening | p. 109 |
| Attend | p. 108 | Respond | p. 109 |

### Listening Styles
p. 109

Each person develops a preferred listening style. The four listening styles are relational, analytical, critical, and task oriented. Knowing your listening style can help you adapt your listening approach for maximum listening effectiveness.

#### Terms to Know

| | | | |
|---|---|---|---|
| Listening Style | p. 109 | Critical Listeners | p. 111 |
| Relational Listeners | p. 110 | Second Guessing | p. 111 |
| Analytical Listeners | p. 110 | Task-Oriented Listeners | p. 111 |

### Listening Barriers
p. 112

Many people struggle with the skill of listening. Barriers to effective listening include (1) self barriers—self-focus, emotional noise, criticism; (2) information-processing barriers—processing rate, information overload, receiver apprehension, shifting attention, cultural differences; and (3) context barriers—time barriers and place barriers.

#### Terms to Know

| | | | |
|---|---|---|---|
| Emotional Noise | p. 113 | Anticipatory Communication | p. 116 |
| Receiver Apprehension | p. 115 | Noise | p. 117 |

## Improving Your Listening Skills                    p. 118

To become a better listener, consider three simple steps that may sound easy to do but are challenging to put into practice: stop, look, and listen. To stop means to be mindful of the message and avoid focusing on your own distracting inner "talk," which may keep you from focusing on the messages of others. To look is to listen with your eyes—to focus on nonverbal information. To listen involves the skill of capturing the details of a message while also connecting those details to a major idea.

### Terms to Know

| | |
|---|---|
| Social Decentering    p. 119 | Meta-Message    p. 119 |

## Responding Skills                    p. 124

The other half of listening is responding to others accurately and appropriately. To respond thoughtfully means to consider the needs of the other person. Check the accuracy of your listening skills by reflecting your understanding of what your partner has said. To respond effectively, be descriptive, timely, brief, and useful.

## Responding with Empathy                    p. 125

Empathy is the process of feeling what another person is feeling. To listen with empathy is to understanding your partner's feelings, ask appropriate questions, paraphrase message content, and paraphrase emotions.

### Terms to Know

| | |
|---|---|
| Paraphrasing    p. 127 | Social Support    p. 128 |

# APPLYING Principles for a Lifetime

**Principle Four:**
**Listen and respond thoughtfully to others.**

- Stop: Work to turn off competing mental messages that distract your listening focus.
- To overcome self barriers to listening effectively, consciously become aware of your drifting attention. Then, to get back in sync, use self-talk skills and emotion management skills (such as deep breathing) to remain calm and focused on the message, not the messenger.
- To overcome information-processing listening barriers, make mental summaries of the message you hear, recognize when you are tired and not at your listening best, take effective notes, and remain focused.
- To overcome context listening barriers, become aware of your best and worst times of the day for listening; consciously intensify your concentration if you know you're not at your listening best; and assertively take action, such as closing a door or a window, to reduce external noise when listening.
- Look: Listen with your eyes to discern nonverbal information that provides important information about emotions, attitudes, and relationship cues.
- Listen: Work to link facts and details with major ideas you hear.
- Respond: Use effective responding skills by providing feedback that is descriptive, timely, brief, and useful while remaining an active listener.

- Be empathic: Try to imagine how you would feel in a situation like the one your communication partner is in. To confirm your interpretation of his or her message, ask appropriate clarifying questions and then paraphrase both the content and the emotions expressed.
- Paraphrase by briefly summarizing the message in your own words while trying to accurately capture the essence of what your listening partner said; don't add to the information presented when paraphrasing.

# ASSESSING Your Skill

## Listening Journal

Keep a listening journal for a day. During your waking hours, keep a notebook handy and note what you have been listening to each hour of the day. You may have been listening to several different sources or people during the course of an hour. Was it primarily a lecture? Were you listening to music or TV? Were you listening to someone during conversation? In addition to providing an entry of *what* you were listening to, also evaluate *how effectively* you listened. Rate your listening on a scale of 1 to 10 (1 = not effective, 10 = very effective) for each one-hour interval. Write a short summary describing what you listened to, how much time you spent listening, and your self-assessment of how effectively you listened during the day.

## Assessing Your Listening Style

Complete the following brief assessment of your listening style.[92] After you have noted your style, reread the material in the chapter about listening styles and then write a short summary of the implications of your listening style for you and your listening behavior. For additional insight, ask a close friend, family member, spouse, or significant other to assess his or her listening style, too. You can then discuss the implications of your listening styles upon your relationship and how you could enhance communication between you.

**Relational Listeners**

1. I am most comfortable listening to people's feelings and emotions. I like to empathize and search for common areas of interest with others when listening; I seek strong interpersonal connections with others.

| 1 | 2 | 3 | 4 | 5 | 6 | 7 | 8 | 8 | 10 |
|---|---|---|---|---|---|---|---|---|----|

Low                                                                         High

**Analytical Listeners**

2. I wait until all the facts are presented before I reach a conclusion or judgment; I like to see all sides of an issue. I am good at analyzing information that I hear.

| 1 | 2 | 3 | 4 | 5 | 6 | 7 | 8 | 8 | 10 |
|---|---|---|---|---|---|---|---|---|----|

Low                                                                         High

### Critical Listeners

3. I am good at critically evaluating the information that I hear; I find inconsistencies and errors in what others say. I listen for the underlying logic and reasoning of what others are saying.

| 1 | 2 | 3 | 4 | 5 | 6 | 7 | 8 | 8 | 10 |
|---|---|---|---|---|---|---|---|---|----|

Low                            High

### Task-Oriented Listeners

4. I listen to determine what I need to do to accomplish a task. I like clear, brief messages so that I can efficiently achieve the work that needs to be done.

| 1 | 2 | 3 | 4 | 5 | 6 | 7 | 8 | 8 | 10 |
|---|---|---|---|---|---|---|---|---|----|

Low                            High

Source: These scales are based on the work of Debra Worthington, Graham D. Bodie, and Christopher Gearhart, "The Listening Styles Profile Revised (LSP-R): A Scale Revision and Validation," paper presented at the Eastern Communication Association, Arlington, VA (April 2011).

## Assessing Listener Apprehension

Take the following test to assess your level of receiver apprehension. Indicate how much each of the statements describes you, using a 5-point scale: 5 = Strongly agree, 4 = Agree, 3 = Uncertain or sometimes, 2 = Disagree, 1 = Strongly disagree.

1. ____ When I am listening, I feel nervous about missing information.

2. ____ I worry about being able to keep up with the material presented in lecture classes.

3. ____ Sometimes I miss information in class because I am writing notes.

4. ____ I feel tense and anxious when listening to important information.

5. ____ I am concerned that I won't be able to remember information I've heard in lectures or discussions.

6. ____ Although I try to concentrate, my thoughts sometimes become confused when I'm listening.

7. ____ I worry that my listening skills aren't very good.

8. ____ I regularly can't remember things that I have just been told.

9. ____ I feel anxious and nervous when I am listening in class.

10. ____ I prefer reading class material rather than listening to it so that I don't have to be stressed about catching all the information the first time.

Scores range from 10 to 50. The higher your score, the more you're likely to experience some anxiety when you listen to others and the harder you'll have to work at developing strategies to improve your listening comprehension.

Source: L. Wheeles, "An Investigation of Receiver Apprehension and Social Context Dimensions of Communication Apprehension," *Speech Teacher* 24 (1975): 261–268. <http://www.tandf.co.uk/journals>. Used by permission: National Communication Association, www.natcom.org

## WEB RESOURCES for More Review, Application, and Assessment

Several websites provide a wealth of information about how to improve your listening, responding, and paraphrasing skills. Here are a few that we recommend:

- **MyCommunicationLab** Highlights of this chapter of MyCommunicationLab include self-tests of memory and a web activity that encourages you check others' perceptions of your own listening. <www.mycommunicationlab.com> (Access code required.)

- **International Listening Association** This organization is dedicated solely to the study of listening. <www.listen.org>

- **Emotional Intelligence Quiz** Discovery Health and the self-quiz site Queendom offer you a very short self-test to help you gauge your emotional intelligence. <http://discoveryhealth.queendom.com/eiq_abridged_access.html>

- **Listening: The "Lost" Communication Skill** Part of the American Communication Association's Open Knowledge Guide to Public Speaking. <http://textcommons.org/node/110>

- **Listening Coach** Read articles on listening and take a self-quiz to score your own listening habits at this site from "Dr. Rick," a professional listening and leadership coach. <http://www.listen-coach.com/>

- **Active Listening** This brief but thorough tutorial from Colorado University can help you improve your listening skills. <http://www.colorado.edu/conflict/peace/treatment/activel.htm>

There are no ordinary people.

C. S. LEWIS

# Chapter OUTLINE

- Understanding Diversity
- Culture and Communication
- Barriers to Bridging Differences and Adapting to Others
- Adapting to Others Who Are Different from You
- Study Guide: Review, Apply, and Assess Your Knowledge and Skill

# Chapter OBJECTIVES

After studying this chapter, you should be able to

1. Describe how differences of gender, sexual orientation, ethnicity, and age influence communication.
2. Define *culture*.
3. Describe, compare, and contrast high-context and low-context cultures.
4. Describe five cultural values.
5. Illustrate five barriers that inhibit communication between individuals.
6. Describe six strategies that will help bridge differences between people and help them adapt to differences.

Jupiterimages/Thinkstock.com

# 6 | Adapting to Others: Diversity and Communication

As C. S. Lewis observed, there are no ordinary people—which implies that each of us is unique. And the not-so-startling fact that people *are* different from one another provides the context for discussion of our final Communication Principle for a Lifetime: *Effective communicators appropriately adapt their messages to others.* We introduce this principle last because often people learn how to adapt only after they have learned the other communication principles. Figure 6.1 presents our now-familiar model, which includes this final principle of appropriately adapting messages to others.

Being able to adapt to others suggests that you already have a sense of who you are and a consciousness of the presence of others—self-awareness and other-awareness, the components of the first principle we presented.[1] We learn to use verbal and nonverbal messages as infants, though it may take several years to develop sophistication in using language and nonverbal symbols. Hearing and listening also develop early in our lives. Studies in developmental communication suggest that the ability to appropriately adapt our behavior to others evolves after we have become aware that there is a "me," after we have learned to use verbal and nonverbal symbols to communicate, and after we have developed an ability to hear and listen to others. To adapt to others requires a relatively sophisticated understanding of the communication process.

One of life's unprofound principles with profound implications for human communication is this: *We each have different backgrounds and experiences.*[2] As you read in Chapter 2, we each see, hear, and experience the world differently. To some degree, we are each estranged from others.

The goals of this chapter are to identify human differences that may inhibit communication with others and to suggest adaptive strategies that can improve the quality and effectiveness of our communication with others. Our premise: To live comfortably in the 21st century, we must learn ways to appreciate and understand human differences rather than ignore them, suffer because of them, or wish they would disappear. But simply understanding that there are differences is not enough to improve communication; it is important to learn how to use effective communication skills to adapt to those differences.

The phrase "survival of the fittest" is attributed to evolution theorist Charles Darwin, but what Darwin *actually* said was, "It is not the strongest of the species that survives, nor the most intelligent that survives. It is the one that is the most adaptable to change."[3] We think that Darwin was correct: The ability to adapt is a quintessential communication principle that will serve you well for a lifetime.

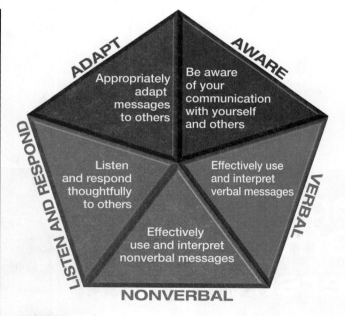

**Figure 6.1
Communication Principles
for a Lifetime**

# Understanding Diversity

Unless you have an identical twin, you look different from everyone else. Although you may have some things in common with a larger group of people (such as skin color, where you grew up, or language), you nonetheless are a unique individual, not only in your appearance but also in your personality and other ways. There is no one exactly like you. Communication researchers have studied several major differences among humans that affect the way we interact with one another. To frame our discussion of diversity and communication, we'll note differences in gender, sexual orientation, ethnicity, and age and the implications these differences have on communication. Some of these differences are learned, some are based on biology—or, in the case of age differences,

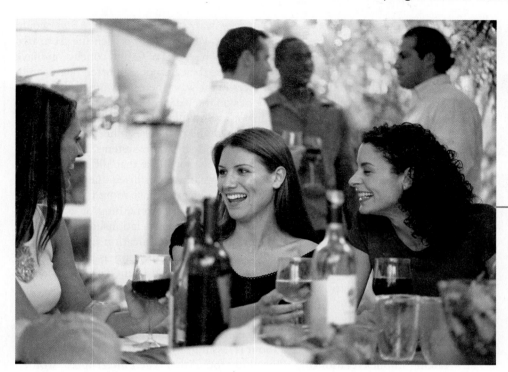

simply how long someone has lived—but they all have an effect on how we perceive and interact with others. Following our discussion of some of the classic ways we are diverse, we'll turn our attention to cultural differences and then note how human differences create communication barriers. We'll conclude the chapter by identifying strategies to enhance the quality of communication with others by appropriately adapting to our differences.

## Sex and Gender

Perhaps the most obvious form of human diversity is gender—the division of human beings into female and male. As pointed out in Chapter 2, a person's sex is determined by biology; gender is the culturally constructed and psychologically based perception of one's self as feminine, masculine, or **androgynous** (having both feminine and masculine traits). One's gender is learned and is socially reinforced by others, as well as by one's life experience and genetics.

At one time or another, you have probably thought, "Why doesn't she (or he) act like people of *my* sex?" Have you ever heard yourself or someone else say, "You men are all alike" or "If women would just be more reasonable, like men are, life would be simpler"? You may not think of yourself as stereotyping others based only on their sex or gender, but there is evidence that many of us do make snap judgments about someone's behavior based on their sex. One study found that, because of the limited cues, you are even more likely to form rigid, inaccurate stereotypes of someone if you're communicating with them via an electronically mediated channel such as e-mail, text, or Facebook.[4] You may also have heard (or said) "Vive la différence"—a French expression that celebrates that men and women are different. Why celebrate? Because that difference makes us fascinating and mysterious, and it keeps the world from being awfully dull. Whatever your view of the relationship between the sexes, your day-to-day interaction with members of both sexes is a fact of life (unless you're a hermit). Women and men work, live, and play together, so it's important to explore the effects of gender on communication to improve our ability to relate to one another.

**androgynous**
Exhibiting both masculine and feminine characteristics.

John Gray, author of the book *Men Are from Mars, Women Are from Venus*, would have us believe that the sexes are so different that we actually approach life from two distinct "planets," or spheres of perspective.[5] Although several of Gray's conclusions have been challenged by communication scholars because they are not supported by research, there are some research-documented differences in the ways men and women communicate.[6] Deborah Tannen, author of several books on the behavior of the sexes, views men and women as distinctly different cultural groups.[7] She suggests that female–male communication is cross-cultural communication, with all the challenges inherent in exchanging messages with persons of very different backgrounds and value systems. Perhaps these viewpoints are a bit extreme, and the sexes are actually more alike than different.

Research using multiple methods and originating in various disciplines consistently shows that differences in men's and women's communication have more to do with *why* we communicate than *how*. Men tend to talk to accomplish something or complete a task. Women often use conversation to establish and maintain relationships.

Research also reveals that men tend to approach communication from a content orientation, meaning that they view the purpose of communication as primarily goal oriented. You talk when you have something to say. This is consistent with the tendency for men to base their relationships, especially their male friendships, on sharing activities rather than talking.

Women, research suggests, tend to use communication for the purpose of relating or connecting to others, of extending themselves to other persons to know them and be known by them. What you talk about is less important than that you're talking, because talking implies relationship. One study found that when interrupted, women are more likely to simply smile, agree, politely nod, and laugh, actions that suggest, according to the researchers, a greater effort, even when interrupted, to maintain a positive relationship and facilitate the flow of conversation.[8] To summarize this difference: *Men often communicate to report; women often communicate to establish rapport.*[9] So the point of difference isn't in the way the sexes actually communicate but in the motivations or reasons for communicating. The *how* may not be that different; the *why* may be very different.[10] Our instrumental and expressive orientations to the world translate into our communication behavior.

To bridge the gap, here's what we suggest you do:

- First, work to understand the differences that may exist.
- Second, make an insightful examination of your own behavior in light of the differences discussed and then determine how you conform to and differ from the description of members of your sex.
- Third, be a gender researcher yourself. Note differences as well as similarities between you and members of the opposite sex. Be careful not to ascribe differences in communication only to gender, but to consider a host of other reasons such as age, personality, or culture.
- Finally, make a conscious effort to adapt your behavior appropriately; be mindful of how you interact with others to enhance the quality of your relationships with them.

One reason adaptation is a premium skill is that by understanding both approaches to communication (content and relational) and by developing the ability to accomplish both, you broaden what you can do. Just because you're female doesn't mean that you have to take an expressive approach to every interaction; just because you're male doesn't mean that conversations are always about information exchange. In a conversation with a member of the opposite sex, try to assess the person's communication motivation. Analyze what the other person must view as the purpose for the conversation, and adjust your response accordingly. Sometimes it's wise simply to ask the person what he or she wants.

## Sexual Orientation

The gay, lesbian, bisexual, and transgender (GLBT) community is an important subculture within the larger U.S. culture. Being gay has become a source of pride for some, but it is still a social stigma for others. There is evidence that GLBT individuals continue to be judged negatively based solely on their sexual orientation.[11] Research further suggests that heterosexuals who have negative perceptions of gays and lesbians are more likely to have rigid views about gender roles and will assume that their peers also hold such rigid views and negative impressions of gays and lesbians.[12] In addition, those who hold negative attitudes toward gays and lesbians are less likely to communicate with them than are others. It is because of the persistence of these negative attitudes toward gays and lesbians, as well as antigay violence and harassment, that some gays and lesbians continue to live in the closet (conceal their sexual orientation).[13]

An effective and appropriate communicator is aware of and sensitive to issues and attitudes about sexual orientation in contemporary society. **Homophobia,** the fear of being labeled or perceived as gay or lesbian, continues to exist among many people. Just as you have been taught to avoid racially biased expressions that degrade someone's race or ethnicity, it is equally important to avoid using language that demeans a person's sexual orientation. Telling stories and jokes whose point or punch line relies on cruelly ridiculing a person because of his or her sexual orientation lowers perceptions of your credibility not only among gay and lesbian people, but also among people who dislike bias against gays and lesbians.

What seems helpful is to create a communication climate in which gays and lesbians can be themselves and comfortably talk about who they are without fearing rejection or discrimination. Creating a climate of openness and acceptance is important for any human relationship. Family members who have a gay, lesbian, bisexual, or transgender member report more overall relational satisfaction if their family doesn't avoid a discussion of homosexuality. In addition, there is less anxiety and negativity if issues of sexuality, specifically sexual orientation, are openly and appropriately discussed. Many universities offer training courses, known as *ally training*, to help faculty and staff members create safe, accepting relationships. Participants are informed about GLBT culture and taught how to provide appropriate support. A faculty or staff member who has completed ally training may post a sign on his or her door to indicate that it's safe to be yourself in that person's office or classroom.[14]

Sometimes we unintentionally offend someone through subtle use or misuse of language. For example, gays and lesbians typically prefer to be referred to as *gay* or *lesbian*, rather than as *homosexual*.[15] And the term *sexual orientation* is preferred over *sexual preference* in describing a person's sexual orientation. Our language should reflect and acknowledge the range of human relationships that exist. The key point is this: It is important to be aware of the range of human sexual expression and to be sensitively other oriented as you interact with those whose sexual orientation is different from your own.

## RECAP

### GENDER-BASED APPROACHES TO COMMUNICATION

| Masculine Approach | Feminine Approach |
|---|---|
| • More instrumental; often characterized by assertiveness and getting things done | • More expressive; often characterized by an emphasis on connecting with others and fostering harmonious relationships |
| • Usually more emphasis on the content of messages | • Usually more emphasis on the relational elements of messages |
| • More focus on the information being exchanged (the *what*) rather than on relational elements (the *how*) in the message | • More focus on the quality of the relationship between communicators than on information exchanged |
| • More attention given to verbal than nonverbal messages | • More attention given to nonverbal elements, *how* something is said rather than *what* is said |

## Age

Because different generations have experienced different cultural and historical events, they often view life differently. If your grandparents or great-grandparents experienced the Great Depression of the 1930s, they may have different attitudes about bank savings accounts than you or even your parents do. Today's explicit song lyrics may shock older Americans who grew up with such racy lyrics as "makin' whoopee." The generation gap is real and has implications for how we communicate with others.

**homophobia**
Fear of, aversion to, or discrimination against gays or lesbians.

There is considerable evidence that people hold stereotypical views of others based on others' perceived age.[16] You may see someone with graying or thinning hair and wrinkles and make assumptions about that person's preferences in music, food, or even politics. And older people who see someone with tattoos, piercings, and wildly colored hair may make stereotypical assumptions about a host of preferences of the younger person. (Even our example of old and young draws on stereotypes that run the risk of contributing to stereotypical images of appearance and a person's age.)

Regardless of the accuracy of the assumptions we make about others based on perceived age, a person's age has an influence on his or her communication with others, including how messages are processed. For example, one study found that older adults have greater difficulty in accurately interpreting the nonverbal messages of others than do younger people.[17] Older adults don't like to be patronized or talked down to (who does?).[18] And younger people seem to value social support, empathic listening, and being mentored more than older people do.[19]

Authors Neil Howe and William Strauss, researchers who have investigated the role of age and generation in society, define a generation as "a society-wide peer group, born over a period roughly the same length as the passage from youth to adulthood, who collectively possess a common persona."[20] *Baby boomers* is the label for one such generation, of people born between 1943 and 1960, during the postwar years. Perhaps your parents or grandparents are "boomers." *Generation X* is the term used for people born between 1961 and 1981. If you were born between 1982 and 2002, you and other members of your generation have been labeled *millennials*. Researchers Howe and Strauss suggest that, as a group, "Millennials are unlike any other youth generation in living memory. They are more numerous, more affluent, better educated, and more ethnically diverse. More importantly, they are beginning to manifest a wide array of positive social habits that older Americans no longer associate with youth, including a focus on teamwork, achievement, modesty, and good conduct."[21] And millennials are more comfortable with technology than other age groups because the Internet, cell phones, and personal computers have always been part of their lives.[22] Table 6.1 summarizes the labels and common characteristics and values of several generational types. The newest generation—people born since 2002—has been labeled *postmillennials*. Because postmillennials are just emerging, there is less research that identifies the specific attributes of this generation. One clear observation is that postmillennials view technology as an even more seamless method of interacting with others than do millennials. For them, technological tools to connect socially have always been a way of relating to others.

Your generation of origin has important implications for communication, especially as you relate to others in both family and work situations. Each generation has developed its own set of values, anchored in social, economic, and cultural factors stemming from the times in which the generation has lived. Our values—core conceptualizations of what is fundamentally good or bad and right or wrong—color our way of thinking about and responding to what we experience. Generational and age differences may create barriers and increase the potential for conflict and misunderstanding. For example, one team of researchers, after investigating the role of generations in the workforce, suggests that Generation X workers are paradoxically both more individualistic (self-reliant) and more team oriented than boomers.[23] In contrast, boomers are more likely to have a sense of loyalty to their employers, expect long-term employment, value a pension plan, and experience job burnout from overwork. Generation Xers, on the other hand, seek a more balanced approach between work and personal life, expect to have more than one job or career, value working conditions over other job factors, and have a greater need to feel appreciated.[24] Of course, these broad generalizations do not apply to all people in these categories.

## Ethnicity

**ethnicity**
A social classification based on factors, such as nationality, religion, and language as well as biological ancestral heritage, that are shared by a group of people with a common geographic origin.

**Ethnicity** is a *social classification* based on a variety of factors, such as nationality, religion, and language as well as biological ancestral heritage (race), that are shared by a group of people with a common geographic origin. Simply stated, an ethnic group is

## Table 6.1
## Summary of Generation Characteristics[25]

| GENERATION NAME | BIRTH YEARS | TYPICAL CHARACTERISTICS |
| --- | --- | --- |
| Matures | 1925–1942 | • Work hard<br>• Have a sense of duty<br>• Are willing to sacrifice<br>• Have a sense of what is right<br>• Work quickly |
| Baby Boomers | 1943–1960 | • Value personal fulfillment and optimism<br>• Crusade for causes<br>• Buy now/pay later<br>• Support equal rights for all<br>• Work efficiently |
| Generation X | 1961–1981 | • Live with uncertainty<br>• Consider balance important<br>• Live for today<br>• Save<br>• Consider every job as a contract |
| Millennials | 1982–2002 | • Are close to their parents<br>• Feel "special"<br>• Are goal oriented<br>• Are team oriented<br>• Focus on achievement |

a group of people who have identified themselves as such, based on a variety of factors that may or may not include ancestral heritage or biological characteristics such as skin color.

Ethnicity fosters common bonds that affect communication patterns. While ethnic groups bring vitality and variety to American society, members of these groups may experience persecution or rejection by members of other groups in our society.

A concept closely related to ethnicity is **race,** which is based on the genetically transmitted physical characteristics of a group of people who are also classified together because of a common history, nationality, or geographical location.[26] Skin color and other physical characteristics affect our responses and influence the way people of different races interact. A person's racial classification is typically based on such visible physiological attributes as phenotypes, which include skin color and other physical features including body type, hair color and texture, and facial attributes.

Although it may seem easy to classify individuals genetically as belonging to one race or another, it's not quite that simple. One geneticist has concluded that there is much more genetic variation *within* a given racial category than *between* one race and another.[27] There really aren't vast genetic differences between the people assigned to two racial categories.[28] That's why many scholars suggest that we think of race as a category that includes not only biological or genetic characteristics, but also such factors as cultural, economic, social, geographic, and historical elements.[29] The term *race* therefore is a fuzzy, somewhat controversial way of classifying people.

Making distinctions between race and ethnicity, communication scholar Brenda Allen proposes that *ethnicity* be used to refer to "a common origin or culture based on shared activities and identity related to some mixture of race, religion, language

**race**
Genetically transmitted physical characteristics of a group of people.

and/or ancestry."[30] She suggests that ethnicity may include race, but that race is a separate category based on more genetic or biological factors that are not clear-cut.[31] A key distinction between race and ethnicity is that ethnicity is a *socially constructed* category that emphasizes culture (learned behaviors, attitudes, beliefs, values, and norms shared by a group of people) and factors other than racial or genetic background.[32] Not all Asians (race), for example, have the same socially constructed cultural background (ethnicity). Nationality and geographical location are especially important in defining an ethnic group. Those of Irish ancestry are usually referred to as an ethnic group rather than as a race. The same could be said of Britons, Norwegians, and Spaniards.

One of the most significant problems stemming from attempts to classify people by racial or ethnic type is the tendency to discriminate and unfairly, inaccurately, or inappropriately ascribe stereotypes to racial or ethnic groups. **Discrimination** is the unfair or inappropriate treatment of people based on their group membership. One of the goals of learning about diversity and becoming aware of both differences and similarities among groups is to eliminate discrimination and stereotypes that cause people to rigidly and inappropriately pre-judge others.

# Culture and Communication

Overheard from a student before class:

> I've had it with all this cultural diversity and gender stuff. It seems like every textbook in every class is obsessed with it. My music appreciation class is trying to force the music of other cultures down my throat. What's wrong with Bach, Beethoven, and Brahms? In English lit, all we're reading is stuff by people from different countries. And it seems my history prof talks only about obscure people I've never heard of before. I'm tired of all this politically correct nonsense. I mean, we're all Americans, aren't we? We're not going off to live in Africa, China, or India. Why don't they just teach us what we need to know and cut all this diversity garbage?

Have you heard this kind of sentiment expressed before? Perhaps you've encountered this kind of "diversity backlash" among some of your classmates, or you may harbor this attitude yourself. It may seem unsettling to some that school curricula and textbooks are focusing on issues of culture and gender differences. But these changes are not motivated by an irrational desire to be politically correct. They are taking place because there is increased diversity. The Communication & Diversity feature "Diversity Almanac" documents how diverse the United States is now and will continue to become in the future. There is evidence that the trend toward greater diversity will continue.[33] With this growing diversity comes a heightened awareness that learning about culture and gender differences can affect every aspect of our lives in positive ways. You may not plan to travel the world, but the world is traveling to you. Your employers, teachers, religious leaders, best friends, or romantic partners may have grown

**discrimination**
The unfair or inappropriate treatment of people based on their group membership.

# Communication&DIVERSITY

## Diversity Almanac

1. Two-thirds of the immigrants on this planet come to the United States.[34]

2. One in seven marriages occurs between spouses of different races or ethnicities.[35]

3. It is estimated that more than 40 million U.S. residents learned something other than English as their first language, including 18 million people for whom Spanish is their first language.[36]

4. Almost one-third of U.S. residents under the age of 35 are members of minority groups, compared with one-fifth of those age 35 or older. According to U.S. Census Bureau population projections, by the year 2023, nearly half of all young adults in this country will come from minority groups.[37]

5. If the current trend continues, by the year 2050 the proportion of the U.S. population composed of non-Hispanic whites will decrease to 53 percent, down from the current 72 percent. Asians will increase to 16 percent, up from 4.5 percent; Hispanics will more than double their numbers, to more than 25 percent, up from just over 11.5 percent; and African Americans will increase their proportion slightly from the current 12 percent.[38]

6. "About one in three U.S. residents is a minority," said Census Bureau Director Louis Kincannon. "To put this into perspective, there are more minorities in this country today than there were people in the United States in 1910. In fact, the minority population in the U.S. is larger than the total population of all but eleven countries."[39]

7. One out of every eight U.S. residents speaks a language other than English at home, and one-third of children in urban U.S. public schools speak a first language other than English.[40]

8. California has a minority population of 20.7 million—21 percent of the nation's total. Texas has a minority population of 12.2 million—12 percent of the nation's total.[41]

9. Non-Hispanic whites constitute a minority of the population in Texas, New Mexico, and California.[42]

10. Sixty percent of the residents of Miami, Florida, are foreign-born.[43]

11. Studies on gay and lesbian populations in the United States offer estimates that vary from 1 to 9 percent of the general male population, and from 1 to 5 percent of the general female population.[44]

12. There are more millennials (born between 1982 and 2002) than any other age group. The U.S. population in 2003 included 100 million millennials, 44 million Generation Xers (1961–1981), and 78 million baby boomers (1943–1960).[45]

up with cultural traditions different from your own. School textbooks and courses are *reflecting* the change, not *initiating* it.

One statistician notes that if the world were a village of 1,000 people, the village would have 590 Asians, 122 Africans, 96 Europeans, 84 Latin Americans, 55 members of the former Soviet Union, and 53 North Americans.[46] Clearly, a global economy and the ease with which technology permits us to communicate with others around the world increase the likelihood that you will establish relationships with people who are different from you and who have cultural traditions different from your own. You need not travel abroad to encounter cultural differences; the world is here.

**Globalization,** the integration of economics and technology that is contributing to a worldwide, interconnected business environment, is changing the way we work and relate to people around the world.[47] Globalization has increased the probability that you will communicate with someone today who has a cultural background different from your own. For example, when you call to get technical assistance with your computer or advice on fixing your TV, you are more likely to talk to someone in India than in Indiana. Although some suggest that because of globalization and the merging of cultural traditions the concept of a "national culture" is obsolete, nonetheless cultural differences do exist. To ignore the range of human cultural differences is to ignore a significant factor, which can mean the difference between effective communication and ineffective communication. Our point is not to debate the advantages or disadvantages of globalization, but only to suggest that one implication of a "flat" world is that you will increasingly communicate with people who have cultural backgrounds different from your own.

**globalization**
The integration of economics and technology that is contributing to a worldwide, interconnected business environment.

## Defining Culture

**Culture** is a learned system of knowledge, behavior, attitudes, beliefs, values, and norms that is shared by a group of people and shaped from one generation to the next.[48] Communication and culture, says anthropologist Edward T. Hall, are inseparable—you can't talk about one without the other.[49] There is ample evidence that documents the influence of culture on how we work and live.[50] In the broadest sense, culture includes how people think, what they do, and how they use things to sustain their lives. Researcher Geert Hofstede says culture is the "mental software" that helps us understand our world.[51] Like the software and operating system in a computer, our culture provides the framework within which we interpret the data and information that enter our life.

Cultures are not static; they change as new information and new technologies modify them.[52] We no longer believe that bathing is unhealthy or that we should use leeches as the primary medical procedure to make us healthy. Through research, we have replaced both of these cultural assumptions with the values of personal hygiene and modern, sophisticated methods of medical care.

Some groups of individuals can best be described as a **co-culture**—a cultural group within a larger culture. Examples of co-cultures include people with physical disabilities, different age groups, and various religious groups. Different Christian denominations, such as the Amish or members of the Church of Jesus Christ of Latter-day Saints (Mormons), have distinct traditions and cultural norms. A person's gender places her or him in one of the co-cultures that researchers have used to analyze and investigate the influence of communication on our relationships with others. Gay, lesbian, bisexual, and transgendered people constitute another example of an important co-culture in our society.

**culture**
A learned system of knowledge, behavior, attitudes, beliefs, values, and norms that is shared by a group of people and shaped from one generation to the next.

**co-culture**
A culture that exists within a larger cultural context (e.g., GLBT cultures, Amish culture).

# Communication&TECHNOLOGY

## Adapting to Differences When Making E-Connections

It is increasingly likely that you communicate with people who are far from where you work and live. It's not unusual to e-mail, text, or instant message people from another culture. With the advent of Facebook, Skype, and other easy-to-use videoconference methods, it's also not surprising to see and hear the person you're talking with. According to a *Business Week* survey, most people believe that they will be working with someone in an international location by 2017.[53]

A team of communication researchers points out that when we communicate via e-mail or phone, it takes a bit longer to interpret information about relationships, because often there are fewer nonverbal cues available.[54] In the case of e-mail, we can't see or hear the person we're exchanging messages with. With a telephone call, we can hear a person, but we miss facial expressions and body posture information. Even during a videoconference, we're not able to see all a person's body posture or watch everyone participating 100 percent of the time. The potential for misunderstanding, already present because of cultural differences, is compounded by the lack of nonverbal information. Evidence also shows that we are more likely to inaccurately stereotype others when interacting via electronic channels than when communicating face to face.[55]

Given the importance and prevalence of e-communication and the increased potential for misunderstanding, how can you enhance the quality of your relationships online? Consider these suggestions:

- If you are using a "lean" communication channel, such as e-mail or texting, to interact with a person who is from a high-context culture, you may need to provide more explicit references to your feelings and emotions. You may need to use emoticons more liberally or describe your emotional responses more explicitly or in writing.
- When appropriate, consider asking more questions to clarify meanings.
- Consciously make more "small talk" about the weather or other topics that may not directly be related to the task at hand. Such interaction helps connect you to others, makes the interaction less task oriented, and provides a balance of relational information that humanizes the communication.
- Use paraphrasing to confirm that you understand what others are saying.
- Finally, you simply may need to be more patient with others; relationships may take longer to develop because of the diminished nonverbal cues. Be mindful of the differences and consciously develop other-oriented skills.

**Intercultural communication** occurs when individuals or groups from different cultures communicate. The transactional process of listening and responding to people from different cultural backgrounds can be challenging. As stressed earlier, the greater the difference in culture between two people, the greater the potential for misunderstanding and mistrust. That's why it is important to understand the nature of culture and how cultural differences influence our communication with others. Such understanding helps us develop strategies to make connections and adapt to others with different "mental software."[56]

When you encounter a culture that has little in common with your own, you may experience **culture shock,** a sense of confusion, anxiety, stress, and loss.[57] If you are visiting or actually living in the new culture, your uncertainty and stress may take time to subside as you learn the values and message systems that characterize the culture. If you are trying to communicate with someone from a background quite different from yours—even on your home turf—it is important to consider the role of culture as you interact.

Our culture and life experiences determine our **worldview**—the general cultural perspective that shapes how we perceive and respond to what happens to us. A culture's worldview, according to intercultural communication scholar Carley Dodd, encompasses "how the culture perceives the role of various forces in explaining why events occur as they do in a social setting."[58] These beliefs shape our thoughts, language, and actions. Your worldview permeates all aspects of how you interact with society; it's like a lens through which you observe the world. Since, as noted in Chapter 1, communication is how we make sense out of the world and share that sense with others, our worldview is one of the primary filters that influence how we make sense out of the world. Two frameworks for describing how culture influences our worldview include cultural contexts and cultural values.

## Cultural Contexts

The **cultural context** of any communication consists of the nonverbal cues that surround and give added meaning to the message. In this sense, *all* nonverbal cues are part of a cultural context. Some cultures give more weight to the surrounding nonverbal context than to the explicit verbal message when interpreting the overall meaning of a message. Other cultures place less emphasis on the nonverbal context and greater emphasis on what someone says.

For example, when you interview for a job, you may be scanning the face of your interviewer and looking for nonverbal messages to provide cues about the impression you are making on the interviewer. These contextual cues (in this case, the nonverbal messages) give meaning to help you interpret the message of your interviewer. Edward T. Hall helped us understand the importance of cultural context when he categorized cultures as either high- or low-context.[59]

**High-Context Cultures**    In **high-context cultures,** nonverbal cues are extremely important in interpreting messages. Communicators rely heavily on the context of subtle information such as facial expression, vocal cues, and even silence in interpreting messages—hence the term *high-context cultures,* to indicate the emphasis placed on the context. Asian, Arab, and southern European peoples are more likely to draw on context for message interpretation.

**Low-Context Cultures**    People in **low-context cultures** rely more explicitly on language and the meaning of words and use fewer contextual cues to send and interpret information. Individuals from low-context cultures, such as North Americans, Germans, and Scandinavians, may perceive people from high-context cultures as less attractive, knowledgeable, and trustworthy, because they violate unspoken low-context cultural rules of conduct and communication. Individuals from low-context cultures often are less skilled in interpreting unspoken contextual messages.[60]

---

**intercultural communication**
Communication between people who have different cultural traditions.

**culture shock**
Feelings of confusion, loss, stress, and anxiety that a person may experience when encountering a culture different from his or her own.

**worldview**
A perspective shared by a culture or group of people about key beliefs and issues, such as death, God, and the meaning of life, which influences interaction with others; the lens through which people in a given culture perceive the world around them.

**cultural context**
Additional information about a message that is communicated through nonverbal and environmental cues rather than through language.

**high-context culture**
A culture in which people derive much information from nonverbal and environmental cues and less information from the words of a message.

**low-context culture**
A culture in which people derive much information from the words of a message and less information from nonverbal and environmental cues.

## Figure 6.2 A Scale of High-Context and Low-Context Cultures

**Low-Context Cultures**
Place emphasis on words

- Are less aware of nonverbal environment and situation
- Need detailed background information
- Tend to segment and compartmentalize information
- Control information and share it on a "need to know" basis
- Prefer explicit and careful directions from someone who "knows"
- Consider knowledge an important commodity

**High-Context Cultures**
Place emphasis on nonverbal expressions and surrounding context

- Consider nonverbal cues important
- Take into account the environment and situation
- Observe a communication partner's gestures, facial expressions, tone of voice, and overall mood
- Maintain extensive information networks

Figure 6.2 describes differences in communication style between high-context and low-context cultures.

## Cultural Values

Ancient Egyptians worshiped cats. The Druids of England believed they could tap into spiritual powers in the shadow of the mysterious rock circle of Stonehenge at the summer solstice. Some would say contemporary Americans place a high value on accumulating material possessions and making pilgrimages to sports arenas on weekends. By paying attention to what a culture values, we can get important clues about how to respond to communication messages, establish relationships, and avoid making embarrassing errors when interacting with people from a given culture. Identifying what a given group of people values or appreciates can give us insight into the behavior of an individual raised within that culture. Although there are considerable differences among the world's **cultural values**—clearly, not all cultures value the same things—Geert Hofstede has identified five categories for measuring values that are important in almost every culture.[61] These generalizations are based on several surveys that he developed and administered to more than 100,000 people. We'll consider each of these five categories of values in more detail. Even though his data were collected more than thirty-five years ago and only sampled employees (predominantly males) who worked at IBM—a large international company with branch offices in many countries—Hofstede's research remains one of the most comprehensive studies to help us describe what people from a culture may value.

According to Hofstede's research, every culture establishes values relating to (1) individualism versus collectivism, (2) distribution of power (either centralized or shared), (3) avoidance of uncertainty versus tolerance for uncertainty, (4) masculine or feminine cultural perspectives, and (5) long-term and short-term orientation to time. An overview of Hofstede's research conclusions for several countries is included in Table 6.2.

As we discuss the five cultural values, keep in mind that we are applying generalizations to a cultural group; certainly not all the people within the cultural group will hold the cultural values we will discuss. Think of these values as explaining cultural *group* differences viewed from an anthropological perspective, rather than *individual* differences viewed from a psychological perspective. There are vast differences *within* a culture as well as between cultural groups.[62]

**cultural values**
Whatever a given group of people values or appreciates.

## Table 6.2
## Countries That Illustrate Five Categories of Cultural Values

| CULTURAL VALUE | COUNTRIES THAT HAVE PEOPLE WHO SCORED HIGHER ON THIS CULTURAL VALUE | COUNTRIES THAT HAVE PEOPLE WHO SCORED LOWER ON THIS CULTURAL VALUE |
|---|---|---|
| **Individualism:** Societies with higher individualism scores generally value individual accomplishment rather than the collective or collaborative achievement valued by societies with lower scores. | United States, Australia, Great Britain, Canada, Netherlands, New Zealand, Italy, Belgium, Denmark, Sweden, France | Guatemala, Ecuador, Panama, Venezuela, Colombia, Indonesia, Pakistan, Costa Rica, Peru, Taiwan, South Korea |
| **Power Distribution:** Societies with higher power distribution scores generally value greater power differences between people; they are generally more accepting of fewer people having authority and power than are those with lower scores on this cultural dimension. | Malaysia, Guatemala, Panama, Philippines, Mexico, Venezuela, Arab countries, Ecuador, Indonesia, India | Australia, Israel, Denmark, New Zealand, Ireland, Sweden, Norway, Finland, Switzerland, Great Britain |
| **Uncertainty Avoidance:** Societies with higher uncertainty avoidance scores generally prefer to avoid uncertainty; they like to know what will happen next. Societies with lower scores are more comfortable with uncertainty. | Greece, Portugal, Guatemala, Uruguay, Belgium, Japan, Peru, France | Singapore, Jamaica, Denmark, Sweden, Hong Kong, Ireland, Great Britain, Malaysia, India, Philippines, United States |
| **Masculinity:** Societies with higher masculinity scores value high achievement, men in more assertive roles, and more clearly differentiated sex roles than people with lower scores on this cultural dimension. | Japan, Australia, Venezuela, Italy, Switzerland, Mexico, Ireland, Jamaica, Great Britain | Sweden, Norway, Netherlands, Denmark, Costa Rica, Finland, Chile, Portugal, Thailand |
| **Orientation to Time:** Societies with higher scores have a longer-term orientation to time; they tend to value perseverance and thrift. Societies with lower scores have a shorter-term orientation to time; they value the past and present, respect for tradition, saving "face," and spending rather than saving. | China, Hong Kong, Taiwan, Japan, Vietnam, South Korea, Brazil, India, Thailand, Hungary, Singapore, Denmark, Netherlands | Pakistan, Czech Republic, Nigeria, Spain, Philippines, Canada, Zimbabwe, Great Britain, United States, Portugal, New Zealand |

Source: Adapted with permission from Geert Hofstede, Gert Jan Hofstede, Michael Minkov, *Cultures and Organizations, Software of the Mind*, Third Revised Edition, (New York: McGraw Hill, 2010). ISBN 0-07-166418-1 © Geert Hofstede BV.

**Individualistic and Collectivistic Cultural Values**   Which of the following two sayings better characterizes your culture: "All for one and one for all" or "I did it my way"? If you chose the first one, your culture is more likely to value group or team collaboration—it is what researchers call a **collectivistic culture.** Collectivistic cultures champion what people do together and reward group achievement. In contrast, the "I did it my way" phrase emphasizes the importance of the individual over the group.[63]

A culture that celebrates individual achievement and in which individual recognition is important is an **individualistic culture.** The United States—with its Academy Awards; its reality TV shows in which contestants vie for the title of "American Idol" or try to be the lone "Survivor"; its countless sports contests; and its community awards to firefighters for dedicated service, to winners of spelling bees, to chefs for their barbecue recipes—perhaps epitomizes the individualistic culture.

Some researchers believe that the values of individualism and collectivism are the most important values of any culture—they determine the essential nature of every

**collectivistic culture**
A culture that places a high value on collaboration, teamwork, and group achievement.

**individualistic culture**
A culture that values individual achievement and personal accomplishments.

other facet of how people behave.[64] Other researchers, however, caution that cultures are complex and that it is dangerous to label an entire culture as "individualistic" or "collectivistic."[65] We agree—obviously, not everyone in a given culture fits a single label. But in trying to understand the role of culture and its effect on human communication, we believe that Hofstede's concept of cultural values, with special emphasis on individualism and collectivism, helps explain and predict how people may send and interpret communication.[66] Using Hofstede's five cultural values to describe a given culture or geographic region is a bit like flying over a country at 35,000 feet; at that height, you can't see the details and notice nuances of difference, but you can gain a broad overview of the cultural landscape.

Traditionally, North Americans place a high value on individual achievements. People from Asian cultures are more likely to value collective or group achievement. Hofstede summed up the American value system this way:

> Chief among the virtues claimed . . . is self-realization. Each person is viewed as having a unique set of talents and potentials. The translation of these potentials into actuality is considered the highest purpose to which one can devote one's life.[67]

In a collectivistic culture, conversely, people strive to accomplish goals for the benefit of the group rather than the individual. Here's a description of the Kenyan culture's emphasis on group or team collaboration:

> Nobody is an isolated individual. Rather, his [or her] uniqueness is a secondary fact. . . . In this new system, group activities are dominant, responsibility is shared and accountability is collective. . . . Because of the emphasis on collectivity, harmony and cooperation among the group tend to be emphasized more than individual function and responsibility.[68]

### Decentralized and Centralized Approaches to Power and Cultural Values

Some cultures are more comfortable with a broad distribution of power than other cultures. People from such cultures prefer a decentralized approach to power. Leadership is not vested in just one person. Decisions in a culture that values decentralized power distribution are more likely to be made by consensus rather than by decree.

Cultures that place a high value on centralized power are more comfortable than other cultures with a more structured form of government and with managerial styles that feature clear lines of authority. Hierarchical bureaucracies are common, and the general assumption is that some people will have more power, control, and influence than others.

### Uncertainty and Certainty and Cultural Values

"Why don't they tell me what's going on?" exclaims an exasperated student. "I don't know what my grades are. I don't know what my SAT score is. I'm in a complete fog." Many people like to know "what's going on." They like to avoid uncertainty and to have a general sense of what's going to happen. Too much uncertainty makes them uncomfortable.

Some people tolerate more ambiguity and uncertainty than others. Cultures in which people need certainty to feel secure are likely to develop and enforce more rigid rules for behavior and establish more elaborate codes of conduct. People from cultures with a greater tolerance for uncertainty have more relaxed, informal expectations for others. "It will sort itself out" and "Go with the flow" are phrases that characterize their attitudes.[69]

Again, we remind you that although there is evidence for the existence of the general cultural value of uncertainty avoidance, not all people in a given culture or country find this cultural value equally important. There is considerable variation within a culture as to how people respond to uncertainty.

### Masculine and Feminine Cultural Values

Some cultures emphasize traditional male values such as getting things done and being assertive; other cultures

People in masculine cultures tend to value achievement, heroism, and wealth, and to prefer traditional roles for men and women. How can a person from such a culture appropriately adapt their communication with people from feminine cultures, who are more likely to value sensitivity and caring for others?

Viorel Sima /Shutterstock.com

place greater emphasis on traditional female values such as building relationships and seeking peace and harmony with others. These values are not really about biological sex differences but about general assumptions that underlie the values of interacting with others. These values are not only about biological differences; they are general approaches to interacting with other people. People from **masculine cultures** also tend to value more traditional roles for men and women. People (both men and women) from masculine cultures value achievement, heroism, material wealth, and making things happen. Men and women from **feminine cultures** tend to value such things as caring for the less fortunate, being sensitive toward others, and enhancing the overall quality of life.[70] Later in this chapter, we will discuss how gender contributes to the development of a culture, but for now it is enough to realize that whole cultures can be typified by whether they identify with or emphasize masculine or feminine values.

We caution you to avoid making sweeping generalizations about every person in any cultural group. Just as there are differences between and among cultures, there are differences within a cultural group. For centuries, most countries have had masculine cultures. Men and their conquests are featured in history books and all aspects of society more than women are. But today's cultural anthropologists see some shift in these values. There is some movement toward the middle, with greater equality between masculine and feminine roles.

# RECAP
## CULTURAL VALUES

| | |
|---|---|
| Individualistic vs. Collectivistic | • Individualistic cultures value individual accomplishments and achievement.<br>• Collectivistic cultures value group and team collaboration. |
| Decentralized vs. Centralized Power | • Centralized power cultures value having power in the hands of a smaller number of people.<br>• Decentralized power cultures favor more equality and a more even distribution of power in government and organizations. |
| Uncertainty vs. Certainty | • Cultures that value certainty do not like ambiguity and value feeling secure.<br>• Cultures with a greater tolerance for uncertainty are comfortable with ambiguity and less information. |
| Masculine vs. Feminine | • Masculine cultures value achievement, assertiveness, heroism, material wealth, and more traditional sex roles.<br>• Feminine cultures value relationships, caring for the less fortunate, overall quality of life, and less traditional distinctions between sex roles. |
| Long-Term vs. Short-Term Orientation to Time | • Cultures with a long-term orientation to time tend to be future oriented and value perseverance and thrift.<br>• Cultures with a short-term orientation to time tend to value the past and present, respecting tradition, preserving "face," and fulfilling social obligations. |

## Long-Term and Short-Term Time Orientation and Cultural Values

A culture's orientation to time falls on a continuum between long-term and short-term.[71] People from a culture with a long-term orientation to time place an emphasis on the future and tend to value perseverance and thrift because these are virtues that pay off over a long period of time. A long-term time orientation also implies a greater willingness to subordinate oneself for a larger purpose, such as the good of society or the group.

In contrast, a culture that tends to have a short-term time orientation values spending rather than saving (because of a focus on the immediate rather than the future), tradition (because of the value placed on the past), and preserving "face" of both self and others (making sure that an individual is respected and that his or her dignity is upheld) and has an expectation that results will soon follow the actions and effort expended on a task. Short-term cultures also place a high value on social and status obligations.

As shown in Table 6.2, cultures or societies with a long-term time orientation include many Asian cultures such as China, Hong Kong, Taiwan, and Japan. Cultures with a short-term time orientation include Pakistan, Czech Republic, Nigeria, Spain, and the Philippines. Both Canada and the United States are closer to the short-term time orientation than the long-term time orientation, which suggests an emphasis on valuing quick results from projects and greater pressure toward spending rather than saving, as well as a respect for traditions.[72]

**masculine culture**
A culture that values achievement, assertiveness, heroism, material wealth, and traditional male and female roles.

**feminine culture**
A culture that values being sensitive toward others and fostering harmonious personal relationships with others.

# Barriers to Bridging Differences and Adapting to Others

Now that we've paid attention to some of the ways people are different from one another, let's identify barriers that increase the differences that exist between people. Differences, whether based in culture or gender, often breed misunderstanding, which can lead to feelings of distrust, suspicion, and even hostility. Among the most common reasons for a woman to end up in an emergency room in the United States today is bodily harm inflicted by a man whom she knows.[73]

The headlines continue to chronicle the prevalence of terrorism, war, and conflict around the globe, which are due, in part, to different cultural perspectives. Our hopes for harmony in our own country erode when we learn of hate crimes committed against members of co-cultural groups within the larger American culture. Our hopes for peace and prosperity among all the world's peoples are often dashed when we read of violent clashes between people of different religions, sexual orientations, and ethnicities.

Is it possible to develop effective relationships with people who are different from ourselves? The answer is "Of course." Although almost every relationship experiences some degree of conflict, most of the world's people do not witness annihilating destruction each day. Bridging culture and gender differences is possible. To develop effective strategies to adapt to others who are different from ourselves, we'll examine some of the barriers that often separate us from one another.

## Assuming Superiority

One of the most powerful barriers to adapting to others is the belief that one's own culture or gender is better than that of others. **Ethnocentrism** is the attitude that our own cultural approaches are superior to those of other cultures.[74] Extreme ethnocentrism is the opposite of being other oriented. When fans from two rival high schools at a Friday night football game scream, "We're number one!" they are hardly establishing quality communication. Competition is, of course, expected in sports; but when the mind-set of unquestioned superiority is created through cultural or religious identification, the resulting mistrust and suspicion are breeding grounds for conflict. Ethnocentrism and cultural snobbery create a barrier that inhibits rather than enhances communication.

It would probably be impossible to avoid feeling most comfortable with our own culture and people who are like us. In fact, some degree of ethnocentrism can play a useful role in perpetuating our own cultural traditions; we form communities and groups based on common traditions, beliefs, and values. A problem occurs, however, if we become so extremely biased in favor of our own cultural traditions that we fail to

**ethnocentrism**
The belief that one's own cultural traditions and assumptions are superior to those of others.

recognize that people from other cultural traditions are just as comfortable with their approach to life as we are with ours. And when we mindlessly attack someone else's cultural traditions (which may be a prelude to physical aggression), we erect communication barriers.

A person who assumes superiority may also assume greater power and control over others. Conflicts are often about power—who has it and who wants more of it. Differences in power are therefore breeding grounds for mistrust and conflict. Nineteenth-century British scholar Lord Acton said that absolute power corrupts absolutely; although this may not always be the case, an ethnocentric mind-set that assumes superiority may add to the perception of assumed power over others. Although it's true that there are cultural differences in attitudes toward power (whether power is centralized or decentralized), world history documents that those who are consistently pushed and pulled and pummeled eventually revolt and seek greater equity of power.

## Assuming Similarity

Just as it is inaccurate to assume that all members of the opposite sex or all people who belong to other social groups or classes are worlds apart from you, it is also wrong to assume that others will act and think just like you. Even if they appear to be like you, all people do not behave the same way.[75] Anthropologists Clyde Kluckhohn and Henry Murray suggested that every person is, in some respects, (1) like all other people, (2) like some other people, and (3) like no other people.[76] Our challenge when meeting others is to sort out how we are alike and how we are unique. Focusing on superficial factors such as appearance, clothing, and even a person's occupation can lead to false impressions. Instead, we must take time to explore the person's background and cultural values before we can determine what we really have in common.

On meeting a new acquaintance, we usually explore what we may have in common. "Do you know so and so?" "Oh, you're from Missouri. Do you know Mamie Smith from Buckner?" The search for similarities helps us develop a common framework for communication. But even when we find a few similarities, it's a mistake to make too many assumptions about our new friend's attitudes and perceptions. Because of our human tendency to develop categories and use words to label our experiences, we may lump people into a common category and assume similarity where no similarity exists.

Our cultural worldview has a profound effect on how we describe ourselves and those in other cultures. Research has found that English-speaking people describe themselves and others by identifying individual personality traits ("Matt is friendly") rather than merely describing behavior ("Matt brings snacks to the meeting").[77] Each of us perceives the world through our own frame of reference. As one ancient Greek sage put it, "Every tale can be told in a different way." We not only see the world differently, but also express those differences in the way we talk, think, and interact with others. If we fail to be mindful that each of us is unique, we may take communication shortcuts, use unfamiliar words, and assume that our communication will be more effective than it is.

## Assuming Differences

Although it may seem contradictory to say so, given what we just noted about assuming similarities, another barrier that may keep you from bridging differences between yourself and someone else is to automatically assume that the other person will be different from you. It can be just as detrimental to communication to assume that someone is essentially different from you as it is to assume that someone is just like you. The fact is, human beings *do* share common experiences and characteristics despite their differences. So we suggest that although you don't want to assume that everyone is just like you, it also hinders communication to assume that you have nothing in common with others.

Cultural anthropologists have spent considerable effort to identify cultural differences among people. The gist of this entire chapter is that people are different—in culture, gender, and factors such as personality, age, sexual orientation, and innate talents. Yet if we don't seek to connect with those factors that make us all members of the human family, we may miss opportunities for bridging the real differences that exist.

The point of noting that humans have similarities as well as differences is not to diminish the role of culture as a key element that influences communication, but to recognize that despite cultural differences we are all members of the human family. The words *communication* and *common* resemble each other. We communicate effectively and appropriately when we can connect to others based on discovering what we hold in common. Identifying common cultural issues and similarities can also help you establish common ground with your audience.

How are we all alike? Cultural anthropologist Donald Brown has compiled a list of hundreds of "surface" universals of behavior.[78] According to Brown, people in all cultures

- Have beliefs about death.
- Have a childhood fear of strangers.
- Have a division of labor by sex.
- Experience certain emotions and feelings, such as envy, pain, jealousy, shame, and pride.
- Use facial expressions to express emotions.
- Have rules for etiquette.
- Experience empathy.
- Value some degree of collaboration or cooperation.
- Experience conflict and seek to manage or mediate conflict.

Of course, not all cultures have the same beliefs about death or the same way of dividing labor according to sex, but all cultures address these issues.

Communication researcher David Kale believes that the dignity and worth of other people are universal values. Thus, he suggests that all people can identify with the struggle to enhance their own dignity and worth, although different cultures express it in different ways.[79] Another common value that Kale notes is world peace.

Intercultural communication scholars Larry Samovar and Richard Porter assert that there are other common elements that cultures share.[80] They note that people from all cultures seek physical pleasure, both emotional and psychological pleasure,

People from many different cultures similarly value close, happy families, but they may have different ideas about what makes a family close and happy. How can you discover the similarities and differences in your values when you communicate with someone from another culture?

Karan Kapoor/Getty Images

# Communication & ETHICS

## Can Stereotyping Others Ever Be a Good Idea?

We've pointed out that being prejudiced toward others, as well as stereotyping people into predetermined, rigid categories (especially because of sexual orientation or racial, ethnic, or cultural backgrounds), can hinder effective communication. Reaching conclusions about someone before you get to know him or her can result in a dishonest relationship. Most people are taught not to be prejudiced toward others. Yet might stereotypes sometimes serve a useful purpose, especially when a quick decision is needed and you have only partial information?

Imagine, for example, that you are driving your car late at night and have a flat tire in a neighborhood that's known to have a high crime rate. While wondering what to do, you see two people who have observed your plight and are moving toward you. Do you hop out of your car and seek their help? Or do you lock your doors and be thankful that you have your cell phone to call for assistance?

Are there times when prejudging a situation and reaching stereotypical conclusions about others may make common sense? Could a case be made that the ability to respond stereotypically may be useful in times of stress when quick thinking is needed?

We never know all the facts about a situation, and we sometimes (maybe even often) have to respond with only the partial information we have at hand. Some might argue that we sometimes need to make stereotypical, snap judgments. Malcolm Gladwell, author of *Blink: The Power of Thinking Without Thinking,* describes how people often make quick, snap decisions and argues that sometimes these "thin-sliced," momentary decisions can be quite accurate.[82] Of course, sometimes snap judgments can be way off base. What do you think? Is it ever appropriate to hold stereotypical views of others and to make judgments about them without knowing all the facts? When do stereotypical evaluations hinder communication? When is it preferable to avoid stereotypical decisions?

and seek to avoid personal harm. It's true that each culture and each person decides what is pleasurable or painful; nonetheless, argue Samovar and Porter, all people operate within this pleasure–pain continuum.

Another advocate for common human values was Oxford and Cambridge professor and widely read author C. S. Lewis. In his book *The Abolition of Man,* Lewis argued for the existence of universal, natural laws, which he called the Tao, that serve as benchmarks for all human values.[81] Lewis identified such common values as do not murder; be honest; hold parents, elders, and ancestors with special honor; be compassionate to those who are less fortunate; keep your promises; and honor the basic human rights of others.

What are the practical implications of trying to identify common human values or characteristics? If you find yourself disagreeing with another person about a particular issue, identifying a larger common value such as the value of peace and prosperity or the importance of family can help you find common ground so that the other person will at least listen to your ideas. It's useful, we believe, not just to categorize our differences but also to explore how human beings are similar to one another. Discovering how we are alike can provide a starting point for human understanding. Yes, we are all different; but we share things in common as well. Communication effectiveness is diminished when we assume that we're all different from one another in every aspect, just as communication is hindered if we assume that we're all alike. We're more complicated than that.

## Stereotyping and Prejudice

Closely related to ethnocentrism and feelings of cultural and gender superiority is the barrier of making a rigid judgment against a class or type of people.

All Russians like vodka.
All men like to watch wrestling.
All Asians are good at math.
All women like to go shopping.

# RECAP

## BARRIERS TO BRIDGING DIFFERENCES AND ADAPTING TO OTHERS

| | |
|---|---|
| Assuming Superiority | Becoming ethnocentric—assuming that one's own culture and cultural traditions are superior to those of others |
| Assuming Similarity | Assuming that other people respond to situations as we respond; failing to acknowledge and consider differences in culture and background |
| Assuming Differences | Assuming that other people are always different from ourselves; failing to explore common values and experiences that can serve as bridges to better understanding |
| Stereotyping and Prejudice | Rigidly categorizing others and prejudging others based on limited information |

These statements are stereotypes. They are all inaccurate. To **stereotype** someone is to place him or her in an inflexible, all-encompassing category. The term *stereotype* started out as a printing term to describe a process in which the typesetter uses the same type to print text again and again. When we stereotype, we "print" the same judgment over and over again, failing to consider the uniqueness of individuals, groups, or events. Such a "hardening of the categories" becomes a barrier to effective communication and inhibits our ability to adapt to others.

A related barrier, **prejudice,** is a judgment based on the assumption that we already know all the information we need to know about a person. To prejudge someone as inept, inferior, or incompetent based on that person's ethnicity, race, sexual orientation, gender, or some other factor is a corrosive practice that can raise significant barriers to effective communication. Some prejudices are widespread. Although there are more women than men in the world, one study found that even when a man and a woman held the same type of job, the man's job was considered more prestigious than the woman's.[83] Even though it is illegal in the United States to discriminate because of a person's gender, race, or age in offering employment or promotions, women and members of minority groups may still be discriminated against. In the workplace, stereotyping and prejudice are still formidable barriers to communicating effectively with others.

Mark Twain once said, "It is discouraging to try and penetrate a mind such as yours. You ought to get out and dance on it. That would take some of the rigidity out of it." Learning how to break rigid stereotypes and overcome prejudice is an important part of the process of learning how to adapt to others.

**stereotype**
To place a person or group of persons into an inflexible, all-encompassing category.

**prejudice**
A judgment of someone based on an assumption that you already know relevant facts or background information about the person.

# Adapting to Others Who Are Different from You

It is not enough simply to identify some of the common barriers that highlight our differences. Although becoming "consciously competent" about what may keep us from adapting and connecting with others is important, there are also some strategies that can help in our quest to adapt to others. Eleanor Roosevelt once said, "We have to face the fact that either we, all of us, are going to die together or we are going to live together, and if we are to live together we have to talk."[84] In essence, she was saying that we need effective communication skills to overcome our differences. It is not enough just to point to the barriers we have identified and say, "Don't do that." Identifying the causes of misunderstanding is a good first step, but most people need more concrete advice with specific strategies to help them overcome these barriers.[85]

# Aim for Intercultural Communication Competence

To have **intercultural communication competence** is to be able to adapt your behavior toward another person in ways that are appropriate to the other person's culture. As we've stressed, intercultural competence involves more than merely being aware of what is appropriate or being sensitive to cultural differences.[86] The interculturally competent person *behaves* appropriately toward others. One team of intercultural communication researchers has developed a framework for describing the stages of interpersonal communication competence. Prior to behaving appropriately toward others, an individual needs to have knowledge about other cultures and the motivation to adapt or modify his or her behavior[87]; this framework has six stages, progressing from least to most competent behavior.[88]

| | |
|---|---|
| **Stage One: Denial** | In this stage, a person believes that there is only one real, authentic culture—his or her own culture. The interculturally incompetent person, characterized by extreme ethnocentrism, denies that there are other ways of doing things or other ways of behaving. The individual is oblivious that other people have a different cultural approach to the world. |
| **Stage Two: Defense** | In this stage, a person acknowledges the presence of other cultures, but still believes that his or her culture has the best way of doing things. The person believes that his or her own view of the world is best and other culturally based views are wrong. So, the person defends his or her own culture as the best culture. |
| **Stage Three: Minimization** | In this stage, a person recognizes that there are other cultural perspectives, but suggests that there are no real differences in the way people behave and interact. He or she simply doesn't see the nuances or the major differences reflected in culture. Thus, cultural differences are minimized. |
| **Stage Four: Acceptance** | In this stage, a person begins to realize that there are other culturally based ways of behaving. The person's ethnocentrism (perception of cultural superiority) is diminished, and he or she recognizes and accepts cultural differences. |
| **Stage Five: Adaptation** | In this stage, intercultural competence emerges in full blossom. A person consciously seeks to appropriately adapt his or her behavior in response to cultural differences. |
| **Stage Six: Integration** | At this highest stage of intercultural competence, a person moves freely in and out of his or her own cultural mind-set while adapting to others. The person skillfully modifies his or her behavior to appropriately adapt to other cultures because the person's own cultural identity is minimized; the focus is on others. |

The first three stages of this six-stage framework reflect an **ethnocentric cultural perspective**, in which a person assumes that her or his own culture is superior to all

**intercultural communication competence**
The ability to adapt one's behavior toward another person in ways that are appropriate to the other person's culture.

**ethnocentric cultural perspective**
The view that one's own culture is superior to all other cultures.

other cultures. The last three stages of cultural competence reflect a more **ethnorelative cultural perspective**. This perspective requires an appreciation for and sensitivity to cultural differences; one's own cultural perspective is not viewed as always superior to other cultural perspectives.[89]

To become competent at any task, you need three things: knowledge, motivation, and skill. The remaining portion of this chapter presents the following specific strategies to help you develop your intercultural communication competence:[90]

To increase your knowledge about others,

- Seek information about a culture.
- Ask questions and listen to the responses.

To motivate yourself to adapt when communicating with others who are different from you,

- Be patient.
- Strive to tolerate ambiguity and uncertainty.
- Become mindful of differences.

To develop your communication skill set,

- Become other oriented.
- Learn appropriate ways to adapt your communication.

# **RE**CAP

## A MODEL OF THE STAGES OF INTERCULTURAL COMPETENCE

| **Stage One: Denial** | **Stage Two: Defense** | **Stage Three: Minimization** |
|---|---|---|
| A person denies that there are other cultural approaches to behavior beyond that of his or her own culture. | A person believes that his or her own culture is best. | A person minimizes cultural differences between himself or herself and others. |

| **Stage Four: Acceptance** | **Stage Five: Adaptation** | **Stage Six: Integration** |
|---|---|---|
| A person begins to realize that there are other culturally based ways of behaving. | A person consciously seeks to appropriately adapt his or her behavior in response to cultural differences. | A person is integrated into several cultures and minimizes his or her own cultural identity. |

**ethnorelative cultural perspective**
An appreciation for and sensitivity to cultural differences.

## Seek Information

Philosopher André Gide said, "Understanding is the beginning of approving." Prejudice often is the result of ignorance. Learning about another person's values, beliefs, and culture can help you understand his or her messages and their meaning. Researchers have found, not surprisingly, that if you have increased contact and experience interacting with someone from another culture then you will be more sensitive, mindful, and other oriented when communicating with that person.[91] The more you know about someone and can comfortably anticipate how he or she will respond, the more interculturally competent you are likely to be. As you speak to a person from another culture, think of yourself as a detective, watching for implied, often unspoken messages that provide information about the values, norms, roles, and rules of that person's culture.

You can also prepare yourself by studying other cultures. If you are going to another country, start by reading a travel guide or another general overview of the culture. You may then want to learn more detailed information by studying the history, art, or geography of the culture. The Internet offers a wealth of information about the cultures and traditions of others. In addition, talk to people from other cultures. If you are trying to communicate with someone closer to home who is from a different background, you can learn about the music, food, and other aspects of the culture. Given the inextricable link between language and culture, the more skilled you become at speaking another language, the better you will understand the traditions and customs of the culture where it is spoken.[92]

## Ask Questions and Listen

When you talk with people who are different from you, you may feel some discomfort and uncertainty. This is normal. We are more comfortable talking with people we know and who are like us. Communication, through the give-and-take process of listening, talking, and asking questions, helps reduce the uncertainty present in any relationship. When you meet people for the first time, you are typically not certain about their likes and dislikes, including whether they like or dislike you. When you communicate with a person from another culture or co-culture, the uncertainty level escalates. As you begin to talk, you exchange information that helps you develop greater understanding. If you continue to ask questions, eventually you will feel less anxiety and uncertainty. You will be more able to predict how the person will behave. When you meet a person who is different from you, ask thoughtful questions, and then pause to listen. This is a simple technique for gathering information and also for confirming the accuracy of your expectations and assumptions.

Just asking questions and sharing information about yourself is not sufficient to remove communication barriers and bridge differences in culture and background, but it is a good beginning. The skills of stopping (focusing on the message of the other person), looking (observing nonverbal cues), and listening (noting both details and major ideas) presented in the last chapter will serve you well in enhancing communication with people from cultural traditions different from your own.

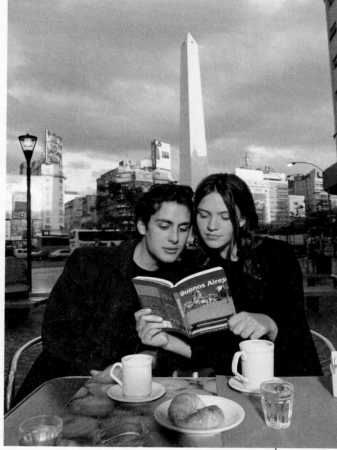

## Tolerate Ambiguity

Many people become uncomfortable when faced with uncertainty and ambiguity—especially if they are from a low-context culture such as those in North America. As discussed earlier in the chapter, people from low-context cultures prefer a more direct approach to getting information. North Americans, for example, often say things like "Tell it to me straight," "Don't beat around the bush," or "Just tell me what you want."

Communicating with someone from a culture that does not value such directness produces uncertainty. It may take time and several exchanges to clarify a message. If you are from a cultural tradition that values certainty and you are uncomfortable with uncertainty, you may have to acknowledge the cultural difference. Be patient and work at tolerating more ambiguity. Don't be in a hurry to have all the details nailed down. Remind yourself that the other person does not have the same attitudes about knowing the future or appreciating details.

A good way to understand people from other cultures is to learn all you can about their culture. If you were planning a visit to another country, how would you find out about its culture and people?

Creatas/Thinkstock

## Develop Mindfulness

To be **mindful** is to be aware of how you communicate with others. A mindful communicator puts into practice the first communication principle presented in this book: *Be aware of your communication with yourself and others.* To be a mindful communicator, you should constantly remind yourself that other people are not like you. Also, you should be aware that other people do not use different communication strategies to offend or to be rude; they just have different culturally based strategies of interacting with others. Intercultural communication scholar William Gudykunst and Young Kim suggest that being mindful is one of the best ways to approach any new cultural encounter.[93] Mindfulness is a conscious state of mind, a realization of what is happening to you at a given moment. If you are not mindful, you are oblivious to the world around you. You are on mental cruise control.[94]

**mindful**
Aware of what you are doing and how you are communicating with others.

How can you cultivate the skill of being mindful? You can become more mindful through **self-talk,** something discussed earlier in the book. Self-talk consists of messages you tell yourself to help you manage your discomfort, emotions, or negative thoughts about situations. For example, acknowledging cultural differences through self-talk, rather than emotionally and mindlessly becoming offended, can help you maintain your composure and communicate in a manner appropriate to the circumstances.

## Become Other Oriented

**Other-oriented communication** is communication in which we take into account the needs, motives, desires, and goals of our communication partners while still maintaining our own integrity. In the choices we make in forming messages and selecting the time and place to deliver them, we should consider the thoughts and feelings of others.

Scholars of evolution might argue that our tendency to look out for number one is what ensures the continuation of the human race. But if we focus exclusively on ourselves, it is very unlikely that we will be effective communicators. As we noted earlier, assuming superiority is a major barrier to communicating with others. Most of us are **egocentric**—focused on ourselves.[95] Our first inclination is to focus on meeting our own needs before addressing the needs of others.[96]

In this chapter, we have emphasized the principle of adapting to others. If we fail to adapt our message to listeners, especially listeners who are different from us (and isn't everyone different from you?), it is less likely that we will achieve our communication goal. As noted earlier, adapting messages to others doesn't mean that we tell others only what they want to hear. That would be unethical, manipulative, and ineffective. Nor does being considerate of others mean we abandon all concern for our own interests.

Becoming other oriented is not a single skill but a family of skills anchored in a willingness to try to understand others' thoughts and feelings. Research in emotional intelligence documents that focusing on the needs and interests of others is essential to adapting communication messages to others.[97]

Research also suggests that the level of empathy and social support we prefer is culturally determined. Research has found, for example, that people from western European countries respond more positively to emotional support than do people from eastern European nations and that people from Asian nations respond even less.[98] So, when providing empathic social support it's important to consider not our own need for emotional support, but the preferences of others.

How do you become other oriented? We suggest a two-stage process, using skills discussed previously. The first stage, which we previewed in Chapter 5, is called social decentering—consciously *thinking* about another's thoughts and feelings. The second stage is developing empathy, a set of skills we also discussed in the last chapter. To empathize is to respond *emotionally* to another's feelings and actions. We'll discuss each of these two stages in more detail.

**Social Decentering**   **Social decentering** is a *cognitive process* through which we take into consideration another person's thoughts, values, background, and perspectives. It is seeing the world from the other person's point of view. To socially decenter is not to be a mind reader but to use past experiences and the ability to interpret the clues of others to understand what others may be thinking or how they may be perceiving issues or situations. According to Mark Redmond, a scholar who has extensively studied the process of social decentering, there are three ways to socially decenter.[99]

1. *Consider how you have responded in the past.* Develop an understanding of the other person based on how you have responded when something similar has happened to you.[100] For example, when someone you know says that he or she feels frazzled because he or she was late for a major meeting, you can think about what would be going through your mind if the same thing happened to you.

**self-talk**
Inner speech; communication with the self; the process of mentally verbalizing messages that help a person become more aware or mindful of how he or she is processing information and reacting to life situations.

**other-oriented communication**
Communication in which we focus on the needs and concerns of others while maintaining our personal integrity; achieved through the processes of socially decentering and being empathic.

**egocentric**
Focused on oneself and one's importance.

**social decentering**
A cognitive process through which we take into account another person's thoughts, values, background, and perspectives.

2. *Consider how the other person has responded in the past.* Base your understanding of what another person might be thinking on your knowledge of how that person has responded in similar situations. In communicating with someone who is different from you, the more direct experience you have interacting with that person, the better able you usually are to make predictions about how that person will react and respond. For example, suppose that you have never known a particular friend to be late for a meeting; you know that this friend is generally punctual. You can therefore guess that your friend would be quite frustrated by being late for a meeting.

3. *Consider how most people respond to similar situations.* If your roommate is from France, you probably have some general sense of the cultural differences between you two. You may harbor some general theories or assumptions about other French people. The trick, however, is to avoid rigid stereotypes or prejudices that confine or limit your perceptions. The more you can learn about others' cultural or gender perspectives, the more accurate you can become in socially decentering. It is important, however, not to develop inaccurate, inflexible stereotypes and labels for others or to base your perceptions of others only on generalizations.

**Develop Empathy** Socially decentering involves attempting to understand what another person may be thinking. Developing **empathy,** a second strategy for becoming other oriented, is feeling the *emotional* reaction that the other person may be experiencing. When we feel empathy, we feel what another person feels.

Empathy is different from sympathy. When you offer **sympathy,** you tell others that you are sorry that they feel what they are feeling. When you sympathize, you acknowledge someone's feelings. When you empathize, however, you experience an emotional reaction that is similar to the other person's; as much as possible, you strive to feel what he or she feels.

As discussed in the last chapter, you develop the ability to empathize by being sensitive to your own feelings, assessing how you feel during certain situations, and then projecting those feelings onto others.[101]

To develop empathy, we suggested the following steps:

1. *Stop* focusing on only your own messages and thoughts, and focus instead on the messages of others.
2. *Look* for information about the emotional meanings of messages by focusing on nonverbal cues.
3. *Listen* by concentrating on what someone is telling you.
4. *Imagine* how you would feel if you were in your communication partner's position.
5. *Ask* appropriate questions, if you need to, to gain additional information.
6. *Paraphrase* your partner's message content and feelings, and monitor his or her reactions to what you communicate.

The late author and theologian Henri J. M. Nouwen suggested that empathy lies at the heart of enhancing the quality of our relationships with others. As Nouwen phrased it, to bridge our differences we need to "cross the road for one another":

We become neighbors when we are willing to cross the road for one another. There is so much separation and segregation: between black people and white people, between gay people and straight people, between young people and old people, between sick people

**empathy**
An emotional reaction that is similar to the reaction being experienced by another person.

**sympathy**
An acknowledgment that someone is feeling a certain emotion, often grief; compassion.

# **RE**CAP

## HOW TO BECOME OTHER ORIENTED

| | |
|---|---|
| Socially Decenter | View the world from another person's point of view. |
| | • Develop an understanding of someone, based on your own past experiences. |
| | • Consider what someone may be thinking, based on your previous association with the person. |
| | • Consider how most people respond to the situation at hand. |
| Develop Empathy | Consider what another person may be feeling. |
| | • Stop: Avoid focusing only on your own ideas or emotions. |
| | • Look: Determine the emotional meaning of messages by observing nonverbal messages. |
| | • Listen: Focus on what the other person says. |
| | • Imagine: Consider how you would feel in a similar situation. |
| | • Paraphrase: Summarize your understanding of the other person's thoughts and feelings. |

and healthy people, between prisoners and free people, between Jews and Gentiles, Muslims and Christians, Protestants and Catholics, Greek Catholics and Latin Catholics.

There is a lot of road crossing to do. We are all very busy in our own circles. We have our own people to go to and our own affairs to take care of. But if we could cross the road once in a while and pay attention to what is happening on the other side, we might indeed become neighbors.[102]

## Ethically Adapt to Others

Adapting to others gets to the bottom line of this chapter. After you have thought about how you may be different from others and even identified potential barriers to communication, you reach this question: So now what do you *do*? What you do is appropriately and ethically adapt.

To **adapt** is to adjust your behavior in response to the other person or people you are communicating with. You don't just keep communicating in the same way you always did. Make an effort to change how you communicate, to enhance the quality of communication.

Several research studies document the importance and value of skillfully being able to adapt your communication behavior.[103] Whether you are in an interpersonal interaction, a group, or a presentational speaking situation, adapting your message to others makes common sense. Even so, being sensitive to others and wisely adapting behaviors to others are often not so common.

Adapting to others does not mean that you only do or say what others expect or that your primary goal in life is always to please others. You do not have to abandon your own ethical principles and positions. In fact, it would be unethical to change your opinions and point of view just to avoid conflict and keep the peace—like a politician who only tells audiences what they want to hear. As President Harry Truman said, "I wonder how far Moses would have gone if he'd taken a poll in Egypt?"[104] When we encourage you to adapt your messages to others, we are not recommending that you become a spineless jellyfish and say things only to make others happy, but you can be sensitive and mindful of how your comments may be received by others.

You have a responsibility to *ethically* adapt your messages to others. To be ethical is to be truthful and honest while also observing the rights of others. Ethical communication is responsible, honest, and fair; enhances human dignity; and maintains listener options rather than coerces or forces someone to behave against his or her will. Ethically adapting

**adapt**
To adjust behavior in response to someone else.

Today's technology can help you adapt your communication. Your phone can translate your words or show a map when you don't speak the local language, for example. But, you must still be aware of what adaptations are appropriate and ethical.

Image Source/Getty Images

your communication to others does not mean that you manipulate a conversation so that only *you* can accomplish your goals. Ideally, both (or all) parties' goals are met. We do not advocate a form of adapted communication that is false or manipulative.

How can you appropriately and ethically adapt your message to others? We adapt messages to others for several reasons: to enhance their understanding of the message, to help us achieve the goal or intended effect of our communication, to ensure that we are ethical in our communication with others, and to establish and develop satisfying relationships. Your goal can help you choose from among the following adaptation strategies.

| TO . . . | YOU MAY NEED TO . . . |
|---|---|
| Enhance understanding | • Slow down or speed up your normal rate of speech. |
| | • Use more examples. |
| | • Speak in a very structured, organized way. |
| Meet your own communication goals | • Use evidence that is most valuable to your listener; statistics may prove your point to some listeners, but others may be more moved by a story that poignantly illustrates your point. |
| Ensure ethical communication | • Give your partner choices and identify options for them, rather than coercing them or making demands. |
| | • Tell the truth, without withholding information. |
| Establish and develop relationships | • Use communication that generates positive feelings. |
| | • Clearly demonstrate your regard for others. |

It is not possible to prescribe how to adapt to others in all situations, but you can draw on the other four Communication Principles for a Lifetime presented in this book:

1. *Be aware of your communication with yourself and others.* You will be more effective in adapting to others if you are aware of your own cultural traditions and gender-related behavior and how they are different from those of other people.
2. *Effectively use and interpret verbal messages.* To be able to interpret spoken information accurately is a linchpin of competence in adapting to others.
3. *Effectively use and interpret nonverbal messages.* Being able to "listen with your eyes" to unspoken messages will increase your ability to adapt and respond to others.
4. *Listen and respond to others thoughtfully.* The essential skills of listening and responding to others are key competencies in being able to adapt to others—to be oriented toward others.

Can the skills and principles we have suggested here make a difference in your ability to communicate with others? The answer is a resounding "yes."[105] Communication researcher Lori Carrell found that students who had been exposed to lessons in empathy as part of their study of interpersonal and intercultural communication improved their ability to empathize with others.[106] There is evidence that if you master these principles and skills, you will be rewarded with greater ability to communicate with others who are different from you—which means everyone.[107]

# RECAP

## ADAPTING TO OTHERS

**Develop Knowledge**

| | |
|---|---|
| Seek Information | Learn about a culture's worldview. |
| Ask Questions and Listen | Reduce uncertainty by asking for clarification and listening to the answer. |

**Develop Motivation**

| | |
|---|---|
| Tolerate Ambiguity | Take your time and expect some uncertainty. |
| Develop Mindfulness | Be consciously aware of cultural differences, rather than ignoring the differences. |

**Develop Skill**

| | |
|---|---|
| Become Other Oriented | Put yourself in the other person's mental and emotional frame of mind; socially decenter and develop empathy. |
| Adapt to Others | Listen and respond appropriately. |

# Study Guide:
# Review, Apply, and Assess
# Your Knowledge and Skill

## REVIEWING What You Know

### Understanding Diversity                                    p. 138

Human differences result in the potential for misunderstanding and miscommunication. Differences in gender, sexual orientation, age, and ethnicity contribute to the challenge of communicating with others. The relevant communication principle is Principle Five: *Effective communicators appropriately adapt their messages to others.*

**Terms to Know**

| | | | |
|---|---|---|---|
| Androgynous | p. 139 | Race | p. 143 |
| Homophobia | p. 141 | Discrimination | p. 144 |
| Ethnicity | p. 142 | | |

### Culture and Communication                                 p. 144

Culture is a system of knowledge that is shared by a group of people. Because of the powerful role culture plays in influencing our values, culture and communication are clearly linked. Cultural values reflect how individuals regard masculine perspectives (such as achieving results and being productive) and feminine perspectives (such as consideration for relationships), their tolerance of uncertainty or preference for certainty, their preference for centralized or decentralized power structures, the value they place on individual or collective accomplishment, and their long-term or short-term orientation to time.

**Terms to Know**

| | | | |
|---|---|---|---|
| Globalization | p. 145 | High-Context Culture | p. 147 |
| Culture | p. 146 | Low-Context Culture | p. 147 |
| Co-Culture | p. 146 | Cultural Values | p. 148 |
| Intercultural Communication | p. 147 | Collectivistic Culture | p. 149 |
| Culture Shock | p. 147 | Individualistic Culture | p. 149 |
| Worldview | p. 147 | Masculine Culture | p. 151 |
| Cultural Context | p. 147 | Feminine Culture | p. 151 |

### Barriers to Bridging Differences and Adapting to Others     p. 152

Several barriers inhibit effective communication.

- *Assuming superiority.* When one culture or gender assumes superiority or is ethnocentric, communication problems often occur.
- *Assuming similarity.* It is not productive when individuals or groups from different backgrounds or cultures assume that others behave with similar responses.
- *Assuming differences.* Don't automatically assume that other people are different from you.
- *Stereotyping and being prejudice.* We stereotype by placing a group or person into an inflexible, all-encompassing category. Stereotyping and prejudice can keep us

from acknowledging others as unique individuals and therefore can hamper effective, open, and honest communication.

### Terms to Know

| | | | |
|---|---|---|---|
| Ethnocentrism | p. 152 | Prejudice | p. 156 |
| Stereotype | p. 156 | | |

## Adapting to Others Who Are Different from You                                      p. 156

You develop intercultural communication competence when you are able to adapt your behavior toward another person in ways that are appropriate to the other person's culture. Specific strategies for becoming interculturally competent include the following:

- Seek information.
- Ask questions and listen.
- Tolerate ambiguity.
- Be mindful.
- Become other oriented by socially decentering and empathizing with others.
- Appropriately and ethically adapt your communication to others.

### Terms to Know

| | | | |
|---|---|---|---|
| Intercultural Communication Competence | p. 157 | Other-Oriented Communication | p. 160 |
| Ethnocentric Cultural Perspective | p. 157 | Egocentric | p. 160 |
| Ethnorelative Cultural Perspective | p. 158 | Social Decentering | p. 160 |
| Mindful | p. 159 | Empathy | p. 161 |
| Self-Talk | p. 160 | Sympathy | p. 161 |
| | | Adapt | p. 162 |

### Principle Five:
### Appropriately adapt messages to others.

Appropriately adapt messages based on gender differences in communication by doing the following: (1) seek to understand differences between genders as well as acknowledge similarities; (2) consider your own preferences, needs, and communication goals; (3) avoid assuming that differences you observe are solely the result of gender; and (4) consider both your needs and goals and those of the other person.

- Appropriately adapt your messages, paying particular attention to your verbal messages, to reflect differences in sexual orientation.
- Appropriately adapt your messages to respond to differences in age and ethnicity.
- Appropriately adapt messages to others based on whether an individual is from a high-context culture (in which an emphasis is placed on nonverbal messages and the surroundings) or a low-context culture (in which an emphasis is placed on words and explicitly communicated messages).
- Appropriately adapt messages to others based on the cultural value of individualism versus collectivism, preference for certainty

## APPLYING
## Principles
## for a
## Lifetime

versus tolerance of uncertainty, tendency to emphasize masculine versus feminine values, preference for centralized or decentralized power, and a long-term or short-term orientation to time.

- Avoid being ethnocentric—always assuming that your cultural traditions and approaches are superior to other cultural traditions.
- Acknowledge differences. Don't assume that everyone does things the same way you do or holds the same attitudes, beliefs, or values that you hold.
- Seek to explore and establish common ground with others. Don't assume that because someone is from another culture or geographic area, you don't have anything in common with the person.
- Avoid making rigid, inflexible stereotypes and prejudgments of others based on limited information.
- Seek to bridge differences between yourself and others who speak a different language or have different interpretations for nonverbal expressions; learn the language of others.
- Bridge cultural differences by learning as much as you can about another culture.
- Listen and ask questions to enhance your understanding of others.
- Be patient and tolerate some ambiguity and uncertainty when you communicate with people who are different from you.
- Become mindful, or aware that differences will exist, to help yourself better tolerate differences.
- Develop your skills at being other oriented. Focus on the needs and concerns of others while maintaining your personal integrity.
- Socially decenter. Think about how your communication partner would respond to information and situations; take into account people's thoughts, values, background, and perspectives.
- Empathize. Try to imagine how you would feel if you were in the other person's position.

# ASSESSING Your Skill

## Assessing Your Ethnocentrism

To assess your self-perceived level of ethnocentrism, complete the following Generalized Ethnocentrism (GENE) Scale.

### Directions

Read the following statements concerning your feelings about your culture and other cultures. In the space provided and using a 5-point scale, indicate the degree to which each statement applies to you by marking whether you (5) Strongly agree, (4) Agree, (3) Are undecided, (2) Disagree, or (1) Strongly disagree with the statement.

There are no correct or incorrect answers. Some of the statements may seem very similar. Remember that everyone experiences some degree of ethnocentrism. Be honest. Work quickly and record your first response.

1. _____ Most other cultures are backward compared with my culture.
2. _____ My culture should be the role model for other cultures.
3. _____ People from other cultures act strangely when they come to my culture.
4. _____ Lifestyles in other cultures are just as valid as those in my culture.
5. _____ Other cultures should try to be more like my culture.
6. _____ I'm not interested in the values and customs of other cultures.
7. _____ People in my culture could learn a lot from people in other cultures.
8. _____ Most people from other cultures just don't know what's good for them.

9. _____ I respect the values and customs of other cultures.

10. _____ Other cultures are smart to look up to our culture.

11. _____ Most people would be happier if they lived like people in my culture.

12. _____ I have many friends from different cultures.

13. _____ People in my culture have just about the best lifestyles anywhere.

14. _____ Lifestyles in other cultures are not as valid as those in my culture.

15. _____ I am very interested in the values and customs of other cultures.

16. _____ I apply my values when judging people who are different.

17. _____ I see people who are similar to me as virtuous/good.

18. _____ I do not cooperate with people who are different.

19. _____ Most people in my culture just don't know what is good for them.

20. _____ I do not trust people who are different.

21. _____ I dislike interacting with the values and customs of other cultures.

22. _____ I have little respect for the values and customs of other cultures.

## Scoring

To determine your ethnocentrism score, complete the following four steps:

1. Add your responses to items 4, 7, and 9.

2. Add your responses to items 1, 2, 5, 8, 10, 11, 13, 14, 18, 20, 21, and 22.

3. Subtract the sum from step 1 from 18 (i.e., 18 minus Step 1 sum).

4. Add results from step 2 and step 3. This is your generalized ethnocentrism score.

Higher scores indicate higher ethnocentrism. Scores higher than 55 points are considered to reflect high ethnocentrism.

Source: The GENE Scale, developed by J. Neuliep and. J. C. McCroskey. See. J. W. Neuliep, *Intercultural Communication: A Contextual Approach* 2e (Boston: Houghton Mifflin, 2003), 29–30.

## Assessing Your Culture Values and Adapting to Others

Based on the descriptions of cultural values described on pages 148–151, use the scales below to indicate your own assessment of your cultural values.

Individualistic ___ ___ ___ ___ ___ ___ ___ Collectivistic
Decentralized ___ ___ ___ ___ ___ ___ ___ Centralized
Uncertainty ___ ___ ___ ___ ___ ___ ___ Certainty
Masculine ___ ___ ___ ___ ___ ___ ___ Feminine
Long Term ___ ___ ___ ___ ___ ___ ___ Short Term

After assessing your cultural values, think of a friend, teacher, classmate, family member, or colleague who may have a different cultural value profile than yourself. Based on the discussion of ways to enhance intercultural competence presented on pages 157–163, what specific strategies could you use to adapt to someone whose cultural values are different from your own?

You need not travel to a foreign destination to experience another culture; opportunities to experience cultural differences may be as close as talking with your roommate, an instructor, or a good friend. To learn more about the role of culture in communication, check out one of the following websites, which offer more information about intercultural communication.

- **Awesome Library** Once you're at this site, type the words "intercultural communication" into the search box to access information and resources about intercultural communication skills and principles. <www.awesomelibrary.org>

- **Taking It Global** This website provides resources that focus on student travel, including cultural trips and ideas to facilitate better understanding between people from different cultures. <www.takingitglobal.org/home.html>

# WEB RESOURCES for More Review, Application, and Assessment

The best of life is conversation, and the greatest success is confidence, or perfect understanding between sincere people.

**RALPH WALDO EMERSON**

# Chapter OUTLINE

- What Is Interpersonal Communication?
- Initiating Relationships
- Maintaining Relationships
- Study Guide: Review, Apply, and Assess Your Knowledge and Skill

# Chapter OBJECTIVES

After studying this chapter, you should be able to

1. Define interpersonal communication and discuss its three unique attributes.

2. Define interpersonal attraction and provide examples of verbal and nonverbal ways we reveal our attraction to others.

3. Describe communication strategies to embrace and avoid when initiating relationships.

4. Discuss self-disclosure and explain its role in maintaining face-to-face and online relationships.

5. Discuss how emotional expression, as a form of self-disclosure, affects relationship maintenance.

Digital Vision/Thinkstock

# 7 | Understanding Interpersonal Communication

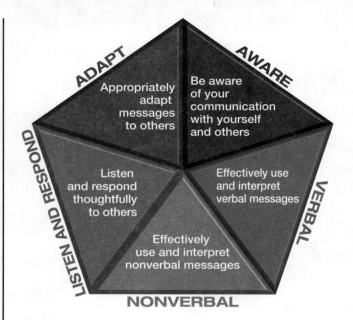

**Figure 7.1**
**Communication Principles for a Lifetime**

"Hi. I'm ____. Nice to meet you." This simple statement can strike fear in the heart of even the most outgoing individual. Yet we know that meeting and getting to know people, as well as becoming known, are some of the most rewarding experiences in this life. If we cannot break out of our comfort zones to communicate with others, we won't survive.

Interpersonal communication is the form of communication we experience most often in our lives, and it involves all five of our Communication Principles for a Lifetime (see Figure 7.1). *In the remaining chapters of the book, you will see a small version of the communication principles model in the margin to highlight our reference to one or more of the communication principles that we discuss.*

Effective interpersonal communication begins with an *awareness* of oneself. As you interact with people in your life, you make mental notes of what works well and not so well. You learn from these experiences and develop a personal style of communication. We continue this process by reassessing and reshaping our communication styles throughout our lives, with the goal of becoming better communicators. The second and third principles involve the *effective use of verbal and nonverbal messages*. We experiment with verbal and nonverbal communication as we interact with people, form relationships, develop those relationships, and, in some cases, let go of those relationships. A major element that enhances relationships is the ability to *listen and respond thoughtfully* to others, our Principle Four. Finally, few interpersonal relationships last without *adaptation*. We live in an extremely diverse world. It's imperative to learn to adapt our communication to others—to their cultural backgrounds and values, personalities, communication styles, needs, and goals—so that we form satisfying relationships that help us enjoy our lives to the fullest.

# What Is Interpersonal Communication?

**interpersonal communication**
Communication that occurs between two people who simultaneously attempt to mutually influence each other, usually for the purpose of managing relationships.

**mediated communication**
Communication that is carried out using some channel other than those used in face-to-face encounters.

**mediated interpersonal communication**
Communication that occurs when two people attempt to mutually influence each other through the use of a mediated channel, usually for the purpose of managing relationships.

**Interpersonal communication** is a special form of human communication that occurs when two people interact simultaneously and attempt to mutually influence each other, usually for the purpose of managing relationships. Traditionally, interpersonal communication research has focused primarily on the face-to-face (FtF) encounter, as researchers have attempted to better understand how people use conversation and nonverbal cues to initiate and maintain relationships. However, given greater accessibility, affordability, and the ease of using technology, it's important to also study how interpersonal communication occurs through mediated channels, such as cell phones and computers.[1]

In Chapter 1, we defined **mediated communication** as communication that is carried out using some channel other than those used in face-to-face encounters. It then follows that **mediated interpersonal communication** is communication that occurs when two people attempt to mutually influence each other through the use of a mediated channel, usually for the purpose of managing relationships. As we proceed through various topics related to interpersonal communication, we will explore the similarities and differences between mediated interpersonal communication and FtF interpersonal communication.

Let's begin by considering three attributes that help us better understand the nature of interpersonal communication.

Attraction is fascinating to observe, as well as to feel for another person. How do you typically communicate the attraction you feel for someone? Do your nonverbal cues reveal your attraction, or do you use language to convey your feelings?

Anton Gvozdikov/Shutterstock.com

- *Interpersonal communication involves quality.* If you're having dinner with a friend, let's hope your communication with your friend is different from your communication with your waiter. The *quality* of the communication makes the difference. Interpersonal communication occurs not just when we interact with someone, but when we treat the other as a unique human being. Conversely, **impersonal communication** occurs when we treat people as objects or respond to their roles rather than to who they are as unique people.[2] In terms of mediated interpersonal communication, e-mailing or texting a friend is interpersonal communication; responding to a mass text or e-mail message is impersonal communication because you likely don't know all the receivers of your message.

- *Interpersonal communication involves mutual influence.* We don't mean to imply that interpersonal communication exclusively involves persuasion—changing someone's mind or swaying someone's opinion. We simply mean that people who interact affect each other in some way. During that dinner with a friend, you might ask your friend where he or she grew up, and you assume that your friend hears you. If so, you've both been affected by the question—there's something you want to know and information your friend can provide. But what if your friend doesn't hear you because of a distracting noise in the restaurant? In this case, interpersonal communication hasn't really occurred because there is no mutual interaction; only you have been affected by your attempt at communication.

- *Interpersonal communication helps manage relationships.* **Relationships** are ongoing connections we make with others through interpersonal communication. For some people, the term *relationship* signals something serious and usually romantic, but we use the word in a much broader sense in this text. You probably have a wide variety of relationships, like with family members, coworkers, classmates, friends, and romantic interests. Some relationships are formed and maintained solely through mediated channels; others involve a combination of FtF and mediated interaction.

**impersonal communication**
Communication that treats people as objects or that responds only to their roles rather than to who they are as unique people.

**relationship**
An ongoing connection made with another person.

## RECAP

### WHAT IS INTERPERSONAL COMMUNICATION?

- High quality: It is superior to impersonal communication.
- Mutually influential: Both people in the relationship are affected.
- Relationship managing: We use it to help start, maintain, and sometimes end our interpersonal relationships.

# Initiating Relationships

Relationships form for different reasons. **Relationships of circumstance** form situationally—simply because our lives overlap with others' lives in some way or because a situation brings us into contact. Relationships with family members, teachers, classmates, and coworkers typically fall into this category. In contrast, relationships that we seek out and intentionally develop are termed **relationships of choice**. These relationships typically include those with friends, lovers, and spouses or relational partners. These categories of relationships are not mutually exclusive. Relationships of circumstance can change into relationships of choice; your sister or brother can turn out to be your best friend. Probably most of your online relationships are relationships of choice. An online relationship of circumstance might be formed between members of a group, such as students enrolled in a class or employees of a company with several corporate locations, who interact online to discuss course topics or current projects.

We communicate differently in these two types of relationships because the stakes are different. Generally, relationships of choice are more important to us and central to our sense of well-being than relationships of circumstance. Also, we tend to be more intimate in relationships of choice, choosing to reveal more sensitive things about ourselves only with our closest friends or lovers. With less intimate acquaintances or family members who have known us for some time, we might get away with some behaviors that would be intolerable or a source of conflict within a relationship of choice.

Some people make relationships look easy; they just seem to meet people and make positive impressions effortlessly. For others, meeting and getting to know people is a huge challenge. We'll let you in on a little secret: Initiating relationships really isn't all that easy for anyone. Let's explore the nature of attraction—what draws us into a conversation in the first place.

## Interpersonal Attraction: Why We Like Whom We Like

**relationship of circumstance**
A relationship that forms situationally, simply because one life overlaps with another in some way.

**relationship of choice**
A relationship that is sought out and intentionally developed.

**attraction**
A motivational state that causes someone to think, feel, and behave in a positive manner toward another person.

**interpersonal attraction**
The degree to which one desires to form or maintain an interpersonal relationship with another person.

**short-term initial attraction**
The degree of potential for developing an interpersonal relationship with someone.

**long-term maintenance attraction**
The level of liking or positive feeling that motivates one to maintain or escalate a relationship.

What does it mean to say that you are attracted to another person? Most of the time, we tend to think of physical or sexual attraction. But there are many forms of attraction besides physical and sexual, including intellectual, spiritual, and personality attraction. **Attraction**, in general, is a motivational state that causes someone to think, feel, and behave in a positive manner toward another person.[3] More specifically, **interpersonal attraction** is the degree to which you desire to form and possibly maintain an interpersonal relationship with another person.

Interpersonal attraction occurs in both early and later stages of relational development:

- **Short-term initial attraction** is the degree to which you sense a potential for developing an interpersonal relationship. For instance, you might find one of your classmates interesting and think about introducing yourself. Or you might interact with someone online and then decide that the person's comments attract you enough to set up a face-to-face encounter.
- **Long-term maintenance attraction** is the type that sustains relationships like best friendships, marriages, or committed partnerings. It refers to a level of liking or positive feeling that motivates you to maintain or escalate a relationship. Short-term attraction typically gives way to long-term attraction as a relationship progresses. Rarely do you maintain a long-term intimate relationship solely on the basis of what you initially found attractive.[4] You usually need something more as you develop an interpersonal attraction and deepen a relationship.

Several factors come into play when you decide to act on your attraction and establish a relationship.

# Communication&DIVERSITY

### Friendships: Thinking Outside the Race

How many friends do you have who are of a different racial or ethnic background than you? How many are a mixture of ethnic backgrounds? Whatever the numbers in your answers to these questions, they are probably quite a bit higher than those a college student like you would have given a few decades ago. We're not saying that previous generations of students were racists—political and social forces greater than the individual were at play, affecting the potential for interracial friendships to occur. Times certainly have changed.

Researchers offer helpful information about how interracial relationships develop and progress, as well as about special challenges the relational partners face.[5] Mark Orbe and Tina Harris are communication scholars and authors of the book *Interracial Communication*.[6] They write about the evolution of relationships—friendships as well as romantic relationships—between members of different races in the United States. Interracial friendships are on the rise, but they are complex because our society is still "racialized" (meaning that it still draws distinctions among the races), although to a lesser degree than ever before in our country's history.

Think about your own circle of friends. How many very close friends do you have who are of a different race than you? Now move out a bit in terms of closeness. How many casual friends, meaning people you're friendly with but don't spend much time with, are of a different race than you? When you strike up a friendship with someone, does race or ethnicity play a factor? You might not consider race a factor when deciding with whom to become friends, but it might be enlightening to look at your circle of friends to see how much ethnic diversity your group actually reflects.

**Similarity**   What about the idea that "opposites attract"? Opposites certainly do attract, and differences between people can be interesting. They can also form the basis for a good friendship or coworker relationship—after all, we learn a great deal from people who are unlike us. But we like to add another phrase to the "opposites attract" cliché: "Opposites attract, but dramatic opposites seldom last." People who are opposites or significantly different in dispositions and preferences may intrigue each other and teach each other something in the short run, but similarity appears to be a more important factor in highly committed, long-term relationships than in short-term, noncommittal relationships.[7]

In general, you are attracted to people with whom you have **similarity**—those whose personality, values, upbringing, experiences, attitudes, or interests are similar to yours.[8] You may also be attracted more to people who are similar to you in age, intelligence, and life goals. The Internet allows people with similar interests to find one another easily and form online relationships.[9] In the initial stages of an online or FtF relationship, we try to emphasize positive information about ourselves to create a positive and attractive image. We reveal those aspects of ourselves that we believe we have in common with the other person, and the other person does the same.[10]

**Physical and Sexual Attraction**   Volumes have been written about the role that physical and sexual attraction play in the formation of relationships.[11] While these forms of attraction are often lumped together or viewed as the same thing, they actually are different. In FtF situations, the degree to which we find another person's physical self appealing represents our **physical attraction** to that person, which is a powerful nonverbal cue. That appeal might be based on height, size, skin tone and texture, clothing, hairstyle, makeup, vocal qualities, gestures, and so forth. By this definition, even if you are heterosexual, you can still be attracted to a person of your own sex because you admire her or his physical attributes.

Is physical attraction a factor in establishing online relationships? Research reveals that many online communicators find the *lack* of emphasis on physical appearance and attractiveness in online relationships to be one of the most positive features of this approach to relationship development.[12] One set of researchers described the Internet as "a world where what you write, not how you look or sound, is who you are."[13]

**similarity**
The degree to which one's characteristics, values, attitudes, interests, or personality traits are like those of another person.

**physical attraction**
The degree to which one finds another person's physical self appealing.

**Sexual attraction** has been defined as "the desire to engage in sexual activity with someone," a desire that "typically is accompanied by feelings of sexual arousal in the presence of the person."[14] You may be physically attracted to someone but not sexually attracted, as we stated before. But can you be sexually attracted but not physically attracted? We're not sure about the answer to that one because it may be a uniquely individual judgment. You may find another person's online communication sexually arousing, even if you've never seen the person in the flesh. Suffice it to say that these two forms of attraction usually operate in tandem, even though they represent different kinds of appeal.

Our perceptions about others' physical attractiveness reduce relationship possibilities. In general, while we may be attracted to a range of persons, we tend to seek out individuals who represent the same level of physical attractiveness we do.[15] In research, this tendency is termed the **matching hypothesis**.[16] Perhaps you perceive yourself to be average looking, not model-beautiful but not unattractive either. You may be physically or sexually attracted to extremely good-looking people; but if you are average looking, you are more likely to seek someone who is also average looking to date, and even marry or become partners with.

**Proximity**   In a traditional sense, the principle of **proximity** in interpersonal relationships refers to the fact that we are more likely to be attracted to people who are nearer to us physically and geographically than to those who are farther away.[17] In your classes, you're more likely to form relationships with classmates sitting on either side of you than with someone seated at the opposite end of the room. Physical proximity increases communication opportunities, and opportunities to interact are likely to increase our attraction to those with whom we communicate.

Technology has turned the notion of proximity on its head, however, with virtual access to people around the globe in almost an instant. Those of you who are "digital natives" grew up in a world of computers where online information was always easily found at your fingertips. You have a different sense of boundaries, geographic limitations, and globalism than previous generations—those known as "digital immigrants," who discovered and adopted technology along the way.[18]

High-school friends who leave their hometowns to attend different colleges can easily stay current in one another's lives through e-mailing, text messaging, using web-cam technology such as FaceTime or Skype on their smart phones or computers, instant messaging, posting on Facebook, tweeting on Twitter, and so forth.[19] College

**sexual attraction**
The desire to have sexual contact with a certain person.

**matching hypothesis**
The theory that one tends to seek out individuals who represent the same level of physical attractiveness as oneself.

**proximity**
The likelihood of being attracted to people who are physically close rather than to those who are farther away.

Video chats, Facebook usage, texts, and other technological innovations have redefined the meaning of proximity in attraction. How do your face-to-face relationships compare to your mediated ones, in terms of proximity?
© i love images/Alamy

students are able to meet their future dorm roommates before moving in together, easing the anxiety of that first move-in day on campus.[20] People who have never (and may never) meet in the physical world can come to feel a sense of proximity and develop relationships with people in the virtual world. Some scholars contend that the instantaneous and pervasive nature of online communication bridges physical distance, creating a virtual closeness that FtF relationships may not achieve.[21] So, the effect of proximity on relationship development, or the very way we conceive of proximity, is changing as we speak.

**Complementarity**   While we tend to like people with whom we have much in common, most of us wouldn't find it very exciting to spend the rest of our lives with someone who had identical attitudes, needs, and interests. We may tend to be attracted to someone similar to us in important things like human values, but for other things we may be more interested in someone with whom we share **complementarity** of abilities and needs.[22] For example, if you are highly disorganized by nature (and that's fine by you), you might be attracted to someone who is very organized because you appreciate that person's sense of structure.

Social psychologist Will Schutz identified three interpersonal needs that motivate us to form and maintain relationships with others: inclusion, control, and affection.[23] **Inclusion** is the need to include others in our activities or to be included in theirs. **Control** is the need to make decisions and take responsibility or the level of willingness to accept others' decision making. **Affection** is the need to be loved and accepted by others or the willingness to give love and acceptance to others. Most people are attracted to those whose interpersonal needs complement their own.

# RECAP

## ELEMENTS OF INTERPERSONAL ATTRACTION

| | |
|---|---|
| Short-Term Initial Attraction | This form of attraction involves a judgment of potential for an interpersonal relationship to develop with someone. |
| Long-Term Maintenance Attraction | This form of attraction is deeper and more long lasting than short-term initial attraction and involves positive feelings that cause us to choose to maintain and escalate relationships. |
| Similarity | Attraction increases if our characteristics, values, attitudes, interests, and personality traits are similar to those of another person. |
| Physical Attraction | This form of attraction is based on another person's physical self. |
| Sexual Attraction | This form of attraction is based on the desire to have sexual contact with another person. |
| Proximity | We are more likely to be interpersonally attracted to people who are physically close to us. |
| Complementarity | We may be attracted to someone whose abilities, interests, and needs differ from but balance or round out our own. |

If you resent it when someone you're dating spends time away from you with his or her friends, you're likely to be less attracted to that person over time because you may have different, noncomplementary inclusion needs. If you have a high need to control and make decisions and a general disrespect for or mistrust of others' decision making, you will be more compatible with someone whose need for control is minimal—a person who wants others to make decisions for her or him.

In essence, we can view pairs of individuals as teams in which each person's needs complement those of the other person in some way. In reality, there are no perfect matches, only degrees of compatibility.

## Communicating Our Attraction

According to research, we can size up a potential romantic partner or good future friend within the first three minutes of meeting them.[24] That's impressive as well as daunting. What kind of impression do you make in the first three minutes of meeting someone? What kind of "vibe" do you get from someone in the first three minutes that lets you know whether you'd like to talk with them further or whether there's a chance of something more meaningful developing?

When we're attracted to people, we use both verbal and nonverbal strategies to communicate our liking. Verbally, we ask questions to show interest, listen responsively, probe for details when others share information, and refer to information

**complementarity**
The degree to which another person's different abilities, interests, and needs balance or round out one's own.

**inclusion**
The need to involve others in one's activities or to be involved in the activities of others.

**control**
The need to make decisions and take responsibility or the level of willingness to accept others' decision making.

**affection**
The need to be loved and accepted by others or the willingness to give love and acceptance to others.

shared in past interactions in an attempt to build a history with people. But we most often communicate our attraction nonverbally, through indirect cues referred to as **immediacy.** As described in Chapter 4, immediacy behaviors reduce the physical and psychological distance between people.[25] Research on speed dating shows that nonverbal immediacy is a primary factor in determining whether a future date is desired.[26] Some examples of nonverbal immediacy cues include the following:

- Sitting in closer proximity
- Increasing our eye contact
- Increasing our use of touch
- Leaning forward
- Keeping an open body orientation rather than a closed-off position
- Using more vocal variety or animation
- Smiling more often than we do normally
- Preening (adjusting clothing, playing with our hair) as a means of attracting attention.[27]

How do we convey attraction in an online or mediated context? It's not as if you could reach through your phone and hug someone. One study asked approximately 6,000 people how they flirt in person as well as online.[28] The majority of people in the study reported that flirting was accomplished online similarly to how it's done in person; people simply translate physical actions into text for mediated communication. For instance, body movements such as laughing translate into acronyms like LOL. Eye behaviors associated with flirting such as winking can be communicated through emoticons such as ;).

## Getting That First Conversation Going

In some ways, online interpersonal relationships have an advantage over FtF relationships in that they develop out of conversation, meaning that an online conversation is probably what launched the relationship in the first place. In an FtF situation, the various steps of noticing someone interesting, realizing that you're interested

**immediacy**
Nonverbal cues, such as eye contact, forward lean, touch, and open body orientation, that communicate feelings of liking, pleasure, and closeness.

(physically, sexually, or interpersonally), finding a way to meet the person (by introducing yourself or through a third-party introduction), and starting up the first conversation can all be nerve-racking.[29] But these steps don't happen the same way in online interactions. Initial online interactions are critical in that they make or break future exchanges. With repeated virtual contact, online topics of discussion often become very personal, and intimacy often develops at a more rapid pace than it typically does in FtF relationships. If rapport develops, it may lead to telephone conversations or FtF meetings.[30]

In FtF settings, once you realize you're attracted to someone (and that realization usually happens very quickly), what do you do next? Research indicates that people who meet and have that all-important first conversation feel enduring effects of the encounter even months later, no matter what direction the relationship took (if it took any direction at all).[31] We have some practical suggestions for how to approach those first conversations so that you feel confident and keep your self-esteem intact while communicating effectively to impress the other person positively.

**Reducing Uncertainty**   Even though most of us like surprises from time to time, human beings are much more comfortable with certainty than with uncertainty. We prefer the known to the unknown, the predictable to the chaotic. Both FtF and online relationships involve uncertainty. One communication research team developed **uncertainty-reduction theory**, an explanation of how we use information as we endeavor to reduce our uncertainty, especially as it relates to communicating with people we don't know (or know well). Communication researchers Charles Berger, Richard Calabrese, and James Bradac contend that this driving motivation among humans to reduce our uncertainty prompts us to communicate.[32]

We typically respond to uncertainty in three ways:

- **Passive strategy:** We seek information by observing people, scoping out situations, and so forth before more actively working to reduce uncertainty. Suppose you just started a new job, a transition that creates a level of uncertainty in most of us. One way to begin to reduce your uncertainty is to simply observe how your coworkers and supervisors interact.
- **Active strategy:** After making our passive observations, we might decide to check our perceptions of things with a third party. You might ask a coworker about something associated with your new job or colleagues, for example. Finding out others' perceptions increases your knowledge, reduces your uncertainty, and helps you decide how to behave.
- **Interactive strategy:** The final strategy is going "straight to the horse's mouth"— communicating directly with the person who has the most potential to reduce our uncertainty. At your new job, this person might be your boss or a coworker who's been on the job a while, or perhaps someone in personnel or human relations.

These strategies don't necessarily have to be used in order. You might bypass the active strategy and head to interactive, deeming it better to get the "straight scoop" from a direct source. We also don't always need to use all three strategies. In some cases, uncertainty can be reduced enough through passive and active strategies; there may be no cause for an interactive approach.[33]

Interactive strategies are frequently used in online relationships, because starting up an online conversation or exchanging e-mails with someone tends to evoke less uncertainty than FtF first conversations. Online exchanges usually happen in private, with less potential for embarrassment than in FtF situations, when such factors as physical appearance and nervousness are in play. But one element can inject uncertainty into the online situation: the potential for deception. Since you stare at a computer monitor rather than into someone's eyes when you "meet" online, you really don't know whom you're talking to. Research has shown people's tendencies to give false information or to omit pertinent facts in their online communication.[34] Subjects in studies reported lying about age, weight, details of physical appearance, marital status, and even their sex, meaning that some gender-bending experimentation certainly

**uncertainty-reduction theory**
A driving human motivation to increase predictability by reducing the unknown in one's circumstances.

**passive strategy**
A noncommunicative strategy for reducing uncertainty by observing others and situations.

**active strategy**
A communicative strategy for reducing uncertainty by getting information from a third party.

**interactive strategy**
A strategy of communicating directly with the source who has the greatest potential to reduce one's uncertainty.

occurs. The uncertainty caused by the relative ease of online deception makes some computer users gun-shy about getting involved with people through the Internet.

**What Do You Say First?**    In some contexts, the first words you exchange with someone may be fairly scripted or expected. For example, in a job interview, introductions and ritualistic greetings typically take up the first few minutes. (See Appendix A for helpful information on communicating in interviews.) But what about situations in which there are no prescribed, explicit rules or expectations for behavior? Our students tell us that the official "date" is a dying institution—they just don't date much anymore. More common than dating is "hanging out," in which two people meet somewhere or a group of people gather together, many of whom are "talking," "seeing each other," or have a special connection that goes beyond what they have with other people. An even newer form of pairs socializing has emerged on some college campuses: Ever heard of "frugaling"? Author Donna Freitas documented the practice, which is just short of dating but more romantic than being friends.[35] (Being "just short of dating" may explain the term because it's more frugal or thrifty not to date.) Freitas explains that frugaling involves hanging out in public with one other person *a lot*, but with no public declaration of connection or relational definition. There's no "determine-the-relationship" conversation, because that would be too intense for the casualness of this form of relationship. There are no PDAs (public displays of affection) or private intimacy either. Nevertheless, people know that a special connection exists.

This first-conversation business used to be easier in the past, but perhaps not particularly satisfying. Men were schooled at their fathers' knees on how to use opening or pickup lines to attract women; women were schooled by their mothers about how to respond (and ignore).[36] Although you may think such opening lines as "Come here often?" "Haven't I met you before?" and (the all-time favorite) "What's your sign?" are relics of the past, recent research has examined how well opening lines work to get a conversation going.[37] Researchers tested the effectiveness of three categories of opening lines said by men to women: (1) flippant and flirtatious, such as "You must be tired, because you've been running through my mind all day"; (2) direct and complimentary, such as "It took a lot of courage to approach you, so can I at least ask your name?"; and (3) innocuous, meaning that the line masked the man's interest, as in "What do you think of the band?" The women in the study liked the direct complimentary line the most, believing that it conveyed more trustworthiness and intelligence than other forms.

Mark Stivers

We don't recommend the "one-size-fits-all" approach to first conversations that is the stereotypical use of a pickup line. Instead, rely on our fifth Communication Principle for a Lifetime, which encourages communicators to appropriately adapt their messages to others. Each situation and the unique qualities of each person you meet should dictate how you communicate.

**The Art and Skill of Asking Great Questions**   When students ask us, as they frequently do, "What makes someone a good conversationalist?" a variety of things come to mind. All five of our Communication Principles for a Lifetime could be reflected in our answer, but one important element is the ability to ask a great question of another person. This skill doesn't just magically appear—it takes time, maturity, and experience with a variety of people and relationships to develop fully.[38]

What do we mean by "asking great questions"? We don't mean tossing rapid-fire, superficial questions at someone, as though you were in the first five minutes of a job interview or gathering data for the census. Asking a great question means, first, tailoring the question to the person as much as possible. Use what you've observed and learned from other sources to formulate your questions. Online, it's typical to ask basic information just to break the ice, but the use of too many "yes/no" questions or questions requiring one-word responses doesn't advance a conversation. Avoid questions that might be too personal or probing in the early stages of developing FtF and online relationships.

A second, very critical skill to develop is really listening to the person's answers to your questions. Then pose a follow-up question based on the person's response to your question. You can offer your opinion on something, but opinions work best when followed up with "Do you agree?" or "That's what I think, but what do you think?" Great conversationalists are great because they listen and then form responses that show they're listening—responses that are designed to draw other people out and let them shine.

**Avoiding Self-Absorption**   Too many people think the best way to be conversationally impressive is by talking glibly, smoothly, confidently, and virtually nonstop *about themselves.* In an online context, when one person's messages are consistently five times as long as the other's and the content rambles on and on about the person, it's a definite turnoff. **Conversational narcissism** or a **self-absorbed communicator style** may be an outgrowth of a personality trait—a belief in oneself as the center of the universe.[39] Other times, it is a *state*, not a *trait*, meaning a temporary style of interacting rather than a more pervasive characteristic of a person. We can all be self-absorbed from time to time, but if the self-absorbed communication continues, if it moves from a temporary state into a more permanent trait or style of a person, the likelihood that the person will be positively perceived seriously declines.

Some verbal indications of self-absorption include the number of times a person uses the pronoun *I* instead of *you* or *we.* Narcissistic communicators converse mostly about themselves and typically provide more detail in their narratives than necessary (because they enjoy the sound of their own voice).[40] They talk more in statements than questions and constantly try to top someone's story or to draw the topic of conversation toward themselves, as in "Oh, you think *you're* tired—let me tell you about the kind of day *I* had." No one's day is as bad, no one's opinion as valuable or information as correct as the self-absorbed communicator's. The person may feign empathy in a conversation: "Oh, I know exactly how you feel." This usually leads to "The same thing happened to me," followed by a long story that takes attention away from the original communicator. Another indication of self-absorption is talking ad nauseam on topics about which one has some particular knowledge or expertise but that bore the socks off listeners. Many times, these types of communicators are driven by insecurity and uncertainty, rather than a belief that they truly are the center of the universe.

In FtF encounters, nonverbally self-absorbed communicators use vocal cues (such as increasing volume) and dominant body postures to hold their turns at talk and

**conversational narcissism (self-absorbed communicator style)**
A dominating communication style in which one focuses attention on oneself.

stave off interruptions from others. They may even physically block another person from attempting to leave the conversation and are generally insensitive to others' nonverbal cues. Online, self-absorbed chatters attempt to dominate the contributions of other chatters, make their postings more frequent and lengthier, and control the topic of conversation. People with self-absorbed personalities soon find themselves with few FtF or online friends, because few of us can tolerate such an out-of-balance relationship.

In sum, the best conversationalists aren't great talkers—they're great listeners and responders (as articulated in Principle Four). In other words, it's not what *you* say, but how you respond to what *others* say that makes you a good conversationalist.

**The Art and Skill of Giving and Receiving Compliments**    Sometimes it seems as though people don't comment about one another unless it's to criticize. That's unfortunate, because positive reinforcement and support from others is central to our self-esteem. Are you a person who compliments others? If so, what do you tend to compliment people for—their appearance, hard work, scholarly achievement, athletic prowess? If you are a person who tends not to compliment others, why is that the case?

British linguistic scholar Janet Holmes calls compliments "social lubricants."[41] She explains that the most common purpose of a compliment is to make someone feel good by offering praise and encouragement, but an important by-product is a sense of increased goodwill and solidarity between the complimenter and the receiver. Research shows that compliments between romantic partners can enhance self-esteem and are viewed as a form of intimate talk, and that the sharing of positive feelings is linked to how satisfied partners are with the relationship.[42]

Giving compliments is a tricky business, because some attempts at flattery can be taken in ways other than you intend. For example, many female professionals tire of receiving workplace compliments on their appearance while their male coworkers are more often complimented on their work-related achievements. Some compliments are too personal and can make people feel uncomfortable. A pattern of personal compliments may be grounds for a claim of sexual harassment. But these are extreme examples. We encourage you to think about complimenting as a communication skill and a strategy particularly useful in first conversations, whether online or face to face. You don't want to come across as a phony or a predator, but a well-thought-out compliment can open the door to further conversation.

It's also important to know how to receive a compliment graciously—not by agreeing with the complimenter (and sounding cocky) or by disagreeing or attempting to talk the person out of his or her compliment, as in "This old outfit? I've had it for years—I just threw it on today." The best response is a simple "thank you" that acknowledges that something nice was said about you.[43]

# Maintaining Relationships

Not only do relationships bring us life's greatest joy, but they also dramatically improve our physical health. Research examining data from more than 300,000 people found that a lack of strong relationships increased one's risk of premature death by 50 percent; this statistic represents a health risk comparable to smoking up to fifteen cigarettes a day, and a greater risk than obesity or physical inactivity.[44]

Many forms of interpersonal communication are necessary to maintain successful, satisfying relationships. Relationship experts John Harvey and Ann Weber describe relationship maintenance as "minding the close relationship," which they define as "thought and behavior patterns that interact to create stability and feelings of closeness in a relationship."[45] In this section, we explore forms of communication most central to relationship maintenance, which also represent some of the most heavily researched topics in the communication discipline.

# Self-Disclosure: Revealing Yourself to Others

Imagine you're hanging out or on a first date and things are going fairly well. But as you're talking, your date starts describing sexual details about his or her last date or romantic partner—information that is just too intimate and private for a first date or, by some people's standards, for *any* date. How would you react?

**Self-disclosure**, originally studied by psychologist Sidney Jourard, occurs when we voluntarily provide information to others that they would not learn unless we told them.[46] Communication scholar David Johnson provides eight reasons why people self-disclose:

- We begin and deepen a relationship by sharing reactions, feelings, personal information, and confidences.
- Self-disclosure improves the quality of relationships.
- Self-disclosure allows us to validate our perceptions of reality.
- Self-disclosure clarifies our understanding of ourselves.
- The expression of feelings and reactions is a freeing experience.
- We may disclose or withhold information about ourselves as a means of social control.
- Self-disclosing is an important part of managing stress and adversity.
- Self-disclosure fulfills a human need to be known intimately and accepted.[47]

## Properties of Self-Disclosure

Because self-disclosure is a building block of intimacy and greater intimacy generally leads to enhanced relationships, we need to understand this unique form of interpersonal communication. Three properties characterize self-disclosure.

- *Reciprocity.* When we share information about ourselves with others, we expect them to share information similar in risk or depth about themselves, or to provide **reciprocity**. What if you share one of your insecurities with someone but the person doesn't reciprocate? You might feel embarrassed or resentful. Sharing information about yourself gives others a certain amount of power over you. If the other person reciprocates by disclosing similar information, it helps maintain a balance of power. Over time, unreciprocated self-disclosure may cause someone to end a relationship.

- *Appropriateness.* Some information is inappropriate to disclose at an early stage of relationship development but is appropriate to disclose at a later stage, but people vary a good deal on this judgment. It's sometimes hard to gauge what's appropriate to talk about and what's not while you're in the process of getting to know someone.[48] Unwanted disclosures may emerge because one person misjudges the nature of the relationship, assuming or wanting a greater level of intimacy than his or her partner assumes or wants. Be sensitive when you choose what and when to disclose; consider how the recipient of your disclosure will react. Conversely, when someone reveals information to you, try to determine whether it's highly personal to her or him and respond appropriately.

- *Risk.* Self-disclosure can be extremely rewarding because of its potential to deepen a relationship and enhance trust. But it's not without its risks because, in our increasingly open culture, protecting our privacy is a challenge.[49] For example, even in a society that is becoming more accepting of homosexuality, bisexuality, and transgenderism, "coming out of the closet" as a form of self-disclosure is still a risky prospect. Relationships with family members and friends can be hurt at the revelation, and the potential for rejection of and hostility toward the discloser is very real.[50] When we disclose, we make ourselves vulnerable and forfeit control of information. We might offend, hurt, or insult another person by our disclosure, thus damaging the relationship. In relationships, we typically seek a balance between the potential risks and rewards of disclosing personal information.

**self-disclosure**
Voluntarily providing information to others that they would not learn if one did not tell them.

**reciprocity**
Sharing information about oneself with another person, with the expectation that the other person will share information that is similar in risk or depth.

# Communication & TECHNOLOGY

## How Much of ME Do THEY Know? Online Self-Disclosure

When you create a profile for an online dating service or a social networking site such as Facebook, you typically have a choice about what information you'll provide and what you'll keep private. You likely don't include your most personal data, because even though you can exert some control over who reads or sees your information, it's still *out there* in a public domain. (We've all no doubt heard horror stories of people who thought their information was sent to only one intended receiver, when in fact it went to a much wider circle.) But many people include things like personality traits, likes and dislikes, hobbies and interests, and opinions and attitudes on their profiles; people have differing opinions about including relationship status, with some choosing to keep that detail private. Once you are "friended" on Facebook or contacted by a potential on-line date, you enter a social network where you can read people's postings, view their photos, follow links to other information, and generally get to know the people better. Revelations of this kind are a form of self-disclosure.[51]

Reciprocity is a factor in the online arena, but it operates a bit differently than in FtF contexts. Author Katrina Shonbeck explains, "If you do not perceive that the other person is reciprocating—replying in an appropriate length of time, staying on topic, responding to your away message, 'poking' you on Facebook, sending you e-cards, e-vites, and so on—chances are you will discontinue or greatly reduce the amount of time devoted to that person."[52]

Some "upsides" or benefits to online disclosure also exist:

- Reading people's profiles or postings or viewing their photos reduces uncertainty about them because it provides more information. If you do meet face to face, text, or talk on the phone, you may have a "leg up" because of your online exposure to them.
- Feelings of isolation may decrease because of online connections with people—a wider variety of people than may be possible to meet face to face.
- For some people, self-disclosure in person is difficult because they're too shy to share information about themselves face to face; online disclosure serves as a relatively safe way to practice self-disclosure and develop disclosure abilities so they can more readily share information in FtF situations.[53]
- The general benefits of mediated interpersonal communication apply to online self-disclosure: It's relatively inexpensive to accomplish; easily accessible for most people; and spans across time, geography, and culture to reach receivers we're unable or unlikely to meet face to face.

Serious downsides also exist.

- Inappropriate information may be shared, on purpose or inadvertently, or information can be used in ways not foreseen by the originator.

Stephanie Piro

"I'm a private person. I never talk about you to anyone we know. I do, however, discuss certain aspects of our relationship online with total strangers!"

- Privacy and boundary issues emerge, as in those instances when people gain access to your online profile, postings, or photos when you didn't mean for them to or didn't want them to. (Photos of people in full "party hearty" mode have damaged many a relationship and a person's credibility.)[54]
- On occasion, poorly chosen words, personal information, or inappropriate photos posted online, often innocently, have cost someone a job or chance at advancement.[55]

You probably don't need to be warned about the need to retain your privacy; college students are very much in the know on that front. But watch out for the lure of social networking sites and other online outlets—the semblance of privacy (just you and your computer or phone, right?), the ease of access, and an "everyone is using it" mentality—as you make conscious decisions about how much THEY should know about YOU.

# Two Models of Self-Disclosure

Research has explored the way in which self-disclosure works to move a relationship toward intimacy. Here we examine two of the more prominent models that illustrate the process by which this happens.

**The Social Penetration Model**  One pair of researchers, Irwin Altman and Dalmas Taylor, developed the **social penetration model**, which illustrates how much and what kind of information we reveal in various stages of a relationship.[56] According to their theory, interpersonal communication in relationships moves gradually from the superficial to the more intimate. Two aspects of this communication increase: the breadth of the information (the variety of topics discussed) and the depth (the personal significance of what is discussed).

As shown in Figure 7.2, the Altman and Taylor model is a configuration of rings, or concentric circles. The outermost circle represents breadth, or all the potential information about yourself that you could disclose to someone—information about athletic activities, spirituality, family, school, recreational preferences, political attitudes and values, and fears. Then there are a series of inner circles, which represent the depth of information you could reveal about yourself. The innermost circle represents your most personal information.

As an online or FtF relational partner interacts with you, that interaction can be seen as a wedge that is at first narrow (few topics are discussed) and shallow (topics are fairly superficial). People who have just started dating might talk about commonalities (like being students at the same college), hobbies, interests, and favorite activities. As the relationship progresses, the wedge becomes broader (as more topics are discussed) and deeper (as more personal topics are discussed). After several dates or conversations about hobbies and interests, topics might turn more to values, like the importance of family and friendships or attitudes about politics or social issues. Self-disclosure causes your layers to be penetrated as you penetrate the layers of the other person.

Each of your relationships exhibits a certain degree of social penetration, determined by the extent to which the other person has entered your concentric circles. Some relationships, such as those with professors, distant family members, and acquaintances,

**social penetration model**
A model of self-disclosure that asserts that both the breadth and the depth of information shared with another person increase as the relationship develops.

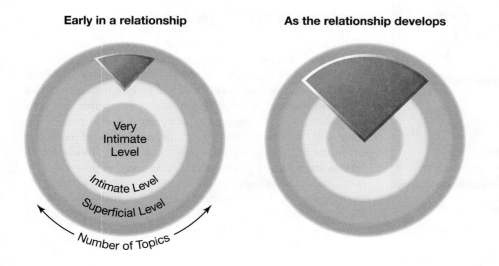

**Early in a relationship**

**As the relationship develops**

Very Intimate Level

Intimate Level

Superficial Level

Number of Topics

**Figure 7.2
Altman and Taylor's Model of Social Penetration**

may reflect a narrow, shallow wedge. The relationship doesn't involve a great deal of personal disclosure. A few relationships represent almost complete social penetration, the kind you achieve in an intimate, well-developed relationship in which a large amount of in-depth self-disclosure has occurred. But many contend that no one can ever completely know another person, that complete social penetration is unattainable. This model is a helpful way to assess your relationships in terms of whom you allow or encourage to get close to you and why. It may also help you diagram the level of intimacy you have in online and FtF relationships with others as you attempt to penetrate their layers.

**The Johari Window**   The **Johari Window** in Figure 7.3 is another model of how self-disclosure varies from relationship to relationship. It reflects various stages of relational development, degrees of self-awareness, and others' perceptions of us. Its name comes from the first names of the two men who developed it (Joe Luft and Harry Ingham) and from its windowlike appearance.[57] The large square window, like the circles in the social penetration model, represents your self. This self encompasses everything about you, including things you don't see or realize. A vertical line divides the square into what you have come to know about yourself and what you don't yet know about yourself. A horizontal line divides the square into what another person knows about you and doesn't know about you. The intersection of these lines divides the Johari Window into the following four quadrants:

- *The Open quadrant.* The part of yourself that you know and have revealed to another person is the Open quadrant. As a relationship becomes more intimate, the Open quadrant grows larger.
- *The Blind quadrant.* Information that another person knows about you but that you fail to recognize is in your Blind quadrant. For example, your closest friends may be able to tell when you're attracted to someone even before you acknowledge the attraction yourself. Before someone knows you well, the Blind quadrant is usually small; it grows larger as that person observes more information that's in your Unknown quadrant.
- *The Hidden quadrant.* Information that you know about yourself, but haven't shared with another person makes up the Hidden quadrant. Initially fairly large, the Hidden quadrant shrinks and the Open quadrant grows as you disclose more and more.
- *The Unknown quadrant.* Information about yourself that you—as well as other people—have yet to discover or realize makes up the Unknown quadrant. People who aren't very introspective and who don't have a very well-developed sense of self have larger Unknown areas than do those who have made a concerted effort to get to know themselves. This quadrant shrinks as you learn more about yourself or as others learn more about you.

**Johari Window**
A model that explains how self-disclosure varies from relationship to relationship; the model reflects various stages of relational development, degrees of self-awareness, and others' perceptions.

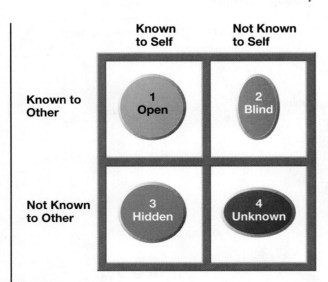

**Figure 7.3
Johari Window**

## Expressing Emotions

"Emotion is the fuel of human communication," says scholar Paul Bolls.[58] Expressing emotions is another powerful way we reveal ourselves to others and deepen our relationships. Such expression comes more easily to some people than others, but it's a skill that can be improved in both your online and your FtF relationships.[59] However, there are cultural barriers to achieving this skill in that many cultures designate particular emotions as appropriate for only some people to display in certain situations.[60] If you placed emotional expression on a continuum according to cultural groups, with one end being an open approach to emotional display and the other end being the suppression of emotional display, American culture would fall somewhere in the middle.[61]

# Communication & ETHICS

## PostSecret: Postcards in Strange Places

In 2004, Frank Warren wanted to do a community art project, so he began leaving blank postcards in public places and giving them to strangers, with the simple request that they write a secret on the card that they haven't told anyone, make sure not to sign their name, and mail the card to him. What resulted was an overwhelming response that has now grown into somewhat of a global phenomenon. Within the first year, Warren received more than 10,000 postcards carrying secrets. He has published multiple books, including *PostSecret: Confessions on Life, Death, and God* and *The Secret Lives of Men and Women*, all filled with pages and pages of anonymous people's secrets submitted on personally decorated, highly artistic postcards. The secrets range from fairly low-level, humorous confessions like "I waste office supplies because I hate my boss" to private passions and eccentricities to humiliating accounts of abuse and suffering. If you'd like to see a sampling, visit <www.postsecret.blogspot.com>.

Since people submit postcards to Warren anonymously and willingly, there's no ethical breach in sharing the secrets with readers, but this "movement" started us thinking about secrets as a unique form of self-disclosure and the ethics involved in keeping secrets. Is it safe to assume that everyone has at least one secret that he or she has never told anyone? What is it about the very nature of secrets that makes many of us want to *tell* them? That's the beauty of Warren's work—the release that *PostSecret* provides in that someone can tell a secret to the world without the risk involved in telling a friend or family member. As Warren writes in his introduction to *PostSecret*, "Secrets have stories; they can also offer truths. After seeing thousands of secrets, I understand that sometimes when we believe we are keeping a secret, that secret is actually keeping us."[62]

Families teach children very specific rules about the appropriateness of emotional display and perpetuate gender distinctions regarding emotions.[63] Many American men are taught to contain their emotions for fear that emotional expression may make them appear weak. Men are allowed to show anger and jealousy (short of physical violence), but it is usually frowned on for men to reveal sadness, fear, or great joy—unless they reveal it in a sporting context. In fact, the male tendency to suppress emotion is so pronounced that it led Sidney Jourard (who first studied self-disclosure) to entitle one of his book chapters "The Lethal Aspects of the Male Role."[64] Jourard found that men who had difficulty expressing their feelings had high levels of stress-related disease.

Women in American culture, in most settings, are allowed the emotional display of crying that can be prompted by sadness, fear, or joy. But many women receive negative reactions when they display anger. The view persists that an angry woman is "out of control" or "hormonal," whereas an angry man is behaving more in line with societal expectations for members of his sex. While these trends and expectations have changed somewhat with recent generations, there is still a significant tendency for men (and many women as well) to believe that emotional expression of any kind is more appropriate in women than men.[65]

As relationships become more intimate, we have a greater expectation that our partner will disclose emotions openly. The amount of risk associated with such emotional disclosure varies from person to person. Most of us are comfortable sharing the emotions of happiness and joy but are more reserved or hesitant about sharing fear or disappointment. While emotional expression can sometimes be difficult to handle, we generally want to know how our partners in intimate relationships are feeling, even if those feelings are negative.

In this chapter, we've explored several aspects of interpersonal communication, yet we've only scratched the surface of the complexities of relationships—those connections that give us life's greatest joys, as well as challenges. In the next chapter, we examine key aspects of communication that are critical to ongoing relationships with regard to our five Communication Principles for a Lifetime.

Many American men learn at an early age to mute their expressions of most emotions, whereas American women often learn to express a wide range of feelings. What were you taught about emotional expression that affects the way you communicate in relationships today?

IKO/Shutterstock.com

# STUDY GUIDE:
# Review, Apply, and Assess Your Knowledge and Skill

## REVIEWING
## What You Know

### What Is Interpersonal Communication? p. 170

Interpersonal communication occurs when two people interact simultaneously and attempt to mutually influence each other, usually for the purpose of managing relationships. Interpersonal communication research has traditionally focused on the face-to-face relationship, but more recently studies have investigated how online relationships are initiated and maintained through mediated interpersonal communication.

Interpersonal communication has three attributes:

- Interpersonal communication involves quality, which can be contrasted with impersonal communication, in which people are treated as objects or are communicated with based on the roles they hold.
- Interpersonal communication involves mutual influence.
- Interpersonal communication helps manage relationships of choice and circumstance.

**Terms to Know**

| | | | |
|---|---|---|---|
| Interpersonal Communication | p. 170 | Impersonal Communication | p. 171 |
| Mediated Communication | p. 170 | Relationship | p. 171 |
| Mediated Interpersonal Communication | p. 170 | | |

### Initiating Relationships p. 172

We are drawn to other people because of similarity; physical, sexual, and interpersonal attraction; proximity; and complementarity. We use nonverbal immediacy cues to convey our attraction and communicate to reduce uncertainty as we initiate and develop relationships. Besides listening, adapting, and being sensitive to nonverbal cues, good interpersonal communicators ask great questions, avoid self-absorbed communication, and give and receive compliments graciously.

**Terms to Know**

| | | | |
|---|---|---|---|
| Relationship of Circumstance | p. 172 | Complementarity | p. 175 |
| Relationship of Choice | p. 172 | Inclusion | p. 175 |
| Attraction | p. 172 | Control | p. 175 |
| Interpersonal Attraction | p. 172 | Affection | p. 175 |
| Short-Term Initial Attraction | p. 172 | Immediacy | p. 176 |
| Long-Term Maintenance Attraction | p. 172 | Uncertainty-Reduction Theory | p. 177 |
| Similarity | p. 173 | Passive Strategy | p. 177 |
| Physical Attraction | p. 173 | Active Strategy | p. 177 |
| Sexual Attraction | p. 174 | Interactive Strategy | p. 177 |
| Matching Hypothesis | p. 174 | Conversational Narcissism (Self-Absorbed Communicator Style) | p. 179 |
| Proximity | p. 174 | | |

### Maintaining Relationships p. 180

Many forms of interpersonal communication are necessary to maintain successful, satisfying relationships. An important communication skill is self-disclosure, or voluntarily providing information to others that they wouldn't learn if you didn't tell them. Self-disclosure is characterized by three aspects: (1) reciprocity, (2) appropriateness, and (3) risk.

Two models of self-disclosure help us understand how relationships progress toward intimacy. Social penetration suggests that interpersonal communication in relationships moves gradually from the superficial to the more intimate. The breadth and depth of communication increase as intimacy increases in relationships. The Johari Window depicts various stages of relational development, degrees of self-awareness, and others' perceptions.

Emotional expression is another powerful mechanism for revealing ourselves to others and deepening our relationships.

### Terms to Know

| | | | |
|---|---|---|---|
| Self-Disclosure | p. 181 | Social Penetration Model | p. 183 |
| Reciprocity | p. 181 | Johari Window | p. 184 |

## Principle One:
### Be aware of your communication with yourself and others.

- Attraction emerges in several different forms; it's important to discover what traits in other people are attractive to you.
- Early in an online or FtF relationship, be aware of aspects of your personality that you want to emphasize to another person to create a positive and attractive image.
- One strategy to reduce uncertainty in interpersonal contexts is to be aware of your surroundings and situation as you passively observe others' interactions.
- The Johari Window and the social penetration model can help you become more aware of your relationships and your interpersonal communication.

## Principle Two:
### Effectively use and interpret verbal messages.

- In initial interactions, honest, direct approaches are preferable to "canned" opening lines.
- When initiating online or FtF relationships, use questions that will engage and draw out another person.
- You may verbally reveal your liking for another person by using informal, personal, and inclusive language.
- You may verbally reveal your liking for another person by asking questions, probing for further information, and directly expressing your feelings.
- An active strategy to reduce uncertainty in interpersonal contexts is to ask third parties for their perceptions and knowledge.
- An interactive information-seeking strategy involves direct communication with the source who has the greatest potential for reducing your uncertainty.
- Asking great questions in a conversation draws a person out and helps a communicator avoid creating a perception of being self-absorbed.
- Practice giving sincere compliments generously and receiving others' compliments graciously.
- One of the key variables in relationship development is self-disclosure.
- As relationships grow more intimate, the expectation of deeper, more personal self-disclosure increases.
- As online and FtF relationships grow more intimate, the expectation of emotional expression increases.

# APPLYING Principles for a Lifetime

### Principle Three:
**Effectively use and interpret nonverbal messages.**

- Physical attraction is the degree to which you find another person's physical self appealing, whereas sexual attraction is the desire to have sexual contact with a certain person.
- In an FtF relationship, you may nonverbally reveal your liking for another person through the display of immediacy cues.
- Certain nonverbal behaviors like increasing volume to ward off interruptions or sending lengthy texts can signal a self-absorbed communication style.

### Principle Four:
**Listen and respond thoughtfully to others.**

- Early in online and FtF relationships, it's important to concentrate on and listen to your partner's responses to your questions so that you can offer an appropriate follow-up response.
- You may verbally reveal your attraction and liking for other people by listening, asking questions to elicit more detail, and then responding appropriately and sensitively to the added information.
- The best conversationalists aren't great talkers; they're great listeners and responders.
- The formulation of great questions in conversation requires listening carefully and responding appropriately to someone's communication.
- It's important to attend carefully to someone's self-disclosure because it comes with an expectation of reciprocity, meaning that the receiver is expected to self-disclose in response to the sender's self-disclosure.

### Principle Five:
**Appropriately adapt messages to others.**

- Adapt to others' communication, especially in first conversations, by attending to what is said and following up with great questions.
- Self-absorbed communication involves little adaptation.
- Adapt your self-disclosure to the other person and the context so that your revelations are appropriate.

# ASSESSING Your Skill

## Learning to Ask Great Questions

Because we think that learning to ask great questions is so important, we want to provide an opportunity for you to practice this art and skill. For each of the situations and snippets of conversation that follow, generate effective follow-up questions that would deepen and extend the conversation. We've provided an example to get you started.

*Sample Situation and Conversation:* The situation is a first conversation between two classmates who have never met; they are seated in the classroom before class begins.

> *Bob:* Hi. My name's Bob. What's yours?
>
> *Sue:* Hi. I'm Sue.
>
> *Bob:* I've never taken a philosophy course before, have you? What do you think this course will be like?
>
> *Sue:* Well, I've never taken one either, but I expect lots of reading. And I've heard the professor's tests are tough.
>
> *Bob:* Oh, great; is it too late to drop?! When you say the tests are tough, tough in what way? Do you mean they cover lots of material, the prof's a hard grader, or what?

1. *Practice Situation:* At a fraternity/sorority mixer, a woman and a man are introduced to each other for the first time by other members of their organizations.

2. *Practice Situation:* After a staff meeting, two new coworkers who will be working on the same important project introduce themselves to each other.

## Too Private to Talk About, Unless It's on Facebook?

For the following topics, check the column to indicate in which situation you would freely disclose the information to another person you were trying to get to know face to face versus online. Then analyze your answers. What information would you share anytime? What information are you unlikely reveal to anyone, in either context?

| Topic | Would Disclose FtF | Would Disclose Online |
|---|---|---|
| Weight | | |
| Racial/ethnic background | | |
| Sexual history | | |
| Family details | | |
| Relationship status | | |
| Weaknesses/Strengths | | |
| Religious/spiritual beliefs | | |
| Political views | | |

**WEB RESOURCES** for More Review, Application, and Assessment

- **MyCommunicationLab** Take the Metacommunication Challenge with a friend or partner, evaluate what a student's blog reveals about him or her, or simply review the contents of this chapter at the website <www.mycommunicationlab.com> (Access code required.)

- **Online dating advice** Many online dating sites exist, and most of them offer suggestions, including the following, for keeping dating fun and safe.[66]

1. Browse multiple services to find the one that best suits you.

2. Do a free trial to see if you like the process before paying a fee.

3. Once you choose to invest time and money in a site, be honest. Don't create a profile as you'd like to *think* you are; describe how you *really* are.

4. Provide a recent, realistic, yet flattering picture of yourself, even if you feel insecure doing so. You will receive more replies than if you choose not to include a picture (which can set off alarms for some people).

5. Don't be discouraged by the responses you receive; it's typical to receive some rude or inappropriate messages from people whose motives are questionable.

6. If you do make a connection with someone and begin to exchange e-mail or text messages, pay attention to what is communicated as well as what is *not* communicated.

7. If you decide to meet face to face with someone you've been e-mailing or texting, be careful. Meet in a public place and have your own transportation so that you can make a safe departure if need be. Make sure that a friend or family member knows what you're doing, where you're going, and when you're meeting the person.

8. Once you meet, if you don't feel a romantic connection, don't be shy about telling the person that you're really not interested. Be assertive and firm, but not rude, in expressing your desire not to pursue things further. No one likes to be strung along.

- **Mindtools** The Mindtools Communication Toolkit provides a variety of questions and helpful hints about how to ask them without sounding like you're conducting a job interview or a census survey. <www.mindtools.com>

Relationship is a pervading and changing mystery . . . brutal or lovely, the mystery waits for people wherever they go, whatever extreme they run to.

EUDORA WELTY

# **Chapter** OUTLINE

- The Importance of Relationships: Friends, Family, and Colleagues
- Stages of Relationship Development
- Tensions in Relationships: The Dialectical Perspective
- Managing Interpersonal Conflict
- Study Guide: Review, Apply, and Assess Your Knowledge and Skill

# **Chapter** OBJECTIVES

After studying this chapter, you should be able to

1. Explain how the five Communication Principles for a Lifetime apply to interpersonal communication among friends, family members, and colleagues.
2. Identify and describe the stages of relational escalation and de-escalation.
3. Discuss relational dialectics and three primary tensions in relationships.
4. Define interpersonal conflict and identify eight types of conflict.
5. Explain the key characteristics of nonconfrontational, confrontational, and cooperative styles of conflict management.

sima/Shutterstock.com

# 8 | **Enhancing Relationships**

What makes you happy? Staring at a computer screen? Working on a project for your job? Reading a great book? Playing a video game? Being by yourself, writing in your journal? Taking a long walk? Let us venture a guess: While any one of these things might bring some level of pleasure into your life, none of them could be considered *the* thing in life that gives you the most enjoyment. Probably most of us would answer that question with some response that involves other people or, perhaps, only one other person.

In Chapter 7, we examined some fundamental aspects of interpersonal communication that help us initiate online and face-to-face relationships. In this chapter, we move forward to discuss interpersonal communication as it occurs in ongoing relationships. Where appropriate, we discuss online relationships, but our primary focus in this chapter is how our five Communication Principles for a Lifetime apply to the good old-fashioned face-to-face relationship.

# The Importance of Relationships: Friends, Family, and Colleagues

These two friends may have met just moments ago; our earliest friendships are usually based on momentary sharing of activities. How long does it take now for you to decide someone is your friend? What influences that decision?

© Getty Images/Thinkstock

Our family members, friends, and coworkers are very important to us. To some degree, we all come from dysfunctional families—there is no such thing as a perfect, or "functional," family. As Leo Tolstoy said, "Happy families are all alike; every unhappy family is unhappy in its own way." But no matter how imperfect our families are, how crazy our siblings used to make us (or still make us), or how far apart we feel we may have grown from family members, almost all of us would agree that family relationships are extremely important. Likewise, when people talk about their jobs and what they like best about where they work, most often they talk about the people they work with. So, disregarding the few true hermits out there, most of us are "people who need people."

## Friendship Matters

One of the best definitions of a friend, attributed to Aristotle, is "a soul that resides in two bodies." A friend is someone we like and who likes us. We trust our friends and share good and bad times with them. We enjoy being with them, so we try to make time for that purpose. We expect a certain level of sacrifice from our friends. For example, you know you've got a good friend when that person gives up something (like a hot date) just to help you through a tough time.

Researchers have examined some differences among friendships at four stages in life: childhood, adolescence, adulthood, and old age.[1] When we start to talk (around the age of two), we begin to play and interact with others and perceive playmates as those who can help meet our needs. Our first friendships are typically superficial, self-centered, and fleeting, because they are based on momentary sharing of activities.[2] As we grow, we develop more of a give-and-take in friendships. During adolescence, we move away from relationships with parents and toward greater intimacy with our peers. At this point in our development, peer relationships are the most important social influence on our behavior.

Adult friendships are among our most valued relationships, even though they may be few in number. Research has found that, on average, adults have ten to twenty casual friends, four to six close friends, and only one to two best friends.[3] Rather than progressing through a series of stages in which intimacy deepens, which is typical of romantic relationships, friendships often alternate between periods of development and deterioration.[4] As Americans continue to spend more hours at work each year, we often find that our closest friends are also our coworkers.[5]

One type of friendship that continues to receive attention from researchers and the popular press is the "friends with benefits" relationship (FWBR), also referred to as the "booty call." Sexual liaisons between people who are "just friends" have been popularized through such movies as *No Strings Attached* and *Friends with Benefits*. Communication scholars Mikayla Hughes, Kelly Morrison, and Kelli Jean Asada define the friends with benefits relationship as one that emerges from a pre-existing friendship but that evolves to include sexual activity. The sexual contact doesn't change the friendship into a romantic relationship or imply a commitment; in fact, the people involved in an FWBR don't want anything more from their partners than what they have. These researchers explain that "these types of relationships are distinct in that they combine . . . the benefits of friendship with the benefits of a sexual relationship, yet avoid the responsibilities and commitment that romantic sexual relationships typically entail."[6]

The FWBR differs from a "hookup" (a casual one-night sexual encounter), which has also been observed among college student populations, in that it is more long-lasting and stable because it builds on a pre-existing friendship.[7] Hughes and her colleagues discovered that FWBRs are relatively common on college campuses today, that participants in such relationships perceive them as important, and that the relationships function effectively, provided both participants adhere to the following rules:

1. FWBR participants must maintain their original friendship, meaning that sexual activity doesn't change the friendship and the participants continue to do things together that they typically did as friends.
2. Emotions don't become involved, or the FWBR will be at risk.
3. The FWBR is maintained in secret, even if, for some people, it means that their romantic/sexual partners don't know about the FWBR.
4. The relationship may be renegotiated, with either participant opting out at any time.[8]

Friendships are extremely important in old age.[9] During retirement, when many individuals have more time for socializing, friendships become increasingly critical. Older adults tend to rely on enduring friendships and to maintain a small, highly valued network of friends.

## Communication Principles for a Lifetime: Enhancing Friendships

Like many other things, friendship development begins with an awareness of yourself—Principle One. Knowing your own interests, likes, and dislikes is a first step if you are trying to expand your circle of friends. If, for example, you consider yourself a spiritual person, you're more likely to make new friends with those kinds of people at a church gathering or in a yoga and meditation class than in some other setting.

We need communication to initiate and maintain friendships. Principles Two and Three, which involve the effective use of verbal and nonverbal communication, are essential in friendship. Our verbal communication tends to become more frequent and to deepen as friendships develop. We also use nonverbal immediacy cues to establish friendships—behaviors that reveal our liking of other people, such as leaning forward, moving closer, making eye contact, smiling, and nodding.

Listening and responding are important communication skills in friendship. Most of us don't stay friends with people who don't seem to listen to us or who listen but respond inappropriately. Probably no other communication skill develops a friendship more than the ability to listen and respond appropriately.

Finally, we learn to adapt to our friends or they probably don't stay our friends for very long (Principle Five). We extend different parts of ourselves and communicate differently with various friends. You may enjoy your dancing buddies because you can let a creative, wilder side of yourself show with them, while you communicate more seriously as you study with a group of classmates who have become your friends.

## Family Matters

Of all the relationships we experience in our lifetimes, none are more complicated than family relationships. Family members have more power to shape our self-concepts and affect self-esteem than other people do. Granted, at some point we can choose to stop or lessen the effect family members can have on our lives. But for most of us, those early messages we received as children still remain in our psyches and affect who we are today.

To say that family life has changed is an understatement. Family units are dramatically different than they were when the predominant profile was a two-parent, father-as-bread-winner, mother-as-homemaker arrangement.[10] In the 1980s, the New York Supreme Court provided a very broad definition of a family, stating, "The best description of a family is a continuing relationship of love and care, and an assumption of responsibility for some other person."[11] The most common profile of the American family in the 21st century is the step-family, or blended family, with rising rates of extended family or multigenerational arrangements.[12]

## Communication Principles for a Lifetime: Enhancing Family Relationships

Growing up in families, we begin to discover who we are and how we should communicate with others. Virginia Satir has conducted extensive research on family communication. She suggests that, in healthy families, "the members' sense of self-worth is high; communication is direct, clear, specific, and honest; rules are flexible, humane, and subject to change; and the family's links to society are open and hopeful."[13] In such families, Satir notes, people listen actively; they look *at* one another, not *through* one another or at the floor; they treat children as people; they touch one another affectionately regardless of age; and they openly discuss disappointments, fears, hurts, angers, and criticism, as well as joys and achievements. The degree to which parents and children can reveal what they are thinking and feeling is a measure of family cohesiveness. Another aspect Satir highlights corresponds to our Principle Four, that of listening and responding. Healthy family relationships are built on foundations of trust, which involves listening to one another and responding helpfully. Many conflicts arise because family members don't listen well to one another and respond based on that faulty listening.

Finally, family relationships involve a good deal of adaptation, particularly when, as adults, we visit our parents. Sometimes our parents and extended family members talk a certain way mainly because they've always talked that way.[14] But if, for example, you're the family member who's moved away, attended college, and adapted your communication to meet the changing times, connect with friends, and demonstrate professionalism at work, it can be quite awkward to be immersed once again in the family setting and realize how much you've changed. Adaptation can be challenging in such a situation, but it's necessary if your goal is effective communication.

## Colleagues Matter

For many of us, our work is our livelihood, our most time-consuming activity. In fact, many Americans are working longer hours—10 percent more time on the job in the 21st century than thirty years ago. And according to the website of the AFL-CIO, Americans are already working almost a full week's worth of hours more per year than they were at the beginning of the 21st century.[15] Many things make a job worthwhile and rewarding, but most people say that relationships with people they work with make the most difference between job satisfaction and dissatisfaction.

What are the most important skills people need to be successful on the job? Year after year, the number-one skill employers look for in new hires is the ability to communicate effectively with others.[16] You land your job through an interview; you keep your job based on your ability to do the work and get along with coworkers and bosses, which usually involves a large amount of interpersonal interaction.

## Communication Principles for a Lifetime: Enhancing Workplace Relationships

Getting accustomed to a new job takes a while. There are the rudimentary things to discover and adjust to, such as finding out where to park or which subway to take, learning what makes the organization function, and observing general office protocol. Then there are the more important things, like learning how to do your job well, ascertaining the chain of command, and discovering which colleagues have the potential to develop into friends.

When most of us start a new job, we experience uncertainty. Our uncertainty will most likely be reduced by those who hired us, those who are assigned to train or orient us to the new situation, and coworkers who are at our same level within the organization. We're most likely to observe our surroundings and how people interact on the job, as a way of becoming more aware so that we'll know how to behave appropriately (Principle One). Perception checking with colleagues also increases awareness. For example, after attending your first staff meeting, you might want to ask a few colleagues whether the gathering was typical of the kind of staff meetings the organization holds.

As we begin to interact with people of varying status in the organization, we draw on our most effective verbal and nonverbal communication skills so that we make positive impressions on others (Principles Two and Three). The higher you go in an organization, the more your job involves communicating with others, both online and in person.

One skill that makes for an effective worker is the ability to listen and respond effectively to colleagues (Principle Four). It's important to listen patiently, fully, and nonjudgmentally at work and to exercise caution before responding so that you respond appropriately.

Finally, our Principle Five about adaptation is critical to successful coworker relationships. You cannot hope to be successful on the job if you communicate the same way to your boss as you do to your peers on the job, your subordinates, and others in your life—including long-term friends, intimates, and family members.[17] This may seem obvious, but we find that people sometimes experience isolation on the job because they cannot get along with coworkers. They don't adapt to the situation, and it often costs them their jobs.

# Stages of Relationship Development

In this chapter, we explore aspects of communication that are critical to the successful functioning of ongoing relationships, but it is helpful to first understand that relationships tend to develop in discernible stages.[18] While the research on relational stages is most often applied to dating or romantic relationships, the information can also apply to other types of relationships.

Understanding relationship stages is important for the following reasons:

- Interpersonal communication is affected by the stage of a relationship. For instance, people in advanced stages discuss topics and display nonverbal behaviors that rarely appear in the early stages of a relationship.
- Interpersonal communication facilitates movement between the various stages. Ongoing relationships change and are constantly renegotiated by those involved. Interpersonal communication moves a relationship forward—possibly from friends to romantic partners to marital or committed partners. Ideally, communication should also move a relationship back to a previous stage, although regressing a relationship or changing a relationship's definition is difficult to accomplish.[19]

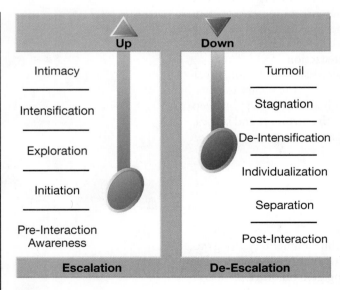

## Figure 8.1
## Relationship Stages

Source: From Steven A. Beebe, Susan J. Beebe, and Mark V. Redmond, *Interpersonal Communication: Relating to Others*, 6th edition. Reprinted and Electronically reproduced by permission of Pearson Education, Inc., Upper Saddle River, New Jersey. Copyright © 2011.

Think of relational stages as floors in a high rise (see Figure 8.1). The bottom floor represents a first meeting; the penthouse is intimacy. Relational development is an elevator that stops at every floor. As you ascend, you might get off the elevator and wander around for a while before going to the next floor. Each time you get on, you don't know how many floors up the elevator will take you or how long you'll stay at any given floor. In fact, sometimes you never get back on the elevator, electing instead to stay at a particular stage of relational development. This may represent stability or stagnation. Stability is not the same as stagnation; it may simply mean that a relationship has reached a comfortable point for both partners. But if one partner believes that the relationship has stabilized and the other partner believes that it has stagnated, dissatisfaction and conflict are often the result.

If you fall head over heels in love, you might want to escalate quickly from floor to floor toward intimacy, possibly even skipping some floors. In contrast, the process of de-escalating a relationship doesn't always occur, but if it does, it may be a slow or a quick descent through various floors. The best approach to relationship development is to share this elevator with your partner or friend so that the two of you make decisions about how high you will ride, how long to stay at each floor, and whether to take the elevator back down. Often partners don't share decisions about movement within the relationship. Sometimes one of the partners rides the elevator alone.

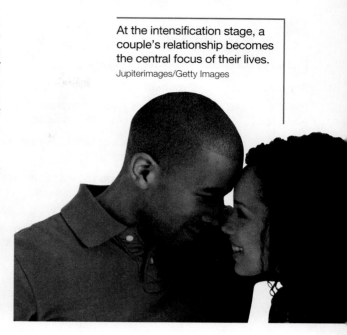

At the intensification stage, a couple's relationship becomes the central focus of their lives.
Jupiterimages/Getty Images

## Relational Escalation

According to Mark Knapp and Anita Vangelisti, the communication scholars who developed the model of developmental stages within relationships, relational escalation occurs in the following five stages:[20]

- **Pre-interaction awareness** is the first stage, one in which potential partners or friends observe each other and talk with other people about each other without having any direct interaction. If your impressions of a potential friend or relational partner aren't favorable or circumstances aren't right, you might not move beyond this first stage.
- In the **initiation stage**, first conversations occur between potential friends or romantic partners, with each person responding to the other's questions as both try to determine what they have in common. Nonverbal cues are important at this stage because they signal interest.
- The **exploration stage** occurs next as partners or friends begin to share more in-depth information. Minimal physical contact is typical, and the amount of time people spend together tends to be fairly limited as the relationship begins to build.
- If people proceed to the **intensification stage**, they start to depend on each other for self-confirmation, meaning that each partner's or friend's opinion of or feeling about the other weighs more heavily than the opinions of other people. Partners spend more time together in a wider variety of activities, adopt more intimate physical distance and contact, and personalize their language. The frequency and level of shared personal information increase, and the two people may decide to label their connection. (Friends may move to "best friend" status.)
- The top level of relationship escalation is the **intimacy stage**, in which partners provide primary confirmation of each other's self-concept and communication is highly personalized and synchronized. Partners talk about anything and everything, and a commitment to maintaining a romantic relationship might even be formalized and socially recognized, such as with a decision to marry or form a legal union. Romantic partners share an understanding of each other's language

**pre-interaction awareness stage**
The stage of becoming aware of one's attraction to another person and observing that person but not actually interacting.

**initiation stage**
The first contact with a person with whom one desires a relationship; usually characterized by asking and answering questions.

**exploration stage**
The stage that involves more in-depth interactions.

**intensification stage**
The stage in which partners begin to depend on each other for self-confirmation; characterized by more shared activities, more time spent together, more intimate physical distance and contact, and personalized language.

**intimacy stage**
The stage in which partners provide primary confirmation of each other's self-concept; characterized by highly personalized and synchronized verbal and nonverbal communication.

# RECAP

## RELATIONAL ESCALATION

| Stage | Explanation |
|---|---|
| Pre-Interaction Awareness | You become aware of your attraction to someone and begin to observe that person. |
| Initiation | You initiate contact with the person with whom you want a relationship. |
| Exploration | Interactions deepen as questions and answers elicit more information from partners. |
| Intensification | Partners begin to depend on each other for confirmation of their self-concepts. They spend more time together, engage in more intimate touch, and personalize their language. |
| Intimacy | Partners provide primary confirmation of each other's self-concept. Verbally, language is highly personalized; nonverbal behaviors are synchronized. |

and nonverbal cues and have a great deal of physical contact. Reaching this stage takes time—time to build trust, share highly personal information, observe each other in various situations, and create an emotional bond and commitment.

What we've described is a nice and tidy model of what *may* happen as a relationship progresses, but we all know that many times relationships are messier than this. Some people move through relational stages very quickly. We probably all know people whose relationships were extremely physical and perhaps sexual from the very start. Are those relationships doomed because they didn't follow set or prescribed paths for development? No; some relationships may just proceed through stages faster than others. Relationships that are extremely physical or sexual may burn out quickly, however, because they lack the emotional foundation necessary to survive; partners may have difficulty developing an emotional connection or finding things in common once the physical "spark" wanes.

## Relational De-Escalation

Sometimes relationships begin to unravel, which can happen for a variety of reasons. Some unravel to the point of termination. But as you may already know, ending a relationship is not as simple as going down the same way you came up; it's not a mere reversal of the escalation process.[21] Relational de-escalation contains the following six stages:

**turmoil stage**
The stage characterized by increased conflict, less mutual acceptance, a tense communication climate, and an unclear relationship definition.

- The **turmoil stage** comes first in relationship demise and is characterized by increased conflict as partners find faults in each other. The definition of the relationship loses clarity, and mutual acceptance declines. Conversations are tense, difficult, and forced.

**stagnation stage**
The stage in which a relationship loses its vitality, partners begin to take each other for granted, and communication and physical contact decline.

- The **stagnation stage** occurs when the relationship loses its vitality and partners become complacent, taking each other for granted. Communication and physical contact decrease; partners or friends spend less time together but don't necessarily engage in conflict. People in a stagnating relationship go through the motions of an intimate relationship without the commitment or joy. But a stagnating relationship can be salvaged; people can repair, redefine, or revitalize their relationship and return to intimacy.

**de-intensification stage**
The stage involving significantly decreased interaction, increased distance, and decreased dependence on one's partner for self-confirmation.

- If turmoil or stagnation continues, friends or partners will likely experience the **de-intensification stage**, which involves significantly decreased interaction; increased physical, emotional, and psychological distance; and decreased dependence on each other for self-confirmation. Partners might discuss the definition of their relationship, question its future, and assess each other's level of dissatisfaction.

**individualization stage**
The stage in which partners define their lives more as individuals and less as a couple.

- After de-intensification, the **individualization stage** occurs, in which partners tend to define their lives more as individuals and less as a couple or unit. Interactions are limited; both partners tend to turn to others for self-concept confirmation. For romantic partners, physical intimacy is at an all-time low, if not nonexistent, and nonverbal distance is easily detected.

**separation stage**
The stage in which individuals make an intentional decision to minimize or eliminate further interpersonal interaction.

- In the **separation stage**, individuals make an intentional decision to minimize or eliminate further interpersonal interaction. If they share custody of children, attend

# Communication & ETHICS

## Pain, Stress, and the (Responsible) Breakup

Anyone who's been through a breakup knows how tough it is on one's psyche and self-esteem, but do you know what a breakup is likely to do to your physical health? Neurobiologists explain that the supply of "feel-good" chemicals in your body diminishes after a breakup, leaving you more vulnerable to the effects of stress hormones.[22] Those stress hormones cause swollen muscles, headaches, a stiff neck, a squeezing sensation in your chest, a disturbed digestive system, and a compromised immune system that can leave you susceptible to bacteria and viruses. Not a pretty picture!

If you deem breaking up with someone in your best interest (perhaps because you've been experiencing those negative health effects while *in* the relationship), are there more sensitive and ethical ways to accomplish it, ways that will lessen the psychological and physical aftereffects? Yes, and here are some things to keep in mind.

- Simply expanding distance—not calling someone back (ever), ignoring text messages or e-mails, avoiding places and situations where you might run into the person, hoping the person will get the hint—is ill-advised. These methods generate confusion and ambiguity, causing undue hurt to the target of the breakup.[23] Relational fuzziness can also keep both parties from getting past the breakup and moving on.

- Using a mediated channel such as a text, e-mail, or voice mail message may make it easier on the "dumper," but is terrible (some would argue, unethical) for the "dumpee." When the dumpee's reply messages go unread or without response, the person is cut off from a full explanation, a chance at negotiation, and the opportunity to express her or his feelings.[24]

- Research shows that most people actually prefer to break up and be broken up with in person, through a conversation that lets both parties air their issues and generate a definite ending.[25] We might fear the conflict and emotional display that might typify such a conversation, but this method is preferable for most people over "what are we now" uncertainty.

- Avoid the dreaded and trite "let's still be friends" line. For most people in the position of being dumped, the *last* thing they want to do or can even conceive of is being friends with a former romantic partner.[26] It's understandable for a dumper to try to soften the blow or retain some kind of connection to the dumpee, but it's selfish to expect the other person to change relationship definition easily or quickly. Maybe, with time, something can be salvaged that works for both parties.

---

mutual family gatherings, or work at the same place, the nature of their interaction noticeably changes. They divide property, resources, and friends. Interactions in this stage are increasingly tense and difficult, especially if the relationship has been intimate.

- The final level in de-escalation is termed the **post-interaction stage**. It represents the lasting effects the relationship has on the self and therefore on other interactions and relationships. Relationships—even failed ones—are powerful experiences in our lives, so the effects continue even after the relationship has ended. In this stage, partners engage in "grave dressing," meaning that they create a public statement for people who ask why they broke up or why they're no longer friends.[27] Sometimes self-esteem gets battered during the final stages of a relationship, so we have to work hard to regain a healthy sense of self.

Here's a final note about relationship endings: Research has begun to investigate how people create or reinvent some sort of connection once they've broken up. Yes, some people actually want to "still be friends" or have a relationship of some form with an ex, as

**post-interaction stage**
The bottom, or final, stage in relational de-escalation, which represents the lasting effects of a relationship on the self.

# RECAP

## RELATIONAL DE-ESCALATION

| Stage | Explanation |
|---|---|
| Turmoil | Partners take each other for granted and have more conflict. They exhibit less mutual acceptance, their communication climate is tense, and their relationship definition is unclear. |
| Stagnation | The relationship loses its vitality, partners begin to take each other for granted, and communication and physical contact decline. |
| De-Intensification | Partners significantly decrease their interaction and their dependence on each other for self-confirmation; they increase their physical distance. |
| Individualization | Partners define their lives more as individuals and less as a couple. |
| Separation | Partners make an intentional decision to minimize or eliminate further interpersonal interaction. |
| Post-Interaction | This is the bottom or final level in relational de-escalation; it represents the lasting effects of a relationship on the individuals. |

challenging as that may be. The **postdissolutional relationship** has been defined as "the relationship formed between dating partners after their romance terminates."[28] (The term doesn't apply to divorced couples who negotiate a connection once their marriage has ended.) These relationships are characterized by a high amount of general satisfaction with the relationship, a moderate amount of emotional intimacy and interpersonal communication, and a low amount of sexual intimacy. In terms of the success of these relationships, what seems to make the difference are how much the partners like each other, how long the partners were together romantically (the longer the romantic relationship, the less successful the postrelationship), and how much the partners hope they will get back together, romantically.[29]

# Tensions in Relationships: The Dialectical Perspective

Relationships are living, breathing, dynamic entities, and no two relationships are the same. Relationships are constantly changing, in both small and large ways. One way to approach relationships, known as **relational dialectics** or the dialectical perspective, was developed by communication scholars Leslie Baxter and Barbara Montgomery (and extended by other researchers).[30] Dialectics help us understand the up-and-down, ebb-and-flow, messy, oftentimes illogical nature of interpersonal relationships. The theory describes a set of tensions that people in relationships commonly face—but by *tensions*, we don't mean to imply something that is necessarily negative. A dialectical perspective suggests that relationship issues are better understood in terms of push–pull dynamics or points on a continuum rather than as opposite poles or fixed entities. While tensions can occur in all sorts of relationships—among family members, between coworkers, within friendships—they are arguably most revealing of the romantic relationship.

Romantic relationship tensions arise from the decision making a couple faces in developing and defining their relationship, not necessarily because of the individuals in the relationship. With each tension, it's not a matter of "either/or" ("either we're committed or we're not"), but a matter of degree or "both/and" ("we're both committed and independent"). If partners can recognize the presence and shifting nature of the tensions, they can talk about them and either resolve them or decide that, as partners, they just aren't suited for each other.

While multiple tensions have been identified in research, for our purposes we will focus on the following three primary issues that most relational partners face:

- *Integration–separation: Autonomy versus connection.* Although people want to be connected to others and feel they're part of a couple or group, they also want to be self-sufficient and independent. The amount of autonomy partners desire varies widely within the partners themselves and over the course of a relationship, making this tension one of the most difficult to confront. Early on, relational partners tend to spend as much time together as possible, but when a time-consuming activity or work project intrudes, friends or family members demand some time, or a "night out without you" is desired, autonomy versus connection conflict can arise.[31] Partners can benefit from honest, open, nondefensive communication about this tension, proactively negotiating how much time they expect to spend together and apart. Even the amount of cell phone contact may need to be negotiated between partners, as research shows that calling, texting, and general over use of mobile phones between partners can heighten this tension.[32]

- *Stability–change: Predictability versus novelty.* Although people are drawn to stability and consistency in a relationship, we're also drawn to excitement and unpredictability, so becoming comfortable with the ebb

**postdissolutional relationship**
The relationship formed between dating partners after their romance terminates.

**relational dialectics**
A perspective that views interpersonal relationships as constantly changing rather than stable and that revolves around how relational partners manage tensions.

At the start of their relationship, this woman may have admired her boyfriend's regular habit of playing lengthy video games with his father. As the novelty wears off in relationships, however, we may find that we are bored with the predictability of our partner. How can you balance stability and change in your own relationships?

© Getty Images/Thinkstock

and flow of these aspects can be a challenge.[33] Typically, at the start of a relationship, people are happy with the status quo, emphasizing a partner's positive points and glossing over personality traits or behaviors that are less desirable. Over time, however, as the novelty wears off, people may have more difficulty accepting each other as they are, and one partner may try to change the other. Being aware that this tension is likely to emerge at some point—or several points—within a relationship is key, because the amount of persuasion or influence that goes on in a relationship is associated with satisfaction.

- *Expression–privacy: Openness versus closedness.* Each of us is different in how open we wish to be (or are comfortable being) and our need for privacy. If relational partners are dramatically different on this count, they'll need to be proactive and work hard to manage this tension, or it might be a deal breaker. Couples, friends, even

**cyberinfidelity**
Online sexual activity outside of one's in-person, monogamous relationship.

# Communication&TECHNOLOGY

## Infidelity in Cyberspace: Is It Cheating If You Don't Actually Touch?

One primary use for computers is keeping in touch with family members and friends.[34] Another is to establish "liaisons" outside one's primary relationship.[35] As one source suggests, "Fueling our sexual freedom is our ability to pursue a fling without even opening the front door; we can simply open a laptop."[36] Typically, such liaisons don't begin as sexual relationships and may form through common interests, but a cyberrelationship can escalate to another level of intimacy and meaning.

Many people have negative reactions to in-person relational infidelity, whether they have experienced it themselves or know someone who has; even those who haven't experienced it say that they would respond negatively to a partner's infidelity.[37] But few people in committed, monogamous relationships think much about **cyberinfidelity** (online sexual activity outside of one's in-person, monogamous relationship)—unless it happens to them.

According to research, part of online deception is escape, so in some people's view, "cybersex is not actual infidelity because the relationship is never physically consummated; because cybersex is virtual, it cannot be real."[38] If no physical contact is made and sexual activity is accomplished through verbal exchanges in virtual reality, how different is cybersex from one's own sexual fantasies? What if the cybersex involves webcams or technology in smartphones that allows callers to see each other? Is that somehow more egregious, now qualifying as infidelity because people can see each other being sexual, whereas text is just words that spark the imagination?

Researchers have asked people about their online sexual activity, including what initially motivated them to engage in cybersex, why they continued to engage in it, the role it played in their lives, and the effects it had on them.[39] Interestingly enough, in one study, 41 percent of respondents didn't believe online sexual activity was cheating on a partner under any circumstances. Fourteen percent deemed it cheating only if a person engaged in cybersex repeatedly with the same person. Smaller percentages of participants believed it was cheating only if webcams were used or the online sex led to phone sex. Thirty-three percent of subjects believed that online sex was cheating and that it was just as much an act of infidelity as in-person sex with someone other than one's partner.

Here are some contentions from the "cybersex isn't cheating" point of view:

- Some people form sexual liaisons online because the anonymity and privacy of the Internet allows them to explore their sexuality with little concern that friends, coworkers, and relational partners will discover their activity.[40]
- People may feel sexually hindered in their face-to-face relationships, so the Internet becomes the arena in which their "true" sexual selves find expression.
- For people whose in-person relationships are in turmoil or decline, online liaisons offer opportunities for sexual expression and gratification.
- Cybersex is advantageous because it avoids concerns about STDs and unwanted pregnancies.
- If a virtual sexual involvement goes awry, participants don't suffer such consequences as in-person retribution or confrontation because online exchanges, for the most part, remain anonymous.

Here's the main argument from the "cheating is cheating, so cybersex is cheating" point of view: Any form of "stepping out" on one's romantic partner without his or her knowledge is cheating, period. No matter whether it occurs in virtual reality or in-person reality, sexual connections outside of one's committed relationship represent infidelity, and infidelity has serious consequences for any relationship.

One final wrinkle: What if your committed, monogamous romantic partner is an online-only relationship, meaning that you're not in each other's face-to-face world? Do the standards somehow shift? Can you cheat online with someone other than your online partner? These questions could make for some interesting discussion among your circle of friends.

family members may feel a push–pull, with one person in the relationship wanting complete openness and equating openness with trust, and the other wanting to retain a degree of privacy and connecting privacy with individual identity.[41] One topic in particular—the discussion between romantic relational partners of past relationships, especially sexual ones—best illustrates this tension. One partner may want to reveal all and know all, whereas the other may not wish to bring the past into the present. Both positions—and all points in between—are legitimate, but they're indicative of a relational tension that typically has to be addressed for a relationship of any kind to flourish.

# Managing Interpersonal Conflict

## A World of Conflict

We live in a world full of conflict. You can hardly watch the news on TV, listen to a radio talk show, or read news online without being confronted with another story of conflict. Whether it's the Middle East, a political coup in a country in Africa, or a disturbance generated by extremist groups right here at home, conflict on a global scale seems inevitable. While conflicts have always existed throughout the world, the events of September 11, 2001, launched the United States into a series of intense conflicts across the globe. How can we understand conflict on such a scale? What can we learn about conflict that might help mediate its destructive effects across the world? Developing an understanding of conflict and effective communication skills to manage it begins one on one, in our day-to-day relationships. Conflict is rooted in interpersonal communication.

**Interpersonal conflict** is a struggle that occurs when two people cannot agree on a way to meet their needs. If needs or goals are incompatible, if there are too few resources to satisfy them, or if individuals opt to compete rather than to cooperate to satisfy them, conflict occurs. The intensity of a conflict usually relates to the intensity of the unmet needs. The bedrock of all conflict is differences—different goals, experiences, expectations, and so forth.[42] Your goal collides head-on with someone else's, and you feel as if you've lost control of the situation. Before we explore how to better manage and resolve conflict, let's first examine the nature of conflict and how it functions in interpersonal relationships.

## Types of Conflict

While we all probably know people who enjoy conflict for conflict's sake, most of us want to better understand conflict so that we're more fully equipped to manage it rather than letting it manage us. Realizing that several forms of conflict exist is a first step.

Conflict can be constructive or destructive.[43] To construct something is to build or make something new. Characterized by cooperation in dealing with differences, **constructive conflict** can help identify which elements of a relationship need to change or be improved so that new patterns are established. Here's an example:

Jake: You know, I'm getting tired of always going to your mother's on Sundays. It's like we're in a rut or something. Just one weekend, I'd like to have a Sunday with no schedule or agenda.

Julie: Jake, I thought you liked going over there, because my mom's such a good cook and you and dad are working on that project together. Plus, it's one of the few times I get to spend time with my folks.

Jake: Well, I do like going over there, but not every weekend.

Julie: I didn't realize you were starting to resent it or feel like you were in a rut. Let's figure something out.

**interpersonal conflict**
A struggle that occurs when two people cannot agree on a way to meet their needs.

**constructive conflict**
Conflict characterized by cooperation in dealing with differences; helps build new insights and patterns in a relationship.

Notice that Julie transforms the issue of disagreement into a topic for discussion and relational adjustment. If Jake hadn't expressed his dissatisfaction, the issue might have taken on larger proportions. He might have expressed his feelings of being in a rut in a more hurtful way later on. A well-managed disagreement that includes expressing one's own needs or revising goals can lead people to examine and then revitalize their relationship. Constructive conflict enables both people to view a disagreement from different perspectives, even if the information shared seems negative at first.

A rapidly spiraling **destructive conflict** can do a great deal of damage. A conflict may start over a seemingly small issue but can increase in intensity as other issues and differences are brought into the discussion. Such destructive escalation blocks off options for managing differences and makes a win–win solution more elusive. The primary characteristic of destructive conflict is a lack of flexibility in responding to others.[44] Combatants view their differences from a win–lose perspective rather than looking for solutions that allow each individual to gain. This form of conflict dismantles relationships without restoring them. If both individuals are dissatisfied with the outcome of the conflict, it's been more destructive than constructive.

In their book on interpersonal conflict, William Wilmot and Joyce Hocker discuss six hallmarks of constructive conflict:[45]

1. *People change.* In relationships, people are involved with each other. In conflict, people must work hard to stay involved with each other, because an interaction that escalates into conflict can pull people apart. Flexibility and a willingness to change are key.
2. *People interact with an intent to learn instead of an intent to protect themselves.* You can learn a great deal about yourself, your partner, and your relationship if you approach conflict as a learning experience—one that will take your relationship forward instead of allowing it to stagnate or regress. Protecting yourself against conflict doesn't help a relationship grow.
3. *People don't stay stuck in conflict when the conflict is constructive.* Destructive conflict can make you feel stuck in one place in a relationship. Constructive conflict is a dynamic process that emerges, plays out, and recedes.
4. *Constructive conflict enhances self-esteem in the participants.* You probably don't associate conflict with enhanced self-esteem, because most of us think of conflict as negative and destructive. However, constructive conflict brings energy and productivity to a relationship and provides each partner with a more honest, complete picture of himself or herself.
5. *Constructive conflicts are characterized by a relationship focus instead of a purely individualistic focus.* If parties in a conflict focus on the relationship instead of themselves, the conflict will more likely be constructive than destructive. Participants should emphasize the "we" over the "I" so that conflict is seen as an experience that builds the relationship.
6. *Constructive conflict is primarily cooperative.* Conflict built on competition, power struggles, and self-interest will destroy a relationship. Conversely, a cooperative, win–win approach to conflict will open the door for greater growth.

Communication scholars Gerald Miller and Mark Steinberg categorize conflict as having three forms:[46]

- **Pseudoconflict** reflects a basic lack of understanding; one person misunderstands the meaning in a message.
- **Simple conflict** stems from differences in ideas, definitions, perceptions, or goals.
- **Ego conflict** occurs when conflict gets personal such that people attack each other's self-esteem.

Let's use an example to help distinguish these types. Two people start out with a simple misunderstanding about the time they were supposed to meet (pseudoconflict). If the misunderstanding escalates, they might argue over their varying perceptions of what being "on time" means (simple conflict), especially if they come from different cultural backgrounds. If the disagreement degenerates and becomes personal, such as

**destructive conflict**
Conflict characterized by a lack of cooperation in dealing with differences; dismantles relationships without restoring them.

**pseudoconflict**
Conflict stemming from a lack of understanding.

**simple conflict**
Conflict over differences in ideas, definitions, perceptions, or goals.

**ego conflict**
Conflict based on personal issues in which people attack each other's self-esteem.

# Communication & DIVERSITY

## Coping with Conflict Across Cultures

Interpersonal conflict is difficult to manage, but cross-cultural conflict can be even more overwhelming. Some people are trained in negotiation and mediation techniques so that they can facilitate peaceful relations between nations and peoples. But what if you're not planning to become an international negotiator? What if you simply want to know a few things to keep from being tossed in jail in a foreign country?

Intercultural communication scholars have written extensively on this subject and produced some insightful information that can help you anticipate and avoid intercultural conflict.[47] People from individualistic cultures, such as the United States, emphasize the importance of the individual over the group. Those in collectivistic cultures, such as Japanese people, emphasize group rather than individual

achievement. These differing values contribute to intercultural conflict.

So what should members of individualistic cultures know when interacting with members of collectivistic cultures? Below are seven assumptions about conflict that individualistic cultures hold; compare this list with seven assumptions about conflict that collectivistic cultures hold, assessing the differences.

Members of different cultural groups not only have different views of conflict, but they also have different ways of dealing with or managing conflict. It's wise to do some research on the country you will be visiting or moving to so that you understand how basic cultural values differ from those of your home country.

### Individualistic Cultures

1. The purpose of conflict is to air major differences and problems.
2. Conflict can be either functional or dysfunctional.
3. Repressed, unconfronted problems can lead to dysfunctional conflict.
4. Functional conflict provides an opportunity for solving problems.
5. Substantive and relational issues in conflict should be handled separately.
6. Conflict should be handled directly and openly.
7. Effective conflict management should be a problem-solving activity with a win–win outcome.

### Collectivistic Cultures

1. Conflict is damaging to self-respect and relational harmony; it should be avoided as much as possible.
2. For the most part, conflict is dysfunctional.
3. Conflict signals emotional immaturity and a lack of self-discipline.
4. Conflict provides a testing ground for skillful negotiation and "face-saving."
5. Substantive and relational issues are always intertwined.
6. Conflict should be handled discreetly and subtly.
7. Effective conflict management should be a face-saving negotiation game with a win–win outcome.

---

**serial arguments**
Argumentative episodes focused on the same issue that occur at least twice.

**irresolvable (intractable) conflict**
A conflict that one or both parties deem impossible to resolve.

one person accusing the other of something deeper than mere misunderstanding (as in, "You did this on purpose" or "You're *always* like this"), an ego conflict has erupted out of a simple conflict.

Two other types of conflict are worthy of note. First, people in ongoing relationships often have **serial arguments**, defined as "argumentative episodes focused on a given issue that occur at least twice."[48] How many times have you heard someone complain, "We have this same argument over and over"? Serial arguments typically involve repetitious, highly negative verbal communication (such as name calling) and negative nonverbal cues (yelling, aggressive movements). They usually spiral and are rarely productive; they engender mutual hostility in the partners and create a pattern that is very hard to break. Over time, unchecked serial arguments have an adverse effect on relationships and can erode self-esteem.

Another form of conflict that occurs within interpersonal relationships is what communication scholars term the **irresolvable** or **intractable conflict**.[49] In such a conflict, one or both of the parties deem the conflict impossible to resolve. A person who holds the view that an argument is irresolvable may not necessarily state that view out in the open, choosing simply to believe that compromise is impossible. She or he may adopt a "go along to get along" approach if relationships with people in an ongoing conflict are worth managing through appeasement or tolerance rather than confrontation.

# How Conflict Functions in Relationships

Conflict is a normal, inevitable element within relationships. One of the most important topics to learn about to enhance relationships of all sorts is conflict—how conflict functions; how each person in a relationship approaches, processes, and responds to conflict; and how we can better manage conflict when it inevitably arises.[50]

It's surprising (and disconcerting) when people in relationships say, "We just get along so well; we belong together because we've never even had a fight." While we don't advocate staging or picking a fight with a partner as an experiment, we do believe that it's worrisome to commit to a person when you don't know how she or he handles conflict. If your partner or close friend is a "screamer" and you prefer to walk away from a conflict in silent protest, your relationship is headed for very rough waters. People's responses to conflict should be known quantities if a relationship is to be successful.

Speed Bump

I DON'T FEEL LIKE HAVING THIS ARGUMENT AGAIN, TOM. STANDING IN FOR ME TONIGHT WILL BE SARA, MY UNDERSTUDY.

Dave Coverly/The Cartoonist Group

**Conflict Involves Power**   One of the most significant elements within interpersonal relationships is power.[51] We might not realize it, but distributing power between partners requires a lot of subtle negotiation. Without this negotiation, conflict can become rampant. Power has been defined in a variety of ways, but for our purposes, **interpersonal power** means the ability to influence another in the direction we desire—to get another person to do what we want.[52] It also involves the ability to resist others' influences on us.[53] Perhaps it is easier to think of it in terms of who has more *control* in a relationship rather than to use the term *power*.

Most interactions, including conflicts, involve some level of power or control. If you ask a friend to go to a movie with you, you attempt to influence him or her. If the answer is no, your friend is mustering resistance and demonstrating power over you. If you don't like the negative response, you might attempt to assert control once more, perhaps by offering to buy your friend's ticket or to drive.

Power dynamics can emerge to typify three forms of romantic relationships:[54]

- In a **complementary relationship**, one partner willingly and continuously cedes power to the other. Historically, in traditional marriages in the United States, husbands tended to be the dominant decision makers, with wives ceding control over such decisions as money matters and child discipline to their husbands. Sometimes a complementary arrangement works because the roles are clearly defined and conflict is minimal, but often the person who rarely makes a decision becomes dissatisfied with the imbalance of power.

- **Symmetrical relationships** are characterized by similar degrees of control on the part of each person. Partners may compete in an effort to dominate the other and assert control, or both may relinquish control to avoid making decisions or committing to something they may later regret. Power struggles are common among independent, strong-willed people. But when both partners cede power, they're often reluctant to express preferences, instead engaging in endless "I don't know—whatever you want" exchanges. This kind of constant negotiation can be time-consuming, fatiguing, paralyzing, and ineffective when quick decisions are needed.

- In a **parallel relationship**, power continually shifts from one partner to the other, depending on the nature of the interaction or situation. Partners alternate being in control according to their strengths and weaknesses. One person may take control because he or she is more experienced or equipped to handle a particular circumstance. In many modern marriages, one spouse is better at handling family finances, while the other handles childcare issues. This form of give and take works extremely well in relationships, but partners need to agree on who is really better suited to take control in a given situation.

**interpersonal power**
The ability to influence another in the direction one desires; getting another person to do what one wants.

**complementary relationship**
A relationship in which one partner willingly and continuously cedes power to the other.

**symmetrical relationship**
A relationship characterized by similar control behaviors in partners; partners compete to dominate each other or both relinquish control to the other to avoid making decisions.

**parallel relationship**
A relationship in which power continually shifts from one partner to the other.

### Conflict May Involve Assertive or Aggressive Communication

Sometimes our emotions cause us to communicate aggressively when assertive communication would be preferable. You may think of assertive and aggressive communication as being the same thing, but they're actually different. **Assertive communication** takes the other person's feelings and rights into account; **aggressive communication** doesn't. Let's say that you experience a mix-up with a close friend over plans for the weekend. You get your signals crossed and don't end up going out together. When you next see your friend, you have the choice of responding to your frustration over the situation in a passive, assertive, or aggressive manner. You could be passive and say nothing about the mix-up. While this may sound like an unrealistic response, some people choose not to communicate even when they have been wronged, a phenomenon known as self-silencing.[55] Such a passive approach tends merely to internalize frustration, which may build into a destructive rage that later erupts.

Another option is to blow up at your friend. This is an aggressive, self-oriented approach because it doesn't take into account the rights of the recipient of such communication. Unfortunately, this is the tactic of choice for some people, especially if they have a great deal of anxiety and feel justified taking out their frustrations on others. An aggressive approach rarely achieves one's objectives.

Clearly, an assertive approach to conflict is best—for ourselves and for the people we interact with. It's important to assert yourself and express your perception of a problem to the person who can best correct or clear it up rather than blowing off steam to an innocent bystander or third party. Communicating assertively means that you explain your concerns or cause for disagreement in a direct and firm manner, staying in control of your emotions but not allowing yourself to be bullied or discounted as you take the receiver's rights into account.[56]

An assertive response to the mix-up with your friend might be something like this: "Hey, we were supposed to get together last weekend, but you never called. What happened?" In this statement, you express your perception of the situation, but ask the other person for her or his perception, rather than aggressively saying something in an angry tone that would make the other person defensive, such as "Why did you leave me hanging when we made definite plans?" If the person offers a lame excuse, an assertive follow-up might be, "Well, I just want you to know that I don't like what happened; it's no big deal, but I just hope it doesn't happen again." If you communicate in this manner, you're far more likely to reach a positive resolution to any conflicts than if you behave passively or aggressively.[57]

## Styles of Managing Conflict

Scholars in the communication discipline like to talk about conflict in terms of *management*, meaning that interpersonal communication can help people work through and handle conflict so that something positive results. What's your approach to managing interpersonal conflict: fight or flight? Do you tackle conflict head on or seek ways to remove yourself from it? Most of us don't have a single way of dealing with disagreements, but we do have a tendency to manage conflict by following patterns we learned early in life and have used before.[58]

Researchers have attempted to identify styles of conflict management. One widely accepted approach organizes conflict styles into three types: (1) nonconfrontational; (2) confrontational or controlling; and (3) cooperative (also known as a *solution orientation*).[59]

**Nonconfrontational Style**   One approach to managing conflict is to back off, either avoiding the conflict or giving in to the other person. Such a style often perpetuates a conflict cycle that leads to a chilling or silencing effect in a relationship.[60] Research shows that when conflict arises during problem-solving discussions, people who exhibit a **nonconfrontational style** of responding to the conflict are perceived as

**assertive communication**
Communication that takes a listener's feelings and rights into account.

**aggressive communication**
Self-serving communication that does not take a listener's feelings and rights into account.

**nonconfrontational style**
A conflict management style that involves backing off, avoiding conflict, or giving in to the other person.

incompetent.[61] Five types of responses may be enacted by people who take a nonconfrontational approach to conflict management:

- A *placating* response is an attempt to please. Placaters seek approval, so they typically default into this approach to conflict management because they fear rejection. Because they're uncomfortable with negative emotions, they rarely seem to get angry, quickly agreeing with others to avoid confrontation.
- Another nonconfrontational style is *distracting*, in which people change the subject or make a joke to avoid conflict or stress rather than face the issues directly. They hope that the problem will eventually go away if it can be put off long enough.
- In the style called *computing*, people remove themselves from conflict by remaining aloof and cool. They avoid emotional involvement and refuse to be provoked or ruffled, even under intense pressure. Their detachment allows them to avoid expressing genuine feelings; instead, they respond to emotional situations with impersonal words and phrases rather than with empathy and engagement in the issues at hand.
- *Withdrawing* from conflict, either physically or psychologically, involves something like an "I don't want to talk about it," "It's not my problem," or one-word "Whatever" kind of response. This approach tends to shut down interpersonal communication in conflict situations rather than fostering discussion and negotiation.
- Some people simply *give in* when faced with conflict, believing that surrendering before the conflict escalates is the best option.

David Sipress/Cartoon Bank

*"Well, if it doesn't matter who's right and who's wrong, why don't I be right and you be wrong?"*

## Confrontational Style

Each of us has some need to control others, but some people always want to dominate and make sure that their objectives are achieved. In managing conflict, people with a **confrontational style** have a win–lose philosophy. They want to win at the expense of the other person, to claim victory over their opponents, and to control others. They focus on themselves and usually ignore the needs of others. Confronters often resort to blaming or seeking a scapegoat rather than assuming responsibility for a conflict. "I didn't do it," "Don't look at me," and "It's not my fault" are typical responses. If this strategy doesn't work, confronters may try hostile name calling, personal attacks, or threats.

## Cooperative Style

Those who have a **cooperative style** of conflict management view conflict as a set of problems to be solved rather than as a competition in which one person wins and another loses. They work to foster a win–win climate by using the following techniques:[62]

- *Separate the people from the problem.* Leave personal grievances out of the discussion. Describe problems without making judgmental statements about personalities.
- *Focus on shared interests.* Emphasize common interests, values, and goals by asking such questions as "What do we both want?" "What do we both value?" "Where do we already agree?"
- *Generate many options to solve the problem.* Use brainstorming and other techniques to generate alternative solutions.
- *Base decisions on objective criteria.* Try to establish standards for an acceptable solution to a problem. These standards may involve costs, timing, and other factors.

VERBAL

**confrontational style**
A win–lose approach to conflict management in which one person wants control and to win at the expense of the other.

**cooperative style**
A conflict management style in which conflict is viewed as a set of problems to be solved rather than as a competition in which one person wins and another loses.

# **RE**CAP

## CONFLICT MANAGEMENT STYLES

| Nonconfrontational | A person avoids conflict by placating (agreeing), distracting, computing (becoming emotionally detached), withdrawing from conflict, or giving in to another person. |
|---|---|
| Confrontational | A person wants to manipulate others by blaming and making threats; this approach sets up a win–lose framework. |
| Cooperative | A person seeks mutually agreeable resolutions to manage differences and works within a win–win framework. A cooperative approach<br>• Separates people from problems.<br>• Focuses on shared interests.<br>• Generates many options to solve problems.<br>• Bases decisions on objective criteria. |

## Conflict Management Skills

As we saw in the previous section, nonconfrontational and confrontational styles of conflict management do not solve problems effectively, nor do they foster healthy long-term relationships. The skills we review here are those we touched on in our discussion of the cooperative style.[63]

Managing conflict, especially emotionally charged conflict, isn't easy. Even with a fully developed set of skills, you shouldn't expect to melt tensions and resolve disagreements instantaneously. The following skills can, however, help you generate options that promote understanding and provide a framework for cooperation.

**Manage Emotions**   For weeks, you've been working on a group project for an important class; your group has a firm deadline that the professor imposed. You submitted your portion of the project to your group members two weeks ago. Today you check in with the group for a progress report and discover that very little has been done. The project isn't much further along than when you completed your portion two weeks ago. Your grade is on the line; you feel angry and frustrated. How should you respond? You may be tempted to march into the next group meeting and scream at your classmates. You might consider going to the professor and complaining. Our best advice is this: Try to avoid taking action when you're in such an emotional state. You may regret what you say, and you will probably escalate the conflict, making the situation worse.

Often the first sign that we're in a conflict situation is a combined feeling of anger, frustration, and fear that sweeps over us. Emotions aroused in us during conflict situations are understandable and to be expected. As psychotherapist Jeffrey Rubin explains, "Your feelings are your reality," meaning that the feelings conflict generates are real and shouldn't be ignored.[64] In actuality, anger is not the predominant emotion generated by conflict. Many of us are unprepared for the aching, lonely, sad, and forlorn feelings that can emerge in conflict.[65] As tall an order as it is, it's important to try to understand the other person's feelings and to take the emotion of the situation seriously.[66] Here are some specific strategies you can draw on when an intense emotional response to conflict clouds your judgment and decision-making skills:[67]

- *Select a mutually acceptable time and place to discuss a conflict.* If you're upset or tired, you're at risk for an emotion-charged confrontation. If you ambush someone with an angry attack, you can't expect her or him to be in a productive frame of mind. Give yourself time to cool off before you try to resolve a conflict. In the case of the group project, you could call a meeting for later in the week. By that time, you could gain control of your feelings and think things through.
- *Plan your message.* If you approach someone to discuss a disagreement, take care to organize your message, perhaps even on paper. Identify your goal and determine what outcome you would like; don't barge in unprepared and dump your emotions on the other person.
- *Monitor nonverbal messages.* Your nonverbal communication plays a key role in establishing an emotional climate. Monitor nonverbal messages—your own and those of others—to help defuse an emotionally charged situation. Speak calmly, use direct eye contact, and maintain a calm facial expression and body position to signal that you wish to collaborate rather than control.

- *Avoid personal attacks, name calling, profanity, and emotional overstatement.* Threats and derogatory language can turn a small conflict into an all-out war. When people feel attacked, they usually respond by becoming defensive in an effort to protect themselves. It's also important to avoid exaggerating your emotions. If you say you're irritated or annoyed rather than furious, you can still communicate your feelings, but you will take the sting out of your description.

- *Use self-talk.* Let's go back to the problem of the group project. At the next meeting, what if a member lashes out at you, suggesting that you're a big part of the problem? Instead of lashing back at that person, the best course would be to pause, take a slow deep breath, and say to yourself, "I could get really mad, but that won't make things better. I'll respond calmly and coolly, so we keep the problem in proportion." You may think that talking to yourself is an eccentricity, but thoughts are directly linked to feelings. The messages we tell ourselves play a major role in how we feel and respond to others.[68]

**Manage Information**  Because uncertainty, misinformation, and misunderstanding are often by-products of conflict and disagreement, skills that promote mutual understanding are important components of cooperative conflict management. The following skills can help you enhance the quality of communication during conflict:

- *Clearly describe the conflict-producing events.* Instead of blurting out complaints in random order, try to deliver a brief, well-organized presentation. Public speaking teachers recommend that, for certain speech topics, you describe events in chronological order. The same technique works well when describing a conflict. In our example of the group project situation, you could offer your perspective on what created the conflict, sequencing the events and describing them dispassionately so that your fellow group members end up sharing your understanding of the problem.

- *"Own" your statements by using descriptive "I" language.* Use "I" language instead of "you" language to create a supportive climate. "I feel upset when it seems as if little is getting done and we're running the risk of not making our deadline" is an example of an "I" statement you could say to your group members. The statement describes your feelings as your own and keeps the issue manageable. Saying

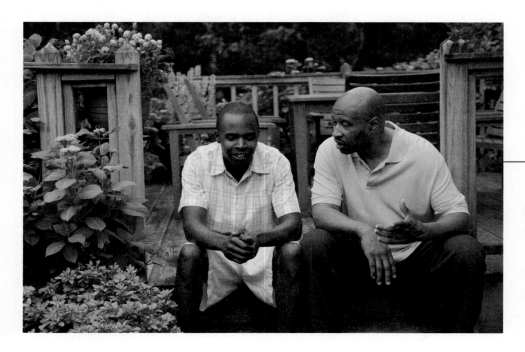

Managing your emotions by monitoring your self-talk, verbal messages, and nonverbal cues can help you resolve conflict more productively. How do you ethically communicate your position in a conflict while adapting your emotional messages to the other person and the situation?

Jack Hollingsworth/Thinkstock

"You folks aren't pulling your weight and you're gonna blow our deadline" has an accusatory sting that will likely make members defensive, escalating the conflict. Also notice that, in the second statement, you don't take any responsibility for the problem but suggest that it belongs to several other people. This "ganging-up" approach almost always heightens people's defensiveness.

- *Use effective listening skills.* Managing information is a two-way process. Whether you're describing a conflict situation to someone or that individual is bringing a conflict to your attention, good listening skills are invaluable. Give your full attention to the speaker and make a conscious point of tuning out your internal messages. Harvard psychologist Howard Gardner suggests that people "listen charismatically," which involves paying careful attention to what is not said (nonverbal cues) and rephrasing what conflict partners say in a tentative, nonthreatening manner.[69]

- *Check your understanding of what others say and do.* Checking perceptions is vital when emotions run high. If you're genuinely unsure about facts, issues, or major ideas addressed during a conflict, ask questions to help you sort through them instead of barreling ahead with solutions. Then summarize your understanding of the information, checking key points to make sure that you comprehend the message.

**Manage Goals**    Conflict is goal-driven; both individuals involved in an interpersonal conflict want something. And, for some reason—competitiveness, scarce resources, or lack of understanding—the goals appear to be in conflict. To manage conflict, it's important to seek an accurate understanding of these goals and identify where they overlap. Here are a couple of techniques to help you accomplish just that:

- *Identify your goal and your partner's goal.* After you describe, listen, and respond, your next task should be to identify what you would like to have happen. What is your goal? Most goal statements can be phrased in terms of wants or desires. Continuing with the group project example, you express to your fellow group members your goal of turning the project in on time. Next, it's useful to identify the goals of other people involved in the conflict. Use effective describing, listening, and responding skills to determine what each conflict partner wants. Obviously, if goals are kept hidden, it will be difficult to resolve the conflict.

- *Identify where your goals and your partner's goals overlap.* Authorities on conflict negotiation stress the importance of focusing on shared goals when seeking to manage differences.[70] Suppose that after you explain your goal about the project deadline, another group member states that her or his goal is to make the project the best it possibly can be. These goals may be compatible, so you've identified a commonality that can help unify the group rather than keep it splintered. But what if that goal of making the project the best means that your group will have to ask the professor for an extension on the deadline? Now you may have competing goals, but at least you've identified a central part of the problem. Framing the problem as "how can we achieve our mutual goal" rather than arguing over differences of opinion moves the discussion to a more productive level.

**Manage the Problem**    If you can view conflicts as problems to be solved rather than battles to be won or lost, you will better manage the issues that confront you in your relationships with others. Of course, not all conflicts can be easily managed and resolved. But using a rational, logical approach to conflict management is more effective than emotionally flinging accusations and opinions at someone. Structuring a disagreement as a problem to solve helps manage emotions that often erupt; a problem-solving orientation to conflict also helps keep the conversation focused on issues rather than personalities.

The problem-solving process is relatively simple: Define the problem, analyze the problem, generate possible solutions, evaluate the pros and cons of the solutions under consideration, and then select the solution that is agreeable to all concerned. The best solution is one that meets the goals of the persons involved in the conflict. As you apply the problem-solving approach to managing conflict, consider the following suggestions:

- *Define the problem before trying to solve it.* When a problem needs to be solved, we typically want to head directly for solutions. Resist that temptation. Before blurting out solutions, realize that you're more likely to reach agreement on the solution to a problem if you each understand the specific issues that trigger the problem.

- *Think of lots of possible solutions. The more possible solutions you identify and consider, the greater the likelihood that the conflict will be managed successfully.* If you're just batting around one or two solutions, you're limiting your options in managing the conflict. Rather than making the conflict a tug of war with only two ends of the rope pulling against each other, consider multiple creative strategies for achieving what you both want.

- *Systematically discuss the pros and the cons of the possible solutions together.* After you have a list of possible solutions, honestly identify advantages and disadvantages of each solution. How do you know which is the best solution? If you discussed the goals that each of you seeks to achieve, you're on your way to developing a vision of the future that can help you sort out the advantages and disadvantages of the solutions you're considering. Determine which solution or combination of solutions best achieves the goals you and your feuding partner are trying to accomplish.

We emphasize again that there are no surefire techniques that will manage or resolve the interpersonal conflicts that will inevitably occur even in the best of relationships. In reality, you don't simply manage your emotions and then march easily on to coolly communicate your ideas, followed by neatly sorting out goals and then rationally solving the problem that created the conflict. Conflict management is messier than this step-by-step process suggests. Our suggestions for managing emotions, information, goals, and the problem won't eliminate conflict from your life. Turning conflicts into problems to solve and seeking mutually agreeable solutions may, however, provide the structure necessary to help you manage conflict constructively.

# STUDY GUIDE:
## Review, Apply, and Assess Your Knowledge and Skill

## REVIEWING What You Know

### The Importance of Relationships: Friends, Family, and Colleagues
p. 192

Relationships of all types are important in our lives, but those with friends, family, and colleagues are most critical to our overall enjoyment. The five Communication Principles for a Lifetime can be applied to each form of relationship and can improve how we communicate interpersonally with others.

### Stages of Relationship Development
p. 196

Research has determined that relationships, particularly intimate or romantic ones, tend to develop in stages of escalation and de-escalation. Interpersonal communication is affected by the stage of a relationship; in turn, movement through the stages is facilitated by interpersonal communication.

The five stages of relational escalation are (1) pre-interaction awareness, (2) initiation, (3) exploration, (4) intensification, and (5) intimacy.

The six stages of relational de-escalation are (1) turmoil, (2) stagnation, (3) de-intensification, (4) individualization, (5) separation, and (6) post-interaction.

#### Terms to Know

| | | | |
|---|---|---|---|
| Pre-Interaction Awareness Stage | p. 197 | Stagnation Stage | p. 198 |
| Initiation Stage | p. 197 | De-Intensification Stage | p. 198 |
| Exploration Stage | p. 197 | Individualization Stage | p. 198 |
| Intensification Stage | p. 197 | Separation Stage | p. 198 |
| Intimacy Stage | p. 197 | Post-Interaction Stage | p. 199 |
| Turmoil Stage | p. 198 | Postdissolutional Relationship | p. 200 |

### Tensions in Relationships: The Dialectical Perspective
p. 200

One approach to studying interpersonal communication in relationships is the relational dialectics perspective, which examines sets of tensions that emerge in ongoing relationships, especially romantic or intimate ones. Three tensions are particularly critical:

- Integration–separation: Autonomy versus connection
- Stability–change: Predictability versus novelty
- Expression–privacy: Openness versus closedness.

#### Terms to Know

| | | | |
|---|---|---|---|
| Relational Dialectics | p. 200 | Cyberinfidelity | p. 201 |

### Managing Interpersonal Conflict
p. 202

Conflict is inevitable in relationships and is rooted in interpersonal communication. Interpersonal conflict occurs when two people cannot agree on a way to meet their needs. Conflict can be constructive or destructive in a relationship, and it occurs in multiple forms: pseudoconflict, simple conflict, ego conflict, serial arguments, and irresolvable (intractable) conflict.

Conflict may manifest itself in assertive communication or aggressive communication. Conflict involves power, which can lead to three forms of relationships: complementary, symmetrical, and parallel.

Three general styles of managing conflict—nonconfrontational, confrontational, and cooperative—have emerged in research. When managing conflict, it's important to manage your emotions, manage the information surrounding the dispute at hand, manage competing goals that may be the root of the problem, and manage the problem rather than the emotion of the situation or the people involved in the conflict.

### Terms to Know

# APPLYING Principles for a Lifetime

### Principle One:
### Be aware of your communication with yourself and others.

- Know your own interests, likes, and dislikes as you expand your circle of friends.
- Awareness and an understanding of self begin in your family.
- Perception checking with colleagues increases your awareness of yourself and your workplace.
- The first stage of relational escalation, the pre-interaction awareness stage, begins with an awareness of the self and the other person you're interested in.
- Be aware that relationships continue to affect our self-concepts even after they end.
- It's important to know your conflict management style, especially if your style differs from other conflict partners'.
- Self-talk is appropriate in conflict, because it can help you manage your emotions and think clearly.
- Check your perceptions of a conflict with trusted others.
- Be aware of your own and others' goals in conflict situations.

### Principle Two:
### Effectively use and interpret verbal messages.

- Language patterns we learn as children in our families stay with us into adulthood.
- People in advanced stages of relationships tend to use verbal communication to discuss topics that typically aren't discussed in early stages.
- Relational partners should use effective verbal communication to work through relational dialectics, or tensions in a relationship.
- Assertive communication takes a receiver's rights into account; aggressive communication doesn't.
- Managing the verbal expression of your emotions in conflict situations is an important skill.
- Plan your message carefully in a conflict situation.
- Avoid personal attacks, name calling, profanity, and emotional overstatements in conflict situations.
- Use "I" language instead of "you" language in a conflict so as to lessen defensiveness.

## Principle Three:
### Effectively use and interpret nonverbal messages.

- Nonverbal immediacy behaviors, such as eye contact and forward body lean, are important in the maintenance of friendships, family relationships, and workplace relationships.
- People in advanced stages of relationships tend to display nonverbal behaviors that typically aren't in evidence in early stages.
- Nonverbal skills are important in your first conversations with people as you attempt to establish and escalate relationships.
- Nonverbal immediacy cues diminish when a relationship is in de-escalation.
- Monitor and adapt your nonverbal behaviors in conflict situations.
- Monitor the nonverbal cues of conflict partners.

## Principle Four:
### Listen and respond thoughtfully to others.

- Listening is important in friendships and family relationships.
- Listening and responding appropriately are key skills that potential employers value.
- Destructive conflict is characterized by a lack of listening.
- Conflict often escalates because the parties don't listen to one another; continue to listen, even if you feel yourself becoming emotional in the conflict.

## Principle Five:
### Appropriately adapt messages to others.

- It's important to learn to adapt our communication in friendships, family relationships, and workplace relationships.
- Adaptation is critical for couples who face relational tensions.
- In conflict situations, partners often have to adapt to each other and admit that they were wrong. Destructive conflict often involves a reluctance to adapt to the other person and see the problem from her or his point of view.
- Be flexible and adapt to other cultures' approaches to conflict; don't assume that your home culture's approach to conflict management is applicable in conflicts with members of other cultural groups.
- After checking your perceptions of a conflict with trusted others, adapt your communication accordingly.
- One way to adapt in a conflict is to look for overlaps between your goals and the goals of your conflict partner.

# ASSESSING
## Your Skill

## Am I an Aggressive or an Assertive Communicator?

Sometimes it's hard to discern the difference between assertive and aggressive communication. To gain some practice, consider the following situations. For each one, first generate aggressive and inappropriate communication. Then rethink the situation and generate an assertive form of communication that would be more effective. We've provided an example to get you started.

*Sample Situation:* You're expecting a raise at work but find out that a coworker, who has less time on the job than you, received a raise and you didn't.

*Aggressive Communication:* You interrupt a staff meeting that your boss is holding, storm about the room, and demand an explanation of why you didn't receive the expected raise.

*Assertive Communication:* You make an appointment with your boss for a meeting. At the meeting, you calmly ask the boss to assess your value to the company, leading up to the question of why you didn't receive the expected raise.

*Situation:* Two people have been in a monogamous dating relationship for several months when one partner finds out that the other person has cheated.

*Situation:* A student receives a disappointing grade on a paper. After reading the papers of a few other classmates and finding that lesser quality papers received higher grades, the student decides to confront the teacher about the grade.

## What's My Style?

In intimate relationships where a great deal is on the line, knowing how you usually tend to handle conflict, as well as how your partner handles it, can save you some major heartbreak. Below, we give you a sample situation and three conflict responses corresponding to the three conflict styles: nonconfrontational, confrontational, and cooperative. Then we list other hypothetical conflict situations, and you should provide responses to the situations for each category of conflict management style. (If you're really brave, pose these same situations to your relational partner and compare your responses to hers or his. That exercise can lead to a constructive, proactive discussion about how to handle conflict in your relationship.)

## Conflict Situation 1

Your roommate is *wild*, partying every night, coming home late, and disrupting your study time and your sleep. This behavior is starting to affect your ability to get your schoolwork done and concentrate on your studies. You're not a fuddy-duddy, but you're not a nightly partier either. How do you communicate in response to this conflict situation?

## Nonconfrontational Response

Ignore it. It's not my problem; it's my roommate's life to live as he (she) pleases. If I bring up my objections to my roommate's behavior, the situation will escalate and get worse, and I'll regret mentioning anything in the first place.

## Confrontational Response

I have rights; I live in this place and pay my fair share of the rent, so I should be able to have some peace and quiet so at least one of us doesn't flunk out of college. When my roommate comes home, I'm going to lay down the law on the late-night partying. If the problem persists, I'll threaten to move out.

## Cooperative Response

My roommate and I both have rights because we both live in this apartment. When my roommate is sober and alone here at the apartment, not with a group of his (her) partying friends, I'll bring up the problem and ask for solutions we can both live with. I want to respect my friend's right to enjoy life, but set limits so my goals can also be reached.

## Conflict Situation 2

You work part time at a restaurant near campus. Thus far the managers have been flexible and understanding about your class schedule and commitments at the university, but now—just when you've got three exams and two papers coming up—they decide to load you up with extra hours. You need this job and want to keep it, so how do you communicate to address the conflict between what you can do and what management wants you to do?

**Nonconfrontational Response:**

**Confrontational Response:**

**Cooperative Response:**

## Conflict Situation 3

You've been dating someone fairly steadily for a few months, but have recently developed a romantic interest in a classmate. You'd like to keep dating your current relational partner, but renegotiate your relationship so that you can start hanging out with other people, like the attractive classmate. How do you communicate to manage this situation?

**Nonconfrontational Response:**

**Confrontational Response:**

**Cooperative Response:**

- **MyCommunicationLab** Watch videos related to this chapter, including *Raised by Wolves*; review the material; and complete an exercise in letting go of past conflict. <www.mycommunicationlab.com> (Access code required.)

- **Mediation** Perhaps you've heard of someone "going to mediation." Centers for mediation services are springing up with increasing frequency across the country. When people in conflict cannot resolve that conflict, they may turn to mediation before taking a more formal (and expensive) step, such as going to court. Many universities now offer mediation services for students, faculty, and staff members. The Ombuds Office at Stanford University defines mediation as a "voluntary meeting of disputing parties to attempt to reach their own solution with the help of a neutral person." Texas State University's Mediation Program works with such issues as roommate grievances, problems within student organizations, and graduate student issues. This program engages trained faculty and staff from the university as mediators. To read more about sample university mediation programs and services, visit these websites:

    <www.fss.txstate.edu> or <www.hr.txstate.edu> (Texas State University–San Marcos)
    <www.student.virginia.edu/~mediate> (University of Virginia)
    <www.oscr.umich.edu/~sdrp> (University of Michigan)
    <www.campus-adr.org> (Wayne State University)

# WEB RESOURCES for More Review, Application, and Assessment

The best way to have a good idea is to have a lot of ideas.

LINUS PAULING

# **Chapter** OUTLINE

- Groups and Teams Defined
- Group and Team Types
- Group and Team Dynamics
- Group and Team Development
- Study Guide: Review, Apply, and Assess Your Knowledge and Skill

# **Chapter** OBJECTIVES

After studying this chapter, you should be able to

1. Define and note similarities and differences between a group and a team.
2. Identify and describe types of small groups.
3. Identify and appropriately perform task and social roles in groups and teams.
4. Describe group rules and norms.
5. Define and differentiate between status and power.
6. List strategies to enhance group cohesiveness.
7. Recognize group and team interaction patterns.
8. Identify the four stages of group development.

© Corbis Bridge/Alamy

# 9 | **Understanding Group and Team Performance**

Do you like working with others in groups? Although you may be one of those people who relish working on team projects and going to meetings, many people don't like collaborating with others. Here are some typical sentiments people sometimes have about working in groups:

> To be effective, a committee should be made up of three persons. But to get anything done, one member should be sick and another absent.

> A committee is a group of people who individually can do nothing and who collectively decide nothing can be done.

> A group task force is a collection of the unfit chosen from the unwilling by the incompetent to do the unnecessary.

Whether you are one of those people who likes group work or one who finds it frustrating and a waste of time, evidence suggests that groups are here to stay. Human beings collaborate.[1] We are raised in groups, educated in groups, and entertained in groups; we worship in groups and work in groups. Today's technology makes it easier for us to collaborate in teams, even when we're not meeting face to face. There is evidence that most of you reading this book will spend about one-third of your time on the job working in groups or teams and attending meetings or preparing for meetings.[2] And if you aspire to upper-management leadership positions, you'll spend up to two-thirds of your time in meetings.[3] One study found that more than 80 percent of organizations use teams to accomplish a major portion of the work.[4] Your work will be based on that kindergarten skill called "getting along with others."

To help you with the inevitable group and team projects that will come your way, this chapter offers descriptions of how groups and teams work. In the next chapter, we'll offer specific strategies for improving group and team performance. As we examine concepts and strategies of group skills and theories, we'll remind you how the core of group communication research can be discussed in terms of the five principles we've used to frame our presentation of human communication:

1. *Be aware of your communication with yourself and others.* Your awareness of your own behavior and the behavior of other group members is often the first step in understanding why you and other group members behave as you do and adjusting your behavior for improved group performance.
2. *Effectively use and interpret verbal messages.* The verbal messages you and other group members use are pivotal in shaping the roles you assume and how the group accomplishes its work.

We are raised and educated in groups, and continue to communicate in groups and teams throughout our lives, so strengthening your group communication skills now will provide lasting benefits.

© Tetra Images/Alamy

3. *Effectively use and interpret nonverbal messages.* The social climate of a group is influenced by the way group members behave nonverbally; eye contact, tone of voice, facial expression, and the use of space and time influence what it feels like to be in a group.
4. *Listen and respond thoughtfully to others.* How group members interact (or don't interact) is directly shaped by group members' skill in listening and responding to what others say and do. One survey found that effective listening was the skill most valued by those who work in groups and teams.[5]
5. *Appropriately adapt messages to others.* The ability to modify messages and adjust to the behavior of others is especially important when communicating with three or more people in a small group.

# Groups and Teams Defined

What makes a group a group? Is a collection of people waiting for an elevator a group? How about students assigned to a class project—do they meet the technical definition of a group? And what about the term *team*? Teams are often viewed as a management innovation that can improve both productivity and morale. Is there a difference between a group and a team? By exploring these questions, you can better understand what groups and teams do and develop strategies for improving group and team performance.

## Communicating in Small Groups

A **small group** consists of three to fifteen people who share a common purpose, feel a sense of belonging to the group, and exert influence on one another.[6] Let's look at this definition more closely.

**A Group Consists of a Small Number of People**  A small group generally needs at least three people. Two people do not usually exhibit the characteristics of group behavior. A group is not *small* anymore when more than fifteen people meet together, however. In a larger group, it can become difficult for all members to participate, and a few members often will monopolize the discussion. A large group frequently operates as a collection of subgroups rather than as a single body. Large groups need formal rules, such as parliamentary procedure, to provide structure that will help the group stay focused on the task at hand.

**A Group Has a Common Purpose**  To be a group, people need to be united by a common goal or purpose. They must all seek the same thing. A collection of people waiting for an elevator may all want to go somewhere, but they probably haven't organized their efforts so that they all are going to the same place. If you are assigned to a class project by an instructor, your classmates do have a common goal—to complete the project and earn a good grade. This class-project group would meet our definition of a group.

**Group Members Feel a Sense of Belonging**  To be a group, the members must realize that they are part of the group. Again, people waiting for the elevator doors to open probably do not feel an obligation to others around them. Group members develop a sense of identity with their group. They know who is in their group and who is not in the group.

**Group Members Exert Influence on Others in the Group**  When you are in a group, your presence and participation influence other people in the group. Group members are interdependent; what one group member says or does affects other group members. Your comments and even your silence help shape what the group does next. Your nonverbal messages have a powerful effect on personal

**small group**
Three to fifteen people who share a common purpose, feel a sense of belonging to the group, and exert influence on one another.

relationships. Each member of a group potentially has some influence on others. Even silence, facial expressions, and eye contact (or lack of it) affect what the group does.

**Small group communication** is the transactive process of creating meaning among three to fifteen people who share a common purpose, feel a sense of belonging to the group, and exert influence on one another. Communicating in small groups is sometimes a challenge because of the potential for misunderstanding. But don't assume that working in a group will inevitably be a frustrating experience. People accomplish much when working together. As anthropologist Margaret Mead said, "Never doubt that a small group of concerned citizens can change the world. Indeed, it's the only thing that ever has." In this chapter and the next, we'll provide concepts and strategies to enhance the quality of your collaborations with others.

## Communicating in Teams

Most of us have participated on a sports team at some time. The goal of a sports team is to win the game or competition. A work team has some of the same characteristics as a sports team.[7] Instead of winning the game, the goal may be to get the contract, build the best mousetrap, or achieve some other objective. A **team** is a coordinated group of people organized to work together to achieve a specific, common goal.[8]

Often the terms *team* and *group* are used interchangeably. Is there a difference? Yes. Given the increased importance teams have in the workforce today, it's important to know precisely how groups and teams are different from each other.[9] Although both groups and teams are made up of a small number of people who work to achieve a goal, teams are often structured deliberately to achieve the goal. Also, teams spend a great deal of time coordinating their efforts to accomplish the goal.[10] Every team is a group, but not every group is highly organized or coordinated enough to meet the definition of a team. Let's consider several specific characteristics of teams.

### Teams Develop Clearly Defined Responsibilities for Team Members
On a sports team, most team members have specifically assigned duties, such as shortstop, pitcher, quarterback, or fullback. On a work team, team members' duties and roles are usually explicitly spelled out. Team members may perform more than one function or role, but they nonetheless have well-defined duties.[11]

### Teams Have Clearly Defined Rules for Team Operation
Team members develop explicit rules for how the work should be done. A rule is a followable prescription for acceptable behavior.[12] Just as there are written rules in the game of Monopoly, there are usually explicit rules for how a team will function. For example, a team may establish a rule that a member who will be absent from a meeting must tell another team member beforehand. Team members know what the rules are and know how those rules affect the team.

### Teams Develop Clear Goals
A third way to characterize a team is to look at the importance and specificity of the team goal.[13] A team goal is usually stated in such a way that the goal can be measured: to win the game, to sell more cornflakes than the competition, or to get to the North Pole before anyone else, for example.

### Teams Develop a Way of Coordinating Their Efforts
Team members spend time discussing how to accomplish the goals of the team. Their work is coordinated to avoid duplication of effort.[14] A sports team spends considerable time practicing how to work together. Watching a sports team at work is like watching a choreographed dance. Team members have developed a system of working together rather than at cross-purposes. Just as a football team develops a list of the plays to get the ball down the field, a work team develops collaborative strategies to achieve its goal.

Although we have differentiated between groups and teams, don't get the idea that they are completely exclusive entities. Both groups and teams are made up of

**small group communication**
The transactive process of creating meaning among three to fifteen people who share a common purpose, feel a sense of belonging to the group, and exert influence on each other.

**team**
A coordinated group of people organized to work together to achieve a specific common goal.

# Communication&ETHICS

## How Far Would You Go to Achieve a Team Goal?

Teams have a strong sense of purpose and a well-structured, clear, and coordinated plan to achieve the goals of the team. Without a clear goal, teams falter. But sometimes you may be part of a team whose goal or means of achieving the goal you don't support. Suppose, for example, that you are a valued and skilled member of a soccer team that has a "win at all costs" mentality. The team wants to win so badly that team members bend some of the rules to enhance their chance of winning: They knowingly allow someone to play who, because of poor grades, is not eligible. Team members let the person play because the person's skill will increase the team's chances of winning. You're the only person who seems concerned about the rule violation. What would you do? Would you continue to participate on the team and not let the other members of the team down, even though permitting an illegal player to participate violates your own ethical standards? Do the ends justify the means? Is winning more important than following the rules?

Here's another example: What if it's not a sports team but a work group? Assume that you're a salesperson and part of a sales team. To get a raise in salary, everyone on the team has to meet the sales goal assigned to the team. One team member consistently lies to customers about the company's product to get a sale; that team member's sales success helps make the whole team look good in terms of sales, but look bad in terms of ethics. What would you do? Would you keep quiet and enjoy the benefits of being part of a "successful" sales team? Or would you bring the unethical behavior of the team member to the attention of your supervisor, even though it would place other team members in jeopardy for knowingly "going along to get along"? Are team goals more important than individual ethical standards?

a small number of people striving to achieve a goal. Since every team is a small group, whenever we refer to a team we are also suggesting that it's a group as well. Think of groups and teams as existing on a continuum; some deliberations will make the people seem more like a group, whereas other behavior—a more coordinated and structured process, with clear rules and explicit goals—will make the people appear to be a team.

## When Not to Collaborate in Groups and Teams

Although we've joined the chorus singing the praises of working in groups and teams, at times one head may be better than two or more. In what situations may it be best to not collaborate? The following are four situations in which it is better to work individually rather than collectively:[15]

- *When the group or team has limited time.* If a very quick decision must be made, delegating an individual to make the decision may be better than convening a group. Sometimes you may not have time to gather a group together to discuss options; action may be needed immediately. In times of extreme crisis or emergency, it may be best to have a leader ready to provide some initial direction.
- *When an expert already has the answer.* You don't need a group to hash through the process of finding an answer if an individual already has the answer. If you want to know what tomorrow's weather will be, ask a meteorologist. Don't collaboratively puzzle through questions that can be readily answered by someone else.

# RECAP

## COMPARING GROUPS AND TEAMS

| | Groups | Teams |
|---|---|---|
| Roles and Responsibilities | Individual responsibilities of group members may not always be explicitly defined. | Expectations, roles, and responsibilities of team members are clearly developed and discussed. |
| Rules | Rules are often not written down or formally developed; rules evolve, depending on the group's needs. | Rules and operating procedures are clearly identified to help the team work efficiently and effectively. |
| Goals | Group goals may be discussed in general terms. | Clearly spelled out goals are the focus of what the team does. |
| Methods | Group members may or may not decide to divide the work among group members. | Team members develop clear methods of collaborating and coordinating their efforts to achieve the team's goals. |

- *When the information is available from other research sources.* Using the power of the Internet, you can find vast amounts of information. If you want a bit of data, a specific date, or more information about something, doing individual research may be better than commissioning a group, team, or task force to get the answers. Some groups find it useful for individual members to gather information and then meet with the rest of the group to analyze and discuss the information. But if you just need information and need it fast, click your mouse or head to the library.

- *When the group or team is entrenched in unmanageable conflict.* We don't suggest that you avoid group and team conversations just because they may arouse conflict and disagreement. In fact, it's normal for groups to experience conflict. An absence of conflict can be a sign of an ineffective group. But if the conflict is so entrenched that group members can't listen and thoughtfully respond, it may be advisable to take a break from group deliberations. Convening a dysfunctional group or team that can't or won't work together may not be the best way to reach a decision. What may be needed is a more structured conversation, such as mediation or negotiation with a trained facilitator, to help sort things out. Don't give up on a group or team just because there is conflict. But if the conflict is so pervasive that no progress is likely, seek other ways of moving forward rather than having the group engage in more contentious talk.

# Group and Team Types

**primary group**
A group, such as a family, that exists to fulfill basic human needs.

**social group**
A group that exists to provide opportunities for group members to enjoy an activity in the company of others.

Most groups can be classified into two general categories—primary and secondary. Groups can further be described within these broad categories in terms of their goals and functions.

## Primary Groups

A **primary group** exists to fulfill basic human needs. It's called a primary group because the group meets a primary human need to socialize or just be together. Two types of primary groups are family groups and social groups.

Universal UClick

**Family Groups**  Family groups are the most basic of all primary groups. They help us meet primary survival needs for food, shelter, and social contact with others. Although some families may have a family business or have other goals, in most family discussions one person does not whip out an agenda while the rest of the group follows a process to achieve a specific outcome. As in other primary groups, family communication is informal. People talk just because they are together.

**Social Groups**  A **social group** meets just for the enjoyment of interacting with other group members. You undoubtedly have a group of friends who get together just for fun. Like a family group, a social group typically has no formal agenda or schedule. A social group gathers to do something enjoyable; it could be just to talk or something more structured such as to watch a movie. In most cases, people in a social group could still do the activity (eat, travel, play music) without being in a group, but a group makes the experience more enjoyable.

## Secondary Groups

**Secondary groups** are more focused on accomplishing a specific task or goal than are primary groups. Although working in a secondary group can be pleasant, the group's key function is to achieve some task-oriented outcome. Specifically, secondary groups include study groups, therapy groups, problem-solving groups, and focus groups.

**Study Groups**   As a college student, you probably don't need a study group defined for you. A **study group** meets to learn new ideas. Learning theory suggests that you are more likely to learn when you actively participate in the learning process. Students sometimes form study groups because they know that by participating in the give and take of a discussion, they'll be more likely to remember what is discussed. Teachers, too, often assign students to groups as a means of accomplishing what is called *collaborative learning*. Assigning students to small groups and inviting participation is a time-proven strategy to help students learn.

**Therapy Groups**   *Therapy* is treatment designed to solve a personal concern or problem or to resolve an issue. A **therapy group** exists to provide treatment for the personal problems that group members may have. Weight Watchers, Alcoholics Anonymous, and Gamblers Anonymous are examples of therapy groups. The feedback people receive from the therapy group leader and other group members is an important part of the treatment. People gain insight by being in a group with others who have similar needs. We learn about ourselves from the perceptions of others. Therapy groups can be virtual groups. Research has found that therapy-group members who only interact via the Internet still report finding the help they need.[16]

**Problem-Solving Groups**   A **problem-solving group** exists to resolve an issue or overcome an unsatisfactory situation or obstacle and achieve a goal. Problem-solving groups are the most common type of groups in businesses and other organizations. In business, the problem on which a group often focuses is, "How can we overcome

**secondary group**
A group formed to accomplish a specific task or goal.

**study group**
A group that exists to help group members learn new information and ideas.

**therapy group**
A group that provides treatment for problems that group members may have.

**problem-solving group**
A group that meets to seek a solution to a problem and achieve a goal.

Many people find that participating in therapy groups helps them with their problems. What benefits do you get from the primary and secondary groups to which you belong? Do the benefits balance the challenges of group participation for you?

Manchan/Getty Images

# Communication&TECHNOLOGY

## Virtues (and Vices) of Virtual Groups

Chances are that you will work in a **virtual group or team**—a group or team that doesn't meet face to face but is instead connected via some electronic channel. What pluses and minuses might you experience as a member of a virtual team?[17]

### BENEFITS OF WORKING IN VIRTUAL TEAMS

- Virtual teams can save members travel time and expense. Thus, technology can help connect people who might not be able to participate otherwise.
- Virtual teams can develop the same degree of trust among members as face-to-face groups.[18]
- In computer-mediated meetings, ideas can be captured and recorded quickly and accurately.
- Technology can help structure a group's process and keep the group focused.
- Some team members may feel more comfortable sharing ideas electronically—or even anonymously—than they do in person.

### CAUTIONS ABOUT WORKING IN VIRTUAL TEAMS

- Developing trust among group members can take longer than with in-person groups.[19]
- When only some members participate virtually in a team, a special effort must be made to integrate these long-distance members into the fabric of the team.
- The increased speed of information transfer can allow little time for reflection. Thus, technology may sometimes help us make mistakes faster.
- Some group members do not thoroughly evaluate the pros and cons of alternatives when using computer-mediated technology.
- The application of technology does not inherently result in better solutions and decisions. Problems are solved and decisions are made by people.[20]

---

an obstacle to make more money?" A problem-solving group or team in a hospital or health clinic will focus on ways to make people healthy. Most problems boil down to something you want more of or less of. The problem-solving group goal is therefore often to figure out *how* to get more or less of something, such as time, money, or help from others.

**Focus Groups**   A **focus group** is a small group of people who are asked to discuss a particular topic or issue while others, the people who brought the group together, listen. In some ways, a focus-group discussion is like a group interview: The purpose is to listen to group members' ideas and responses to the subject being discussed. One person usually acts as the moderator or facilitator, asking open-ended questions and giving group members a chance to share their views on the subject. Many advertising agencies will present a new advertising campaign to a focus group and then listen to the group members' responses to assess the effectiveness of the campaign. Before launching a new kind of potato chip, for instance, a snack company may use reactions from a focus group to guide it in marketing the new product. Politicians often use focus groups to determine the effectiveness of a political strategy or new policy.

These categories give you a general idea of the goals different groups develop during the course of their existence, but they are not mutually exclusive. In fact, the types of groups we've identified often overlap. You could, for example, be in a study group for a class but, during your conversation, discuss a problem and recommend solutions.

## Working in Real Groups and Teams

Textbooks have a tendency to describe things in tidy ways, which may make it appear as if the world were neatly organized into clear categories and clear-cut definitions. Although we've defined groups and teams and have described distinctly different types of groups—as they operate in real-world businesses and other organizations—real groups and teams don't always neatly fit textbook categories.

**virtual group or team**
A group or team whose members are not together in the same physical location but who are typically connected via an electronic channel such as the Internet, a telephone, or a video conference.

**focus group**
A group that is asked to discuss a particular topic or issue so that others can better understand how the group members respond to the topic or issue presented to them.

It is likely that in today's multitasking workforce *you will be participating in many different types of teams and groups at the same time*. Most people do not belong to just one team at a time or focus all their energy and talent on one primary task. The **bona fide perspective** of groups suggests that the context and boundaries for the groups in which we participate move and change. The term *bona fide* simply means authentic, true, or genuine. Thus, a bona fide perspective is concerned with how groups actually operate in work, school, and other real-world situations.

According to communication scholar Linda Putnam, who has done extensive research and writing about bona fide groups, we need to be more sensitive to how groups really operate in natural settings.[21] Most groups and teams do not work in isolation from other groups; they are connected to and genuinely influenced by what else is happening in the larger organization. If, for example, an organization is losing money and is on a tight budget, the lack of money will affect how a group operates within the organization. Or, if you're working on a group project in your college or university, group members are doing more than just working on one group project. They have lives and are communicating in a number of groups (family, social, study, work) simultaneously. Therefore, Putnam suggests that two elements need to be addressed when considering bona fide groups: (1) how the group is connected to other groups and the organization and (2) how the group operates in relationship to its external context.

How can you apply a bona fide perspective to help you with groups and teams to which you belong? Consider these observations:

- If you're a group or team leader, a bona fide perspective suggests that you need to be aware that the people who work with you have multiple roles and multiple jobs. Just as your instructor needs to remember that you're likely taking more than one class, so should a group or team leader realize that her or his fellow members are working on multiple projects (both individual and collaborative projects) at the same time.
- Remember that the teams you're working with today may not be the same teams you'll be working with tomorrow. Team membership changes. The changing composition of the group may require that the group go through numerous periods of reorientation as new group members come and other go.
- When some members participate in a virtual team via e-mail, video conference (such as Skype), or phone rather than face to face, special effort must be made to integrate these long-distance group members into the fabric of the team.
- Remember that when you work on a group or team task, you're bound by the constraints of the larger organization in which you work. You're not just working in isolation—you're connected to the whole, although all you may experience is the interaction in the group or team in which you're working.

Naturally occurring groups are complex, with changeable boundaries and changeable group members. The bona fide, or authentic, approach reminds us to be realistic when we apply definitions, principles, and practices of group theory to groups and teams.

**bona fide perspective**
A perspective that focuses on how groups actually operate within organizations.

Group members and leaders need to adapt to real-world constraints, including group members' commitments outside the group, and the context in which the group is acting. What adaptations can you suggest to add to those listed here in your text?
BananaStock/Thinkstock

# Group and Team Dynamics

Groups and teams are dynamic; their structure changes. The study of group dynamics includes a discussion of the roles, norms, status, power, and cohesiveness of groups. We'll examine each concept and note how it is related to the five Communication Principles for a Lifetime.

# Roles

Your **role** is the consistent way you communicate with others in a group. It is based on your expectations of yourself and the expectations others place on you. Do you often become a leader of a group, or are you more comfortable just blending in and taking directions from others? Or are you the one who makes sure the group gets the work done instead of just having a good time? There are also group members who seem especially gifted at smoothing conflict and disagreement. Or perhaps there is no typical pattern to what you do in a group; your role depends on the group and who else is in it.

The following are three classic categories of group roles.

### Types of Roles

- **Task roles** are behaviors that help the group achieve its goal and accomplish its work; gathering and sharing research conclusions with the group, taking minutes of meetings, and writing ideas on a chalkboard are examples of task-role behaviors.
- **Social roles** focus on behavior that manages relationships and affects the group climate; these roles help resolve conflict and enhance the flow of communication. Smoothing hurt feelings and helping the group celebrate its accomplishments are examples of social-role behavior.
- **Individual roles** focus attention on the individual rather than the group. They do *not* help the group; they emphasize individual accomplishments and issues rather than those of the entire group. Dominating group discussions to talk about personal issues or concerns, telling frequent jokes that get the group off track, and constantly complaining or whining about how one's individual needs aren't being met are examples of individual roles.

**Leadership Roles**    The role of leader, a person who influences others in the group, is a special kind of role, and more than one person can assume it. Some leaders focus on assisting with the team's task and therefore assume more task roles to get the job accomplished. Other leaders assume more social roles to help manage the quality of relationships in the group. Usually, a person who assumes an individual, self-focused role doesn't emerge as a natural leader. Being overly dominant or aggressive or blocking the team's progress may focus attention on an individual, but such self-focused behavior doesn't wear well over time, and people who focus on themselves rather than the team aren't perceived as effective leaders.

**Specific Roles**    More than sixty-five years ago, Kenneth Benne and Paul Sheats came up with a list of group roles that remains a classic way of dividing up the roles that group and team members typically assume.[22] Table 9.1 (pages 227 and 228) presents a summary of these roles. As you review the roles and their descriptions, note whether you usually assume roles in the task, social, or individual category. Or perhaps you'll see yourself in a variety of roles in all three categories.

As you look at the list of roles in Table 9.1, you may think, "Yes, that's what I usually do. That's the role I usually take." You can probably see roles that fit other group members. Most group members don't assume only one or two roles during group meetings. Most of us assume several roles when we interact in a group. A role is worked out jointly between us and the group, and the roles we assume change depending on which group we're in. There is also evidence that your personality and the personality characteristics of other team members have major influences on team role development.[23] Effective group members adapt their behavior to what is happening or needed in the group. In some groups, your expertise may give you the confidence to give information and share your opinions freely. In other groups, you may assume a role to maintain social harmony and peace.

**Balancing Roles**    What are the best or worst roles to assume? We don't recommend that you assume any individual role; by definition, these roles focus attention on an individual rather than the group. The group needs a balance of task and social roles,

**role**
The consistent way a person communicates with others in a group.

**task role**
A role that helps a group achieve its goal and accomplish its work.

**social role**
A role that helps a group manage relationships and affects the group climate.

**individual role**
A role that focuses attention on the individual rather than on the group.

# Table 9.1
# A Classification of Group Roles

| TASK ROLES | DESCRIPTION | EXAMPLE |
| --- | --- | --- |
| Initiator/contributor | Offers new ideas or approaches to the group; suggests ways of getting the job done. | "How about developing an agenda to help us organize our work?" |
| Information seeker | Asks for additional clarification, facts, or other information that helps the group with the issues at hand. | "Can anyone tell me how many times the university has threatened to close the fraternities and sororities on campus because of the problem of underage drinking?" |
| Opinion seeker | Asks group members to share opinions or express a personal point of view. | "So, what do you all think of the new dress code the school board is proposing?" |
| Information giver | Provides facts, examples, statistics, or other evidence that relates to the task confronting the group. | "Within the past year, the vice president for student affairs has given a special award to three fraternities and one sorority for developing a program to combat underage drinking." |
| Opinion giver | Offers opinions or beliefs about what the group is discussing. | "I think the new school dress code proposed for first graders is unworkable." |
| Elaborator | Provides comments or examples to extend or add to the comments of others. | "Tom, that's a good point. I had the same thing happen to me when my children were attending a private school in New York last year." |
| Coordinator | Clarifies and notes relationships among the ideas and suggestions that have been offered by others. | "Tyrone, your ideas sound a lot like Juanita's suggestion. Juanita, why don't you elaborate on your idea so that Tyrone can decide whether he agrees or disagrees with you?" |
| Orienter | Summarizes what has occurred and seeks to keep the group focused on the task at hand. | "I think we're getting a bit off track here. Let's go back to the issue on the agenda." |
| Evaluator/critic | Assesses the evidence and conclusions that the group is considering. | "How recent are those statistics? I think there are newer figures for us to consider." |
| Procedural technician | Helps the group accomplish its goal by handling tasks such as distributing reports, writing ideas on a chalkboard, or performing other tasks. | "I'll write your ideas on the board as you suggest them. After the meeting, I'll copy them and summarize them in an e-mail message to each of you." |
| Recorder | Makes a written record of the group's progress by writing down specific comments, facts, or the minutes of the meeting. | "I'll take the minutes of today's meeting." |

| SOCIAL ROLES | DESCRIPTION | EXAMPLE |
| --- | --- | --- |
| Encourager | Offers praise and support and confirms the value of other people and the ideas they contribute. | "You're doing a wonderful job." |
| Harmonizer | Manages conflict and mediates disputes among group members. | "Tynesha, you and Mandy seem to be agreeing more than you are disagreeing. Both of you want the same goal. Let's brainstorm some strategies that can help you both get what you want." |

*(continued)*

**Table 9.1** (*continued*)

| SOCIAL ROLES | DESCRIPTION | EXAMPLE |
|---|---|---|
| Compromiser | Resolves conflicts by trying to find an acceptable solution; seeks new alternatives. | "Jane, you want us to meet at 7:00 p.m., and Sue, you'd like us to start at 8:00. What if we started at 7:30? Would that work?" |
| Gatekeeper | Encourages people who talk too much to contribute less and invites those who are less talkative to participate. | "Tim, we've not heard what you think. What do you suggest we do?" |
| Follower | Goes along with the suggestions and ideas of other group members. | "I can support that option. You have summarized the issues about the same way I see them." |
| Emotion expresser | Verbalizes how the group may be feeling about a specific issue or suggestion. | "We seem to be frustrated that we are not making more progress." |
| Group observer | Summarizes the group's progress or lack of progress. | "We are making great progress on all the issues except how much salary we should offer." |
| Tension reliever | Monitors stress within the group and offers suggestions for breaks, using humor or other appropriate strategies. | "Hey, what we need is a good laugh. Here's a joke I saw on the Internet today." |

| INDIVIDUAL ROLES | DESCRIPTION | EXAMPLE |
|---|---|---|
| Aggressor | Deflates or disconfirms the status of other group members or tries to take credit for the work of others. | "Lee, your idea is the pits. We all know that what I suggested two meetings ago is the only way to go." |
| Blocker | Is negative, stubborn, and disagreeable without an apparent reason. | "I just don't like it. I don't have to tell you why. I just don't like it." |
| Recognition seeker | Seeks the spotlight by dwelling on his or her personal accomplishments; seeks the praise of others. | "Don't you remember this was my idea? And say, did you see my picture in the paper? I won the grand prize at the science fair." |
| Self-confessor | Uses the group as a forum to disclose unnecessary personal feelings and personal problems unrelated to the group's task. | "Let me tell you how my parents are so unfair. They won't let me live off campus next year. My parents just don't understand me." |
| Joker | Wants to crack jokes, tell stories, and just have fun instead of focusing on the task or what the group needs. | "Hey, let's forget this project and go to the mall. Then I'll tell you the gossip about Professor Smith. What a kook!" |
| Dominator | Tries to take control of the group, talks too much, and uses flattery or aggression to push his or her ideas off on the group. | "Now, here's what we're going to do: Marcie, you will take notes today; Phil, you go get us some pizza; and Russ, I want you to just sit there in case I need you to run an errand." |
| Special-interest pleader | Seeks to get the group to support a pet project or personal agenda. | "My service club would like it if we would support the new downtown renovation project. I'll stand a good chance at club president if I can get you on board." |
| Help seeker | Seeks to evoke a sympathetic response from others; often expresses insecurity stemming from feelings of low self-worth. | "I don't know if I can participate in this project. I'm not very good with people. I just feel like I don't relate well to others or have many friends." |

instead of attention drawn to an individual. At the same time, however, don't ignore the contributions of group members. One study found that one of the most negative things a group member can do is ignore comments another group member makes, isolating a group member.[24]

What is the proper balance between task and social concerns? Some experts recommend a 60-40 balance between task and social roles.[25] Groups seem to operate most effectively when they avoid an "all work and no play" approach. Conversely, an out-of-balance group that focuses just on having a good time is not going to achieve its task goals. In general, more comments need to be about getting the work done than about having fun or managing the social climate, but also make sure that there are good working relationships among group members. If your group seems unduly focused on the task and members are insensitive to the harmony of the group relationships, the group will not be as effective as it might be.

Use two of the Communication Principles for a Lifetime to help you balance roles.

| | |
|---|---|
| *Principle 1: Be aware of your communication:* | Monitor what roles are being assumed and not assumed in your group. |
| *Principle 5: Adapt appropriately:* | Adapt your behavior to the group's needs by helping meet a need or fill an unfilled role. |

## Rules

As noted both in Chapter 1 and earlier in this chapter, *rules* are followable prescriptions that indicate what behavior is expected or preferred.[26] Rules also clearly specify what behavior is inappropriate. Leaders or members of groups and teams often develop rules that specify how people should behave.

In particular, teams often develop ground rules that help them function more smoothly. **Team ground rules** are a way to talk about the behaviors that are expected of group members. They are important to help manage uncertainty when working with others. Rules are needed to ensure that a team is both efficient and effective. Although most informal groups do not develop explicit, written rules, more formal, highly structured teams may take time to develop such rules as that everyone should attend all meetings, meetings will start on time, and each member should follow through on individual assignments. By college, most students are quite familiar with rules. Making the rules explicit makes it easier to foster appropriate behavior and prevent inappropriate behavior.

## Norms

Although not all groups develop explicit rules, most groups and teams develop norms. **Norms** are general standards that determine what is appropriate and inappropriate behavior in a group. As their name implies, norms reflect what's normal behavior in the group; they influence a variety of group member behaviors, such as the type of language that is acceptable, the casualness of members' clothing, or the acceptability of using first names. Is it normal for group members to raise their hands before speaking in your group? Is it acceptable to move around while the group is in session or to get a cup of coffee while someone is talking?

**Norms and Rules**  How do norms differ from rules? Rules are more explicit. Group and team rules are written down or at least verbalized. Here's an example of a rule: Any member of this team who does not pay his or her dues on time will pay an extra $5 in dues. Norms, on the other hand, are more general standards or expectations that are not as clearly spelled out. It may be a norm in your group that no one uses four-letter words; there's probably no written policy that prohibits expletives and

**team ground rules**
The behaviors that are expected of team members, often spelled out in explicit rules of acceptable behavior developed by team members working together.

**norms**
Standards that determine what is appropriate and inappropriate behavior in a group.

Cultural norms about the use of time are just one source of diversity you may encounter when communicating in groups or teams. How can you start a discussion about group norms?
Evangelos/Shutterstock.com

group members may never have said, "No one should ever use a curse word during our discussions," but even without such specific admonitions, group members don't use offensive or obscene words.

**Sources of Norms**   Norms develop based on norms that you and other team members have experienced in other groups as well as on behavior that occurs naturally as group members interact. If after a couple of meetings no one is uttering a swear word, a norm has begun to gel.

The norms that emerge in a group are also strongly influenced by the larger cultural context in which group members live. Norms relating to how attentive the group is to deadlines and punctuality, for example, are anchored in the overall cultural expectations. Some people approach time from a **monochronic time perspective**; they are more likely to develop norms to do only one thing at a time, to pay attention to deadlines and schedules, and to make plans to use time efficiently. Others prefer a **polychronic time perspective**; they do many things at a time, don't worry about deadlines and schedules, believe relationships are more important than work, change plans frequently, and are less concerned about deadlines than are monochronic individuals.[27] Many people from North America and northern Europe tend to be monochronic; deadlines and timelines are valued.[28] People from Latin America, southern Europe, and the Middle East often tend to be polychronic; deadlines and strict adherence to schedules are less important.[29]

If you find yourself in a group whose members have cultural approaches to time or other norms that are different from yours, what should you do? Consider these suggestions:

- Take time to talk about those differences. Share your concerns and assumptions.
- Don't pounce on other team members and accuse them of being laggards or taskmasters.
- Make the issue a group concern rather than an issue between just one or two people.

Conversation and compromise can accomplish a lot when you find yourself facing cultural differences.

**monochronic time perspective**
Preferring to do one thing at a time, to pay attention to deadlines and schedules, and to use time efficiently.

**polychronic time perspective**
Preferring to do many things at once, to place less emphasis on deadlines and schedules, and to consider relationships to be more important than work and meeting deadlines.

**Enforcing Norms**   Noticing when someone breaks a norm can also help you spot a norm. If a member waltzes into a meeting twenty minutes late and several folks grimace and point toward the clock on the wall, that's a sure sign that a norm has been violated. The severity of the punishment for violating a norm corresponds to the significance of the norm.[30] Mild punishment is usually unspoken—such as silent glances or frowning stares. More serious punishment might include a negative comment about the behavior in front of other group members or even expulsion from the group.

You don't have to worry about whether your group will have norms or not; norms happen. You should, however, monitor the group norms to ensure that your behavior doesn't distract from the work of the group and to notice the possible development of any unproductive group norms (such as spending too much time socializing) that the group should talk about.

## Status

As she walks into the room, all eyes are fixed on her. Group members watch every move. As the chairperson, she has much influence. Without her support, no new issues will come before the board. She has high status. **Status** refers to an individual's importance and prestige. Your status in a group influences to whom you talk, who talks to you, and even what you talk about. Your perceived importance affects both your verbal and your nonverbal messages. A person with high status typically

- Talks more than low-status members.
- Directs comments to other high-status group members.
- Has more influence on the decisions the group makes.
- Is listened to by group members.
- Addresses more comments to the entire group than to individuals.[31]

Because high-status people enjoy more privileges, most people want to be in the "in group"—the group with status and influence. Being aware of status differences can help you predict who talks to whom. If you can discern status differences, you'll also be better able to predict the type of messages communicated. Although some people underestimate their perceived level of status and influence in a group, research suggests that you are probably quite perceptive at knowing your own status level when communicating with others.[32]

But just because a person has status doesn't mean that his or her ideas are good. Some groups get into trouble because they automatically defer to the person with more status without reviewing the validity of the ideas presented. Status influences group communication, but don't let status differences influence your perceptions of and critical thinking about the merit of the ideas presented. Conversely, don't dismiss ideas simply because the person who suggested them doesn't have status or prestige. Focus on the quality of the message, not on the messenger.

## Power

Status refers to perceived importance, whereas power refers to whether the status influences behavior. **Power** is the ability to influence others' behavior. Although status and power often go hand in hand, a group member can have status and still not be able to influence how others behave. People have power if they can affect what

**status**
An individual's importance and prestige.

**power**
The ability to influence other people's behavior.

others do. Their power stems from the resources available to them to influence others. Who does and doesn't have power in a group influences how people relate to one another.

A power struggle often creates ripples of conflict and contention through a group. Power struggles also often focus attention on individual group members rather than on the group as a whole. People with less power tend to participate less in group discussion unless they're trying to gain power. A group that is not power balanced may have problems; the "power people" may dominate the discussion. In any group or team, when one or more members dominate the discussion, the group loses the contributions and insights of others. Research supports the conclusion that groups with equal power distribution usually have better quality outcomes than other groups.[33]

According to a classic discussion of how individuals become powerful, there are five power bases: legitimate, referent, expert, reward, and coercive power. These power bases explain why certain people have power and why others don't.[34]

**Legitimate Power**    You have **legitimate power** if someone elected or appointed you to a position of power. Your power source comes from holding a position of responsibility. The president of your university or college has the legitimate power to establish and implement school policy. U.S. senators and police officers are other examples of people who have legitimate power. A group or team member who has been elected chair or president of the group is given legitimate power to influence how the group operates.

**Referent Power**    You have **referent power** if people like you. Put simply, people we like have more power over us than people we do not like. If you are working on a committee with your best friend, your friend exerts power over you in the sense that you will tend to give more credence to what your friend recommends than to other recommendations. Just the opposite occurs if you are working with someone you don't like; you will be more likely to ignore the advice that comes from someone you don't admire than from someone you do.

**Expert Power**    Knowledge is power. People who have **expert power** are perceived as informed or knowledgeable. They have more influence in a group or team than do people who are perceived as uninformed. Suppose you are working with a group to develop strategies to clean up the river that runs through your town. Your colleague who is majoring in aquatic biology will probably have more power than other, less knowledgeable group members.

**legitimate power**
Power that stems from being elected or appointed to a position of authority.

**referent power**
Power that stems from being liked.

**expert power**
Power derived from having expertise and information.

**reward power**
Power that comes from the ability to provide rewards or favors.

**coercive power**
Power that stems from being able to punish others.

**Reward Power**    People who can grant favors, money, or other rewards have more power than people who can't provide such rewards; those who can bestow rewards have **reward power**. People who have greater power to reward are typically sent more positive, supportive messages than people who don't have the ability to reward others. Someone also has reward power if he or she can take away a punishment or other unpleasant experience. But reward power is effective only if the person being rewarded finds the reward satisfying or useful. What is rewarding to one person may not be rewarding to another person.

**Coercive Power**    You have coercive power if you can punish others. **Coercive**

# RECAP

## TYPES OF POWER

| | |
|---|---|
| Legitimate Power | Power that results from being elected, appointed, or ordained to lead or make decisions for a group or a team. |
| Referent Power | Power that results from being popular and well liked. |
| Expert Power | Power that results from having information or being knowledgeable about issues or ideas. |
| Reward Power | Power that results from having the resources to bestow gifts, money, recognition, or other rewards that group members value. |
| Coercive Power | Power that results from having the ability to punish others. |

**power** is the flip side of reward power. The ability to influence comes from the ability to make others uncomfortable. If someone can cut your salary, lower your grade, demote you, or force you to do unpleasant jobs, that person has coercive power. The power results from the perception that the person with the power will actually use the power. If a person has the authority to punish but group members don't perceive that the person will use this power, there really is no coercive power.

Even though we have categorized power into five different types, don't get the idea that group members may exert just one type of power. In reality, group or team members often have more than one type of power. For example, because a group member may be the elected leader (legitimate power), he or she may also be able to offer more rewards (reward power) or punishments (coercive power).

## Cohesiveness

If you have ever read about the Three Musketeers or seen a movie about them, you know that their motto was "One for all, and all for one." They were a cohesive group—they liked to be around one another. **Cohesiveness** is the degree of attraction that members of a group feel toward one another and the group. In a highly cohesive group, the members feel a high degree of loyalty to one another; the goal of the group is also the goal of the individual. Cohesive group members listen to one another. Members of a cohesive group are more likely to use words and phrases that have a unique meaning to group members than all members of less cohesive groups; they are also more likely to tell "inside jokes"—jokes that mean something only to them.[35]

Groups become cohesive because of a variety of forces that attract people to the group and to one another. Similarity of goals, feelings of genuine liking, and similarity of backgrounds and culture are variables that influence group cohesiveness.

What makes groups and teams cohesive? Table 9.2 summarizes some strategies that enhance group cohesiveness and other strategies that make a group less cohesive. The common element in cohesive groups is the manner in which group members communicate with one another. Cohesiveness is more likely to occur if group members have the opportunity to talk with one another freely about a goal all members have in common and if this interaction increases group members' affection and liking for one another. Teams that have greater control over how they conduct their work are also likely to be more cohesive than other teams.[36]

**cohesiveness**
The degree of attraction group members feel toward one another and toward their group.

## Table 9.2
## Suggestions for Enhancing Group Cohesiveness[37]

| COHESIVE GROUPS | UNCOHESIVE GROUPS |
| --- | --- |
| Talk about the group in terms of "we" rather than "I"; stress teamwork and collaboration. | Emphasize the individual contributions of group members; stress individual accomplishment. |
| Reinforce good attendance at group meetings. | Make little effort to encourage group members to attend every meeting. |
| Establish and maintain group traditions. | Make little effort to develop group traditions. |
| Set clear short-term and long-term goals. | Avoid setting goals or establishing deadlines. |
| Encourage everyone in the group to participate in the group task. | Allow only the most talkative or high-status members to participate in the group task. |
| Celebrate when the group accomplishes either a short-term or a long-term goal. | Discourage group celebration; make sure group meetings are all work and little or no fun. |

Can a group be too cohesive? Yes. If group members are focused only on developing a positive, cohesive relationship to the exclusion of getting their work done, group productivity can suffer. If the group becomes obsessed primarily with having fun and enjoying one another's company, it will produce *less* work. Although usually cohesiveness is a good thing, a group can have too much of a good thing. Strive for group cohesiveness, but balance it with concern for accomplishing the group's task.

## Communication Interaction Patterns

Do you have a Facebook page? If you do or if you're connected to someone else's page, you have a sense of how we form connections with other people. Sometimes you're invited to join someone else's social network. Or you may discover that you have a lot in common with some people and just naturally connect to their pages. Just as you may interact with some people's Facebook pages more than others, when not communicating in cyberspace you communicate with some people more than others. When you participate in a group or team, you'll find that you talk more with some people than with others. Group communication scholars have studied and classified the various distinct patterns that emerge when people talk to one another in groups.[38] A **communication interaction pattern** is a consistent pattern of who talks to whom. Some groups have an equal distribution of interaction among group members, whereas others develop distinct patterns of interaction.[39]

In most groups, we often speak to specific people in the group rather than to the group as a whole. We also tend to speak to people who have power and status, more often directing communication to those in leadership positions than to those who have less influence in the group. In addition, we talk to people we like more than people we don't like.[40] However, there will also be more communication directed toward someone in the group who holds an opinion different from that of the rest of the group. This person is called a **group deviate**. Other group members may spend considerable time trying to change that person's opinion.

A group in which everyone talks to everyone else is called an all-channel network. All channels are open and used, as you can see in Figure 9.1. There is considerable interaction, and no cliques or small subgroups emerge. A **clique** is a smaller group of people within a group who form a common bond among themselves. Perhaps in your social, service, or religious groups you have special friends whom you seek out and who seek you out when you attend meetings. During meetings, you probably sit together, share private jokes and stories, and talk about other members. Although there is nothing wrong with having special friends and colleagues, cliques can become detrimental to a group or team if they foster rivalries within the group or if they inhibit the flow of communication with others. Groups should avoid dividing into subgroups or cliques that can develop divisive power plays that foster conflict. You don't want cliques or groups to ratchet up the emotional tension as the group seeks to deliberate rationally. How do you avoid being in a clique? You become aware that you are in a subgroup that could be detrimental to the larger group.

The chain network in Figure 9.2 illustrates a form of group communication in which people convey a message to one person at a time rather than communicating with all group members at once. In organizations, it is typical to find a hierarchical chain communication pattern. Here's an example: The president of the company sends a message to the vice

**communication interaction pattern**
A consistent pattern of who talks to whom.

**group deviate**
A group member who holds an opinion, attitude, or belief that is different from that of other group members.

**clique**
A smaller, cohesive group within a group.

**Figure 9.1**
**All-Channel Small Group Communication Network**

**Figure 9.2
Chain Small
Group
Communication
Network**

president, who talks to the director. The director then talks to the manager, who eventually gives the message to the other employees. As you might suspect, passing a message through many different ears and minds often results in misunderstanding by the time the message reaches the last person in the chain.

The wheel network pattern shown in Figure 9.3 occurs when one group member receives most of the messages. This pivotal communicator is also the prime source of information to other group members. Perhaps one member of your family always seems to know what's going on. The wheel pattern emerges when there is a strong leader or when the group members do individual tasks and need someone to keep them informed of what others are doing, without interacting with those others. Overall, having a central leader is helpful if a group is performing routine, everyday tasks that don't require much coordination. For more complex work that calls for greater interaction and creativity, however, a decentralized communication pattern (one in which all group members are encouraged to communicate, or an all-channel network) results in overall the greatest team member satisfaction with the result.

What's the best interaction pattern? It depends. The most effective leaders and group members adapt their interaction pattern to fit the task and the time constraints of the project at hand. Sometimes, the efficiency and structured nature of the chain or wheel pattern may be called for. For example, during the huddle before a football play, the quarterback usu-ally does most of the talking while others listen (wheel network). But most teams function best if there is an all-channel pattern of communication, especially when the group is trying to generate new, creative ideas.[41] Breaking into smaller groups can be a useful divide-and-conquer strategy and enhances efficiency for some tasks. If the group is not too large, the all-channel pattern serves most groups well. As you participate in or lead group meetings, be aware of the general pattern of communication. Are all members participating? Do some people whisper their ideas only to a few and not share with the rest of the group? Is a group deviate monopolizing the conversation? By being observant of interaction patterns, you can help the group enhance cohesiveness and develop appropriate roles to get the work done.

# Group and Team Development

Sometimes, small group communication can be a disorganized, messy process—especially if the all-channel network is the predominant communication pattern. Although the free flow of ideas is a good thing, it may seem as though there is no order or structure to the way group members interact. But what may look like chaotic talk may, in fact, be just a normal aspect of how groups behave.

Researchers have found that some groups go through certain phases or sequences of talk when they meet to solve a problem or make a decision.[42] Some researchers have found three phases; most

**Figure 9.3
Wheel Small Group Communication
Network**

have found four. One of the most descriptive four-phase models was developed by communication researcher Aubrey Fisher.[43] His four phases of group talk are (1) orientation, (2) conflict, (3) emergence, and (4) reinforcement. To understand the sequence of these four phases can be like having a group map. By listening to what people are saying, you can identify where the group is. We will describe these phases so that you can identify them when they occur in your group.

## Orientation

As you might suspect, when people first get together in a group, they enter the **orientation phase**, in which they adjust to at least two things: who's in the group (group process) and what they will be doing (group task).

When you join a group for the first time, you have high uncertainty about how the group will be organized, who's in charge, and exactly how things will work. Research on the orientation phase suggests that your earliest communication is directed at orienting yourself to others, as well as to the group's task. What happens during this first phase is often referred to as **primary tension**. This tension results from the uncertainty and discomfort people experience when they meet for the first time.[44] Just as you may have some anxiety when you give a speech, some uncertainty and anxiety occur in a group when group members are trying to figure out who is supposed to do what, who's in charge, and why they are there. Some group members who don't like uncertainty at all and are eager to start sorting things out will suggest an agenda: "Hello, my name is Steve. Let's each introduce ourselves." Other group members are quite content to sit quietly in the background and let others take the lead. As people begin to become acquainted and start talking about the group's purpose, typical groups experience the second phase—conflict.

**orientation phase**
The first phase of group interaction, in which members become adjusted to one another and to the group's task.

**primary tension**
Tension arising from the uncertainty and discomfort that occur when a group first meets.

## Conflict

As pointed out, people are different—and nowhere is that more evident than in a group discussion after the group gets down to business. As group members become more comfortable and oriented toward the task and one another, they start asserting

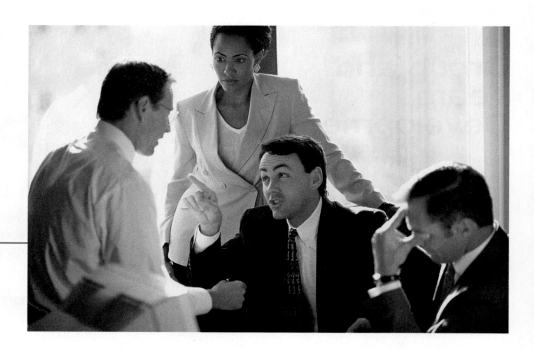

Taking a "time out" might help to resolve this team's conflict. What other strategies have you found useful for dealing with conflict in groups?
Stockbyte/Thinkstock

opinions about what the group should be doing and who should be doing it. They have tested the water in the first phase and are now ready to jump in. This second phase, which is characterized by increased disagreement, is known as the **conflict phase**, and the conflict that arises in the phase is sometimes called **secondary tension**. This tension or conflict occurs when there is a struggle for leadership or when group members disagree with one an other.

Conflict is not always bad—it occurs when people are honest about sharing their opinions. If there is no conflict, it usually means that people aren't honest about how they really feel.[45] As journalist Walter Lippman once said, "When we all think alike, then no one is thinking." The conflict phase is necessary for solving problems and maintaining group relationships. When ideas aren't challenged and tested, groups are more likely to make unwise decisions. We are not suggesting that you celebrate when you have conflict, only that you take some comfort in knowing that conflict is an expected part of group deliberations. The amount and intensity of the conflict vary, depending on how important the issues are to the group. The more important the issues are to group members, the greater the intensity of the conflict is likely to be.

Research suggests that when intense conflict arises in your group, especially conflict that results in heightened emotions and tension because of cultural differences, it may be best to "cool it."[46] Taking time to back off rather than continuing to hash out issues verbally may be helpful in managing the tension. Regardless of the issue or trigger for the conflict, when emotions are aroused, rational discussion is hard to achieve. Especially if the group you're in includes people from a variety of cultural backgrounds, letting the group "breathe" rather than continuing to hammer out meaning with more talk may be best. We're not suggesting that all conflict should be managed by avoiding it; we are suggesting that when emotions become aroused it's difficult to make headway on the issues with words that may expand the conflict.

When conflict in virtual groups and teams stems from differences in cultural values or perceptions, it's important that team members feel connected to the team and empowered to participate rather than feel marginalized or discounted. Research suggests that having virtual team members vote on decisions or the value and importance of contributions is a useful way to keep them engaged with the team.[47]

## Emergence

You know you are in the **emergence phase** when the group begins to solidify a common point of view. Decisions emerge; conflict is reduced. Although conflict is still evident in this third phase, what sets the emergence phase apart from the conflict phase is the way in which group members manage conflict. Norms, roles, and leadership patterns that have been established in the group now help the group get work accomplished. In the emergence phase, the group settles on norms and moves closer to agreement. The group begins to get a clearer glimpse of how issues will be resolved and what the group outcome will be.

Not all of what emerges may be productive. The group could decide that the conflict is so intense that the best decision is to disband the group, or an individual could decide to leave the group.

## Reinforcement

Group members become more unified in the **reinforcement phase**. During the orientation, conflict, and emergence phases, group members struggle through getting acquainted, developing cohesiveness, competing for status and prominence, and puzzling over action the group could take. The group eventually emerges from those struggles and develops a new sense of direction. This accomplishment results in a

**conflict phase**
The second phase of group interaction, in which group members experience some degree of disagreement about social and task issues.

**secondary tension**
The conflict that occurs, after the members of a group have become acquainted with one another, over group norms, roles, leadership, and differences among member opinions.

**emergence phase**
The third phase of group interaction, in which conflict or disagreement is managed, decisions are made, and group problems begin to be solved or managed.

**reinforcement phase**
The fourth phase of group interaction, in which group members express positive feelings toward one another and toward the group.

# Communication & DIVERSITY

## The Impact of Individualism and Collectivism on Groups and Teams

As mentioned in Chapter 6, individualistic cultures tend to focus on individual achievement. Most North Americans value individual accomplishment over group or team achievement. In general, people from the dominant cultural groups in the United States, Great Britain, and Australia savor and celebrate individual accomplishment. Collectivistic cultures emphasize group or team accomplishment rather than individual achievement. Research suggests that the collectivist mind-set is prevalent in Asian countries, Latin America, and some parts of eastern Europe.[48]

These two perspectives have important implications for group and team collaboration. People who hold individualistic cultural values may find it more difficult to work collaboratively than people from collectivistic cultures. The following summary compares individualistic assumptions with collectivistic assumptions about working in groups and teams.[49] These differences can sometimes explain why groups and teams have difficulty accomplishing their tasks. If you're from a culture that places a high value on individual achievement, you may find it challenging to work collaboratively with others.

| Individualistic Assumptions | Collectivistic Assumptions |
|---|---|
| The best decisions are made by individuals. | The most effective decisions are made by teams. |
| Planning should be done by leaders. | Planning is best done by the entire group. |
| Individuals should be rewarded. | Groups or teams should be rewarded. |
| Individuals should work primarily for themselves. | Individuals should work primarily for the team. |
| Healthy competition among group and team members is more important than teamwork. | Teamwork is more important than competition. |
| Meetings are for sharing information with others. | Meetings are for making group or team decisions. |
| To get something accomplished, you should work with individual people. | To get something accomplished, you should work with the entire group or team. |
| The prime objective of meetings is to advance your own ideas. | The prime objective of meetings is to reach consensus or agreement. |
| Group or team meetings are often a waste of time. | Group or team meetings are the best way to achieve a quality goal. |

more positive feeling about the group. The group more clearly develops a sense of "we." In fact, one way you can identify the reinforcement phase is when group members use more collective pronouns (*we, us, our*) than personal pronouns (*I, me, my*) to talk about the group.

## The Process Nature of Group Phases

Even though we have identified four distinct phases that groups can experience, don't get the idea that all groups progress neatly through these phases in exactly the same way. They don't.[50] Some researchers have found that only about one-third of all groups experience these distinct stages.[51] Other studies have difficulty identifying four phases and find just one or two. Even if you have trouble identifying these phases in your group, you will probably see some elements of the four phases during your group meetings. Some groups get stuck in one of the phases. For example, have you ever participated in a group that could never quite figure out what it was supposed to do? It was stuck in the orientation phase.

Some groups remain in the conflict phase for long periods of time, perhaps bouncing between orientation and conflict. The group either seems torn by personal conflict between group members or just can't reach agreement or make a decision.

Eventually something will emerge from the group (phase three), even if it is not a wise decision or quality solution. The group may decide, for example, to disband and never meet again because it is so dysfunctional. Although not the original objective of the group, something emerged—the group members quit.

Reinforcement is likely to occur because we like to make sense out of what happens to us. Even if the group disbands, we are likely to celebrate its demise or reinforce the decision to disband. Because of our culture's emphasis on efficiency and productivity, many groups quickly gloss over the reinforcement aspects of group celebration. Wise group leaders and participants make sure that accomplishments are celebrated and both group and individual efforts are recognized. The cohesiveness and positive feelings that result from such celebrations will be helpful as the group prepares for its next task.

# **RE**CAP

## A MAP OF GROUP PHASES

| Phase One: Orientation | • What are we doing here? |
| | • What is our goal? |
| | • Who are these people? |
| | • What is my role? |
| **Phase Two: Conflict** | • Who put that person in charge? |
| | • I see the goal differently. |
| | • I have different ideas. |
| | • I have different strategies. |
| **Phase Three: Emergence** | • Something happens. |
| | • Decisions are made. |
| | • Issues are managed. |
| | • The group moves forward. |
| **Phase Four: Reinforcement** | • The group is aware it is making progress. |
| | • Members seek to justify their actions. |
| | • Members reward others. |
| | • The team celebrates its success or rationalizes its failure. |

# STUDY GUIDE:
## Review, Apply, and Assess Your Knowledge and Skill

**REVIEWING**
What You
Know

### Groups and Teams Defined                                    p. 219

Small group communication is the transactive process of creating meaning among a small number (three to fifteen) of people who share a common purpose, feel a sense of belonging to the group, and exert influence on one another. Groups and teams are similar in that they are collections of a small number of people who meet to achieve a goal. A team can be differentiated from a group in that it is more highly organized and the members' collaborative efforts are more coordinated to achieve the team goal.

**Terms to Know**

| | | | |
|---|---|---|---|
| Small Group | p. 219 | Team | p. 220 |
| Small Group Communication | p. 220 | | |

### Group and Team Types                                        p. 222

There are two fundamental types of groups: primary groups and secondary groups. Primary groups, such as family groups and social groups, exist to fulfill primary human needs to socialize and live together. Secondary groups form to achieve a specific goal. Types of secondary groups include study groups, therapy groups, focus groups, and problem-solving groups.

**Terms to Know**

| | | | |
|---|---|---|---|
| Primary Group | p. 222 | Problem-Solving Group | p. 223 |
| Social Group | p. 222 | Focus Group | p. 224 |
| Secondary Group | p. 223 | Virtual Group or Team | p. 224 |
| Study Group | p. 223 | Bona Fide Perspective | p. 225 |
| Therapy Group | p. 223 | | |

### Group and Team Dynamics                                     p. 225

Groups and teams are dynamic. A variety of factors influence the ever-changing nature of members' interactions in groups and teams. One factor is the role you assume in a group—the consistent way you communicate with others. There are three primary types of roles in small groups and teams: (1) task roles help the group do its work, (2) social roles help the group members relate to one another, and (3) individual roles inappropriately divert the group's focus to individual concerns rather than group concerns. Other factors that affect the dynamic nature of groups and teams include norms (standards of what is normal or expected), rules (explicit statements about appropriate and inappropriate behavior), status (a person's importance or prestige), power (the ability to influence others), cohesiveness (the degree of loyalty and attraction the group members feel toward one another), and interaction patterns (the consistent communication networks that emerge based on who talks to whom).

### Terms to Know

## Group and Team Development                              p. 235

Group communication may sometimes seem chaotic, but researchers have noted that many (though not all) groups experience predictable phases. During the orientation phase, group members get acquainted with both the task and one another. The second phase, conflict, occurs when group members recognize that they have differing ideas and opinions about both the group's task and its procedures for accomplishing the task. The third phase, emergence, is evident when the group begins to make decisions and starts to complete the task. The reinforcement phase occurs when the group has accomplished its task and takes some time to recognize and confirm the group's actions.

### Terms to Know

#### Principle One:
#### Be aware of your communication with yourself and others.

- Be aware of your role and the roles of others in groups and teams.
- Be aware of how you and your group develop and maintain group norms.
- Be mindful of how your power and the power of others influence group interaction.
- Be aware of the forces that affect group and team cohesiveness.
- Be aware of and sensitive to the stages of orientation, conflict, emergence, and reinforcement that influence group interaction.

#### Principle Two:
#### Effectively use and interpret verbal messages.

- Be verbally supportive of other team members so as to foster a collective sense of team spirit.
- Verbally help clarify team goals; clear, elevating goals are the hallmark of an effective team.
- Express realistic optimism when working with others in groups and teams; groups and teams with a positive outlook are more effective than those with a pessimistic perspective.
- Help the group or team set clear ground rules and clarify norms that may be ambiguous.
- Talk about your group or team in terms of "we" rather than "I."

# APPLYING Principles for a Lifetime

### Principle Three:
### Effectively use and interpret nonverbal messages.

- Nonverbal cues help you understand group and team norms.
- Observe group and team members' use of space, touch, and eye contact to pick up clues about status and power.
- Be supportive of other group members nonverbally as well as verbally; reinforce statements with positive facial expressions, eye contact, and head nods to indicate agreement when appropriate.

### Principle Four:
### Listen and respond thoughtfully to others.

- Listening well is a very important way to help a group; listening skills help you identify your roles and the roles of others.
- Listen to others to help identify group and team norms and rules.
- Listen attentively to other group members to help foster a climate of cohesiveness.

### Principle Five:
### Appropriately adapt messages to others.

- Adapt to group roles, norms, rules, and status differences.
- Adapt to help the group become oriented to the task, manage conflict, facilitate emergent decisions, and reinforce group behavior.
- Adapt appropriately to cultural differences within the group.

# ASSESSING Your Skill

## Agree–Disagree Statements

Read each of the following statements once. Take four or five minutes to do so. Then, in small groups, try to reach consensus about each statement (everyone either agreeing or disagreeing with the statement). Try especially to find reasons for differences of opinions. If your group cannot reach consensus, you may change the wording in any statement enough to promote unanimity. Write *A* on the line preceding a statement if you agree or *D* if you disagree.[52]

1. _____ Despite its flaws, a meeting is the best way to get work done in an organization.

2. _____ There are often occasions when an individual who is a part of a working team should do what he or she thinks is right, regardless of what the group has decided to do.

3. _____ Sometimes it is necessary to move people in the direction you yourself think is right, even if they object.

4. _____ It is sometimes necessary to ignore the feelings of others to reach a group decision.

5. _____ When the leader is doing his or her best, one should not openly criticize or find fault with his or her conduct.

6. _____ In most team conflicts, someone must win and someone must lose. That's the way conflict is.

7. _____ Much time is wasted in talk when everybody in the group has to be considered before making a decision.

8. _____ Almost any job that can be done by a committee can be done better by having one individual responsible for the job.

9. _____ Body language and nonverbal messages are more important than verbal messages when communicating with others in team meetings.

10. _____ If people spend enough time together, they will find something to disagree about and will eventually become upset with one another.

11. _____ Most hidden agendas are probably best kept hidden to ensure a positive social climate and manage conflict.

12. _____ If you disagree with someone in a group, it is usually better to keep quiet than to get the group off-track with your personal difference of opinion.

13. _____ When a team can't reach a decision, members should abide by the decision of the group leader if the leader is qualified and competent.

14. _____ Some people produce more conflict and tension than others. These people should be restricted from decision-making meetings.

## Assessing Group Communication Skills

Communication researchers Katherine Hawkins and Bryant Fillion surveyed personnel managers to find out what the managers considered the most important skills necessary for successful groups and teams. The items in the following list of skills are among those the personnel managers deemed important. Rate each member of a group you are in on the following skills, using a scale from 1 to 5 (1 = not at all effective, 2 = generally not effective, 3 = uncertain, 4 = effective, and 5 = very effective).

*Scoring:* Total the score for each group member. A perfect score is 65; the lowest possible score is 13. Your instructor may invite you to share your ratings of other group members anonymously. Or, if you don't share your ratings, simply note how you evaluate your skill in comparison to your ratings of other group members.

| | Group Member | | | | |
|---|:---:|:---:|:---:|:---:|:---:|
| **Skill** | **A** | **B** | **C** | **D** | **E** |
| 1. Listens effectively | ___ | ___ | ___ | ___ | ___ |
| 2. Understands roles and responsibilities | ___ | ___ | ___ | ___ | ___ |
| 3. Actively contributes to the group | ___ | ___ | ___ | ___ | ___ |
| 4. Asks clear questions | ___ | ___ | ___ | ___ | ___ |
| 5. Establishes and maintains rapport with others | ___ | ___ | ___ | ___ | ___ |
| 6. Is sensitive to people with different cultural backgrounds | ___ | ___ | ___ | ___ | ___ |
| 7. Uses clear, concise, accurate, and professional language | ___ | ___ | ___ | ___ | ___ |
| 8. Communicates well with people who have different professional backgrounds | ___ | ___ | ___ | ___ | ___ |
| 9. Gives clear and accurate instructions | ___ | ___ | ___ | ___ | ___ |
| 10. Presents a positive professional image nonverbally (through appropriate grooming and attire) | ___ | ___ | ___ | ___ | ___ |
| 11. Helps resolve conflicts | ___ | ___ | ___ | ___ | ___ |
| 12. Accurately summarizes information for the group | ___ | ___ | ___ | ___ | ___ |
| 13. Gives brief, clear, well-organized, and informative presentations to the group when appropriate | ___ | ___ | ___ | ___ | ___ |
| **Total** | ___ | ___ | ___ | ___ | ___ |

Learn more about groups and teams at these websites, created by the publisher of your textbook.

- **MyCommunicationLab** In addition to reviewing the chapter with flash cards, self-tests, and more, you can watch and critique a video that explores different ways of approaching conflict and another that shows a challenging virtual team meeting. <www.mycommunicationlab.com> (Access code required.)

- **Pearson's Introduction to Communication Study Site** For a collection of resources and strategies to help you work with others in small groups and teams, check out the small group section provided by the publisher of your book. You can also participate in an interactive activity or take a quick quiz to test your knowledge of groups and teams. <www.pearsonintrocommunication.com>

# WEB RESOURCES for More Review, Application, and Assessment

Never doubt that a small group of concerned citizens can change the world; it's the only thing that ever has.

MARGARET MEAD

© Fancy/Alamy

# Chapter OUTLINE

- What Effective Group Members Do
- Structuring Group and Team Problem Solving
- Enhancing Group and Team Leadership
- Enhancing Group and Team Meetings
- Study Guide: Review, Apply, and Assess Your Knowledge and Skill

# Chapter OBJECTIVES

After studying this chapter, you should be able to

1. Identify six functions that effective group members perform.
2. List and describe the five steps of group problem solving (reflective thinking).
3. Compare and contrast the trait, functional, styles, situational, and transformational approaches to understanding leadership.
4. Develop and use an agenda to ensure that meetings have appropriate structure.
5. Use strategies to maintain appropriate discussion and dialogue to ensure that meetings include appropriate interaction.

# 10 | Enhancing Group and Team Performance

What's so great about groups? Why does every organization, from the U.S. Congress to the local Parent Teacher Association, use groups, teams, and committees to get something done? The simple fact is: Groups work. Collaborating with others produces clear benefits that just don't happen when you give a task to an individual. Research clearly supports the following conclusions:

- Groups and teams come up with more creative solutions to problems than a person does working alone.
- Working with others in groups improves group members' comprehension of the ideas presented.
- Group and team members are more satisfied with the group's conclusions and recommendations if they participated in the discussion than if they did not.
- Groups have access to more information when they tap into the experience of group members.[1]

All these advantages sound wonderful. But these benefits of collaboration don't occur automatically when people work in groups and teams. Sometimes there are significant disadvantages to working collaboratively.

- Overly talkative or insensitive, overbearing people may speak too much. The advantage of working collaboratively is lost when one or more people dominate the conversation.
- Group members sometimes feel pressure to conform to what other group members are doing and saying. It can be difficult to stick up for your own ideas when everyone else sees issues differently.
- Some group members just sit back and wait for others to do the work. It may be easy for some people to loaf and not do their share of the work. If not enough people carry part of the load, the advantages of working together as a group don't materialize.
- Working in groups and teams takes more time than working individually. It takes time to talk and listen.[2]

This chapter is designed to help you achieve the advantages of working in groups and minimize the disadvantages of working collaboratively. We can't claim that by following all the strategies we suggest your life will be free of unpleasant and unproductive

Groups offer a lot of advantages when trying to solve problems, so it pays to learn how to overcome some of the challenges to effective group communication.

Tom Ackerman/Stockbyte/Thinkstock

group experiences. We do believe, however, that group members who both understand how groups work (see Chapter 9) and know principles and strategies for enhancing the quality of group work are much more likely to avoid the pitfalls and reap the benefits of working in groups. Working in groups will usually involve more time than working by yourself, but the benefit of improved decision quality can far outweigh the disadvantage of investing more time.

Underpinning all the suggestions we offer in this chapter are the same five Communication Principles for a Lifetime that we introduced in Chapter 1 and have been discussing throughout the book. Effective group members are aware of what they are doing. They effectively use verbal and nonverbal messages, listen and respond, and then appropriately adapt their messages to others.

# What Effective Group Members Do

"I hate groups," mutters an exasperated group member who has just finished a two-hour meeting in which nothing was accomplished. "Not me," chirps another group member. "Meetings and team projects are fun. I like the energy and productivity that occur when we work together." What is it the second person knows that the first one doesn't? As we noted at the start of the last chapter, working in groups can be frustrating, but it doesn't have to be if you and other group members learn some fundamental ways to perform effectively as group members.

## Identify and Implement Key Functions to Achieve Results

Effective group and team members help ensure that key functions or communication behaviors that enhance the overall quality of the group are put into practice. Researchers have found that when these critical functions are not performed, the group is less effective. This **functional approach** to group communication describes the kinds of behaviors or functions that lead to better solutions and decisions in group deliberations.[3]

Researchers have spent several years trying to identify the key functions of high-performing groups and teams so that you can make sure that you enact them in your group. The primary means by which researchers have identified these functions is by comparing the way group members in high-performing groups talk with the way group members in low-performing groups talk.

The essence of these functions involves group members being vigilant thinkers.[4] **Vigilant thinkers** pay attention to the *process* of how problems are solved. A vigilant thinker assesses, evaluates, and tests ideas; he or she effectively uses verbal messages and listens to what others are saying. Communication researcher Randy Hirokawa and his colleagues identified four essential questions that vigilant-thinking group members should consider:

**functional approach**
An approach to group problem solving that assumes that, to achieve a group goal, group members should perform certain communication functions.

**vigilant thinker**
A group member who pays attention to the process of how problems are solved, is sensitive to the need to make changes, identifies the goal of the group, identifies options the group has, and evaluates the positive and negative implications of the options.

1. What goal does the group want to achieve?
2. Does something in the current situation need to be changed to achieve the goal?
3. What options does the group have that will help achieve the goal?
4. What are the positive and negative implications of the options?[5]

Even though these questions are usually discussed in the order listed, some productive, vigilant-thinking groups don't always follow this sequence.[6] What is clear, however, is that if these critical questions are not discussed, the group is less effective in solving problems and making wise decisions. These questions lead to the achievement of the following six critical functions that effective groups need to consider.

## Identify a Clear, Elevating Goal

Among the first questions that a vigilant-thinking group asks relates to the group's goal: What are we trying to do?[7] According to one research team, the goal should be not only clear, but also *elevating*, or exciting to the group.[8] The group needs to know that it is pursuing a goal that is significant; the group goal needs to be something more exciting and important than anything a group member could achieve individually. A professional baseball team during spring training camp may hang up signs in the locker room that say "World Series Champs!" A professional football team may see itself as a Super Bowl contender at the beginning of summer training camp. Groups, too, need to identify a clear, exciting, yet realistic goal that drives all aspects of what the group does.[9] Without a goal and a results-driven structure to achieve the goal, group performance sputters. Research has found that it's important not only to set goals, but to develop contingency plans in case the goal is not reached as expected. Being able to react and adjust team plans to achieve a goal is especially important.[10]

## Develop a Results-Driven Structure

A group or team may have a clear goal, such as winning the Super Bowl, getting an "A" on a group assignment, or selling more widgets than other groups in the company—but just having a clear, elevating goal doesn't mean that the group will achieve what it wants to achieve. Results-driven action has to follow a goal-setting structure. If you want to win the Super Bowl, you have to invest time in becoming physically fit and working on executing successful football plays. If you want to get an "A" on the assignment, you need to be doing what the instructor wants you do to rather than socializing and just having fun.

A group with a **results-driven structure** is organized around the action steps it needs to take to achieve its goal.[11] To be driven by results means that you "keep your eye on the prize" and then develop a group or team structure to achieve the prize. Perhaps you've been part of a group or team that was quite busy but didn't seem to accomplish much; that kind of activity reflects a non–results-driven structure. A group that structures itself for results makes sure that its work is clearly linked to the desired outcome. Results-driven groups focus on verbs—action words—that provide the road map to success.

## Gather and Share Appropriate Information

Another question that vigilantly thinking groups ask is, "Does something need to be changed?" To answer that question, high-performing groups and teams don't just rely on the unsupported opinions of group members. Instead, they gather information and analyze the situation.[12]

To analyze an issue, an effective group should do at least three things:

1. *Gather the information the group members need.* Computer programmers are familiar with the acronym GIGO: "Garbage in, garbage out." If you develop a computer program using bad information or a bad program command (garbage), you're likely to come out with low-quality output (more garbage). Information is the fuel that makes a group function well.[13]

2. *Share the information among group and team members.* Group members have a tendency to share information with other group members that everyone already knows. Research has found, however, that better decisions are made when group members make an effort to share information that others may *not* know.[14] So, if you are uncertain whether other group members know what you know, don't hesitate to share that information with the entire group.

3. *Draw accurate conclusions from the information.* Having too little evidence—or no evidence at all—is one reason groups sometimes fail to analyze their current situation correctly.[15] Even if group members do have plenty of evidence, however,

**results-driven structure**
A structure that causes a group to focus its efforts on the actions it needs to take to achieve its goals.

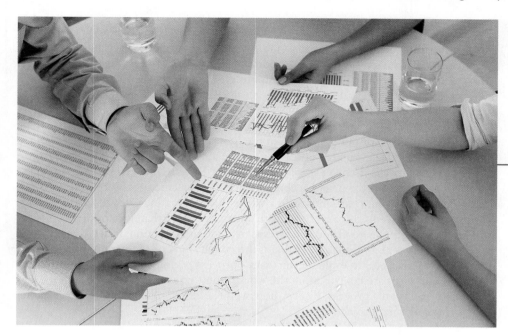

it may be bad evidence; or perhaps they may not have tested the evidence to see whether it is true, accurate, or relevant. Group members who use evidence to support their well-reasoned arguments are more likely to have their conclusions accepted by the entire group than group members who do not.[16]

One team of researchers found that when there is missing or unknown information, effective group members will do their best to make inferences or to find the missing or unknown information.[17] Group members who don't gather and use information effectively are more likely to make bad decisions than others. Here are some tips for gathering and using information effectively:

- In group deliberations, ask for expert advice sooner rather than later. Seeking expert advice results in better group outcomes.
- If you find that just a few people are doing the talking and sharing information, invite quieter group members to participate. Groups that have more equal participation by all group members generally are more effective than other groups.
- Don't rush to make a quick decision. To reach a better outcome, take your time and sift through the information you have.

## Develop Options

Another hallmark of a vigilantly thinking group is that the members generate many ideas and potential solutions after gathering information and analyzing a situation. Effective groups don't just settle on one or two ideas and then move on. They list multiple creative approaches.

Sometimes groups get stuck and ideas just don't flow. If that happens to your group, you may want to take a break from the difficult issues or problems rather than continue to hammer away at them. Taking a break gives you a chance to thrash through the issues. You may generate a breakthrough solution when you are not actively trying to; perhaps you've had a great idea come to you when you were taking a walk or driving. The principle of self-awareness operates here: As a group member, you have a responsibility to become aware of the group's ability to generate high-quality ideas. Be sensitive to the group's need to take a fresh look at the problem or issue.

## Evaluate Ideas

High-performing groups know a good idea when they see it. They are able to evaluate evidence, opinions, assumptions, and solutions to separate good ideas from bad ones. Low-performing groups are less discriminating. A group that is too eager to make a decision just so it can get a job done and that does not critically evaluate ideas usually comes up with low-quality decisions.

As we've seen, a group of vigilant thinkers examines the advantages and disadvantages of an idea, issue, or opinion.[18] When the group is zeroing in on a particular course of action, the effective group has at least one member who suggests, "Let's consider the positive and negative consequences of this decision." Research reveals that it's especially important to talk about the negative consequences of a specific proposal.[19] Some groups use a chalkboard or flip chart and make a written list comparing the pros and the cons. Groups that do so are likely to come up with a better decision than groups that don't systematically evaluate the good and bad aspects of a potential solution or decision.

Not only is it a good idea to evaluate the conclusions of the group, but research suggests that it is useful to evaluate the team's process periodically and talk about how well team members are coordinating the work. Don't wait until the project is finished to evaluate the team's process; discuss how well the team is achieving its goals as the team is working on a project.[20]

## Develop Sensitivity Toward Others

Most of the functions we've described so far focus on getting work done effectively and efficiently, but group success is about more than just focusing on the task. Being solely task oriented is not beneficial to the way that a group functions. Effective group members balance concern for the task with concern for the feelings of others.

Fostering a climate of fairness and supportiveness is essential to developing a well-functioning team.[21] In groups that function effectively, members are aware of how their comments might be perceived by others. Effectively functioning group members make comments that confirm the value of others' contributions and nonverbally show that they are genuinely interested in what others are saying. Group members also listen to what each group member has to say—even members who hold a minority opinion. One benefit of working in a group is that you can hear a variety of ideas. If opinions of others are quickly squelched because they are not what most other group

Members of high-performing groups and teams are likely to enjoy spending time together. A good balance of social and task focus makes it more fun for group members to be together. How else can you make group membership more enjoyable for yourself and other members?

Yuri Arcurs/Shutterstock.com

members think or believe, the group loses the power of many different points of view.

A recent study found that one sign of a competent group is that group members simply like spending time with one another.[22] They also explicitly talk about the importance of trusting one another, clarify misunderstandings by collaboratively defining key terms, listen effectively, consciously talk about what makes the group effective, share personal information, and use humor and laugh together. In summary, competent group members are sensitive to how individual members relate to one another.

## Develop a Positive Personal Style

You may have heard the story about a boy who awoke on the morning of his birthday to find only a large pile of manure where he'd hoped to find birthday presents. Undaunted, he smiled and said, "With this much horse manure, there's got to be a pony here somewhere!" Effective team members are optimistic like that boy: Even in bad times, they find something to be positive about.

One thing effective team members are optimistic about is themselves. Researchers have found that effective teams and effective team members *believed* that they were effective, that they had the skills and resources to accomplish their task. Teams that were less effective *thought* that they were less effective.[23] Was the team effective because of a self-fulfilling prophecy (just expecting to be effective caused the team to act effectively)? Or did team members think that they were effective because they really were a top-notch team? We're not quite sure what the precise cause-and-effect relationship is between self-perceptions of being effective and actually being effective. Teams that have a positive, can-do attitude, however, perform better than teams whose members have doubts, worries, and uncertainties about whether they will get the job done. The bottom line is that optimism enhances effectiveness.

## WHAT EFFECTIVE GROUP AND TEAM MEMBERS DO

| Group Function | Description of Function |
|---|---|
| Identify and Implement Key Functions to Achieve Results | Getting a handle on key functions helps the group<br>• Identify the goal.<br>• Identify what needs to be changed.<br>• Identify options.<br>• Identify positive and negative implications of the options. |
| Identify a Clear, Elevating Goal | A clear, elevating, or important goal anchors the purpose of group discussion. |
| Develop a Results-Driven Structure | Structure helps the group stay on task and do those things that will help it achieve its goal. |
| Gather Appropriate Information | Conducting research and using accurate information are important elements in the deliberation of any group or team. |
| Share Information | Effective groups ensure that all group members have access to the information available to the group. |
| Develop Options | Effective groups expand the number of alternatives or options before choosing a course of action. |
| Evaluate Ideas | Effective groups or teams examine the pros and cons of an option before implementing the strategy. |
| Develop Sensitivity Toward Others | Group members do more than focus on the task; they express sensitivity to the needs and concerns of group members by using appropriate verbal and nonverbal messages, listening, responding, and adapting messages to others. |
| Develop a Positive Personal Style | Effective group members are optimistic and have a positive yet realistic attitude about the prospects for overall group success. |

As we've seen, being driven by results also makes a group member more productive. Furthermore, and perhaps not surprisingly, team members also like colleagues who are encouraging, patient, enthusiastic, and friendly. To be perceived as an ineffective team member, argue with others frequently, be intolerant and impatient, and cultivate skills that will help you win the "pain-in-the-neck" award. To be an effective team member, do the opposite.

You may wonder whether these attributes of team effectiveness can be enhanced through study and training. There's good news: Evidence suggests that, by learning more about teams and participating in training development courses you can indeed improve your team skills.[24]

# Structuring Group and Team Problem Solving

How many of us have uttered the plea, "Just tell me what to do"? When we do, we are usually looking for simple techniques or steps to help us achieve our goal. One approach to group problem solving is based on a similar goal. This structural approach is more prescriptive than the functional approach to group problem solving that we just discussed. Just as a prescription from your doctor is based on the assumption that a specific dose of medicine will help remedy an ailment, a prescriptive approach to problem solving is based on the assumption that you can do specific things to enhance the communication health of the group.

As shown in Table 10.1 and as explained by communication researcher Arthur VanGundy, problems can be classified on a continuum from *structured* to *unstructured*.[25] Unstructured problems generate a great deal of uncertainty for groups charged with solving them. In VanGundy's view, the less structured the problem, the greater the need for a structured approach to help the group manage its uncertainty. Leaders who give the group structure by setting goals, keeping track of the time, and suggesting procedures enhance the group's perceived effectiveness.

More than seventy methods or sequences of prescriptive steps and techniques have been identified for structuring problem solving in groups and teams.[26] Several researchers have sought to identify the sequence that works best. They have discovered that there are no magic techniques that enable a group of team members to always come up with the right solution to a problem. No single prescriptive method or series of steps works best in every situation. There is some hope, though: Research shows that *having some structured sequence of steps or questions works better than having no structure.*[27]

An important conclusion of group researchers is that structure must be balanced with interaction in a group.

**structure**
The way a group or team discussion is organized, focusing on the group's agenda and the task that needs to be achieved.

**interaction**
The give-and-take discussion and responsiveness to other group members.

- **Structure** is the way a group or team discussion is organized to follow a prescribed agenda. Groups and teams need structure to keep them on task and on track. According to research, groups that engage in free-ranging discussion without an agenda change topics about once a minute.[28] Besides having difficulty staying focused, without adequate structure or focus, a group will take more time to do its work, the group is more likely to jump at the first solution recommended, it's more likely that one or more people will dominate the discussion, and conflict is more likely to go unmanaged.[29]
- **Interaction** includes give-and-take discussion and the responsiveness of group members to the comments of others. In an interactive group, there are fewer long utterances, more people contribute, and more people take turns talking. People

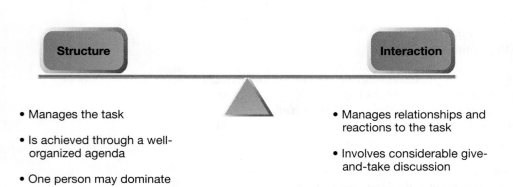

**Structure**
- Manages the task
- Is achieved through a well-organized agenda
- One person may dominate

**Interaction**
- Manages relationships and reactions to the task
- Involves considerable give-and-take discussion
- There is much talk and participation from the group or team members

**Figure 10.1**
**Groups Need a Balance of Structure and Interaction**

## Table 10.1
## Structured and Unstructured Problems

|  | STRUCTURED PROBLEMS | UNSTRUCTURED PROBLEMS |
|---|---|---|
| **Solution** | One single, best solution exists. | There is more than one acceptable solution. |
| **Process** | Solving the problem causes little uncertainty. | There is a lot of uncertainty about how to solve the problem. |
| **Example** | Mathematics problems | How to reform government programs |

listen and thoughtfully respond to one another. In a highly structured meeting, there is more control over who talks, about what, and for how long; overly structured meetings include less interaction.

As suggested in Figure 10.1, the key is to find the right balance between structure and interaction. When there is too much interaction, the group experiences the chaos of unbridled talk, which may not be focused; group and team members may need help focusing on one idea at a time rather than bouncing from topic to topic. When there is too much structure, however, the group loses the freedom to listen and respond with sensitivity to what others are saying.

In the pages that follow, we present a set of steps that can help you develop a sequence of things group members should be talking about. These five steps are inspired by educator and philosopher John Dewey, who in 1910 wrote a book called *How We Think*.[30] His book described how individuals go about the problem-solving process; in essence, he described the scientific method that scientists still use to solve problems: defining and analyzing a problem, identifying solutions, picking a solution, and putting the solution into practice. He called this process **reflective thinking**. We present these steps here, not as a one-size-fits-all prescription that you should always follow, but as a way of structuring the problem-solving process to manage uncertainty and also to ensure that the key functions we talked about earlier are accomplished during your discussion. In addition to describing each step of the reflective thinking process, we present several techniques to help you structure discussion.

## Step 1: Identify and Define the Problem

"What's your problem?" Groups work best when they have identified a clear, elevating goal that unites their problem-solving effort. To reach a clear statement of the problem, consider asking the following questions:

- What is the specific problem that concerns us?
- What do we want more of or less of?
- What terms, concepts, or ideas do we need to define so as to understand the problem?
- Who is harmed by the problem?
- When do the harmful effects of the problem occur?

Whatever method or technique a group uses, it is essential that group members know precisely what problem they are trying to solve.

**Develop a Question**    Most group experts recommend that an effective way to give your problem-solving task appropriate structure is to phrase your problem in the form of a policy question. A policy question is phrased so that the group will recommend

**reflective thinking**
A problem-solving process based on the scientific method.

One way to help your group fully identify and define a problem is to use these six questions, about the problem.
iQoncept/Shutterstock.com

some action (policy) to eliminate, reduce, or manage the problem. Policy questions begin with the words "What should be done about . . ." or "What could be done to improve . . . ."

Here are some examples:

- What should be done to lower the cost of tuition at our university?
- What could be done to decrease property taxes in our state?
- What should be done to make health care more affordable for all U.S. citizens?

**Clarify the Problem**   One specific technique for clarifying the problem is to use the journalists' six questions method.[31] Most news reporters are taught to include the answers to six questions—who, what, when, where, why, and how—when writing a news report. Answering each of these six questions about the problem the group has identified can help further define and limit the problem. These answers can also help the group move to the next step in the process—analyzing the problem.

## Step 2: Analyze the Problem

To analyze something is to break it down into smaller pieces; to analyze a problem is to consider the causes, effects, symptoms, history, and other information that will inform the group about how to best solve the problem. Many groups want to "cut to the chase" quickly and start spinning out solutions without taking the time to analyze the problem thoroughly. Resist this temptation. Analyzing a problem well is an important prerequisite to finding an effective solution. When analyzing a problem, group members will need to spend time in the library or on the Internet to gather information and determine how experts view the problem. Essential questions that can help you analyze problems include the following:

- How long has the problem been in existence?
- How widespread is the problem?
- What are the causes of the problem?
- What are the effects of the problem?
- What are the symptoms of the problem?
- Who is harmed by the problem?
- What methods already exist for managing the problem?
- What are the limitations of existing methods?
- What obstacles keep the group from achieving the goal?

**criteria**
Standards for an acceptable solution.

**force field analysis technique**
A method of analyzing a problem or issue by identifying forces that increase the likelihood that the desired goal will occur (driving forces) and forces that decrease the probability that the goal will occur (restraining forces).

**Establish Criteria**   In addition to considering these questions, group members should develop criteria for an acceptable solution. **Criteria** are standards for an acceptable solution to a problem. Identifying clear criteria can help you spot a good solution when you see one. Sample criteria for solutions include the following:

- The solution should be inexpensive; the cost should not exceed a specified percentage of the budget.
- The solution should be implemented by a certain date.
- The solution should be agreed on by all group members.
- The solution should be agreed on by all persons affected by the recommendations.

Don't rely on your memory when you verbalize criteria. Write down on a chalkboard or flip chart the list of criteria your group has identified and include the list in the minutes or notes that summarize the meeting.

**Analyze Problem Elements**   After you have gathered information and developed criteria, your group may need to develop a systematic way of analyzing the information you've gathered. One technique that can help structure the analysis of your problem and also help your team identify criteria is the **force field analysis technique** shown in Figure 10.2.[32] This technique works best when your group has

## Figure 10.2
## Force Field Analysis

This analysis was conducted by a group that wanted to increase the number of students who volunteer for community projects. The goal is written on the top. *Driving Forces*, shown on the left, are factors that increase the group's chance of achieving its goal. *Restraining Forces*, listed on the right, are factors that reduce the group's ability to get more students to volunteer.

Source: Adapted from Julius E. Etington, *The Winning Trainer* (Houston: Gulf Publishing, 1989).

identified a clear goal and needs to assess what is happening now that would increase the probability that the goal will be achieved.

After identifying a goal, the group lists all the driving forces currently at work that would help achieve the goal. Then the group does just the opposite: It identifies the restraining forces that are keeping the group from achieving the goal. When complete, the task of the group in developing solutions is now clear: Increase the driving forces and decrease the restraining forces.

We offer two final cautions:

- *Avoid analysis paralysis.* Be careful not to spend so much time overanalyzing data that you forget that the purpose of the group is to solve the problem.
- *Beware of the "killer inch" problem.* This problem occurs when group members agree on the major points but are distracted by minor details; they've traveled a long way to reach their goal, but they get distracted in the last inch of the journey.

## Step 3: Generate Creative Solutions

Now that you've identified a specific problem, analyzed its causes and history, and established clear criteria for solutions, you're ready to generate creative options to solve the problem. **Creativity** is the generation, application, combination, and extension of new ideas. Researchers have found that your entire group is more likely to be creative if individual group members are creative; it's important not to rely on others to be creative, but to develop your own creative skill. It's simply not true that only a few gifted and talented people are creative; creative ideas can come from anyone. Author Malcolm Gladwell believes that our powers of intuition and creativity harbor the

**creativity**
The generation, application, combination, and extension of new ideas.

greatest potential for generating the breakthrough ideas that can change the world.[33] Your group is more likely to be creative if you do the following things:[34]

- Make sure everyone knows the precise nature of the problem.
- Review and summarize the analysis of the problem.
- Promote a climate of freedom; let people experiment and play with ideas.
- Don't judge and evaluate the ideas of others prematurely.
- Listen to minority points of view; you never know who may have the next great insight.
- Provide enough time for creativity to occur; don't rush the creative process.

**Brainstorming** is the classic technique for identifying possible solutions to a problem. This technique was developed by an advertising executive about fifty years ago to encourage a group to be creative.[35] You've probably used brainstorming before. Many groups, however, don't use the technique effectively.

### Problems with Brainstorming

The key to making brainstorming work—to generating many creative ideas—is to *separate the generation of ideas from the evaluation of ideas.* This means that group members are supposed to feel free to offer ideas without fear of criticism, snickering, or being made to feel foolish. Reality, however, may be quite different. When group members start suggesting ideas, there may be either verbal or, more likely, nonverbal evaluation of ideas. People may laugh at the more offbeat suggestions; or, when someone announces a suggestion, others may frown, sneer, or voice an editorial comment. Another subtle form of evaluation occurs when some group ideas are praised and some are not. Group members whose ideas are not praised may feel that their ideas are considered stupid. Clearly, when ideas are evaluated as soon as they're offered, brainstorming doesn't work well; members may be reluctant to share ideas. This is especially true of group members who are shy or uncomfortable talking in a group; these people, however, may have great ideas that are worth sharing.

**brainstorming**
A technique for generating many possible solutions to a problem by withholding evaluation while group members suggest ideas; ideas are evaluated after suggestions have been offered.

**silent brainstorming (nominal group technique)**
A method of generating creative ideas; group members brainstorm individually and write down their ideas before meeting together to share them.

### Better Brainstorming

One solution to this problem is to have a period of **silent brainstorming** before members share their ideas verbally. Another name for silent brainstorming is the nominal group technique.[36] For a few moments, people work individually—for that period of time, they are a group in name only (hence the name *nominal*). After group members have brainstormed individually, they share their ideas with the group.

The same rules apply, whether you are brainstorming out loud or silently:

- Set aside judgments and criticism when people offer ideas.
- Think of as many ideas as possible; volume is important.
- Piggyback someone else's idea.
- Try to identify one or more zany or wild ideas—this triggers creativity and may lead to a less zany but workable idea.

- Record the ideas on a flip chart or chalkboard when people share them. It's usually best to go around the group one at a time to have group members share what they have written down.
- Evaluate the ideas *after* all the group members have finished sharing.

You may ask group members to do some individual brainstorming before they come to the group meeting. For example, you could say, "Each group member should bring five or ten suggestions for solving our problem." Or you could just invite group members to brainstorm ideas silently for a few minutes and then move into small groups to share and piggyback ideas. Ask group members to do some private brainstorming and e-mail their responses to either the group leader or other group members. Another creative way to generate ideas is to have group members first write each idea or suggestion on a sticky note.[37] Once the ideas are on the sticky notes, group members can stick them to the wall and then arrange them in groups. Seeing other group members' ideas may trigger additional creative ideas from the group. The goal is to separate generating or listing ideas from critiquing the ideas. When those two parts of brainstorming get mixed together, fewer ideas flow because of group members' fear of being criticized.

## Step 4: Select the Best Solution

The next step is to evaluate the ideas your group has identified and pick the best solution. The group members now take the long list of ideas generated and determine which ones best meet the criteria they identified when they analyzed the problem. They also determine which solutions best achieve the clear, elevating goal they identified. It's really important that group members have both a clear goal and specific criteria—without them, they will have difficulty recognizing a good solution when they see it.

It is usually easier for groups to expand alternatives (brainstorm) than to narrow alternatives. The methods used by groups to whittle a long list down to a manageable number for more serious debate include these five approaches:

## RECAP

### BRAINSTORMING STEPS

1. Select a problem that needs to be solved.
2. Discuss the history, causes, and background of the problem. Make sure the group knows precisely what options are needed.
3. Tell the group to develop a creative mind-set:
   - Put aside judgments and evaluations.
   - Stress quantity of ideas.
   - Avoid criticizing ideas, including your own.
   - Try to come up with one or more wild ideas–stretch your imagination; it's easier to modify wild ideas.
   - Piggyback someone else's ideas.
4. Start brainstorming. Give the group a time limit.
5. To reduce the possibility that people will evaluate ideas, consider using a period of silent brainstorming before having people verbalize their ideas.
6. Write all the ideas on a chalkboard or flip chart.
7. Keep reminding the group not to evaluate the ideas of others when they are first expressed.
8. Evaluate the ideas after all ideas have been presented.

1. *Decision by expert.* Let someone who has high credibility narrow the list.
2. *Rank.* Tell group members to rank their top five choices from 1 to 5.
3. *Rate.* Ask group members to evaluate each solution on a scale from 1 to 5; the solutions rated best get the most serious discussion.
4. *Majority vote.* Group members vote for the ideas they like.
5. *Consensus.* Group members seek a solution that all group or team members can accept.

**Develop Consensus**   **Consensus** occurs when there is enough agreement that group members will all support a decision. Consensus doesn't mean that everyone agrees enthusiastically and completely with what the group has decided—but at least group members won't stand in the way of what the group has decided. Reaching a consensus decision has the advantage that all group members can verbalize support for the decision. But reaching consensus takes time.

**consensus**
Agreement among all members of a group or team to support an idea, proposal, or solution.

## Table 10.2
## Suggestions for Reaching Group and Team Consensus[38]

| EFFECTIVE GROUP MEMBERS | INEFFECTIVE GROUP MEMBERS |
| --- | --- |
| **Keep the Group Oriented Toward Its Goal** | |
| Remind the group what the goal is. | Go off on tangents and do not stay focused on the agenda. |
| Write facts and key ideas on a flip chart or chalkboard. | Fail to summarize or rely on oral summaries to keep group members focused on the goal. |
| Talk about the discussion process; ask questions that keep the group focused on the agenda. | Do little to help clarify group discussion. |
| **Listen to the Ideas of Others** | |
| Clarify misunderstandings. | Do not clarify misunderstandings or check to see whether others understand their message. |
| Emphasize areas of agreement. | Ignore areas of agreement. |
| Maintain eye contact when listening to someone and remain focused on the speaker without interrupting. | Do not have eye contact with the speaker, and do not focus attention on the speaker; interrupt the speaker. |
| **Promote Honest Dialogue and Discussion** | |
| Seek out differences of opinion. | Do not seek other opinions from group members. |
| Do not change their minds quickly to avoid conflict. | Quickly agree with other group members to avoid conflict. |
| Try to involve everyone in the discussion. | Permit one person or just a few people to talk too much and dominate the conversation. |

The three primary strategies summarized in Table 10.2 can help groups reach consensus:

1. Be goal oriented.[39]
2. Listen.
3. Promote honest dialogue and discussion.

**Avoid Groupthink**   Be cautious if all group members agree too quickly. You may be experiencing groupthink instead of consensus. **Groupthink** occurs when group members seem to agree but primarily just want to avoid conflict. On the surface, it seems as though group members have reached consensus—but it's an illusion of agreement. Another way of describing groupthink is to call it faulty consensus; too little disagreement often reduces the quality of group decisions. If a group does not seriously examine the pros and cons of an idea, it's likely that the quality of the decision it makes will suffer because the group has not used its full power to analyze and evaluate ideas.

Failure to test ideas and the resulting groupthink can have serious consequences in the form of wrong, dangerous, or stupid decisions. The following list identifies a few well-known disasters or problems in which groupthink was a key factor.

**groupthink**
A faulty sense of agreement that occurs when members of a group fail to challenge an idea; a false consensus reached when conflict is minimized and group members do not express concerns or reservations about an idea or proposal.

- In 1986, American viewers watched in horror as the *Challenger* space shuttle, carrying the first teacher in space, exploded on live TV. The tragedy resulted from both faulty engineering and groupthink: Some people knew that the shuttle wouldn't fly in cold temperatures, but because of pressure to stay on schedule decided not to stop the launch.[40]
- In 1999, several students were killed in a traditional pre-football game bonfire at Texas A&M University in College Station. Some thought the bonfire construction

# Communication & ETHICS

## When Is It Wrong to Get Along?

Some people think of conflict as bad and detrimental to a group, yet, being too uncritical and failing to raise reservations about group conclusions can breed a climate of groupthink. How do you know when to challenge ideas?

Is it ethical to remain silent because you want to maintain peace when you actually disagree with an idea suggested? When is it best to keep quiet rather than express disagreement that could escalate to more intense conflict? What are your personal criteria for expressing disagreement with others in a group or team? Specifically, when do you speak up, and when do you avoid creating a fuss?

unsafe before the accident occurred, but because of tradition the bonfire continued to be built, and tragedy was the result.[41]

- The commission that investigated the September 11, 2001 terrorist attacks concluded that groupthink was one of the factors contributing to the nation's not being prepared for the attacks.[42] The commission believed that there was pre-existing evidence of a terrorist threat, yet not enough action was taken to address the problem fully.
- 2003, the *Columbia* space shuttle disintegrated on re-entry into the earth's atmosphere because of damage sustained during takeoff. Some thought that there might be a problem but didn't speak up, so no corrective action was attempted.

The headlines are not the only places to look for examples of groupthink. If you think about it, you'll find plenty of examples in groups and teams you've worked with.

What causes groupthink? Sometimes it occurs because group members are not particularly interested in the topic or are tired and want to get on with other work. If a group has a highly revered leader, someone with high status whom all group members respect, the group is likely to agree with the leader rather than test and challenge the leader's ideas. Groupthink also occurs when group members believe that they can do no wrong. Rather than take time to test and evaluate ideas, the group that feels invincible may quickly decide that their decision is a good one. Groupthink can also occur when (1) the group feels apathetic about its task, (2) group members don't expect to be successful, (3) one group member has very high credibility—group members tend to believe what he or she says, (4) one group member is very persuasive, and (5) group members don't usually challenge ideas—it's expected that group members will agree with one another.[43] Be on the lookout for these symptoms in your groups and teams.

Of course, as the saying goes, "Hindsight is 20/20." After the fact, it can be easy to spot an example of groupthink. The hard part is to be aware of groupthink when it occurs in your

Henry Martin/Cartoon Bank

"All those in favor say 'Aye.'"   "Aye."   "Aye."   "Aye."   "Aye."   "Aye."

# RECAP

## TOP SIX REASONS GROUPS AND TEAMS SOMETIMES MAKE STUPID DECISIONS

| | |
|---|---|
| No Common Goal | Group does not begin with the end in mind—no collective vision. |
| Analysis Paralysis | Team members overanalyze unimportant details; talk is valued more than action. |
| Jumping to Solutions | People propose solutions before the facts are known. |
| Topic Hopping | There is a lack of agenda and structure; discussion is not focused on the goal. |
| Killer Inch | People agree on major points but argue over minor details. |
| Groupthink | Group and team members agree too quickly; ideas are not questioned or challenged. |

**Figure 10.3
T-Chart**

| Pros | Cons |
|------|------|
|      |      |

group. Knowing the causes and symptoms of groupthink can help you spot it if it occurs in your group and then put an end to it.

To overcome groupthink, consider the following strategies.[44]

- Don't agree with someone just because he or she has high status; examine the ideas of others carefully, regardless of their position.
- Consider asking someone from outside the group to evaluate the group's decisions and decision-making process.
- Assign someone to be a devil's advocate—to look for disadvantages to a proposed idea.
- Ask group members to break into smaller teams or pairs to consider both the pros and the cons of a proposed solution.

An easy way to structure the discussion suggested in the last item above is to use a T-chart like the one in Figure 10.3. Write the possible solution at the top of the chart (on a flip chart, chalkboard, or transparency using an overhead projector) and then list both the pros and the cons. This technique will help you look at the positive and negative consequences of an action before you leap into a specific recommendation.

# RECAP

## REFLECTIVE-THINKING STEPS AND TECHNIQUES

| Steps | Techniques |
|-------|-----------|
| 1. Identify and define the problem. | • Phrase the problem as a policy question.<br>• Use the journalists' six questions (Who? What? When? Where? Why? How?) to help define the issues. |
| 2. Analyze the problem. | • Use force field analysis to identify driving and restraining forces.<br>• Develop clear criteria that clarify the issues and can help in evaluating solutions. |
| 3. Generate creative solutions. | • Use brainstorming.<br>• Use silent brainstorming (nominal group technique) or electronic brainstorming. |
| 4. Select the best solution. | • Narrow alternatives using ranking, rating, majority vote, or expert decision.<br>• Reach consensus by being goal oriented, by listening, and by promoting honest dialogue. |
| 5. Take action. | • Develop a clear action plan.<br>• Make a written list of who should do what. |

## Step 5: Take Action

Once you have identified your solution(s), your group needs to consider the question "Will it work?" You may want to do a pilot test (practice test) or ask a small group of people what they think of your idea before you "go public" with it. Bouncing your proposed solution off an expert and checking to see if the solution has been successful when others have adopted it can help you test the solution's effectiveness.

If your group has to not only identify a solution but also put it into action, your group will need structure to make sure that details don't get overlooked in getting the job done. Perhaps you know the people in the following story:

This is a story about four people: Everybody, Somebody, Anybody, and Nobody. There was an important job to be done, and Everybody was asked to do it. Everybody was sure Somebody would do it. Anybody could have done it, but Nobody did it. Somebody got angry about that because it was Everybody's job. Everybody thought

Anybody could do it, but Nobody realized that Everybody wouldn't do it. It ended up that Everybody blamed Somebody when actually Nobody asked Anybody.

Make a written list of who should do what. Follow up at the next group meeting to see whether the assignments have been completed. Effective groups and teams develop an action plan and periodically review it to make sure Anybody asked Somebody.

# Enhancing Group and Team Leadership

**Leadership** is the ability to influence others through communication. Some view a leader as someone who delegates and directs the group. Others see a leader as someone who is primarily responsible for ensuring that whatever task is assigned or designed by the group is completed. Actually, most groups have many leaders—not just one person who influences others. In fact, each group or team member undoubtedly influences what the group does or does not achieve. Regardless of who serves as leader, research suggests that the quality of group and team leadership has a significant effect on how satisfied team members are.[45] Members of an effectively led team feel greater satisfaction, are more productive, and are less likely to be absent than members of less effective groups.[46] The quality of team leadership influences virtually every aspect of what it feels like to be a team member. The prevailing approaches to analyzing the behavior of effective leaders are the trait, functional, styles, situational, and transformational approaches to leadership.

## Trait Approach

Are leaders born or made? The **trait approach to leadership** suggests that there are certain attributes or traits that make leaders. According to this approach, if you are born with these traits or if you cultivate leadership skills, you will be a leader. Research has identified intelligence, confidence, social skills, general administrative skill, physical energy, and enthusiasm as some of the traits effective leaders possess.[47] Researchers have also found that effective leaders develop persuasive arguments and are comfortable expressing their ideas to others.[48] Although many leaders do seem to have traits or special skills that can enhance their ability to influence others, just having these traits does not mean that you will be an effective leader. Many of these attributes that researchers have found may be important, but they are not sufficient to make a leader effective. Another research study found support for two of the Communication Principles for a Lifetime presented in this book: Effective leaders are self-aware and adapt to the people they lead and the context in which they lead.[49] But these traits alone will not ensure effective leadership behavior. Leadership is more complicated than that.

## Functional Approach

Rather than identifying personality characteristics or other traits, the **functional approach to leadership** categorizes the essential leadership behaviors or functions that need to be performed to enhance the workings of a group. According to the functional approach, there are two broad leadership functions: (1) task functions and (2) process functions. These two functions should look familiar. They are similar to the types of group roles discussed in the last chapter.

**Task functions** include behaviors that help the group or team get the work done. Whether the leader is appointed or elected, one of the responsibilities of leaders is to ensure that the group completes the task it is tackling. The functional approach to leadership suggests that several people can share the leadership functions. These are some of the jobs that often need to be done:

- Helping set the group's agenda
- Recording what the group does

**leadership**
The ability to influence the behavior of others through communication.

**trait approach to leadership**
A view of leadership that identifies specific qualities or characteristics of effective leaders.

**functional approach to leadership**
A view of leadership that identifies the key task and process roles that need to be performed in a group.

**task function**
A leadership behavior that helps a group accomplish its job.

- Determining when meetings begin and end
- Preparing and distributing handouts
- Initiating or proposing new ideas
- Seeking and giving information
- Suggesting options
- Elaborating on the ideas of others
- Evaluating ideas

In most groups, these key functions are assumed by many if not most group members. A group member who rarely helps with any of these tasks often earns the uncoveted title of "slacker."

**Process functions** are the second major type of function leaders assume in groups. Process leaders seek to maintain a friendly environment that promotes honest, frank discussion. Process leaders have "people skills." They listen sensitively to others and are observant of nonverbal cues. They focus on managing relationships by adapting to the needs of individual members. Another key process leadership task is to seek support from people and resources outside the team. An effective team leader keeps the team informed about how external influences affect the team's work goals.[50] Although a single person can perform all these functions, just as with task leadership, it is more than likely that several people will help maintain the group's process. Specific process roles include the following:

- Energizing the team by encouraging team members to keep at it
- Mediating conflict
- Compromising or helping others to compromise
- Gatekeeping: monitoring discussion to ensure that some members don't talk too much and others too little

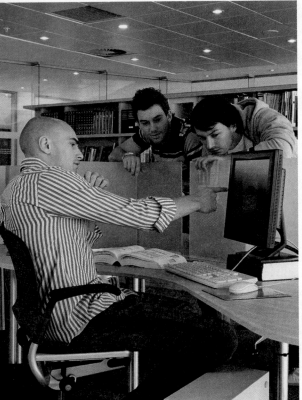

Giving information, suggesting options, and evaluating the ideas of group members are among the task functions involved in leading a group. Which task and process functions of leadership do you feel best equipped to carry out, and for which do you need to further develop your skills?
Goodshoot/Thinkstock

In most groups or teams, these process roles are not formally assigned. Although some of the task functions may be explicitly assigned to others ("Daria, would you make copies of this report?"), process roles are assumed when needed; they emerge based on the needs of the group and the personality, skills, sensitivity, and past experiences of the group members who are present. It is unlikely that you will start a meeting by saying, "Okay, Janice, you're in charge of settling the arguments between Ken and Daryl. And Carl, you try to encourage Muriel and Russell to talk more." Effective leaders look for opportunities to enhance the overall climate of the group; they try to catch people doing something right and then offer sincere praise and recognition.

## Styles Approach

The **styles approach to leadership** suggests that leaders operate in one of three primary styles: (1) authoritarian, (2) democratic, or (3) laissez-faire. The methods used to influence group members usually fall into one of these broad categories, outlined in Table 10.3.[51]

**Authoritarian leaders** influence by giving orders and controlling others. Dictators and military officers assume this leadership style. But you don't have to be in the military or living in a dictatorship to experience an authoritarian leadership style. Perhaps you've felt like mumbling, "Who put *her* in charge?" during a group meeting. Or maybe you have observed that some action needed to be taken and asked someone in the group to do what you thought was needed. As we discussed, groups need a certain amount of structure. The authoritarian leader assumes that he or she knows the type and amount of structure the group needs and proceeds to tell others what to do. Authoritarian leaders may be self-aware and may use appropriate verbal and nonverbal messages, but they are not always known for listening and responding to others; they also may not be worried about adapting their messages to those whom they lead. They often speak and expect others to follow. Of the three primary leadership styles, the

**process function**
A leadership behavior that helps maintain a positive group climate.

**styles approach to leadership**
A view of leadership that identifies three methods of interacting when leading others: authoritarian, democratic, and laissez-faire.

**authoritarian leader**
One who leads by directing, controlling, telling, and ordering others.

## Table 10.3
## Leadership Styles

| AUTHORITARIAN | DEMOCRATIC | LAISSEZ-FAIRE |
|---|---|---|
| The leader makes all policy decisions. | The leader discusses all policy decisions with group members. The group makes decisions by consensus. | The leader gives minimal direction to discussions of policy decisions. Group members must initiate discussions about policy and procedures. |
| The leader determines what will happen one step at a time; future steps are unclear or uncertain. | The group discusses what steps need to be taken. Group members work together to develop both short-term and long-term action steps. | The leader may supply information about what steps need to be taken, if asked. The leader does not volunteer information. |
| The leader tells people what to do. | The leader serves as a facilitator to develop a collaborative approach to accomplishing the group's work. | The leader does not participate in making work assignments. |

authoritarian leader is least effective over a long period of time.[52] Yet when a group or team experiences increased stress, a decisive leader is perceived as more charismatic than other types of leaders.[53] Group members don't like an authoritarian leader all the time, but they may tolerate or even appreciate a bold, charismatic leader when there's a need for someone to make an important decision quickly.

The **democratic leader**, as you might guess from the name, consults with the group before issuing edicts. The democratic leader listens and adapts messages to others. This type of leader seeks to join in the process of influencing without bulldozing or shoving the group into action it may resent. Sometimes formal votes are taken in larger groups or assemblies; but in smaller groups, the leader or leaders gauge the reaction of the group through dialogue and nonverbal cues. The democratic leader leads by developing a consensus rather than telling people what to do or think.

The **laissez-faire leader** takes a hands-off, laid-back approach to influencing. This type of leader shies away from actively influencing the group. He or she influences only when pushed to lead. Like the authoritarian leader, this type of leader often does not adapt to the needs of the group. A laissez-faire approach is easiest to spot when an elected or appointed leader simply won't lead. Some laissez-faire leaders fear making a mistake. Others just want to be liked and don't want to ruffle anyone's feathers. But as the slogan goes, "Not to decide is to decide." The laissez-faire leader is influencing the group by his or her silence or inactivity. The team may have a problem to unravel, but the laissez-faire leader is reluctant to act.

Which leadership style works best? It depends on the situation.

- During times of crisis, a group needs a decisive leader who can help manage uncertainty and provide appropriate structure. An authoritarian style may be acceptable.[54]
- If the group's task is to solve a problem or make a decision collaboratively, the democratic leadership style is what the group needs.
- If a group's goal is primarily social or creative, a laissez-faire leader may be best.

It also depends on the leader and the members. One study found that a democratic, collaborative leadership style works best when the leader is perceived as credible and charismatic.[55] A more directive, authoritarian style of leadership is generally more effective when group members believe that they can effectively accomplish the work and value direct assistance and guidance.

The effective leader adapts his or her style to fit the needs of the group and the task at hand. The principle of adapting to others gives rise to the situational approach

**democratic leader**
One who leads by developing a consensus among group members; a leader who asks for input and then uses the input when leading and making decisions.

**laissez-faire leader**
One who fails to lead or who leads or exerts influence only when asked or directed by the group.

to leadership. Remember that leadership in groups and teams is usually shared by several people. Even when someone has been appointed or elected to be "the leader," leadership roles are often assumed by several group members.

## Situational Approach

The **situational approach to leadership** views leadership as an interactive process in which such factors as culture, time limitations, group member personalities, and the work the group needs to do determine a particular style of leadership. Sometimes a group needs a strong, authoritarian leader to make decisions quickly so that the group can achieve its goal. Although a democratic leadership style is preferred by most groups, leaders sometimes need to be more assertive, especially in times of crisis or high uncertainty.

Groups with highly structured goals and a high level of stress may operate best with a more authoritarian leadership style. For example, firefighters who are battling a house fire with a family of five people inside have a clearly structured goal—save lives. In this situation, the group needs decisive authoritarian leadership. But a book club that is trying to select its next reading selection has less structured goals (there are many possible options) and a less stressful situation (there is no fire!). This less structured and less stressful task calls for a more participative democratic style of leadership. So, according to the situational approach, the answer to the question "What's the best leadership style?" is "It depends."[56]

The readiness of the group also plays a major role in which leadership style would work best.[57] *Readiness* refers to a group member's ability to assume responsibility to accomplish a task, their overall knowledge, background, and experience, and their general level of motivation. As shown in Figure 10.4, a directive, "telling" style of leadership seems to work best when groups have a low level of readiness. A high degree

**situational approach to leadership**
A view of leadership as an interactive process in which a leader gauges how to lead based on such factors as the quality of the relationships among group members, the power of the leader, the nature of the task, and the maturity of the group.

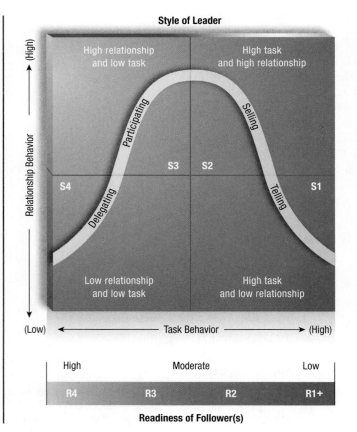

## Figure 10.4
## Group Member Readiness and Leadership Style

As the continuum of follower readiness shows, leaders should be more direct in groups where followers have less ability or willingness to accomplish tasks. The four quadrants of the graph show how much task guidance and interaction support different leaders offer. Delegating leaders take a laissez-faire approach, handing off problems and offering little interaction or guidance. Participating leaders encourage a lot of interaction but refrain from taking control. Selling leaders provide a lot of guidance and encourage interaction, explaining the reasoning for their instructions. Telling leaders simply tell people what to do and do not spend much time discussing their directives.

Source: "Situational Leadership Behavior." From *Management of Organizational Behavior* 8e, 2001. Reprinted with permission of Center for Leadership Studies, Escondido, CA 92025. www.situational.com All rights reserved.

of readiness would suggest that a more delegating style of leadership would help the group function well.

One simple rule for determining your leadership style is that when the leader emerges naturally from the group or leads a one-time-only group, the group will permit him or her to be more directive. If the group will be together for some time and the quality of group relations is important to the functioning of the group, a more participative, democratic leadership style is in order.[58]

## Transformational Leadership

One of the newer leadership approaches to emerge is called the **transformational approach to leadership**.[59] The transformational leader influences the group or organization by *transforming* the group—giving it a new vision, energizing or realigning the group culture, or giving the group a new structure. The leader leads by helping the group see all the possibilities within the group. The transformational leader also develops a relationship with those whom he or she leads.[60] Author Peter Senge suggests three fundamental skills of transformational leadership: (1) Build a shared vision, (2) challenge existing ways of thinking, and (3) be a systems thinker—help a group or team see that everything is connected to everything else.[61] Emerging research suggests that transformational leaders can enhance team cohesiveness and improve perceptions of team performance.[62] They achieve these benefits by linking with other groups and teams either inside or outside the organization; they help the group span boundaries and stay connected with issues and forces that influence the group.[63] Another skill of transformational leaders is the ability to help a team or organization grow and develop by encouraging new ideas. Transformational leaders help teams adopt new ideas and

**transformational approach to leadership**
A view of leadership that defines a leader as one who leads by shaping the vision of the group and by developing trust through quality interpersonal relationships with group members.

**surface-level diversity**
Human differences that are easily visible to us, such as differences in ethnicity, race, age, sex, gender, and other social and observable features.

**deep-level diversity**
Human differences that aren't always visible on the surface, such as differences in attitudes, opinions, values, information, culture, and other factors that take time to become evident in groups.

# Communication & DIVERSITY

## Deep and Surface Diversity: Which Differences Make a Difference?

People work in groups because "two heads are better than one." Multiple "heads" are better than one because our differences result in more varied approaches to solving a problem or illuminating an issue. But are all differences created equal?

Researchers have found that some differences among group members are more significant than others.[66] **Surface-level diversity** encompasses the human differences that are easily visible to us, such as differences in ethnicity, race, age, sex, gender, and other social and observable features. **Deep-level diversity** involves differences that aren't always visible on the surface, such as differences in attitudes, opinions, values, information, culture, and other factors that take time to become evident in groups. Group communication researcher Ralph Rodriguez has found that these differences in underlying values or approaches to problems affect a group's performance more than do differences in such surface characteristics as race, gender, and ethnicity. Rodriguez also suggests that groups can enhance the quality of their outcomes if they discuss their differences.[67]

- *Be cautious of making sweeping generalizations about those who are from a culture that appears to be similar*

*to yours.* Researchers have found that we often expect people who look like us at the surface level to agree with us. Yet the deep-level differences may be the best predictors of whether someone agrees or disagrees with our perspective.[68]

- *Take time to explore group members' deep-level differences in perspectives and approaches.* These deep-level differences are noticed only after people spend time with one another and are engaged in conversation.

- *Encourage people to share ideas and information via e-mail or text messages.* Because some members of a group may be quieter than others, responding individually rather than orally in the presence of others may bring out more differences in perspective that can help a group reach a better outcome.

- *Group members need the benefit of different perspectives.* If you're in the surface-level minority or the deep-level minority in a group, make sure that you tactfully, yet assertively, express your ideas, opinions, facts, and information to the group.

information. Teams that emphasize learning do a better job of both accomplishing the task and fostering positive, supportive interpersonal relationships.[64]

Articulating a collective vision is an important part of what a transformational leader does. An authoritarian leader would just tell the group, "Here's your vision; now get to work." The democratic leader would ask, "What vision do you want?" The laissez-faire leader would do nothing about a vision unless asked to do something. The situational leader would say, "Let me see what type of group I'm leading and listen to group members, and then I'll share a vision." The transformational leader paints a picture of the future for the group by getting to know individual members in the group. Drawing on the approaches of both the democratic leader and the situational leader, the transformational leader leads by establishing quality interpersonal relationships with others. Transformational leaders provide inspiration, motivation, and intellectual stimulation for the group by being aware of individual needs. A wise leader will also consider the cultural backgrounds of those whom she or he leads. Research supports the important role of culture in influencing the style of leadership that seems to be best suited to a team.[65] A group with a collective cultural framework seems to appreciate more participative styles of leadership.

Transformational leadership is less a set of prescribed skills or techniques than a general philosophy that says people can be trusted and can be motivated to achieve important goals if they have someone they can trust to help them see the possibilities. Transformational leaders like to think of themselves as coaches or mentors rather than leaders who dictate or even just facilitate interaction; they are sometimes viewed as the "guide on the side" rather than the "sage on the stage."

Can transformational leadership skills—or any leadership skills—be taught, the way you can teach someone to drive a car? Some suggest that experience is the best teacher.[69] You can learn how to communicate, listen, relate, and solve problems, but having an opportunity to practice these skills in real-life settings may be the best way to develop your leadership skills. Whether you learn leadership skills and principles from a book or from the "school of life," the role of a good leader is that of a servant, helping others accomplish a goal. This ancient description of a wise leader offers considerable insight into what makes a leader great:

> The wicked leader the people despise.
> The good leader the people revere.
> Of the great leader the people say,
> "We did it ourselves."
>
> —Lao Tsu

# Enhancing Group and Team Meetings

Humor columnist Dave Barry said, "If you had to identify, in one word, the reason why the human race has not achieved, and never will achieve, its full potential, that word would be

## RECAP

### LEADERSHIP APPROACHES

| Approach to Leadership | Guiding Principle |
|---|---|
| Trait | Leaders possess certain traits or characteristics that contribute to leadership effectiveness. |
| Functional | Leaders influence others through two primary functions:<br>• Task functions, which help accomplish the work<br>• Process functions, which help establish a positive climate |
| Styles | Leadership is enacted in three primary styles:<br>• Authoritarian leaders direct and control others.<br>• Democratic leaders solicit input from others and seek to lead by involving others in the decisions.<br>• Laissez-faire leaders intentionally influence others only when asked or directed by others to lead. |
| Situational | Leadership is an interactive process in which a leader adapts his or her approach based on such factors as<br>• The quality of group member relationships.<br>• The nature of the task.<br>• Time limitations. |
| Transformational | A leader influences others by<br>• Developing a shared vision.<br>• Using listening and relationship-building skills to create a climate of trust. |

*meetings.*[70] Meetings are an inescapable fact of life for most people and will undoubtedly be inescapable for you as well.

Why does meeting participation inspire such a negative reaction—not only from Dave Barry, but from many people? Often, it's because meeting leaders and participants have not mastered the principles we've stressed as fundamental to communication success in any context. Meetings are more productive if participants are aware of their behaviors and the behavior of others. Using and interpreting verbal and nonverbal messages effectively are also vital for meeting effectiveness, as are listening and responding to messages with sensitivity. Because of the complexity and uncertainty that arise when people collaborate, being able to adapt message content and message structure is essential. We conclude this chapter by providing some tips for managing one of the most likely collaborative contexts you'll encounter—meetings.

What specific problems occur most frequently in meetings? Based on a survey of meeting participants, the most common meeting "sin" is getting off the subject.[71] The second biggest problem is not having clear goals or a meeting agenda. Meeting goers also reported that often meetings were too long, people weren't prepared, nothing really happened, meetings started late, and there were no follow-up action plans.

Meetings need two essential things to be effective: *structure* and *interaction*. Sound familiar? As noted earlier in this chapter, groups also need a balance of these two things.

## Manage Meeting Structure

The essential weapon to combat disorganized, rambling meetings is a clear, well-developed agenda. An **agenda** is a list of the key issues, ideas, and information that will be discussed, in the order of discussion. How do you develop a well-crafted agenda? Consider these three steps.

**Step One: Determine Your Meeting Goals**   Every meeting seeks to accomplish something. (If you don't have something to accomplish, don't hold a meeting!) Most meetings have one or more of the following three goals: (1) giving information, (2) discussing information, and (3) taking action.

- *Giving information.* An information-giving meeting is like a briefing or a series of short speeches. If the only task is to share information, you may not really need a meeting at all—a written memo or an e-mail message will suffice. If you want to share information with others face to face to emphasize its importance, giving information is an appropriate primary meeting goal.
- *Discussing information.* An information-discussion meeting is one in which there is considerable give and take. The key to this type of meeting is not to let it become a series of long-winded speeches. Also, if you're not careful, discussions digress from the topic. The meeting leader or meeting participants should be aware of the goals of the discussion so that the comments remain relevant.

**agenda**
A written plan for achieving the goals during a group meeting, which typically includes items for discussion, action, and information.

- *Taking action.* A meeting may involve making a decision, solving a problem, or implementing a decision or solution. If the purpose of the meeting is to take action, it's helpful if group members know before they arrive for the meeting that they will be asked to take some action.

### Step Two: Identify What Needs to Be Discussed to Achieve the Goal

After you have determined your goal(s), you need to determine how to structure the meeting to achieve the goal. What topics need to be covered to achieve the goal? What information do you need? What issues do you need to focus on? Brainstorm answers to these questions, but don't worry about the precise order of the items yet; focus on organizing the agenda after you know what you need to discuss.

### Step Three: Organize the Agenda

Once you have identified your meeting goals (giving information, discussing information, taking action) and assessed what you need to talk about, take time to arrange the items in the most effective way to achieve your goals. There are several strategies for organizing effective meetings.[72]

- Organize the agenda around your meeting goals. If you're meeting to solve a problem, you could use the five problem-solving steps as an agenda-setting guide: (1) identify and define the problem, (2) analyze the problem, (3) generate creative options, (4) select the best option, and (5) take action. A single meeting may focus on only one or two of those steps; don't feel that you have to cram all five problem-solving steps into every meeting.
- Use subheads of "Information Items," "Discussion Items," and "Action Items" as you construct your agenda to signal to group members the goal of the discussion, as shown in the sample meeting agenda.
- Consider putting your most important agenda item first, because usually what is introduced first takes the most time.
- There may be times when you will want to put your most challenging issue for discussion in the middle of the meeting; this gives the group a chance to get oriented at the beginning and ease out of the discussion at the end.[73]
- Consider making your first agenda item something that will immediately involve all meeting participants in active discussion. If you start with routine reports (a common practice), you establish a norm of passivity, and boredom is the usual result.
- If you are going to discuss a conflict-producing topic, you may want to put that agenda item after an issue on which you think the group will reach agreement; groups may be more likely to reach agreement on a contentious issue if they have already reached agreement on another point.
- Start the meeting by asking meeting participants if they have any other agenda items to consider. That way you aren't as likely to be surprised by people who want to add something after you've planned the meeting agenda.
- After you've prepared your agenda, estimate how long you think the group will take to discuss each agenda item. Most groups take more time than you would expect to talk about issues and ideas.

# RECAP

## MAKING MEETING AGENDAS USEFUL

| Potential Meeting Agenda Problem | Suggested Meeting Agenda Strategy |
|---|---|
| Meeting participants tend to spend more time on the first or second agenda item than on later items. | Make sure that the early agenda items are something the group needs to spend time on. |
| Meeting participants want to talk, even if the meeting leader wants them to just listen. | Take advantage of the desire to participate by inviting input and discussion early in the meeting rather than trying to squelch discussion or interrupt group members. |
| Meeting participants aren't prepared. They haven't done their "homework." | Take a few minutes for silent reading. Let members get up to speed by reviewing information or quickly looking at key pieces of data. |
| Meeting participants won't stick to the agenda. | Continue to remind the group of the agenda and the overall goal of the meeting. Make sure to distribute a written agenda ahead of the meeting. |
| There is an agenda item that may produce conflict and disagreement. | Help the group develop a sense of success by putting one or more non-controversial items on the agenda ahead of the item that may produce conflict. Build on the group's ability to reach agreement. |

A sample agenda is shown here. Notice that the meeting has clear goals. Also notice how many of the agenda items are phrased as questions. Questions give an agenda focus and help to manage discussion.

When your job is to lead the meeting, you have several specific tasks to perform, including the following:

1. Call the group together; find out when is the best time to meet (finding time is often a major problem for busy people).
2. Develop an agenda, using the steps already described.
3. Determine whether there is a **quorum**— the minimum number of persons who must be present at a meeting to conduct business.
4. Call the meeting to order.
5. Use a flip chart, chalkboard, or dry-erase board to summarize meeting progress; written notes of the meeting become the "group mind" and help keep the group structured.
6. Decide when to take a vote.
7. Prepare a final report or delegate to a group member the preparation of a report or minutes.

## SAMPLE MEETING AGENDA

Meeting Goals:

1. Discuss new product proposal: evaluate the pros and cons
2. Decide whether to implement the personnel policy and mentor program
3. Receive updates from committees
   I. Discussion Items
      A. How should we revise today's agenda?
      B. Identify new problems: What new issues or problems have you identified?
      C. React to new product team proposal (distributed by e-mail): What are the pros and cons of the proposal?
   II. Action Items
      A. Should we approve the new personnel policy (distributed by e-mail)?
      B. Issue: Should we implement the new mentor program? If so, what should the program policies be?
   III. Information Items
      A. New employee orientation report
      B. Planning committee report
      C. Finance committee report
      D. Announcements

## Manage Meeting Interaction

Interaction, as you recall, is the back-and-forth dialogue and discussion in which participants engage during meetings. Without interaction, meetings would be like a monologue, a speech, or a seminar rather than a lively discussion. It's important for people in a meeting to be involved in the discussion. Research has found that meetings that have a more equal participation by all participants generally are more effective than meetings dominated by a few people.[74] But too much unfocused interaction can result in a disorganized, chaotic discussion. To keep a meeting on track, meeting leaders and participants need facilitation skills. The most important facilitation skills include being a gatekeeper, using metadiscussion, monitoring discussion time, and structuring discussion techniques to keep discussion focused.

**Use Gatekeeping Skills**    A gatekeeper encourages less-talkative members to participate and tries to limit long-winded contributions by other group members. Gatekeepers need to be good listeners so that they can help manage the flow of conversation. Gatekeepers make such comments as "Ashley, we haven't heard your ideas yet. Won't you share your thoughts with us?" or "Mike, thanks for sharing, but I'd like to hear what others have to say." Polite, tactful invitations to talk or limit talk usually work. You may need to speak privately with a chronic oververbalizer to let him or her know that you'd appreciate a more balanced discussion.

**Use Metadiscussion**    **Metadiscussion** literally means "discussion about discussion."[75] It's a comment about the discussion process rather than about the topic under consideration. Metadiscussional statements include "I'm not following this conversation. What is our goal?" "Can someone summarize what we've accomplished so far?" and "Peggy, I'm not sure I understand how your observation relates to our meeting goal." These comments contain information and advice about the communication *process* rather than about the issues being discussed.

**quorum**
The minimum number of persons who must be present at a meeting to conduct business.

**metadiscussion**
Discussion about the discussion process; comments that help the group remain focused on the goals of the group or that point out how the group is doing its work.

Metadiscussional phrases are helpful ways to keep the team or group focused on the task. Obviously, metadiscussional statements should not be phrased to personally attack others. Don't just blurt out "You're off task" or "Oh, let's not talk about that anymore." Instead, use tactful ways of letting other group members know that you'd like to return to the issues at hand. Use "I" messages rather than "you" messages to bring the group back on track. An **"I" message** begins with the word *I*, such as "I am not sure where we are in our discussion" or "I am lost here." A **"you" message** is a way of phrasing a message that makes others feel defensive—for example, "You're not following the agenda" or "Your point doesn't make any sense." Another way to express these same ideas, but with less of a negative edge, is to use "I" messages such as "I'm not sure where we are on the agenda" or "I'm not sure I understand how your point relates to the issue we are discussing." The ability to carry on metadiscussion is an exceptionally powerful skill, because you can offer metadiscussional statements even if you are not the appointed leader.

**"I" message**
A message in which you state your perspective or point of view.

**"you" message**
A message that is likely to create defensiveness in others because it emphasizes how another person has created a problem rather than describing the problem from one's own perspective ("I" message).

**Monitor Time**   Being sensitive to the time the group is spending on an issue is yet another skill necessary to manage meeting interaction. Think of your agenda as a map, helping you plan where you want to go. Think of the clock as your gas gauge, telling you the amount of fuel you have to get where you want to go. In a meeting, keeping one eye on the clock and one eye on the agenda is analogous to focusing on the map and the gas gauge on a car trip. If you are running low on fuel (time), you will need to either get more gas (budget more time) or recognize that you will not get where you want to go. Begin each meeting by asking how long members can meet. If you face two or three crucial agenda items and one-third of your group has to leave in an hour, you may need to reshuffle your agenda to make sure that you can achieve your goals.

# Communication & TECHNOLOGY

## Virtual Meeting Tips

A virtual meeting occurs when you use the Internet or some other electronic means of connecting with others rather than meeting face to face. Increased globalization of the economy, rising travel costs, and technological advances in electronic collaboration make it likely that you will hold meetings in cyberspace. What are ways to maximize your e-collaboration? Here are several research-supported tips to help you make the most of mediated meetings.[76]

- *Start live.* If at all possible, make your first meeting a face-to-face meeting. Getting to know your team members live and in person helps develop positive relationships at the outset of a longer project in which you will be interacting over a period of time.[77]
- *Develop communication ground rules.* When not communicating during a planned virtual meeting, determine how and when you will communicate with other team members.[78] Will you call someone on the phone? Skype? Only use e-mail? Clarify communication expectations about the method of communication and when it's best to reach your fellow team members.
- *Communicate frequently.* One ground rule we suggest is to contact team members when questions or issues arise even if you're not in a scheduled meeting.

Don't hesitate to send virtual meeting members short notes and messages. Resist the temptation to hold on to information until you have a longer message. Frequent communication helps virtual meeting participants get to know one another.

- *Use technology to monitor team progress.* Invite team members to provide periodic reports via e-mail or on the team home page. Also distribute meeting minutes via e-mail very soon after the group has held a virtual meeting.
- *Encourage the development of relationships.* Virtual meetings have a tendency to be task oriented. To foster good team relationships, at the beginning of a virtual meeting allow time for relationship building; encourage meeting participants to engage in "off-task" talk, communicating personal information. During the meeting, ensure that every person is heard from and that all are engaged and participating in the meeting.
- *Be positive.* Research also suggests that virtual group members who have a positive perception of their own abilities to achieve results, whether in a face-to-face or a computer-mediated virtual group, are, in fact, more effective. So, fostering a "can-do" spirit in a group or team is a good thing to do.[79]

**Use Structure to Manage Interaction** Another way to manage interaction is to use some of the prescriptive structures talked about earlier. For example, using silent brainstorming is a way to gain maximum participation from everyone. Yet another strategy is to ask people to come to the meeting with written responses to questions you posed in the agenda, which group members received in advance of the meeting. This signals that you want people to prepare for the meeting rather than doing their "homework" at the meeting. An essential task of the meeting facilitator is to orchestrate meaningful interaction during the meeting so that all group or team members have the opportunity to share. Another structured method of inviting involvement is to have group members first write individually and then share their ideas with the group. Having members write before speaking is like providing them with a script, which can be effective in garnering contributions from *all* group members—not just the people who talk the most or who aren't shy about speaking up.

One of the best ways to ensure appropriate interaction as a meeting participant when you are not assigned the specific role of leader is to consider the following suggestions from Roger Mosvick and Robert Nelson in their book *We've Got to Start Meeting Like This!*[80]

- Organize what you say. Don't ramble.
- Speak to the point. Make sure that your contributions are relevant to the goal.
- Make one point at a time.
- Speak clearly and forcefully. Weak, timid suggestions mumbled to the group will probably not be listened to.
- Support your ideas with evidence. Don't just assert opinion without data or expert opinion backing you up.
- Listen. Listen. Listen. Connect your comments to those of others.

What are the best strategies to make yourself a valuable meeting leader or participant? The five Communication Principles for a Lifetime emphasized throughout the book will serve you well. In general, be aware of your own behavior and the behavior of others. Monitor your verbal and nonverbal messages to make sure that you are making comments relevant to the task at hand, but also be sensitive to the needs of the people in your group. You develop that sensitivity by listening to others and thoughtfully responding. Ineffective meeting participants make little effort to link their comments to what others are saying. They also don't adapt to the messages of others. Effective communicators adapt what they say and do to help achieve the goals of the group.

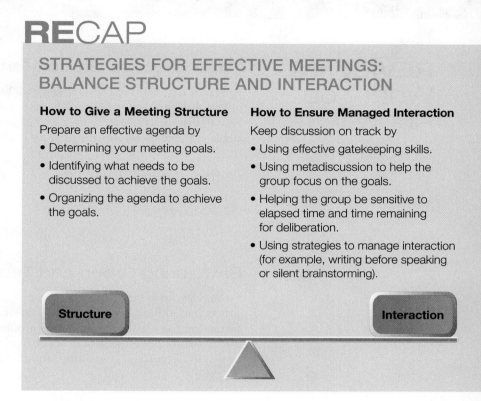

# RECAP

## STRATEGIES FOR EFFECTIVE MEETINGS: BALANCE STRUCTURE AND INTERACTION

### How to Give a Meeting Structure
Prepare an effective agenda by
- Determining your meeting goals.
- Identifying what needs to be discussed to achieve the goals.
- Organizing the agenda to achieve the goals.

### How to Ensure Managed Interaction
Keep discussion on track by
- Using effective gatekeeping skills.
- Using metadiscussion to help the group focus on the goals.
- Helping the group be sensitive to elapsed time and time remaining for deliberation.
- Using strategies to manage interaction (for example, writing before speaking or silent brainstorming).

**Structure**      **Interaction**

# STUDY GUIDE:
# Review, Apply, and Assess Your Knowledge and Skill

**REVIEWING**
What You
Know

## What Effective Group Members Do        p. 247

Research has identified several essential functions that, when carried out in a group, enhance group performance. Effective group members identify the goal; develop a results-driven structure; gather, share, and use information effectively; develop options; evaluate ideas; and are sensitive to group social and relationship concerns.

### Terms to Know

| | | | |
|---|---|---|---|
| Functional Approach | p. 247 | Results-Driven Structure | p. 248 |
| Vigilant Thinker | p. 247 | | |

## Structuring Group and Team Problem Solving  p. 252

Groups perform best if they have appropriate structure to make a sometimes bumpy process smoother. Although there is no single series of steps that will ensure high performance, five classic steps can help groups organize the problem-solving process: (1) identify and define the problem, (2) analyze the problem, (3) generate creative solutions, (4) select the best solution, and (5) take action.

### Terms to Know

| | | | |
|---|---|---|---|
| Structure | p. 252 | Brainstorming | p. 256 |
| Interaction | p. 252 | Silent Brainstorming (Nominal | |
| Reflective Thinking | p. 253 | Group Technique) | p. 256 |
| Criteria | p. 254 | Consensus | p. 257 |
| Force Field Analysis Technique | p. 254 | Groupthink | p. 258 |
| Creativity | p. 255 | | |

## Enhancing Group and Team Leadership        p. 261

High-performing groups have competent group leaders. Researchers have devised several approaches to analyzing leadership. The trait approach to leadership seeks to identify certain characteristics or traits that all leaders possess. The functional approach to leadership suggests that leaders need to be concerned with both task functions and group process functions. A third approach to understanding leadership, the styles approach, identifies leaders as authoritarian, democratic, or laissez-faire. No one style seems to work all the time. The situational leadership approach suggests that the best leadership style depends on a variety of factors, including the readiness of the group, the urgency of the problem, and the type of issue the group is discussing. Finally, transformational leadership is an approach that encourages leaders to help shape the vision and goals of the group by being in touch with followers.

**Terms to Know**

## Enhancing Group and Team Meetings    p. 266

An effective meeting needs a balance of structure and interaction. Groups maintain appropriate structure if meeting planners develop and use an agenda to keep the discussion focused and on track. Meetings also need appropriate amounts of dialogue and discussion. Effective meeting participants monitor the amount of participation from other group or team members and serve as gatekeepers to ensure that ooververbalizers don't monopolize the discussion and quiet members don't feel intimidated.

**Terms to Know**

**Principle One:**
**Be aware of your communication with yourself and others.**
- Be sensitive to your group's need for appropriate structure to organize and focus the discussion or interaction and to encourage dialogue.
- Be aware of the appropriate leadership style to meet your group's needs.

**Principle Two:**
**Effectively use and interpret verbal messages.**
- Clearly describe the goal of the group.
- Evaluate the merits of ideas by verbalizing both the pros and the cons.
- Use verbal "I messages" to express your need for information and your sensitivity to other group members' feelings.
- Develop and use written agendas to give meetings structure.
- Manage the amount of interaction in a group by encouraging quiet members to participate and overly dominant members to let others express ideas.
- Use metadiscussion to keep a meeting on track.

**Principle Three:**
**Effectively use and interpret nonverbal messages.**
- Use appropriate nonverbal messages to establish and maintain a positive group climate.
- When brainstorming, do your best to avoid expressing your evaluation of others' ideas nonverbally.

**APPLYING**
Principles
for a
Lifetime

- Communicate your sensitivity to other group members through your nonverbal behavior.
- Use appropriate eye contact and other nonverbal cues to regulate the flow of interaction in group and team meetings.

### Principle Four:
### Listen and respond thoughtfully to others.

- Listen to other group members to determine whether your group is accomplishing the appropriate group functions.
- Listen and respond to others to express your sensitivity to others' ideas and opinions.
- To be an effective leader, listen and thoughtfully respond to all members.
- Listen and respond to provide appropriate contributions to group meetings and problem-solving discussions.

### Principle Five:
### Appropriately adapt messages to others.

- Adapt your leadership and group membership styles to achieve the goals of the group.
- Adapt your messages to help the group identify, define, and analyze the problem; create solutions; select the best solution; and take action.
- Adapt your messages to give group meetings appropriate structure and to foster interaction.

# ASSESSING Your Skill

## Assessing Group and Team Problem-Solving Competencies[81]

Use the evaluation form on pages 276–277 to assess the presence or absence of small group communication competencies in a group or team discussion. *Competencies* are specific behaviors that group and team members perform. The assessment form includes nine competencies organized into four general categories. Here's how to use the form:

1. Observe a group or team that is attempting to solve a problem. Write the names of the group members at the top of the form. (If the group includes more than five group members, photocopy the form so that each group member can be evaluated.)

2. When using the form, first decide whether each group member has performed each competency. Circle NO if the group member was not observed performing the competency. Circle YES if you did observe the group member performing the competency (for example, defining the problem, analyzing the problem, identifying criteria).

3. For each competency for which you circled YES, determine how effectively the competency was performed. Use a scale from 0 to 3:

   0 = The group member performed this competency but did so inappropriately or inadequately. For example, the person observed tried to define the problem but did so poorly.

   1 = Overall, the person's performance of this competency was adequate.
   2 = The person performed this competency twice.
   3 = The person performed this competency three or more times.

4. Total the score for each group member in each of the following four categories.

   *Problem-oriented competencies* consist of items 1 and 2. These are behaviors that help the group or team define and analyze the problem. If a group member performed the competencies, his or her total number of points range from 0 to 6. The more points he or she scores, the better the individual performed this competency.

*Solution-oriented competencies* include items 3, 4, and 5; the total number of points for this category range from 0 to 9. These competencies focus on how well the group or team member helped develop and evaluate a solution to the problem.

*Discussion management competencies*, competencies that helped the group or team remain focused or helped the group manage interaction, are items 6 and 7. The total points for this category range from 0 to 6.

*Relational competencies* are behaviors that focus on dealing with conflict and developing a positive, supportive group climate. Items 8 and 9 reflect this competency; points for this category range from 0 to 6.

5. You can also assess the group's or team's overall ability to perform these competencies. The column marked "Group Assessment" can be used to record your overall impressions of how effectively the group or team behaved. Circle NO if no one in the group performed a particular competency. Circle YES if at least one person in the group or team performed this competency. Then evaluate how well the entire group performed this competency, using the scale already described.

Sometimes it is difficult to make so many judgments about group competencies by just viewing a group discussion once. Many people find that it's easier to make a video recording of the group discussion so that they can observe it more than once.

- **MyCommunicationLab** Highlights of this chapter of MyCommunicationLab include a web activity exploring groupthink and a video about virtual miscommunication. Be sure to use the self-quizzes to review chapter material, too. <www.mycommunicationlab.com> (Access code required.)

- **Meeting Tips** For a summary of meeting strategies and tactics, go to <http://www.etu.org.za/toolbox/docs/building/webmeetings.html>

- **Virtual Meetings** A commercial site, GoToMeeting will let you sign up for a thirty-day free trial subscription to practice your virtual meeting skills. Consider signing up with friends or colleagues to gain experience in using virtual meeting software. <http://www.gotomeeting.com/fec/online_meeting>

- **Robert's Rules of Order** Parliamentary procedure is a standard set of rules helpful for organizing large group meetings. For the classic guide to parliamentary procedure, consult the website. <http://www.rulesonline.com>

## WEB RESOURCES for More Review, Application, and Assessment

# Competent Group Communicator

| PROBLEM-SOLVING GROUP COMMUNICATION COMPETENCIES | GROUP MEMBER A | | GROUP MEMBER B | |
|---|---|---|---|---|

**COMPETENCIES**

## Problem-Oriented Competencies

| | GROUP MEMBER A | | GROUP MEMBER B | |
|---|---|---|---|---|
| 1. **Defined the problem** the group attempted to solve. | NO | YES 0 1 2 3 | NO | YES 0 1 2 3 |
| 2. **Analyzed the problem** the group attempted to solve. Used relevant information, data, or evidence; discussed the causes, obstacles, history, symptoms, or significance of the problem. | NO | YES 0 1 2 3 | NO | YES 0 1 2 3 |

## Solution-Oriented Competencies

| | | | | |
|---|---|---|---|---|
| 3. **Identified criteria** for an appropriate solution to the problem. | NO | YES 0 1 2 3 | NO | YES 0 1 2 3 |
| 4. **Generated solutions** or alternatives to the problem. | NO | YES 0 1 2 3 | NO | YES 0 1 2 3 |
| 5. **Evaluated solution(s):** Identified positive or negative consequences of the proposed solutions. | NO | YES 0 1 2 3 | NO | YES 0 1 2 3 |

## Discussion Management Competencies

| | | | | |
|---|---|---|---|---|
| 6. **Maintained task focus:** Helped the group stay on or return to the task, issue, or topic the group was discussing. | NO | YES 0 1 2 3 | NO | YES 0 1 2 3 |
| 7. **Managed group interaction:** Appropriately initiated and terminated discussion, contributed to the discussion, or invited others to contribute to the discussion. Didn't dominate or withdraw. | NO | YES 0 1 2 3 | NO | YES 0 1 2 3 |

## Relational Competencies

| | | | | |
|---|---|---|---|---|
| 8. **Managed conflict:** Appropriately and constructively helped the group stay focused on issues rather than personalities when conflict occurred. | NO | YES 0 1 2 3 | NO | YES 0 1 2 3 |
| 9. **Maintained climate:** Offered positive verbal comments or nonverbal expressions that helped maintain a positive group climate. | NO | YES 0 1 2 3 | NO | YES 0 1 2 3 |

## Scoring

NO = Not observed   YES

| 0 = Overall inappropriate or inadequate performance of competency | 1 = Overall adequate performance of competency | 2 = Person performed this competency twice | 3 = Person performed this competency three or more times |
|---|---|---|---|

| GROUP MEMBER C | | GROUP MEMBER D | | GROUP MEMBER E | | GROUP ASSESSMENT | |
|---|---|---|---|---|---|---|---|
| NO | YES<br>0 1 2 3 | NO | YES<br>0 1 2 3 | NO | YES<br>0 1 2 3 | NO | YES<br>0 1 2 3 |
| NO | YES<br>0 1 2 3 | NO | YES<br>0 1 2 3 | NO | YES<br>0 1 2 3 | NO | YES<br>0 1 2 3 |
| NO | YES<br>0 1 2 3 | NO | YES<br>0 1 2 3 | NO | YES<br>0 1 2 3 | NO | YES<br>0 1 2 3 |
| NO | YES<br>0 1 2 3 | NO | YES<br>0 1 2 3 | NO | YES<br>0 1 2 3 | NO | YES<br>0 1 2 3 |
| NO | YES<br>0 1 2 3 | NO | YES<br>0 1 2 3 | NO | YES<br>0 1 2 3 | NO | YES<br>0 1 2 3 |
| NO | YES<br>0 1 2 3 | NO | YES<br>0 1 2 3 | NO | YES<br>0 1 2 3 | NO | YES<br>0 1 2 3 |
| NO | YES<br>0 1 2 3 | NO | YES<br>0 1 2 3 | NO | YES<br>0 1 2 3 | NO | YES<br>0 1 2 3 |
| NO | YES<br>0 1 2 3 | NO | YES<br>0 1 2 3 | NO | YES<br>0 1 2 3 | NO | YES<br>0 1 2 3 |
| NO | YES<br>0 1 2 3 | NO | YES<br>0 1 2 3 | NO | YES<br>0 1 2 3 | NO | YES<br>0 1 2 3 |

Problem-Oriented Competencies (0–6)

Solution-Oriented Competencies (0–9)

Discussion Management Competencies (0–6)

Relational Competencies (0–6)

Freedom of speech is of no use to a man who has nothing to say.

FRANKLIN D. ROOSEVELT

## **Chapter** OBJECTIVES

After studying this chapter, you should be able to

1. List the nine components of the audience-centered public speaking model.

2. Define speaker anxiety, explain what causes it, and offer at least three suggestions for building confidence.

3. Write an audience-centered specific-purpose statement.

4. Generate main ideas from a central idea.

5. Describe four sources and seven types of supporting material for a presentation, and offer guidelines for using each type effectively.

Bronwyn Photo/Shutterstock.com

# 11 | **Developing Your Presentation**

A good friend of ours who has lived in Hong Kong for several years recently remarked that she found traveling back to the United States exhausting. Her reason? It was not so much the long plane trip or the thirteen-hour time difference, but, as she explained, "When I begin to hear airport public announcements in English instead of Cantonese, I suddenly feel compelled to pay attention to every word. All that listening wears me out!"

Few of us can take for granted that others will listen to us merely because we are speaking their native language. When we study the presentational speaking process and learn its component skills and principles however, we certainly increase the likelihood that others will listen to us out of genuine, compelling interest.

Far from being a rare talent possessed only by an inspired few, **public speaking**, or **presentational speaking**, is a teachable, learnable process—a process of developing, supporting, organizing, and orally presenting ideas. The skills you will develop as you learn and practice the presentational speaking process will be of practical use in the future. They will give you an edge in other college courses that require oral presentations. They may help you convince a current or future boss that you deserve a raise. And they may even land you a job.

Let's begin our discussion with an overview of the presentational speaking process. Then we will offer suggestions for building your confidence as a presentational speaker. In the final pages of this chapter, we will focus more closely on the first five stages of the presentational speaking process—discovering and narrowing your topic, identifying your purpose, developing a central idea, generating main ideas, and gathering supporting material for your presentation—all firmly grounded in the five Communication Principles for a Lifetime.

# Overviewing the Presentational Speaking Process

Chances are that you didn't complete a driver-education course before you got behind the wheel of a car for the first time. Similarly, you don't have to read an entire book on public speaking before you give your first presentation. An overview of the presentational speaking process can help you with your early assignments, even if you have to speak before you have a chance to read Chapters 12 through 15.

Figure 11.1 illustrates the presentational speaking process. View the model as a clock, with "Select and narrow topic" at 12 o'clock. From this stage, the process proceeds clockwise in the direction of the arrows, to "Deliver presentation." Each stage is one of the tasks of the public speaker:

1. Select and narrow topic.
2. Identify purpose.
3. Develop central idea.
4. Generate main ideas.
5. Gather supporting material.
6. Organize presentation.
7. Rehearse presentation.
8. Deliver presentation.

Note that a ninth component, "Consider the audience," appears at the center of the model. Double-headed arrows connect this center with every other stage, illustrating that at any point you may revise your ideas or strategies as you learn more about your audience. Your audience influences every decision you make.

**Audience-centered presentational speakers** are inherently sensitive to the diversity of their audiences. While guarding against generalizations that might be offensive, they acknowledge that cultural, ethnic, and other traditions affect the way

**public speaking (presentational speaking)**
A teachable, learnable process of developing, supporting, organizing, and orally presenting ideas.

**audience-centered presentational speaker**
Someone who considers and adapts to the audience at every stage of the presentational speaking process.

people process messages. They apply the fundamental principle of appropriately adapting their messages to others. How? They might choose to use pictures to help them communicate. They might select topics and use illustrations with universal themes such as family and friendship. They might adjust the formality of their delivery and even their dress to whatever is expected by the majority of the audience members. The fundamental communication principle of adapting to the audience is the key to the success of any presentation.

# Building Your Confidence

The above overview of the stages of the public speaking process should help you understand how to prepare for your first speaking assignment, but if you still feel nervous at the prospect, you are definitely not alone.[1] One study found that more than 80 percent of us feel anxious when we speak to an audience.[2] Another survey discovered that people are more afraid of public speaking than of death![3]

Increasingly, researchers are concluding that communication apprehension may have a genetic or biological basis: Some people may inherit a tendency to feel anxious about speaking in public.[4] Yet even if you are predisposed by genetics to experience **speaker anxiety**, you can learn strategies to help you manage your apprehension. If, on the other hand, the prospect of giving a presentation makes you feel a sense of heightened excitement rather than fear, you can use these same strategies to make your excitement help rather than distract you.

## Figure 11.1
## An Audience-Centered Model of the Presentational Speaking Process

**speaker anxiety**
Also known as stage fright; anxiety about speaking in public that is manifested in physiological symptoms such as rapid heartbeat, butterflies in the stomach, shaking knees and hands, quivering voice, and increased perspiration.

# DEVELOPING YOUR PRESENTATION
## stepbystep

### Considering Your Audience

A well-known Chinese proverb says that a journey of a thousand miles begins with a single step. Developing and delivering a presentation may seem like a daunting journey. If you take it one step at a time and keep your focus on your audience, however, we believe that you'll be rewarded with a well-crafted and well-delivered message.

To help you see how the audience-centered presentation process unfolds, this Developing Your Presentation Step-by-Step feature will provide a window through which you can see how one student prepared and delivered a presentation. Tony

Longoria, a student and teaching assistant at Texas State University–San Marcos, developed the informative presentation entitled "Excessive Facebooking: What You Need to Know" that is outlined in Chapter 12.[5] In the pages ahead, we'll walk through the process Tony used to develop his speech.

Tony thought about his audience even before selecting his topic. Realizing that his listeners would include both university students and faculty, he knew that he could discuss complex issues, using a fairly advanced vocabulary. His concern, however, was to find a topic that would interest both groups.

Harry Potter creator J. K. Rowling has admitted experiencing speaker anxiety; we all need to take positive steps to control anxiety before a performance.

AP Photo/Seth Wenig

**illusion of transparency**
The mistaken belief that the physical manifestations of a speaker's nervousness are apparent to an audience.

## Understand Speaker Anxiety

It is important to understand first that speaker anxiety results from your brain signaling your body to help with a challenging task. Your body responds by increasing your breathing rate and blood flow and by pumping more adrenaline, which in turn result in the all-too-familiar symptoms of a rapid heartbeat, butterflies in the stomach, shaking knees and hands, quivering voice, and increased perspiration.

Although these physical symptoms may annoy and worry you, they indicate that your body is trying to help you with the task at hand. The same increased oxygen, blood flow, and adrenaline that cause the uncomfortable symptoms can actually be helpful. For example, you may find that you speak with heightened enthusiasm. Your brain thinks faster and more clearly than you would have believed possible. Your state of increased physical readiness can help you speak better.

Keep in mind, too, that most speakers feel more nervous than they look. Although the antiperspirant advertising slogan "Never let 'em see you sweat" suggests that our increased perspiration, along with our shaking hands and knocking knees, is likely to be visible to our audience, rarely is that true. Communication researchers call this mistaken belief the **illusion of transparency** and have found that simply informing speakers that their nervousness is not as apparent as they think can improve the quality of their speeches.[6]

## Know How to Develop a Presentation

Communication researchers have found that public speaking instruction decreases students' perception of their own speaker anxiety.[7] If you have read the first part of this chapter, you have already taken this first step toward managing anxiety—learning about the public speaking process. Just knowing what you need to do to develop an effective presentation can boost your confidence in being able to do it.

## Be Prepared

Being well prepared will decrease anxiety. Communication researchers have found that one way for speakers to manage anxiety is to follow the recommended steps for preparing a speech, which include developing a logical and clear outline.[8] Being prepared also involves discovering an appropriate topic and researching that topic thoroughly. Perhaps most important, it includes rehearsing your presentation. Research suggests that people who spend more time rehearsing experience less speaker anxiety than do people who rehearse less.[9]

When you rehearse your presentation, imagine that you are giving it to the audience you will actually address. Stand up. If you cannot rehearse in the room where you will deliver the presentation, at least imagine that room. Practice rising from your seat, walking to the front of the room, and beginning your presentation. Speak aloud rather than rehearsing silently. Thorough preparation that includes realistic rehearsal will increase your confidence when it is time to deliver your presentation.

## Focus on Your Audience

The fundamental communication guideline of being centered on your audience is key to reducing speaker anxiety. As you prepare your presentation, consider the needs, goals, and interests of your audience. As you rehearse your presentation, visualize your audience members and imagine how they may respond; practice adapting your presentation to the responses you imagine. The more you know about your listeners and how they are likely to respond to your message, the more comfortable you will feel about delivering that message. And as you finally deliver your presentation, focus on connecting to your audience. Look especially for positive, reinforcing feedback from audience members.[10] The more you concentrate on your audience, the less you attend to your own nervousness.

## Focus on Your Message

Focusing on your message can be another anxiety-reducing strategy. Like focusing on your audience, it keeps you from thinking too much about how nervous you are. In the few minutes before you begin your presentation, think about what you are going to say. Mentally review your main ideas. Silently practice your opening lines and your conclusion. Once you are speaking, maintain your focus on your message and your audience, rather than on your fears.

## Give Yourself a Mental Pep Talk

Even if you focus primarily on your audience and your message, you are bound to have some lingering thoughts about your performance. Rather than allowing yourself to dwell on how worried or afraid you are, make a conscious effort to think positively. Remind yourself that you have chosen a topic you know something about. Give yourself a mental pep talk before getting up to speak: "I know I can give this presentation. I have prepared and practiced, and I'm going to do a great job." Researchers have suggested that such "prespeaking exercises" may be the most effective antidotes for anxiety both before and during the speech.[11]

## Use Deep-Breathing Techniques

Two physical symptoms of nervousness are shallow breathing and rapid heart rate. To counter these symptoms, take a few slow, deep breaths before you get up to speak. As you slowly inhale and exhale, try to relax your entire body. These simple strategies will increase your oxygen intake and slow your heart rate, making you feel calmer and more in control.

## Take Advantage of Opportunities to Speak

As you gain public speaking experience, you will feel more in control of your nervousness. Communication researchers have found that most public speakers become progressively more comfortable as they speak, a phenomenon they call **habituation**.[12] Past successes build confidence. Your communication course will provide opportunities for frequent practice, which will increase your skill and confidence.

## Seek Professional Help

For a few people, the above strategies may not be enough help. These people may still experience a level of speaker anxiety that they consider debilitating. If you believe that you may be such a person, ask your communication instructor where you might turn for additional help. Some college or university departments of communication maintain communication labs that teach students additional strategies to help manage counterproductive anxiety.

One such strategy is **systematic desensitization**, which helps you learn to manage anxiety through a combination of general relaxation techniques and visualization of successful and calm preparation and delivery of a presentation.[13] Another proven strategy is **performance visualization**: viewing a videotape of a successful, effective speaker, becoming familiar enough with the videotaped presentation that you can imagine it, and eventually visualizing yourself as the speaker. This process may offer one of the best long-term strategies for managing speaker anxiety. Studies suggest that student speakers who practice performance visualization view themselves as more positive, vivid, and in-control

**habituation**
The process of becoming more comfortable as you speak.

**systematic desensitization**
An anxiety management strategy that includes general relaxation techniques and visualization of success.

**performance visualization**
An anxiety management strategy that involves viewing a videotape of a successful presentation and imagining oneself delivering that presentation.

**RE**CAP

### BUILDING YOUR CONFIDENCE

- Understand speaker anxiety.
- Know how to develop a presentation.
- Be prepared.
- Focus on your audience.
- Focus on your message.
- Give yourself a mental pep talk.
- Use deep-breathing techniques.
- Take advantage of opportunities to speak.
- Seek professional help.

speakers both immediately after performance visualization and up to several months later than those who did not practice this method.[14]

These or other services may be available through university counseling or other student support services. If you believe that you might benefit from professional help, find out what is available and use it.

# Selecting and Narrowing Your Topic

Sometimes a speaker is invited or assigned to speak on a certain topic and doesn't have to think about selecting one. Other times, however, a speaker is given some guidelines—such as time limits and perhaps the general purpose for the presentation—but otherwise is free to choose a topic. When that happens to you—as it almost certainly will in your communication class—your task may be made easier by exploring three questions: Who is the audience? What is the occasion? What are my interests and experiences?

## Who Is the Audience?

As we have noted several times throughout this book, the principle of appropriately adapting messages to others is central to the communication process. In presentational speaking, that adaptation begins with topic selection. Who are the members of your audience? What interests and needs do they have in common? Why did they ask you to speak?

One professional speaker calls the answers to such questions "actionable intelligence"—information that you can use as you select your topic.[15] Your college classmates are likely to be interested in such topics as college loans and the job market. Older adults might be more interested in hearing a speaker address such topics as the cost of prescription drugs and investment tax credits. Thinking about your audience can often yield an appropriate topic.

## What Is the Occasion?

You might also consider the occasion for which you are being asked to speak. A Veterans' Day address calls for such topics as patriotism and service to one's country. A university centennial address will focus on the successes in the institution's past and a vision for its future.

## What Are My Interests and Experiences?

Self-awareness, another communication principle you already know, can also help you discover a topic. Exploring your own interests, attitudes, and experiences may suggest topics about which you know a great deal and feel passionately, resulting in a presentation you can deliver with energy and genuine enthusiasm. One speaker's thinking about her own interests and experiences quickly produced the following list of possible topics:

> San Diego, California: city of cultural diversity
> Hybrid cars
> The reconstructed Globe Theatre
> Working at Six Flags
> What a sociologist does

Even after considering audience, occasion, and personal interests and experiences, you may still find yourself facing a speaking assignment for which you just cannot come up with a satisfactory topic. When that happens, you might try silent brainstorming, scanning web directories and web pages, or listening and reading for topic ideas.

## Conducting Silent Brainstorming

*Silent brainstorming*, discussed in Chapter 10 as a technique used by small groups to generate creative ideas, is a useful strategy for generating possible topics for presentations. A silent brainstorming session of about three minutes yielded the following list of eleven potential topics:

Gargoyles
Gothic architecture
Notre Dame
French food
Disney's *The Hunchback of Notre Dame*
Collecting Disney movie celluloids
Grammy Award–winning movie themes
Academy Award–winning movies of the 1940s
The Motion Picture Academy's Lifetime Achievement Award
John Wayne
The California Gold Rush

Having generated a list of topics, you can now go back and eliminate topics that don't have much promise or that you know you would never use. For example, you may not have any real interest in or reason for discussing the California Gold Rush. However, perhaps your film course has given you good background for discussing Academy Award–winning movies of the 1940s or some other decade. Keep the topics you like in your class notebook. You can reconsider them for future assignments.

## Scanning Web Directories and Web Pages

You know how addicting it can be to surf the web, following various categories and links out of interest and curiosity. What may seem an idle pastime can actually be a good way to discover potential speech topics. For example, a recent random search on Yahoo! Everything at <everything.yahoo.com>, starting with the general menu heading All Yahoo!, yielded the following categories and possible topics, arranged from broad to narrow:

Green
Living green
Environmental news
Bacteria may unlock mysteries of human body

An additional advantage of this strategy is that you now have both a broad topic and one or more potential sources for your presentation.

## Listening and Reading for Topic Ideas

It is not unusual to see on television or read in a news source something that triggers an idea for a presentation. For example, the following list of quite varied topics was suggested by the headlines in a recent daily newspaper:

Medical radiation safety
*E. Coli* outbreaks
Voice of America broadcasts in the age of Twitter
Arizona wildfires
Cosmic explosions and new classes of supernova

You might also discover a topic in material you have studied for a class. Perhaps you recently had an interesting discussion about minimum mandatory sentencing in your criminology class. It might make a good topic for a presentation, and your instructor would probably be happy to suggest additional resources.

# DEVELOPING YOUR PRESENTATION
## stepbystep

### Selecting and Narrowing Your Topic

While on Facebook one Sunday afternoon, Tony runs across a statistic that catches his interest: By December 2010, Facebook had more than 400 million active users worldwide—100 million more people than the population of the United States (www.facebook.com/press/info.php?timeline).

Tony is surprised. He had no idea that Facebook was such an international phenomenon. As he ponders the statistic, another thought goes through his mind: Maybe Facebook would make a good topic for his upcoming informative presentation. Based on his own recent experience, perhaps he could focus on the excessive use of Facebook.

Even a subject that comes up in casual conversation with friends may make a good speech topic. Perhaps everyone in your dorm seems to be sniffling and coughing all at once. "It's sick-building syndrome," gasps one. Sick-building syndrome might be an interesting topic for a presentation.

The point is to keep your eyes and ears open. You never know when you might see or hear a potential topic. If you do, write it down. Nothing is as frustrating as knowing that you had a good idea for a topic but now can't remember what it was!

Even if you discover potential topics through brainstorming, surfing the web, or listening or reading, you should still consider the communication principles of adapting to your audience and being aware of your own interests and experiences before you make your final topic selection. You will also need to consider the time limits of the speaking assignment. Many good topics need to be narrowed before they are appropriate for a given assignment.

One strategy for narrowing topics is to construct the kinds of categories and subcategories created by web directories. Write your general topic at the top of a list, making each succeeding word or phrase more specific and narrow:

Animals
Pets
Reptiles
Bearded dragons
Caring for a pet bearded dragon

If you have ten minutes for your presentation, you might decide that the last topic is too narrow. If so, just go back one step. In ten minutes, you may be able to discuss the characteristics and habits of bearded dragons, as well as how to care for them as pets.

# RECAP

## SELECTING AND NARROWING YOUR TOPIC

- Consider the audience, the occasion, and your interests and experiences.
- Practice silent brainstorming.
- Scan web directories and web pages.
- Listen and read for topic ideas.
- Narrow your topic by generating increasingly specific categories and subcategories.

# Identifying Your Purpose

Now that you have a topic in mind, you need to determine your purpose for your presentation. A clear purpose can help you select main ideas, an organizational strategy, and supporting material, and it can even influence how you deliver your presentation. You should determine both your general purpose and your specific purpose for every presentation you give.

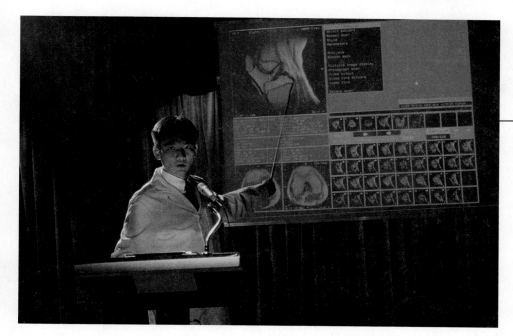

## General Purpose

Your **general purpose** is the broad reason for giving your presentation: to inform, to persuade, or to entertain.

- **To inform.** When you inform, you teach. You define, describe, or explain a thing, person, place, concept, or process. You may use some humor in your presentation; you may encourage your audience to seek out further information about your topic. Your primary purpose for speaking, however, is to give information.
- **To persuade.** If you are using information to try to change or reinforce your audience's ideas or convictions or to urge your audience to do something, your general purpose is persuasive. The insurance representative who tries to get you to buy life insurance, the candidate for state representative who asks for your vote, and the coordinator of Habitat for Humanity who urges your school organization to get involved in building homes all have persuasive general purposes. They may offer information about life expectancy, the voting record of an incumbent opponent, or the number of people in your community who cannot afford decent housing, but they use this information to convince you or to get you to do something. Their primary purpose is persuasive.
- **To entertain.** The speaker whose purpose is to entertain tries to get the members of his or her audience to smile, laugh, and generally enjoy themselves. For the audience members, learning something or being persuaded about something is secondary to having a good time. Most after-dinner speakers speak to entertain, as do most stand-up comedians and storytellers.

In your speech class, the general purpose for each assignment will probably be set by your instructor. Because the general purpose influences the way you develop and organize your presentation, as well as the way you deliver it, it is important to be aware of your general purpose throughout the process of developing and delivering your presentation.

## Specific Purpose

Knowing whether you want to inform, persuade, or entertain clarifies your general purpose for speaking. You also need to determine your specific purpose. A **specific purpose** is a concise statement of what your listeners should be able to do by the

**general purpose**
The broad reason for giving a presentation: to inform, to persuade, or to entertain an audience.

**specific purpose**
A concise statement of what listeners should be able to do by the time the speaker finishes the presentation.

## Table 11.1
## Examples of General and Specific Purposes

| GENERAL PURPOSES | SPECIFIC PURPOSES |
| --- | --- |
| To inform | At the end of my presentation, the audience will be able to list two benefits for adults of learning to play a musical instrument. |
| To persuade | At the end of my presentation, the audience will enroll in a music appreciation course. |
| To entertain | At the end of my presentation, the audience will be laughing at my misadventures as an adult cello student. |

time you finish your presentation. In other words, a specific purpose is an audience-centered behavioral goal for your presentation. Table 11.1 shows examples of general and specific purposes.

A specific-purpose statement is not intended to become part of your speech, but to guide your own preparation of the speech. You can begin a specific-purpose statement for any presentation with the words

At the end of my presentation, the audience will . . .

Then you can specify a behavior. For example, if you are giving an informative presentation on eating disorders, you might state:

At the end of my presentation, the audience will be able to explain the causes and most successful treatments for anorexia and bulimia.

If your topic is Zen meditation and your general purpose is to persuade, you might say:

At the end of my presentation, the audience will try Zen meditation.

# DEVELOPING YOUR PRESENTATION
## stepbystep

### Identifying Your Purpose

Tony's assignment is to prepare and deliver an informative presentation, so he knows that his general purpose is to inform. He will explain how Facebook use can become excessive and how users can manage their time on Facebook.

Tony also knows that his specific purpose should begin with the phrase "At the end of my presentation, the audience will. . . ." So he jots down,

At the end of my presentation, the audience will know about excessive Facebook use.

As Tony thinks further about his draft specific purpose, he sees some problems with it. How can he determine what his audience "knows" at the end of his presentation? And just what might his listeners learn about excessive Facebook use that they do not already know? He edits his purpose statement to read,

At the end of my presentation, the audience will minimize the time they spend on Facebook.

This version is more specific, but perhaps more appropriate for a persuasive speech than an informative one. He wants his audience to demonstrate their understanding of new information, but not necessarily to take action. Maybe a better statement would be

At the end of my presentation, the audience will be able to explain the growing and serious phenomenon of Facebook addiction and list four strategies for managing it.

Tony is pleased with this third version. It specifies what he wants his audience members to understand at the end of his speech and how they can demonstrate that understanding. He is ready to move to the next step of the process.

Wording your specific purpose as in the examples above will help you keep your audience foremost in your mind during the entire presentation preparation process.

Every subsequent decision you make while preparing and delivering your presentation should be guided by your specific purpose. As soon as you have formulated it, write it on a note card and keep it with you while you are working on your presentation. Think of it as a compass pointing true north—toward your audience. Refer to it often.

# Developing Your Central Idea

Your specific purpose indicates what you want your audience to know or do by the end of your presentation, but your **central idea** makes a definitive point *about* your topic. It focuses on the content of the speech.

Sometimes, as in the following example, wording the central idea can be as simple as copying the part of the specific purpose statement that specifies what the audience should be able to do.

| | |
|---|---|
| TOPIC: | Foreign-language education |
| SPECIFIC PURPOSE: | At the end of my presentation, the audience will be able to explain two reasons foreign-language education should begin in the elementary grades. |
| CENTRAL IDEA: | Foreign-language education should begin in the elementary grades. |

But even though they may seem similar, the specific purpose and central idea are used in quite different ways.

**Specific Purpose**
- Guides the speaker in preparing a presentation
- Is not stated in the presentation

**Central Idea**
- Guides the audience in listening to a presentation
- Is stated at or near the end of the speech introduction

Professional speech coach Judith Humphrey explains the importance of a central idea:

Ask yourself before writing a speech . . . "What's my point?" Be able to state that message in a single clear sentence. Everything else you say will support that single argument.[16]

To be most useful to both speaker and listeners, the "single clear sentence" to which Humphrey refers should be an audience-centered sentence; reflect a single topic; be a complete declarative sentence; and use direct, specific language.

## An Audience-Centered Idea

If your specific purpose is focused on your audience, your central idea probably will be, too. It should reflect a topic in which the audience has a reason to be interested and should provide some knowledge that they do not already have or make some claim about the topic that they may not have previously considered. Consider the appropriateness of these central ideas for an audience of college students.

**RE**CAP

## IDENTIFYING YOUR PURPOSE

**General Purpose**

- To inform        To define, describe, or explain a thing, person, place, concept, or process

- To persuade    To change or reinforce audience members' ideas or convictions, or to urge them to do something

- To entertain    To amuse an audience

**Specific Purpose**

- Specifies what you want audience members to be able to do by the end of your presentation
- Guides you in developing your presentation
- Uses the words "At the end of my presentation, the audience will. . . ."

**central idea**
A definitive point *about* a topic.

| | |
|---|---|
| INAPPROPRIATE: | Taking Advanced Placement classes in high school can help fulfill your general education requirements. *(Inappropriate because taking Advanced Placement classes is something college students either did or did not do in the past. They cannot make any decisions about them at this point.)* |
| APPROPRIATE: | Taking web-based classes can help fulfill your general studies requirements. *(Appropriate because students are probably looking for various options for completing required courses. They can choose to take courses on the web.)* |

## A Single Topic

A central idea should reflect a single topic. Trying to cover more than one topic, even if the multiple topics are related, only muddles your presentation and confuses the audience.

| | |
|---|---|
| MULTIPLE TOPICS: | Clubbing and running in marathons are two activities that appeal to many college students. |
| SINGLE TOPIC: | Clubbing appeals to many college students. |

## A Complete Declarative Sentence

**declarative sentence**
A complete sentence that makes a statement as opposed to asking a question.

Your central idea should be more than just the word or phrase that is your topic; it should also make a claim about your topic. Questions may help you come up with a central idea, but because they don't make any kind of claim, questions themselves are not good central ideas. A central idea should be a complete **declarative sentence**, not a topic and not a question.

| | |
|---|---|
| TOPIC: | Study abroad |
| QUESTION: | Should students consider opportunities to study abroad? |
| CENTRAL IDEA: | Study abroad provides significant advantages for students in most fields of study. |

## Direct, Specific Language

A good central idea uses direct, specific language rather than qualifiers and vague generalities.

| | |
|---|---|
| VAGUE: | Crop circles are not what they seem to be. |
| SPECIFIC: | Although they have been attributed to alien forces and unknown fungi, crop circles are really just a clever hoax. |

## DEVELOPING YOUR PRESENTATION
### stepbystep

### Developing Your Central Idea

Tony knows from reading Chapter 11 of this book that his central idea should be a complete declarative sentence that states a single audience-centered idea. He knows, too, that sometimes you can develop your central idea by copying the part of your specific purpose statement that specifies what the audience should do. So, he writes,

> The growing and serious phenomenon of Facebook addiction can be managed by implementing four strategies.

## RECAP

### THE CENTRAL IDEA SHOULD . . .

Be audience-centered.

Reflect a single topic.

Be a complete declarative sentence.

Use direct, specific language.

# Generating Main Ideas

If the central idea of a presentation is like the thesis statement of a paper, the **main ideas** of a presentation correspond to the paragraph topics of a paper. They support or subdivide the central idea and provide more detailed points of focus for developing the presentation.

Getting from the central idea to related but more specific main ideas can seem challenging, but actually you can use the central idea to generate main ideas. Here's how.

Write the central idea at the top of a sheet of paper or a word-processing document. Then ask yourself three questions:

1. Does the central idea have *logical divisions*?
2. Can I think of several *reasons* the central idea is true?
3. Can I support the central idea with a series of *steps* or a *chronological sequence*?

You should be able to answer yes to one of these questions and to write down the corresponding divisions, reasons, or steps. Let's apply this strategy to several examples.

**main ideas**
Subdivisions of the central idea of a presentation that provide detailed points of focus for developing the presentation.

## Does the Central Idea Have *Logical Divisions*?

Suppose that your central idea is "Most accomplished guitarists play three types of guitars." The phrase *three types* is a flag that indicates that this central idea does indeed have logical divisions—in this case, the three types of guitars. You list the three that come to mind:

1. Acoustic
2. Classical
3. Electric

You don't need to use Roman numerals or to worry particularly about the order in which you have listed the types of guitars. Right now, you are simply trying to generate main ideas. They aren't set in concrete, either. You may revise them—and your central idea—several times before you actually deliver the presentation. For example, you may decide that you need to include steel guitars in your list, so you revise your central idea to read "four types of guitars" and add "steel" to your list. If your central idea has logical divisions, you may organize those logical divisions topically, spatially, or according to cause–effect or problem–solution, organizational strategies that will be discussed in Chapter 12.

Identifying main ideas will help you to make the logic of your speech clear to your audience. You can divide your central idea into main ideas by asking yourself whether the central idea has logical divisions, whether there are several reasons the central idea is true, or whether the central idea can be supported with a sequence or series of steps.
R. Gino Santa Maria /Shutterstock.com

## Can You Think of Several *Reasons* the Central Idea Is True?

If your central idea is "Everyone should study a martial art," you may not be able to find readily apparent logical divisions. Simply discussing judo, karate, and taekwondo would not necessarily support the argument that everyone should study one of them. However, the second question is more productive: You can think of a number of *reasons* everyone should study a martial art. You quickly generate this list:

1. Martial arts teach responsibility.
2. Martial arts teach self-control.
3. Martial arts teach a means of self-defense.

Unlike the list of types of guitars, this list is written in brief complete sentences. You may or may not use full sentences in your own list. The purpose of your first list of main ideas is just to get the ideas in written form, whether words, phrases, or sentences. You can and will revise them later. If your main ideas are reasons your central idea is true, you will probably organize them according to effect–cause.

## Can You Support the Central Idea with a Series of *Steps* or a *Chronological Sequence*?

"The events of September 11, 2001, were the climax of a decade of deadly terrorist attacks against the United States." This sentence seemed like a pretty good central idea when you came up with it, but now what do you do? It doesn't have any logical divisions. You couldn't really develop reasons that it is true. You could, however, probably support this central idea with a chronological sequence or a history of the problem. You jot down the following list:

1. 1993—Bomb explodes in the underground parking garage of the World Trade Center, killing six people.
2. 1995—Car bomb in Riyadh, Saudi Arabia, kills seven people, five of them U.S. military and civilian National Guard advisors.
3. 1996—Bomb aboard a fuel truck explodes outside a U.S. Air Force installation in Dhahran, Saudi Arabia, killing nineteen U.S. military personnel.
4. 1998—Bombs destroy the U.S. embassies in Nairobi, Kenya, and Dar es Salaam, Tanzania. Three hundred one people are killed, including thirteen Americans.
5. 2000—Bomb damages the *USS Cole* in the port of Aden, Yemen, killing seventeen American sailors.
6. 2001—Hijacked airliners crash into the World Trade Center in New York, the Pentagon outside Washington, D.C., and a field in Pennsylvania, killing more than 3,000.[17]

These six fatal terrorist attacks, arranged in chronological order, could become the main ideas of your speech.

How many main ideas should you have? Your topic and time limit will help you decide. A short presentation (three to five minutes) might have only two main ideas. A longer one (eight to ten minutes) might have four or five. If you have more potential

# DEVELOPING YOUR PRESENTATION
## stepbystep

## Generating Your Main Ideas

With his central idea in hand, Tony knows that he next needs to generate main ideas for his presentation. He asks three questions:

- Does the central idea have logical divisions?
- Can I think of several reasons the central idea is true?
- Can I support my central idea with a series of steps or a chronological sequence?

Tony recognizes that because his central idea contains a number ("four"), it likely has logical divisions. He jots down his central idea:

The growing and serious phenomenon of Facebook addiction can be managed by implementing four strategies.

Then he lists the four strategies:

1. Admit the problem.
2. Write down how much time you spend every day on Facebook.

3. Give yourself a set amount of time every day on Facebook.
4. Turn off Facebook e-mail notifications.

At first, Tony thinks that these four points might make good main ideas for his speech. Then he realizes that before he can talk about managing Facebook addiction, he needs to explain what it is and why it is significant. He inserts another sentence at the top of his previous list:

1. Facebook addiction is a growing and serious phenomenon.

He then gathers all four strategies for managing Facebook addiction under a second main idea:

2. Facebook addiction can be managed by implementing four strategies.

Now Tony has two main ideas that both support his central idea and fulfill his specific purpose.

main ideas than you can use, decide which main ideas are likely to be most interesting, relevant, and perhaps persuasive to your audience or combine two or more closely related ideas.

# Gathering Supporting Material

By the time you have decided on your main ideas, you have a skeleton presentation. Your next task is to flesh out that skeleton with **supporting material**, both verbal and visual. Verbal supporting material includes illustrations, explanations, descriptions, definitions, analogies, statistics, and opinions—material that will clarify, amplify, and provide evidence to support your main ideas and your thesis. Visual supporting material includes objects, charts, graphs, posters, maps, models, and computer-generated graphics. You can also support your speech with audio aids such as music or sounds from your iPod or laptop. The speaker who seeks out strong verbal and visual supporting material is adhering to the fundamental communication principles of using verbal and nonverbal messages effectively.

**supporting material**
Verbal or visual material that clarifies, amplifies, and provides evidence to support the main ideas of a presentation.

**vertical search engine**
A website that indexes information on the World Wide Web in a specialized area.

## Sources of Supporting Material

Like a chef who needs to know where to buy high-quality fresh fruits and vegetables for gourmet recipes, you need to know where to turn for supporting material that will effectively develop your presentation and achieve your specific purpose. We will discuss four potential sources of supporting material: yourself, the Internet, online databases, and the library.

**Yourself**   If you were self-aware as you selected your topic, you may be your own source. You may have chosen a topic based on your passionate interest in collecting CDs, raising cockatiels, or cooking. You may have chosen a topic with which you have had some personal experience, such as undergoing plastic surgery or negotiating a favorable apartment lease. You may have chosen a topic for which you have conducted an online survey among your classmates, using simple, free software such as SurveyMonkey. Or you may have conducted a live interview with an expert. (Appendix A provides information and guidelines for participating in an information-gathering interview.)

A smart phone lets you do Internet research for your speech anywhere, but there are also times you may need to visit a library or interview someone to get information for your speech.
scyther5/Shutterstock.com

The point is that you don't necessarily need to consult the Internet or run to the library for every piece of supporting material on every topic on which you speak. It is true that most well-researched presentations will include some objective material gathered from the Internet or from library resources, but your listeners will respect your authority if they realize that you have firsthand knowledge of, or have consulted primary sources about, your topic.

**The Internet**   Only a few years ago, the Internet was more of a research curiosity than a serious source of supporting material. Now it is the first place most of us turn when faced with a research task.

You have probably accessed material on the Internet with Google or Yahoo! Although easy to use and generally helpful, these and other general search engines can yield an overwhelming number of resources. The following relatively simple strategies can help you narrow thousands or even millions of hits to a more workable number:

**Vertical search engines.**   One way you can narrow your search is to use a **vertical search engine**, a specialized tool that may index, for example, only academic sources (Google Scholar) or job websites (Indeed).

# Communication&TECHNOLOGY

## Check Facts from the Internet . . . or Else

In the spring of 2010, NBC Today Show anchor Ann Curry was invited to deliver the commencement address at Wheaton College in Norton, Massachusetts. She writes about how her research strategy for that speech led to her most embarrassing moment:

> Last year I gave a commencement address at Wheaton College. I prepared this strong speech that I thought would be compelling to the graduates. At the last moment, after dinner with my family, I decided to include a mention of all the great people who graduated from the school.

I went to the computer and added the names: Dennis Hastert, Billy Graham, Wes Craven. It was only later that I discovered that none of those people had gone to Wheaton College in Norton, Mass. They had graduated from Wheaton College in Wheaton, Ill.[18]

Curry acknowledged her mistake and wrote a letter of apology to the school. The lesson? Don't assume that the hits produced by Internet search engines necessarily yield the information you are seeking. Check your facts.

**Boolean search**
A web search that ties words together so that a search engine can hunt for the resulting phrase.

**Boolean searches.**  Another way to narrow a search is to conduct a **Boolean search,** which allows you to enclose phrases in quotation marks or parentheses so that a search yields only those sites on which all words or the phrase appear in that order and eliminates sites that contain the words at random. Boolean searches also let you exclude words or phrases from your search or restrict the dates of documents to a specified time frame.

**Criteria for evaluating web resources.**  A third strategy for sorting through information you discover on the Internet has to do with the principles of appropriately interpreting verbal and nonverbal messages. Specifically, you need to evaluate the sites you discover according to a consistent standard. The six criteria in Table 11.2 can serve as such a standard.[19]

## Table 11.2
## Six Criteria for Evaluating Internet Resources

| CRITERION | APPLYING THE CRITERION | DRAWING CONCLUSIONS |
|---|---|---|
| *ACCOUNTABILITY*: Who is responsible for the website? | • Look to see whether the website is signed.<br><br>• Follow hyperlinks or search the author's name to determine the author's expertise and authority.<br><br>• If the website is unsigned, check "Sponsor Links" (Google) or "Sponsored Results" (Yahoo!) to determine what individual or organization is responsible for the site. | • If you cannot identify or verify an author or sponsor, be wary of the website. |
| *ACCURACY*: Is the information correct? | • Consider whether the author or sponsor is a credible authority.<br><br>• Assess the care with which the website has been written. | • If the author or sponsor is a credible authority, the information is more likely to be accurate than inaccurate.<br><br>• A website should be relatively free of writing errors. |

*(continued)*

| CRITERION | APPLYING THE CRITERION | DRAWING CONCLUSIONS |
|---|---|---|
| | • Conduct additional research into the information on the site. | • You may be able to verify or refute the information by consulting another resource. |
| *OBJECTIVITY*: Is the website free of bias? | • Consider the interests, philosophical or political biases, and source of financial support of the author or sponsor of the website. | • The more objective the author and sponsor of the website, the more credible the information. |
| | • Does the website include advertisements that might influence its content? | |
| *DATE*: Is the site current? | • Look at the bottom of the website for a statement of when the site was posted and when it was last updated. | • In general, when you are concerned with factual data, the more recent, the better. |
| | • If you cannot find a date on the website, click on the View menu at the top of your browser screen and go down to Page Info. When you click on Page Info, you will find a Last Modified date. | |
| | • Enter the title of the website in a search engine. The resulting information should include a date. | |
| *USABILITY*: Do the layout and design of the website facilitate its use? | • Does the website load fairly quickly? | • Balance graphics and any fees against practical efficiency. |
| | • Is a fee required to gain access to any of the information on the website? | |
| *DIVERSITY*: Is the site inclusive? | • Do language and graphics reflect and respect differences in gender, ethnic, racial, and sexual preference? | • A website should be free of bias, representative of diverse perspectives, and accessible by people with disabilities. |
| | • Do interactive forums invite divergent perspectives? | |
| | • Is the website friendly to people with disabilities (e.g., offering a large-print or video option)? | |

# Communication&ETHICS

## Is It Ethical to Buy a Speech?

An online "speech mill" advertises that for $13 per page "highly qualified writers" will prepare a custom presentation for you. The ad goes on to claim that the speeches are "original" and "from scratch," designed to "let you escape the whole preparation process."

Would it be ethical to use this or a similar website to prepare a presentation for a class assignment? Are you comfortable with the site's "plagiarism-free guarantee"? Would it be ethical to buy a speech from such as site for a personal occasion, such as a great-aunt's funeral or your cousin's wedding? How do online speechwriters for hire compare, ethically, with professional speechwriters, who are commonly hired by executives and politicians?

**Online Databases**   **Online databases** provide access to bibliographic information, abstracts, and full texts for a variety of resources, including periodicals, newspapers, government documents, and even books. Like websites, online databases are accessed via a networked computer. Unlike websites, however, most databases are restricted to the patrons of libraries that subscribe to them. Your library may subscribe to several or all of the following popular full-text databases:

- **ABI/Inform Global.** This resource offers many full-text articles in business and trade publications from 1971 to the present.
- **Academic Search Complete.** This popular database offers many full-text articles from 1865 to the present, covering a wide variety of subjects.
- **JSTOR.** This multisubject full-text database offers journal articles from the first volume to fairly recent—although not usually the most current—ones.
- **LexisNexis Academic.** Focusing on business, industry, and law, this database provides many full-text articles from newspapers, magazines, journals, newsletters, and wire services. Dates of coverage vary.

**Traditional Library Resources**   Despite the explosion of Internet and database resources in recent years, the more traditional holdings of libraries, both paper and electronic, remain rich sources of supporting material. Spend some time becoming familiar with your library's services and layout so that you know how and where to access books, periodicals, newspapers, and reference materials.

- **Books.** Libraries' collections of books are called the **stacks**. The stacks are organized by call numbers, which are available on electronic catalog entries like the one shown in Figure 11.2. A location guide can tell you the floor or section of the stacks that houses books with the call numbers in which you are interested.
- **Periodicals.** Although full texts of many magazine and journal articles are provided by databases, publishers may not make their most recent issues available online. Finding a current article may require a trip to the library.

  A **periodical index** can help you decide what articles might be useful. Formatted as large bound volumes for many years, most periodical indexes today are provided via databases. Some of the best-known indexes include the *Readers' Guide* and the *Public Affairs Information Service.*

  Most periodicals are housed in a section of the library dedicated to periodicals, where bound volumes of past issues and single copies of current issues are arranged by call number. Some may be available on microfilm. Don't let microfilm intimidate you. Microfilm readers are easy to use, and most librarians or aides will be glad to show you how to set up the reader with the film you need.

- **Newspapers.** Like periodicals, most newspapers are available on databases, but the library may be the only place you can find smaller local papers, yesterday's or today's papers, or very old editions if you are looking for articles about a historical

**online database**
A subscription-based electronic resource that may offer access to abstracts or the full texts of entries, in addition to bibliographic data.

**stacks**
The collection of books in a library.

**periodical index**
A listing of bibliographical data for articles published in a group of magazines or journals during a given time period.

## Figure 11.2
## Entry from an Electronic Card Catalog

Courtesy of Albert B. Alkek Library, Texas State University–San Marcos.

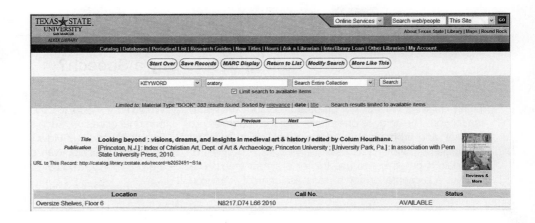

# DEVELOPING YOUR PRESENTATION
## stepbystep

### Gathering Supporting Material

With a draft of his specific purpose, central idea, and main ideas in hand, Tony begins to research Facebook addiction. Facebook itself is one resource he can use.

While he is online, he decides to do a search, using Yahoo! He discovers a column in the Duke University *Chronicle*, written by a student who describes her own Facebook addiction. Next he enters the keyword "Facebook" in the database Academic Search Complete and finds a relevant article in the journal *Engineering and Technology*.

Tony records the essential bibliographical information for these sources. Then he begins to read carefully and take notes. As he does, he puts quotation marks around any material he copies verbatim and makes sure that he has copied it accurately.

---

event. Most of a library's back newspaper holdings will likely be on microfilm. In addition, newspaper databases such as *Newspaper Source* not only index but provide full texts of selected articles from newspapers and transcripts from news organizations.

- **Reference resources.** Print **reference resources**—which include encyclopedias, dictionaries, atlases, almanacs, and books of quotations—are indexed in a library's card catalog with a *ref* prefix on their call numbers to show that they are housed in the reference section of the library. Like periodicals, newspapers, and microfilm, print reference resources are usually available only for in-house research and cannot be checked out.

- Reference librarians are specialists in the field of information science. They are often able to suggest additional print or electronic resources that you might otherwise overlook. If you plan to use the reference section, visit the library during daytime working hours. A full-time reference librarian is more likely to be on hand and available to help you at that time than in the evenings or on weekends.

## RECAP

### SOURCES OF SUPPORTING MATERIAL

1. *You.* Take advantage of your own expertise.

2. *The Internet.* Use vertical search engines, conduct Boolean searches, and apply evaluation criteria to choose the best information.

3. *Online databases.* For access to abstracts and full texts for a variety of resources, explore the databases to which your library subscribes.

4. *Libraries.* Get to know your librarian for help mining traditional library resources.

## Types of Supporting Material

If you have explored your own knowledge and insights and those of people you know, discovered material on the Internet, consulted databases, and examined a variety of library resources, you probably have a wealth of potential supporting material. Now you will need to decide what to use in your presentation. Keeping in mind your listeners' knowledge, interests, and expectations will help you determine where an illustration might stir their emotions, where an explanation might help them to understand a point, and where statistics might convince them of the significance of a problem. Let's discuss these and other types of supporting material and consider suggestions for using them effectively.

**Illustrations**    **Illustrations** offer an example of or tell a story about an idea, issue, or problem a speaker is discussing. They can be as short as a word or phrase or as long as a well-developed paragraph. Sometimes speakers will offer a series of brief illustrations, as President George W. Bush did in his final state of the union address in January 2008:

**reference resources**
Material housed in the reference section of a library, such as encyclopedias, dictionaries, atlases, almanacs, and books of quotations.

**illustration**
A story or anecdote that provides an example of an idea, issue, or problem the speaker is discussing.

In the past seven years, we've also seen images that have sobered us. We've watched throngs of mourners in Lebanon and Pakistan carrying the caskets of beloved leaders taken by the assassin's hand. We've seen wedding guests in blood-soaked finery staggering from a hotel in Jordan, Afghans and Iraqis blown up in mosques and markets, and trains in London and Madrid ripped apart by bombs. On a clear September day, we saw thousands of our fellow citizens taken from us in an instant.[20]

Other speakers offer longer and more detailed illustrations. And still others will use instead a **hypothetical illustration**—one that has not actually occurred. If you decide to use a hypothetical illustration, it is important to make clear to your audience that the scene you describe never really happened. Notice how Matthew uses the word *imagine* to make clear to his audience that his illustration is hypothetical:

> Imagine an evening outing: You and your two children decide to have a fun night out. You look up to your rearview mirror to see a car slam into the back of your car—WHAM—killing your children. You survive the crash and so does the individual who rear-ended you.[21]

Whether you choose to use brief or extended illustrations, true or hypothetical ones, remember this principle: Everybody likes to hear a story. An illustration almost always ensures audience interest. In addition, communication researchers have found that listeners are less likely to generate counterarguments to a persuasive message supported by examples and personal narratives than one not so supported.[22]

The following suggestions should help you use illustrations effectively in your presentations:

- Be sure that your illustrations are directly relevant to the idea or point they are supposed to support.
- Choose illustrations that are typical, not exceptions.
- Make your illustrations vivid and specific.
- Use illustrations with which your listeners can identify.
- Remember that the most effective illustrations are often personal ones.

**hypothetical illustration**
An example or story that has not actually occurred.

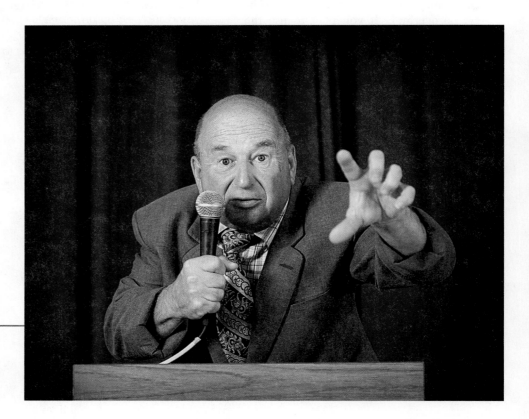

Everybody loves a good story. Do you think this speaker's illustration is keeping the attention of his audience?
© MichaelJay/iStockphoto.com

**Descriptions and Explanations** Probably the most commonly used forms of supporting material are descriptions and explanations. A **description** provides detailed images that allow an audience to see, hear, smell, touch, or taste whatever you are describing. Descriptions can make people and scenes come alive for an audience. In her Nobel Prize acceptance speech, writer Doris Lessing described Africa as she remembered it:

> the banks of the Zambesi, where it rolls between pale grassy banks, it being the dry season, dark-green and glossy, with all the birds of Africa around its banks . . . . elephants, giraffes, lions and the rest . . . the sky at night, still unpolluted, black and wonderful, full of restless stars.[23]

An **explanation** of how something works or why a situation exists can help an audience understand conditions, events, or processes. Speaking to an audience of supervisors about managing stress and increasing personal productivity, author Jeff Davidson explained why people tend to be most productive in the morning:

> Doctor Norbert Myslinski, a neuroscience professor at the University of Maryland, found that cortisol peaks around the time you wake up. Cortisol, a naturally occurring stress hormone that affects your ability to respond to challenges, increases your blood-sugar level, better enabling you to handle tasks energetically and with enough momentum to carry you through their completion. Most importantly, tackling tough tasks in the morning generally enhances your confidence level. By increasing productivity at the beginning of your day, you are motivated to perform better and accomplish more throughout the rest of your afternoon and evening.[24]

Although descriptions and explanations are part of most presentations, they lack the inherent interest factor that illustrations have. The following suggestions may help you keep audiences from yawning through your descriptions and explanations:

- Avoid too many descriptions and explanations.
- Keep your descriptions and explanations brief.
- Describe and explain in specific and concrete language.

**Definitions** Speakers should offer **definitions** of all technical or little-known terms in their presentations, but they do not need to define terms that most or all audience members are likely to find familiar. If you determine that you should define a word or phrase for your audience, consider whether you can best define it by **classification**, the format of a standard dictionary definition, or by an **operational definition**, explaining how the word or phrase works or what it does. Discussing his role in an investigation of unlawful interrogation practices, New York attorney Scott Horton used this operational definition of *torture*:

> The following techniques were the focus of our concern: waterboarding, long-time standing, hypothermia, sleep deprivation in excess of two days, the use of psychotropic drugs and the sensory deprivation/sensory overload techniques first developed for the CIA at McGill University.[25]

To use definitions effectively, consider the following suggestions:

- Use definitions only when necessary.
- Be certain that your definitions are understandable.
- Be sure that any definition you provide accurately reflects your use of the word or phrase throughout the presentation.

**Analogies** An **analogy** demonstrates how unfamiliar ideas, things, and situations are similar to something the audience already understands. Speakers can use two types of analogies in their presentations. The first is a **literal analogy**, or comparison of two similar things. Kristen uses a literal analogy to offer a solution to America's complex income tax system:

**description**
A word picture.

**explanation**
A statement that makes clear how something is done or why it exists in its present or past form.

**definition**
A statement of what something means.

**classification**
A type of definition that first places a term in the general class to which it belongs and then differentiates it from all other members of that class.

**operational definition**
A definition that shows how a term works or what it does.

**analogy**
A comparison between two ideas, things, or situations that demonstrates how something unfamiliar is similar to something the audience already understands.

**literal analogy**
A comparison between two similar things.

According to many experts, following in Europe's fiscal footsteps could bring the American tax system up to speed. With a flat income tax, the U.S. could keep fairness while gaining simplicity and efficiency in its taxing burden.[26]

The second type of analogy is a **figurative analogy**, a comparison of two seemingly dissimilar things that in fact share a significant common feature. In his much-acclaimed "Last Lecture," Carnegie Mellon professor Randy Pausch created a memorable figurative analogy between one's outlook on life and the outlooks of two beloved characters from *Winnie the Pooh*:

> You just have to decide if you're a Tigger or an Eeyore. I think I'm clear where I stand on the great Tigger/Eeyore debate. Never lose the childlike wonder. It's just too important.[27]

Two suggestions can help you use analogies more effectively in your presentations:

- Be certain that the two things you compare in a literal analogy are very similar.
- Make the similarity between the two things compared in a figurative analogy apparent to the audience.

**Statistics** **Statistics**, or numerical data, can represent hundreds or thousands of illustrations, helping a speaker express the significance or magnitude of a situation. Statistics can also help a speaker express the relationship of a part to the whole. In this brief excerpt from a presentation on bogus airline parts, Jon uses both types of statistics:

> 26 million parts are installed on airplanes every year in the U.S., and the FAA estimates that at least 2% of these parts are counterfeits.[28]

Skilled speakers learn how to use statistics to their greatest advantage. For example, they try to make huge numbers more dramatic for their audiences. AFL-CIO president John J. Sweeney dramatized the danger of unsafe bridges in the United States by making a statistic personal:

> Since I was coming to work from Washington to New Rochelle this morning, I asked my staff to check out my route.
> We found that traveling the I-95 corridor between Washington, D.C. and New York City, I would cross or come within two-tenths of a mile of 30 bridges that are rated either functionally obsolete or structurally deficient.[29]

**figurative analogy**
A comparison between two seemingly dissimilar things that share some common feature on which the comparison depends.

**statistics**
Numerical data that summarize examples.

**exploding**
Adding or multiplying related numbers to enhance their significance.

A student speaker heightened the effect of the incredible 300-mile distances run by the Tarahumaran tribes of northern Mexico by comparing comparing that statistic with another figure familiar to her listeners:

> To put that into perspective, that's like running 12 marathons back to back to back to back . . . to back to back to back to back . . . to back to back to back to back.[30]

And another student speaker dramatized a statistic by **exploding** it to enhance its significance:

> Every 20 minutes, a person is killed or badly wounded by a land mine, which translates to . . . approximately 20,000 people annually.[31]

In addition to dramatizing statistics, you can use statistics more effectively if you apply the following suggestions:

- Round off large numbers.
- Use visual aids to present your statistics.
- Cite the sources of your statistics.

**Opinions** The opinions of others can add authority, drama, and style to a presentation. A speaker can use three types of opinions: expert testimony, lay testimony, and literary quotations.

**Expert testimony** is the type of opinion most frequently employed by speakers. If you lack authority on your topic, cite someone who can offer such expertise. In preparing her speech on the college credit card crisis, Jeni realized that her audience might not believe that the misuse of credit cards by college students is a widespread problem. So Jeni quoted an expert:

> Ruth Suswein, executive director of the Bankcard Holders of America, told the . . . *Pittsburgh Post Gazette*, "I defy you to go on any college campus and find any student who doesn't know some other student who has messed up using credit cards."[32]

After an F5 tornado ravaged Joplin, Missouri, in May 2011, television audiences were moved by the compassionate reporting of Weather Channel journalist Mike Bettes, who was one of the first reporters on the scene. For a speaker, as well as a news organization, such **lay testimony** can provide the most memorable moments of a presentation, stirring an audience's emotions.

Finally, speakers may wish to include **literary quotations** in their presentations. Salem State College Professor Robert Brown quoted architect Buckminster Fuller to make a point about how the English language has become increasingly visual and kinesthetic:

> As the architectural visionary Buckminster Fuller was fond of saying, "I am a verb." In English, with every innovation that comes to market, we transform things into actions, and nouns into verbs, as when I say: "Let me friend you. Let me cell phone you."[33]

Whether you use expert testimony, lay testimony, or literary quotations, consider the following suggestions for using opinions effectively in your presentations:

- Be certain that any authority you cite is actually an expert on the subject you are discussing.
- Identify your sources.
- Cite unbiased authorities.
- Cite opinions that are representative of prevailing opinion. If you cite a dissenting viewpoint, identify it as such.
- Quote or paraphrase your sources accurately and note the context in which the remarks were originally made.
- Use literary quotations sparingly.

As you select your illustrations, descriptions, explanations, definitions, analogies, statistics, and opinions, be guided not only by the suggestions provided in this chapter for each type of supporting material but also by the five Communication Principles for a Lifetime:

- **Be aware of your communication with yourself and others.** The best supporting material reflects self-awareness, taking advantage of your own knowledge and experience.
- **Effectively use and interpret verbal messages.** Effective verbal supporting material is appropriately worded, concrete, and vivid enough that your audience can visualize what you are talking about.
- **Effectively use and interpret nonverbal messages.** Use visual aids to present statistics.
- **Listen and respond thoughtfully to others.** If listeners find a presentation boring, it is probably because the speaker has not used the fundamental principles of communication as criteria for selecting supporting material.
- **Appropriately adapt messages to others.** Sensitivity to your audience will help you choose the verbal and visual supporting material that is most appropriately adapted to them.

**expert testimony**
The opinion of someone who is an acknowledged expert in the field under discussion.

**lay testimony**
The opinion of someone who experienced an event or situation firsthand.

**literary quotation**
A citation from a work of fiction or nonfiction, a poem, or another speech.

## Acknowledgment of Supporting Material

In the United States and most other Western cultures, using the words, sentence structures, or ideas of another person without crediting the source is a serious breach of ethics. Once you have supporting material in hand, you must decide whether and how to acknowledge the source.

**Determining What Should Be Acknowledged**   Some information is so widely known that you may not need to acknowledge a source. For example, you need not cite a source if you say that former FBI official Mark Felt was identified as the long-anonymous Watergate informant "Deep Throat." This fact is general knowledge and is widely available in a variety of sources. If you decide to use any of the following, however, you must acknowledge the source:

# **RE**CAP

## SUPPORTING YOUR SPEECH

| Type of Supporting Material | Guidelines for Use |
| --- | --- |
| Illustrations | • Make illustrations directly relevant to the idea or point they support. |
| | • Choose illustrations that are typical. |
| | • Make illustrations vivid and specific. |
| | • Use illustrations with which your listeners can identify. |
| | • Remember that the most effective illustrations are often personal ones. |
| Descriptions and Explanations | • Avoid too many descriptions and explanations. |
| | • Keep descriptions and explanations brief. |
| | • Describe and explain in specific and concrete language. |
| Definitions | • Use definitions only when necessary. |
| | • Be certain that definitions are understandable. |
| | • Be sure that a definition accurately reflects your use of the word or phrase. |
| Analogies | • Be certain that the two things you compare in a literal analogy are very similar. |
| | • Make apparent to the audience the similarity between the two things compared in a figurative analogy. |
| Statistics | • Round off large numbers. |
| | • Use visual aids. |
| | • Cite your sources. |
| Opinions | • Be certain that any authority you cite is actually an expert on the subject you are discussing. |
| | • Identify your sources. |
| | • Cite unbiased authorities. |
| | • Cite representative opinions, or identify dissenting viewpoints as such. |
| | • Quote or paraphrase accurately and in context. |
| | • Use literary quotations sparingly. |

- Direct quotations, even if they are only brief phrases
- Opinions, assertions, or ideas of others, even if you paraphrase them rather than quote them verbatim
- Statistics
- Any nonoriginal visual materials, including graphs, tables, and pictures

**Understanding Plagiarism and Its Consequences**   Presenting someone else's words or ideas without acknowledging the source constitutes **plagiarism**, a breach of academic honesty that can have dire consequences.

A few years ago, one of your authors heard a student's excellent speech on the importance of detecting cancer early. The only problem was that she heard the same speech again in the following class period! On finding the "speech"—actually a *Reader's Digest* article that was several years old—both students were certain that they had discovered a shortcut to an A. Instead, they failed the assignment, ruined their course grades, and lost their instructor's trust. The consequences of plagiarism in other arenas can be even more severe, including the loss of a job or the end of a promising career.

**Acknowledging Sources in Oral Citations**   To acknowledge your source, you can integrate an **oral citation** into your presentation. For example, you might say:

> In *The New York Times* of June 10, 2011, University of Chicago historian Adam Green explains that "public parks and beaches, places of fun and play, have also been places that serve as a kind of barometer of the full social condition at any moment in time."[34]

**plagiarism**
The presentation of someone else's words or ideas without acknowledging the source.

**oral citation**
The oral presentation of such information about a source as the author, title, and publication date.

# Communication&DIVERSITY

## How to Adapt to Your Diverse Audience

One of the principles we've stressed throughout this book is the importance of adapting your message to others. Many, if not most, of the presentations you give will be to audiences that represent a mix of cultures and backgrounds rather than a single cultural tradition. In this speaking situation, it is important to realize that not all audience members expect information to be presented as *you* prefer. Here are some ideas to help you adapt when you speak to an audience of people who have cultural backgrounds different from your own.[35]

- *Adapt your supporting materials.* Telling a good story to illustrate your ideas is an especially effective strategy to appeal to a wide range of audience preferences. Most audiences value a good story with a point or moral that is relevant to the point you want to make.
- *Adapt your visual support.* You might want to use more visual aids to illustrate your talk. Pictures and images can communicate universal messages, especially emotional ones.
- *Adapt your speech organization.* People from the predominant culture in North America usually prefer

a structured presentation that follows an outlined pattern; they also prefer an introduction that previews the ideas you'll present and a conclusion that crisply summarizes the essential points you've made. A Russian or Eastern European audience would expect a less tightly structured presentation, however. When you're in doubt about listener preferences, we recommend being structured and organized.

- *Adapt your delivery style.* One study found that members of some cultures prefer a more formal oratorical style of delivery than the conversational, extemporaneous style that is usually taught in American presentational speaking classes.[36] For example, Japanese speakers addressing a predominantly Japanese audience begin a presentation by making respectful references to their audience.

Our overarching suggestion is to be aware of who will be in your audience. Before you design or deliver your presentation, if you're unsure of your listeners' speaking-style preferences, ask for tips and strategies from audience members or people you trust.

## REVIEWING What You Know

### Overviewing the Presentational Speaking Process $\qquad$ p. 280

The stages of the public speaking process center on consideration of audience members, who influence every decision a speaker makes. A speaker's tasks include selecting and narrowing a topic, identifying a general and specific purpose for speaking, developing the central idea of the presentation, generating main ideas, gathering supporting material, organizing the presentation, and rehearsing and delivering the presentation.

**Terms to Know**

| | |
|---|---|
| Public Speaking (Presentational Speaking) p. 280 | Audience-Centered Presentational Speaker p. 280 |

### Building Your Confidence $\qquad$ p. 281

Focusing on your audience and message and giving yourself mental pep talks can help you become a more confident speaker, as can knowing how to develop a presentation, being well prepared, and seeking out opportunities to speak.

**Terms to Know**

| | | | |
|---|---|---|---|
| Speaker Anxiety | p. 281 | Systematic Desensitization | p. 283 |
| Illusion of Transparency | p. 282 | Performance Visualization | p. 283 |
| Habituation | p. 283 | | |

### Selecting and Narrowing Your Topic $\qquad$ p. 284

As you begin to prepare your presentation, you will first have to select and narrow your topic, keeping in mind the audience, the occasion, and your own interests and experiences. You may find helpful such strategies as silent brainstorming, scanning web directories and websites, and listening and reading for topic ideas.

### Identifying Your Purpose $\qquad$ p. 286

Once you have a topic, you need to identify both your general purpose and your specific purpose. General purposes include to inform, to persuade, and to entertain. Specific purposes are determined by the general purpose, the topic, and the audience.

**Terms to Know**

| | |
|---|---|
| General Purpose p. 287 | Specific Purpose p. 287 |

## Developing Your Central Idea   p. 289

Your central idea will focus on the content of your speech. It should be centered on your audience; reflect a single topic; be a complete declarative sentence; and use direct, specific language.

**Terms to Know**

## Generating Main Ideas   p. 291

The main ideas of a presentation support or subdivide the central idea. They are usually logical divisions of the central idea, reasons the central idea is true, or a series of steps or a chronological sequence that develops the central idea.

**Terms to Know**

## Gathering Supporting Material   p. 293

You have at least four potential sources of supporting material: yourself, the Internet, online databases, and traditional library resources. Personal knowledge and experience increase the likelihood that the audience will find you a credible speaker. To supplement your own knowledge and experience, you can turn to the vast resources of the Internet. Online databases provide both bibliographic information and full texts to subscribers. And most likely, you will still use traditional library resources—books, periodicals, newspapers, and reference resources—as sources of supporting material.

The types of supporting material you can use in a presentation include illustrations, descriptions and explanations, definitions, analogies, statistics, and opinions. Simple guidelines can help you use each type of supporting material effectively and cite your sources correctly.

**Terms to Know**

**Principle One:**
**Be aware of your communication with yourself and others.**
- Understand that speaker anxiety results from your body working to help you perform better.
- Give yourself a pep talk before getting up to speak.
- Consider your own interests and experiences when selecting a topic.
- Remember that the best supporting material often draws on your own knowledge and experience.

**APPLYING**
Principles
for a
Lifetime

### Principle Two:
### Effectively use and interpret verbal messages.

- Focus on your message to help you become a more confident speaker.
- Search for topics on the Internet, in the media, and in books.
- Word your specific purpose in terms of your audience to help you keep your focus on them.
- Make sure that your central idea reflects a single topic, is a complete declarative sentence, and uses specific language.
- Consider the accountability, accuracy, objectivity, date, usability, and sensitivity to diversity of verbal material you find on websites.
- Make your illustrations vivid and specific.
- Keep descriptions and explanations brief.
- Describe and explain in specific and concrete language.
- Make your definitions readily understandable, and be certain that they accurately reflect how you use the word or phrase in the speech.
- Round off large numbers to make them more understandable.
- Cite unbiased authorities who represent prevailing opinion.
- Quote or paraphrase accurately and in context.
- Integrate oral citations of your sources into your presentation.

### Principle Three:
### Effectively use and interpret nonverbal messages.

- Remember that nonverbal indicators of speaker anxiety are rarely visible to an audience.
- Consider the accountability, accuracy, objectivity, date, usability, and sensitivity to diversity of pictures and graphics you find on websites.
- Use visual aids to make statistics more readily understandable to your listeners.

### Principle Four:
### Listen and respond thoughtfully to others.

- To increase your confidence when speaking in public, seek out information about your listeners and how they are likely to respond to your message.
- Listen for topic ideas in the course of casual conversation with friends.

### Principle Five:
### Appropriately adapt messages to others.

- As you learn more about your audience, you can revise ideas or strategies for your presentation at any point in your preparation process.
- Be centered on your audience to increase your confidence.
- Be sensitive to and adapt to the diversity of your audience.
- Consider your audience's interests and expectations as you select the topic for your presentation.
- Keep in mind your audience's knowledge, interests, and expectations as you select supporting material for your presentation.

## ASSESSING Your Skill

### Personal Report of Communication Apprehension (PRCA-24)

The best known and most frequently used measure for assessing communication apprehension is James C. McCroskey's Personal Report of Communication Apprehension, which assesses anxiety in the context of a number of communication activities, including public or presentational speaking.

*Directions:* This instrument is composed of twenty-four statements concerning your feelings about communication with other people. Please indicate in the space provided the degree to which each statement applies to you by marking whether you (1) Strongly Agree, (2) Agree, (3) Are Undecided, (4) Disagree, or (5) Strongly Disagree with each statement. There are no right or wrong answers. Many of the statements are similar to other statements. Do not be concerned about it. Work quickly and just record your first impression.

1. ____ I dislike participating in group discussions.
2. ____ Generally, I am comfortable while participating in a group discussion.
3. ____ I am tense and nervous while participating in group discussions.
4. ____ I like to get involved in group discussions.
5. ____ Engaging in a group discussion with new people makes me tense and nervous.
6. ____ I am calm and relaxed while participating in group discussions.
7. ____ Generally, I am nervous when I have to participate in a meeting.
8. ____ Usually I am calm and relaxed while participating in meetings.
9. ____ I am very calm and relaxed when I am called upon to express an opinion at a meeting.
10. ____ I am afraid to express myself at meetings.
11. ____ Communicating at meetings usually makes me uncomfortable.
12. ____ I am very relaxed when answering questions at a meeting.
13. ____ While participating in a conversation with a new acquaintance, I feel very nervous.
14. ____ I have no fear of speaking up in conversations.
15. ____ Ordinarily I am very tense and nervous in conversations.

16. ____ Ordinarily I am very calm and relaxed in conversations.
17. ____ While conversing with a new acquaintance, I feel very relaxed.
18. ____ I'm afraid to speak up in conversations.
19. ____ I have no fear of giving a speech.
20. ____ Certain parts of my body feel very tense and rigid while giving a speech.
21. ____ I feel relaxed while giving a speech.
22. ____ My thoughts become confused and jumbled when I am giving a speech.
23. ____ I face the prospect of giving a speech with confidence.
24. ____ While giving a speech I get so nervous, I forget facts I really know.

SCORING:

Group = 18 − (1) + (2) − (3) + (4) − (5) + (6)
Meeting = 18 − (7) + (8) + (9) − (10) − (11) + (12)
Dyadic = 18 − (13) + (14) − (15) + (16) + (17) − (18)
Public = 18 + (19) − (20) + (21) − (22) + (23) − (24)
Overall CA = Group + Meeting + Dyadic + Public

Source: J. McCroskey, *An Introduction to Rhetorical Communication* 9th Ed., © 2006. Reprinted and electronically reproduced by permission of Pearson Education, Inc., Upper Saddle River, New Jersey.

- **MyCommunicationLab** In addition to flash cards and self tests for this chapter, MyCommunicationLab offers a video tutorial on overcoming nervousness and an interactive review of avoiding plagiarism. <www.mycommunicationlab.com> (Access code required.)
- **Idea Generator** These special projects from the Directors Bureau, an award-winning production company, are sources of possible presentation topics. <www.tdbspecialprojects.com/#169515/Idea-Generator>
- **Total News** The Total News Network provides news reports from a number of major news providers, including the Associated Press, Google News, Yahoo! News, BBC, and NPR. In addition to the site's value as a source of supporting material, the "Top News Trends" column is a possible source of presentation topics. <http://totalnewschannel.com/>
- **Statistics from the U.S. Census** The official home page for the U.S. Census provides statistics that address a wide range of U.S. and world demographics and issues. <www.census.gov>

**WEB RESOURCES** for More Review, Application, and Assessment

Don't agonize. Organize.

FLORYNCE R. KENNEDY

# Chapter OUTLINE

- Organizing Your Main Ideas
- Organizing Your Supporting Material
- Organizing Your Presentation for the Ears of Others
- Introducing and Concluding Your Presentation
- Outlining Your Presentation
- Study Guide: Review, Apply, and Assess Your Knowledge and Skill

# Chapter OBJECTIVES

After studying this chapter, you should be able to

1. List and explain the six functions of a presentation introduction.
2. List and explain the four functions of a presentation conclusion.
3. Discuss the purpose and characteristics of a preparation outline.
4. Outline a presentation according to standard outline format.
5. Prepare speaking notes.

Digital Vision/Thinkstock

# 12 | Organizing and Outlining Your Presentation

One study found that college students report spending, on average, nearly half of their total speech preparation time outlining and revising their speeches.[1] This chapter will be key in helping you use that preparation time effectively.

You have already completed the first five stages of audience-centered presentation preparation:

- Select and narrow a topic.
- Determine your purpose.
- Develop your central idea.
- Generate main ideas.
- Gather supporting material.

Now it is time to put your presentation together. You will need to consider first how best to organize your main ideas. Then you will organize your supporting material for maximum effect, and devise signposts to lead your audience through your presentation. You will develop an effective introduction and conclusion. Finally, once you have made the necessary decisions about these component parts, you will be ready to outline the entire presentation and prepare your speaking notes.

# Organizing Your Main Ideas

A logically organized speech includes an introduction, a body, and a conclusion. The body presents the most important content of the presentation—the main ideas that you generated with the help of your central idea. At least five strategies can help you determine an effective order in which to present those main ideas.

## Organizing Ideas Topically

**topical organization**
Organization determined by the speaker's discretion or by recency, primacy, or complexity.

If your main ideas are logical divisions of your central idea, you will probably arrange them according to **topical organization**, the strategy used most frequently. Topical organization may be simply an arbitrary arrangement of main ideas that are fairly equal in importance. For example, if you are giving an informative presentation on the various instrument families in the modern symphony orchestra, your main ideas will probably be strings, woodwinds, brass, and percussion. The order in which you discuss these instrument groups may not really matter.

Hugh MacLeod/Gapingvoid.com

At other times, topical organization is less arbitrary. Three principles may help you arrange your main ideas effectively.

**Recency**    The principle of **recency** suggests that audiences remember best what they hear last. If you want to emphasize the string section of an orchestra, you will purposefully place that instrument family last in your informative presentation.

**Primacy**    Another principle that can help guide your topical organization is **primacy**, which suggests that you discuss your most convincing or your least controversial idea first. To adapt to an audience who may be skeptical of some of your ideas, discuss first those points on which you all agree. If you are speaking to an anti-gun-control audience about ways to protect children from violence in schools, don't begin by advocating gun control. Instead, begin by affirming family values and education in the home, perhaps move on to the importance of an anti-violence curriculum and adequate counseling in schools, and only then discuss gun control as a possible preventive measure.

**Complexity**    Organization according to **complexity** moves moves from simple ideas and processes to more complex ones. You have learned many life skills in order of complexity. In first grade, you learned to read easy words first and then moved on to more difficult ones. In third grade, you learned single-digit multiplication tables before moving on to more complex double- and triple-digit multiplication problems. Similarly, if you are giving a presentation on how to trace your family's genealogy, you might discuss readily available, user-friendly Internet sources before explaining how to access old courthouse records or parish registries of births, deaths, and baptisms.

## Organizing Ideas Chronologically

If you determine that you can best develop your central idea through a series of steps, you will probably organize those steps—your main ideas—chronologically. **Chronological organization** is based on time or sequential order according to when each step or event occurred or should occur. If you are explaining a process, you will want to organize the steps of that process from first to last. If you are providing a historical overview of an event, movement, or policy, you might begin with the end result and trace its history backward in time. Topics that lend themselves to chronological organization include the process for stripping and refinishing a piece of furniture, the three deadliest U.S. tornadoes on record, and the history of higher education for women.

**recency**
Arrangement of ideas from least important to most important or from weakest to strongest.

**primacy**
Arrangement of ideas from most important to least important or from strongest to weakest.

**complexity**
Arranging ideas from simple to more complex.

**chronological organization**
Organization by time or sequence.

Spatial organization is the best choice for this boat-tour guide's instructional presentation about Chicago architecture. If the speaker were on land, what other organizational patterns might work for a speech on this topic?

© Jason Lindsey/Alamy

## Organizing Ideas Spatially

"Go down the hill two blocks and turn left by the florist. Then go three blocks to the next stoplight and turn right. The place you're looking for is about a block farther, on your right." When you offer someone directions, you organize your ideas spatially. **Spatial organization** means arranging items according to their location, position, or direction. It is another strategy by which you might organize main ideas that are logical divisions of your central idea.

Presentations that rely on description are especially good candidates for spatial organization. For example, a discussion of the route taken by Sir Edmund Hillary and Tenzing Norgay when climbing Mount Everest in 1953 or of the molecular structure of DNA would lend itself to spatial organization. You might choose to organize your presentation on the three deadliest U.S. tornadoes spatially (according to where each tornado occurred) rather than chronologically (by year).

## Organizing Ideas to Show Cause and Effect

**Cause–and–effect organization** actually refers to two related patterns: identifying a situation and then discussing the resulting effects (cause–effect), and presenting a situation and then exploring its causes (effect–cause).

If your main ideas are logical divisions of your central idea, you might organize them according to cause–effect. A speaker discussing the consequences of teenage pregnancy might use a cause–effect pattern, first establishing that teenage pregnancy is a significant social issue and then discussing various consequences or effects.

If your main ideas are reasons your central idea is true, you will probably organize them according to effect–cause. A speaker who wanted to explore the reasons for the high rate of teen pregnancy would probably use an effect–cause pattern, first discussing teenage pregnancy as an effect and then exploring its various causes.

As the recency principle would suggest, a cause–effect pattern emphasizes effects; an effect–cause pattern emphasizes causes.

## Organizing Ideas by Problem and Solution

If, instead of exploring causes or consequences of a problem or issue, you want either to explore how best to solve the problem or to advocate a particular solution, you will probably choose **problem–solution organization**. This strategy is appropriate for organizing logical divisions of a central idea. For example, if you are speaking on how listeners can protect themselves from mountain lion attacks in the U.S. West, you might first establish that a significant problem exists, and then talk about solutions to that problem. Or, if you are talking about ending discrimination against overweight people, you could first establish that such discrimination exists and then talk about solutions that would end the discrimination.

You can use problem–solution organization for either informative or persuasive presentations. When your general purpose is to persuade, you will go on to urge your audience to support or adopt one or more of the solutions you discuss.

Both the mountain lion and the weight discrimination topics also lend themselves to organization by cause and effect. You could, for example, discuss mountain lion attacks as

**spatial organization**
Organization according to location, position, or direction.

**cause–and–effect organization**
Organization by discussing a situation and its causes, or a situation and its effects.

**problem–solution organization**
Organization by discussing first a problem and then various solutions.

# RECAP

## ORGANIZING YOUR MAIN IDEAS

| Strategy | Description | Applicable to main ideas that are . . . |
|---|---|---|
| Topical | Arbitrary arrangement of topics or organization according to recency, primacy, or complexity | Logical divisions |
| Chronological | Organization by time or sequence | Steps or a chronological sequence |
| Spatial | Organization according to location or position | Logical divisions |
| Cause and effect | Organization by discussing a situation and its causes (effect–cause) or a situation and its effects (cause–effect) | Reasons (effect–cause)  Logical divisions (cause–effect) |
| Problem and solution | Organization by discussing a problem and then various solutions | Logical divisions |

an effect and explore why the frequency of such attacks has increased in recent years (causes), or you could talk about discrimination against overweight people as a cause and discuss the harmful effects of such discrimination. In such instances, how do you decide which organizational pattern to use? Return to your specific purpose. If you want your audience to be able to explain how to end discrimination against overweight people, select the problem-and-solution organizational strategy. If you want your audience to be able to explain the harmful effects of discrimination against those who are overweight, use the cause-and-effect strategy. Let both your general and your specific purpose continue to guide your presentation as you organize your main ideas.

# Organizing Your Supporting Material

Once you have organized your main ideas, you are ready to organize the supporting material for each idea. Suppose you have two brief illustrations, a statistic, and an opinion in support of your first main idea. How should you organize these materials to communicate your verbal message most effectively?

The now-familiar strategies for organizing main ideas can also help you organize your supporting material. For example, you might arrange a group of brief illustrations *chronologically*. At other times, you might apply the principle of *recency* and save your most convincing statistic for last. If you decide to present first the opinion with which you are certain your audience will agree, you apply the principle of *primacy*. Or you might arrange two explanations according to the principle of *complexity*, presenting the simplest one first and working up to the more complex one.

Two additional organizational principles are specific to the organization of supporting material.

- **Specificity.** Sometimes your supporting material includes both specific illustrations and more general explanations or statistics. The principle of **specificity** suggests that you group your specific information and either offer it first, followed by your general explanation or statistics, or give your general explanation or statistics first and then follow with your specific illustrations. In a presentation to raise awareness about poverty, Kerlin provides general statistics before moving to a specific illustration:

  > In New Orleans, 38% of children live in poverty, which is more than double the national child poverty rate of 17%. In the state of Louisiana, 13% of children live not in poverty—but extreme poverty. Let me tell you about the 6-year-old hero in the aftermath of Katrina. Deamonte Love was born and raised in a poor family. According to the *Los Angeles Times* of September 5, 2005, that 6-year-old boy walked down the road, holding a 5-month-old infant. He had no clues whatsoever where his parents were, while surrounded by five toddlers, and one was wearing only diapers.[2]

**specificity**
Organization from specific information to a more general statement or from a general statement to specific information.

# Communication & ETHICS

## The Ethics of Primacy and Recency

Nico knows that according to the principle of recency, he should discuss last what he wants his audience to remember best. In his presentation on the risk of counterfeit prescription drugs, however, Nico thinks that it may be more ethical to reveal immediately to his audience how costly the problem is in terms of both dollars and human lives. Is it ethical for Nico to save that important statistic for last?

# Communication & DIVERSITY

## Acknowledging Cultural Differences in Organizing Messages

What's the shortest distance between two points? Why, going in a straight line, of course. In organizing a message, it may seem that the most logical strategy is to develop a structure that moves from one idea to the next in a logical, "straight" way. But not every culture organizes ideas using that logic. In fact, each culture teaches its members unique patterns of thought and organization that are considered appropriate for various occasions and audiences.

In general, speakers in the United States tend to be more linear and direct than do Semitic, Asian, Romance, or Russian speakers.[3] Semitic speakers support their main points by pursuing tangents that might seem "off topic" to many U.S. listeners. Asians may allude to a main point only through a circuitous route of illustrations and parables.

And speakers from Romance and Russian cultures tend to begin with a basic principle and then move to facts and illustrations that only gradually are related to the main point. The models in Figure 12.1 illustrate these culturally diverse patterns of organization.[4]

Of course, these generalizations are very broad. As an effective speaker who seeks to adapt to your audience, you should investigate and perhaps acknowledge or even consider adopting the customary organizational strategy of your particular audience. In addition, when you are listening to a presentation, recognizing the existence of cultural differences can help you appreciate and understand the organization of a speaker from a culture other than your own.

**U.S.**     **Semitic**     **Asian**     **Romance**     **Russian**

### Figure 12.1
### Organizational Patterns by Culture

Lieberman, Devorah, *Public Speaking in the Multicultural Environment,* 2nd Ed., © 1997. Reprinted and Electronically reproduced by permission of Pearson Education, Inc., Upper Saddle River, New Jersey.

# RECAP

## ORGANIZING YOUR SUPPORTING MATERIAL

| Strategy | Description |
| --- | --- |
| Chronology | Organization by time or sequence |
| Recency | Most important material last |
| Primacy | Most convincing or least controversial material first |
| Complexity | From simple to more complex material |
| Specificity | From specific information to general overview or from general overview to specific information |
| "Soft" to "hard" evidence | From hypothetical illustrations and opinions to facts and statistics |

- **"Soft" to "Hard" Evidence.** Another principle that can help you organize your supporting material is moving from "soft" to "hard" evidence. Illustrations, descriptions, explanations, definitions, analogies, and opinions are usually considered **soft evidence**, whereas statistics are **hard evidence.** In his speech on providing asylum to victims of systematic rape, Samin moves from soft evidence to a hard statistic:

  > On New Year's Eve, the Congolese army went to the village of Fizi and raped 62 women from 7 p.m. to 6 a.m. . . . The 2010 International Statistics on Crime and Justice Report laments that nearly 200,000 women worldwide face the threat of repeated rape by their government or military in countries such as Zimbabwe, Sudan, and Guatemala.[5]

# Organizing Your Presentation for the Ears of Others

You now have a fairly complete, logically organized plan for your presentation, but if you tried to deliver it at this point, your audience would probably become confused. What are your main ideas? How is one main idea related to the next? What supporting material develops which main idea? To adapt your logically organized message to your audience, you need to provide **signposts**, organizational cues for the audience's ears. You do so by adding previews, transitions, and summaries that allow you to move smoothly from one idea to the next throughout the presentation.

## Previews

A **preview** "tells them what you're going to tell them"; it is a statement of what is to come. Previews help your audience members anticipate and remember the main ideas of your presentation. They also help you move smoothly from the introduction to the body of your presentation and from one main idea to the next.

**Initial Preview**  The **initial preview** is usually presented in conjunction with, and sometimes as part of, the central idea. Consider Kevin's presentation calling for an end to the FBI practice of making information requests without first getting search warrants. Notice how he states his central idea and then previews his three main ideas near the end of the introduction:

> It is imperative that we stop the use of warrantless requests of records by the federal government for mere convenience of information. We will first examine the reasons for the FBI's abuse of power; next, explore the damage the bureau's dangerous activities have done; before finally, we discover solutions to abolish a system that . . . allows the FBI to make sending you a subpoena for information as easy as writing a request on a Post-it note.[6]

**Internal Preview**  In addition to offering an initial preview, a speaker may also offer an **internal preview** at various points throughout a presentation. Internal previews introduce and outline ideas that will be developed as the presentation progresses. Meleena provides an internal preview just before the final main idea of her presentation on sexual harassment in schools:

> Now . . . we can look at some things that we can all do, as parents, teachers, and students, to stop sexual harassment in our schools. There are two ways to prevent these causes from recurring. The first is education and the second is immediate action.[7]

When Meleena delivers this preview, her listeners know that she is going to talk about two possible solutions to the problem she has been discussing. Their anticipation increases the likelihood that they will hear and later remember these solutions.

## Verbal and Nonverbal Transitions

A **transition** signals to the audience that a speaker is moving from one idea to the next.

**Verbal Transition**  To use verbal messages effectively, include **verbal transitions**, words or phrases that show relationships between ideas in your presentation. They include simple enumeration (*first, second, third*); synonyms or pronouns that refer to earlier key words or ideas (the word *they* at the beginning of this sentence refers to the phrase "verbal transitions" in the previous sentence); and words and phrases that show relationships between ideas (*in addition, not only . . . but also, in other words, in summary, therefore, however*). As you begin to rehearse your presentation, you might need to experiment with various verbal transitions to achieve a flow that seems natural and logical to you. If none of the verbal alternatives seems quite right, consider a nonverbal transition.

**soft evidence**
Illustrations, descriptions, explanations, definitions, analogies, and opinions.

**hard evidence**
Statistics.

**signpost**
A verbal or nonverbal organizational signal.

**preview**
A statement of what is to come.

**initial preview**
First statement of the main ideas of a presentation, usually presented with or near the central idea.

**internal preview**
A preview within the speech that introduces ideas still to come.

**transition**
A word, phrase, or nonverbal cue that indicates movement from one idea to the next or the relationship between ideas.

**verbal transition**
A word or phrase that indicates the relationship between two ideas.

**Nonverbal Transition** Sometimes used alone and sometimes in combination with verbal transitions, an effective **nonverbal transition** might take the form of a facial expression, a pause, a change in vocal pitch or speaking rate, or movement. Most good speakers will use a combination of verbal and nonverbal transitions to help them move from one idea to the next throughout their presentations.

## Summaries

Like previews, a **summary**—a recap of what has been said—provides an additional opportunity for the audience to grasp a speaker's most important ideas. Most speakers use two types of summaries: internal summaries and a final summary.

**Internal Summary** Like internal previews, **internal summaries** occur within and throughout a presentation. After you have discussed two or three main ideas, you might want to use an internal summary to ensure that the audience keeps them firmly in mind before moving on to another main idea. You can combine an internal summary with an internal preview. In his "Last Lecture," Carnegie Mellon professor Randy Pausch combined an internal preview and summary in this way:

> All right, so now the third part of the talk. Lessons learned. We've talked about my dreams. We've talked about helping other people enable their dreams. Somewhere along the way there's got to be some aspect of what lets you get to achieve your dreams.[8]

**Final Summary** In your conclusion, you may want to provide your audience with a final opportunity to hear and remember your main ideas. Whereas your initial preview gave your audience members their first exposure to your main ideas, your **final summary** will give them their last exposure to those ideas. Near the end of Stephanie's presentation on cruise ship violence, she provides this final summary of her three main ideas:

> Today we outlined violence on cruise ships and the need for recourse; we then discussed the nature of these criminal environments and lack of laws; and finally, we explored solutions for handling or avoiding these crimes even if the authorities are not supportive.[9]

**nonverbal transition**
A facial expression, vocal cue, or physical movement that indicates that a speaker is moving from one idea to the next.

**summary**
A recap of what has been said.

**internal summary**
A recap within the presentation of what has been said so far.

**final summary**
A recap of all the main points of a presentation, usually occurring just before or during the conclusion.

Professor Randy Pausch effectively used signposts in his now-famous "Last Lecture," delivered shortly before his death. How can you use verbal transitions to show the relationship between ideas in your presentation?

AP Images/Daily Progress, Kaylin Bowers

Adding previews, transitions, and summaries to your well-organized presentation applies the fundamental principles of using both verbal and nonverbal messages effectively and of adapting your message to others. It increases the likelihood that your audience will grasp your main ideas and the logic of your organizational strategy.

# Introducing and Concluding Your Presentation

At this point, you have developed and organized the ideas and content of the body of your presentation, but you might not have thought about how you are going to begin and end the presentation. That's okay. Even though you will deliver your introduction first, you usually plan it last. You need to know what you're introducing—especially your central idea and main ideas. Once you do, it is time to plan how you will introduce and conclude your presentation. Although your introduction and conclusion make up a relatively small percentage of the total presentation, they provide your audience with first and final impressions of you and your presentation. They are important considerations in adapting your message to others.

## Introductions

Your **introduction** should convince your audience to listen to you. More specifically, it must perform six functions: get the audience's attention, introduce the topic, give the audience a reason to listen, establish your credibility, state your central idea, and preview your main ideas. Let's briefly consider each of these functions.

**Get the Audience's Attention**   If an introduction does not capture the attention of audience members, the rest of the presentation may be wasted on them. You have to use verbal messages effectively to wake up your listeners and make them want to hear more.

There are several good ways to gain an audience's attention. One commonly used and quite effective way is to open with an illustration. Buey Ruet opens his speech on the bloodshed in Sudan with this moving personal illustration:

> On October 15, 1994, a woman by the name of Workinsh Admasu opened a letter, which required her 8- and 13-year-old boys to immediately report to military training camp. Three weeks after basic training, the boys, along with another 300,000 8- to 14-year-olds, strapped on AK47s that were half of their body weight and headed off to fight in Sudan's civil war. . . . That 8-year-old boy was me. . . . My 13-year-old brother and I were forced to experience things that no other child should ever have to experience.[10]

Other strategies are to ask a rhetorical question, relate a startling fact or statistic, quote an expert or a literary text, tell a humorous story, or refer to historical or recent events. Comedian Conan O'Brien used humor in the introduction to (and throughout) his 2011 commencement address at Dartmouth College:

> New Hampshire is such a special place. When I arrived, I took a deep breath of this crisp New England air and thought, "Wow, I'm in the state that's next to the state where Ben and Jerry's ice cream is made."[11]

Barack Obama combined references to place and historical event in the opening words of his March 2008 address in Philadelphia:

> "We the people, in order to form a more perfect union."
>
> Two hundred and twenty-one years ago, in a hall that still stands across the street, a group of men gathered and, with these simple words, launched America's improbable experiment in democracy.[12]

**introduction**
Opening lines of a presentation, which must catch the audience's attention, introduce the topic, give the audience a reason to listen, establish the speaker's credibility, state the central idea, and preview the main ideas.

Conan O'Brien used humor to catch the audience's attention in his 2011 commencement address at Dartmouth College. If you are thinking of a humorous introduction, be sure to evaluate its appropriateness for the audience, occasion, and your own ability to be funny.

AP Photo/Jason R. Henske

Still other speakers might get their audience's attention by referring to a personal experience, the occasion, or something said by a preceding speaker. Although not all these strategies will work for all presentations, at least one of them should be an option for any presentation you make. With a little practice, you may be able to choose from several good possibilities for a single presentation.

**Introduce the Topic**    Within the first few seconds of listening to you, your audience should have a pretty good idea of what your topic is.

**Give the Audience a Reason to Listen**    Not only do you have to get your audience's attention and introduce your topic, but you also have to motivate your listeners to continue to listen. Show the listeners how your topic affects them and those they care about. Catherine uses rhetorical questions to drive home to her audience the relevance and importance of her speech on a healthy diet:

> What if I told you that, by decreasing one food item in your and your loved ones' diet, you could significantly lessen the chance for metabolic syndrome (or obesity); heart disease; coronary artery disease; osteoporosis due to calcium depletion; high blood pressure; colon, kidney, breast, prostate, and liver cancer? Would you change the menu at your and your loved ones' next meal?[13]

By the end of your introduction, your audience should be thinking, "This concerns *me*!"

**Establish Your Credibility**    A credible speaker is one whom the audience judges to be believable, competent, and trustworthy. Be aware of the skills, talents, and experiences you have had that are related to your topic. You can increase your credibility by telling your audience about your expertise. For example, in your introduction to a persuasive presentation on studying abroad, you might say:

> I know firsthand how studying abroad can broaden your worldview, increase your understanding of another culture, and enrich your academic studies. Last fall, I studied at the Sorbonne in Paris.

**State Your Central Idea**   Your central idea usually appears at or near the end of your introduction, as in the following example from Aaron's speech on post-traumatic stress disorder:

> Hundreds of combat veterans . . . are being dismissed from the Armed Services without the medical benefits needed to treat combat stress.[14]

**Preview Your Main Ideas**   Previewing your main ideas allows your listeners to anticipate and begin to listen for those main ideas. You can provide your initial preview immediately after your central idea. Here is the initial preview of main ideas that follows Aaron's central idea, quoted above:

> So in today's speech we will uncover the problems associated with the denial of benefits to discharged veterans suffering from Post-traumatic Stress Disorder. Next we will investigate the causes of these problems before finally understanding what can be done to solve this flaw in the policies of the VA.[15]

## Conclusions

Your introduction creates a critically important first impression, and your **conclusion** leaves an equally important final impression. Long after you finish speaking, your audience will hear the echo of effective final words. An effective conclusion serves four functions: to summarize the presentation, to reemphasize the main idea in a memorable way, to motivate the audience to respond, and to provide closure. Let's consider each of these functions.

**conclusion**
Closing lines of a presentation, which leave a final impression.

**closure**
The sense that a presentation is finished.

**Summarize the Presentation**   The conclusion offers a speaker a last chance to repeat his or her main ideas. Most speakers summarize their main ideas between the body of the presentation and its conclusion or in the first part of the conclusion.

**Reemphasize the Central Idea in a Memorable Way**   The conclusions of many famous speeches contain many of the lines we remember best:

> that government of the people, by the people, for the people, shall not perish from the earth. (*Abraham Lincoln*)[16]

> Old soldiers never die; they just fade away. (*General Douglas MacArthur*)[17]

> Free at last! Free at last! Thank God almighty, we are free at last! (*Martin Luther King Jr.*)[18]

Use your final verbal message effectively. Word your thoughts so that your audience cannot help but remember them.

**Motivate the Audience to Respond**   Think back to your specific purpose. What do you want your audience to be able to do by the end of your presentation? If your purpose is to inform, you may want your audience to think about your topic or seek more information about it. If your purpose is to persuade, you may want your audience to take some sort of action, such as write a letter, make a phone call, or volunteer for a cause. Your conclusion is where you can motivate your audience to respond. Travis closes his presentation on sleep deprivation with this admonition:

> Before we are all, literally, dead on our feet, let's take the easiest solution step of all. Tonight, turn off your alarm, turn down your covers, and turn in for a good night's sleep.[19]

**Provide Closure**   You may have experienced listening to a presentation and not being certain when it was over. If so, you were listening to a speaker who did not achieve the last purpose of an effective conclusion: providing **closure**, or a sense that the presentation is finished.

You can provide closure by referring back to your introduction and finishing a story, answering a rhetorical question, or reminding your audience of where you started. Steven had opened his presentation on reducing DUI occurrences with an

A good introduction should "tell them what you are going to tell them," letting the audience know your purpose, central ideas, and main ideas. How can your nonverbal cues help your audience to understand the organization of your main ideas?

photobank.ch/Shutterstock.com

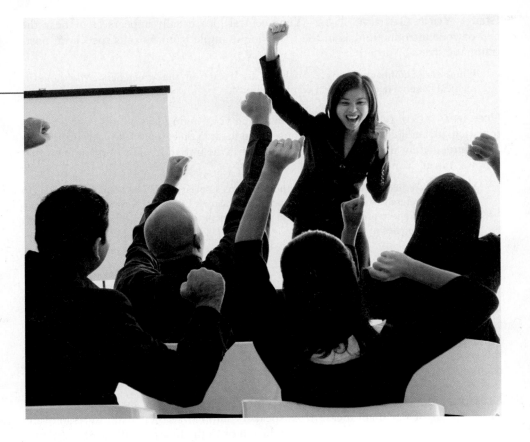

Effective speakers often save their most important idea—the one they want the audience to walk away with—for last.

Ron Chapple/Photolibrary

extended illustration about a Wyoming highway patrol officer forced to kill a woman in self-defense after the inebriated woman brutally attacked him. He provides memorable closure to his presentation by finishing the story:

> Whenever I heard about someone being killed during an alcohol-related traffic incident, I used to shrug it off, thinking, "How does this affect me?" . . . When the Wyoming highway patrolman took the life of Alyssa Harriet, I learned how drinking and driving affects me, because that highway patrolman is my brother.[20]

You can also achieve closure by using verbal and nonverbal signposts. For example, you might use such transitions as *finally* and *in conclusion* as you move into your conclusion. You might pause before you begin the conclusion, slow your speaking rate as you deliver your final sentence, or signal by falling vocal inflection that you are making your final statement. Experiment with these strategies until you are certain that your presentation "sounds finished."

# RECAP

## THE PURPOSES OF INTRODUCTIONS AND CONCLUSIONS

| | |
|---|---|
| Your introduction should . . . | Get your audience's attention. |
| | Introduce your topic. |
| | Give your audience a reason to listen. |
| | Establish your credibility. |
| | State your central idea. |
| | Preview your main ideas. |
| Your conclusion should . . . | Summarize your presentation. |
| | Reemphasize your central idea in a memorable way. |
| | Motivate your audience to respond. |
| | Provide closure. |

# Outlining Your Presentation

With your introduction and conclusion planned, you are almost ready to begin rehearsing your presentation. By this point, you should have your preparation outline nearly complete. A **preparation outline** is a fairly detailed outline of your central idea, main ideas, and supporting material. It may also include your specific purpose, introduction, and conclusion. A second outline, which you will prepare shortly, makes up the speaking notes from which you will eventually deliver your presentation.

## Preparation Outline

Although few presentations are written in manuscript form, most speakers develop a fairly detailed preparation outline to help them ensure that their main ideas are clearly related to their central idea and are logically and adequately supported. A speaker who creates a preparation outline is applying the first fundamental principle of communication: becoming increasingly aware of his or her communication. In addition to helping the speaker judge the unity and coherence of the presentation, the preparation outline also serves as an early rehearsal outline and is usually handed in as part of a class requirement.

Instructors who require students to turn in a preparation outline will probably have their own specific requirements. For example, some instructors ask for the introduction and conclusion as part of the outline, whereas others ask for an outline only of the body of the presentation. Some ask that you incorporate signposts into the outline or write your specific purpose at the top of the outline. Be certain that you carefully listen to and follow your instructor's specific requirements regarding which elements to include.

Almost certainly, your instructor will require that you use **standard outline format**. Standard outline format lets you become more aware of the exact relationships among various main ideas, subpoints, and supporting material in your presentation. Even if you haven't had much experience with formal outlines, the following guidelines can help you produce a correct outline.

**Use Standard Numbering**   Outlines are numbered with Roman and Arabic numerals and uppercase and lowercase letters followed by periods, as follows.

I. First main idea
   A. First subdivision of I
   B. Second subdivision of I
      1. First subdivision of B
      2. Second subdivision of B
         (a) First subdivision of 2
         (b) Second subdivision of 2

II. Second main idea

You will probably not need to subdivide beyond the level of lowercase letters in most presentation outlines.

**preparation outline**
A detailed outline of a presentation that includes the central idea, main ideas, and supporting material, and may also include specific purpose, introduction, and conclusion.

**standard outline format**
Conventional use of numbered and lettered headings and subheadings to indicate the relationships among parts of a presentation.

# Communication&TECHNOLOGY

## Using Outlining Software

Word-processing programs such as Microsoft Word have features that allow you to set the style of, and various levels within, an outline. The feature will then apply the appropriate number, letter, and indentation to each heading you provide.

If you are using MyCommunicationLab in your communication course, that site gives you online access Outline icons that allow you to create customized, specific outlines of your presentations.

Try using one or both of these outlining resources to prepare either your preparation outline or your speaking notes for your next presentation. Then evaluate whether using the tool made outlining easier or harder for you than outlining by hand.

**Use at Least Two Subdivisions, If Any, for Each Point**   You cannot divide anything into fewer than two parts. On an outline, every I should be followed by a II, every A should be followed by a B, and so on. If you have only one subdivision, fold it into the level above it.

**Line Up Your Outline Correctly**   Main ideas, indicated by Roman numerals, are written closest to the left margin. The *periods* following these Roman numerals line up so that the first letters of the first words also line up:

> I. First main idea
> II. Second main idea
> III. Third main idea

Letters or numbers of subdivisions begin directly underneath the first letter of the first *word* of the point above:

> I. First main idea
>   A. First subdivision of I
>   B. Second subdivision of I

If a main idea or subdivision takes up more than one line, the second line begins under the first letter of the first word of the preceding line:

> I. First main idea
>   A. A rather lengthy subdivision
>      that runs more than one line
>   B. Second subdivision

**Within Each Level, Make the Headings Grammatically Parallel**
Regardless of whether you write your preparation outline in complete sentences or in phrases, be consistent within each level. In other words, if I is a complete sentence, II should also be a complete sentence. If A is an infinitive phrase (one that begins with *to* plus a verb, such as "to guarantee greater security"), B should also be an infinitive phrase.

A sample preparation outline for the presentation we've been watching Tony Longoria prepare in the Developing Your Presentation Step-by-Step feature is shown on page 323.[21] Your instructor may have additional or alternative requirements for what your preparation outline should include or how it should be formatted.

## Speaking Notes

As you rehearse your presentation, you will need to look at your preparation outline less and less. You have both the structure and the content of your presentation quite well in mind. At this point, you are ready to develop a shorter outline to serve as your speaking notes.

Your speaking notes should provide all the information you will need to make your presentation as you have planned, but not be so detailed that you will be tempted to read rather than speak to your audience. Here are a few suggestions for developing speaking notes.

**Use Note Cards**   Note cards don't rustle as paper does, and they are small enough to hold in one hand. Type or print neatly on one side only, making sure that the letters and words are large enough to be read easily. Plan your note cards according to logical blocks of material, using one note card for your introduction, one or two for the body of your presentation, and one for your conclusion. Number your note cards in case they get out of order while you are speaking.

**Use Standard Outline Form**   Standard outline form will help you find your exact place when you glance down at your speaking notes. You will know, for example, that your second main idea is indicated by "II."

# Sample Preparation Outline

## Purpose

At the end of my presentation, the audience will be able to explain the growing and serious phenomenon of Facebook addiction and list four strategies for managing it.

## Introduction

Hi, my name is Tony, and I'm a Facebook addict. In the past, my excessive use of Facebook has interfered with my work and my studies.

For those of you who may not know, Facebook is an ultrapopular social networking site used by students and people all over the world to communicate and socialize with family, friends, and organizations.

When I began using Facebook in 2006, I originally started using it for the college courses that I teach. I successfully incorporated Facebook into four of my communication classes, and my students loved it. In fact, they preferred to communicate on Facebook rather than on Bobcatmail or TRACS. But for me, it became a problem.

## Central Idea

The growing and serious phenomenon of Facebook addiction can be managed by implementing four strategies.

## Preview

Today I'm going to be talking with you about some Facebook facts. I'm then going to offer you some warning signs that can help you determine whether or not you're a Facebook addict. And finally, I'll be sharing with you some tips that helped me reduce my own excessive Facebook use.

*Signpost:* So let's start with some Facebook facts.

## Body

I.  Facebook addiction is a growing and serious phenomenon.
    A.  Facebook has been growing at an incredible pace since Mark Zuckerberg and some friends started Facebook in their Harvard dorm room in February of 2004.
        1.  By December of that year, Facebook had already reached 1 million active users.
        2.  Today, Facebook has over 400 million active users world-wide—100 million more people than the entire population of the United States.
        3.  There is more than one way now to access Facebook. In 2007, Facebook made it possible to connect through a smartphone or a hand-held mobile device, making Facebook accessible from anywhere at any time.

*Signpost:* Now that you have been updated on some Facebook facts, let's talk about excessive Facebook use and some warning signs that you could be a Facebook addict.

    B.  Facebook addiction is a serious issue, with specific warning signs.
        1.  Chris Edwards, an author in the *Engineering and Technology* journal, says that Facebook is the number one site that people visit to waste time.

---

*Writing the purpose statement at the top of the outline helps the speaker keep it in mind, but always follow your instructor's specific requirements for how to format your preparation outline.*

*Tony catches his listeners' attention by introducing himself with the greeting traditionally used by Alcoholics Anonymous and other twelve-step groups.[22] Other strategies for effectively getting audience attention were discussed earlier in the chapter.*

*Tony writes out and labels his central idea and preview. Again, follow your instructor's requirements.*

*The first main idea of the presentation is indicated by the Roman numeral I. This main idea has two subpoints, indicated by A and B.*

*Subpoints 1, 2, and 3 provide supporting material for A.*

*This signpost summarizes Tony's first idea—that Facebook is a growing phenomenon—and previews his second idea—that Facebook addiction has become a serious issue with distinct warning signs.*

*(continued)*

## Sample Preparation Outline *(continued)*

*Tony should have written citations of his sources available for his instructor or any other audience member who might want them.*

Edwards also suggests that Facebook is a "gateway drug" that leads people to other online time-wasters such as YouTube and other social networking sites.

2. Facebook.com reports that the average user is on Facebook for an hour and a half each day. Personally, I was on Facebook for a few hours a day, and I know people who spend even more time on it. Some of my students admit that they never disconnect from Facebook throughout the day.

3. Ashley Sarpong, a columnist for the Duke University *Chronicle*, wrote about her Facebook addiction. In one of her articles she confessed to "frequent all-nighters" for school due to "wasted afternoons on Facebook." Can any of you relate to Ashley and me?

4. Now let's talk about the warning signs that you could be a Facebook addict:
   a. You are late to meetings because you were on Facebook.
   b. Your friends and family comment on your excessive Facebook use.
   c. You constantly check Facebook from your computer and/or mobile device.

*Signpost:* Now I'd like to talk to you about some tips that have helped me reduce my excessive time on Facebook.

*Here Tony offers solutions to the problem he has presented: strategies that helped him deal with his own Facebook addiction.*

II. Facebook addiction can be managed by implementing four strategies.
   A. I had to first admit that I had a problem.
   B. The second thing I did was write down how much time I spent on Facebook—that's when I discovered that I was spending hours online every day.
   C. I gave myself a set time every day to visit Facebook.
   D. I turned off e-mail notifications.

*In his conclusion, Tony brings closure to his presentation by restating his central idea and summarizing his main ideas. His final sentence drives home the importance of his topic to his student audience and "sounds finished."*

## Conclusion

Today I have told you some interesting facts about Facebook and given you some warning signs of Facebook addiction. I have also discussed with you the tips that helped me minimize my Facebook usage. If you are a student whose grades are suffering from Facebook addiction, remember this: Sometimes, the difference between an "A" and an "F" is Facebook.

**Include Your Introduction and Conclusion in Abbreviated Form**   Even if your instructor does not require you to include your introduction and conclusion on your preparation outline, include shortened versions of them on your note cards. You might even feel more comfortable delivering the presentation if you have your first and last sentences written out in front of you.

**Include Your Central Idea, but Not Your Purpose Statement**   Be sure to include your central idea in your speaking notes. Do not include your purpose statement because you will not actually say it during your presentation.

**Include Supporting Material and Signposts**   Write out in full any statistics and direct quotations and their sources. Write your key signposts—your initial preview, for example—to ensure that you will not grope awkwardly as you move from one idea to another.

**Include Delivery Cues**   Writing on your note cards such cues as "Louder," "Pause," or "Walk two steps left" will remind you to communicate the nonverbal messages you have planned. Write your delivery cues in a different-color ink so that you don't confuse them with your verbal content.

Figure 12.2 illustrates speaking notes for Tony's presentation on Facebook addiction.

# RECAP

## TWO TYPES OF PRESENTATION OUTLINES

| Type | Purpose |
|---|---|
| Preparation Outline | Allows speaker to examine presentation for completeness, unity, coherence, and overall effectiveness. May serve as first rehearsal outline. |
| Speaking Notes | Include supporting material, signposts, and delivery cues. |

**Figure 12.2
Sample
Speaking Notes**

**Introduction**
- Hi, my name is Tony & I'm a Facebook addict.
- Excessive use has interfered w/ work & studies.
- Facebook =
  - Ultra-popular social networking site.
  - Used by students & people all over the world.
  - Communicate & socialize w/ family, friends, & organizations.
- 2006: started using Facebook for college courses I teach.
  - Successful — students loved, preferred it.
  - But problem.

**Central Idea**
The growing & serious phenomenon of Facebook addiction can be managed by implementing four strategies.

**Preview**
Today,
- (hold up 1 finger) Talk w/ you about Facebook facts.
- (hold up 2 fingers) Offer warning signs to determine whether Facebook addict.
- (hold up 3 fingers) Share tips that helped me reduce use.

**Signpost:** So let's start w/ some Facebook facts.
(Pause)

**Body**
I. Growing & serious phenomenon.
  A.  Growing @ incredible pace since Mark Zuckerberg & friends started in Harvard dorm room, Feb. 2004.

## REVIEWING
## What You
## Know

### Organizing Your Main Ideas                                p. 310

Once you have found supporting material, you are ready to organize your ideas and information. Depending on your topic, purpose, and audience, you can organize the main ideas of your presentation chronologically, topically, spatially, by cause and effect, or by problem and solution.

#### Terms to Know

| | | | |
|---|---|---|---|
| Topical Organization | p. 310 | Chronological Organization | p. 311 |
| Recency | p. 311 | Spatial Organization | p. 312 |
| Primacy | p. 311 | Cause-and-Effect Organization | p. 312 |
| Complexity | p. 311 | Problem–Solution Organization | p. 312 |

### Organizing Your Supporting Material                       p. 313

You can often organize supporting material according to one of the same patterns used to organize main ideas. Supporting material can also be organized according to the principle of recency, primacy, complexity, or specificity; or from soft to hard evidence.

#### Terms to Know

| | | | |
|---|---|---|---|
| Specificity | p. 313 | Hard Evidence | p. 314 |
| Soft Evidence | p. 314 | | |

### Organizing Your Presentation for the
### Ears of Others                                            p. 315

With your presentation organized, you will want to add signposts—previews, transitions, and summaries—to make your organization clearly apparent to your audience.

#### Terms to Know

| | | | |
|---|---|---|---|
| Signpost | p. 315 | Verbal Transition | p. 315 |
| Preview | p. 315 | Nonverbal Transition | p. 316 |
| Initial Preview | p. 315 | Summary | p. 316 |
| Internal Preview | p. 315 | Internal Summary | p. 316 |
| Transition | p. 315 | Final Summary | p. 316 |

### Introducing and Concluding Your
### Presentation                                              p. 317

A carefully planned introduction will get your audience's attention, introduce your topic, give the audience a reason to listen, establish your credibility, state your central idea, and preview your main ideas. An equally carefully planned conclusion will summarize your presentation, reemphasize the central idea in a memorable way, motivate your audience to respond, and provide closure.

### Terms to Know

| | | | |
|---|---|---|---|
| Introduction | p. 317 | Closure | p. 319 |
| Conclusion | p. 319 | | |

## Outlining Your Presentation    p. 320

A final step before beginning to rehearse your presentation is to prepare a detailed preparation outline and speaking notes. Your preparation outline should follow the instructions provided by your instructor.

### Terms to Know

| | | | |
|---|---|---|---|
| Preparation Outline | p. 321 | Standard Outline Format | p. 321 |

### Principle One:
### Be aware of your communication with yourself and others.
- Be aware of the skills, talents, and experiences you have that can enhance your credibility with your listeners.
- Use a preparation outline to demonstrate to yourself that your main ideas are clearly related to your central idea and are logically and adequately supported.

### Principle Two:
### Effectively use and interpret verbal messages.
- To communicate your verbal message effectively, organize your presentation logically.
- Use verbal transitions to show relationships between ideas in your presentation.
- Introduce your topic and preview your main ideas in your introduction.
- Use stories, examples, illustrations, statistics, a quotation, or other techniques to capture your listeners' attention when you begin your talk.
- In your conclusion, summarize your presentation and reemphasize your main idea in a memorable way.

### Principle Three:
### Effectively use and interpret nonverbal messages.
- Use nonverbal transitions—pauses, facial expression, altered vocal pitch or speaking rate, and movement—to indicate when you are moving from one idea to the next.
- Use nonverbal cues—such as pausing, slowing your rate of speech, and letting your vocal inflection fall—to signal closure in the final sentence or two of your conclusion.
- Add delivery cues and reminders to your final speaking notes.

## APPLYING Principles for a Lifetime

### Principle Four:
### Listen and respond thoughtfully to others.

- As you listen to presentations, consider that their organization may reflect patterns considered appropriate in cultures other than your own.

### Principle Five:
### Appropriately adapt messages to others.

- Investigate and consider using the customary organizational strategy of your audience's culture.
- In most cases, discuss last the idea that you most want your audience to remember.
- If you know your audience members will be skeptical of some of your ideas, present first those ideas on which you can agree.
- Provide signposts as organizational cues for your audience.
- Use your introduction and conclusion to help adapt your presentation to your audience.

# ASSESSING
## Your Skill

## Listening to and Outlining a Presentation

Take notes as you listen to a presentation, either live or recorded. Then organize your notes into an outline that you think reflects both the speaker's organization and the intended relationship among ideas and supporting material.

## Analyzing the Organization of a Speech

Read one of the speeches in Appendix B. Answer the following questions.

1. How are the main ideas organized?
2. Look closely at the supporting materials. If two or more are used to support any one main idea, what strategy do you think the speaker used to organize them?
3. Is there an initial preview statement? If so, what is it?
4. Is there a final summary? If so, what is it?
5. Find at least one example of each of the following:
   - A transition word or phrase
   - An internal preview
   - An internal summary

## Developing a Practice Introduction

Draft an introduction for a presentation on one of the following topics:

- Strategies for surviving a tornado
- Private-school vouchers
- Mars up close
- Celebrities and the press

In addition to introducing the topic and previewing your main ideas, be sure to plan strategies for getting the attention of audience members and giving them a reason to listen. Also devise a way to establish your own credibility as a speaker on that topic.

- **MyCommunicationLab**  MyCommunicationLab offers an online tool for outlining your presentation. <www.mycommunicationlab.com> (Access code required.)

- **Five Tips for Introducing Your Presentation**  This advice on developing an introduction includes five fairly simple but helpful tips. <www.speech-topics-help.com/speech-introduction.html>

- **Developing an Outline**  Purdue University's Online Writing Lab provides you with detailed guidance on how to develop and format an outline. <http://owl.english.purdue.edu>

- **Using Speaking Notes**  This brief video emphasizes the difference between speaking notes and a script. <http://www.ehow.com/video_4976823_public-speaking-using-notes.html>

**WEB RESOURCES** for More Review, Application, and Assessment

O the orator's joys! To inflate the chest, to roll the thunder of the voice out from the ribs and throat, to make the people rage, weep, hate, desire.

WALT WHITMAN

# Chapter OUTLINE

- Methods of Delivery
- Effective Verbal Delivery
- Effective Nonverbal Delivery
- Effective Presentation Aids
- Some Final Tips for Rehearsing and Delivering Your Presentation
- Criteria for Evaluating Presentations
- Study Guide: Review, Apply, and Assess Your Knowledge and Skill

# Chapter OBJECTIVES

After studying this chapter, you should be able to

1. List and describe the four methods of delivery and provide suggestions for effectively using each one.
2. List and explain five criteria for using words well.
3. Identify and illustrate characteristics of effective nonverbal delivery.
4. Discuss how to prepare and use presentation aids effectively.
5. Understand and apply criteria for evaluating speeches.

© Yuri Arcurs/Alamy

# 13 | Delivering Your Presentation

Which is more important, the content of a presentation or the way it is delivered? Speakers and speech teachers have argued about the answer to this question for thousands of years. In the fourth century BCE, the Greek rhetorician Aristotle declared delivery "superfluous." On the other hand, when his contemporary and fellow Athenian Demosthenes was asked to name the three most important elements for a speaker to master, he is reported to have replied, "Delivery, delivery, delivery."

The debate continues. Which is more important, content or delivery? One researcher has concluded that delivery is almost twice as important as content when students give self-introduction presentations and three times as important when students give persuasive presentations.[1] Other scholars have found that delivery provides important information about a speaker's feelings and emotions and will in turn affect listeners' emotional responses to the speaker.[2] Most speech teachers today agree that both content and delivery contribute to the effectiveness of a presentation. As a modern speechwriter and communication coach suggests

> In the real world—the world where you and I do business—content and delivery are always related. And woe be to the communicator who forgets this.[3]

In this chapter, we will discuss how you can apply the five Communication Principles for a Lifetime to delivery. We will talk about both verbal and nonverbal delivery skills. We will consider how important it is to be aware of the words you use and of such nonverbal cues as gestures, eye contact, and facial expression. We will also discuss how to determine what presentation aids might be effective for your audience, and we'll offer guidelines for both preparing and using various presentation aids.

# Methods of Delivery

Audiences today generally expect speakers to use clear, concise, everyday language and conversational delivery style, as opposed to the flowery language and dramatic, choreographed gestures used by speakers a century ago. Different audiences, however, expect and prefer variations of this general delivery style. For example, if you are using a microphone to speak to an audience of 1,000 people, your listeners may expect a relatively formal delivery style. On the other hand, your communication class would probably find it odd if you delivered a formal oration to your twenty-five classmates.

This speaker's posture, gesture, and facial expression all help to convey his message. How can you make sure that your delivery effectively reinforces your verbal message?

Jupiterimages/Thinkstock

People from different cultures also have different expectations of speakers' delivery. Listeners from Japan and China, for example, prefer subdued gestures to a more flamboyant delivery. British listeners expect a speaker to stay behind a lectern and use relatively few gestures.

Speakers should consider and adapt to their audience's expectations, their topic, and the speaking situation as they select from four basic methods of delivery: manuscript speaking, memorized speaking, impromptu speaking, and extemporaneous speaking.

## Manuscript Speaking

Perhaps you remember the first presentation you ever had to give, maybe as long ago as elementary school. Chances are that you wrote your speech out and read it to your audience.

Unfortunately, **manuscript speaking** is rarely done well enough to be interesting. Most speakers who rely on a manuscript read it in either a monotone or with a pattern of vocal inflection that makes the presentation sound as if it were being read. They are so afraid of losing their place that they keep their eyes glued to the manuscript and seldom look at the audience. These challenges are significant enough that most speakers should avoid reading from a manuscript most of the time.

There are some exceptions, though. Sometimes effective verbal messages depend on careful and exact phrasing. For example, because an awkward statement made by the U.S. secretary of state could cause an international crisis, he or she usually has remarks on critical issues carefully scripted. If you ever have to speak on a sensitive, critical, or controversial issue, you too might need to deliver a manuscript presentation. If so, consider the following suggestions:[4]

- Type your manuscript in short, easy-to-scan phrases on the upper two-thirds of the paper so that you do not have to look too far down the page.
- If possible, practice with your manuscript before you speak.
- If you're afraid that you'll lose your place in the manuscript, unobtrusively use your index finger to keep your place in the text.
- Use appropriate nonverbal messages. Try to take in an entire sentence at a time so that you can maintain eye contact with your audience throughout each sentence.
- Do not read the manuscript too quickly. Use a slash mark (/) or some other symbol to remind you to pause in strategic places.
- Vary the rhythm, inflection, and pace of your delivery so that the presentation does not sound as if it is being read.
- Use gestures and movement to add further nonverbal interest and emphasis to your message.

## Memorized Speaking

After that first speech you read in elementary school, you probably became a more savvy speaker, and the next time you had to give a speech, you decided to write it out and memorize it. You thought that no one would be able to tell. What you didn't know then, but probably do now, is that most **memorized speaking** sounds stiff and recited. In addition, you run the risk of forgetting parts of your speech and having to search awkwardly for words in front of your audience. By doing so, you forfeit the ability to adapt to your audience while you are speaking.

On occasion, speaking from memory is justifiable. If you must deliver a short presentation within narrowly proscribed time limits, memorizing and rehearsing it will allow you to time it more accurately. Three guidelines can help you use nonverbal messages effectively when you deliver a presentation from memory:

- Do not deliver your memorized speech too rapidly.
- Avoid patterns of vocal inflection that make the speech sound recited. Focus on what you are saying, and let your voice rise and fall to emphasize important words and phrases and to reflect the structures of your sentences. Consider recording

**manuscript speaking**
Reading a presentation from a written text.

**memorized speaking**
Delivering a presentation word for word from memory without using notes.

your presentation beforehand and listening to it to ensure that your vocal delivery sounds like a conversation rather than a recitation.

- Use gestures and movement to add interest and emphasis to your message.

## Impromptu Speaking

In 1993, when President Bill Clinton was delivering his first state of the union address, the teleprompter scrolled the wrong text of his speech for nine minutes. What Clinton did next as millions of people watched on television has become what political advisor and commentator Paul Begala calls "part of the Clinton legend." Drawing on his years of experience, the president kept speaking. As Begala marvels, "Nine minutes the guy went without a note, and no one could tell."[5]

Although you plan your presentations, there are times—as illustrated by Clinton's experience—when the best plans go awry. A more likely possibility is that you will be asked to answer a question or respond to an argument without advance warning or time to prepare. At such times, you will have to call on your skills in **impromptu speaking**, or speaking "off the cuff."

Along with having a solid grasp of the topic on which you are asked to speak can help you in such instances, five additional guidelines can help you avoid fumbling for words or rambling:

- Consider your audience. A quick mental check of who your audience members are and their interests, expectations, and knowledge can help ensure that your impromptu remarks are centered on them.
- Be brief. One to three minutes is probably a realistic time frame for most impromptu presentations. As one leadership consultant points out, "You're merely expected to hit a theme, say a few nice words, and then depart."[6]
- Organize. Think quickly about an introduction, body, and conclusion. If you want to make more than one point, use a simple organizational strategy such as chronological order—past, present, and future. Or construct an alphabetical list in which your main ideas begin with the letters A, B, and C.[7]
- Draw on your personal experience and knowledge. Audiences almost always respond favorably to personal illustrations, so use any appropriate and relevant ones.
- Use gestures and movement that arise naturally from what you are saying.
- Be aware of the potential impact of your communication. If your subject is at all sensitive or your information is classified, be noncommittal in what you say.

## Extemporaneous Speaking

We have saved for last the method of speaking most appropriate for most circumstances, preferred by most audiences, and most often taught in public speaking classes: **extemporaneous speaking**. The extemporaneous presentation is a well-developed and well-organized message delivered in an interesting and vivid manner. It reflects your understanding of how to use both verbal and nonverbal messages effectively and your ability to adapt these messages to your audience.

Although the presentational speaking chapters in this book offer numerous guidelines for extemporaneous speaking, consider these four when you reach the rehearsal and delivery stages:

- Use a full-content preparation outline when you begin to rehearse your extemporaneous presentation. Be aware of your growing confidence in delivering it, and continue to decrease your reliance on your notes.
- Prepare speaking notes. Using this new outline, continue to rehearse.
- Even as you become increasingly familiar with your message, do not try to memorize it word for word. Continue to vary the ways in which you express your ideas and information.
- As you deliver your presentation, adapt it to your audience. Use gestures and movement that arise naturally from what you are saying.

**impromptu speaking**
Delivering a presentation without advance preparation.

**extemporaneous speaking**
Delivering a well-developed, well-organized, carefully rehearsed presentation without having memorized exact wording.

# Effective Verbal Delivery

In an examination of some 125 years' worth of student speeches prepared for intercollegiate competition, researchers Leah White and Lucas Messer found remarkable consistency in students' use of stylized language. White and Messer explain,

> Style and delivery are often tightly connected. Speeches rich in language strategies lend themselves to engaging deliveries.[8]

Although you will not write out most presentations word for word, you will want to plan and rehearse words, phrases, and sentences that accurately and effectively communicate your ideas. At the same time, you will want to give your message a distinctive and memorable style. Let's examine some guidelines for effectively using and understanding words and word structures in a presentation.

## Using Words Well

The most effective words are specific and concrete, unbiased, vivid, simple, and correct. Building on our discussion in Chapter 3 of the power of verbal messages, we'll examine each of these characteristics in turn.

**Specific, Concrete Words**  A **specific word** refers to an individual member of a general class—for example, *ammonite* as opposed to the more general term *fossil*, or *sodium* as opposed to *chemical*. Specific words are often **concrete words**, appealing to one of the five senses and communicating an image clearly. For example, which word in each of the following pairs creates a more specific mental picture?

| | |
|---|---|
| dog | poodle |
| utensil | spatula |
| toy | building block |

In each case, the second word is more specific and concrete than the first and better communicates the image the speaker intends. For maximum clarity in your presentations, use more specific, concrete words than general, abstract ones.

**Unbiased Words**  **Unbiased words** do not disparage, either intentionally or unintentionally, either gender or any racial, cultural, or religious group, nor do they offend any audience member who may belong to one of these groups.

Although a speaker can fairly easily avoid overtly offensive language, it is more difficult to avoid language that subtly stereotypes or discriminates. As we noted in Chapter 3, the once-acceptable use of a masculine noun (*man, mankind*) to refer generically to all people may now be offensive to many audience members. Other words that reflect gender bias include *chairman, waiter,* and *congressman*. Even if you yourself do not consider these terms offensive, a member of your audience might. When possible, you should adapt to your audience by choosing instead such unbiased gender-neutral alternatives as *chairperson* or *chair, server,* and *member of Congress*.

**Vivid Words**  **Vivid words** add color and interest to your language. Like concrete words, they help you communicate mental images more accurately and interestingly.

**RE**CAP

## METHODS OF DELIVERY

| Manuscript | Reading a presentation from a written text |
|---|---|
| Memorized | Giving a presentation word for word from memory without using notes |
| Impromptu | Delivering a presentation without advance preparation |
| Extemporaneous | Speaking from a written or memorized outline without having memorized the exact wording of the presentation |

**specific word**
A word that refers to an individual member of a general class.

**concrete word**
A word that refers to an object or describes an action or characteristic in the most specific way possible.

**unbiased word**
A word that does not stereotype, discriminate against, or insult either gender or any racial, cultural, or religious group.

**vivid word**
A colorful word.

This word cloud visualizes the frequency with which President Obama used different words in his 2009 inaugural address. Note that many of the larger words, which are those the president used most, are simple words that tend to evoke vivid emotions among Americans. How can you use simple, specific words to drive home your messages?
Wordle.com

# **RE**CAP

## USING WORDS WELL

Use specific, concrete words to communicate clearly and specifically.

Use unbiased words to avoid offending people of either gender or from any racial, cultural, or religious group.

Use vivid words to add color and interest to your language.

Use simple words to be understood readily.

Use correct words to enhance your credibility.

**thesaurus**
A list of synonyms.

**simple word**
A word known to most people who speak the language.

**correct word**
A word that means what the speaker intends and is grammatically correct in the phrase or sentence in which it appears.

Most speakers who try to make their language more vivid think first of adding adjectives to nouns—for example, *distressed oak table* instead of *table*, *scruffy tabby cat* instead of *cat*—and certainly the first phrase of each example is more vivid than the other. Less frequently considered is the potential power of substituting vivid verbs for "blah" verbs—for example, *sprout* instead of *grow*, *devour* instead of *eat*.

When searching for a vivid word, you might want to consult a **thesaurus**, or collection of synonyms, but do not assume that the most obscure or unusual synonym you find will necessarily be the most vivid. Sometimes a simple word can evoke a vivid image for your audience.

**Simple Words**   **Simple words** are generally an asset to a speaker. They will be immediately understood by an audience. In his classic essay "Politics and the English Language," George Orwell includes this prescription for simplicity:

> Never use a long word where a short one will do. . . . Never use a foreign phrase, a scientific word, or a jargon word if you can think of an everyday English equivalent.[9]

Selected thoughtfully, simple words can communicate with both accuracy and power.

**Correct Words**   Finally, and perhaps most obviously, you should use **correct words** when you speak. Grammatical and usage errors communicate a lack of preparation and can lower your credibility with your audience. Be aware of errors that you make habitually. If you are uncertain about how to use a word, look it up in a dictionary or ask someone who knows. If you are stumped by whether to say "Neither the people nor the president *knows* how to solve the problem" or "Neither the people nor the president *know* how to solve the problem," seek assistance from a good English handbook. (By the way, the first sentence is correct!)

## Crafting Memorable Word Structures

We have discussed the importance of using words that are concrete, unbiased, vivid, simple, and correct. Now we will turn our attention to word structures—phrases and sentences that create the figurative language, drama, and cadences needed to provide what one marketing communication specialist calls "ear appeal."[10]

**Figurative Language**   One way to make your presentation memorable is to use **figurative language**, including **metaphors** (implied comparisons), **similes** (overt comparisons using *like* or *as*), and **personification** (the attribution of human qualities to nonhuman things or ideas). Such language is memorable because it is used in a way that is a little different from its ordinary, expected usage.

Nineteenth-century Missouri senator George Graham Vest used all three types of figurative language to good advantage in his short but memorable "Tribute to the Dog," delivered in Warrensburg, Missouri, in 1870, and nominated by columnist William Safire as one of the greatest speeches of the second millennium.[11] Memorable at least in part because of the figurative language Vest employs, this speech is available online in the Great Speeches collection at the History Place <www.historyplace.com/speeches/vest.htm>.

**Metaphors**   Vest makes the abstract concept of malice more concrete with the metaphor "the stone of malice."

**Similes** Vest uses a simile to compare the dog's master to a prince: "He guards the sleep of his pauper master as if he were a prince."

**Personification** Finally, Vest personifies death, which "takes [the dog's] master in its embrace."

**Drama** Another way to make your word structures in your presentation more memorable is to use language to create **drama** by phrasing something in an unexpected way. Three specific devices that can help you achieve verbal drama are omission, inversion, and suspension:

**Omission** When you strip a phrase or sentence of nonessential words that the audience expects or with which they are so familiar that they will mentally fill them in, you are using **omission**. Journalist Bill Moyers described modifications in the format of a major American newspaper with the succinct phrase

More money, less news.[12]

**Inversion** Inversion—reversing the normal order of words in a phrase or sentence—can also create drama in a presentation. John F. Kennedy inverted the usual subject–verb–object sentence pattern to object–subject–verb to make this brief declaration memorable:

This much we pledge.[13]

**Suspension** A third way to create drama through sentence structures is to employ verbal **suspension**, saving an important word or phrase for the end of a sentence rather than placing it at the beginning. Speaking to the Democratic National Convention in July 2004, former president Jimmy Carter used suspension to dramatize the importance of the global role of the United States:

At stake is nothing less than our nation's soul.[14]

**Cadence** A final way to create memorable word structures is to create **cadence**, or language rhythm. A speaker does so not by speaking in a sing-song pattern, but by using such stylistic devices as parallelism, antithesis, repetition, and alliteration:

**Parallelism** Parallelism occurs when two or more clauses or sentences have the same grammatical pattern. Addressing supporters during the 2008 U.S. presidential campaign, Republican candidate John McCain used parallel verb phrases to declare his intent to

deliver health care services, support retirees, fuel our transportation network, stimulate research and development, and harness new technologies.[15]

**Antithesis** Similar to parallelism, except that the two structures contrast in meaning, **antithesis** is often marked by the conjunctions "not only . . . but (also)." In a presentation marking the fiftieth anniversary of John F. Kennedy's "Moon Shot" speech, Vice President Joe Biden noted that Kennedy's character

was a reflection not only of his generation, but of America's character.[16]

**Repetition** Repetition of an important word or phrase can add emphasis to a key idea and memorability to your message. In her moving convocation address to

"Nice speech, except that the term is 'trickle-down,' not 'tinkle-down.'"

Baloo-Rex May/CartoonStock

**figurative language**
Language that deviates from the ordinary, expected meaning of words to make a description or comparison unique, vivid, and memorable.

**metaphor**
An implied comparison between two things.

**simile**
An overt comparison between two things that uses the word *like* or *as*.

**personification**
The attribution of human qualities to inanimate things or ideas.

**drama**
A characteristic of a speech created when something is phrased in a way that differs from the way the audience expects.

**omission**
Leaving out a word or phrase the audience expects to hear.

**inversion**
Reversing the normal word order of a phrase or sentence.

**suspension**
Withholding a key word or phrase until the end of a sentence.

**cadence**
The rhythm of language.

**parallelism**
Using the same grammatical structure for two or more clauses or sentences.

**antithesis**
Contrasting the meanings of the two parts of a parallel structure.

**repetition**
Emphasizing a key word or phrase by using it more than once.

# RECAP

## CRAFTING MEMORABLE WORD STRUCTURES

To make your message memorable, use . . .

**Figurative Language**

| | |
|---|---|
| Metaphor | Making an implied comparison |
| Simile | Making a comparison using *like* or *as* |
| Personification | Attributing human qualities to nonhuman things or ideas |

**Drama**

| | |
|---|---|
| Omission | Leaving nonessential words out of a phrase or sentence |
| Inversion | Reversing the normal order of words in a phrase or sentence |
| Suspension | Withholding the key words in a phrase or sentence until the end |

**Cadence**

| | |
|---|---|
| Parallelism | Using two or more clauses or sentences with the same grammatical structure |
| Antithesis | Using a two-part parallel structure in which the second part contrasts in meaning with the first |
| Repetition | Using a key word or phrase more than once |
| Alliteration | Repeating a consonant sound |

a grieving Virginia Tech community after the April 2007 campus shootings, poet and Virginia Tech professor Nikki Giovanni repeated five times the stirring affirmation

> We are Virginia Tech.[17]

**Alliteration**    A final strategy for creating cadence is to use **alliteration**, the repetition of an initial consonant sound several times in a phrase, clause, or sentence. In his 2011 state of the union address, President Barack Obama used the alliterative phrase

> poised for progress.[18]

Repeating the *p* sound added cadence—and memorability—to the passage.

# Effective Nonverbal Delivery

At this point, you understand how important it is to deliver your presentation effectively and what delivery style most audiences today prefer. You are familiar with the four methods of delivery and know how to maximize the use of each one. You also have some ideas about how to use effective and memorable language. Still, you may wonder, "What do I do with my hands?" "Is it all right to move around while I speak?" "How can I make my voice sound interesting?" To help answer these and similar questions, and to help you use nonverbal messages more effectively, we'll examine five major categories of nonverbal delivery: eye contact, physical delivery, facial expression, vocal delivery, and personal appearance. This discussion further develops the fundamental principle of using and interpreting nonverbal messages that we introduced in Chapter 4.

**alliteration**
The repetition of a consonant sound (usually the first consonant) several times in a phrase, clause, or sentence.

**eye contact**
Looking at an audience during a presentation.

## Eye Contact

Of all the nonverbal delivery variables discussed in this chapter, the most important one in a presentational speaking situation for North Americans is **eye contact**. Eye contact with your audience members lets them know that you are interested in and ready to talk to them. It also permits you to determine whether they are responding to you. In addition, most listeners will think that you are more capable and trustworthy if you look them in the eye than if you avoid eye contact. Some studies document a relationship between eye contact and speaker credibility, as well as between eye contact and listener learning.[19]

How much eye contact do you need? One study found that speakers with less than 50 percent eye contact are considered unfriendly, uninformed, inexperienced, and even dishonest by their listeners.[20] On the other hand, is there such a thing as too much eye contact? For North American audiences, the answer is probably not. Be aware, though, that not all people from all cultures prefer as much eye contact as North Americans do. Asians, for example, generally prefer less.

The following suggestions can help you use eye contact effectively when you speak in public:

- Establish eye contact with your audience before you say anything. Eye contact sends listeners a message to tune in as you start your talk.
- Maintain eye contact with your audience as you deliver your opening sentence without looking at your notes.
- Try to establish eye contact with people throughout your audience, not just with the front row or only one or two people. Briefly look into the eyes of an individual, and then transfer your eye contact to someone else.
- Do not look over your listeners' heads! They will notice if you do so and may even turn around to try to find out what you are looking at.

## Physical Delivery

Gestures, movement, and posture are the three key elements of **physical delivery**. A good speaker knows how to use effective gestures, make meaningful movements, and maintain appropriate posture while speaking to an audience.

**Gestures**  The hand and arm movements you use while speaking are called **gestures**. Nearly all people from all cultures use some gestures when they speak. In fact, research suggests that gesturing is instinctive and that it is intrinsic to speaking and thinking.[21] Yet even if you gesture easily and appropriately in the course of everyday conversation, you may feel awkward about what to do with your hands when you are in front of an audience. To minimize this challenge, consider the following guidelines:

- Focus on the message you want to communicate. As in ordinary conversation, when you speak in public, your hands should help emphasize or reinforce your verbal message. Your gestures should coincide with what you are saying.
- Again, as in conversation, let your gestures flow with your message. They should appear natural, not tense or rigid.
- Be definite. If you want to gesture, go ahead and gesture. Avoid minor hand movements that will be masked by the lectern or that may appear to your audience as accidental brief jerks.
- Vary your gestures. Try not to use the same hand or one all-purpose gesture all the time. Think of the different gestures you can use, depending on whether you want to enumerate, point, describe, or emphasize ideas.
- Don't overdo your gestures. You want your audience to focus not on your gestures, but on your message.
- Make your gestures appropriate to your audience and situation. When speaking to a large audience in a relatively formal setting, use bolder, more sweeping, and more dramatic gestures than when speaking to a small audience in an informal setting. Also consider the culture-based expectations of your audience. Americans in general tend to use more gestures than do speakers from other cultures. If you are speaking to a culturally diverse audience, you may want to tone down your gestures.

**Movement**  Another element of physical delivery is **movement**. You may wonder, "Should I walk around during my presentation, or should I stay in one place?" "Should I stay behind the lectern, or could I stand beside or in front of it?" "Can I move around among the audience?" The following criteria may help you determine the answers to the preceding questions:

- Like gestures, any movement should be purposeful. It should be consistent with the verbal content of your message; otherwise, it will appear to be aimless wandering. You might signal the beginning of a new idea or major point in your speech with movement, or you might move to signal a transition from a serious idea to a more humorous one. The bottom line is that your use of movement should make sense to your listeners. No movement at all is better than random, distracting movement.

**physical delivery**
A person's gestures, movement, and posture, which influence how a message is interpreted.

**gestures**
Movements of the hands and arms to communicate ideas.

**movement**
A change of location during a presentation.

This speaker's gesture acknowledging his fellow graduates is simple, natural, and definite. Focusing on your audience and your message during rehearsals can help you to gesture effectively when you deliver your presentation to an audience.

Comstock/Thinkstock

- If a physical barrier such as a lectern, a row of chairs, or an overhead projector makes you feel cut off from your listeners, move closer to the audience. Studies suggest that physical proximity enhances learning.[22]
- Adapt to the cultural expectations of your audience. British listeners, for example, have commented to us that American lecturers tend to stand too close to an audience when speaking. If you think that movement will make your audience uncomfortable, stay in one carefully chosen spot to deliver your presentation.

**Posture**    **Posture** is the third element of physical delivery to consider when delivering a presentation. One study suggests that your posture may reflect on your credibility as a speaker.[23] Another study suggests that "fear contagion," the spread of fear throughout a crowd, is largely a response to posture cues.[24] Certainly, slouching lazily across a lectern does not communicate enthusiasm for or interest in your audience or your topic. On the other hand, you should adapt your posture to your topic, your audience, and the level of formality of the speaking occasion. For example, during a very informal presentation it may be perfectly appropriate, as well as comfortable and natural, to lean against the edge of a desk.

Few speech teachers or texts advocate specific speaking postures. Instead, you should observe some commonsense guidelines about posture:

- Avoid slouching, shifting from one foot to the other, or drooping your head.
- Unless you have a disability, do not sit while delivering a presentation. An exception might be perching on or leaning against the edge of a desk or stool (which would still elevate you slightly above your audience) during a very informal presentation.

Like your gestures and movement, your posture should not call attention to itself. Rather, it should reflect your interest in and attention to your audience and your presentation.

**posture**
A speaker's stance.

**facial expression**
An arrangement of the facial muscles to communicate thoughts, emotions, and attitudes.

## Facial Expression

Your **facial expression** plays a key role in expressing your thoughts, emotions, and attitudes.[25] Your audience sees your face before they hear what you are going to say, giving you the opportunity to set the tone for your message even before you begin to speak.

Social psychologist Paul Ekman has found that facial expressions of primary emotions are virtually universal, so even a culturally diverse audience will be able to read your facial expressions clearly.[26]

Throughout your presentation, your facial expression, like your body language and eye contact, should be appropriate to your message. Present somber news wearing a serious expression. Relate a humorous story with a smile. To communicate interest in your listeners, keep your expression alert and friendly. To ensure that you are maximizing the use of this important nonverbal delivery cue, rehearse your presentation in front of a mirror; better yet, video yourself rehearsing your presentation. Consider as objectively as possible whether your face is reflecting the emotional tone of your ideas.

## Vocal Delivery

We have already discussed the importance of selecting words and phrases that will most effectively communicate your ideas, information, and images. We referred to this element of delivery as verbal delivery. **Vocal delivery**, on the other hand, involves nonverbal vocal cues—not the words you say, but the way you say them. Effective vocal delivery requires you to speak so that your audience can understand you and will remain interested in what you are saying. Nonverbal vocal elements include volume, pitch, rate, and articulation.

**Volume**   **Volume** is the softness or loudness of your voice. It is the most fundamental determinant of audience understanding. If you do not speak loudly enough, even the most brilliant presentation will be ineffective, because the audience simply will not hear you. In addition, volume can signal important ideas in your presentation; for example, you can deliver a key idea either more loudly or more softly than you have been speaking. Consider these guidelines to help you appropriately adapt the volume of your voice to your audience's needs:

- Speak loudly enough so that the members of your audience farthest from you can hear you without straining. Doing so will ensure that everyone else in the room can hear you, too.
- Vary the volume of your voice in a purposeful way. Indicate important ideas by turning your volume up or down.
- Be aware of whether you need a microphone to amplify your volume. If you do and one is available, use it.

**vocal delivery**
Nonverbal voice cues, including volume, pitch, rate, and articulation.

**volume**
The softness or loudness of a speaker's voice.

# Communication & DIVERSITY

## The Academic Quarter

When speaking at a Polish university a few years ago, one of your authors expected to begin promptly at 11:00 a.m as announced in the program and on posters. By 11:10, it was clear that the speech would not begin on time, and your author began to despair of having any audience at all.

In Poland, it turns out, both students and professors expect to adhere to the "academic quarter." In other words, most lectures begin at least fifteen minutes, or a quarter of an hour, after the announced starting time.

If your author had asked a Polish professor about the audience's expectations, he would have known about this custom in advance. One way to avoid such misunderstandings is to talk with people you know who are familiar with the cultural expectations. Try to observe other speakers presenting to similar audiences. Ask specific questions, including the following:

1. Where does the audience expect me to stand while speaking?
2. Do listeners expect direct eye contact?
3. When will the audience expect me to start and stop my talk?
4. Will listeners find movement and gestures distracting or welcome?
5. Do listeners expect presentation aids?

Keep cultural differences in mind as you rehearse and deliver presentations to diverse audiences.

There are three kinds of microphones, only one of which demands much technique:

**Lavaliere.** The *lavaliere microphone* is a clip-on microphone often used by news reporters and interviewees. Worn on the front of a shirt or a jacket lapel, it requires no particular care other than not thumping it or accidentally knocking it off.

**Boom.** A *boom microphone* is used by makers of movies and TV shows. It hangs over the heads of the speakers and is controlled remotely, so the speakers need not be particularly concerned with it.

**Stationary.** A *stationary microphone* may be attached to a lectern, sit on a desk, or stand on the floor. Generally, today's stationary microphones are multidirectional. Even so, you will have to keep your mouth at about the same distance from the microphone at all times to avoid distracting fluctuations in the volume of sound. You can turn your head from side to side and use gestures, but you will have to limit other movements.

Under ideal circumstances, you will be able to practice with your microphone. If you have the chance, figure out where to stand for the best sound quality and to determine how sensitive the mike is to extraneous noise. Practice will accustom you to any voice distortion or echo that might occur so that these sound qualities do not surprise you during your presentation.

**Pitch**    Whereas volume is the loudness or softness of your voice, **pitch** refers to how high or low your voice is. To some extent, pitch is determined by physiology. The faster the folds in your vocal cords vibrate, the higher the habitual pitch of your voice. In general, female vocal folds vibrate much faster than do those of males. You can, however, raise or lower your habitual pitch within a certain range.

Variation in pitch, called **inflection**, is a key factor in communicating the meaning of your words. You know that a startled "Oh!" in response to something someone has told you communicates something quite different from a lower-pitched, questioning "Oh?" Your vocal inflection indicates your emotional response to what you have heard.

Vocal inflection also helps keep an audience interested in your presentation. If your pitch is a monotone, the audience will probably become bored quickly. To help you monitor and practice your pitch and inflection as you prepare to speak, record and play back your presentation at least once as you rehearse. Listen carefully to your pitch and inflection. If you think that you are speaking in too much of a monotone, practice again with exaggerated variations in pitch.

**Rate**    Another vocal variable is **rate**, or speed. How fast do you talk? Most speakers average between 120 and 180 words per minute but vary their rate to add interest to their delivery and to emphasize key ideas. To determine whether your speaking rate is appropriate and purposeful, become conscious of it. Record your presentation during rehearsal and listen critically to your speech speed. If it seems too fast, make a conscious effort to slow down. Use more **pauses** after questions and before important ideas. If you are speaking too slowly, make a conscious effort to speed up.

**Articulation**    **Articulation** is the enunciation of sounds. As a speaker, you want to articulate distinctly to ensure that your audience can determine what words you are using. Sometimes we fall into the habit of mumbling or slurring—saying *wanna* instead of *want to, chesterdrawers* instead of *chest of drawers*. Some nonstandard articulation may be part of a speaker's **dialect**, a speech style common to an ethnic group or a geographic region. One dialect with which most of us are familiar is the dialect of the southern United States, characterized by a distinctive drawl.

Although most native speakers of English can understand English dialects, studies have shown that North American listeners assign more favorable ratings to, and can recall more information presented by, speakers with dialects similar to their own.[27] If your dialect is significantly different from that of your listeners, or if you suspect that it could be potentially distracting, you may want to work to improve or standardize your articulation.

---

**pitch**
How high or low a speaker's voice is.

**inflection**
Variation in vocal pitch.

**rate**
How fast or slowly a speaker speaks.

**pause**
A few seconds of silence during a presentation, used both to slow a fast pace and to signal a key idea.

**articulation**
The production of clear and distinct speech sounds.

**dialect**
A consistent style of pronunciation and articulation that is common to an ethnic group or geographic region.

# DEVELOPING YOUR PRESENTATION
## Step by Step

### Rehearsing Your Presentation

Tony begins to rehearse his presentation. From the beginning, he stands and speaks aloud, practicing gestures and movement that seem appropriate to his message.

At first, Tony rehearses from his preparation outline (pp. 323–324). These early rehearsals go quite well, but the speech runs a little short. Tony knows that he tends to speak fairly rapidly, so

he decides to plan more pauses throughout the speech—some to allow his listeners to think about an important point he has just made, and others to provide nonverbal transitions. When he prepares his speaking notes, Tony writes the delivery cue "Pause" in several strategic places.

---

To do so, be aware of words or phrases that you have a tendency to drawl, slur, or chop. Once you have identified them, practice saying them distinctly and correctly.

**appearance**
A speaker's dress and grooming.

## Appearance

What would you wear to deliver a presentation to your class? To address your city council? The fact that you would probably wear something different for each of these occasions suggests that you are already aware of the importance of a speaker's **appearance**. There is considerable evidence that your personal appearance affects how your audience will respond to you and your message. If you violate your audience's expectations, you will be less successful in achieving your purpose. The following guidelines may make selecting a wardrobe a bit easier when you are next called on to speak:

- Never wear anything that is potentially distracting, such as a T-shirt with writing on it. You want your audience to listen to you, not read you.
- Consider appropriate clothing as a presentation aid. For example, if you are a nurse or emergency technician, wear your uniform when you speak about your profession. (We'll discuss presentation aids in more detail shortly.)
- Take cues from your audience. If you know that they will be dressed in business attire, dress similarly. If anything, you want to be a bit more dressed up than members of your audience.
- When in doubt about what to wear, select something conservative.

**presentation aid**
Any tangible item used to help communicate ideas to an audience.

# Effective Presentation Aids

We have already discussed two elements of delivery: verbal delivery and nonverbal delivery. A third element used with increasing frequency in this era of sophisticated computer presentation software is the **presentation aid.** The term *presentation aid* refers to anything your audience

## **RE**CAP

### CHARACTERISTICS OF EFFECTIVE NONVERBAL DELIVERY

- **Eye contact** should be established before you say anything and sustained as much as possible throughout your presentation.
- **Gestures** should be relaxed, definite, varied, and appropriate to your audience and the speaking situation.
- **Movement** should be purposeful and adapted to the audience's cultural expectations.
- **Posture** should feel natural and be appropriate to your topic, your audience, and the occasion.
- **Facial expression** should be alert, friendly, and appropriate to your message.
- **Volume** should be loud enough that you can be easily heard and should be purposefully varied.
- **Pitch** should be varied so that the inflection in your voice helps sustain your audience's interest.
- **Rate** should be neither too fast nor too slow and can be varied to add interest and emphasize key ideas.
- **Articulation** should be clear and distinct.
- **Appearance** should conform to what the audience expects.

can listen to or look at to help them understand your ideas. Charts, photographs, posters, drawings, graphs, audio and video recordings, and PowerPoint™ slides are some of the types of presentation aids frequently used by speakers.

As long as they *aid* the speaker, rather than *replace* the speaker, presentation aids can be invaluable. They help you gain and maintain your audience's attention.[28] They communicate your organization of ideas. They illustrate sequences of events or procedures. They help your audience understand and remember your message. In addition, chances are that for at least one of the assignments in your communication class you will be required to use a presentation aid. Because presentation aids are valuable supplements to your speeches and because students of communication are so often required to use them, let's discuss first the types of available presentation aids, including computer-generated ones. Then we will discuss guidelines for preparing presentation aids and provide some general suggestions for using them effectively.

## Types of Presentation Aids

If you are required to use a presentation aid for an assignment or think that a presentation aid might enhance your message, you have a number of options from which to select. You might decide to use an object or a model; a person; two-dimensional presentation aids such as drawings, photographs, maps, charts, or graphs; or audiovisual aids.

**Objects**   The first type of presentation aid you ever used—perhaps as long ago as preschool "show and tell"—was probably an object. You took to school your favorite teddy bear or the new remote-control car you got for your birthday. Remember how the kids crowded around to see what you had brought? Objects add interest to a talk because they are real. Whether the members of your audience are in preschool or college, they like tangible, real things. If you use an object as a presentation aid, consider these guidelines:

- Make certain that the object can be handled easily. If it is too large, it may be unwieldy; if it is too small, your audience won't be able to see it.
- Don't use dangerous or illegal objects as presentation aids. They may make your audience members uneasy or actually put them at risk.

**Models**   If it is not possible to bring an object to class, you may be able to substitute a model. You cannot bring a 1956 Ford Thunderbird into a classroom, but you may be able to construct and bring a model. You could probably not acquire a dog's heart to bring to class, but you might be able to find a model to use for your explanation of how heartworms damage that vital organ. If you use a model as a presentation aid, be sure that the model is large enough to be seen by all members of your audience.

**People**   You might not think of people as potential presentation aids, but they can be. George W. Bush used ordinary people as visual aids for some of his most important presidential speeches, "asking them to stand and then telling stories of their sacrifices or heroism . . . a way of coming down from the stage, as it were, and mingling with the crowd."[29] In other instances, people can model costumes, play a sport with you, or demonstrate a dance. If you are going to ask someone to assist you by acting as a presentation aid for a speech, consider the following guidelines:

- Rehearse with the person who will be helping you.
- Don't have the person stand beside you doing nothing. Wait until you need your presentation aid to have your assistant come to the front.
- Don't let your presentation aid steal the show. Make his or her role specific and fairly brief. As the speaker, you should remain the "person of the hour."

**Drawings**   You can use simple drawings to help illustrate or explain ideas that you are talking about. For example, you could sketch the tunnels of a fire ant mound to show your audience why it is so difficult to eradicate an entire ant colony. You could sketch the plants and animals crucial to the life cycle of the Florida Everglades. If you use a drawing as a visual aid, consider these suggestions:

- Keep your drawings large and simple. Line drawings are often more effective than more detailed ones.
- One way to show the audience your drawing is to scan it and then put it into a PowerPoint slide.
- Your drawing does not have to be original artwork. You could ask a friend to help you prepare a drawing, or you could use computer software to generate a simple image. Just be sure to credit your source if you use someone else's sketch.

**Photographs**   If you are giving a speech on urban forestry, you might want to show your audience good color pictures of trees appropriate for urban sites in your area. In this case, photographs would show color and detail that would be nearly impossible to achieve with drawings.

The biggest challenge to using photographs as presentation aids is size; most printed photos are simply too small to be seen clearly from a distance. If you want to use photographs, store them on a flash drive. Then, when you want the photos, you can bring them up on a computer screen and use a video projection system to enlarge them for your audience.

**Maps**   Like photographs, most maps are too small to be useful as presentation aids; to be effective, they must be enlarged in some way. Consider these suggestions for using maps effectively in a presentation:

- Enlarge your map by transferring it to a PowerPoint slide.
- Highlight on your map the areas or routes you are going to talk about in your presentation.

**Charts**   Charts can summarize and organize a great deal of information in a small space. Consider using a chart anytime you need to present information that could be organized under several headings or in several columns. The chart in Figure 13.1 displays the numbers and percentages of males age 18 to 24 living at home in the United States over a thirty-year period.[30] You can prepare charts quite easily by using the Table feature in your word-processing program. Keep in mind these guidelines:

- Be certain that your chart is big enough to be seen easily.
- Keep your chart simple. Do not try to put too much information on one chart. Eliminate any unnecessary words.

**Graphs**   Graphs are effective ways to present statistical relationships to your audience and help make data more concrete. You are probably already familiar with the three main types of graphs:

| Males Age 18–24 Living at Home in the U.S.: 1985–2005 | | |
|---|---|---|
| Year | Number | Percent of Total 18–24-Year-Old Population |
| 1985 | 8,172,000 | 60% |
| 1995 | 7,328,000 | 58% |
| 2005 | 7,448,000 | 53% |

**Figure 13.1 Chart**

**Males Age 18–24 Living at Home in the U.S.: 1985–2005**

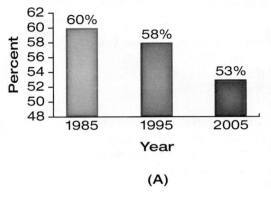

(A)

**Percent of Males Age 18–24 Living at Home in the U.S.: 2005**

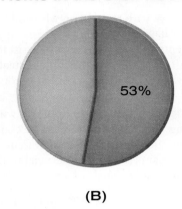

(B)

**Males Age 18–24 Living at Home in the U.S.: 1985–2005**

(C)

## Figure 13.2
## Three Types of Graphs: (A) Bar Graph, (B) Pie Graph, and (C) Line Graph

**Bar graph.**   A **bar graph** consists of bars of various lengths that represent percentages or numbers. It is useful for making comparisons.

**Pie graph.**   A round **pie graph** shows how data are divided proportionately.

**Line graph.**   A **line graph** can show both trends over a period of time and relationships among variables.

Figure 13.2 illustrates all three types of graphs, displaying the percentages from the chart in Figure 13.1. All three graphs were generated by Microsoft Excel.

The following guidelines will help you use graphs more effectively in your presentations:

- Keep your graphs simple and uncluttered.
- Remember that many computer programs will generate graphs from statistics. You often don't need to find graphs already prepared or draw your own.

**Audio and Video**   If you want to use audio presentation aids—say, music or excerpts from speeches or interviews—you might want to play a CD or MP3 file. Both are readily available, and their sound can be amplified. Similarly, modern video technolo-

**bar graph**
A graph consisting of bars of various lengths that represent numbers or percentages.

**pie graph**
A circular graph that shows how a set of data is divided proportionately.

**line graph**
A graph that shows trends over a period of time and relationships among variables.

# Communication&ETHICS

## Profanity in an Audio Presentation Aid

Matt wants to talk to his college classmates about the use of profanity in rap music. He plans to play sound clips of several profane lyrics from current hits to illustrate his point. Should Matt play these songs, even though doing so might offend several members of his audience?

gies allow you to show scenes from a movie, an excerpt from a training film, or a brief original video. Recordings stored on DVDs, computer devices, or streamed from the Internet generally offer good picture and sound quality and permit freeze-frame viewing. Most audio and video devices also allow you to replay a scene several times if you want your audience to listen or watch for different specific elements.

If you plan to use an audio or video presentation aid, consider these suggestions:

- Be certain that the equipment you need will be available in the room in which you are going to speak. Have the equipment set up and ready to go.
- Be certain that the volume of any audio is amplified enough so that your audience can hear it without straining.
- If you have an audience of twenty-five to thirty people, you can use a twenty-five-inch screen for video. For larger audiences, you will need several television monitors or projection technology.
- Use only brief clips and excerpts. Audio and video should always supplement, rather than supplant, your speech.

**PowerPoint**   Not too many years ago, if you wanted to use a drawing or graph as a visual aid, you had to draw it by hand on a chalkboard, flip chart, or overhead transparency. If you wanted to use a photograph or map, you had to have it professionally enlarged. Although speakers still occasionally use overheads, chalkboards, flip charts, and posters, most speakers today use PowerPoint slides.

With PowerPoint, you can develop a list of your main points for audience members to refer to as you speak, as illustrated in Figure 13.3 on page 348. You can present graphs and charts. You can use clip art, or you can scan or electronically cut and paste photographs, maps, or drawings. You can even incorporate video and audio clips. Although PowerPoint helps you adapt your message to audiences who increasingly expect sophisticated technical support, don't let your PowerPoint slides become your presentation. Use them to supplement it. In addition, keep the following tips in mind:[31]

- Don't use too many slides.
- Make certain that the slides you do use contain significant information in a simple, uncluttered style.
- Don't overuse bulleted text. Some experts suggest no more than seven lines of text on any single slide.
- Make informed decisions about fonts, color, and layout. A light background with darker-colored words in a simple 28-point-or-larger font usually works well.
- Finally, practice with your PowerPoint slides so that you can time them to coincide with your oral presentation.

# Guidelines for Preparing Presentation Aids

In addition to the specific guidelines for preparing and using various types of presentation aids, four general guidelines can help you prepare all types of presentation aids more effectively.

**Figure 13.3**
**PowerPoint Slide**

Source: Photo of Paul Laurence Dunbar from the Ohio Historical Society, Dunbar House web page, 2011, <http://ohsweb.ohiohistory.org>.

# Paul Laurence Dunbar
## 1872–1906

- Known as the "poet laureate of his people"
- Wrote popular poetry in African–American dialect
- Wrote significant poetry in standard English: "We Wear the Mask"

# RECAP

## TYPES OF PRESENTATION AIDS

- Use *objects* that you can handle easily and that are safe and legal.
- Be sure that any *models* you use are large enough to be seen easily.
- Rehearse with *people* who will serve as presentation aids, and don't let them steal the show.
- Keep *drawings* simple and large.
- Be sure that *photographs* are large enough to be seen easily.
- Highlight on a *map* the geographic areas you will discuss.
- Limit the amount of information you put on any single **chart**.
- Keep **graphs** simple and uncluttered.
- Use only brief **audio and video** clips, make sure they can be easily seen or heard, and have equipment ready to go before you speak.

**Select the Right Presentation Aids** As is evident from the above discussion, you have a number of options for presentation aids. If you are trying to decide which to use, consider these suggestions:

1. Be constantly aware of your specific purpose. Be certain that your presentation aid contributes to it.
2. Adapt to your listeners. Let their interests, experiences, and knowledge guide your selection of presentation aids. For example, an audience of accountants would readily understand arbitrage charts that might be incomprehensible to a more general audience. If you will be speaking to a large audience, be certain that everyone will be able to see or hear your presentation aid.
3. Consider your own skill and experience. Use equipment with which you have had experience, or allow yourself ample time to practice.
4. Take into account the room in which you will speak. If it has large windows and no shades, for example, do not plan to use a visual presentation aid that will require a darkened room. If you plan to use PowerPoint slides, be sure that both hardware and software are available and in good working order.

**Make Your Presentation Aids Easy to See** You have probably experienced the frustration of squinting and straining to read a speaker's too-small presentation aid. If you are going to remember only one thing about using a presentation aid, remember to make it big!

**Keep Your Presentation Aids Simple**    Don't cram too much information on any single presentation aid. Limit text to key words or phrases. Leave plenty of white space.

**Use Presentation Aids Thoughtfully**    One speechwriter and presentation coach warns against this bleak but all-too-common scenario:

> The presenter says, "And now, I'd like to talk about quality." And lo and behold . . . the word *quality* flashes on a screen. Now, folks, does this slide offer any new information? Does it clarify a complex point? Does it strengthen the bond between presenter and audience? You know the answer: a resounding "no."[32]

Be sure that the aids you use help you communicate your message.

## Guidelines for Using Presentation Aids

Once you have prepared potentially effective presentation aids, you will want to use them effectively as well. In addition to the guidelines offered earlier in this chapter, the following suggestions will help you adapt various types of presentation aids to your audience more effectively.

**Rehearse with Your Presentation Aids**    The day of your speech should not be the first time that you deliver your presentation while holding up your model, advancing your PowerPoint slides, or cueing your MP3 player. Practice setting up and using your presentation aids until you feel at ease with them. Consider during rehearsal what you would do at various stages of the speech if you had to carry on without a particular presentation aid. Electricity fails, equipment fails to show up, and bulbs burn out. Have contingency plans.

**Maintain Eye Contact with Your Audience, Not with Your Presentation Aids**    You can glance at your presentation aids during your talk, but do not talk to them. Keep looking at your audience.

**Explain Your Presentation Aids**    Always talk about and explain your presentation aids. Do not assume that the audience will understand their relevance and how to interpret them.

**Time the Display of Your Presentation Aids to Coincide with Your Discussion of Them**    Don't put a presentation aid in front of your audience until you are ready to use it. Likewise, remove or cover your presentation aid after you are finished with it. Keeping presentation aids in front of an audience before or after you use them will only serve to distract from your message.

**Do Not Pass Objects, Pictures, or Other Small Items Among Audience Members**    Passing things around distracts audience members. Either people are focused on whatever they are looking at, or they are counting the number of people who will handle the object before it reaches them. If the item is too small for everyone to see it when you hold it up, it is not a good presentation aid.

**Use Handouts Effectively**    Handing out papers during your presentation can also distract your audience. If possible, wait to distribute handouts until after you have spoken. If your audience needs to refer to the material while you are speaking about it, go ahead and pass out the handouts; then, at various points in your presentation, tell audience members where in the handout they should focus.

**Use Small Children and Animals with Caution**    Small children and even the best-trained animals are unpredictable. In a strange environment, in front of an audience, they may not behave in their usual way. The risk of having a child or animal detract from your presentation may be too great to justify using either as a presentation aid.

Although this speaker has developed a compelling PowerPoint presentation aid, he is losing eye contact with his audience as he presents it. How can you learn to handle your presentation aids with confidence, while maintaining effective eye contact with your audience?

David Young-Wolff/PhotoEdit

# Some Final Tips for Rehearsing and Delivering Your Presentation

Throughout this chapter, we have described and offered suggestions for effective verbal and nonverbal delivery and use of presentation aids. In addition to those tips, the following suggestions will help you make the most of your rehearsal time and ultimately deliver your presentation successfully:

- Finish your preparation outline several days before you must deliver the presentation. Begin to rehearse from the preparation outline. Revise the presentation as necessary, and then outline your speaking notes. Continue to rehearse and modify your speaking notes as necessary.
- Practice, practice, practice. Rehearse aloud as often as possible. Only by rehearsing will you gain confidence in both the content of the presentation and your delivery.
- Use good delivery skills while rehearsing. Rehearse your presentation standing up. Pay attention to your gestures, posture, eye contact, facial expression, and vocal delivery, as well as the verbal message. Rehearse with your presentation aids.
- If possible, practice your presentation for someone. Researchers in one study found that students who practice their speeches before an audience score higher on evaluation instruments than do students who practice without an audience.[33]
- Use audio or video technology to record your presentation, but try not to be overly critical when you listen to or watch yourself, as many of us tend to be. Notice whether you use too many filler sounds or words, such as "uh," "er," "okay," "you know," and "like." Realize, however, that you're developing a delivery style unique to you, so don't try to change too much.
- Re-create the speaking situation in your final rehearsals. Try to rehearse in a room similar to the one in which you will deliver the presentation. Use the speaking notes you will use the day you deliver the presentation. Give the presentation without stopping. The more realistic the rehearsal, the more confidence you will gain.

# Communication&TECHNOLOGY

### The Um Counter

A $0.99 app compatible with iPhone, iPod Touch, and iPad is designed to help a speaker rehearse his or her presentation or, as the app maker points out, "to, like, help eliminate, y'know, those irritating non-words from your vocabulary." A similar app called Word Counter is available for other smartphones.

Marco Benassi, http://umlikeyknow.com

- Get plenty of rest the night before you speak. Being well rested is more valuable than squeezing in a frantic, last-minute rehearsal.
- Arrive early. If you don't know for certain the location of the room in which you'll make your presentation, give yourself plenty of time to find it. Rearrange any furniture or equipment, and set up and check your presentation aids.
- Review and apply the suggestions offered in Chapter 11 for becoming a more confident speaker. As the moment for delivering your presentation nears, remind yourself of the effort you have spent preparing it. Visualize yourself delivering the presentation effectively. Silently practice your opening lines. Think about your audience. Breathe deeply. Relax.
- If something unforeseen (a ringing cell phone, for example) briefly interrupts your presentation, remain composed as you pause briefly and then pick up where you left off. If the incident is amusing, you can laugh along with your audience. When the presidential seal fell off Obama's lectern and crashed to the stage during a speech, he quipped,

  That's all right, all of you know who I am.[34]

- After you have delivered your presentation, seek feedback from members of your audience. Use the information you gain to improve your next presentation.

When the presidential seal fell off the lectern during one of his talks, President Barack Obama briefly and humorously acknowledged the glitch, before smoothly resuming his presentation. How can you prepare to deliver your speech with similar confidence?
REUTERS/Jason Reed

# Criteria for Evaluating Presentations

What makes a presentation successful? Our purpose here is not to take you through the centuries of dialogue and debate about this issue, but rather to offer practical ways to evaluate your own presentation as well as those of others.

Your instructor will probably use a rubric or evaluation form that lists precise criteria. Underlying any list of what a successful speaker should do, however, are two fundamental goals: A successful presentation should be *effective*, and it should be *ethical*.

- **Effective**   To be effective, a presentation should be understandable to listeners and should achieve the speaker's intended purpose.[35]

# DEVELOPING YOUR PRESENTATION
## Step by Step

### Delivering Your Presentation

The long-awaited day of Tony's presentation has arrived at last. He got a full night's sleep last night and ate a light breakfast before setting out for class.

As he waits to speak, Tony visualizes himself delivering his speech calmly and confidently. When his name is called, he rises, walks to the front of the room, and establishes eye contact with his audience before he begins to speak.

During his speech, Tony focuses on adapting his message to his listeners. He looks at individual members of his audience, uses purposeful and well-timed gestures, and speaks loudly and clearly.

Even before he hears his classmates' applause, Tony knows that his presentation has gone well.

- **Ethical**   A good speaker is an ethical speaker—one who tells the truth, cites sources for nonoriginal words and ideas, and is sensitive and responsive to listeners. Even if a message can be understood clearly and achieves the speaker's purpose, if the speaker has used unethical means to achieve that purpose, the presentation is not successful.

More specific criteria for determining whether a presentation is effective and ethical, presented within the context of the model of audience-centered presentational speaking, are presented in the resources at the end of this chapter.

# STUDY GUIDE:
## Review, Apply, and Assess Your Knowledge and Skill

## Methods of Delivery                                        p. 332

As you consider how you will deliver your presentation, you will select from four methods of delivery: manuscript speaking, memorized speaking, impromptu speaking, and extemporaneous speaking. Extemporaneous speaking is the style taught today in most presentational speaking classes and preferred by most audiences.

**Terms to Know**

| | | | |
|---|---|---|---|
| Manuscript Speaking | p. 333 | Impromptu Speaking | p. 334 |
| Memorized Speaking | p. 333 | Extemporaneous Speaking | p. 334 |

## Effective Verbal Delivery                                  p. 335

Once you know what method of delivery you will use, you should think about and rehearse words, phrases, and sentences that will best communicate your intended message and give it a distinct and memorable style. The most effective language is concrete, unbiased, vivid, simple, and correct. You can also make your presentation memorable by using figurative language and language that creates drama and cadence.

**Terms to Know**

| | | | |
|---|---|---|---|
| Specific Word | p. 335 | Personification | p. 336 |
| Concrete Word | p. 335 | Drama | p. 337 |
| Unbiased Word | p. 335 | Omission | p. 337 |
| Vivid Word | p. 335 | Inversion | p. 337 |
| Thesaurus | p. 336 | Suspension | p. 337 |
| Simple Word | p. 336 | Cadence | p. 337 |
| Correct Word | p. 336 | Parallelism | p. 337 |
| Figurative Language | p. 336 | Antithesis | p. 337 |
| Metaphor | p. 336 | Repetition | p. 337 |
| Simile | p. 336 | Alliteration | p. 338 |

## Effective Nonverbal Delivery                               p. 338

Nonverbal variables are also critical to effective delivery. Physical delivery includes a speaker's gestures, movement, and posture. Eye contact is perhaps the most important delivery variable, determining to a large extent your credibility with your audience. Facial expression plays a key role in expressing thoughts, emotions, and attitudes. Vocal delivery includes such elements as volume, pitch, rate, and articulation. Finally, your personal appearance can also affect how your audience responds to you and your message.

**Terms to Know**

| | | | |
|---|---|---|---|
| Eye Contact | p. 338 | Gestures | p. 339 |
| Physical Delivery | p. 339 | Movement | p. 339 |

## Effective Presentation Aids

Presentation aids include objects or models, people, drawings, photographs, maps, charts, graphs, and audio or video presentations. Today, most presentation aids can be created and displayed by using PowerPoint slides. Guidelines for using any type of presentation aid include selecting the right one for the audience, occasion, and room, and making the presentation aid easy to see and simple. Be sure to rehearse with your presentation aid, maintain eye contact with your audience, explain your presentation aid, time your use of your presentation aid, refrain from passing things around or using handouts indiscriminately, remember that small children and animals are unpredictable presentation aids, and use technology thoughtfully.

### Terms to Know

## Some Final Tips for Rehearsing and Delivering Your Presentation

Final suggestions for rehearsing your presentation include allowing ample time, rehearsing aloud and standing as often as possible, practicing your presentation for someone, recording and listening to or watching your presentation, and re-creating in your final rehearsals the actual speaking situation. Final tips for delivering your presentation include getting plenty of rest the night before you speak, arriving early, and applying the suggestions offered in Chapter 11 for becoming a more confident speaker.

## Criteria for Evaluating Presentations

Underlying any list of what a successful speaker should do are two fundamental goals: A successful presentation should be effective, and it should be ethical.

## APPLYING Principles for a Lifetime

**Principle One:**
**Be aware of your communication with yourself and others.**

- If your subject is sensitive or your information classified, be cautious and noncommittal in any impromptu remarks you make.
- As you become increasingly comfortable rehearsing an extemporaneous presentation, you can decrease your reliance on your notes.
- Usage and articulation errors communicate a lack of preparation. If you are uncertain how to use or pronounce a word or phrase, look it up or ask someone.

- Use a microphone if you need one and one is available. Be sure to rehearse with it.
- Be aware of your speaking rate, and adjust it if necessary.
- Be certain that your presentation aids, especially those that use technology, contribute to your specific purpose.
- Pay attention to your nonverbal delivery when you rehearse your presentation.
- During rehearsal, record your presentation; objectively and critically observe your gestures, posture, eye contact, facial expression, and vocal delivery, as well as your verbal message; and make necessary adjustments.
- When you deliver your presentation, apply the suggestions offered in Chapter 11 for becoming a more confident speaker.

### Principle Two:
### Effectively use and interpret verbal messages.
- When exact wording is critical, you may want to deliver a manuscript or memorized presentation.
- Do not try to memorize an extemporaneous presentation word for word; vary the ways in which you express ideas and information.
- Phrase your ideas so that they will be clear, accurate, and memorable.
- Use words that are concrete, unbiased, vivid, simple, and correct.
- Make your presentation memorable with figurative images, drama, and cadence.

### Principle Three:
### Effectively use and interpret nonverbal messages.
- When you deliver a manuscript speech, try to look at an entire sentence at a time so that you can maintain eye contact as you deliver the sentence.
- Do not read a manuscript speech too rapidly; vary the rhythm, inflection, and pace of delivery so that the speech does not sound as though it is being read.
- Deliver a memorized speech at a moderate pace, and avoid patterns of vocal inflection that make the speech sound recited.
- Use gestures and movement to add interest and emphasis to both manuscript and memorized speeches.
- To heighten your credibility and increase listener learning, use eye contact to let your audience know that you are interested in and ready to talk to them.
- Use gestures to reinforce your verbal message.
- Move during your presentation to signal the beginning of a new idea or major point or to signal a transition between a serious idea and a humorous one.
- Speak loudly enough to be heard easily by all members of your audience.
- Vary the volume of your voice to emphasize ideas and sustain the audience's interest.
- Vary your speaking rate to add interest to your delivery and emphasize key ideas.
- Articulate your words clearly.

### Principle Four:
### Listen and respond thoughtfully to others.
- Use eye contact to help you determine how your audience members are responding to you.
- If possible, rehearse your presentation for someone and seek feedback about both your content and your delivery.

**Principle Five:**
## Appropriately adapt messages to others.

- Although audiences today generally expect speakers to use everyday language and a conversational delivery style, you will need to adapt your delivery to audiences of different sizes and from different cultures.
- Consider your audience and speaking context when you select a method of delivery.
- Consider your audience members' interests, expectations, and knowledge to ensure that your impromptu presentation is centered on them.
- As you deliver an extemporaneous presentation, adapt it to your audience.
- Avoid any language that might be offensive to a member of your audience.
- Adapt your gestures to your audience. Use bolder, more sweeping, and more dramatic gestures with large audiences. Tone down gestures if you are speaking to a culturally diverse audience who might prefer a more subdued style.
- Adapt your movement during a presentation to the cultural expectations of your audience. It is better to stay in one carefully chosen spot than to make your audience uncomfortable.
- Assume a posture that seems natural to you in light of the topic, audience, and formality of the occasion.
- Adapt the amount of eye contact you use to the expectations of your audience. North Americans prefer as much eye contact as possible; Asians generally prefer less.
- To communicate your interest in your listeners, keep your facial expression alert and friendly.
- Adapt the volume of your voice to your audience's needs.
- Adapt your appearance to meet your audience's expectations.
- Let your audience's interests, experiences, and knowledge guide your preparation and selection of presentation aids.

---

# ASSESSING
## Your Skill

### Evaluating a Presentation

The following questions, linked to the audience-centered model first presented in Chapter 11 and included in Figure 13.4 on the next page, can help you evaluate any presentation, whether your own or another speaker's.

---

# WEB RESOURCES
## for More Review, Application, and Assessment

- **MyCommunicationLab** Under the Resources tab on MyCommunicationLab, you will find a file of 100+ Classic & Contemporary Speeches. In this file are links to transcripts; audio files; and, for a number of the more recent speeches, video files. <www.mycommunicationlab.com> (Access code required.)

- **how*j*say: A Talking Pronunciation Dictionary** This site is one of a number of readily available talking dictionaries of English pronunciation. <www.howsjsay.com>

- **Six Power Principles for Speech Editing** Moving from macroconcerns to microconcerns, the editing strategies offered on this site can help you achieve more effective verbal delivery. <http://sixminutes.dlugan.com/speech-preparation-5-editing/>

- **Online Tutorial for Effective Use of PowerPoint** This site, from the Digital Media Library at Baruch College, offers an interactive online tutorial for preparing and delivering effective PowerPoint presentations. <www.baruch.cuny.edu/dml/engine.php?action=viewAsset&mediaIndex=432>

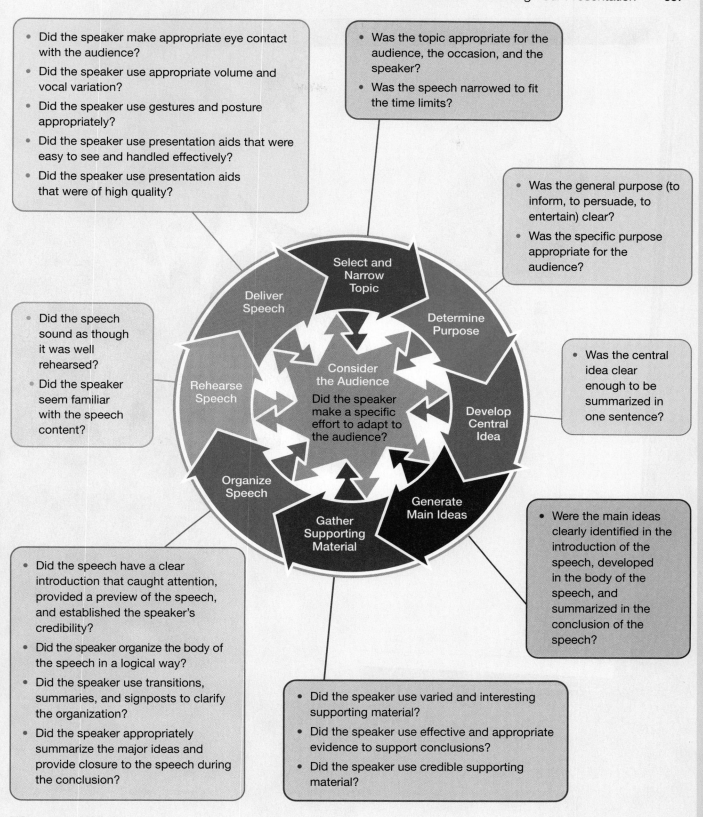

- Did the speaker make appropriate eye contact with the audience?
- Did the speaker use appropriate volume and vocal variation?
- Did the speaker use gestures and posture appropriately?
- Did the speaker use presentation aids that were easy to see and handled effectively?
- Did the speaker use presentation aids that were of high quality?

- Was the topic appropriate for the audience, the occasion, and the speaker?
- Was the speech narrowed to fit the time limits?

- Was the general purpose (to inform, to persuade, to entertain) clear?
- Was the specific purpose appropriate for the audience?

- Did the speech sound as though it was well rehearsed?
- Did the speaker seem familiar with the speech content?

- Was the central idea clear enough to be summarized in one sentence?

- Did the speech have a clear introduction that caught attention, provided a preview of the speech, and established the speaker's credibility?
- Did the speaker organize the body of the speech in a logical way?
- Did the speaker use transitions, summaries, and signposts to clarify the organization?
- Did the speaker appropriately summarize the major ideas and provide closure to the speech during the conclusion?

- Were the main ideas clearly identified in the introduction of the speech, developed in the body of the speech, and summarized in the conclusion of the speech?

- Did the speaker use varied and interesting supporting material?
- Did the speaker use effective and appropriate evidence to support conclusions?
- Did the speaker use credible supporting material?

Deliver Speech · Select and Narrow Topic · Determine Purpose · Develop Central Idea · Generate Main Ideas · Gather Supporting Material · Organize Speech · Rehearse Speech · Consider the Audience · Did the speaker make a specific effort to adapt to the audience?

## Figure 13.4
**Asking yourself these questions will help you evaluate any speech.**

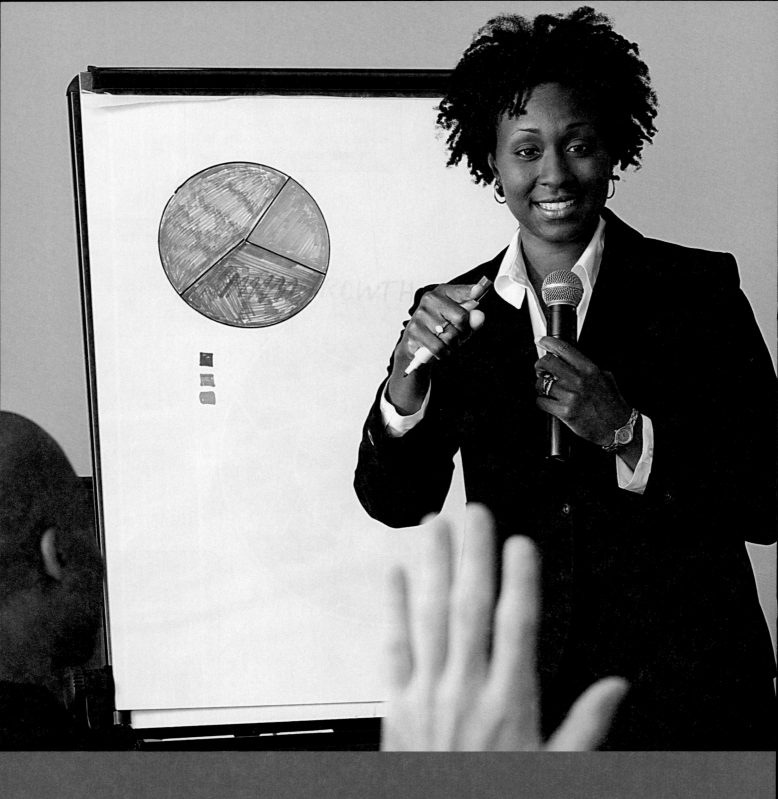

If you think education is expensive, try ignorance.

DEREK BOK

# Chapter OUTLINE

- Types of Informative Presentations
- Strategies for Organizing Your Informative Presentation
- Strategies for Making Your Informative Presentation Clear
- Strategies for Making Your Informative Presentation Interesting
- Strategies for Making Your Informative Presentation Memorable
- Study Guide: Review, Apply, and Assess Your Knowledge and Skill

# Chapter OBJECTIVES

After studying this chapter, you should be able to

1. Describe and illustrate five types of informative presentations.
2. Identify and use appropriate strategies for organizing informative presentations.
3. Identify and use strategies for making informative presentations clear.
4. Identify and use strategies for making informative presentations interesting.
5. Identify and use strategies for making informative presentations memorable.

Comstock Images/Getty Images/Thinkstock

# 14 | Speaking to Inform

© Mike Baldwin / Cornered

Michael Baldwin/CartoonStock

"I don't have any yet. We just opened."

One survey of both speech teachers and students who had taken a communication course found that the single most important skill taught in a presentational speaking class is how to give an informative presentation.[1] Given the importance in our lives of sending and receiving information, this finding is not surprising.

The purpose of a message to **inform** is to share information with others to enhance their knowledge or understanding of the material you present, be it information, concepts, or ideas. When you inform someone, you assume the role of a teacher by defining, illustrating, clarifying, or elaborating on a topic.

Informing or teaching others can be a challenge because of a simple fact: *Presenting information does not mean that communication has occurred.* Communication happens when listeners make sense of the information.

Another challenge of speaking to inform is to keep your informative message from becoming a persuasive one. It cannot be denied that informing and persuading are interrelated. Indeed, information alone may persuade someone to think or do something in a different way. If you intentionally try to change or reinforce your listeners' feelings, ideas, or behavior, however, your speech may become more persuasive than informative.

In this chapter, we will examine different types of informative tasks and identify specific strategies to help you organize your messages and make them clear, interesting, and memorable. Throughout our discussion, we will continue to apply the five Communication Principles for a Lifetime.

# Types of Informative Presentations

Identifying the type of informative presentation you will deliver can help you select and narrow your topic, organize your message, and select appropriate supporting material.

## Presentations About Objects

A speech about an object might be about anything tangible—anything you can see or touch. You may or may not show the actual object to your audience while you are talking about it. Objects that could form the basis of an interesting presentation include the following:

Items from your own collection (antiques, CDs, baseball cards)
The Eiffel Tower
Cellos
Digital cameras
The Roosevelt Memorial in Washington, D.C.
Toys

**inform**
To share information with others to enhance their knowledge or understanding of the information, concepts, and ideas you present.

# Presentations About Procedures

A presentation about a procedure discusses how something works (for example, how blood travels through the human circulatory system) or describes a process that produces a particular outcome (such as how grapes become wine). At the close of such a presentation, your audience should be able to describe, understand, or perform the procedure you have described. Here are some examples of procedures that could be topics of effective informative presentations:

> How to access television network programming on your iPad
> How state laws are made
> How to refinish furniture
> How to select a cell phone
> How to plant an organic garden
> How to select and purchase stocks

Notice that all these examples start with the word *how*. A presentation about a procedure usually focuses on how a process is completed or how something can be accomplished. Presentations about procedures are often presented in workshops or other training situations in which people learn skills.

One good way to teach people a skill is to follow the acronym T-E-A-C-H, which stands for Tell-Example-Apply-Coach-Help.[2]

- *Tell:* Describe what you want your listeners to know.
- *Example:* Show them an example of how to perform the skill.
- *Apply:* Give them an opportunity to apply the knowledge by performing the skill.
- *Coach:* Provide positive coaching to encourage them.
- *Help:* Help them learn by correcting mistakes.

Many presentations about procedures include visual aids. Whether you are teaching people how to install a WiFi router or how to give a presentation, showing them how to do something—*the Example* step of the T-E-A-C-H acronym—is almost always more effective than just telling them how to do it.

# Presentations About People

Most of us enjoy hearing about the lives of real people, whether famous or unknown, living or dead, who have some special quality. The key to making an effective biographical presentation is to be selective. Don't try to cover every detail of your subject's life. Relate the key elements in the person's career, personality, or other significant life features so that you build to a particular point, rather than just recite facts about the individual. One speaker gave a memorable presentation about his friend:

> To enter Charlie's home was to enter a world of order and efficiency. His den reflected his many years as an Air Force officer; it was orderly and neat. He always knew exactly where

# Communication & ETHICS

## Confidential or Potentially Dangerous Information

Mike, a computer engineering major, understands how a computer hacker recently accessed confidential personal information files on faculty members at his university. The procedure is actually simple enough that even people without sophisticated technical ability could understand and replicate it. Mike thinks that the procedure might be a good topic for an interesting informative presentation. Meanwhile, Mike's classmate Paul, a chemistry major, considers whether to give an informative presentation on how to create homemade explosives. If you are privy to confidential or potentially dangerous information, is it ethical to share it with others in an informative presentation?

If you've been either a spectator of, or participant in, bicycle racing at any level, you might have a good topic for an informative speech. How could your speech bring to life the crowded start of a race, like this one?

Digital Vision/Thinkstock

everything was. When he finished reading the morning paper, he folded it so neatly by his favorite chair that you would hardly know that it had been read. Yet for all of his efficiency, you knew the minute you walked into his home that he cared for others, that he cared for you. His jokes, his stories, his skill in listening to others drew people to him. He never met a stranger. He looked for opportunities to help others.

Notice how these details capture Charlie's personality and charm. Presentations about people should give your listeners the feeling that the person is a unique, authentic individual.

One specific type of presentation about a person is an introduction of another speaker and his or her topic. There are two cardinal rules for introducing another speaker: Be brief and be accurate. Remember that the audience has come to hear the main speaker, not you. In addition, be certain that you know how to pronounce the speaker's name and that you have accurate information about him or her.

## Presentations About Events

Have you experienced a natural disaster such as an earthquake, hurricane, or tornado? Have you witnessed the inauguration of a president, governor, or senator? A major event, whether one you have experienced firsthand or one you have researched, can form the basis of a fascinating informative presentation. Your goal as a speaker is to describe the event in concrete, tangible terms, bringing the experience to life for your audience.

You may have seen a recording of the CBS news bulletin on the assassination of John F. Kennedy. Legendary newscaster Walter Cronkite's ability to describe the event while reflecting the incredible emotion of the moment has made that broadcast a classic. Just as Cronkite was able to do, your purpose as an informative speaker describing an event is to make that event come alive for your listeners.

## Presentations About Ideas

By nature, presentations about ideas are more abstract than other types of presentations. The following principles, concepts, and theories might be topics of idea presentations:

Principles of time management
Freedom of speech
Evolution
Theories of communication
Buddhism
Animal rights

As you look at this list, you may think that those topics seem boring, but as the British writer G. K. Chesterton once said, "There is no such thing as an uninteresting topic; there are only uninterested people." The selection and use of illustrations, examples, and anecdotes to make an otherwise abstract idea seem both interesting and relevant to your listeners are keys to gaining and maintaining interest in your presentation about an idea.

# Strategies for Organizing Your Informative Presentation

As with any presentation, your audience will better understand your informative presentation if you organize your ideas logically. Regardless of the length or complexity of your message, you must follow a logical pattern to be understood. As summarized in Table 14.1 on page 365, the topic of your informative presentation may lend itself to a particular organizational pattern.

## Organizing Presentations About Objects

Presentations about objects may be organized topically; a topical pattern is structured around the logical divisions of the object you're describing. Here's a sample topical outline for a speech about an object—a nuclear power plant:

I. The reactor core
   A. The nuclear fuel in the core
   B. The placement of the fuel in the core
II. The reactor vessel
   A. The walls of a reactor vessel
   B. The function of the coolant in the reactor vessel
III. The reactor control rods
   A. The description of the control rods
   B. The function of the control rods

Presentations about objects may also be organized chronologically. A speaker might, for example, focus on the history and development of nuclear power plants, and such a presentation would probably be organized chronologically. Or, depending on the speaker's specific purpose, the presentation could be organized spatially, describing the physical layout of a nuclear power plant.

## Organizing Presentations About Procedures

Speeches about procedures are usually organized chronologically, according to the steps involved in the process. Anita chose a chronological organization for her explanation of how to develop a new training curriculum in teamwork skills:

I. Conduct a needs assessment of your department.
   A. Identify the method of assessing department needs.
   B. Implement the needs assessment.
II. Identify the topics that should be presented in the training.
   A. Specify topics that all members of the department need.
   B. Specify topics that only some members of the department need.
III. Write training objectives.
   A. Write objectives that are measurable.
   B. Write objectives that are specific.
   C. Write objectives that are attainable.
IV. Develop lesson plans for the training.
   A. Identify the training methods you will use.
   B. Identify the materials you will need.

Notice that Anita grouped the tasks into steps. Her audience members will remember the four general steps much more easily than they could have hoped to recall the curriculum development process had each individual task been listed as a separate step.

## Organizing Presentations About People

One way to talk about a person's life is in chronological order—birth, school, career, family, professional achievements, death. If, however, you are interested in presenting a specific theme, such as "Winston

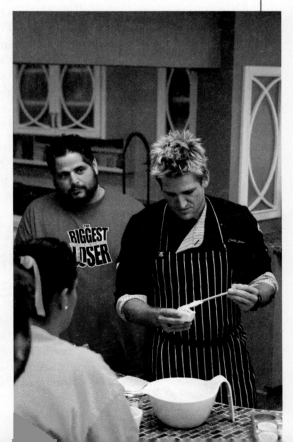

Television chefs such as Curtis Stone, shown here teaching contestants from *The Biggest Loser* how to make healthier meals, often arrange their presentations chronologically, to show the procedure of following a recipe from start to finish. What procedures could you describe to an audience?
NBC/NBCU Photo Bank via AP Images

Churchill, master of English prose," you may decide instead to organize Churchill's life experiences topically:

I. Journalist
II. Author
III. Orator

## Organizing Presentations About Events

Most speeches about an event follow a chronological arrangement, but a presentation about an event might also describe the complex issues or causes behind it and be organized topically. For example, if you were to talk about the Civil War, you might choose to focus on three causes of the war:

I. Political
II. Economic
III. Social

Although these main points are topical, specific subpoints may be organized chronologically. However you choose to organize your speech about an event, remember that your goal should be to ensure that your audience is enthralled by your vivid description.

## Organizing Presentations About Ideas

Most presentations about ideas are organized topically (by logical subdivisions of the central idea) or according to complexity (from simple ideas to more complex ones). The following example illustrates how Thompson used a topical organization for his informative presentation about philosophy:

I. Definition of philosophy
  A. Philosophy as viewed in ancient times
  B. Philosophy as viewed today
II. Three branches of the study of philosophy
  A. Metaphysics
    1. The study of ontology
    2. The study of cosmology
  B. Epistemology
    1. Knowledge derived from thinking
    2. Knowledge derived from experiencing
  C. Logic
    1. Types of reasoning
    2. Types of proof

Thompson decided that the most logical way to give an introductory talk about philosophy was first to define it and then to describe three branches of philosophy. Because of time limits, he chose to describe only three.

# Strategies for Making Your Informative Presentation Clear

Think of the best teacher you ever had. He or she probably possessed a special talent for making information clear, interesting, and memorable. Some speakers, like some teachers, are better than others at presenting information clearly.

A message is clear when the listener understands it in the way the speaker intended. Phrased in baseball terminology, a message is clear when what I throw is

**Table 14.1**
## Organizing Informative Presentations

| PRESENTATION TYPE | DESCRIPTION | TYPICAL ORGANIZATIONAL PATTERNS | SAMPLE TOPICS |
|---|---|---|---|
| Objects | Present information about tangible things | Topical<br>Spatial<br>Chronological | The Rosetta Stone<br>MP3 players<br>International space station<br>The U.S. Capitol |
| Procedures | Review how something works or describe a process | Chronological<br>Topical<br>Complexity | How to . . .<br>    Clone an animal<br>    Operate a nuclear power plant<br>    Use a computer<br>    Trap lobsters |
| People | Describe either a famous person or a personal acquaintance | Chronological<br>Topical | Rosa Parks<br>Nelson Mandela<br>Indira Gandhi<br>Your grandmother<br>Your favorite teacher |
| Events | Describe an actual event | Chronological<br>Topical<br>Complexity<br>Spatial | Chinese New Year<br>Inauguration Day<br>Cinco de Mayo |
| Ideas | Present abstract information or information about principles, concepts, theories, or issues | Topical<br>Complexity | Communism<br>Economic theory<br>Tao Te Ching |

what you catch. As described in the Communication & Diversity box on page 366, translating your speech into the audience's language is a basic step toward helping listeners understand.

How else do you make your messages clear to others?[3] Be aware (mindful) of what you intend to communicate. Say to yourself, "If I were hearing this message for the first time, would it make sense to me?" Three ways you can help your audience make sense of your message are to express your ideas simply, present information at a reasonable pace, and relate new information to what the audience already knows.

## Simplify Ideas

Your job as a presentational speaker is to communicate with your audience, not to see how many complex words and ideas you can cram into your speech. The simpler your ideas and phrases, the greater the chance that your audience will understand and remember them.

Let's say that you decide to talk about state-of-the-art tablet computers. That's a fine topic, but don't try to make your audience as sophisticated as you are about tablets in a five-minute presentation. Discuss only major features and name one or two leaders in the field. Don't load your presentation with complex details. Edit ruthlessly.

# Communication & DIVERSITY

## Using an Interpreter

It is quite possible that you may at some time be asked to speak to an audience of people who do not understand English or who cannot hear. In such a situation, you will need an interpreter to translate your message so that your audience can understand you. When using an interpreter, consider the following tips:

1. Edit your message to make sure that it fits within the time limit. A presentation that may take you thirty minutes to deliver without an interpreter will take at least an hour to present with an interpreter.
2. Even with an experienced interpreter, you'll need to slow your speaking rate a bit. Also, be sure to pause after every two or three sentences to give the interpreter time to translate your message.
3. Don't assume that your audience doesn't understand you just because

Vladimir Mucibabic/Shutterstock.com

you're using an interpreter. Don't say anything that you don't want your audience to hear.
4. If you have many facts, figures, or other detailed data, write this information down before you speak, and give it to your interpreter.
5. Humor often doesn't translate well. Be cautious of using a joke that was a real knee-slapper when you told it to your colleagues in your office; it may not have the same effect on people with a different cultural background and different language. Also, even a very skilled interpreter may have difficulty communicating the intended meaning of your humor.
6. Avoid using slang, jargon, or terms that will be unfamiliar to your listeners or the interpreter.
7. When possible, talk with your interpreter before you deliver your presentation. Tell him or her the general points you will present. If possible, give the interpreter an outline or a transcript if you are using a manuscript.

## Pace Your Information Flow

Arrange your supporting material so that you present an even flow of information rather than bunch up many significant details around one point. If you present too much new information too quickly, you may overwhelm your listeners, and their ability to understand may falter. Signposts can also help you pace your informative speech, and they offer your listeners both a break from listening to new information and help in processing that information.

## Relate New Information to Old

Most of us learn by building on what we already know. We try to make sense out of our world by associating the new with the old. When you meet someone for the first time, you may be reminded of someone you already know. It's like learning math: Your understanding of calculus is based on your knowledge of algebra.

When presenting new information to a group, help your listeners associate your new idea with something that is familiar to them. Use an analogy. Tell bewildered new college students how their new academic life will be similar to high school and how it will be different. Describe how raising cattle is similar to taking care of any animal; they all need food, water, and shelter. By building on the familiar, you help your listeners understand how your new concept or information relates to their experience.

# Strategies for Making Your Informative Presentation Interesting

He had them. Every audience member's eyes were riveted on the speaker. It was as quiet as midnight in a funeral home. Audience members were leaning forward ever so slightly, not wanting to miss a single idea or brilliant illustration. No one moved. They hung on every word. How can you create such interest when *you* speak? Here are several strategies to keep your audiences listening for more.

*Michael Baldwin/CartoonStock*

**The speech was almost interesting. People began to sit up and fake interest.**

## Relate to Your Listeners' Interests

Your listeners may be interested in your topic for a variety of reasons. It may affect them directly, it may add to their knowledge, it may satisfy their curiosity, or it may entertain them. These reasons are not mutually exclusive. For example, if you were giving a lecture on fifteenth-century Benin sculptures to a middle-class audience at a public library, your listeners would be interested because your talk would add to their knowledge, satisfy their curiosity, and entertain them.

Another way to make your message interesting is to think about why you yourself are interested in the topic. Once you are aware of your own interests and background, you can often find ways to establish common bonds with your audience.

## Use Attention-Getting Supporting Material

Consider the following tips for selecting supporting material to best capture and keep your listeners' attention:

- Before providing detailed supporting material, first give listeners the "big picture," conveying the gist of the object, process, person, event, or idea. Research suggests

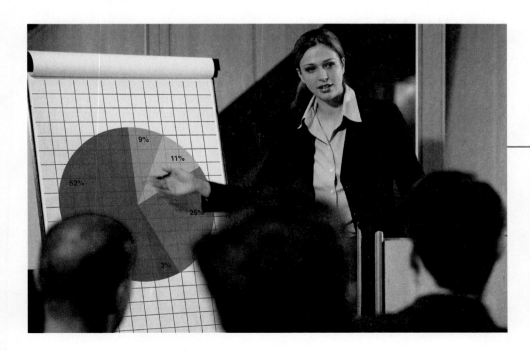

This speaker is presenting information that relates directly to audience members' interests. She is also using attention-getting statistics and colorful, eye-catching presentation aids. When you make informative presentations, you should also incorporate several techniques for keeping the audience focused on your message.

AISPIX/Shutterstock.com

that you can increase audience interest if you first provide a simple overview with an analogy, model, picture, or vivid description.[4]

- As you discuss the object, process, person, event, or idea, keep in mind the *who, what, when, where,* and *why* questions:

*Who* is involved?
*What* is the object, process, event, or idea that you want to describe?
*When* and *where* does or did the object exist, the process take place, the person live, the event occur, or the idea evolve?
*Why* does or did the object, process, event, or idea occur, or *why* is it important to the audience?

## Establish a Motive for Your Audience to Listen to You

Some situations have built-in motives for listeners. A teacher can say, "There will be a test covering my lecture tomorrow. It will count as 50 percent of your semester grade." Such statements may not make the teacher popular, but they will certainly motivate the class to listen. Lacking the power of a teacher to assign grades, you will need to find more creative ways to get your audience to listen to you.

- One way to arouse the interest of your listeners is to ask them a question, such as one of the following:

"How many of you are interested in saving tuition dollars this year?"
"Who would like to save money on their income taxes?"
"How many of you would like to learn an effective way of preparing your next speech?"

These questions could stimulate your listeners' interest and motivate them to give you their attention.

- A second way to get your listeners' interest is to begin your presentation with an anecdote, a startling statistic, or some other attention-getting strategy.
- Finally, you can tell your listeners explicitly how the information you present will be of value to them.

## Use Word Pictures

A **word picture** is a vivid description that helps your listeners form a mental image by appealing to one or more of their senses of sight, sound, smell, touch, and taste. Such powerful images can gain and hold an audience's attention.

Once you have a clear mental image of the person, place, or object you want to describe, use as many of your senses as possible to construct effective word pictures:

- **Sight.** Use lively language to describe the flaws, foibles, bumps, and beauties of the people, places, and things you want your audience to see.
- **Sound.** Use colorful, onomatopoetic words, such as *buzz, snort, hum, crackle,* or *hiss,* to imitate the sound you want your listeners to hear with their "mental ear." For example, instead of saying, "When I walked in the woods, I heard the sound of twigs breaking beneath my feet and wind moving the leaves above me in the trees," you might say, "As I walked in the woods, I heard the *crackle* of twigs underfoot and the *rustle* of leaves overhead."
- **Smell.** What fragrance or aroma do you want your audience to recall? For example, the first day of school may evoke the scents of new shoe leather, unused crayons, and freshly painted classrooms. The associated smells greatly enhance the overall word picture.

**word picture**
A vivid description that invites listeners to draw on their senses.

- **Touch.** Describe how an object feels when touched. Rather than saying that something is rough or smooth, use a simile, such as "the rock was rough as sandpaper" or "the pebble was as smooth as a baby's skin." These descriptions appeal to both visual and tactile senses.
- **Taste.** Thinking about your grandmother may evoke memories of her buttery homemade noodles; her sweet, fudgy nut brownies; or her light, flaky pie crust. Descriptions of these taste sensations would be welcomed by almost any audience, particularly your fellow college students who are subsisting mainly on dormitory food or their own cooking! More important, such description can help you paint an accurate, vivid image of your grandmother.

In addition to describing sensory images, you can enhance a word picture by describing the emotion a listener might feel if he or she were to experience the situation you relate. Use specific adjectives rather than general terms such as *happy* or *sad*. One speaker, talking about receiving her first speech assignment, described her reaction with these words:

> My heart stopped. Panic began to rise up inside. Me? . . . For the next five days I lived in dreaded anticipation of the forthcoming event.[5]

Notice how effectively such words and phrases as "my heart stopped," "panic," and "dreaded anticipation" invoke the speaker's terror at the prospect of giving a speech, much more so than had she simply said, "I was scared."

## Create Interesting Presentation Aids

Research suggests that presentation aids can help you get and maintain audience members' attention, as well as increase their retention of the information you present.[6] Each day, audiences are exposed to a barrage of messages conveyed through such highly visual electronic media as DVDs and streaming video. They have grown to depend on more than words alone to help them remember ideas and information. When you present summaries of data, a well-crafted line graph can quickly and memorably reinforce the words and numbers you cite.

## Use Humor

"Humor is the spice of speeches," says comedian Michael Klepper. "Too little and your message may be bland or lifeless, too much and it can burn the mouth."[7] The

# Communication&TECHNOLOGY

### Using an Electronic Thesaurus

Most word-processing programs include an electronic thesaurus. To use this tool in Microsoft Word, highlight a word in your text for which you would like to find a synonym and then click on "Thesaurus" under the "Tools" menu. You will get a pop-up box with several alternatives for your highlighted word. If one of these synonyms creates a better word picture, you might want to replace your original word with the new one.

A word of caution, however, about using any thesaurus, whether electronic or traditional: Be sure that you know the alternative word well enough to understand its connotations and grammatical usage. A thesaurus should remind you of a word with which you are already familiar, not launch you into an uncharted adventure in diction!

Judicious use of humor will help keep your audience's attention and can help them remember and understand your points. Before using humor, be sure to evaluate carefully whether the joke or story you want to use is appropriate for the occasion and the audience, as well as your ability to tell it well.

Digital Vision/Thinkstock

challenge is to use just the right kind of humor in the right amounts. Use humor wisely by considering the following ideas:[8]

- **Be certain your humor is appropriate to your listeners.** Because it is your audience that "gives attempts at humor their success or failure,"[9] you should avoid topics or language that might offend your listeners and create so much emotional noise for them that they cannot focus on your presentation.

- **Use humor to make a point.** Don't tell a joke just for the sake of getting a laugh. Make sure that your story or punch line relates to your message. Here's an example of how one presenter used a brief joke to make a point about the value of teamwork:

  I read recently about a veterinarian and a taxidermist who decided to share a shop in a small town in Ohio. The sign in the front window read: "Either way, you get your dog back."

  There is an important lesson there. We need to work together to solve our problems. People from marketing need to work with operations people. Designers need to work with engineers. Then, when we find a problem that one part of the organization can't solve, someone else may suggest a solution. It doesn't matter who comes up with the solution. The important thing is to "get your dog back."[10]

- **Make yourself the butt of the joke.** Audiences love it when you tell a funny or embarrassing story about yourself. In addition, if the joke's on you, you don't have to worry about whether you will offend someone else.

- **Use humorous quotations.** You don't have to be a comedy writer to be funny. Quote humorous lines of proverbs, poetry, or sayings from others. Remember, however, that what may be funny to you may not be funny to your audience. Try out your quotes and jokes on others before you present them from behind the lectern. And don't try to pass off a quotation from someone else as one of your own; always give credit for quotations you use.

- **Use cartoons.** A cartoon may be an effective way to make a point. Make sure that your cartoon is large enough to be seen by everyone in the audience. As with any humor, though, don't overdo your use of cartoons.

# Strategies for Making Your Informative Presentation Memorable

If you've made your message clear and interesting, you're well on your way to ensuring that your audience members will remember what you say. You want your ideas to stick in your listeners' minds as if they were made of Velcro, rather than slide off as if they were made of Teflon.

People remember what is important to them, so it is not surprising that one key to making your message memorable is to adapt it to your listeners. Presenting a well-organized message will also help your listeners remember what you say. In this section, we'll discuss several additional strategies for making your presentation memorable.

## Build in Redundancy

Seldom do writers need to repeat themselves. If readers don't quite understand a passage, they can go back and read it again. When you speak, however, it is useful to repeat key points. As we have noted before, audience members generally cannot stop you if a point in your presentation is unclear or if their minds wander; to make sure that the information you want to communicate will get across, you need to build in redundancy. Most speech teachers advise their students to structure their presentations as follows:

1. *Tell them what you're going to tell them.* In the introduction of your presentation, provide a broad overview of the purpose of your message. Identify the major points you will present.
2. *Tell them.* In the body of your presentation, develop each of the main points mentioned during your introduction.
3. *Tell them what you've told them.* Finally, in your conclusion, summarize the key ideas discussed in the body of your presentation.

## Use Adult Learning Principles

If your audience is adult listeners, you should make sure that you deliver your message in the way that adults learn best. **Adult learning principles** suggest that adults prefer the following:[11]

**adult learning principles**
Preferences of adult learners for what and how they learn.

- Relevant information that they can use immediately
- Active involvement in the learning process
- Connections between the new information and their life experiences

Most people with office jobs have in-baskets (or "in-piles") on their desks, where they place work that needs to be done. Similarly, adult learners tend to have "mental in-baskets"; as audience members, they have mental agendas of what they want or need to gain from listening to a presentation. Remember the characteristics of adult learners, as well as the important principle of adapting your message to others. If you tailor your information to address *their* agenda, you will make your message memorable and also have more success in informing your audience.

## Reinforce Key Ideas Verbally

You can reinforce an idea by using a phrase such as "This is the most important point" or "Be sure to remember this next point; it's the most compelling one." Suppose you have four suggestions for helping your listeners chair a meeting, and your last suggestion is the most important one. How can you make sure that your audience knows that? Just tell them: "Of all the suggestions I've given you, this last tip is the most important one. Here it is: Never fail to distribute an agenda before you chair any meeting." Be careful not to overuse this technique. If you claim that every other point is a key point, soon your audience will not believe you.

## Reinforce Key Ideas Nonverbally

You can also signal the importance of a point with nonverbal emphasis. Gestures can accent or emphasize key phrases, just as italics do in written communication.

A well-placed pause can emphasize and reinforce a point. Pausing just before or just after you make an important point will focus attention on your thought. Raising or lowering your voice can also reinforce a key idea.

Movement can help emphasize major ideas. Moving from behind the lectern to tell a personal anecdote can signal that something special and more intimate is about to be said. Remember that your movement and gestures should be meaningful and natural, rather than seeming arbitrary or forced. Your need to emphasize an idea can provide the motivation to make a meaningful movement.

The following presentation on commercial airline travel can be categorized as an informative speech about a process, organized by the problem–solution pattern described in Chapter 12. In the presentation, student speaker Austen Adair applies a number of strategies for making an informative presentation clear, interesting, and memorable:

- **Clear.** Austen make his presentation clear by providing signposts at strategic points to give his audience opportunities to process new information.
- **Interesting.** Austen took an important step in making his presentation interesting when he initially selected his topic. By speaking on a subject to which his listeners can relate (the challenges of post-9/11 commercial air travel), Austen captures and sustains their attention.
- **Memorable.** Finally, Austen makes his presentation memorable with his closing lines, which help his adult listeners connect their life experiences with the new information they have learned.

## RECAP

### STRATEGIES FOR MAKING AN INFORMATIVE PRESENTATION CLEAR, INTERESTING, AND MEMORABLE

**Make Your Presentation Clear**

Simplify ideas.

Pace the information flow.

Relate new information to old.

**Make Your Presentation Interesting**

Relate to your listeners' interests.

Use attention-catching supporting material.

Establish a motive for your audience to listen to you.

Use word pictures.

Create interesting presentation aids.

Use humor.

**Make Your Presentation Memorable**

Build in redundancy.

Use adult learning principles.

Reinforce key ideas verbally.

Reinforce key ideas nonverbally.

# Sample Informative Presentation

## Up in the Air

AUSTEN ADAIR[12]                    *Texas State University-San Marcos*

*Note: You can visit MyCommunicationLab to watch a video of Austen delivering this presentation.*

In his 1960s comedy *Sail Away*, playwright Noah Coward posed the question, "Why do the wrong people travel?" Think about it: When you go to the airport nowadays, what do you see? For example, you may see a horrific long line at security or perhaps even a woman screaming at a gate agent because a flight has been cancelled in the middle of a hurricane. Unfortunately, both of these instances are based on true events. Having worked for a major international airline, I have seen the good, the bad, and the ugly. But it doesn't always have to be that way. Air travel can be a very easy process, even for the common passenger. Today, we will discuss the current state of the aviation industry and identify two ways to easily navigate through the air travel process, which include extensive pre-planning and proper airport etiquette.

Before we can begin to travel, we must first have a good understanding of how a once-booming industry evolved into its current bankrupt state. According to Mark Gottdiener in his book, *Life in the Air: Surviving the New Culture of Air Travel*, there are over two million air travelers on over twenty thousand flights daily in the United States. That number is pretty significant, considering the fact that the industry is less than a hundred years old. In 1914, the first commercial flight took off from Tampa Bay, Florida and landed only a short distance away in St. Petersburg. At this time, the US government had some pretty heavy regulations on the aviation industry, as its primary purpose was to carry US mail. However, as air travel became more and more popular in the 1950s and 1960s, airlines wanted more freedoms and more rights to accommodate their passengers. So in 1978, they got their wish—and the airlines of the United States became deregulated. At this time we saw an exponential growth in the market as ticket prices dropped, and we saw the creation of the first frequent-flier program. Unfortunately, this success would not be everlasting. According to Rigas Doganis in his aptly named book *Airline Business*, he states that in early 2001 the airlines were already on a downward spiral in a falling market and had a problem of over-capacity. In essence, the airlines had too many seats and not enough butts to fill them. And of course after the terrorist attacks on September 11, 2001 everything changed. Today, the airline industry is experiencing or looking forward to a loss of over 2.8 billion dollars in 2010, according to the International Air Transport Association. While that number may seem grim, it can be used to the advantage of the common passenger.

Now that we have a little bit better understanding of the current state of the aviation industry, we can begin to pre-plan our trip, working under the basic assumption that the earlier our trip is planned, the easier and cheaper it will be.

The first thing you want to do is buy a ticket. There are a lot of websites now that offer very low ticket prices but with those cheap prices come very heavy restrictions. So you always want to read the fine print, as well as buy the ticket directly from the air carrier of your preference. Also, you want to be aware of baggage. You used to be able to check up to two bags free of charge in the belly of the aircraft. Unfortunately that is not now the case. Now fees for even the first checked bag range from fifteen to fifty dollars. So you want to make sure to try to consolidate all of your items into your carry-on, if possible. You are allowed two carry-ons on the aircraft. One can be a standard-sized roller, and the other can be a personal item such as a backpack or even a purse. With these carry-ons you want to be aware of

*Austen introduces his presentation with a quotation that is also a rhetorical question.*

*Austen establishes a motive for his audience to listen to him by mentioning his experience working in the airline industry.*

*Austen previews the three main ideas of his presentation.*

*Austen organizes his first main idea chronologically, tracing the history of the airline industry from 1914 to the present.*

*By using the phrase "to the advantage of the common passenger," Austen makes the statistics about airlines' financial losses seem more relevant to his listeners.*

*Austen's second main idea—that effectively planning air travel can make it go more smoothly—includes two tips: buy your ticket thoughtfully and be aware of baggage policies.*

*(continued)*

# Sample Informative Presentation *(continued)*

*Austen provides another signpost to summarize his second main idea and preview his third one.*

*Austen organizes his third main idea chronologically, according to the steps a passenger takes once he or she is in the airport.*

*Drawing on the principle that adult learners prefer to connect their life experiences with the new information they have learned, Austen adapts the familiar mantra delivered by flight attendants just before takeoff.*

the Transportation Security Administration's 3-1-1 rule. This rule states that each passenger may have liquids in 3.4-ounce-or-less size containers, carried in one, one-quart baggie. This can be very important when you are trying to get through the security process.

Now that we've had a chance to pre-plan our trip, we want to make sure we have enough poise and grace to get through the airport with as much ease as possible.

Angela Dahlberg, in her article "Air Rage Post-9/11," states that 53% of passengers are more suspicious of their fellow passengers. Certainly we are living in trying times with the events of September 11th fresh in our minds, so we want to make sure we are composed as we go through the airport. You want to make sure to be there at least and hour to an hour-and-a half before your scheduled departure. This way you ensure that you are there early enough, just in case anything may happen. The first thing you want to do is check in. Go to the ticket counter. Now they have self-service check-in machines that make the check-in process very quick and very easy and geared directly toward the passenger. Once you have your boarding pass in hand, you may go directly to the TSA security checkpoint. At this juncture, you want to make sure to take off your shoes, all jewelry and metal objects, belt, and cell phone, and place them all into the bin they provide for you. This is to ensure that the process is efficient, quick, and easy as possible. Once you are through here, you want to go to the gate. You want to be there at least 45 minutes prior to your originally scheduled departure time, just to make sure you are in the right place at the right time. Now all you have to do is board the aircraft, store your luggage, and you are ready to go.

In conclusion, the air travel process can be very easy once you have a prior knowledge of the commercial aviation industry, you pre-plan your trip, and you implement proper airport etiquette. So, ladies and gentleman, make sure all your seats are locked in the upright position, make sure all tray tables are stowed, be aware of all the emergency exits, sit back, relax, and get ready for takeoff—because literally, the sky's the limit.

# STUDY GUIDE:
## Review, Apply, and Assess Your Knowledge and Skill

### Types of Informative Presentations
p. 360

There are five basic types of informative presentations. Messages about objects discuss tangible things. Messages about procedures explain a process or describe how something works. Messages about people can be about either the famous or the little known. Messages about events describe major occurrences or personal experiences. Messages about ideas are often abstract and generally discuss principles, concepts, or theories.

**Terms to Know**

Inform    p. 360

### Strategies for Organizing Your Informative Presentation
p. 362

Strategies for organizing your informative presentation will vary according to the type of informative presentation and your specific purpose. A presentation about an object may be organized topically, chronologically, or spatially. A presentation about a procedure will usually be organized chronologically. Presentations about either people or events are also usually organized chronologically but can be organized topically. A presentation about an idea will probably be organized topically.

### Strategies for Making Your Informative Presentation Clear
p. 364

To make your message clear, use simple rather than complex ideas, pace the flow of your information, and relate new information to old ideas.

### Strategies for Making Your Informative Presentation Interesting
p. 367

To increase interest in your presentation, relate information to your listeners' interests, find and use attention-getting supporting material, establish a motive for your audience to listen to you, use vivid word pictures, create intriguing and clear presentation aids, and use humor appropriately.

**Terms to Know**

Word Picture    p. 368

### Strategies for Making Your Informative Presentation Memorable
p. 371

To make messages memorable, build in some redundancy (tell them what you're going to tell them, tell them, and then tell them what you've told them), apply principles of adult learning, and reinforce key ideas both verbally and nonverbally.

**Terms to Know**

Adult Learning Principles    p. 371

# APPLYING
## Principles for a Lifetime

**Principle One:**
### Be aware of your communication with yourself and others.

- To determine how best to organize your message, be conscious of the type of informative message you are developing (presentation about an object, a procedure, a person, an event, or an idea).
- Be mindful of strategies that will make your informative messages clear, interesting, and memorable.

**Principle Two:**
### Effectively use and interpret verbal messages.

- Use supporting material such as stories, examples, and illustrations to gain and maintain attention.
- Use word pictures to make images and stories interesting and memorable.
- Pace the flow of the information you present to enhance message clarity.
- Relate new information to old information to increase clarity and retention.
- To help make your message memorable, reinforce ideas verbally.
- Use simple rather than complex ideas to make your message clear.
- Build in message redundancy to enhance message retention.

**Principle Three:**
### Effectively use and interpret nonverbal messages.

- Use presentation aids to make messages clear, interesting, and memorable.
- Observe the nonverbal behavior of your audience to help you determine whether your message has been communicated clearly.
- Nonverbally reinforce ideas to make your message memorable.

**Principle Four:**
### Listen and respond thoughtfully to others.

- Before you deliver your presentation to an audience, talk and listen to audience members to help you customize your message for them.

**Principle Five:**
### Appropriately adapt messages to others.

- To enhance message clarity, adapt the structure and flow of your presentation to your listeners.
- To help gain and maintain interest and attention, adapt your examples and illustrations to your listeners.

# ASSESSING
## Your Skill

### Checklist for an Informative Presentation

The chapter-end materials for Chapter 13 include a list of presentation evaluation questions linked to the audience-centered model. You may also find it useful to refer to the following checklist specific to informative speaking.

| Element | Criteria | Additional Comments |
|---|---|---|
| **Audience** | _____ Adapted to needs, interests, and background of audience. | |
| **Topic** | _____ Appropriate to audience, occasion, and speaker. | |
| | _____ Focused on objects, procedures, people, events, or ideas. | |
| | _____ Narrowed to fit the time limits. | |
| **Purpose** | _____ Informative general purpose—to share information by teaching, defining, illustrating, describing, or explaining. | |
| | _____ Audience-centered specific purpose. | |
| | _____ General and specific purposes achieved. | |
| **Central Idea** | _____ Clear one-sentence declarative summary of the presentation. | |
| **Main Ideas** | _____ Related to central idea as natural divisions, reasons, or chronological steps. | |
| | _____ Previewed in introduction of presentation. | |
| | _____ Developed in body of presentation. | |
| | _____ Summarized in conclusion of presentation. | |
| **Supporting** | _____ Ideas simplified. | |
| **Material** | _____ Information flow appropriately paced. | |
| | _____ New information related to old. | |
| | _____ Use of attention-catching supporting material. | |
| | _____ Use of word pictures. | |
| | _____ Appropriate use of humor. | |
| **Organization** | _____ Introduction caught attention, established motive for audience to listen, stated central idea, previewed main ideas. | |
| | _____ Body organized in a logical way. | |
| | _____ Redundancy and reinforcement of key ideas evident. | |
| | _____ Conclusion restated central idea, summarized main ideas, and provided closure. | |
| **Delivery** | _____ Nonverbal reinforcement of key ideas. | |
| | _____ Eye contact with listeners. | |
| | _____ Appropriate volume and vocal inflection. | |
| | _____ Appropriate gestures, movement, and posture. | |
| | _____ Interesting and effectively prepared presentation aids, if any. | |

# WEB RESOURCES for More Review, Application, and Assessment

- **MyCommunicationLab** Visit Chapter 14 for an interactive step-by-step planning aid for your informative speech. Also remember that MyCommunicationLab provides pretest and posttest questions to help you review this, and every, chapter. <www.mycommunicationlab.com> (Access code required.)
- **Possible Topics for Your Informative Speech** You will find hundreds of possible topics for informative speeches on the site. <www.write-out-loud.com/informational-speech-topics.html>
- **Humorous Quotations** The collection of humorous verbal gaffes at Humorous Quotations includes news reports, classified ads, and signs. If you decide to use humor in your informative presentation, follow the suggestions in the text for using humor wisely. <www.rinkworks.com/said/>

Give me the right word and the right accent and I will move the world.

JOSEPH CONRAD

# Chapter OUTLINE

- Persuasion Defined
- Motivating Your Audience: The Psychology of Persuasion
- Selecting and Narrowing Your Persuasive Topic
- Identifying Your Persuasive Purpose
- Developing Your Central Idea as a Persuasive Proposition
- Supporting Your Persuasive Proposition with Credibility, Logic, and Emotion
- Organizing Your Persuasive Message
- Adapting Ideas to People and People to Ideas
- Study Guide: Review, Apply, and Assess Your Knowledge and Skill

# Chapter OBJECTIVES

After studying this chapter, you should be able to

1. Define persuasion and describe five ways listeners may be motivated.
2. Define and provide examples of inductive, deductive, and causal reasoning and reasoning by analogy.
3. Explain three ways to make emotional appeals in a persuasive presentation.
4. List and explain four ways to organize a persuasive message.
5. Provide specific suggestions for adapting to receptive audiences, neutral audiences, and unreceptive audiences.

Goodshoot/Thinkstock

# 15 | Speaking to Persuade

You don't have to be an attorney, an advertiser, or a politician to use the highly valued skill of persuasion. Whether you're asking your roommate to help you clean the kitchen, seeking an extension on your term paper, or trying to convince the school board not to raise taxes, you, too, need the power to persuade.

In 333 BCE, Aristotle was among the first to write a comprehensive guide to persuasion. His work, *Rhetoric*, was used by other Greek and Roman writers who sought to summarize principles and strategies of persuasion. The chapter you are reading draws on some of that classic advice and updates it with contemporary research. We first define persuasion, noting how it is both similar to and different from informing others, and then describe how persuasion works by explaining how to motivate an audience. We also offer suggestions for developing a persuasive speech; present ideas to help you organize your persuasive message; and provide methods to help you move an audience with your credibility, use of logic, and use of emotional appeals. Finally, although we hope that all the audiences you face are receptive to your persuasive speeches, we'll help you adapt your message not only to receptive audiences but also to those who are neutral or unreceptive.

# Persuasion Defined

**Persuasion** is the process of attempting to change or reinforce attitudes, beliefs, values, or behavior. When we persuade, we are urging someone to modify or maintain the way he or she thinks, feels, or behaves.

In Chapter 14, we described strategies for informing others—presenting new information so that others will understand and remember what is communicated. Like an informative presentation, a persuasive presentation needs to be well organized; have a clear beginning, middle, and end; use interesting supporting material; have smooth transitions; and be skillfully delivered. In a persuasive presentation, however, you will do more than teach; you will try to change or reinforce your listeners' feelings, ideas, or behavior.

Using force to achieve your goal is **coercion**, not persuasion. Weapons, threats, and other unethical strategies may momentarily achieve what you want, but it certainly is not appropriate or ethical to use such means. Efforts to persuade should be grounded in giving people options rather than forcing them to respond in a certain way.

Now that you have an understanding of what persuasion is and isn't, you probably wonder about how to develop a persuasive message. You start your preparation for a persuasive presentation in the same way that you begin preparing for any speech: by considering the needs, interests, and background of your audience. Ethically adapting to listeners is important in any communication situation, but it is especially important when persuading others.

The audience-centered model of public speaking, introduced in Chapter 11 and shown again in Figure 15.1, can help you design and deliver a persuasive presentation, just as it can an informative one. Because audience analysis is at the heart of

**persuasion**
The process of attempting to change or reinforce a listener's attitudes, beliefs, values, or behavior.

**coercion**
The use of force to get another person to think or behave as you wish; coercion is unethical because it takes away free choice.

# Communication & ETHICS

### Hidden Agendas

David is trying to get businesspeople to invest in the new Internet company he works for. He told a group of people at a Chamber of Commerce meeting that he wanted to inform them about some of the new and exciting ideas his company was developing. His real purpose, however, was to get people to invest in his company. Was it ethical of David not to tell his listeners that he really wanted them to become investors?

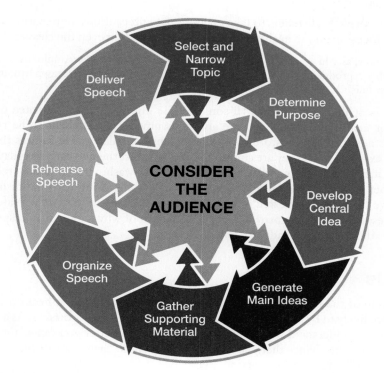

**Figure 15.1
Audience-
Centered
Model of the
Presentational
Speaking Process**

the speech-making process, before we talk about the nuts and bolts of developing a persuasive presentation, we'll discuss the psychology of persuasion—what motivates an audience to respond to your persuasive appeal. Understanding how an audience is likely to respond to your message can help you not only develop your presentation, but also be a smarter consumer of persuasive messages that come your way.

# Motivating Your Audience: The Psychology of Persuasion

How does persuasion work? What makes you dial the phone to have a piping hot pepperoni pizza delivered to your door after watching a television commercial for pizza? What motivates people to do things that they wouldn't do unless they were persuaded to do so? Let's look at five explanations of why people respond to efforts to persuade.

## Dissonance

When you are presented with information that is inconsistent with your current thinking or feelings, you experience a kind of mental discomfort called **cognitive dissonance**. For example, if you frequently drive when you are drowsy and then learn that driving when drowsy is a major contributor to traffic accidents, dissonance theory predicts that you will experience cognitive dissonance. The incompatibility between your behavior and your new knowledge will make you feel uncomfortable. And your discomfort may prompt you to change your thoughts, likes or dislikes, feelings, or behavior so that you can restore your comfort level or sense of balance—in this case, by not driving when drowsy.

Skilled persuasive speakers know that creating dissonance and then offering their listeners a way to restore balance is an effective persuasive strategy. For example, Sean

**cognitive dissonance**
The sense of mental disorganization or imbalance that may prompt a person to change when new information conflicts with previously organized thought patterns.

wants to persuade his listeners to take greater safety precautions in preparing food. He begins by focusing on the health threat posed by bacteria in even the cleanest kitchens:

> Right now, as you sit and listen to me speak about kitchen bacteria, millions of them are probably reproducing in your kitchen, simply waiting for the perfect opportunity to join you for lunch.[1]

Sean is deliberately creating dissonance. He knows that his audience members value their health and that they have always assumed their kitchens to be relatively clean. His next task is to restore his listeners' sense of balance. He assures them that solutions exist and that "they are simple and you can start them as early as today." If the audience members implement such simple actions as washing their hands frequently, using paper towels, and washing sponges and dishcloths along with the dishes, they can resolve their dissonance and once again feel secure about their kitchen safety. The need to resolve dissonance provides one explanation of why people may respond to a speaker's attempts to persuade.

## Needs

Need is one of the best motivators. A shopper who just broke the heel off a shoe is much more likely to buy new shoes than is someone who is just browsing. As a speaker, the better you understand what your listeners need, the better you can adapt to them and the greater the chance that you can persuade them to change an attitude, belief, or value or get them to take some action.

The classic theory that outlines our basic needs was developed by Abraham Maslow.[2] If you've taken a psychology course, you have undoubtedly encountered this theory, which has important applications for persuasion. Maslow suggested that a **hierarchy of needs**, illustrated in Figure 15.2, motivates the behavior of all people:

- *Physiological needs.* At the bottom of the hierarchy are basic physiological needs (such as needs for food, water, and air), which have to be satisfied before we attend to any other concern.
- *Safety needs.* Once our physiological needs are met, we think next about safety needs. We need to feel safe and be able to protect those we love.
- *Social needs.* Comfortable and secure, we attend next to social needs, including the need to be loved and the need to belong to a group.
- *Self-esteem needs.* The next level of need is for self-esteem, or to think well of ourselves.
- *Self-actualization needs.* Finally, if the first four levels of need have been satisfied, we may attend to the need for self-actualization, or achieving our highest potential.

**hierarchy of needs**
Abraham Maslow's classic theory that humans have five levels of needs and that lower-level needs must be met before people can be concerned about higher-level needs.

## Figure 15.2
## Maslow's Hierarchy of Needs

Source: Maslow, Abraham (1954). *Motivation and Personality.* New York: HarperCollins.

As a persuasive speaker, understanding and applying the hierarchy of needs helps you to adapt to your audience. One practical application is to do everything in your power to ensure that your audience's physiological needs are met. For example, if your listeners are sweating and fanning themselves, they are unlikely to be very interested in whether Bigfoot exists or whether the city should reopen River Park. If you can turn on the air conditioning or fans, you will stand a greater chance of persuading them than if you continue in that stifling atmosphere.

Another way you can apply the hierarchy of needs is by appealing to an audience's basic need for safety. For example, Mike knows that most of his audience members have young friends or family members who routinely ride school buses. As he begins to talk about the problem of safety hazards on school buses, he appeals to the audience's need to protect those they love.

## Fear Appeals

One of the oldest ways to convince people to change their minds or their behavior is by scaring them into compliance. Fear works. The appeal to fear takes the form of a verbal message—an "if–then" statement. *If* you don't do X, *then* awful things will happen to you. "If you don't get a flu shot, then you will probably catch the flu." "If you don't wear a seatbelt, then you are more likely to die in an automobile accident." "If you don't vote for me, then my opponent in this election will ruin the country." These statements are all examples of fear appeals. A variety of research studies support the following strategies for effectively using fear as a motivator:[3]

- *A strong threat to a family member or someone whom members of the audience care about will often be more successful than a fear appeal directed at the audience members themselves.* Here's an example: "If your parents don't have a smoke alarm in their house, they are ten times more likely to die in a house fire."
- *The more respected the speaker, the greater the likelihood that the appeal to fear will work.* When trying to motivate with fear, quoting a doctor if you're talking about a health issue or quoting an award-winning teacher if you're talking about an education issue will probably be more effective than just stating your own opinion.
- *Fear appeals are more successful if you convince your audience that the threat is real and will affect them unless they take action.* In trying to convince her audience to eat less fat and exercise more, Sophia said, "An overly fatty diet coupled with lack of exercise is the primary cause of heart disease in the United States. Eat less fat and get more exercise, or you may die prematurely."
- *Increasing the intensity of a fear appeal increases the likelihood that the fear appeal will be effective; this statement is especially true if the listener can take the action the persuader is suggesting.* Research findings suggest that the more fear and anxiety produced by a message, the more likely it is that the listener will respond. If evidence exists to support the claim, strong, credible fear appeals seem to work better than mild fear appeals.

The effectiveness of fear appeals is based on the theory of cognitive dissonance and Maslow's need theory. The fear aroused creates dissonance. Taking action reduces the fear and can meet a need, such as to live a long life, to be safe from harm, to have good friends, or to have a fulfilling career.

Of course, you have an ethical responsibility not to overstate your case or fabricate evidence when using a fear appeal. The persuader always has an ethical responsibility to be truthful when trying to arouse fear in the listener.

## Positive Appeals

A political candidate's TV ad declares: "Vote for me and you'll have lower taxes and higher wages, and your children will be better educated." Does this politician's promise sound familiar? It sounds like what most politicians offer—better days ahead if you'll vote for the person you see on your TV screen. Politicians, salespeople, and most other successful persuaders know that one way to change or reinforce your attitudes, beliefs, values, or behavior is to use a positive motivational appeal.

Positive motivational appeals are verbal messages promising that good things will happen if the speaker's advice is followed. The key to using positive motivational appeals is to know what your listeners value. Most Americans value a comfortable, prosperous life; stimulating, exciting activity; a sense of accomplishment; world, community, and personal peace; and overall happiness and contentment. In a persuasive presentation, you can motivate your listeners to respond to your message by describing what good, positive things will happen to them if they follow your advice.

## The Elaboration Likelihood Model

One of the newest frameworks for understanding persuasion is called the **elaboration likelihood model (ELM)**.[4] ELM theory, which focuses on how audience members interpret persuasive messages, includes a category of factors that researchers call *indirect* or *peripheral*. If you respond to the catchy music, creative logo, or attractive spokesperson in an advertisement, you have been indirectly persuaded. When hearing a presentation by one of your classmates, you may be influenced by the speaker's smart outfit or jazzy PowerPoint template. If you can't identify exactly why you were persuaded, you were probably persuaded by peripheral factors.

Advertisers have long been aware of the effectiveness of indirect persuasion. One researcher points out,

> In current advertising practice, it is rare to find magazine ads that lead off with a direct verbal claim such as "[Brand X] gets clothes clean." Instead of straightforward claims that a brand possesses some attribute or delivers some benefit, one encounters pictures of . . . measuring cups full of blue sky.[5]

Because ELM theory is a more audience-centered model than other persuasive theories, it can be especially valuable in helping you understand how you have been persuaded. It also suggests, however, that as a speaker, you should be aware of and adapt the indirect factors—such as your delivery, appearance, and general impression of preparedness—that can influence your listeners.

# Selecting and Narrowing Your Persuasive Topic

With a basic understanding of how persuasion works, we're ready to focus on the specifics of developing a persuasive talk. As with any presentation, after you've thought about your audience, the next step is to select and narrow your topic. The best persuasive topic is one about which you feel strongly. If your listeners sense that you are committed to and excited about your topic, chances are that they will be interested and involved as well.

The principle of appropriately adapting messages to others can help guide your choice of persuasive topic. Know the local, state, national, and international issues that interest and affect your listeners:

- Should the city build a new power plant?
- Should convicted child molesters be permitted to live in any neighborhood they like?
- Should the United States drop economic sanctions against Cuba?

**elaboration likelihood model (ELM)**
A contemporary theory that people can be persuaded both directly and indirectly.

These and other significant controversial issues make excellent persuasive speech topics. Avoid frivolous topics, such as "why you should make your own potholders," when so many important issues challenge the world and your listeners.

Pay particular attention to electronic and print media so that you remain informed about important issues of the day. Blogs and Internet chat rooms or news sites can provide ideas for persuasive presentations. Other potential sources of persuasive topics include talk radio and daily newspapers. After you have chosen a topic for your persuasive message, keeping up with the latest information from media can help you narrow your topic and help you find interesting and appropriate supporting material for your presentation.

# Identifying Your Persuasive Purpose

Attitudes, beliefs, and values, identified in Chapter 2 as components of a person's self-concept, are also integral to understanding how to persuade. When your general purpose is to persuade, your specific purpose will target your listeners' attitudes, beliefs, or values, or their behavior.

- **Attitude.** An **attitude** is a learned predisposition to respond favorably or unfavorably to something. In other words, attitudes represent likes and dislikes. Because many attitudes are formed quickly and often with little evidence, they are relatively susceptible to change if the person who holds them is exposed to additional evidence or gains more experience. For example, we may like a song we hear on the radio and then decide after we buy it that we don't really like it so well after all. We may think that we don't like spinach and then discover that a friend's Florentine dip is delicious. As a persuasive speaker, you would probably have a good chance to succeed if, for example, your specific purpose targeted audience attitudes about the following issues:

  At the end of my presentation, the audience will favor making downtown streets one-way to regulate traffic flow.

  At the end of my presentation, the audience will agree that the community needs a new elementary school.

- **Belief.** A **belief** is the way in which we structure our perception of reality: It is our sense of what is true or false. Perhaps you believe that the earth is round, that God exists, and that your local bank is a financially sound institution. We base our beliefs on our own past experiences and on those of other people. Beliefs are more difficult to alter than attitudes. If your audience were skeptical, you would need a great deal of evidence to succeed with these specific purpose statements:

  At the end of my presentation, the audience will testify that ghosts exist.

  At the end of my presentation, the audience will acknowledge that the increase in highway traffic deaths is related to the increase in the speed limit for large trucks.

- **Value.** A **value** is an enduring conception of right or wrong, or good or bad. If you value something, you classify it as good or desirable, and you classify its opposite or its absence as bad or wrong. If you do not value something, you are indifferent to it. Values determine your behavior and goals. For example, because you value honesty, you refuse to cheat on a test. Because you value freedom, you support asylum for political refugees. Values are stable and deeply ingrained. Although it is not impossible to change the values of audience members, it is much more difficult than trying to change attitudes or beliefs. Political and religious points of view are especially difficult to modify. If you were speaking to a conservative Republican audience, you would find it difficult to achieve these specific purposes:

According to the Elaboration Likelihood Model, we are often persuaded by indirect factors that are not central to the product or message. What indirect factors do the advertisers of this product hope will persuade shoppers to buy it?
Vladimir Wrangel/Shutterstock.com

**attitude**
A learned predisposition to respond favorably or unfavorably to something; a like or dislike.

**belief**
A sense of what is true or false.

**value**
An enduring conception of right or wrong, or good or bad.

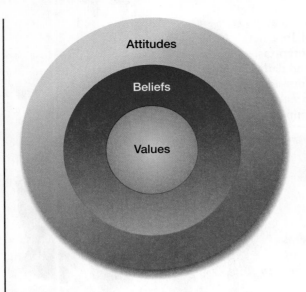

## Figure 15.3
### Comparing Attitudes, Beliefs, and Values

Attitudes—our likes and dislikes—are much more likely to change than are our beliefs or values. Our sense of what is right and wrong—our values—are least likely to change.

**proposition**
A claim with which you want your audience to agree.

**proposition of fact**
A claim that something is or is not the case or that something did or did not happen.

**proposition of value**
A claim that calls for the listener to judge the worth or importance of something.

**proposition of policy**
A claim advocating a specific action to change a regulation, procedure, or behavior.

**rhetoric**
The process of discovering the available means of persuasion.

At the end of my presentation, the audience will campaign for the Democratic ticket in the upcoming election.

At the end of my presentation, the audience will support the right of art museums to show whatever kinds of art the museum directors deem appropriate.

Figure 15.3 illustrates that attitudes lie fairly close to the surface of our convictions, with values the most deeply ingrained in the center of the model. Be aware of whether your specific purpose targets an attitude, a belief, a value, or a behavior, and be realistic in assessing what you will need to do in your presentation to effect change. Recall, too, from our definition of *persuasion* that you can try to *reinforce* attitudes, beliefs, values, and behavior that audience members already hold, or you can try to *change* their attitudes, beliefs, values, or behavior. Reinforcing what listeners already know or think is relatively easy; it's more of a challenge to change their minds.

# Developing Your Central Idea as a Persuasive Proposition

After clarifying their specific purpose, most persuasive speakers find it useful to cast their central idea as a **proposition** or statement with which they want their audience to agree. A well-worded proposition is a verbal message that can help you fine-tune your persuasive objective and develop strategies for convincing your audience that your proposition is true. There are three categories of propositions: propositions of fact, propositions of value, and propositions of policy. Let's examine each type in more detail.

## Propositions of Fact

**Propositions of fact** are claims that something is or is not the case or that something did or did not happen. A speaker who uses a proposition of fact as the central idea of a persuasive presentation focuses on changing or reinforcing the listeners' beliefs—what they think is true. Propositions of fact can become central ideas for persuasive speeches. Here are some examples:

- U.S. foreign embassies and consulates are vulnerable to terrorist attacks.
- Nuclear power plants are safe and efficient.
- People who were abused by their parents are more likely to abuse their own children than people who were not abused as children.

A speech based on one of these propositions would need to include credible evidence to support the accuracy of the conclusion.

## Propositions of Value

As the word *value* suggests, **propositions of value** call for the listener to judge the worth or importance of something. A simple example is "Tattoos are beautiful." Other value propositions compare two ideas, things, or actions and suggest that one is better than the other. Here are two examples:

- Small high schools are better than large high schools.
- Rock music is better than classical music.

## Propositions of Policy

The third type of proposition, the **proposition of policy**, advocates a specific action, such as changing a regulation, procedure, or behavior. Propositions of policy include the word *should*. Here are some examples:

- All first-year college students should have their own laptop computers.
- The honors program should have a full-time faculty coordinator.
- The city should build a new public library.

The speaker who develops a proposition of policy is often likely to go one step beyond influencing an audience's attitudes, beliefs, and values and will urge them to take action.

With your specific purpose and central idea in hand, you are ready to move to the next stages in the presentational speaking process. In most cases, you can draw your main ideas from several *reasons* the persuasive proposition is true. Then you will be ready to begin gathering supporting material.

This persuasive speaker is presenting to her audience a proposition of value, comparing two different options. How can you express the central idea of your persuasive speech as a proposition of fact, value, or policy?

Robert Kneschke/Shutterstock.com

# Supporting Your Persuasive Proposition with Credibility, Logic, and Emotion

Aristotle defined *rhetoric* as the process of "discovering the available means of persuasion."[6] What exactly are those "available means"? They are the various strategies you can use to support your persuasive proposition. Aristotle suggested three: (1) **ethos**, emphasizing the credibility or ethical character of a speaker; (2) **logos**, using logical arguments; and (3) **pathos**, using emotional appeals to move an audience.

## Ethos: Establishing Your Credibility

If you were going to buy a new computer, to whom would you turn for advice? Perhaps you would consult your brother, who is a computer geek, or your roommate, who is a computer science major. Alternatively, you could seek advice from *Consumer Reports*, the monthly publication of studies of various consumer products. You would turn to a source that you consider knowledgeable, competent, and trustworthy, or, in other words, credible.

**Understanding Credibility**   **Credibility** is an audience's perception of a speaker's competence, trustworthiness, and dynamism. Your listeners, not you, determine whether you have credibility.

For centuries, teachers and researchers have sought to understand the factors audiences consider in deciding whether a speaker is credible. Aristotle thought that a public speaker should be ethical, possess good

**ethos**
The credibility or ethical character of a speaker.

**logos**
Logical arguments.

**pathos**
Emotional appeals.

**credibility**
An audience's perception of a speaker's competence, trustworthiness, and dynamism.

# RECAP

## PERSUASIVE PROPOSITIONS

| Type of Proposition | Definition | Example |
|---|---|---|
| Proposition of Fact | A claim that something is or is not the case or that it did or did not happen | Asbestos exists in our elementary school. |
| Proposition of Value | A claim that calls for the listener to judge the worth or importance of something | Using calculators for elementary math is a good idea. |
| Proposition of Policy | A claim advocating a specific action to change a regulation, procedure, or behavior | Casino gambling should be legalized in all states. |

character, display common sense, and be concerned for the well-being of his audience. Quintilian, a Roman teacher of public speaking, advised that a speaker should be "a good man speaking well." These ancient speculations about the elements that enhance a speaker's credibility have been generally supported by modern research.

**Competence.**   One clear factor in credibility is **competence**. A speaker should be informed, skilled, or knowledgeable about the subject he or she is discussing. You will be more persuasive if you can convince your listeners that you know something about your topic. How can you do that?

You can use verbal messages effectively by talking about relevant personal experience with the topic. If you have taken and enjoyed a cruise, for instance, you can tell your audience about the highlights of your trip. You can also cite evidence to support your ideas. Even if you have not taken a cruise yourself, you can be prepared with information about what a good value a cruise is—how much it costs and what is included, versus how much the same trip would cost if one were to travel by air and stay and eat in hotels.

**Trustworthiness.**   A second factor in credibility is **trustworthiness**. While delivering a speech, you need to convey honesty and sincerity to your audience. You can't do so simply by saying, "Trust me." You have to earn trust by demonstrating that you are interested in and experienced with your topic. Again, speaking from personal experience makes you seem to be a more trustworthy speaker. Conversely, having something to gain by persuading your listeners may make you suspect in their eyes, which is why salespeople and politicians often lack credibility; if you do what they say, they will clearly benefit by earning sales commissions or being elected to public office.

**Dynamism.**   A third factor in credibility is a speaker's **dynamism**, or energy. Dynamism is often projected through delivery. If we apply the communication principle of using and understanding nonverbal messages effectively, a speaker who maintains eye contact, has enthusiastic vocal inflection, and moves and gestures purposefully is likely to be seen as dynamic. **Charisma** is a form of dynamism. A charismatic speaker possesses charm, talent, magnetism, and other qualities that make the person attractive and energetic. President Franklin Roosevelt and Pope John Paul II were considered charismatic speakers by many people.

**Enhancing Your Credibility**   You have opportunities before, during, and after your presentation to enhance your credibility.

**competence**
An aspect of a speaker's credibility that reflects whether the speaker is perceived as informed, skilled, and knowledgeable.

**trustworthiness**
An aspect of a speaker's credibility that reflects whether the speaker is perceived as believable and honest.

**dynamism**
An aspect of a speaker's credibility that reflects whether the speaker is perceived as energetic.

**charisma**
Talent, charm, and attractiveness.

**initial credibility**
The impression of a speaker's credibility that listeners have before the speaker begins to speak.

**derived credibility**
The impression of a speaker's credibility based on what the speaker says and does during the presentation.

**terminal credibility**
The final impression listeners have of a speaker's credibility, after the presentation has been concluded.

Audiences often perceive a dynamic, charismatic speaker, such as this one, as credible. What steps can you take to be more dynamic in your delivery, or to assure your audience of your competence or trustworthiness?
Stockbyte/Thinkstock

**Before you speak.**  **Initial credibility** is the impression your listeners have of you before you even begin to speak. They grant you initial credibility based on such factors as your appearance and your credentials. Two strategies for enhancing your initial credibility are dressing appropriately and having a brief summary of your qualifications and accomplishments ready for the person who will introduce you.

**As you speak.**  **Derived credibility** is the perception your listeners form as you deliver your presentation. If you appropriately adapt your message to your audience, you will enhance your derived credibility. Specific strategies include establishing common ground with your listeners, supporting your arguments with evidence, and presenting a well-organized message.

**After you speak.**  The last form of credibility, called **terminal credibility**, is the perception of your credibility that your listeners have when you finish your presentation. A thoughtfully prepared and well-delivered conclusion can enhance your terminal credibility, as can maintaining eye contact through and even after your closing sentence. Also apply the communication principle of listening and responding thoughtfully to others: Be prepared to answer questions after your presentation, regardless of whether a question-and-answer period is planned.

## Logos: Using Evidence and Reasoning

In addition to being considered a credible speaker, you will gain influence with your audience if you can effectively use logically structured arguments supported with evidence. As we noted earlier, Aristotle called logical arguments *logos*, which translated from Greek means "the word." Using words effectively to communicate your arguments to your listeners is vital to persuading thoughtful and informed listeners.[7] The goal is to provide logical **proof** for your arguments. Proof consists of both evidence and reasoning. **Evidence** is another word for the illustrations, definitions, statistics, and opinions that are your supporting material. **Reasoning** is the process of drawing conclusions from your evidence. There are three major ways to draw logical conclusions: inductively, deductively, and causally.

**Inductive Reasoning**  Reasoning that arrives at a general conclusion from specific instances or examples is known as **inductive reasoning**. You reason inductively when you claim that a conclusion is probably true because of specific evidence.

For example, if you were giving a speech attempting to convince your audience that Hondas are reliable cars, you might use inductive reasoning to make your point. You have a 2001 Honda Civic that has 140,000 miles on it and has required little repair other than routine maintenance. Your brother has a Honda Accord and has driven it twice as long as any other car he has ever owned. Your mother just returned from a 3,000-mile road trip in her Honda CR-V, which performed beautifully. Based on these specific examples and bolstered by statistics from many other Honda owners, you ask your audience to agree that your general conclusion is probable: Hondas are reliable cars.

**Reasoning by analogy** is a special type of inductive reasoning. An analogy demonstrates

**proof**
Evidence plus reasoning.

**evidence**
The material used to support a point or premise.

**reasoning**
The process of drawing a conclusion from evidence.

**inductive reasoning**
Using specific instances or examples to reach a probable general conclusion.

**reasoning by analogy**
A special kind of inductive reasoning that draws a comparison between two ideas, things, or situations that share some essential common feature.

## RECAP

### ENHANCING YOUR CREDIBILITY

**Enhancing Your Initial Credibility: Before You Speak**
- Dress appropriately.
- Have a brief summary of your qualifications and accomplishments ready for the person who will introduce you.

**Enhancing Your Derived Credibility: As You Speak**
- Establish common ground with your audience.
- Support your arguments with evidence.
- Present a well-organized message.

**Enhancing Your Terminal Credibility: After You Speak**
- Prepare your conclusion and deliver it well.
- Maintain eye contact through and even after your closing sentence.
- Be prepared to answer questions after your presentation.

how an unfamiliar idea, thing, or situation is similar to something the audience already understands. If you develop an original analogy, rather than quote one you find in a printed source, you are reasoning inductively. Here's an example of reasoning by analogy: Mandatory rear seatbelt laws that were enacted in Missouri saved lives; therefore, Kansas should also develop mandatory rear seatbelt laws. The key to arguing by analogy is to claim that the two things you are comparing (such as driving habits in Missouri and Kansas) are similar, so your argument is sound. Here's another example: England has a relaxed policy toward violence being shown on television and has experienced no major rise in violent crimes; therefore, the United States should relax its policy on showing violence on TV.

**Deductive Reasoning**    Reasoning from a general statement or principle to reach a specific conclusion is called **deductive reasoning**. Deductive reasoning can be structured as a **syllogism**, a three-part argument that consists of a major premise, a minor premise, and a conclusion. In a message in which you are attempting to convince your audience to vote for an upcoming school bond issue, your syllogism might look like the following:

> MAJOR PREMISE: Keeping schools in good repair extends the number of years that school buildings can be used.
>
> MINOR PREMISE: The proposed school bond issue provides money for school repairs.
>
> CONCLUSION: The proposed school bond issue will extend the number of years that we can use our current school buildings.

Contemporary logicians note that when you reason deductively, your conclusion is certain rather than probable. The certainty of the conclusion rests primarily on the validity of the major premise and secondarily on the truth of the minor premise. If you can prove that keeping schools in good repair extends the useful life of school buildings, and if it is true that the proposed bond issue provides money for school repairs, your conclusion will be certain.

**Causal Reasoning**    You use **causal reasoning** when you relate two or more events in such a way as to conclude that one or more of the events probably caused the others. For example, you might argue that public inoculation programs during the twentieth century eradicated smallpox.

**deductive reasoning**
Moving from a general statement or principle to reach a certain specific conclusion.

**syllogism**
A three-part argument, including a major premise, a minor premise, and a conclusion.

**causal reasoning**
Relating two or more events in such a way as to conclude that one or more of the events caused the others.

# Communication&**DIVERSITY**

## "Elementary Reasoning, My Dear Watson"

Although we frequently use the word *diversity* to refer to readily discernible differences in sex, race, culture, and age, *diversity* can also refer to differences in perspective or point of view. As the following narrative shows, people may draw different conclusions from the same evidence.

Sherlock Holmes and Dr. Watson went on a camping trip. After a good meal and a bottle of wine, they lay down for the night and went to sleep. Some hours later, Holmes awoke and nudged his faithful friend.

"Watson, look up at the sky and tell me what you see."

Watson replied, "I see millions and millions of stars."

"What does that tell you?" inquired Holmes.

Watson pondered for a minute. "Astronomically, it tells me that there are millions of galaxies and potentially billions of planets. Astrologically, I observe that Saturn is in Leo. Horologically, I deduce that the time is approximately a quarter past three. Theologically, I can see that God is all powerful and that we are small and insignificant. Meteorologically, I suspect that we will have a beautiful day tomorrow. What does it tell you?"

Holmes was silent for a minute and then spoke. "Watson, you idiot! Someone has stolen our tent!"

As we noted in Chapter 12 when we discussed cause and effect as an organizational strategy, there are two ways to structure a causal argument. One is by reasoning from cause to effect, or predicting a result from a known fact. For example, you know that it has rained more than an inch over the last few days, so you predict that the aquifer level will rise. The inch of rain is the cause, and the rising aquifer is the effect. The other way to structure a causal argument is by reasoning from a known effect to the cause. National Transportation Safety Board accident investigators reason from effect to cause when they reconstruct airplane wreckage to determine the cause of an air disaster.

The key to developing any causal argument is to be certain that a causal relationship actually exists between the two factors you are investigating. A few summers ago, a young science student took part in a project involving counting chimney swifts in a given area just before sunset. He counted the most chimney swifts on the Fourth of July. It would not have been valid, however, to argue that fireworks (or watermelon or hot dogs or anything else connected with the Fourth of July) caused an increase in the number of chimney swifts seen in the area. The Fourth of July holiday and the bird count were not related by cause and effect.

**Logical Fallacies**  Trying to establish a causal link where none exists is a type of **logical fallacy**. Unfortunately, not all people who try to persuade you will use sound evidence and reasoning. Some will try to develop arguments in ways that are irrelevant or inappropriate. To be a better-informed consumer, as well as a more ethical persuasive speaker, you should be aware of some of the following common logical fallacies.

**Causal fallacy.**  Trying to link the Fourth of July with the chimney swift count is an example of a **causal fallacy**, or, to use its Latin term, *post hoc, ergo propter hoc* ("after this; therefore, because of this"). Simply because one event follows another does not mean that the two are related.

**Bandwagon fallacy.**  "Jumping on the bandwagon" is a colloquial expression for thinking or doing something just because everybody else is. Someone who argues that "everybody thinks that, so you should too" is using the **bandwagon fallacy**. Speakers using the bandwagon fallacy often use the word *everybody*:

*Everybody* knows that taxes are too high.
*Everybody* agrees that the government should support a strong military.

**Either–or fallacy.**  "Either we support the bond issue, or we end up busing our students to another school district!" shouts Lupe in a moment of heated debate among the members of the school board. This **either–or fallacy** ignores that there may be

## RECAP

### INDUCTIVE, DEDUCTIVE, AND CAUSAL REASONING

| Type of Reasoning | Reasoning begins with . . . | Reasoning ends with . . . | Conclusion is . . . | Example |
|---|---|---|---|---|
| Inductive | specific examples | a general conclusion | probable or not probable | Dell, Gateway, and IBM computers are all reliable. Therefore, PCs are reliable. |
| Deductive | a general statement | a specific conclusion | certain or not certain | All professors at this college have advanced degrees. Tom Bryson is a professor at this college. Therefore, Tom Bryson has an advanced degree. |
| Causal | something known | a speculation about causes or effects of what is known | likely or not likely | The number of people with undergraduate degrees has risen steadily since 1960. This increasing number has caused a glut in the job market of people with degrees. |

**logical fallacy**
False reasoning that occurs when someone attempts to persuade without adequate evidence or with arguments that are irrelevant or inappropriate.

**causal fallacy**
Making a faulty cause and effect connection between two things or events.

**bandwagon fallacy**
Suggesting that because everyone believes something or does something, it must be valid, accurate, or effective.

GIVE ME LIBERTY OR GIVE ME DEATH!!

©Glenn and Gary McCoy/Distributed by Universal Uclick via CartoonStock.com

Glenn and Gary McCoy/CartoonStock

other solutions to the district's problem of dilapidated buildings (for example, purchasing portable classroom buildings or drawing new attendance zones within the district).

**Hasty generalization.** A person who draws a conclusion from too little evidence or nonexistent evidence is making a **hasty generalization**. For example, one person's failing a math test does not necessarily mean that the test was too difficult or unfair.

**Personal attack.** Using a **personal attack** as a substitute for a refutation of issues is also a logical fallacy. This approach is also known as an ad hominem argument, a Latin phrase that means "to the man." For example, "The HMO bill is a bad idea because it was proposed by that crazy senator" is a personal attack. Don't dismiss an idea solely because you have something against the person who presents it.

**Red herring.** Someone who argues against an issue by bringing up irrelevant facts or arguments is using a **red herring**. This fallacy takes its name from the old trick of distracting dogs who are following a scent by dragging a red herring across a trail. Speakers use a red herring when they want to distract an audience from certain issues. A congressional representative, indicted for misuse of federal funds, would be using a red herring if he called a press conference and spent most of the time talking about a colleague's sexual indiscretions.

**Appeal to misplaced authority.** When advertisers trot out baseball players to endorse breakfast cereal or movie stars to pitch credit cards, they are guilty of an **appeal to misplaced authority**. Although baseball players may know a great deal about the game of baseball, they are no more expert than most of us about breakfast cereal. Movie stars may be experts at acting, but they probably are not experts in the field of personal finance.

**Non sequitur.** If you argue that students should give blood because it is nearly time for final exams, you are guilty of using a **non sequitur** (Latin for "it does not follow") because your reason has nothing to do with your argument.

Persuasive speakers who provide logical proof (evidence and reasoning) for their arguments and who avoid logical fallacies heighten their chances for success with their audience. Good speakers also know that evidence and reasoning are not their only tools. Emotion is another powerful strategy for moving an audience to support a persuasive proposition.

## Pathos: Using Emotion

People often make decisions based not on logic but on emotion. Advertisers know all about it; just think of soft-drink commercials. There is little rational reason that people should spend any part of their food budget on soft drinks that are "empty calories." So soft-drink advertisers turn instead to emotional appeals, striving to connect feelings of pleasure with their product. Smiling people, upbeat music, and good times are usually part of the formula for selling soft drinks.

One way to make an emotional appeal is with emotion-arousing verbal messages. Words such as *mother*, *flag*, *freedom*, and *slavery* trigger emotional responses in listeners.

**either–or fallacy**
Oversimplifying an issue as offering only two choices.

**hasty generalization**
Reaching a conclusion without adequate supporting evidence.

**personal attack**
Attacking irrelevant personal characteristics of someone connected with an idea, rather than addressing the idea itself.

**red herring**
Irrelevant facts or information used to distract someone from the issue under discussion.

**appeal to misplaced authority**
Using someone without the appropriate credentials or expertise to endorse an idea or product.

**non sequitur**
Latin for "it does not follow"; presenting an idea or conclusion that does not logically follow the previous idea or conclusion.

Patriotic slogans, such as "Remember the Alamo" and "Give me liberty, or give me death," are examples of phrases that have successfully aroused emotions in their listeners.

Another way to appeal to emotions is to use concrete illustrations and descriptions. Although illustrations and descriptions are themselves types of evidence or supporting material, their effect is often emotional, as in the following example:

> Michelle Hutchinson carefully placed her three-year-old daughter into her child safety seat. She was certain that Dana was secure. Within minutes Michelle was involved in a minor accident, and the seat belt that was never designed to hold a child safety seat allowed the seat to lunge forward, crushing the three-year-old's skull on the dash. Dana died three days later.[8]

Effective use of nonverbal messages can also appeal to audience members' emotions. Visual aids—pictures, slides, or video—can provide emotion-arousing images. A photograph of a dirty, ragged child alone in a big city can evoke sadness and pain. A video clip of an airplane crash can arouse fear and horror. A picture of a smiling baby makes most of us smile, too. As a speaker, you can use visual aids to evoke both positive and negative emotions.

When you use emotional appeals, you have an obligation to be ethical and forthright. Making false claims, misusing evidence or images, or relying exclusively on emotion without any evidence or reasoning violates standards of ethical presentational speaking.

## RECAP

### TIPS FOR USING EMOTION TO PERSUADE

- Use emotion-arousing words.
- Use concrete illustrations and descriptions to create emotional images.
- Use visual aids to evoke both positive and negative emotions.
- Be ethical and forthright. Avoid making false claims, misusing evidence or images, or relying exclusively on emotion.

# Organizing Your Persuasive Message

As you know, the way that you organize a presentation can affect your listeners' response to your message. Some speakers gather stories, examples, facts, and statistics to achieve their persuasive goal and then develop an organizational structure for these materials. Other speakers organize the presentation first and then collect supporting material. In reality your presentation's structure usually emerges after you have done at least some initial research and thinking about both your message and your audience. An audience-centered speaker adapts the organization of the presentation based on the audience's needs, attitudes, beliefs, behaviors, and background. Most persuasive presentations are organized according to one of four strategies: problem–solution, cause-and-effect, refutation, or the motivated sequence. The first two strategies were also discussed in Chapter 12; the last is a special variation of the problem–solution format.

## Problem–Solution Organization

**Problem–solution organization** is the most basic organizational pattern for a persuasive presentation. The problem–solution strategy works best when a problem can be clearly documented and one or more solutions are proposed to deal with the evils of the problem.

When you use problem–solution organization, apply the principle of appropriately adapting messages to others. If you are speaking to an apathetic audience or one that is not aware that a problem exists, emphasize the problem portion of the message. If your audience is already aware of the problem, emphasize the solution or solutions. In either case, your challenge will be to provide ample evidence that your perception of the problem is accurate and reasonable. You'll also need to convince your listeners that the solution or solutions you advocate are the most appropriate ones to solve the problem.

**problem–solution organization**
Organization by discussing first a problem and then its various solutions.

Notice how Nicholas organizes his presentation, "The Death of Reading," in a problem–solution pattern:[9]

I. PROBLEM: Reading is a dying activity.
 A. Each year more than 500 courts hear arguments to ban books.
 B. Since 1990, more than 2,000 libraries across America have closed.
 C. Leisure reading has decreased more than 50% since 1975.
II. SOLUTIONS:
 A. Teach children that reading as an activity has worth and beauty.
 B. Teach children that books in and of themselves only express ideas and should not be banned.
 C. Support programs such as "One City, One Book" that encourage community involvement and literary discussion.
 D. Give books as gifts.
 E. Allow others to see you read.

The persuasive presentation at the end of this chapter is an example of a message organized by first stating the problem and then presenting some specific solutions.

## Cause-and-Effect Organization

**cause-and-effect organization**
Organization by discussing a situation and its causes, or a situation and its effects.

A speaker who employs **cause-and-effect organization** can either identify a situation and then discuss the resulting effects (cause–effect), or present a situation and then explore its causes (effect–cause).

Regardless of which variation you choose, you should apply the fundamental principle of being aware of your communication with yourself and others. Specifically, you must analyze and then convince your listeners of the critical causal link.

If two or more situations are causally related, a cause and effect strategy can work well for a persuasive presentation. Here is an example of a persuasive outline organized from cause to effect:[10]

I. CAUSE: The foster care system is in crisis.
 A. Since 1987, there has been a 90 percent increase in the number of children placed in foster care nationally.
 B. During that same time, there has been a 3 percent decrease in the number of licensed foster homes.

This speaker uses a graph to persuade the audiences that a new marketing plan has affected profits. How would relating cause and effect help you to persuade your audience?

Thinkstock Images/Getty Images

II. EFFECT: Children in foster care are at risk.
  A. Children in the foster care system are five times more likely to die as a result of abuse than children in the general population.
  B. 80 percent of federal prisoners spent time in the nation's foster care system as children.

An effect may have more than one cause. For example, standardized test scores may be low in your state both because of low per-pupil expenditures and because of a lack of parental involvement in the schools. To argue that only one of the two factors causes the low test scores would not be accurate.

It is also possible for two situations to coexist but not be causally related. Say that standardized test scores are indeed low in your state and that your state has a lottery. Both situations exist, but one does not cause the other.

## Refutation

A third way to organize your efforts to persuade an audience is especially useful when you are facing an unreceptive audience—one that does not agree with your point of view or your specific proposition. **Refutation** is an organizational strategy in which you identify likely objections to your proposition and then refute those objections with arguments and evidence. You will be most likely to organize your persuasive message by refutation if you know your listeners' chief objections to your proposition. In fact, if you do not acknowledge such objections, the audience will probably think about them during your presentation anyway. Credible facts and statistics will generally be more effective in supporting your points of refutation than will emotional arguments.

One speaker organized a persuasive presentation on organ donation by refuting four common misconceptions about the process:[11]

I. Anyone who decides to become a donor can reconsider that decision at any time.
II. Doctors will do everything to save the life of an organ donor that they would do for a non-donor.
III. No one who views the body of an organ donor will be able to tell that organs have been removed.
IV. Families of organ donors do not pay for any procedure related to the organ donation.

## The Motivated Sequence

The **motivated sequence**, devised by Alan Monroe, is a five-step organizational plan that integrates the problem–solution method with principles that have been confirmed by research and practical experience.[12] The five steps are attention, need, satisfaction, visualization, and action.

**Attention**  Your first task in applying the motivated sequence, as well as the first stage in appropriately adapting your message to others, is to get your listeners' attention. You already know attention-getting strategies for introductions: rhetorical questions, illustrations, startling facts or statistics, quotations, humorous stories, and references to historical or recent events. The attention step is, in essence, your application of one of these strategies.

Samin begins his persuasive presentation about landmines with this attention-catching illustration:

In Angola, little Tusnia became yet another one of the town's orphans. She was out in the field playing with her friends when she stumbled onto the ground and screamed. Her mother went running to see what happened, stepped in the wrong place, and was mutilated instantly. Parts from her body were found as far as 30 meters from the explosion site.[13]

**refutation**
Organization according to objections your listeners may have to your ideas and arguments.

**motivated sequence**
Alan H. Monroe's five-step plan for organizing a persuasive message: attention, need, satisfaction, visualization, and action.

**Need**    After getting your audience's attention, establish why your topic, problem, or issue should concern your listeners. Tell your audience about the problem. Adapt your message to them by convincing them that the problem affects them directly. Argue that there is a need for change. During the need step (which corresponds to the problem step in a problem–solution strategy), you should develop logical arguments backed by evidence. At this point, you create dissonance or use a credible fear appeal to motivate listeners to respond to your solution. Samin outlines his need step as follows:

> Citizens of countries with landmines face two major problems: risk of death or serious injury, and disruption of daily routines.

**Satisfaction**    After you explain and document a need or problem, identify your plan (or solution) and explain how it will satisfy the need. You need not go into painstaking detail. Present enough information for your listeners to gain a general understanding of how the problem may be solved. Samin recommends two solutions in his satisfaction step:

> One possible solution is to spread awareness. Luckily, this process has already been started by the United Nations Children Fund or UNICEF. . . . And a second solution is to teach successful de-mining technology to indigenous populations.

**visualization**
A word picture of the future.

**positive visualization**
A word picture of how much better things will be if a solution is implemented.

**negative visualization**
A word picture of how much worse things will be if a solution is not implemented; a fear appeal.

**Visualization**    Now you need to give your audience a sense of what it would be like if your solution were adopted or, conversely, not adopted. **Visualization**—a word picture of the future—applies the fundamental principle of using and understanding verbal messages effectively. An appropriate presentation aid can also help your audience visualize the implications of your persuasive message. With a **positive visualization** approach, you paint a rosy picture of how wonderful the future will be if your satisfaction step is implemented. With a **negative visualization** approach, you paint a bleak picture of how terrible the future will be if nothing changed; you use a fear appeal to motivate your listeners to do what you suggest to avoid further problems. You might also combine both approaches: The problem will be solved if your solution is adopted, but things will get increasingly worse if it is not. An ethical speaker makes sure that the positive or negative visualization message is accurate and not overstated. Samin offers positive visualization to communicate what can happen if his second solution is implemented:

> Perhaps in the future Tusnia can use this technology to start de-mining Angola so that the horrific atrocity that she faced will not happen to anyone else.

**Action**    The final step of the motivated sequence requires you to adapt your solution to your audience. Offer your listeners some specific action they can take to solve the problem you have discussed. Identify exactly what you want them to do. Give them simple, clear, and easy-to-follow steps. At the end of your presentation, provide a phone number to call for more information, an address to which they can write a letter of support, or a petition to sign. Samin suggests a specific action step his listeners can take to solve the problem of landmines:

> First, sign the People's Treaty to Support the Convention on Cluster Munitions, which is a de-mining effort. Second, Help the International Campaign to Ban Landmines by donating money to their cause.

You can adapt the motivated sequence to both your topic and the needs of your audience. For example, if you are speaking to a knowledgeable, receptive audience, you do not need to spend a great deal of time on the need step. Your listeners already know that the need is serious. They may, however, feel helpless to do anything about it. In this case, you would want to emphasize the satisfaction and action steps.

On the other hand, if you are speaking to neutral or apathetic audience members, you will need to spend time getting their attention and proving that a problem exists, is significant, and affects them personally. In this case, you will emphasize the attention, need, and visualization steps.

# Communication & TECHNOLOGY

## The Motivated Sequence in Television Advertising

Strategies for organizing persuasive messages are used not just by presentational speakers but also by advertisers. Many sixty-second TV commercials use the motivated sequence, at least in part, to persuade

The next time you are watching TV, try to pay particular attention to the commercials. How does a commercial get your attention? How does the advertiser establish a need

for the product? What product is being sold? (With some contemporary advertising, the answer to that question is more difficult to discern than you might expect!) What does the commercial suggest will happen if you buy and use the product? If you don't? What action does the advertiser advise you to take? For example, does the commercial suggest where you can go to get the product?

These organizational strategies are summarized in Table 15.1. Is there one best way to organize a persuasive message? The answer is no. The organizational strategy you select must depend on your audience, message, and desired objective. Just remember that your decision can have a major effect on your listeners' response to your message.

## Table 15.1 Organizational Patterns for Persuasive Presentations

| ORGANIZATIONAL PATTERN | DEFINITION | EXAMPLE |
|---|---|---|
| Problem–Solution Organization | Organization by discussing a problem and then its various solutions | I. Tooth decay threatens children's dental health.<br>II. Inexpensive, easy-to-apply sealants make teeth resistant to decay. |
| Cause-and-Effect Organization | Organization by discussing a situation and its causes, or a situation and its effects | I. Most HMOs refuse to pay for treatment they deem "experimental."<br>II. Patients die who might have been saved by "experimental" treatment. |
| Refutation | Organization according to objections your listeners may have to your ideas and arguments | I. Although you may think that college football players get too much financial aid, they work hard for it, spending twenty to thirty hours a week in training and on the field.<br>II. Although you may think that college football players don't spend much time on academics, they have two hours of enforced study every weeknight. |
| Motivated Sequence | Alan H. Monroe's five-step plan for organizing a persuasive message: attention, need, satisfaction, visualization, and action | I. Attention: "An apple a day keeps the doctor busy." What has happened to the old adage? Why has it changed?<br>II. Need: Pesticides are poisoning our fresh fruits and vegetables.<br>III. Satisfaction: Growers must seek environmentally friendly alternatives to pesticides.<br>IV. Visualization: Remember the apple poisoned by Snow White's wicked stepmother? You may be feeding such apples to your own children.<br>V. Action: Buy fruits and vegetables raised organically. |

# Adapting Ideas to People and People to Ideas

Rhetoric scholar Donald C. Bryant's definition of rhetoric emphasizes the principle of appropriately adapting a message to an audience, which he calls the process of adjusting ideas to people and people to ideas.[14] With this thought, we've now come full circle in the process of developing a persuasive message. As we have emphasized throughout our discussion of presentational speaking, analyzing your audience members and adapting to them is at the heart of the speech-making process; it's one of the fundamental Communication Principles for a Lifetime. In a persuasive presentation, adapting begins with identifying your specific purpose and understanding whether you are trying to change or reinforce attitudes, beliefs, values, or behavior. It continues when you select an organizational strategy.

For example, if your audience members are unreceptive toward your ideas, you might organize your speech by refutation and address their objections directly. Both research studies and experienced speakers can offer other useful suggestions to help you adapt to your audience. Let's look at some specific strategies for persuading receptive, neutral, and unreceptive audiences.

## The Receptive Audience

It is usually a pleasure to address an audience that already supports you and your message. In these situations, you can explore your ideas in depth and can be fairly certain of a successful appeal to action.

One suggestion to help you make the most of such a speaking opportunity is to identify with your audience. Emphasize your similarities and common interests. A good place to do so is often in the introduction of your message.

Another suggestion is to state your speaking objective overtly, telling your audience members exactly what you want them to do and asking them for an immediate show of support. If your listeners are already receptive, you don't have to worry that being overt will antagonize them. Rather, it will give you more time to rouse them to passionate commitment and action.

A third suggestion for persuading a receptive audience is to use emotional appeals. If your listeners already support your position, you can spend less time providing detailed evidence and instead focus on using strong emotional appeals to move them to action.

Most audiences will start out fairly neutral toward your persuasive goal. To persuade such an audience, you can establish common ground between their needs and your goals and appeal to their interests.

Digital Vision/Thinkstock

# The Neutral Audience

Many audiences will fall somewhere between being wildly enthusiastic and being hostile and will simply be neutral. The listeners' neutrality may take the form of indifference: They know about the topic or issue, but they don't see how it affects them, or they can't make up their minds about it. Alternatively, their neutrality may take the form of ignorance: They just don't know much about the topic. Regardless of whether they are indifferent or ignorant, your challenge is to get them interested in your message. Otherwise, they may escape by sleeping through your presentation or engaging in such self-distracting activities as texting on their cell phones or surfing the web on their laptops. The following suggestions can help you engage your neutral audience members:

- *Appeal to them early.* "Hook" a neutral audience with an especially engaging introduction or attention step. Brian provided such an introduction to his persuasive presentation about the number of Americans who live with chronic pain:

  "I can't shower because the water feels like molten lava. Every time someone turns on a ceiling fan, it feels like razor blades are cutting through my legs. I'm dying." Meet David Bogan, financial advisor from Deptford, New Jersey; Porsche, boat, and homeowner; and a victim of a debilitating car accident that has not only rendered him two years of chronic leg pain, but a fall from the pinnacle of success. Bogan has nothing now. Life to him, life with searing pain, is a worthless tease of agony and distress.[15]

- *Appeal to common ground.* Another strategy for persuading neutral audiences is to refer to universal beliefs or common concerns. For example, protecting the environment and having access to good health care might be common concerns.
- *Appeal to their interests.* Show how the topic affects not only them but also people they care about. For example, parents will be interested in issues and policies that affect their children.
- *Limit your appeals.* Be realistic about what you can accomplish. People who are neutral at the beginning of your presentation are unlikely to change their opinion in just a few minutes. Persuasion is unlikely to occur all at once or after only one presentation of arguments and issues.

# The Unreceptive Audience

As a speaker, one of your biggest challenges is to persuade audience members who are unreceptive toward you or your message. If they are unreceptive toward you personally, you need to find ways to enhance your credibility and persuade them to listen to you. If they are unreceptive toward your point of view, several strategies may help.

First, don't immediately announce your persuasive purpose. Immediately and explicitly telling your unreceptive listeners that you plan to change their minds can make them defensive. Instead, focus on areas of agreement. As you would with a neutral audience, refer to universal beliefs and concerns. Rather than saying, "I'm here this morning to convince you that we should raise city taxes," you might say, "I think we can agree that we have an important common goal: achieving the best quality of life possible here in our small community."

Second, if you think that your audience may be unreceptive, follow the principle of primacy and advance your strongest arguments first. If you save your best argument for last (the recency principle), your audience may already have stopped listening.

Third, acknowledge the opposing points of view that audience members may hold. Summarize the reasons they may oppose your point of view; then cite evidence and use arguments to refute the opposition and support your conclusion. In speaking to students seeking to hold down tuition costs, a dean might say, "I am aware that many of you struggle to pay for your education. You work nights, take out loans, and live frugally." Then the dean could go on to identify how the university could provide additional financial assistance to students.

Finally, when speaking to an unreceptive audience, be especially aware of and effectively use nonverbal messages. One study suggests that unreceptive audiences may more negatively evaluate speakers who do not gesture than they do those who use gestures.[16]

In the following persuasive presentation on breast cancer, Kailey Slone argues a proposition of policy. She supports her presentation by being a knowledgeable, well-prepared speaker; using evidence and reasoning; and making emotional appeals. She organizes her persuasive presentation according to a problem–solution pattern.

## **RE**CAP

### ADAPTING IDEAS TO PEOPLE AND PEOPLE TO IDEAS

| Persuading the Receptive Audience | Persuading the Neutral Audience | Persuading the Unreceptive Audience |
|---|---|---|
| • Identify with your audience. | • Gain and maintain your audience's attention. | • Don't tell listeners that you are going to try to convince them to support your position. |
| • Emphasize common interests. | • Refer to beliefs and concerns that are important to listeners. | • Present your strongest arguments first. |
| • Provide a clear objective; tell your listeners what you want them to do. | • Show how the topic affects people your listeners care about. | • Acknowledge opposing points of view. |
| • Appropriately use emotional appeals. | • Be realistic about what you can accomplish. | • Use appropriate gestures. |

# Sample Persuasive Presentation

## Real Men *AND* Women Wear Pink

**KAILEY SLONE**[17]              *Texas State University–San Marcos*

*Note: You can visit MyCommunicationLab to watch a video of Kailey delivering this presentation.*

*Kailey captures the attention of her listeners with a hypothetical illustration, indicated by the word "Imagine." She moves from this soft evidence to statistics that include both men and women, communicating to her entire audience that "This issue concerns you."*

Imagine yourself sitting in a cold, stale doctor's office, with sweaty palms and a racing heart. The doctor steps in, you see his face, and your heart sinks. You were just diagnosed with breast cancer. One out of eight women who live to be the age 85 will contract breast cancer. And statistics say that 1,910 new cases were expected to be found in men in the year 2009. These rising statistics show that breast cancer can and will hit close to home. My grandmother was recently diagnosed with and treated for breast cancer. Because I just went through treatment with her, I realize what a breast cancer patient goes through. Because breast cancer is a growing epidemic among men and women each year in the United States, and because a cure for breast cancer has yet to be found, I propose that you participate in the Susan G. Komen Race for the Cure to help contribute to breast cancer research. But before we talk about the solution, we must first understand breast cancer as a problem. The problem is that without a cure, breast cancer will continue to be on the rise in the United States.

According to the Susan G. Komen Foundation, since 1940, breast cancer cases in the United States have increased by 1% each year—which means that over the last seventy years, breast cancer cases have increased by 70%. That's shocking. In 2005, breast cancer cases were 122 in every 100,000 women and 1.2 per 100,000 men. Then, in a more recent study done by clinicians, titled "Cancer Statistics," 180,150 estimated new cases were added to the growing number. Now, college students, this is where breast cancer can affect people like you and me. In college, we are all faced with the opportunity to consume alcohol. (Stick with me here!) One analysis of a combination of fifty-three case studies found that every one alcoholic drink per day increases our chance as women 7%. Having two to three alcoholic drinks per day increases women's risk by 20%. Also, for women who have an immediate family member who has been diagnosed, treated, or affected by breast cancer, the chances for contracting breast cancer double in their lifetime.

*Kailey provides statistics to support her argument that the incidence of breast cancer in the United States is rising.*

*She adds a fear appeal to convince her listeners that the threat of breast cancer is real and could directly affect them.*

As you can see, breast cancer is affecting more and more people, year after year. Thus, it is necessary for us to become involved in the solution.

The solution that I propose is one that requires you and me to take action. It is one that requires us to *be* the change that we want to see in the future. I propose that you participate in the Susan G. Komen Race for the Cure. This solution will work because other foundation fundraisers have been proven to work. I say "proven to work" because research happens with funding, and a cure happens from research. For example, according to an article titled, "Relay for Life, Second Life," Relay for Life has raised 1.5 billion dollars for the American Cancer Society. Another foundation, titled Pink Hair for Hope, brought 375 hair salons together and raised one million dollars for breast cancer. In a study done in Michigan, a fundraiser for Crop Hunger and a walk with over 15,000 participants, sponsored by Church World Service, raised over $250,000 to help feed children in third-world countries.

*Kailey urges her audience to take direct, specific action.*

In conclusion, it should be obvious to us now that breast cancer is affecting more and more people every year in the United States. It should also be apparent that with these rising statistics, breast cancer will likely affect you and me in our future. Therefore, we must take action in making the dream of a cure become a reality. I am urging you to sign up for and participate in the Susan G. Komen Race for the Cure to continue cancer research. I was with my grandmother the day she got the news. I saw the fear in her eyes, and I saw the trembling in her hands. I don't wish this on anyone else. Thankfully, my grandmother today is a breast cancer survivor. As a survivor, she believes in Susan G. Komen's ability to contribute to a cure. And because she does, so should you. Register for a race—and remember that real men *and* women wear pink.

*As Kailey summarizes her main points, she makes a final fear appeal by telling her listeners that "breast cancer will likely affect you and me in our future." Reminding them of her experience with her grandmother, she adds, "I don't wish this on anyone else."*

# STUDY GUIDE:
# Review, Apply, and Assess Your Knowledge and Skill

## REVIEWING What You Know

### Persuasion Defined                                    p. 380

Persuasion is the process of attempting to change or reinforce attitudes, beliefs, values, or behaviors.

**Terms to Know**

| | |
|---|---|
| Persuasion    p. 380 | Coercion    p. 380 |

### Motivating Your Audience: The Psychology of Persuasion                                    p. 381

Several theories suggest how listeners may be motivated to respond to a persuasive message. Cognitive dissonance, a sense of mental disorganization or imbalance that arises when new information conflicts with previously organized thought patterns, may prompt a person to change attitudes, beliefs, values, or behavior. Maslow's classic hierarchy of needs attempts to explain why people may be motivated to respond to persuasive appeals to various levels of need. Both fear appeals and positive motivational appeals can prompt listeners to respond to a persuasive message. The elaboration likelihood model (ELM) explains how listeners may be motivated by such peripheral factors as the speaker's appearance.

**Terms to Know**

| | |
|---|---|
| Cognitive Dissonance    p. 381 | Elaboration Likelihood Model |
| Hierarchy of Needs    p. 382 | (ELM)    p. 384 |

### Selecting and Narrowing Your Persuasive Topic                                    p. 384

Preparing and presenting a persuasive message requires the same general approach as preparing any other kind of presentation. When you have a choice of persuasive topics, select a topic that interests you and your listeners.

### Identifying Your Persuasive Purpose                                    p. 385

Your specific persuasive purpose is to target your audience's attitudes, beliefs, values, or behavior. Attitudes are learned predispositions to respond favorably or unfavorably toward something. A belief is one's sense of what is true or false. Values are enduring conceptions of right or wrong or good or bad. Of the three, attitudes are most susceptible to change, and values are least likely to change.

**Terms to Know**

| | |
|---|---|
| Attitude    p. 385 | Value    p. 385 |
| Belief    p. 385 | |

## Developing Your Central Idea as a Persuasive Proposition      p. 386

After clarifying your specific purpose, you can word your central idea as a proposition of fact, value, or policy.

**Terms to Know**

## Supporting Your Persuasive Proposition with Credibility, Logic, and Emotion      p. 387

A key to persuading others is to establish your credibility as a speaker. Credibility is an audience's perception of a speaker's competence, trustworthiness, and dynamism. Enhancing your initial credibility before you speak, your derived credibility during your presentation, and your terminal credibility after your presentation will help you improve your overall credibility as a presentational speaker.

Reasoning, the process of drawing a conclusion from evidence, is integral to the persuasive process. The three primary types of reasoning are inductive, deductive, and causal. You can also reason by analogy. You can be an effective and ethical persuader by avoiding various reasoning fallacies, such as the causal fallacy, bandwagon fallacy, either–or fallacy, hasty generalization, personal attack, red herring, appeal to misplaced authority, and non sequitur.

In addition to persuading others because of who you are (ethos) or how well you reason (logos), you can also move an audience to respond by using emotional appeals (pathos).

**Terms to Know**

## Organizing Your Persuasive Message      p. 393

Ways to organize your persuasive message include problem–solution organization, cause and effect organization, refutation, and the motivated sequence. The motivated sequence includes five steps: attention, need, satisfaction, visualization, and action.

**Terms to Know**

## Adapting Ideas to People and People to Ideas p. 398

Be prepared to adapt your persuasive messages to receptive, neutral, and unreceptive audiences. If your listeners are receptive, identify with them, be overt in stating your speaking objective, and use emotional appeals. If they are neutral, "hook" them with your introduction, refer to universal beliefs and common concerns, show them how the topic affects them and those they care about, and be realistic about what you can accomplish. If your listeners are unreceptive, focus on areas of agreement rather than telling them that you are going to try to convince them to support your position, present your strongest arguments first, acknowledge opposing points of view, and use appropriate gestures.

# APPLYING Principles for a Lifetime

### Principle One:
### Be aware of your communication with yourself and others.

- Know whether the specific purpose of your presentation is to change or reinforce an attitude, a belief, a value, or a behavior, and be realistic in assessing what you need to do to effect change.
- Relate personal experience to make you seem a more competent and trustworthy speaker.
- To help enhance your initial credibility, have a brief summary of your qualifications and accomplishments ready for the person who will introduce you.
- To be a better informed consumer of persuasive messages, as well as a more ethical persuasive speaker, be aware of and avoid using common logical fallacies.

### Principle Two:
### Effectively use and interpret verbal messages.

- To create negative visualization, describe in detail how bleak or terrible the future will be if your solution is not implemented.
- To create positive visualization, describe in detail how wonderful the future will be if your solution is implemented.
- To select and narrow a topic for a persuasive presentation, stay current on important issues of the day by paying attention to print and electronic media.
- Word your central idea as a proposition to help you fine-tune your speaking objective and develop strategies for persuading your listeners.
- To bolster your audience's opinion of your competence, cite evidence to support your ideas.
- To enhance your terminal credibility, prepare a thoughtful conclusion.
- Provide logical proof (evidence and reasoning) for your arguments and avoid logical fallacies to heighten your chances for success with your audience.
- Use emotion-arousing words and concrete illustrations and descriptions to appeal to an audience's emotions.

### Principle Three:
## Effectively use and interpret nonverbal messages.

- Maintain eye contact, use enthusiastic vocal inflection, and move and gesture purposefully to increase the likelihood that your audience will view you as dynamic.
- Dress appropriately to enhance your credibility.
- To enhance your terminal credibility, maintain eye contact through and even after your closing sentence.
- Use presentation aids to help evoke both positive and negative emotions as well as positive and negative visualization.
- Use gestures when speaking to an unreceptive audience.

### Principle Four:
## Listen and respond thoughtfully to others.

- Be prepared to answer questions after your presentation, regardless of whether there is a planned question-and-answer period.

### Principle Five:
## Appropriately adapt messages to others.

- As you develop your persuasive purpose, consider the background and cultural expectations of your listeners.
- To motivate your listeners, appeal to their basic needs.
- Do everything possible to ensure that your audience's physiological and safety needs are met.
- If you are speaking to an apathetic audience or one that is not even aware that a problem exists, emphasize the problem portion of your problem–solution presentation.
- If your audience is aware of the problem you are discussing, emphasize the solution or solutions in your problem–solution presentation.
- Acknowledge and then refute the opposing points of view held by an unreceptive audience.
- In the need step of your motivated-sequence presentation, establish why your topic, problem, or issue should concern your listeners. Convince audience members that the problem affects them directly.
- In the action step of the motivated sequence, suggest a specific action your listeners can take to solve the problem you have discussed.
- If you are speaking to a knowledgeable, receptive audience, do not spend a great deal of time on the need step of the motivated sequence; instead, emphasize the satisfaction and action steps.
- If you are speaking to a neutral audience, emphasize the attention, need, and visualization steps of the motivated sequence.
- Establish common ground with your audience.
- Make the most of your opportunity to speak to a receptive audience by identifying with them.
- If your audience is receptive, state your speaking objective overtly, tell your listeners exactly what you want them to do, and ask them for an immediate show of support.
- Use emotional appeals with a receptive audience.
- To persuade a neutral audience, appeal to universal beliefs and concerns.
- Show a neutral audience how your topic affects them and those they love.
- Be realistic about what you can accomplish with neutral and unreceptive audiences.
- With an unreceptive audience, focus on areas of agreement.
- If your audience is unreceptive, advance your strongest arguments first.

# ASSESSING
## Your Skill

## Checklist for a Persuasive Presentation

The chapter-end materials for Chapter 13 include a list of presentation evaluation questions linked to the audience-centered model. You may also find it useful to refer to the following checklist specific to persuasive speaking.

| Element | Criteria | Additional Comments |
|---|---|---|
| **Audience** | _____ Adapted to needs, interests, and background of audience. | |
| | _____ Evidence of analyzing and adapting to the receptive, neutral, or unreceptive audience. | |
| **Topic** | _____ Appropriate to audience, occasion, and speaker. | |
| | _____ Focused on an important issue. | |
| | _____ Narrowed to fit the time limits. | |
| **Purpose** | _____ Persuasive general purpose—to change or reinforce listeners' attitudes, beliefs, values, or behavior. | |
| | _____ Audience-centered specific purpose. | |
| | _____ General and specific purposes achieved. | |
| **Central Idea** | _____ Clear one-sentence declarative summary of the presentation. | |
| | _____ A proposition of fact, value, or policy. | |
| **Main Ideas** | _____ Related to central idea as natural divisions, reasons, or chronological steps. | |
| | _____ Previewed in introduction of presentation. | |
| | _____ Developed in body of presentation. | |
| | _____ Summarized in conclusion of presentation. | |
| **Supporting Material** | _____ Ethos evident in speaker's appearance, credentials, preparation, and delivery. | |
| | _____ Logos evident in logically reasoned arguments supported by evidence. | |
| | _____ Pathos evident in emotion-arousing words and phrases, concrete illustrations and descriptions, and evocative presentation aids. | |
| **Organization** | _____ Introduction caught attention, established motive for audience to listen, stated central idea, and previewed main ideas. | |
| | _____ Body organized in a logical way—for example, according to problem–solution, cause and effect, refutation, or the motivated sequence. | |
| | _____ Conclusion restated central idea, summarized main ideas, and provided closure. | |
| **Delivery** | _____ Nonverbal reinforcement of key ideas. | |
| | _____ Eye contact with listeners. | |
| | _____ Appropriate volume and vocal inflection. | |
| | _____ Appropriate gestures, movement, and posture. | |
| | _____ Positive and negative emotions and visualization evoked by presentation aids, if any. | |

- **MyCommunicationLab** MyCommunicationLab provides a feature called The Public Speaker: Quick & Dirty Tips. Among these tips, in a section titled "How to Be Diplomatic," are strategies for persuading people to change without damaging your relationship with them. <www.mycommunicationlab.com> (Access code required.)
- **Maslow's Hierarchy of Needs** This interactive activity tests your ability to apply Maslow's hierarchy of needs to hypothetical but realistic examples. <www.wisc-online.com/objects/ViewObject.aspx?ID=I2P401>
- **Logical Fallacies** One of the most important skills a consumer of persuasive messages can have is the ability to spot faulty reasoning in an argument. This site identifies and provides examples of many types of logical fallacies. <www.philosophypages.com/lg/>

# WEB RESOURCES for More Review, Application, and Assessment

# A | Interviewing

## Appendix OUTLINE

- Types of Interviews
- Phases of an Interview
- How to Be Interviewed for a Job
- How to Be Interviewed in an Information-Gathering Interview
- The Responsibilities of the Interviewer
- Study Guide: Review, Apply, and Assess Your Knowledge and Skill

## Appendix OBJECTIVES

After studying this appendix, you should be able to

1. Describe what an interview is.
2. Identify five different kinds of interviews.
3. Describe the three phases of a well-structured interview.
4. Identify and discuss the important elements of being interviewed for a job.
5. Develop a clear, well-worded resumé.
6. Identify and discuss the important elements of participating in an information-gathering interview.
7. Explain how to conduct an interview.

We imagine that you won't be as unwise as the job applicant who put on his resumé that his work availability was limited because Friday, Saturday, and Sunday were "drinking time," or the one who tried to explain away an arrest found during a background check by admitting, "We stole a pig, but it was a really small pig." Nonetheless, you can still benefit from reading tips, strategies, and suggestions for polishing your interviewing skills.[1]

An **interview** is a form of oral interaction structured to achieve a goal; it often involves just two people who take turns speaking and listening, but it can include more than two people. An effective interview is not a random conversation; rather, the person conducting the interview has carefully framed the objectives of the interview and developed a structured plan for achieving the objectives. The person being interviewed should also prepare by considering the kinds of questions he or she may be asked and being ready to give appropriate responses.

The stakes are often high when you participate in an interview. If you are interviewing for a job, your career and perhaps your future rest on the impression you make. If someone is interviewing you to gather information, the accuracy of what you say can have a powerful effect on others. Or, if you are the person who is conducting the job interview, you have much to gain or lose; your choice of a new employee will affect the success of the organization. If you're interviewing someone to gather information, your credibility is at stake if you pass on or publish information that later proves to be false or inaccurate.

In this introduction to interviewing, we'll discuss communication strategies that can enhance your job interview skills and offer tips about how to participate in an information-gathering interview. We'll conclude the appendix by identifying strategies that can help you polish your talents if you are the person interviewing others. Whether you are a recent high school graduate or have been in the workforce for several years and have come back to school to finish your degree and pursue a new career, the Communication Principles for a Lifetime that we've emphasized in this book can help you enhance your interviewing skills.

# Types of Interviews

The planned or structured nature of the interview sets it apart from other communication situations, yet interviews sometimes include elements of interpersonal, group, and presentational communication. Interviews embody interpersonal communication in that there are two or more people participating in the interview who must establish a relationship. If the goal of the interview is to find a solution to a vexing problem, the interview may resemble elements of a group discussion in which a problem is defined and analyzed and solutions are generated, evaluated, and then implemented. Preparing for a job interview is like a public speaking situation; you focus on your audience (the interviewer), keep your purpose in mind as you research the company you're interviewing with, organize your ideas, and even rehearse your responses to questions you think you may be asked.

When people think of the term *interview*, what most commonly comes to mind is a job interview. Yet interviews can also be means of gathering information, sharing job performance feedback, solving problems, and persuading others. Even though we are focusing primarily on employment and information-gathering interviews, the strategies we present can help you with *any* interview situation.

## Information-Gathering Interview

**Information-gathering interviews**, just as the name suggests, are designed to seek information from the person being interviewed. *Public-opinion polls* are one type of information-gathering interview. When you leave an organization, you may be asked to participate in an *exit interview*, an interview designed to assess why you are leaving the company. A reporter for a newspaper, radio, or TV station interviews people to gather information for a story or broadcast.

**interview**
A form of oral interaction structured to achieve a goal; it involves two or more people who take turns speaking and listening.

**information-gathering interview**
An interview, such as an opinion poll, whose purpose is to seek information from another person.

Those most skilled at conducting information-gathering interviews do their homework before the interview. They come prepared with specific questions and have already conducted background research. In addition to preparing questions, a skilled information-gathering interviewer listens and develops questions that stem from the information that is shared during the interview.

## Appraisal Interview

An **appraisal interview**, sometimes called a performance review, occurs when a supervisor or employer shares information with you about your job performance. Such an interview enables you to see how others perceive your effectiveness and helps you determine whether you are likely to get a promotion or a layoff. During an appraisal interview, you can typically express your observations about the organization and your goals for the future. Usually a supervisor prepares a written report summarizing your strengths and weaknesses, and then meets with you to review it.

When receiving feedback from a supervisor, the best approach is to listen and gather as much objective information about his or her perceptions as possible. In an evaluation situation, especially if the feedback is negative, it is easy to become defensive. Instead, you should try to manage your emotions and use the information to your benefit. If you disagree with your supervisor's evaluation, consider using the conflict management skills we discussed in Chapter 8. In addition, provide specific examples to support your position. Just saying that you don't like the review is likely to do more harm than good.

## Problem-Solving Interview

A **problem-solving interview** is designed to resolve a problem that affects one or both parties involved in the interview. A disciplinary interview to consider corrective action toward an employee or students is one type of problem-solving interview. Grievance interviews are also problem-solving interviews; one person brings a grievance or complaint against another person, and solutions are sought to resolve the problem or conflict.

The strategies presented in Chapter 10 for structuring a problem-solving group discussion can also help you organize a problem-solving interview. Before seeking to solve or manage a problem, first define the issues; then analyze the causes, history, and symptoms of the problem. Rather than focusing on only one solution, brainstorm several possible solutions and then evaluate the pros and the cons of the potential solutions before settling on a single solution.

## Persuasion Interview

During a **persuasion interview**, one person seeks to change or reinforce the attitudes, beliefs, values, or behavior of another person. The sales interview is a classic example of an interview in which the goal is to persuade. A political campaign interview is another example of a persuasion interview.

Our discussion in Chapter 15 of the principles and strategies of persuading others can help you prepare for a persuasion interview. The advantage of trying to persuade someone during an interview rather than in a speech is the size of the audience; during a persuasive interview, you may have an audience of one. It is especially important to analyze and adapt to your listener when seeking to persuade.

## Job Interview

A **job interview** is a focused, structured conversation whose goal is to assess a person's credentials and skills for employment. The job interview may involve elements of each of the types of interviews we've already discussed. Information is both gathered and shared, and a job interview will certainly solve a problem if you're the one looking for

**appraisal interview**
An interview during which a supervisor or employer shares information with an employee about his or her job performance.

**problem-solving interview**
An interview, such as a grievance or disciplinary interview, that is designed to solve a problem.

**persuasion interview**
An interview that attempts to change or reinforce attitudes, beliefs, values, or behavior, such as a sales interview.

**job interview**
A focused, structured conversation whose goal is to assess a person's credentials and skills for employment.

a job and you are hired. Elements of persuasion are also involved in a job interview. If you are seeking a job, you're trying to persuade the interviewer to hire you; if you are the interviewer and you're interviewing an exceptionally talented person, your job is to persuade the interviewee to join your organization.

Regardless of the purpose or format of the interview, the five Communication Principles for a Lifetime that we've used to organize our discussion of interpersonal, group and team, and presentational communication situations will serve you well when you participate in an interview. Whether you are the interviewer or the interviewee, it is important to be aware of how you are coming across to others. Using and interpreting verbal and nonverbal messages are critical to having a successful interview. In our definition of an interview, we noted that all individuals involved both talk and listen. Unless you can adapt your messages to others, you won't be successful. Effective interview participants listen, respond, and speak extemporaneously rather than delivering overly scripted, planned messages. Adapting to others is essential.

# Phases of an Interview

Just as a speech or term paper has a beginning, middle, and end, so does a well-structured interview. No matter what type of interview, most interviews have three phases:

1. *The opening.*   The interviewer tries to put the interviewee at ease and presents an overview of the interview agenda.
2. *The body.*   During the longest part of an interview, the interviewer asks questions, and the interviewee listens and responds. The interviewee may also ask questions.
3. *The conclusion.*   The interviewer summarizes what will happen next and usually gives the interviewee an opportunity to ask any final questions.

It is the responsibility of the interviewer, the person leading the interview, to develop a structure for the interview. But it's also helpful for the interviewee to understand the overall structure in advance to know what to expect both before and during the interview. So, whether you're the interviewer or the interviewee, understanding the interview structure we discuss should be of value to you.

## The Opening

The opening of any interview is crucial because it creates a climate for positive and open communication. When interviewing someone, you should strive to establish rapport and to clarify the goals of the interview.

To establish rapport, start the conversation with something that will put the interviewee at ease. The discussion could be about something as simple as the weather, recent events both of you attended, or other light topics. Making direct eye contact, smiling appropriately, and offering a firm handshake all help establish a warm atmosphere.

Besides making the interviewee comfortable, the interviewer should clarify the goals of the interview by explicitly stating the general purpose for the meeting. After the opening conversation, it may be helpful to provide a general overview of the nature and purpose of the interview and an estimate of how long the interview will last. Clarifying a meeting's purpose helps both parties get their bearings and check their understanding. A good interviewer makes sure that everyone is on the same wavelength before the actual questioning begins.

Both the interviewer and the interviewee should try to arrive a few minutes ahead of the scheduled hour of the interview. Be prepared, however, to wait patiently, if necessary. If you are the interviewer and have decided to use a recorder, set it up. You may keep it out of sight once the interviewee has seen it, but *never* try to hide a recorder at the outset—such a ploy is unethical and illegal. If you are going to take written notes, get out your paper and pen. Now you are ready to begin asking your prepared questions.

# The Body: Asking Questions

Once the interviewee has been put at ease during the opening of the interview, the bulk of the interview will consist of the interviewer asking the interviewee questions. Even though both parties listen and speak, the interviewer has the primary responsibility for questioning. If the interviewer has done a good job of identifying and clarifying his or her objectives and gathering information, the key questions to be asked are usually fairly obvious.

**Question Types** Interview questions fall into one of four categories: open, closed, probing, or hypothetical.[2] A typical interview usually includes some of each type.

**Open Questions** **Open questions** are broad and unstructured questions that allow interviewees considerable freedom to determine the amount and kind of information they will provide. Because they encourage the interviewee to share information almost without restriction, open questions are useful in determining opinions, values, and perspective. Such questions as "What are your long- and short-term career goals?" "Why do you seek employment here?" and "How do you feel about gun control?" prompt personal and wide-ranging responses.

**Closed Questions** **Closed questions** limit the range of possible responses. They may ask for a simple yes or no—"Do you enjoy working in teams?"—or they may allow interviewees to select responses from a number of specific alternatives: "How often do you go to the movies? (1) Less than once a month, (2) Once a month, (3) Twice a month, (4) Once a week." Closed questions enable the interviewer to gather specific information by restricting interviewees' freedom to express personal views or elaborate on responses. Closed questions are most often used when an interviewer is trying to obtain a maximum amount of information in a short period of time.

**Probing Questions** **Probing questions** encourage interviewees to clarify or elaborate on partial or superficial responses. Through the use of these questions, interviewers attempt to clarify or direct responses. Such questions as "Could you elaborate on your coursework in the area of communication?" "Do you mean to say that you already own three vacuum cleaners?" and "Will you tell me more about your relationship with your supervisor?" call for further information in a particular area. Often spontaneous, probing questions follow up on the key questions that interviewers have prepared in advance.

**Hypothetical Questions** Interviewers use **hypothetical questions** when they describe a set of conditions and ask interviewees what they would do if they were in that situation. Such questions are generally used either to gauge reactions to emotion-arousing or value-laden circumstances or to reveal on interviewee's likely responses to real situations. A police officer might ask an eyewitness to a murder, "What if I told you that the man you identified as the murderer in the line-up was the mayor?" During an exit interview, a personnel manager might ask, "If we promoted you to chief sanitary engineer and paid you $4 an hour more, would you consider staying with Bob's Landfill and Television Repair?"

**Questioning Sequences** Open, closed, probing, and hypothetical questions may be used in any combination, as long as their sequence is thoughtfully planned. Depending on the purpose, these questions may be arranged into three basic sequences: funnel, inverted funnel, and tunnel.

**The Funnel Sequence** As shown in Figure A.1, the **funnel sequence** begins with broad, open questions and proceeds to more closed questions. The advantage of this format is that it allows an interviewee to express views and feelings without

**open question**
A question that is broad and unstructured and that allows the respondent considerable freedom to determine the amount and kind of information provided.

**closed question**
A question that limits the range of possible responses and requires a simple, direct, and brief answer.

**probing question**
A question that encourages the interviewee to clarify or elaborate on partial or superficial responses and that usually takes the discussion in a desired direction.

**hypothetical question**
A question used to gauge an interviewee's reaction to an emotion-arousing or value-laden situation or to reveal an interviewee's likely reactions to a real situation.

**funnel sequence**
A questioning sequence that begins with broad, open questions and proceeds toward more closed questions.

Getting at specific pieces of
information through use of
direct questioning

**Figure A.1
The Funnel
Sequence**

restriction, at least early in an interview. For example, it may be more useful to begin a grievance interview with the question "How would you describe your relationship with your supervisor?" than with "What makes you think that your supervisor treats you like an idiot?" The first question allows the free expression of feelings, whereas the second clearly reflects an interviewer's bias, immediately forcing the discussion in a negative direction. The following series of questions provides an example of a funnel sequence that might be used for an information-gathering interview.

1. Why do you find communication interesting?
2. What area of communication are you primarily interested in?
3. How long have you studied interpersonal communication?
4. Why do you think interpersonal attraction theory is useful?
5. What would you do to test interpersonal attraction theory?

Notice that the questions start by asking for general information and then focus on more specific ideas.

**The Inverted Funnel Sequence**   The opposite of the funnel sequence is the **inverted funnel sequence**, shown in Figure A.2, which begins with closed questions and proceeds to more open questions. An interview designed to gather information about a worker grievance might be based on the inverted funnel and might include the following series of questions:

1. Do you believe that your supervisor wants to fire you?
2. What makes you think that you'll be fired soon?
3. What do you think has caused this problem between you and your supervisor?
4. How has this problem affected your work?
5. How would you describe the general working climate in your department?

The relatively closed questions that begin the inverted funnel sequence are intended to encourage an interviewee to respond easily, because they require only brief answers (yes or no, short lists, and the like). As the sequence progresses, the questions become more open and thus require more elaborate answers and greater disclosure.

The inverted funnel sequence is appropriate when an interviewer wants to direct the interview along specific lines and encourage an interviewee to respond with short, easily composed answers. An interviewer can follow up with more general questions to provide increasingly broad information—the "big picture."

**The Tunnel Sequence**   Finally, the **tunnel sequence** consists of a series of related open or closed questions or a combination of the two; the sequence is intended to gather a wide range of information. This sequence does not include probing questions; it goes into less depth than

# RECAP

## TYPES OF INTERVIEW QUESTIONS

|  | **Uses** | **Example** |
|---|---|---|
| **Open Question** | Prompts wide-ranging responses. Answers reveal interviewee's opinions, values, perspectives. | Tell me about your previous job duties. How would you describe your son's problems in school? |
| **Closed Question** | Requests simple yes or no response or forces interviewee to select a response from limited options. | Have you been skiing in the past month? Which one of the following drinks would you buy? a. Coke b. Pepsi c. 7-Up |
| **Probing Question** | Encourages clarification of or elaboration on previous responses. Leads response in a specific direction. | Would you tell me more about the pain in your side? We've talked about your mother. Can you describe how you felt about your father's long absences from home when you were a child? |
| **Hypothetical Question** | Gauges reactions to emotional or value-laden situations. Elicits response to a real or imaginary situation. | How would you support your opponent if she were elected chair of the board? What would you do if your secretary lost an important file? |

the other three sequences. An interviewer may use the tunnel sequence to gather information about attitudes and opinions without regard for the reasons behind an interviewee's answers or the intensity of his or her feelings. The following is a typical tunnel sequence:

1. What are the three major issues in the presidential campaign this year?
2. Which candidate would you vote for if the election were held today?
3. For whom do you think you will vote in the race for U.S. senator?
4. Are you a registered voter in this state?
5. What do you think of the proposition to set up a nuclear waste dump in this state?

The tunnel sequence is most appropriate when an interviewer wants some general information on a variety of topics in a relatively short period of time.

Although these sequences have been discussed as if they were independent and easily distinguishable, good questioning strategy will probably combine one or more question sequences. The key to effective interviewing is to prepare a set of questions that will get the needed kinds and amount of information. An interviewer should remain flexible enough to add, subtract, and revise questions as a discussion proceeds. Such an approach ensures that the objectives of the interview will be accomplished.

As you conduct the interview, use the questions you have prepared as a general guide but not a rigid schedule. If the person you are interviewing mentions an interesting angle you did not think of, don't be afraid to pursue the point. Listen carefully to the person's answers and ask for clarification of any ideas you don't understand.

## The Conclusion

Opinion polls, marketing surveys, and sales pitches often end rather abruptly with a "Thank you for taking the time to help me." Many other kinds of interviews require follow-up meetings or some form of future contact, however. For this reason, and for reasons of common courtesy, the conclusion of an interview is very important. Conclusions can summarize the interview and establish a basis for a continued relationship, as well as bring the meeting to a close.

**Summarizing**   A primary function of the conclusion is to summarize the proceedings. All parties should be aware of and agree on what happened during the meeting. To ensure understanding and agreement, an interviewer summarizes the highlights of the discussion, asking for and offering clarification if necessary.

**Continuing the Relationship**   Another function of the conclusion is to encourage a continued, friendly relationship. The positive communication climate developed during the interview should be carried into the conclusion. The interviewer may need to establish interpersonal harmony if you asked questions that resulted in conflict or made the interviewee uncomfortable. Comments such as "I'm glad we had a chance to talk about this problem" or "Thank you for sharing and listening" enable both parties to feel that they have had a positive and productive encounter.

**Clarifying Expectations**   An interviewer can tell the interviewee when to expect further contact or action, if appropriate. A job applicant wants to know when to expect a phone call about a follow-up interview or a job offer. An expert, interviewed by a journalist, wants to know what will be done with his or her comments and when the story is likely to be published.

**Ending the Meeting**   At the end of virtually any interview, good manners require both the interviewer and the interviewee to say "Thank you." Because an interview is a mutual effort, both parties deserve recognition. One final suggestion: Do not prolong the interview beyond the time limits of your appointment.

Building the "big picture" with repeated questioning, integrating previous responses

**Figure A.2
The Inverted
Funnel Sequence**

**inverted funnel sequence**
A questioning sequence that begins with closed questions and proceeds to more open questions, intended to encourage an interviewee to respond easily early in the interview.

**tunnel sequence**
A way of structuring interview questions so that parallel open or closed questions (or a combination of open and closed questions) are asked to gather a large amount of information in a short amount of time; no probing questions are asked.

# RECAP

## ORGANIZING AN INTERVIEW

| Phase | Goals |
|---|---|
| **Opening** | Put the interviewee at ease. |
| | Review the purpose. |
| | Establish rapport. |
| | Provide an orientation. |
| **Body** | Use questions appropriate to the interview type and objective. |
| | • Use open questions to elicit wide-ranging responses. |
| | • Use closed questions to get specific responses. |
| | • Use probing questions to seek clarification or elaboration. |
| | • Use hypothetical questions to gauge a reaction to an imaginary situation. |
| | Design questioning sequences appropriate to the interview purpose. |
| | • Use the funnel sequence to elicit general comments first and specific information later. |
| | • Use the inverted funnel sequence to elicit specific information first and more general comments later. |
| | • Use the tunnel sequence to gather lots of information without probing too deeply. |
| **Conclusion** | Summarize the proceedings. |
| | Encourage friendly relations. |
| | Arrange further contact(s). |
| | Exchange thank-yous. |

**resumé**
A written, concise, well-organized description of a person's qualifications for a job.

# How to Be Interviewed for a Job

Woody Allen once said, "Ninety percent of life is just showing up." We suggest that you do more than just show up for a job interview, however. Like giving an effective speech, having a successful job interview involves thoughtful preparation and careful planning. According to Career-Builder.com, a popular website for job hunters, it takes an average of seventeen interviews to get one job offer.[3] To increase your odds of getting hired following an interview, we present research-based suggestions and strategies to help you make your first impression your best impression when looking for employment.

## Be Aware of Your Skills and Abilities

The first communication principle we introduced in this book is to be aware of your communication. Before you interview for a job, it is important to be aware not only of your communication as you interact with others, but also of your unique skills, talents, and abilities. Many people select a career because they think that they might like to *be* a lawyer, doctor, or teacher. But rather than thinking about what you want to be, we suggest considering what you like to *do*. Ask yourself these questions:

- What do I like to do in my free time?
- What are my best skills and talents?
- What education and training do I have?
- What experiences or previous jobs have I had?

In addition to answering these questions, write down responses to complete this statement: "I can . . . ." For example, you might respond: "I can cook, write, relate well to others." List as many answers as possible. Here's another statement to complete: "I have . . . ." You might answer: "I have traveled, worked on a farm, sold magazine subscriptions." Responding to the "I can" and "I have" statements will help you develop an awareness of your skills and experiences that will help you respond readily when you are asked about them during the interview. Reflecting on your interests can help you decide which career will best suit your talents; you will also be able to develop a resumé that reflects your best abilities.

## Prepare Your Resumé

A **resumé** is a written, concise, well-organized description of your qualifications for a job. How long should a resumé be? Many employers don't expect a resumé to be longer than two pages; some will look only at a one-page resumé. (Resumés of experienced career professionals may be longer than two pages, however.) Although your resumé is important in helping you land a job, its key function is to help you get an interview—it's how you perform in the interview that determines whether you get the job. Employers rarely hire someone based only on a resumé. Most employers spend less than a minute—and some only a few seconds—looking at each resumé. Therefore, your resumé should be clear and easy to read and should focus on the essential information an employer seeks.

# Sample Resumé

**MARK SMITH**
3124 West Sixth Street
San Marcos, TX 78666
(512) 555-0102
(512) 555-0010

**PROFESSIONAL OBJECTIVE:** Seeking a position in human resources as a training specialist.

**EDUCATION:**
Bachelor of Arts Degree
Major: Communication Studies
Minor: English
Texas State University–San Marcos
Graduation Date: May 20XX

**PROFESSIONAL EXPERIENCE:**
20XX–Present, Intern, GSD&M, Austin, Texas
- Assisted in creating a leadership training program
- Designed flyers and display ads using desktop publishing software
- Made cold calls to prospective clients

20XX–August 20XX, Intern, Target Market, Houston, Texas
- Developed sales training seminar
- Coordinated initial plan for writing advertising copy for Crest Inc.'s advertising campaign

20XX–20XX, Supervisor, S&B Associates, San Marcos, Texas
- Supervised three employees editing training materials

20XX–20XX, Advertising Sales and Reporter, *University Star*, San Marcos, Texas
- Sold ads for university paper and worked as social events reporter

**OTHER EXPERIENCE:**
20XX–20XX, Summer job at Target, San Marcos, Texas
20XX–20XX, Summer job at YMCA, Austin, Texas

**SKILLS:** Team Leadership, Photography, Computer Proficiency, Research and Analysis, Public Speaking, Customer Service

**ACCOMPLISHMENTS & HONORS:** Paid for majority of my college education while maintaining a 3.5 grade point average, Presidential Scholarship, Vice President of Texas State University Communication Club, Editor/Historian of MortarBoard, John Marshall High School Vice President of Junior Class, Yearbook Coordinator

**PROFESSIONAL ORGANIZATIONS:** Lambda Pi Eta, American Society for Training and Development, Communication Club, National Communication Association

**INTERESTS:** Photography, tennis, softball, theater

**REFERENCES:** Available at your request

Under "references," you put "sleeping in".

I thought it said "preferences".

Andy Cowan/King Features Syndicate

Most employers will be looking for standard information on your resumé. (Study the sample resumé that appears on page 417.[4]) Be sure to include the following information on your resumé:

- *Personal information.* Employers will look for your name, address, phone numbers, e-mail address, and web page address (if you have one). Provide phone numbers where you can be reached during both the day and the evening.
- *Career objective.* Many employers will want to see your career objective. Make it brief, clear, and focused. Customize your career objective for each different position you seek.
- *Education.* Include your major, your degree, your graduation date, and the institution you attended.
- *Experience.* Describe your relevant work experience, listing your most recent job first. Include the names of employers, dates when you worked, and a very brief description of your duties.
- *Honors and special accomplishments.* List any awards, honors, offices held, or other leadership responsibilities.
- *Optional information.* If you have volunteer experience, have traveled, or have computer skills or other pertinent experience, be sure to include it if it is relevant to your objective and the job.
- *References.* List the names, phone and fax numbers, and e-mail addresses of people who can speak positively about your skills and abilities. Or you may indicate that your references are available on request.

When developing your resumé, be sure to use specific action verbs to describe your experience. Also use these action words during your interview. Rather than using a general verb such as "I *worked* on a project," use more descriptive action words that clarify the role you assumed. Consider using some of the following words when listing or describing your activities or accomplishments:

| | | |
|---|---|---|
| accelerated | designed | interpreted |
| accepted | developed | maintained |
| accomplished | directed | managed |
| achieved | effected | mastered |
| adapted | eliminated | motivated |
| administered | evaluated | negotiated |
| analyzed | expanded | operated |
| approved | expedited | organized |
| built | facilitated | originated |
| completed | found | participated |
| conceived | generated | planned |
| conducted | guided | promoted |
| controlled | improved | proposed |
| coordinated | increased | provided |
| created | influenced | recommended |
| delegated | initiated | reduced |
| demonstrated | instructed | researched |

| | | |
|---|---|---|
| resulted in | stimulated | translated |
| reviewed | structured | traveled |
| revised | supervised | updated |
| selected | tested | utilized |
| solved | trained | won |

## Identify the Needs of Your Potential Employer

After you have analyzed your skills and abilities and have prepared a well-crafted resumé, you need to anticipate the needs and goals of your potential employer. A good interviewee adapts his or her message to the interviewer.

How do you find information about an organization that will help you adapt your message to fit its needs? In a word, do research. Gather as much information as you can about not only the person who will interview you but also the needs and goals of the organization or company where you seek a job.

Virtually every organization these days has a web presence. Explore the information available on the Internet. Do more than just look at the organization's home page; click on the various hyperlinks that help you learn about what the organization does.

## Look and Communicate Your Best

"When in doubt, look intelligent," said humorist and writer Garrison Keillor. This advice is especially important when you prepare for a job interview. You should also communicate intelligently. The opportunity to assess your appearance and the way in which you express yourself nonverbally is one of the most important reasons an interviewer wants to meet you face to face.

**Dress for Success**   As we discussed in Chapter 1, don't forget about the power of nonverbal messages in making a good impression. Dressing for success is crucial. Regardless of the type or level of the job for which you are applying, most experts suggest that you dress conservatively and give special attention to your grooming. For most professional positions, men will be expected to wear a coat and tie or a suit and well-polished shoes. Women will be expected to wear a dress, suit, or other coordinated attire. There are many jobs, of course, for which wearing a business suit to the interview would be overkill (such as manual labor), but if you're not certain what to wear, it's better to err on the side of dressing up than dressing down.

**Communicate Your Best**   What determines whether you are hired for the job? In short, it's the way you communicate. By the time you get to an interview, your interviewer has already determined that you have at least the minimum qualifications for the job. Your ability to apply the Communication Principles for a Lifetime that we've reiterated throughout the book is key to making a good impression on your interviewer. In Chapter 1, when we discussed why it's important to learn about communication, we noted the key factors that employers look for in a job applicant and the top three factors focus on your communication skill.[5] Your ability to listen, respond, and relate to your interviewer is one of the best predictors of whether you will be hired for a job.

The opportunity to assess your appearance and the way in which you express yourself nonverbally is one of the most important reasons an interviewer wants to meet you face to face. Among the areas an interviewer is trying to assess by observing your behavior are the following:

- *Self-expression.* Are you clear or are you vague when you respond to questions? Do you have effective eye contact? Do you talk too much or too little?
- *Maturity.* Are you likely to make good judgments and effective decisions?
- *Personality.* What's your overall style of relating to people? Are you outgoing, shy, quiet, overbearing, enthusiastic, warm, friendly?

- *Experience.* Can you do the job? Do you have a track record that suggests you can effectively do what needs to be done?
- *Enthusiasm.* Do you seem interested in this job and the organization? Do you seem to be genuine and authentic, or is your enthusiasm phony?
- *Goals.* Where are you heading in life? Are your short-term and long-term goals compatible with the needs of the organization?

Marketing experts know the importance of developing a brand name (such as Coke, Kleenex, or Starbucks) to make a product memorable and distinctive. A **personal brand** works the same way. Your personal brand is the clear impression you leave when the interview has concluded. As career counselor Delores Dean notes, "The goal in branding is to leave behind an impression of you that will be remembered. You must stand out above the rest and be the best."[6] How do you develop yourself as a memorable brand? One way is to use both nonverbal and verbal messages effectively. Nonverbally, you can make sure that you are remembered through your appearance. Pay special attention to what you wear and how you interact nonverbally with the interviewer to leave a positive impression. Verbally, if you project a positive attitude when you speak, you can leave a lasting, positive impression. A memorable, appropriate, and well-told brief story in response to a question can also help you be remembered. The goal of the interview is not only to *make* a positive impression, but also to *leave* a positive impression that will be remembered once the interviewer sifts through the notes and memories of multiple interviews.

## Polish Your Online Appearance

Journalist Andy Simmons noted, "Every American has, at some point, appeared naked, drunk, unconscious, rude, crude or felonious online. Okay, maybe not everyone, but surf the Net and that's the impression you'll get."[7] Simmons's point is that it's important to make sure your online impression is as presentable as your live-and-in-person appearance. If you have a Facebook page, make sure that it contains no embarrassing photos or quotes that might damage your reputation, because employers are surfing the web to see if you are as credible as your resumé or personal impression suggests. According to CareerBuilder.com, when employers checked the facts on people's resumés by using the power of the Internet, here's what they found:

- 31 percent had lied about their qualifications.
- 24 percent had some link to criminal behavior.
- 19 percent had made negative comments about a past employer.
- 19 percent had bragged about drinking or using illegal drugs.
- 15 percent had shared confidential information about their former employers.
- 11 percent had posted unflattering or sexually explicit photos.
- 8 percent had used an obscene or unprofessional online screen name.

So, don't think that no one will find out about something you or a "friend" of yours has posted about you online. Increasingly, employers are using social networks such as Facebook to see if your cyberpersonality is consistent with the well-scrubbed, polished appearance you presented in your interview and with your resumé.

Make sure your Facebook page is switched to "private" so that only those you authorize can review any personal information. Or, better yet, purge your social network files of anything that is unflattering or embarrassing. What's to prevent someone who does have access to your information from sharing it with a wider audience? Keep a close eye on what is posted on the Internet about you. Also, make sure that those who do have access to your e-pages don't post unflattering comments about your socializing habits. When you are in the job-hunting mode, search for your name through Google or another search engine frequently to make sure that nothing negative about you is showing up online. By signing up for Google Alert, you'll find out when your name pops up on the Internet. One final tip: Avoid what you and your friends may think are cute and funny e-mail addresses, such as Imlazyandbored.com or hottotrot .com; a prospective employer is not likely to be amused and is not likely to hire you.

**personal brand**
The clear impression an interviewee leaves when the interview has concluded.

# Communication&TECHNOLOGY

## Tips for E-Resumés

Given the popularity of **e-resumés** (resumes that are submitted in an electronic form via the Internet), chances are that you will send an e-resumé to a prospective employer rather than mailing or hand-delivering a "hard copy."[8] An e-resumé has several advantages:

- You can send your resumé to many people in a short amount of time.
- You can easily customize your resumé for different prospective employers, emphasizing the particular skills that an employer is seeking.
- You can showcase your computer and graphic skills if the job you are applying for requires those skills.[9]

When you develop your e-resumé, you have some decisions to make. First, do you use a "plain text" file, which does not permit you to enhance your resumé with such formatting as boldface, italics, or underlining but uses only unadorned words to sell your credentials? A plain text file is also called an ASCII file. It has the advantage of being easily distributed to many employers, but it can be viewed by anyone, including your current employer, whom you may not want to know that you are job hunting.[10] If you use an HTML resumé, which is basically a web page, you can provide more formatting and direct your resumé to a specific person or organization. Most consultants recommend an HTML format.[11]

Another decision to make is how widely you should distribute your e-resumé. Because it takes only a click of a mouse to send your resumé, you may be tempted to submit it to prospective employers whose job offerings are not quite a match for your skills. Resist this temptation. Because of the ease of submitting e-resumés, employers have been inundated with them, making it a challenge to sort through all the resumes they receive. As in any communication situation, think about your audience. Send your resumé only to those employers who you think are interested in someone with your credentials.

Most employers won't take the time to read attachments that you send along with your resumé. Rather than using attachments to showcase your past work, many experts recommend that you use a **hyperlink** to lead the e-resumé reader to your work samples. A hyperlink is simply the connector between one page and another on the World Wide Web.[12]

Although e-resumés have many advantages, you may still want to follow up with more personal approaches to the job search. Some employers specifically state that they do not want phone calls or visits, but unless you are prohibited from making follow-up contacts, it can be helpful to support your e-contact with personal contact with your prospective employer.

# Listen, Respond, and Ask Appropriate Questions

Because an interview is a structured, planned discussion, it is important to demonstrate effective listening and responding skills. Stay focused on what your interviewer is asking you. Remember to stop, look, and listen for both the details of the questions and the major points of the questions.

When you respond to questions, you should project genuine enthusiasm and competence. Don't put on an act: Be yourself while being professional. Be friendly and pleasant without being overly effusive or giddy. Communication researcher Mary Minto found that *how* you respond to an interviewer's questions could be even more important than *what* you say.[13] Your tone of voice, use of pauses and gestures, and posture are vital in expressing your personality and overall mood. Talking rapidly and nonstop without periodically pausing, for example, communicates that you are not sensitive to others.

One of the best ways to prepare for an interview is to anticipate the interviewer's questions. Table A.1 on page 422 lists typical questions that may be asked during an interview. We don't recommend that you memorize "canned" or overly rehearsed answers, but it may help to think about possible responses to these questions. Also be prepared to answer questions about your unique experiences, such as military service, vocational training, or membership on sports teams.

**e-resumé**
A resumé that is submitted in electronic form via the Internet.

**hyperlink**
An electronic connector between one page and another on the World Wide Web.

## Table A.1
## Typical Questions Asked During a Job Interview[14]

### I. Education

1. Why did you select your major area of study?
2. Why did you select your college/university?
3. If you were starting college again, what would you do differently? Why?
4. What subjects were most and least interesting? Useful? Why?
5. Other than the courses you studied, what is the most important thing you learned from your college experience?
6. How did you finance your college education?

### II. Experience

7. What do you see as your strengths as an employee?
8. You say that a strength you have is _____. Give me some indication, perhaps an example, that illustrates this strength.
9. What special skills would you bring to this position?
10. Describe your last few work experiences. Why did you leave each one?
11. What were the best and worst aspects of your last job?
12. What were some of your achievements and disappointments in your last job?
13. Do you see yourself as a leader/manager of people? Why?
14. What kinds of work situations would you like to avoid? Why?
15. What frustrations have you encountered in your work experience? How have you handled these frustrations?
16. What do you look for in a boss?
17. Most employees and bosses have some disagreements. What are some things that you and your boss have disagreed about?

### III. Position and Company

18. Why did you select this company?
19. Why did you decide to apply for this particular position?
20. How do you see yourself being qualified for this position?
21. Are you willing to relocate?

### IV. Self-Evaluation

22. Tell me a little bit about yourself. Describe yourself.
23. What do you see as your personal strengths? Talents? How do you know that you possess these? Give examples of each.
24. What do you see as your weak points? Areas for improvement? Things you have difficulty doing? What have you done to deal with these weak areas?
25. Describe a specific work problem you had. Tell what you did to solve this problem.
26. What do you consider to be your greatest work achievement? Why?

### V. Goals

27. Where do you see yourself being in your profession in five years? In ten years? How did you establish these goals? What will you need to do to achieve these goals?
28. What are your salary expectations for this position? Starting salary? Salary in five years?

It is important to be sure to get a good night's sleep before the interview and to eat sensibly (don't skip breakfast; don't stuff yourself at lunch) so that you can stay alert. Long interviews can be physically demanding.

Consider the interview an opportunity to ask questions as well as to answer them; toward the end of an interview, most interviewers will give you an opportunity to ask whatever questions you'd like. Asking questions about an organization is a way to display enthusiasm for the job, as well as a means of assessing whether you really want to join the organization. You will want to know the following:

- Will there be any job training for this position?
- What are the opportunities for advancement?
- What is the atmosphere like in the workplace? (You will also be able to observe the workplace during the interview.)
- What hours do people work?
- Is there flexibility in scheduling the work day?
- When do you anticipate making a decision about this position?

The very first question you ask should *not* be "How much does this job pay?" Usually the interviewer will discuss salary and benefits with you during the interview. If it is a preliminary interview and there is a chance that you will be called back for another interview, you may want to defer questions about salary and benefits until you know that the organization is seriously considering you for the position.

During the interview, maintain eye contact and speak assertively. The goal in an interview is to project a positive attitude to the interviewer. As motivational speaker Zig Ziglar once noted, "Your attitude, not your aptitude, will determine your altitude."

## Follow Up After the Interview

After the interview, it is wise to write a brief letter or e-mail to thank the interviewer and to provide any additional information that may have been requested. You may also want to send a thank-you note to others in the organization, such as a secretary or administrative assistant, for helping you arrange the interview. If the interviewer asked for references, make sure to let your references know as soon as possible that they may be contacted. If you are asking them to send letters of recommendation to the organization, expedite the process by providing addressed, stamped envelopes or the appropriate e-mail addresses and a copy of your resumé so that they can personalize their letters with specific information.

Is it appropriate to call the person who interviewed you to ask when a decision will be made about hiring someone? Some employers abide by the philosophy "Don't call us, we'll call you," but many others would interpret your call as a sign of your interest in the position and a testament to your ability to follow through. You may want to take the direct approach and simply ask the interviewer toward the end of the interview, "Would it be all right if I called you in a few days to see if you have made a decision or if you need additional information?" If the interviewer tells you that a decision will be made by a certain date and then that date passes by, it is probably okay to call and find out whether the job has been offered to someone else and to express your continued interest in the position if it hasn't been filled.

# How to Be Interviewed in an Information-Gathering Interview

The bulk of the responsibility for an effective information-gathering interview falls on the person who is doing the interviewing. If you are the interviewer in an information-gathering interview, review the suggestions we offer in this appendix for structuring the interview; most information-gathering interviews follow this general structure.

If you are the person being interviewed, however, your primary responsibilities are to be prepared, to listen carefully, and to respond appropriately to questions. In addition, a good interviewee knows what to expect in an information-gathering interview. You should prepare responses to anticipated questions, pay close attention to requests for specific information, and answer questions directly and accurately.

## Prepare for the Interview

In most cases, interviewees have some advance knowledge of the purpose and objective of interviews, especially if someone is seeking specific information or advice. You can therefore anticipate probable topics of discussion. If you are uncertain what the interview is about, it is appropriate to ask the person who will interview you how to best prepare for the questions he or she plans to ask. Yes, sometimes news programs have an interviewer pop up in an office, thrust a microphone in an interviewee's face, and ask a pointed question; in most cases, however, CBS news anchor Scott Pelley (or his equivalent) is not going to ambush you.

Depending on the nature of the interview, you may want to brush up on the facts you may be asked about. Jot down a few notes to remind you of names, dates, and places. In some cases, you may want to do some background reading on the topic of the interview.

Finally, think about not only what you will say in the interview but also how you will respond nonverbally. Be on time. Maintain an attitude of interest and attentiveness with eye contact, attentive body positions, alert facial expressions, and an appropriately firm handshake.

## Listen Effectively

Interviewing situations require you to listen to determine the amount and depth of information desired. If your responses are to be appropriate and useful, you must know what is being requested. If questions are unclear, ask for clarification or elaboration. By doing so, you can respond more fully and relevantly.

Successful interviewees practice empathy. Interviewers are people, and interviewing situations are interpersonal encounters. Effective interviewees consider situations from interviewers' points of view, listen "between the lines" of what someone says to focus on underlying emotions, and watch for nonverbal cues. When interviewees listen to all facets of the communication, they can better adapt to the situation.

## Respond Appropriately

Just as questioning is the primary responsibility of an interviewer, responding is the primary responsibility of an interviewee. Keep answers direct, honest, and appropriate in depth and relevance. For example, in response to the question "How would you describe the quality of your relationship with your family?" don't give a fifteen-minute speech about your problems with your ex-spouse, keeping the children in clothes, and finding dependable home care for your aging parents. To make sure that you give the best possible answer, listen carefully when a question is posed and, if necessary, take a few moments to think before you answer. A response that is well thought out, straightforward, and relevant will be much more appreciated than one that is hasty, evasive, and unrelated to the question.

Using language and vocabulary appropriate to the situation is also important. The use of too much slang or technical terminology in an attempt to impress an interviewer can easily backfire by distracting the interviewer or distorting communication. Direct and simple language promotes understanding.

Finally, be flexible and adaptable to the needs of the interviewing situation. Some interviewers will ask questions to throw you off guard. If so, take a moment to think before you respond. Try to discover the reason for the question and respond to the best of your ability. Listen carefully for the content *and* intent of questions so that you provide the information requested, especially when the interviewer changes topics. Flexibility and adaptability depend on good listening, empathy, accurate reading and interpretation of nonverbal communication, and practice. Just remember: "Engage brain before opening mouth."

# The Responsibilities of the Interviewer

So far, we've emphasized how to behave when you are the person being interviewed. As you assume leadership positions in your profession and community, you will undoubtedly be called on to interview others. In addition to knowing how to structure the opening, body, and conclusion of an interview, which we discussed earlier, there are several other characteristics of effective interviewers, whether you are seeking a future employee or simply gathering information.

## Be Aware of Biases and Prejudices

First and foremost, an interviewer must be aware of his or her own biases and prejudices. Each person has a set of experiences, beliefs, attitudes, and values that influence how that person receives, interprets, and evaluates incoming stimuli. If accurate and useful information is to be shared in an interview, an interviewer must be aware of his or her own perceptual processes so as to make accurate and objective interpretations. An otherwise qualified candidate for a job shouldn't be eliminated from consideration just because the interviewer has a bias against red-haired people, for example.

## Adapt to an Interviewee's Behavior

Skilled interviewers observe, evaluate, and adapt to the communication behavior of their interviewees. Because no two interviews—and no two interviewees—are exactly alike, interviewers adapt their communication behavior accordingly. A flexible communication style is a necessity. Interviewers should have predetermined plans, but they should not be thrown off balance if an interviewee suddenly turns the tables and asks, "How much money do *you* make for *your* job?"

Adaptability also includes the use of appropriate language and vocabulary. You should consciously choose language and vocabulary that interviewees will understand. Little is gained by the use of technical, ambiguous, or vague terms. Words should be straightforward, simple, and specific, but not so simple that interviewees feel "talked down" to. Empathy is important when determining the most appropriate language and vocabulary to use.

## Deal Wisely with Sensitive Content

When planning questions for an interview, consider possible sensitive topics and topics to be avoided. A question in a grievance interview such as "Why were you fired from your last job?" will provoke a defensive reaction.

Good judgment and choice of words play crucial roles. One ill-chosen question can destroy the positive and open communication developed in an opening. Effective interviewers avoid potentially troublesome topics and attempt to put interviewees at ease. They discuss sensitive issues *if and only if* they are related to the purpose of the interviews. When a sensitive subject must be discussed, experienced interviewers choose their words carefully; thus, the question "Why were you fired?" might be rephrased as "How would you describe your relationship with your previous supervisor?"

## Listen Effectively

The admonition to listen effectively has appeared frequently in this appendix. Effective listening is at the heart of any interview. No matter how well interviewers have prepared, the time will have been wasted if they are poor listeners. They need strong listening skills to make sure that they are receiving the kind and amount of information they need. They must be able to identify partial or irrelevant responses.

Highly developed listening skills also increase the ability to accurately perceive and interpret unintentional messages and beliefs, attitudes, and values. Interviewers learn a great deal from nonverbal, as well as verbal, communication.

## Record Information

The information accumulated from an interview is useless if it is not recorded completely and accurately. A partial or inaccurate report can lead to poor decisions and mistaken actions. Take appropriate, legible, written notes. If you plan to use a tape or digital recorder, ask the interviewee in advance for permission to use it.

## Ask Appropriate Questions

The success of most interviews will be determined by the quality of the questions asked during the conversation. Think of questions as "mental can openers" designed to reveal how the other person thinks and behaves. Earlier we discussed question types (open, closed, probing, and hypothetical) and question sequences (funnel, inverted funnel, and tunnel). Some of your questions should be planned. Other questions may evolve from the discussion. The best questions during an interview emerge from simply listening to what the other person is saying and then probing or following up on information and ideas verbalized.

If you are interviewing a job applicant, be aware that there are certain questions that you should *not* ask. These questions are inappropriate because they ask for information that either laws or court interpretations of laws suggest could lead to illegal discrimination. Here's a list of topics you should not bring up during an employment interview when you're asking the questions:[15]

| | |
|---|---|
| arrest records | insurance claims |
| less-than-honorable discharges | judgments |
| gender and marital status | citizenship or national origin |
| maiden name | mother's maiden name |
| number of children | place of birth |
| ages of children | disabilities |
| number of preschool children | handicap |
| spouse's name | illnesses or accidents |
| spouse's education | hospitalizations |
| spouse's income | current or prior medication/treatment |
| form of birth control | workers' compensation claims |
| family plans | weight |
| child care arrangements | religion |
| car accidents | church affiliation |
| lawsuits | social organizations |
| legal complaints | loans |
| ownership of home | wage assignments or garnishments |
| rental status | bankruptcy |
| length of residence | credit cards |
| date of high school graduation | form of transportation |
| age | ownership of car |
| sexual orientation | |

## Types of Interviews

An interview is a form of oral interaction that is structured to achieve a goal and that involves two or more people who take turns speaking and listening. In this appendix, we have focused on tips and strategies for being interviewed and for interviewing others. We've identified five types of interview situations: the information-gathering interview, the appraisal interview, the problem-solving interview, the persuasion interview, and the job interview.

### Terms to Know

| | | | |
|---|---|---|---|
| Interview | p. 410 | Problem-Solving Interview | p. 411 |
| Information-Gathering Interview | p. 410 | Persuasion Interview | p. 411 |
| Appraisal Interview | p. 411 | Job Interview | p. 411 |

## Phases of an Interview

All interviews have an opening, in which the interviewee is put at ease; a body, during which questions are asked and answered; and a conclusion, which brings the interview to a comfortable close.

### Terms to Know

| | | | |
|---|---|---|---|
| Open Question | p. 413 | Funnel Sequence | p. 413 |
| Closed Question | p. 413 | Inverted Funnel Sequence | p. 414 |
| Probing Question | p. 413 | Tunnel Sequence | p. 414 |
| Hypothetical Question | p. 413 | | |

## How to Be Interviewed for a Job

When you are seeking employment, start by becoming aware of your skills and abilities; then use your personal inventory to develop a well-written resumé. Focus on the needs of your prospective employer: Research the organization where you seek a job. During the interview, listen carefully to the questions asked by the interviewer and respond appropriately. After the interview, it may be appropriate to send a thank-you note to the interviewer.

### Terms to Know

| | | | |
|---|---|---|---|
| Resumé | p. 416 | E-Resumé | p. 421 |
| Personal Brand | p. 420 | Hyperlink | p. 421 |

## How to Be Interviewed in an Information-Gathering Interview

When preparing to be interviewed for an information-gathering interview, remember three primary tasks. First, prepare for the interview by reviewing information you think that the interviewer will ask you about. Second, listen closely to the questions you are being asked. Finally, respond appropriately by keeping answers direct and honest. Don't ramble. Observe the nonverbal responses of the interviewer to determine whether you are appropriately answering the questions.

## The Responsibilities of the Interviewer    p. 425

When you interview others, don't let your own biases and prejudices interfere with your job of listening and responding to the interviewee. Although it's useful to have a list of questions, be prepared to adapt to the interviewee's behavior. The best interviews have a spontaneous flow rather than a rigid structure. Don't ask illegal questions during a job interview and handle sensitive questions with tact and diplomacy. Listening well is the hallmark of an effective interviewer. Develop a strategy to record the information you gather from the interview. Finally, the key to any interview is the quality of the questions asked. As the interviewer, it is your responsibility to ask clear, appropriate, and answerable questions.

# APPLYING Principles for a Lifetime

### Principle One:
**Be aware of your communication with yourself and others.**

- Take inventory of your skills and abilities to help you determine the job opportunities and careers that are best for you.
- Use your analysis of your talents to help you develop your resumé.
- During an interview, monitor your messages to ensure that you are communicating clearly and effectively.

### Principle Two:
**Effectively use and interpret verbal messages.**

- Speak clearly and respond to each question you are asked during an interview.
- Use action-oriented words on your resumé and during an interview to describe your accomplishments.
- Organize your resumé to include key elements of your education, experience, and special qualifications.
- When conducting an employment interview, don't ask illegal or unethical questions.

### Principle Three:
**Effectively use and interpret nonverbal messages.**

- Pay special attention to your appearance when you interview for a job; dress conservatively and appear neat and well groomed.
- Speak with confidence, use appropriate eye contact, and communicate interest and enthusiasm during the interview.
- When you interview someone, monitor your interviewee's nonverbal messages for clues about the individual's personality and ability to work with people.
- As an interviewer, observe, evaluate, and then appropriately adapt to the communication behavior of the interviewee.

### Principle Four:
### Listen and respond thoughtfully to others.
- When you are interviewed for a job, be sure to stop, look, and listen to the questions and comments of the interviewer.
- Listen for both the details of the message and the major points or key ideas.
- When interviewing others, consider listening among your most important tasks.

### Principle Five:
### Appropriately adapt messages to others.
- Learn as much as you can about any prospective employer so that you can describe how your abilities best fit with the needs of the organization to which you are applying.
- Appropriately adapt your communication behavior during an interview, whether you are the interviewer or the interviewee, based on what you learn and observe during the interview.

## ASSESSING Your Skill

1. Resumé checklist. Before submitting your resumé to a prospective employer, use the following checklist to ensure that it meets the criteria of an effective resumé.

     ____ Name, address, and all contact numbers are accurate.

     ____ My career objective matches the advertised need of the employer.

     ____ My employment dates are accurate.

     ____ I've described the projects completed and skills I possess using action verbs.

     ____ My resumé is clearly formatted.

     ____ There are no spelling errors.

     ____ There are no grammar or punctuation errors.

2. Watch an information-gathering interview on *60 Minutes* or another news program. Identify the types of questions that the interviewer asks (open question, closed question, probing question, hypothetical question). Based on the information presented in this appendix, evaluate the effectiveness of both the interviewer and the interviewee.

# Sample Speeches for Discussion and Evaluation

# Informative Speech

## The Tarahumarans

### CHRISTY LIU[1]

On Feb 5, 2011, Belgian Stefaan Engels finished running a marathon every day for an entire year. NPR reports that on Feb 8, 2011, Stefaan the "marathon man" said he just wanted to prove it was possible and make the rest of us look bad. But little did he know that in Mexico, a group of people have made him look like the underachiever for centuries. The March 5, 2011, *New Straits Times* explains that a collection of tribes in northern Mexico, the Tarahumarans, are capable of running a mind-blowing 300 miles—without stopping. To put that into perspective, that's like running 12 marathons back to back to back to back . . . to back to back to back to back. . . . Christopher McDougall notes in his 2009 book *Born to Run* that the Tarahumara population totals about 70,000, and they have lived in complete isolation for over 400 years. Additionally, the tribes have never had a single occurrence of diabetes, cancer, or heart disease. Ever. In contrast, the March 16, 2011, *Wall Street Journal* reports that in this year alone, over two million Americans will die from the very same diseases that Tarahumaran tribes manage to avoid. In order to discover what the Tarahumarans' amazing achievements can teach our society and then reveal what we are all innately capable of, let's examine the characteristics and implications of the running ability, nutrition, and social structure of a tribe that an August 31, 2010, Discovery broadcast claims is "redefining the limits of human endurance."

In 1928, two Tarahumarans were entered in the Olympic marathon, but no one told them the race was only 26 miles, so when the Tarahumarans crossed the finish line, they kept going. When officials finally stopped them, the two men complained, "too short, too short!" Instead of making a "that's what she said" joke, let's examine their amazing running abilities and understand the implications on our innate physical potential. For the Tarahumarans, everyone—men and women, old and young—have the ability to run amazing distances—and they do it barefoot. As the previously mentioned *Born to Run* states, the longest distance ever run by a tribesman was 435 miles, which is about the distance between Normal, Illinois [where this presentation was delivered] and Canada. Furthermore, in 1995, a Tarahumaran named Juan Herrera competed in the Leadville Trail 100, an ultramarathon. Despite having never seen the course before, 55-year-old Juan Herrera *won* the race with a record time that stood for 11 years.

For us, the Tarahumara reveal our potential distance-running abilities. While NPR depicted the marathon man as extraordinary, none of the Tarahumarans had the heart to tell Stefaan that he wasn't that special (they also don't speak Dutch). A TED Talk posted on February 4, 2011, reveals that human beings evolved with sweat glands that cool us specifically to facilitate long-distance running. Thus, the previously cited Discovery Channel broadcast notes, at one point, everyone on the planet had the ability to run hundreds of miles. Yet the development of cars and civilization has turned our running abilities into our appendix: It exists, but we don't really need use it, and so we've lost the potential. Meanwhile, as Christopher McDougall states, the Tarahumarans have "never forgotten what it felt like to love running."

Anthropologist Brian Stross, who recently visited the Tarahumara, reveals in an October 27, 2010, personal interview that tribes gather together, drink gallons of their homemade corn beer, and eventually the women rip each other's tops off and wrestle. With that vivid mental picture, let's examine their diet and its implications for our food model.

The Tarahumara diet baffles most marathon runners. According to the previously cited Discovery Channel broadcast, 80% of their diet is corn, and occasionally, they get their protein by chasing a deer until it collapses from exhaustion. We evolved our unique sweating mechanism so we could do just that: chase prey until they overheat. The Tarahumarans never lost their running ability because they still hunt this way. The *Huffington Post* of March 16, 2011, notes that in a single run, Tarahumarans use more calories than an average Tour de France competitor. To fuel these runs, the Tarahumarans' simple diet of corn and beer provides hydration, calories, and carbs. Essentially, the Tarahumarans drink till they hit the ground, so that the next morning, they can get up and hit the ground running—occasionally topless.

For us, the Tarahumarans show that diet is much more complex than eating a certain number of calories. Michael Pollan laments in his 2008 book *In Defense of Food* that we see nutrition as similar to baking a cake: The right ingredients in the right ratio will magically make us healthy. While we're busy being the fat kids who love cake, the Tarahumarans have combined their food traditions and running abilities. The reason the Tarahumarans can maintain their unconventional diet and extraordinary health is because both evolved together. On the other hand, our solution is to use diet as a reaction to flaws in exercise, or vice versa. Clearly, not only should we seriously consider brewing corn beer, but perhaps we should work to develop a holistic understanding of healthiness, where food and health work cooperatively instead of reactively.

When the Tarahumarans participated in the Leadville 100 marathons, they were given flashlights. Having never before seen a flashlight, they held them straight up, like torches, which made lighting the path . . . difficult. So, in order to shed light on our two cultures, let's examine the Tarahumarans' original social structure, and then see the implications of Western influence.

Before modern society, the Tarahumarans exceeded our standards for social harmony. The *National Geographic* of November 2008 explains that tribes maintained a peaceful life, with a crime rate that was close to zero. Back in 1998, *MexConnect* of July 1 reported that Tarahumaras avoided lying to or cheating a fellow tribesman and exhibited a high standard of social tolerance. For example, in his 1978 book *Tarahumara of the Sierra Madre*, John Kennedy (other Kennedy) notes that a man named Marucio often wore women's clothing and made sexual advances towards men. While his moves were politely rejected, his tribe did not discriminate against his behavior. The Tarahumarans demonstrated a level of social harmony that has yet to be found in our supposedly civilized society.

Over time, modern influences impacted the Tarhumarans' culture. A 2001 documentary, *Voices of the Sierra Tarahumara*, explains that when a railroad built near one village introduced modern delights such as chocolates and cars, tribe members moved from close-knit communities to big cities to afford these luxuries. Today, there are no more long-distance runners in that village. The previously cited *Born to Run* contends that tribesmen affected by modernization were also caught cheating in marathons by taking short cuts. When Tarahumarans were introduced to modern society, it led to the breakdown of their community structure and sense of honesty, and eventually their running ability. Tarahumarans may indicate that close-knit social structures leave more room for honesty and appreciation of the community over the individual.

So the Tarahumara have taught us that it's possible to run down deer, drink gallons of beer, and love our peers. After examining the Tarahumara lifestyle and implications for our society, it is hoped that we have preserved a small piece of their lives and salvaged a part of our own. Our minds might have forgotten what we are physically capable of, but the Tarahumara remind us that from the very beginning, we were *all* born to run.

# Persuasive Speech

## The Misspoken Epidemic

### KYLE AKERMAN[2]

As Marco Melgoza stands with a placard outside of his school, not welcome to protest within its property, he has one wish on his mind: the end of torment by his classmates. At school, Marco is teased, ridiculed, and barraged with homophobic slurs. According to the October 14, 2010, issue of the *Advocate*, school officials believe they are doing all they can. But since reporting the issue, Marco has had his head slammed into the cement on 4 different occasions. And according to the *Christian Science Monitor* of September 29, 2010, Marco is just one of the nearly 85% of GLBT youth who report being physically or verbally harassed in the past year. The Winter 2010 *Palaestra* journal explains that current policies so broadly construe schools' discretion that teachers and administrators may arbitrarily choose not to report instances of abuse. So, while *ABCNews* of September 29, 2010, explains that "42 states . . . have adopted state laws on bullying prevention," these laws are ineffective because of the pervasive connotations associated with the word *bullying*: that bullies are just misguided kids and bullying itself is just a childhood rite of passage. Verbal and physical attacks are addressed under the blanket term *bullying*. And *gay bullying* poses even more definitional challenges because of its politically charged nature. Yet, if these cases had happened when the attackers were a few years older, their actions would be grounds for imprisonment. We must stop treating these attacks as *bullying*, instead calling them what they are: *assault* and *harassment*. In order to redefine *gay bullying* as what it is, let's first examine what has led to the inaccurate definition; next, sift through the results of this misnomer; before finally determining how to overcome what the Human Rights Campaign website on January 27, 2010, describes as "discrimination [that] can lead, and has led to, life-threatening violence and suicide."

The Department of Education's *Stop Bullying* website of September 2, 2010, contends that eight in ten LGBT students have been the victim of verbal harassment, and one in five is the victim of physical assault. Our antiquated definitions of *bullying* leave students without recourse in the face of these malicious attacks for two reasons: inappropriate framing of bullying and lack of school response.

Initially, the entanglement of gay bullying with the political divisiveness of homosexuality makes schools reluctant to act. According to the *Chicago Sun Times* of October 10, 2010, there is pressure from those opposed to gay rights to condemn the identity issues surrounding gay bullying as a "manipulative tactic to sway young people's views of homosexuality." Essentially, gay rights opponents equate protecting gay teens with pushing the perceived gay agenda. Thus, according to *Arizona Central* of January 4, 2011, "administrators often fail to dole out punishment for bullying recommended by handbooks." In focusing on the potential political ramifications of effective policies, we are treating students' safety as a political bargaining chip, rather than ensuring the safety and security that we should expect from our schools.

Additionally, in dealing with juveniles, the emphasis remains on education and rehabilitation of attackers, rather than protection of victims. And new policies, according to the previously cited *Palaestra* journal, reflect this logic by requiring that schools discipline bullies, without specifying what reactions are necessary. The harsh reality is that when bullies remain undeterred by slaps on the wrist from teachers and administrators, we leave the victims to fend for themselves, and GLBT individuals are 40% more likely to be punished than their attackers, according to the December 8, 2010, issue of *The Week*. Giving bullies the benefit of the doubt falsely justifies their actions and sends victims a message that they are less important than their tormentor.

According to the *Minnesota Independent* of December 28, 2010, Alex Merrit is a straight student in Minnesota who was harassed not by peers, but by his teachers. *Queerty* of December 24, 2010, reports two teachers taunted him, insisting that he enjoys wearing women's clothes and has "a thing for older men." Both gay and straight students are being harassed for their perceived sexual identity, to two ends: politically biased reactions and unacceptable learning environments. Initially, as political biases guide the punishment of bullies, victims are undermined, underrepresented, and completely unprotected. The November 9, 2010, school newspaper at St. Charles North High School in Illinois reports that during the school's diversity week, three students wore t-shirts promoting the murder of homosexuals. They weren't even asked by officials to change their clothes. And, the Human Rights Campaign website of October 29, 2010, quotes Clint McChance, a school board official, saying that the only way he would honor the deaths of gay youth is if every gay youth committed suicide. In relying on school officials to serve as the sole arbiters in these cases, we leave too much to political preferences—to the detriment of vulnerable students. Additionally, without other recourse, victims are left to fight for themselves if they are to feel safe, let alone learn, in their schools. *Change.org* of December 10, 2010, tells the story of a 16-year-old student repeatedly harassed with homophobic jeers and slurs until he threatened to attack his tormentors. He was suspended, while his bullies have seen no retribution. But like so many students, inaction by teachers and administrators left him little choice. The October 2, 2010, *New York Times* asserts that victims of bullying "face increased risk for depression, PTSD," and more than a quarter had suicidal thoughts. In forcing victims to stand up for themselves, and then punishing them for it, our schools are no better than the bullies themselves.

The Penn State *Counselor Education Newsletter* of March 2011 states that "youth hear anti-gay remarks approximately 25 times in an average school day, or more specifically, once every 14 minutes." It is time that we take a stand against the mislabeling of assault and harassment as simple bullying in two ways.

First, we need to stop talking about schoolyard bullying and start addressing assault and harassment as what it is. Help me support the Safe Schools Improvement Act introduced by Senator Bob Casey of Pennsylvania, which will provide a steadfast definition for *harassment* and disallow schools to look the other way. It requires schools to report bullying and harassment data to the Department of Education annually, at risk of losing federal funds. I have brought a petition addressed to Senator Casey. Please sign your name to demonstrate that we will not be satisfied with policies that allow school officials to turn a blind eye to the plight of their students.

Second, it's important for victims of bullying to know what their rights are if they are to have any hope of ending their torment. I have brought a handout clarifying what constitutes *assault* and *harassment* under the law, so that students know there are other options if their school administrators refuse to act. Please take one, take it back to your local school district, and insist that these definitions are posted visibly so that students are aware that they have legal rights at school. And, to ensure that administrators are held accountable for action in cases of bullying, we must ensure that each school is furnished with a Coplogic communication system, which allows students to anonymously submit cases of assault and harassment through an e-mail or text message, and automatically forwards this information to local law enforcement. While the police will not intervene without request, Coplogic creates a paper trail that schools cannot sidestep. In your handouts, I have information about this affordable software, which you can re-direct to local schools so we can offer students the legal safeguards they need and deserve.

Marco Melgoza still stands up honorably in defense of himself and his peers. Unfortunately, the names he is called and the tolerance level at his school continue to give him something to fight against. But until we begin to treat this violence as the criminal act it is, we can regretfully only expect more suicides and the continuation of hatred. By looking at the causes, effects, and solutions of this deplorable mislabeling, it is hoped that we can once again offer students a school experience that centers around education rather than survival.

# Endnotes

## Chapter 1

1. E. T. Klemmer and F. W. Snyder, "Measurement of Time Spent Communicating," *Journal of Communication* 20 (1972): 142.
2. We thank Tom Burkholder, University of Nevada, Las Vegas, for this idea.
3. J. C. Humes, *The Sir Winston Method: The Five Secrets of Speaking the Language of Leadership* (New York: William Morrow, 1991).
4. V. Marchant, "Listen Up!" *Time* (June 28, 1999): 72.
5. A. Vangelisti and J. Daly, "Correlates of Speaking Skills in the United States: A National Assessment," *Communication Education* 38 (1989): 132–143.
6. M. Cronin, ed., "The Need for Required Oral Communication Education in the Undergraduate General Education Curriculum," unpublished paper, 1993, available from the National Communication Association, Washington, DC.
7. J. Ayres and T. S. Hopf, "The Long-Term Effect of Visualization in the Classroom: A Brief Research Report," *Communication Education* 39 (1990): 75–78.
8. See J. C. McCroskey and M. Beatty, "The Communibiological Perspective: Implications for Communication in Instruction," *Communication Education* 49 (2000): 1; also see J. C. McCroskey, J. A. Daly, M. M. Martin, and M. J. Beatty, eds., *Communication and Personality: Trait Perspectives* (Cresskill, NJ: Hampton Press, 1998).
9. J. H. McConnell, *Are You Communicating? You Can't Manage without It* (New York: McGraw-Hill, 1995).
10. As quoted from G. N. Toogood, *The New Articulate Executive: Look, Act, and Sound Like a Leader* (New York: McGraw-Hill, 2010), 3.
11. J. L. Winsor, D. Curtis, and R. D. Stephens, "National Preferences in Business and Communication Education: A Survey Update," *Journal of the Association of Communication Administration* 3 (1997): 170–179. For a summary of the values and virtues of studying communication, see S. P. Morreale and J. C. Pearson, "Why Communication Education Is Important: The Centrality of the Discipline in the 21st Century," *Communication Education* 57.2 (2008): 224–240; also see S. P. Morreale, D. W. Worley, and B. Hugenberg, "The Basic Communication Course at Two- and Four-Year U.S. Colleges and Universities: Study VIII—The 40th Anniversary," *Communication Education* 59.4 (2010): 405–430; Hart Research Associates "Raising the Bar: Employers' Views on College Learning in the Wake of the Economic Downturn," Washington, DC Association of American Colleges and Universities (January 10, 2010); D. Sellnow, "Integrated Composition and Communication: Addressing the Needs of the 21st Century," paper presented at the Rhetoric Society of American annual conference, Minneapolis, Minnesota (May 2010).
12. The University of Wisconsin–River Falls, Career Services, "What Skills and Attributes Employers Seek When Hiring Students," <http://www.uwrf.edu/ccslskills/htm>, retrieved June 4, 2007; C. Luckenbaugh and K. Gray, "Employers Describe Perfect Job Candidate," Association of Colleges and Employers Survey, <http://www.naceweb.org/press/display.asp?year=2003&prid=169>, retrieved June 4, 2007; R. S. Hansen and K. Handson, "What Do Employers Really Want? Top Skills and Values Employers Seek from Job Seekers," <http://www.quintcareers.com/job_skills_values.html>, retrieved June 4, 2007. For evidence that communication skills can be developed, see R. F. Brown, C. L. Bylurd, J. A. Gueguen, C. Diamond, J. Eddington, and D. Kissane, "Developing Patient-Centered Communication Skills Training for Oncologists: Describing the Content and Efficacy of Training," *Communication Education* 59.3 (2010): 235–248; G. Sulcas and J. English, "A Case for Focus on Professional Communication Skills at Senior Undergraduate Level in Engineering and the Built Environment," *Southern African Linguistics & Applied Language Studies* 28.3 (2010): 219–226.
13. K. E. Davis and M. Todd, "Assessing Friendship: Prototypes, Paradigm Cases, and Relationship Description," in *Understanding Personal Relationships*, edited by S. W. Duck and D. Perlman (London: Sage, 1985); B. Wellman, "From Social Support to Social Network," in *Social Support: Theory, Research and Applications*, edited by I. G. Sarason and B. R. Sarason (Dordrecht, Netherlands: Nijhoff, 1985); R. Hopper, M. L. Knapp, and L. Scott, "Couples' Personal Idioms: Exploring Intimate Talk," *Journal of Communication* 31 (1981): 23–33.
14. M. Argyle and M. Hendershot, *The Anatomy of Relationships* (London: Penguin Books, 1985), 14.
15. D. Goleman, "Emotional Intelligence: Issues in Paradigm Building," in *The Emotionally Intelligent Workplace*, edited by C. Chemiss and D. Goleman (San Francisco: Jossey-Bass, 2001), 13.
16. V. Satir, *People Making* (Palo Alto, CA: Science and Behavior Books, 1972), 1.
17. M. Argyle, *The Psychology of Happiness* (London: Routledge, 2001).
18. J. Lynch, *The Broken Heart: The Medical Consequences of Loneliness* (New York: Basic Books, 1977).
19. D. P. Phillips, "Deathday and Birthday: An Unexpected Connection," in *Statistics: A Guide to the Unknown*, edited by J. M. Tanur (San Francisco: Holden-Day, 1972); also see F. Korbin and G. Hendershot, "Do Family Ties Reduce Mortality? Evidence from the United States 1968," *Journal of Marriage and the Family* 39 (1977): 737–746; K. Heller and K. S. Rook, "Distinguishing the Theoretical Functions of Social Ties: Implications of Support Interventions," in *Handbook of Personal Relationships* 2e, edited by S. W. Duck, K. Dindia, W. Ickes, R. Milardo, R. S. L. Mills, and B. R. Sarason (Chichester, England: Wiley, 1997); B. R. Samson, L. G. Sarason, and R. A. R. Gurung, "Close Personal Relationships and Health Outcomes: A Key to the Role of Social Support, in *Handbook of Personal Relationships 2e*, edited by S. W. Duck, K. Dindia, W. Ickes, R. Milardo, R. S. L. Mills, and B. R. Sarason (Chichester, England: Wiley, 1997); S. Duck, *Relating to Others* (Buckingham, England: Open University Press, 1999), 1.
20. Pamela Paul, "Does Facebook Make Someone Social Offline?" *New York Times*, (January 30, 2011): Style 8; also see S. Craig Watkins and H. Erin Lee, "Got Facebook? Investigating What's Social About Social Media," University of Texas at Austin (accessed January 31, 2011) <http://www.theyoungandthedigital.com/wp-content/uploads/2010/11/watkins_lee_facebookstudy-nov-18.pdf>.
21. F. E. X. Dance and C. Larson, *Speech Communication: Concepts and Behavior* (New York: Holt, Rinehart and Winston, 1972).
22. Dance and Larson, *Speech Communication*.
23. J. T. Masterson, S. A. Beebe, and N. H. Watson, *Invitation to Effective Speech Communication* (Glenview, IL: Scott, Foresman, 1989).
24. M. Gladwell, *Blink: The Power of Thinking without Thinking* (New York: Little, Brown, 2005).
25. This section is based on Masterson, Beebe, and Watson, *Invitation to Effective Speech Communication*. We are especially indebted to J. T. Masterson for this discussion.
26. See R. P. Wolff, *About Philosophy* (Upper Saddle River, NJ: Prentice Hall, 2000), 308–335.
27. C. S. Lewis, *The Abolition of Man* (New York: Macmillan, 1947); also see A. M. Nicholi Jr., *The Question of God: C. S. Lewis and Sigmund Freud*

*Debate God, Love, Sex, and the Meaning of Life* (New York: Free Press, 2002).

28. C. Christians and M. Traber, *Communication Ethics and Universal Values* (Beverly Hills, CA: Sage, 1997); also see S. Bok, *Common Values* (Columbia: University of Missouri Press, 2002).

29. Christians and Traber, *Communication Ethics and Universal Values.*

30. For an excellent discussion of comparative religions and the common principle of being other-oriented, see W. Ham, *Man's Living Religions* (Independence, MO: Herald Publishing House, 1966), 39–40.

31. See K. Armstrong, *Twelve Steps to a Compassionate Life* (New York: Knopf, 2011), 9.

32. For additional discussion of the ethical values taught in the world's religions, see H. Smith, *The World's Religions* (San Francisco: HarperSanFrancisco, 1991).

33. National Communication Association, "NCA Credo for Communication Ethics," 1999 (Accessed June 27, 2001), <http://www.natcom.org/conferences/Ethicslethicsconfcred099.htm>.

34. H. Lasswell, "The Structure and Function of Communication in Society," in *The Communication of Ideas*, edited by L. Bryson (New York: Institute for Religious and Social Studies, 1948), 37.

35. See V. E. Cronen, W. B. Pearce, and L. M. Harris, "The Coordinated Management of Meaning: A Theory of Communication," in *Human Communication Theory: Comparative Essays*, edited by F. E. X. Dance (New York: Harper & Row, 1982), 61–89.

36. N. S. Baron, *Always On: Language in an Online and Mobile World* (New York: Oxford University Press, 2008); also see D. Crystal, *txtng: The gr8 db8* (Oxford, England: Oxford University Press, 2008); S. Turkle, *Alone Together: Why We Expect More from Technology and Less from Each Other* (New York: Basic Books, 2011); M. A. Dourin, "College Students' Text Messaging, Use of Textese, and Literacy Skills," *Journal of Assisted Learning* 27.1 (2011): 67.

37. Watkins and Lee, "Got Facebook?"

38. A. M. Ledbetter, "Measuring Online Communication Attitude: Instrument Development and Validation," *Communication Monographs* 76.4 (2009): 463–486.

39. Watkins and Lee, "Got Facebook?"

40. Watkins and Lee, "Got Facebook?"

41. Y. Amichai-Hamburger, *The Social Net: Human Behavior in Cyberspace* (Oxford, England: Oxford University Press, 2005); K. Y. A. McKenna and J. A. Bargh, "Plan 9 from Cyberspace: The Implications of the Internet for Personality and Social Psychology," *Personality and Social Psychology Review 4* (2000): 57–75.

42. S. Turkle, *Alone Together*, 1.

43. R. Kraut, M. Patterson, V. Lundmark, S. Kiesler, M. Tridas, and W. Scherlis, "Internet Paradox: A Social Technology That Reduces Social Involvement and Psychological Well-Being?" *American Psychologist* 53 (1998): 1017–1031.

44. R. Kraut, S. Kiesler, B. Boneva, J. Cummings, V. Helgeson, and A. Crawford, "Internet Paradox Revisited," *Journal of Social Issues* 58 (2002): 49–74; P. E. N. Howard, L. Raine, and S. Jones, "Days and Nights on the Internet: The Impact of a Diffusing Technology," *American Behavioral Scientist* 45 (2001): 383–404; M. A. Mazur and R. J. Bums, "Perceptions of Relational Interdependence in Online Relationships: The Effects of Communication Apprehension and Introversion," *Communication Research Reports* 17.4 (2000): 397–406.

45. B. Jin and J. F. Pena, "Mobile Communication in Romantic Relationships: Mobile Phone Use, Relational Uncertainty, Love, Commitment, and Attachment Styles," *Communication Reports* 23.1 (2010): 39–51.

46. L. Barker, R. Edwards, C. Gaines, K. Gladney, and F. Holley, "An Investigation of Proportional Time Spent in Various Communication Activities of College Students," *Journal of Applied Communication Research* 8 (1981): 101–109.

47. D. Barnlund, *Interpersonal Communication: Survey and Studies* (Boston: Houghton Mifflin, 1968).

48. See, for instance, C. R Berger and J. J. Bradac, *Language and Social Knowledge: Uncertainty in Interpersonal Relations* (London: Arnold, 1982).

49. O. Wiio, *Wiio's Laws—and Some Others* (Espoo, Finland: Welin-Goos, 1978).

50. T. Watzlawick, J. B. Bavelas, and D. Jackson, *The Pragmatics of Human Communication* (New York: W. W. Norton, 1967).

51. S. B. Shimanoff, *Communication Rules: Theory and Research* (Beverly Hills, CA: Sage, 1980).

52. For an excellent review of intrapersonal communication theory and research, see D. Voate, *Intrapersonal Communication: Different Voices, Different Minds* (Hillsdale, NJ: Lawrence Erlbaum, 1994).

53. D. Quinn, *My Ishmael* (New York: Bantam Books, 1996).

54. B. Plester and C. Wood, "Exploring Relationships between Traditional and New Media Literacies: British Preteen Texters at School," *Journal of Computer-Mediated Communication* 14 (2009): 1108–1129.

55. Robert Fulghum, *All I Really Need to Know I Learned in Kindergarten* (New York: Ballantine Books, 1988).

56. Barker et al., "An Investigation of Proportional Time."

57. We appreciate and acknowledge our friend and colleague M. Redmond for his contributions to our understanding of interpersonal communication. For more information, see S. A. Beebe, S. J. Beebe, and M. V. Redmond, *Interpersonal Communication: Relating to Others* 6e (Boston: Pearson, 2011).

58. For an excellent discussion of the power of dialogue to enrich the quality of communication, see D. Yankelovich, *The Magic of Dialogue: Transforming Conflict into Cooperation* (New York: Simon & Schuster, 1999).

59. S. A. Beebe and J. T. Masterson, *Communicating in Small Groups: Principles and Practices* 10e (Boston: Pearson, 2012).

60. For a discussion of group size, see Beebe and Masterson, *Communicating in Small Groups.*

61. M. S. Poole and I. Ahmed, "Group Decision Support Systems," in *21st Century Communication: A Reference Handbook*, edited by W. Eadie (Thousand Oaks, CA: Sage, 2010); also see M. C. Poole, "Collaboration, Integration, and Transformation: Directions for Research on Communication and Information Technologies," *Journal of Computer-Mediated Communication* 14 (2009): 753–763.

## Chapter 2

1. S. R. Covey, *The Seven Habits of Highly Effective People* rev. ed. (New York: Simon & Schuster, 2004), 67.

2. D. W. Johnson, *Reaching Out: Interpersonal Effectiveness and Self-Actualization* 10e (Boston: Allyn & Bacon, 2008), 51.

3. S. E. Wood, E. Green Wood, and D. Boyd, *Mastering the World of Psychology* 4e (Boston: Pearson, 2010), 115.

4. R. A. Baron, N. R. Branscombe, and D. R. Byrne, *Social Psychology* 12e (Boston: Allyn & Bacon, 2009).

5. D. Layder, *Social and Personal Identity: Understanding YourSelf* (London: Sage, 2004), 7–19.

6. K. Horney, *Neurosis and Human Growth* (New York: W. W. Norton, 1991), 17.

7. A. Elliott, *Concepts of the Self* 2e (Cambridge, UK: Polity Press, 2007); K. J. Gergen, *The Saturated Self: Dilemmas of Identity in Contemporary Life* (New York: Basic Books, 2000); B. Goss, *Processing Communication: Information Processing in Intrapersonal Communication* (Belmont, CA: Wadsworth, 1982), 72.

8. J. T. Masterson, S. A. Beebe, and N. H. Watson, *Invitation to Effective Speech Communication* (Glenview, IL: Scott, Foresman, 1989).

9. W. James, *Principles of Psychology* (New York: Henry Holt, 1890).

10. G. Bukobza, "The Epistemological Basis of Selfhood," *New Ideas in Psychology* 25 (2007): 37–65.

11. Bukobza, "The Epistemological Basis of Selfhood," 39.

12. For more information on self-concept and culture, see C. Kanagawa, S. E. Cross, and H. R. Markus, "'Who Am I?' The Cultural Psychology of the Conceptual Self," *Personality and Social Psychology Bulletin* 27 (2001): 90–103; S. Kitayama, H. R. Markus, H. Matsumoto, and V. Norasakkunkit, "Individual and Collective Processes in the Construction of the Self: Self-Enhancement in the U.S. and Self-Criticism in Japan," *Journal of Personality and Social Psychology* 72 (1997): 1245–1267; D. Watkins et al., "Cultural Dimensions, Gender, and the Nature of Self-Concept: A 14-Country Study," *International Journal of Psychology* 33 (1998): 17–31.

13. T. Raiten-D'Antonio, *Ugly as Sin: The Truth about How We Look and Finding Freedom from Self-Hatred* (Deerfield Beach, FL: Health Communications Inc., 2010); M. P. Levine and S. K. Murnen, "Everybody Knows That Mass Media Are a Cause of Eating Disorders: A Critical Review of Evidence for a Causal Link Between Media, Negative Body Image, and Disordered Eating in Females," *Journal of Social and Clinical Psychology* 28 (2009): 9–42; J. S. Aubrey, "The Impact of Sexually Objectifying Media Exposure on Negative Body Emotions and Sexual Self-Perceptions: Investigating the Mediating Role of Body Self-Consciousness," *Mass Communication and Society* 10 (2007): 1–23; B. Harper and M. Tiggemann, "The Effect of Thin Ideal Media Images on Women's Self-Objectification, Mood, and Body Image," *Sex Roles* 58 (2007): 649–657; M. Krcmar, S. Giles, and D. Helme, "Understanding the Process: How Mediated and Peer Norms Affect Young Women's Body Esteem," *Communication Quarterly* 56 (2008): 111–130; C. Heldman, "Out-of-Body Image," *Ms.* (Spring 2008), 52–55; H. Dohnt and M. Tiggemann, "The Contribution of Peer and Media Influences to the Development of Body Satisfaction and Self-Esteem in Young Girls: A Prospective Study," *Developmental Psychology* 42 (2006): 929–936; S. Steese, M. Dollette, W. Phillips, E. Hossfeld, G. Matthews, and G. Taormina, "Understanding Girls' Circle as an Intervention on Perceived Social Support, Body Image, Self-Efficacy, Locus of Control, and Self-Esteem," *Adolescence* 41 (2006): 55–74.

14. National Institute on Media and the Family, "Shocking Dieting Statistics," May 19, 2010 <www.healthkicker.com>.

15. S. Grogan, *Body Image: Understanding Body Dissatisfaction in Men, Women, and Children* (New York: Psychology Press, 2007); S. Cahill and A. Mussap, "Emotional Reactions Following Exposure to Idealized Bodies Predict Unhealthy Body Change Attitudes and Behaviors in Women and Men," *Journal of Psychosomatic Research* 62 (2007): 631–639.

16. C. H. Cooley, *Human Nature and the Social Order* (New York: Scribner's, 1912).

17. G. H. Mead, *Mind, Self, and Society* (Chicago: University of Chicago Press, 1934).

18. R. M. Dailey, "Testing Components of Confirmation: How Acceptance and Challenge from Mothers, Fathers, and Siblings Are Related to Adolescent Self-Concept," *Communication Monographs* 77 (2010): 592–617.

19. J. Stewart, K. E. Zediker, and S. Witteborn, *Together: Communicating Interpersonally* 6e (Los Angeles: Roxbury, 2005).

20. M. L. Hecht, M. J. Collier, and S. A. Ribeau, *African American Communication: Ethnic Identity and Cultural Interpretation* (Newbury Park, CA: Sage, 1993).

21. J. N. Martin and T. K. Nakayama, *Experiencing Intercultural Communication* 4e (New York: McGraw-Hill, 2010).

22. D. K. Ivy, *GenderSpeak: Personal Effectiveness in Gender Communication* 5e (Boston: Pearson, 2012); J. E. O. Blakemore and R. E. Centers, "Characteristics of Boys' and Girls' Toys," *Sex Roles* 53 (2005): 619–634; T. L. Kuther and E. McDonald, "Early Adolescents' Experiences with and Views of Barbie," *Adolescence* 39 (2004): 39–51; M. A. Messner, "Barbie Girls versus Sea Monsters: Children Constructing Gender," *Gender and Society* 14 (2000): 765–784.

23. J. E. Stake, "Gender Differences and Similarities in Self-Concept within Everyday Life Contexts," *Psychology of Women Quarterly* 16 (1992): 349–363.

24. S. Lamb, L. M. Brown, and M. Tappan, *Saving Our Sons from Superheroes, Slackers, and Other Media Stereotypes* (New York: St. Martin's, 2009); S. Lamb and L. M. Brown, *Packaging Girlhood: Rescuing Our Daughters from Marketers' Schemes* (New York: St. Martin's, 2006).

25. G. Steinem, *Revolution from Within: A Book of Self-Esteem* (Boston: Little, Brown, 1993), 26.

26. J. D. Campbell, P. D. Trapnell, S. J. Heine, I. M. Katz, L. F. Lavallee, and D. R. Lehman, "Self-Concept Clarity: Measurement, Personality Correlates, and Cultural Boundaries," *Journal of Personality and Social Psychology* 70 (1996): 141–156.

27. For more information on self-concept clarity, see J. D. Campbell, "Self-Esteem and Clarity of the Self-Concept," *Journal of Personality and Social Psychology* 59 (1990): 538–549; A. Hucker, A. J. Mussap, and M. M. McCabe, "Self-Concept Clarity and Women's Sexual Well-Being," *Canadian Journal of Human Sexuality* 19 (2010): 67–77; G. W. Lewandowski, N. Nardone, and A. J. Raines, "The Role of Self-Concept Clarity in Relationship Quality," *Self & Identity* 9 (2010): 416–433; M. N. Bechtoldt, C. K. W. De Dreu, B. A. Nijstad, and D. Zapf, "Self-Concept Clarity and the Management of Social Conflict," *Journal of Personality* 78 (2010): 539–574; J. Lodi-Smith and B. W. Roberts, "Getting to Know Me: Social Role Experiences and Age Differences in Self-Concept Clarity During Adulthood," *Journal of Personality* 78 (2010): 1383–1410; C. K. W. De Dreu and D. van Knippenberg, "The Possessive Self as a Barrier to Conflict Resolution: Effects of Mere Ownership, Process Accountability, and Self-Concept Clarity on Competitive Cognitions and Behavior," *Journal of Personality and Social Psychology* 89 (2005): 345–357.

28. L. Rill, E. Baiocchi, M. Hopper, K. Denker, and L. N. Olson, "Exploration of the Relationship Between Self-Esteem, Commitment, and Verbal Aggressiveness in Romantic Dating Relationships," *Communication Reports* 22 (2009): 102–113; T. DeHart and B. W. Pelham, "Fluctuations in State Implicit Self-Esteem in Response to Daily Negative Events," *Journal of Experimental Social Psychology* 43 (2007): 157–165.

29. Ivy, *GenderSpeak.*

30. G. D. Webster, L. A. Kirkpatrick, J. B. Nezlek, C. V. Smith, and E. L. Paddock, "Different Slopes for Different Folks: Self-Esteem Instability and Gender as Moderators of the Relationship between Self-Esteem and Attitudinal Aggression," *Self and Identity* 6 (2007): 74–94; B. W. Pelham, S. L. Koole, C. D. Hardin, J. J. Hetts, E. Seah, and T. DeHart, "Gender Moderates the Relation between Implicit and Explicit Self-Esteem," *Journal of Experimental Social Psychology* 41 (2005): 84–89.

31. American Association of University Women, *Shortchanging Girls, Shortchanging America* (Washington, DC: AAUW Educational Foundation, 1991).

32. M. Sadker and D. Sadker, *Failing at Fairness: How America's Schools Cheat Girls* (New York: Scribner's, 1994), 77.

33. L. Muehlbronner, "Girls, Sports, and Self-Esteem," April 19, 2011 <www.kidsportsmagazine.com>; J. Frost and S. J. McKelvie, "The Relationship of Self-Esteem and Body Satisfaction to Exercise Activity for Male and Female Elementary School, High School, and University Students," *Athletic Insight: The Online Journal of Sport Psychology* 7 (2005): 36–45; E. Daniels and C. Leaper, "A Longitudinal Investigation of Sport Participation, Peer Acceptance, and Self-Esteem Among Adolescent Girls and Boys," *Sex Roles* 55 (2006): 875–880.

34. L. Smith LeBeau and J. T. Buckingham, "Relationship Between Social Comparison Tendencies, Insecurity, and Perceived Relationship Quality," *Journal of Social and Personal Relationships* 25 (2008): 71–86; C. McFarland, R. Beuhler, R. von Ruti, L. Nguyen, and C. Alvaro, "The Impact of Negative Moods on Self-Enhancing Cognitions: The Role of Reflective versus Ruminative Mood Orientations," *Journal of Personality and Social Psychology* 93 (2007): 728–750; A. M. Guest, "Cultures of Childhood and Psychosocial Characteristics: Self-Esteem and Social Comparison in Two Distinct Communities," *Ethos* 35 (2007): 1–32; B. Butzer and N. A. Kuiper, "Relationships Between the Frequency of Social Comparisons and Self-Concept Clarity, Intolerance of Uncertainty, Anxiety, and Depression," *Personality and Individual Differences* 41 (2006): 167–176; L. Festinger, "A Theory of Social Comparison Processes," *Human Relations* 2 (1954): 117–140.

35. D. Smeesters, T. Mussweiler, and N. Mandel, "The Effects of Thin and Heavy Media Images on Overweight and Underweight Consumers: Social Comparison Processes and Behavioral Implications," *Journal of Consumer Research* 36 (2010): 930–949; S. H. Sohn, "Sex Differences in Social Comparison and Comparison Motives in Body Image Process," *North American Journal of Psychology* 12 (2010): 481–500; K. N. Kubic and R. M. Chory, "Exposure to Television Makeover Programs and Perceptions of Self," *Communication Research Reports* 24 (2007): 283–291.

36. M. M. Martin and J. W. Gentry, "Stuck in the Model Trap," in *Taking Sides: Clashing Views on Controversial Issues in Mass Media and Society* 8e, edited by A. Alexander and J. Hanson (Dubuque, IA: McGraw-Hill/Dushkin, 2005), 52–61.

37. P. M. Valkenburg, J. Peter, and A. P. Schouten, "Friend Networking Sites and Their Relationship to Adolescents' Well-Being and Social Self-Esteem," *CyberPsychology & Behavior* 9 (2006): 484–490.

38. N. B. Ellison, C. Steinfield, and C. Lampe, "The Benefits of Facebook 'Friends': Social Capital and College Students' Use of Online Social Networking Sites," *Journal of Computer-Mediated Communication* 12 (2007): 1143–1168.

39. N. Haferkamp and N. C. Kramer, "Social Comparison 2.0: Examining the Effects of Online Profiles on Social-Networking Sites," *CyberPsychology, Behavior, & Social Networking* 14 (2011): 309–314.

40. A. L. Gonzales and J. T. Hancock, "Mirror, Mirror on My Facebook Wall: Effects of Exposure to Facebook on Self-Esteem," *CyberPsychology, Behavior, & Social Networking* 14 (2011): 79–83.

41. Gonzales and Hancock, "Mirror, Mirror on My Facebook Wall," 81–82.

42. L. Jussim and K. D. Harber, "Teacher Expectations and Self-Fulfilling Prophecies: Knowns and Unknowns, Resolved and Unresolved Controversies," *Personality and Social Psychology Review* 9 (2005): 131–155; L. Jussim, K. D. Harber, J. T. Crawford, T. R. Cain, and F. Cohen, "Social Reality Makes the Social Mind: Self-Fulfilling Prophecy, Stereotypes, Bias, and Accuracy," *Interaction Studies* 6 (2005): 85–102; S. Madon, M. Guyll, R. Spoth, and J. Willard, "Self-Fulfilling Prophecies," *Psychological Science* 15 (2004): 837–845.

43. B. M. DiPaola, M. E. Roloff, and K. M. Peters, "College Students' Expectations of Conflict Intensity: A Self-Fulfilling Prophecy," *Communication Quarterly* 58 (2010): 59–76; J. Hattie, *Self-Concept* (Hillsdale, NJ: Lawrence Erlbaum, 1992).

44. U. Orth, K. H. Trzesniewski, and R. W. Robins, "Self-Esteem Development from Young Adulthood to Old Age: A Cohort-Sequential Longitudinal Study," *Journal of Personality and Social Psychology* 98 (2010): 645–658.

45. A. Eryilmaz and H. Atak, "Investigation of Starting Romantic Intimacy in Emerging Adulthood in Terms of Self-Esteem, Gender, and Gender Roles," *Educational Sciences: Theory & Practice* 11 (2011): 595–600; S. Zhang and L. Stafford, "Perceived Face Threat of Honest but Hurtful Evaluative Messages in Romantic Relationships," *Western Journal of Communication* 72 (2008): 19–39; M. H. Kernis, C. E. Lakey, and W. L. Heppner, "Secure versus Fragile High Self-Esteem as a Predictor of Verbal Defensiveness: Converging Findings Across Three Different Markers," *Journal of Personality* 76 (2008): 477–512.

46. J. M. Twenge, *Generation Me: Why Today's Young Americans Are More Confident, Assertive, Entitled—and More Miserable Than Ever Before* (New York: Free Press, 2006), 2.

47. J. M. Twenge, S. Konrath, J. D. Foster, W. K. Campbell, and B. J. Bushman, "Egos Inflating over Time: A Cross-Temporal Meta-Analysis of the Narcissistic Personality Inventory," *Journal of Personality* 76 (2008): 875–901; S. Konrath, J. M. Twenge, W. K. Campbell, J. D. Foster, and B. J. Bushman, "This Generation Is More Special Than the Others: A Cross-Temporal Meta-Analysis of the Narcissistic Personality Inventory," paper presented at the conference on Educating the Next Generation of College Students, University of San Diego, February 27, 2007.

48. S. Mehdizadeh, "Self-Presentation 2.0: Narcissism and Self-Esteem on Facebook," *CyberPsychology, Behavior, & Social Networking* 13 (2010): 357–364.

49. S. M. Bergman, M. E. Fearrington, S. W. Davenport, and J. Bergman, "Millennials, Narcissism, and Social Networking: What Narcissists Do on Social Networking Sites and Why," *Personality & Individual Differences* 50 (2011): 706–711.

50. For other research as well as popular literature on narcissism and self-esteem, see J. M. Twenge and W. K. Campbell, *The Narcissism Epidemic: Living in the Age of Entitlement* (New York: Free Press, 2011); J. K. Bosson, C. E. Lakey, W. K. Campbell, V. Zeigler-Hill, C. H. Jordan, and M. H. Kernis, "Untangling the Links Between Narcissism and Self-Esteem: A Theoretical and Empirical Review," *Social and Personality Psychology Compass* 2 (2008): 1415–1439; V. Zeigler-Hill, "Discrepancies Between Implicit and Explicit Self-Esteem: Implications for Narcissism and Self-Esteem Instability," *Journal of Personality* 74 (2006): 119–144; E. Hoover, "Here's You Looking at You, Kid: Study Says Many Students Are Narcissists," *The Chronicle of Higher Education*

(March 9, 2007); A. L. Ball, "The New and Improved Self-Esteem," *O: The Oprah Winfrey Magazine* (January 2008): 164–265, 217–219; P. Marx, "Can You Have Too Much Self-Esteem?" *O: The Oprah Winfrey Magazine* (May 2004): 249; C. Sedikides, E. A. Rudich, A. P. Gregg, M. Kumashiro, and C. Rusbult, "Are Normal Narcissists Psychologically Healthy?: Self-Esteem Matters," *Journal of Personality and Social Psychology* 87 (2004): 400–416; R. F. Baumeister, B. J. Bushman, and W. K. Campbell, "Self-Esteem, Narcissism, and Aggression: Does Violence Result from Low Self-Esteem or from Threatened Egotism?" *Current Directions in Psychological Science* 9 (2000): 26–29.

51. Goss, *Processing Communication*, 72.

52. E. J. Oliver, D. Marklan, and J. Hardy, "Interpretation of Self-Talk and Post-Lecture Affective States of Higher Education Students: A Self-Determination Theory Perspective," *British Journal of Educational Psychology* 80 (2010): 307–323; J. Hardy, R. Roberts, and L. Hardy, "Awareness and Motivation to Change Negative Self-Talk," *Sport Psychologist* 23 (2009): 435–450; L. C. Lederman, "The Impact of Gender on the Self and Self-Talk," in *Women and Men Communicating: Challenges and Changes* 2e, edited by L. P. Arliss and D. J. Borisoff (Prospect Heights, IL: Waveland, 2001), 78–89; J. R. Johnson, "The Role of Inner Speech in Human Communication," *Communication Education* 33 (1984): 211–222; J. Ayres, "The Power of Positive Thinking," *Communication Education* 37 (1988): 289–296.

53. A. T. Latinjak, M. Torregrosa, and J. Renom, "Combining Self Talk and Performance Feedback: Their Effectiveness with Adult Tennis Players," *Sport Psychologist* 25 (2011): 18–31; N. Zourbanos et al., "The Social Side of Self-Talk: Relationships Between Perceptions of Support Received from the Coach and Athletes' Self-Talk," *Psychology of Sport & Exercise* 12 (2011): 407–414; A. V. Tovares, "Managing the Voices: Athlete Self-Talk as a Dialogic Process," *Journal of Language & Social Psychology* 29 (2010): 261–277.

54. C. J. Mruk, *Self-Esteem: Research, Theory, and Practice* 3e (New York: Springer, 2006).

55. B. R. Schlenkere, S. A. Wowra, R. M. Johnson, and M. L. Miller, "The Impact of Imagined Audiences on Self-Appraisals," *Personal Relationships* 15 (2008): 247–260; see J. Ayres and T. S. Hopf, "The Long-Term Effect of Visualization in the Classroom: A Brief Research Report," *Communication Education* 39 (1990): 75–78; J. Ayres and T. S. Hopf, "Visualization: Is It More Than Extra-Attention?" *Communication Education* 38 (1989): 1–5.

56. J. Ayres, T. S. Hopf, and D. M. Ayres, "An Examination of Whether Imaging Ability Enhances the Effectiveness of an Intervention Designed to Reduce Speech Anxiety," *Communication Education* 43 (1994): 252–258.

57. P. R. Hinton, *The Psychology of Interpersonal Perception* (New York: Routledge, 1993).

58. E. B. Goldstein, *Sensation and Perception* 8e (Belmont, CA: Wadsworth); A. S. Rancer, F. F. Jordan-Jackson, and D. A. Infante, "Observers' Perceptions of an Interpersonal Dispute as a Function of Mode of Presentation," *Communication Reports* 16 (2003): 35–48; D. A. Kenny, *Interpersonal Perception: A Social Relations Analysis* (New York: Guilford Press, 1994).

59. J. Kornfield, *The Wise Heart: A Guide to the Universal Teachings of Buddhist Psychology* (New York: Bantam Dell/Random House, 2008), excerpted in "The One-Minute Miracle," *O: The Oprah Winfrey Magazine* (June 2008): 140.

60. E. S. Byers, "Beyond the Birds and the Bees and Was It Good for You? Thirty Years of Research on Sexual Communication," *Canadian Psychology* 52 (2011): 20–28; B. Fink, P. J. Matts, S. Roder, R. Johnson, and M. Burquest, "Differences in Visual Perception of Age and Attractiveness of Female Facial and Body Skin," *International Journal of Cosmetic Science* 33 (2011): 126–131; S. F. O'Neil and M. A. Webster, "Adapation and the Perception of Facial Age," *Visual Cognition* 19 (2011): 534–550.

61. D. J. Schneider, A. H. Hastorf, and P. C. Ellsworth, *Person Perception* 2e (Reading, MA: Addison-Wesley, 1979).

62. D. T. Kenrick, S. L. Neuberg, and R. B. Cialdini, *Social Psychology: Goals in Interaction* 5e (Boston: Pearson, 2009).

63. M. L. Shier, M. E. Jones, and J. R. Graham, "Perspectives of Employed People Experiencing Homelessness of Self and Being

Homeless: Challenging Socially Constructed Perceptions and Stereotypes," *Journal of Sociology & Social Welfare* 37 (2010): 13–37; A. J. Kosor and L. Kendal-Wilson, "Older Homeless Women: Reframing the Stereotype of the Bag Lady," *Affilia* 17 (2002): 354–370.

64. M. Muchnik, "Gender Stereotypes in the Language of *Be My Knife* by David Grossman," *Text & Talk* 30 (2010): 553–570; D. L. Oswald, "Gender Stereotypes and Women's Reports of Liking and Ability in Traditionally Masculine and Feminine Occupations," *Psychology of Women Quarterly* 32 (2008): 196–203; C. Hoessler and A. L. Chasteen, "Does Aging Affect the Use of Shifting Standards?" *Experimental Aging Research* 34 (2008): 1–12.

65. C. N. Macrae, G. V. Bodenhausen, A. B. Milne, and J. Jetten, "Out of Mind but Back in Sight: Stereotypes on the Rebound," *Journal of Personality and Social Psychology* 67 (1994): 808–817.

66. This chapter benefited from the fine scholarship and work of M. V. Redmond, coauthor of *Interpersonal Communication: Relating to Others* 6e (Boston: Pearson, 2011).

## Chapter 3

1. "World Briefing, Australia: And It Came 2 Pass," *New York Times* (October 7, 2005): 8.

2. L. D. Rosen, J. Chang, L. Erwin, L. M. Carrier, and N. A. Cheever, "The Relationship between 'Textisms' and Formal and Informal Writing Among Young Adults," *Communication Research* 37 (2010): 420; F-Y. F. Wei and Y. K. Wang, "Students' Silent Messages: Can Teacher Verbal and Nonverbal Immediacy Moderate Student Use of Text Messaging in Class?" *Communication Education* 59 (2010): 475–496; A. Angster, M. Frank, and D. Lester, "An Exploratory Study of Students' Use of Cell Phones, Texting, and Social Networking Sites," *Psychological Reports* 107 (2010): 402–404; R. Rettie, "Texters Not Talkers: Phone Call Aversion Among Mobile Phone Users," *Psychology Journal* 5 (2007): 33–57; D. Harley, S. Winn, S. P. Pemberton, and P. Wilcox, "Using Texting to Support Students' Transition to University," *Innovations in Education and Teaching International* 44 (2007): 229–241; T. Igarashi, J. Takai, and T. Yoshida, "Gender Differences in Social Network Development via Mobile Phone Text Messages: A Longitudinal Study," *Journal of Social and Personal Relationships* 22 (2005): 691–713; C. Thurlow, "Generation Txt? The Sociolinguistics of Young People's Text Messaging," *Discourse Analysis Online* 1 (2003): 1.

3. K. H. Turner, "Flipping the Switch: Code-Switching from Text Speak to Standard English," *English Journal* 98 (2009): 60–65; L. Thompson and J. Cupples, "Seen and Not Heard? Text Messaging and Digital Sociality," *Social and Cultural Geography* 9 (2008): 95–108.

4. "College Graduates Aren't Ready for the Real World," *The Chronicle of Higher Education* (February 18, 2005): B11.

5. B. Spitzberg and J. P. Dillard, "Social Skills and Communication," in *Interpersonal Communication Research: Advances Through Meta-Analysis*, edited by M. Allen, R. W. Preiss, B. M. Gayle, and N. Burrell (Mahwah, NJ: Lawrence Erlbaum, 2002), 89–107.

6. B. L. Whorf, "Science and Linguistics," in *Language, Thought, and Reality*, edited by J. B. Carroll (Cambridge: Massachusetts Institute of Technology Press, 1956).

7. R. F. Verderber and K. S. Verderber, "Elements of Language," in *Making Connections: Readings in Relational Communication* 5e, edited by K. M. Galvin (New York: Oxford University Press, 2011), 51–60.

8. *Oxford Desk Dictionary and Thesaurus, American Edition* (New York: Oxford University Press, 2007).

9. S-T. Kousta, G. Vigliocco, D. P. Vinson, M. Andrews, and E. Del Campo, "The Representation of Abstract Words: Why Emotion Matters," *Journal of Experimental Psychology* 140 (2011): 14–34; D. A. Stapel and G. R. Semin, "The Magic Spell of Language: Linguistics Categories and Their Perceptual Consequences," *Journal of Personality and Social Psychology* 93 (2007): 23–33; A. M. Glenberg, M. Sato, L. Cattaneo, L. Riggio, D. Palumbo, and G. Buccino, "Processing Abstract Language Modulates Motor System Activity," *Quarterly Journal of Experimental Psychology* 61 (2008): 905–919.

10. L. M. Bauer, E. L. Olheiser, and J. Altarriba, "Word Type Effects in False Recall: Concrete, Abstract, and Emotion Word Critical Lures," *American Journal of Psychology* 122 (2009): 469–481; A. Parker and N.

Dagnall, "Concreteness Effects Revisited: The Influence of Dynamic Visual Noise on Memory for Concrete and Abstract Words," *Memory* 17 (2008): 397–410.

11. A. G. Smith, ed., *Communication and Culture* (New York: Holt, Rinehart and Winston, 1966).

12. C. Condon, M. Perry, and R. O'Keefe, "Denotation and Connotation in the Human-Computer Interface: The 'Save As . . .' Command," *Behaviour & Information Technology* 23 (2004): 21–31.

13. H. Tanaka, "Politeness in a Japanese Intra-Organisational Meeting: Honorifics and Socio-Dialectal Code Switching," *Journal of Asian Pacific Communication* 21 (2011): 60–76; A. De Fina, "Code-Switching and the Construction of Ethnic Identity in a Community of Practice," *Language in Society* 36 (2007): 371–392; E. Richardson, "'She Was Workin Like Foreal': Critical Literacy and the Discourse Practices of African American Females in the Age of Hip Hop," *Discourse & Society* 18 (2007): 789–809.

14. R. R. Heredia and J. Altarriba, "Bilingual Language Mixing: Why Do Bilinguals Code-Switch?" *Current Directions in Psychological Science* 10 (2001): 164–168; F. Grosjean and J. L. Miller, "Going In and Out of Languages: An Example of Bilingual Flexibility," *Psychological Science* 5 (1994): 201–206.

15. J. Close Conoley, "Sticks and Stones Can Break My Bones and Words Can Really Hurt Me," *School Psychology Review* 37 (2008): 217–220.

16. Y. Osward, *Every Word Has Power: Switch on Your Language and Turn on Your Life* (New York: Atria Books/Simon & Schuster, 2008); P. Denton, *The Power of Our Words: Teacher Language That Helps Children Learn* (Turners Falls, MA: Northwest Foundation for Children, 2007).

17. D. K. Ivy, *GenderSpeak: Personal Effectiveness in Gender Communication* 5e (Boston: Pearson, 2012).

18. C. M. Frisby, "Sticks 'N Stones May Break My Bones, but Words They Hurt Like Hell: Derogatory Words in Popular Songs," *Media Report to Women* 38 (2010): 12–18; H. A. Schroth, J. Bain-Chekal, and D. F. Caldwell, "Sticks and Stones May Break Bones and Words Can Hurt Me: Words and Phrases That Trigger Emotions in Negotiations and Their Effects," *International Journal of Conflict Management* 16 (2005): 102–127; A. Palayiwa, P. Sheeran, and A. Thompson, "'Words Will Never Hurt Me!': Implementation Intentions Regulate Attention to Stigmatizing Comments About Appearance," *Journal of Social and Clinical Psychology* 29 (2010): 575–598; A. Ellis, *A New Guide to Rational Living* (North Hollywood, CA: Wilshire Books, 1977).

19. C. Peterson, M. E. P. Seligman, and G. E. Vaillant, "Pessimistic Explanatory Style Is a Risk Factor for Physical Illness: A 35-Year Longitudinal Study," *Journal of Personality and Social Psychology* 55 (1988): 23–27.

20. S. Dunn, "Standing Up for 'Bad' Words," *The Chronicle of Higher Education: The Chronicle Review* (March 14, 2008): B28.

21. R. T. Schaefer, *Racial and Ethnic Groups, Census Update* 12e (Boston: Prentice Hall, 2010); B. J. Allen, *Differences Matter: Communicating Social Identity* 2e (Long Grove, IL: Waveland, 2010); D. J. Napoli and V. Lee-Schoenfeld, *Language Matters: A Guide to Everyday Questions About Language* 2e (New York: Oxford University Press, 2010); M. P. Orbe and T. M. Harris, *Interracial Communication: Theory into Practice* 2e (Thousand Oaks, CA: Sage, 2008); J. Perlmann and M. C. Waters, eds., *The New Race Question: How the Census Counts Multiracial Individuals* (New York: Russell Sage Foundation, 2005); R. Harris and B. Rampton, eds., *The Language, Ethnicity, and Race Reader* (New York: Routledge, 2003); D. I. Kertzer and D. Arel, *Census and Identity: The Politics of Race, Ethnicity, and Language in National Censuses* (New York: Cambridge University Press, 2002).

22. G. He, "An Analysis of Sexism in English," *Journal of Language Teaching and Research* 1 (2010): 332–335; J. B. Parks and M. A. Roberton, "Generation Gaps in Attitudes Toward Sexist/Nonsexist Language," *Journal of Language and Social Psychology* 27 (2008): 276–283; J. B. Parks and M. A. Roberton, "Explaining Age and Gender Effects on Attitudes Toward Sexist Language," *Journal of Language and Social Psychology* 24 (2005): 401–411; E. L. Cralley and J. B. Ruscher, "Lady, Girl, or Woman: Sexism and Cognitive Busyness Predict Use of Gender-Biased Nouns," *Journal of Language and Social Psychology* 24 (2005): 300–314.

23. C. Kramarae, "Muted Group Theory and Communication: Asking Dangerous Questions," *Women & Language* 28 (2005): 55–61; S. Ardener, "Muted Groups: The Genesis of an Idea and Its Praxis," *Women & Language* 28 (2005): 50–54; J. K. Swim, R. Mallett, and C. Stangor, "Understanding Subtle Sexism: Detection and Use of Sexist Language," *Sex Roles* 51 (2004): 117–128; J. Briere and C. Lanktree, "Sex-Role Related Effects of Sex Bias in Language," *Sex Roles* 9 (1983): 625–632; L. Brooks, "Sexist Language in Occupational Information: Does It Make a Difference?" *Journal of Vocational Behavior* 23 (1983): 227–232.

24. H. S. O'Donnell, "Sexism in Language," *Elementary English* 50 (1973): 1067–1072, as cited by J. C. Pearson, L. Turner, and W. Todd Mancillas, *Gender and Communication* 3e (Dubuque, IA: William C. Brown, 1995).

25. P. Gygax, U. Gabriel, O. Sarrasin, J. Oakhill, and A. Garnham, "Some Grammatical Rules Are More Difficult Than Others: The Case of the Generic Interpretation of the Masculine," *European Journal of Psychology of Education* 24 (2009): 235–246; M. A. Clason, "Feminism, Generic 'He,' and the *TNIV* Bible Translation Debate," *Critical Discourse Studies* 3 (2006): 23–35; L. Conkright, D. Flannagan, and J. Dykes, "Effects of Pronoun Type and Gender Role Consistency on Children's Recall and Interpretation of Stories," *Sex Roles* 43 (2000): 481–499; J. L. Stinger and R. Hopper, "Generic *He* in Conversation?" *Quarterly Journal of Speech* 84 (1998): 209–221; J. Gastil, "Generic Pronouns and Sexist Language: The Oxymoronic Character of Masculine Generics," *Sex Roles* 23 (1990): 629–641; D. K. Ivy, L. Bullis-Moore, K. Norvell, P. Backlund, and M. Javidi, "The Lawyer, the Babysitter, and the Student: Inclusive Language Usage and Instruction," *Women & Language* 18 (1994): 13–21; W. Martyna, "What Does 'He' Mean? Use of the Generic Masculine," *Journal of Communication* 28 (1978): 131–138.

26. *Publication Manual of the American Psychological Association* 6e (2009), Supplemental Material: Writing Clearly and Concisely, General Guidelines for Reducing Bias, available at <www.apastyle.org>.

27. L. Madson and R. M. Hessling, "Does Alternating Between Masculine and Feminine Pronouns Eliminate Perceived Gender Bias in a Text?" *Sex Roles* 41 (1999): 559–576; D. Kennedy, "Review Essay: She or He in Textbooks," *Women & Language* 15 (1992): 46–49.

28. L. Madson and J. Shoda, "Alternating Between Masculine and Feminine Pronouns: Does Essay Topic Affect Readers' Perceptions?" *Sex Roles* 54 (2006): 275–285; T. Strahan, "'They' in Australian English: Non-Gender-Specific or Specifically Non-Gendered?" *Australian Journal of Linguistics* 28 (2008): 17–29.

29. Ivy, *GenderSpeak*.

30. Ivy, *GenderSpeak*.

31. M. Kantor, *Homophobia: The State of Sexual Bigotry Today* 2e (Santa Barbara, CA: Praeger, 2009); L. A. M. Perry and D. Ballard-Reisch, "There's a Rainbow in the Closet: On the Importance of Developing a Common Language for 'Sex' and 'Gender,'" in *Readings in Gender Communication*, edited by P. M. Backlund and M. R. Williams (Belmont, CA: Wadsworth, 2004), 17–34; G. Griffin, "Understanding Heterosexism—The Subtle Continuum of Homophobia," *Women & Language* 21 (1998): 33–39.

32. Ivy, *GenderSpeak*.

33. N. Updike, "That's So Gay!" September 14, 2000, <salon.com>; Associated Press, "'That's So Gay' Prompts a Lawsuit: Student Sent to Principal's Office Insists It Was Not a Homophobic Putdown," February 28, 2007, <msnbc.com>.

34. T. D. Nelson (Ed.), *Ageism: Stereotyping and Prejudice Against Older Persons* (Cambridge: Massachusetts Institute of Technology Press, 2004); A. Williams and J. F. Nussbaum, *Intergenerational Communication Across the Life Span* (Mahwah, NJ: Lawrence Erlbaum, 2000); E. O'Reilly, *Decoding the Cultural Stereotypes about Aging: New Perspectives on Aging Talk and Aging Issues* (New York: Routledge, 1997).

35. R. K. S. Macaulay, *Talk That Counts: Age, Gender, and Social Class Differences in Discourse* (New York: Oxford University Press, 2005); M. Argyle, *The Psychology of Social Class* (New York: Routledge, 1993).

36. J. S. Seiter, J. Larsen, and J. Skinner, "'Handicapped' or 'Handicapable'? The Effects of Language About Persons with Disabilities on Perceptions of Source Credibility and Persuasiveness," *Communication Reports* 11 (1998): 21–31.

37. J. R. Gibb, "Defensive Communication," Journal of Communication 11 (1961): 141–148. For other research on communication climate, see K. Czech and G. L. Forward, "Leader Communication: Faculty Perception of the Department Chair," *Communication Quarterly* 58 (2010): 431–457; J. M. Reagle, "'Be Nice': Wikipedia Norms for Supportive Communication," *New Review of Hypermedia & Multimedia* 16 (2010): 161–180; J. A. H. Becker, B. Ellevold, and G. H. Stamp, "The Creation of Defensiveness in Social Interaction II: A Model of Defensive Communication among Romantic Couples," *Communication Monographs* 75 (2008): 86–110; L. Cairns, "Reinforcement," in *The Handbook of Communication Skills* 3e, edited by O. Hargie (London: Routledge, 2006), 147–164; J. A. H. Becker, J. R. B. Halbesleben, and H. D. O'Hair, "Defensive Communication and Burnout in the Workplace: The Mediating Role of Leader-Member Exchange," *Communication Research Reports* 22 (2005): 143–150.

38. B. Clark, "50 Trigger Words and Phrases for Powerful Multimedia Content," April 20, 2009, <www.copyblogger.com/trigger-words/>; E. T. Booth, "Assign This: Trigger Words," *Spectra* (Washington, DC: National Communication Association, June/July 2007).

39. A. J. Clark, "Empathy and Sympathy: Therapeutic Distinctions in Counseling," *Journal of Mental Health Counseling* 32 (2010): 95–101; I. Devoldre, M. H. Davis, L. L. Verhofstadt, and A. Buysse, "Empathy and Social Support Provision in Couples: Social Support and the Need to Study the Underlying Processes," *Journal of Psychology* 144 (2010): 259–284; T. G. Cassels, S. Chan, W. Chung, and S. A. J. Birch, "The Role of Culture in Affective Empathy: Cultural and Bicultural Differences," *Journal of Cognition and Culture* 10 (2010): 309–326; J. D. Trout, *The Empathy Gap: Building Bridges to the Good Life and the Good Society* (New York: Viking, 2009); J. Hakansson and H. Montgomery, "Empathy as an Interpersonal Phenomenon," *Journal of Social and Personal Relationships* 20 (2003): 267–284; M. V. Redmond, "The Functions of Empathy (Decentering) in Human Relations," *Human Relations* 42 (1993): 593–606.

40. D. Johnson, "Helpful Listening and Responding," in Galvin, *Making Connections*, 70–76; D. F. Barone, P. S. Hutchings, H. J. Kimmel, H. L. Traub, J. T. Cooper, and C. M. Marshall, "Increasing Empathic Accuracy through Practice and Feedback in a Clinical Interviewing Course," *Journal of Social and Clinical Psychology* 24 (2005): 156–171.

## Chapter 4

1. M. Fox, *Talking Hands: What Sign Language Reveals About the Mind* (New York: Simon & Schuster, 2008); R. B. Grossman and J. Kegl, "Moving Faces: Categorization of Dynamic Facial Expressions in American Sign Language by Deaf and Hearing Participants," *Journal of Nonverbal Behavior* 31 (2007): 23–38.

2. A. Mehrabian, *Nonverbal Communication* (Chicago: Aldine-Atherton, 1972).

3. L. E. Boone and D. L. Kurtz, *Contemporary Business* 13e (New York: Wiley, 2010); V. Quercia, *Internet in a Nutshell* (Cambridge, MA: O'Reilly, 1997).

4. R. Bringhurst, *The Elements of Typographic Style* 3e (New York: Harts and Marks, 2004).

5. N. M. Doering and S. Poeschl, "Nonverbal Cues in Mobile Phone Text Messages: The Effects of Chronemics and Proxemics," in *The Reconstruction of Space and Time: Mobile Communication Practices*, edited by R. Ling and S. Campbell (New Brunswick, NJ: Transaction Publishers, 2009), 109–136; B. Eggen and A. M. Szostek, "I Know That You Know: Ascertaining Mutual Awareness of Recipient's Availability Status in Instant Messaging Applications," *Lecture Notes in Computer Science* 5726 (2009): 182–195; K. K. Stephens, M. L. Houser, and R. L. Cowan, "R U Able to Meat Me: The Impact of Students' Overly Casual Email Messages to Instructors," *Communication Education* 58 (2009): 303–326; E. Dresner and S. C. Herring, "Functions of the Nonverbal in CMC: Emoticons and Illocutionary Force," *Communication Theory* 20 (2010): 249–268; S-K. Lo, "The Nonverbal Communication Functions of Emoticons in Computer-Mediated Communication," *CyberPsychology & Behavior* 11 (2008): 591–593; A. M. Ledbetter and K. A. Larson, "Nonverbal Cues in E-Mail Supportive Communication: Associations with Sender Sex, Recipient Sex, and Support Satisfaction," *Information, Communication, & Society* 11 (2008): 1089–1110.

6. R. L. Birdwhistell, *Kinesics and Context* (Philadelphia: University of Pennsylvania Press, 1970).

7. N. O. Rule and N. Ambady, "She's Got the Look: Inferences from Female Chief Executive Officers' Faces Predict Their Success," *Sex Roles* 61 (2009): 644–652; L. P. Naumann, S. Vazire, P. J. Rentfrow, and S. D. Gosling, "Personality Judgments Based on Physical Appearance," *Personality and Social Psychology Bulletin* 35 (2009): 1661–1671; F. J. Bernieri, "The Expression of Rapport," in *The Sourcebook of Nonverbal Measures: Going Beyond Words*, edited by V. Manusov (Mahwah, NJ: Lawrence Erlbaum, 2005), 347–359.

8. W. E. Chaplin, J. B. Phillips, J. D. Brown, N. R. Clanton, and J. L. Stein, "Handshaking, Gender, Personality, and First Impressions," *Journal of Personality and Social Psychology* 79 (2000): 110–117.

9. G. L. Stewart, S. L. Dustin, M. R. Barrick, and T. C. Darnold, "Exploring the Handshake in Employment Interviews," *Journal of Applied Psychology* 93 (2008): 1139–1146.

10. M. Argyle, *Bodily Communication* (New York: Methuen, 1988).

11. M. Jung and H. N. Fouts, "Multiple Caregivers' Touch Interactions with Young Children Among the Bofi Foragers in Central Africa," *International Journal of Psychology* 46 (2011): 24–32; P. Yang, "Nonverbal Gender Differences: Examining Gestures of University-Educated Mandarin Chinese Speakers," *Text & Talk* 30 (2010): 333–357; P. Szarota, "The Mystery of the European Smile: A Comparison Based on Individual Photographs Provided by Internet Users," *Journal of Nonverbal Behavior* 34 (2010): 249–256; D. Matsumoto, A. Olide, J. Schug, B. Willingham, and M. Callan, "Cross-Cultural Judgments of Spontaneous Facial Expressions of Emotion," *Journal of Nonverbal Behavior* 33 (2009): 213–238; H. A. Elfenbein, "Learning in Emotion Judgments: Training and the Cross-Cultural Understanding of Facial Expressions," *Journal of Nonverbal Behavior* 30 (2006): 21–36; D. Matsumoto and S. H. Yoo, "Culture and Applied Nonverbal Communication," in *Applications of Nonverbal Communication*, edited by R. E. Riggio and R. S. Feldman (Mahwah, NJ: Lawrence Erlbaum, 2005), 255–277.

12. L. A. Samovar, R. E. Porter, and E. R. McDaniel, "Approaches to Intercultural Communication," in *Intercultural Communication: A Reader* 13e, edited by L. A. Samovar, R. E. Porter, and E. R. McDaniel (Belmont, CA: Wadsworth, 2011), 1–3.

13. J. Douglas Jr., "Outside Texas, 'Hook 'em Horns' Gesture Has Different and Unflattering Meanings," *Fort Worth Star Telegram* (January 23, 2005): 2A.

14. See J. K. Burgoon and S. B. Jones, "Toward a Theory of Personal Space Expectations and Their Violations," *Human Communication Research* 2 (1976): 131–146. For discussions and applications of expectancy violations theory, see E. L. Cohen, "Expectancy Violations in Relationships with Friends and Media Figures," *Communication Research Reports* 27 (2010): 97–111; A. Ramirez Jr. and Z. Wang, "When Online Meets Offline: An Expectancy Violations Theory Perspective on Modality Switching," *Journal of Communication* 58 (2008): 20–39; J. K. Burgoon and N. E. Dunbar, "Nonverbal Expressions of Dominance and Power in Human Relationships," in *The Sage Handbook of Nonverbal Communication*, edited by V. Manusov and M. L. Patterson (Thousand Oaks, CA: Sage, 2006), 279–297; S. Campo, K. A. Cameron, D. Brossard, and M. S. Frazer, "Social Norms and Expectancy Violation Theories: Assessing the Effectiveness of Health Communication Campaigns," *Communication Monographs* 71 (2004): 448–470; L. A. Erbert and K. Floyd, "Affectionate Expression as Face-Threatening Acts: Receiver Assessments," *Communication Studies* 55 (2004): 254–270; J. L. Bevan, "General Partner and Relational Uncertainty as Consequences of Another Person's Jealousy Expression," *Western Journal of Communication* 68 (2004): 195–218; J. L. Bevan, "Expectancy Violation Theory and Sexual Resistance in Close, Cross-Sex Relationships." *Communication Monographs* 70 (2003): 68–82; W. A. Afifi and J. K. Burgoon, "The Impact of Violations on Uncertainty and the Consequences for Attractiveness," *Human Communication Research* 26 (2000): 203–233.

15. J. Fast, *Body Language* (New York: M. Evans, 1970).

16. P. Ekman and W. V. Friesen, "The Repertoire of Nonverbal Behavior: Categories, Origins, Usage, and Coding," *Semiotica* 1 (1969): 49–98.

17. P. Sorokowski. "Politicians' Estimated Height as an Indicator of Their Popularity," *European Journal of Social Psychology* 40 (2010): 1302–1309; Open NY, "The Measure of a President," *New York Times*, October 6, 2008, <http://www.nytimes.com/interactive/2008/10/06/opinion/06opchart.html>; E. Tenner, "Political Timber: Glitter, Froth, and Measuring Tape," *The Chronicle of Higher Education* (October 1, 2004): B12–B13.

18. K. Soper, "RateMyProfessor'sAppearance.com," *The Chronicle of Higher Education* (September 17, 2010): B24; T. A. Moriarty, "They Love Me, They Love Me Not," *The Chronicle of Higher Education* (April 24, 2009): A27; R. Toor, "Can't We Be Smart and Look Good, Too?" *The Chronicle Review* (April 3, 2009): B4–B5; C. Edwards, A. Edwards, Q. Qing, and S. T. Wahl, "The Influence of Computer-Mediated Word-of-Mouth Communication on Student Perceptions of Instructors and Attitudes toward Learning Course Content," *Communication Education* 56 (2007): 255–277; A. Edwards and C. Edwards, "The Impact of Instructor Verbal and Nonverbal Immediacy on Student Perceptions of Attractiveness and Homophily," *Journal on Excellence in College Teaching* 12 (2001): 5–16; K. A. Rocca and J. C. McCroskey, "The Interrelationship of Student Ratings of Instructors' Immediacy, Verbal Aggressiveness, Homophily, and Interpersonal Attraction," *Communication Education* 48 (1999): 308–316; G. Montell, "Do Good Looks Equal Good Evaluations?" *The Chronicle of Higher Education: Career Network*, October 15, 2003, <http://chronicle.com>.

19. S. Darlow and M. Lobel, "Who Is Beholding My Beauty? Thinness Ideals, Weight, and Women's Responses to Appearance Evaluation," *Sex Roles* 63 (2010): 833–843; M. S. Richardson and J. S. Paxton, "An Evaluation of a Body Image Intervention Based on Risk Factors for Body Dissatisfaction: A Controlled Study with Adolescent Girls," *International Journal of Eating Disorders* 43 (2010): 112–122; M. Krcmar, S. Giles, and D. Helme, "Understanding the Process: How Mediated and Peer Norms Affect Young Women's Body Esteem," *Communication Quarterly* 56 (2008): 111–130; J. S. Wrench and J. L Knapp, "The Effects of Body Image Perceptions and Sociocommunicative Orientations on Self-Esteem, Depression, and Identification and Involvement in the Gay Community," *Journal of Homosexuality* 55 (2008): 471–503; B. Ackerman, "The Dangers of Body Dysmorphic Disorder: Discover the Dangers Associated with This Unhealthy Behavior," *American Fitness* (2006): 24–26; M. M. Martin and J. W. Gentry, "Stuck in the Model Trap," in *Taking Sides: Clashing Views on Controversial Issues in Mass Media and Society* 8e, edited by A. Alexander and J. Hanson (Dubuque, IA: McGraw-Hill/Dushkin, 2005), 52–61; G. B. Forbes, L. E. Adams-Curtis, B. Rade, and P. Jaberg, "Body Dissatisfaction in Women and Men: The Role of Gender-Typing and Self-Esteem," *Sex Roles* 44 (2001): 461–484.

20. B. Verhulst, M. Lodge, and H. Lavine, "The Attractiveness Halo: Why Some Candidates Are Perceived More Favorably Than Others," *Journal of Nonverbal Behavior* 34 (2010): 111–117; T. H. Feeley, "Evidence of Halo Effects in Student Evaluations of Communication Instruction," *Communication Education* 51 (2002): 225–236; E. Hatfield and S. Sprecher, *Mirror, Mirror. . .: The Importance of Looks in Everyday Life* (Albany: SUNY Press, 1986); C. M. Marlowe, S. L. Schneider, and C. E. Nelson, "Gender and Attractiveness Biases in Hiring Decisions: Are More Experienced Managers Less Biased?" *Journal of Applied Psychology* 81 (1998): 11–21.

21. K. Doss and A. S. Ebesu Hubbard, "The Communicative Value of Tattoos: The Role of Public Self-Consciousness on Tattoo Visibility," *Communication Research Reports* 26 (2009): 62–74; T. Vinciguerra, "AMA Proposal: Lose Lab Coats," *Dallas Morning News* (July 26, 2009): 8A; M. Tiggemann and F. Golder, "Tattooing: An Expression of Uniqueness in the Appearance Domain," *Body Image* 3 (2006): 309–315; J. V. Peluchette, K. Karl, and K. Rust, "Dressing to Impress: Beliefs and Attitudes Regarding Workplace Attire," *Journal of Business and Psychology* 21 (2006): 45–63; S. Breitenbach, "Tattoos and Piercings Can Keep Young People from Jobs," *Frederick News-Post* (November 12, 2005).

22. N. Armstrong and M. Wagner, *Field Guide to Gestures: How to Identify and Interpret Virtually Every Gesture Known to Man* (Philadelphia: Quirk Books, 2003).

23. Ekman and Friesen, "The Repertoire of Nonverbal Behavior."

24. R. E. Axtell, *Gestures: Do's and Taboos of Body Language around the World* (New York: Wiley, 1998).

25. G. Beattie, J. Ross, and K. Webster, "The Fixation and Processing of the Iconic Gestures That Accompany Talk," *Journal of Language and Social Psychology* 29 (2010): 194–213; E. Stevanoni and K. Salmon, "Giving Memory a Hand: Instructing Children to Gesture Enhances Their Event Recall," *Journal of Nonverbal Behavior* 29 (2005): 217–233.

26. J. Holler and K. Wilkin, "Co-Speech Gesture Mimicry in the Process of Collaborative Referring During Face-to-Face Dialogue," *Journal of Nonverbal Behavior* 35 (2011): 133–153; W. G. Woodall and J. P. Folger, "Nonverbal Cue Context and Episodic Memory: On the Availability and Endurance of Nonverbal Behaviors as Retrieval Cues," *Communication Monographs* 52 (1985): 320–333.

27. C. Darwin, *Expression of Emotions in Man and Animals* (London: Appleton; reprinted University of Chicago Press, 1965).

28. M. Gagnon, P. Gosselin, I. Hudon-ven der Buhs, K. Larocque, and K. Milliard, "Children's Recognition and Discrimination of Fear and Disgust Facial Expressions," *Journal of Nonverbal Behavior* 34 (2010): 27–42; J. P. Forgas and R. East, "How Real Is That Smile? Mood Effects on Accepting or Rejecting the Veracity of Emotional Facial Expressions," *Journal of Nonverbal Behavior* 32 (2009): 157–170; D. Matsumoto and B. Willingham, "Attitudes and Social Cognition: Spontaneous Facial Expressions of Emotion of Congenitally and Noncongenitally Blind Individuals," *Journal of Personality and Social Psychology* 96 (2009): 1–10; J. Beavin Bavelas and N. Chovil, "Nonverbal and Verbal Communication: Hand Gestures and Facial Displays as Part of Language Use in Face-to-Face Dialogue," in *The Sage Handbook of Nonverbal Communication*, edited by V. Manusov and M. L. Patterson (Thousand Oaks, CA: Sage, 2006), 97–115; M. Coulson, "Attributing Emotion to Static Body Postures: Recognition Accuracy, Confusions, and Viewpoint Dependence," *Journal of Nonverbal Behavior* 28 (2004): 117–139.

29. L. K. Guerrero, P. A. Andersen, and W. A. Afifi, *Close Encounters: Communicating in Relationships* 5e (Los Angeles: Sage, 2011); J. Hall, M. Cody, G. Jackson, and J. Flesh, "Beauty and the Flirt: Attractiveness and Approaches to Relationship Initiation," paper presented at the meeting of the International Communication Association, Montreal (May 2008); D. D. Henningsen, M. Braz, and E. Davies, "Why Do We Flirt?" *Journal of Business Communication* 45 (2008): 483–502; N. Gueguen, "The Effect of a Woman's Smile on Men's Courtship Behavior," *Social Behavior and Personality* 36 (2008): 1233–1236; S. Metts, "Gendered Communication in Dating Relationships," in *The Sage Handbook of Gender and Communication*, edited by B. J. Dow and J. T. Wood (Thousand Oaks, CA: Sage, 2006), 25–40; P. Collett, *The Book of Tells* (London: Bantam, 2004); L. A. Renninger, T. J. Wade, and K. Grammer, "Getting That Female Glance: Patterns and Consequences of Male Nonverbal Behavior in Courtship Contexts," *Evolution and Human Behavior* 25 (2004): 416–431; D. Singh, "Mating Strategies of Young Women: Role of Physical Attractiveness," *Journal of Sex Research* 41 (2004): 43–54.

30. M. M. Moore, "Nonverbal Courtship Patterns in Women: Context and Consequences," *Ethology and Sociobiology* 6 (1985): 237–247.

31. C. Farris, T. A. Treat, R. J. Viken, and R. M. McFall, "Perceptual Mechanisms That Characterize Gender Differences in Decoding Women's Sexual Intent," *Psychological Science* 19 (2008): 348–354; M. R. Trost and J. K. Alberts, "How Men and Women Communicate Attraction: An Evolutionary View," in *Sex Differences and Similarities in Communication*, edited by K. Dindia and D. J. Canary (Mahwah, NJ: Lawrence Erlbaum, 2006), 317–336; D. J. Henningsen, "Flirting with Meaning: An Examination of Miscommunication in Flirting Interactions," *Sex Roles* 50 (2004): 481–489; M. M. Moore, "Courtship Communication and Perception," *Perceptual and Motor Skills* 94 (2002): 97–105; E. Koukounas and N. M. Letch, "Psychological Correlates of Perception of Sexual Intent in Women," *Journal of Social Psychology* 141 (2001): 443–456; A. Abbey, "Sex Differences in Attributions for Friendly Behavior: Do Males Misperceive Females' Friendliness?" *Journal of Personality and Social Psychology* 42 (1982): 830–838; L. B. Koeppel, Y. Montagne, D. O'Hair, and M. J. Cody, "Friendly? Flirting? Wrong?" *The Nonverbal Communication Reader: Classic and Contemporary Reading* 2e, edited by L. K. Guerrero, J. DeVito, and M. L. Hecht (Prospect Heights, IL: Waveland, 1999), 290–297.

32. A. Abbey, T. Zawacki, and P. O. Buck, "The Effects of Past Sexual Assault Perpetration and Alcohol Consumption on Reactions to Women's Mixed Signals," *Journal of Social and Clinical Psychology* 24 (2005): 129–157; H. J. Delaney and B. A. Gluade, "Gender Differences in Perception of Attractiveness of Men and Women in Bars," *Journal of Personality and Social Psychology* 16 (1990): 378–391.

33. T. Field, J. E. Malphurs, R. Yando, D. Bendell, K. Carraway, and R. Cohen, "Legal Interviewers Use Children's Affect and Eye Contact Cues to Assess Credibility of Their Testimony," *Early Child Development & Care* 180 (2010): 397–404; A. Vrij, S. Mann, S. Leal, and R. Fisher, "'Look into My Eyes': Can an Instruction to Maintain Eye Contact Facilitate Lie Detection?" *Psychology, Crime, & Law* 16 (2010): 327–348; J. Bailly, "The Secret Language of Brows," *O: The Oprah Winfrey Magazine* (June 2009): 180–185; N. M. Tess and S. L. Brodsky, "Expert Witness Credibility as a Function of Eye Contact Behavior and Gender," *Criminal Justice and Behavior* 35 (2008): 1515–1526; L. K. Guerrero and K. Floyd, *Nonverbal Communication in Close Relationships* (Mahwah, NJ: Lawrence Erlbaum, 2006); C. S. Rhys, "Gaze and Turn: A Nonverbal Solution to an Interactive Problem," *Clinical Linguistics and Phonetics* 19 (2005): 419–431; Collett, *The Book of Tells*; M. L. Jensen and J. K. Burgoon, "Interpersonal Deception Theory," in *The Nonverbal Communication Reader* 3e, edited by L. K. Guerrero and M. L. Hecht (Long Grove, IL: Waveland, 2008), 421–431; M. L. Knapp, *Lying and Deception in Human Interaction* (Boston: Pearson/Allyn & Bacon, 2008); L. A. Stromwall, M. Hartwig, and P. A. Granhag, "To Act Truthfully: Nonverbal Behavior and Strategies During a Police Interrogation," *Psychology, Crime, and Law* 12 (2006): 207–219; Vrij, "Nonverbal Communication and Deception"; B. M. DePaulo, J. L. Lindsay, B. E. Malone, L. Muhlenbruck, K. Charlton, and H. Cooper, "Cues to Deception," *Psychological Bulletin* 129 (2003): 74–118; M. Zuckerman and R. E. Driver, "Telling Lies: Verbal and Nonverbal Correlates of Deception, in *Multichannel Integrations of Nonverbal Behavior*, edited by A. W. Siegman and S. Feldstein (Hillsdale, NJ: Lawrence Erlbaum, 1985), 129–148.

34. M. L. Knapp and J. A. Hall, *Nonverbal Communication in Human Interaction* 7e (Belmont, CA: Thomson/Wadsworth, 2010).

35. S. A. Beebe, "Eye Contact: A Nonverbal Determinant of Speaker Credibility," *Speech Teacher* 23 (1974): 21–25.

36. P. Ekman and W. Friesen, *Unmasking the Face* (Englewood Cliffs, NJ: Prentice Hall, 1975); R. L. Birdwhistell, "The Language of the Body: The Natural Environment of Words," in *Human Communication: Theoretical Explorations*, edited by A. Silverstein (New York: Wiley, 1974), 203–220.

37. A. G. Halberstadt, P. A. Dennis, and U. Hess, "The Influence of Family Expressiveness, Individuals' Own Emotionality, and Self-Expressiveness on Perceptions of Others' Facial Expressions," *Journal of Nonverbal Behavior* 35 (2011): 35–50; K. U. Likowski, P. Weyers, B. Seibt, C. Stohr, P. Pauli, and A. Muhlberger, "Sad and Lonely? Sad Mood Suppresses Facial Mimicry," *Journal of Nonverbal Behavior* 35 (2011): 101–117; E. B. Roesch, L. Tamarit, L. Reveret, D. Grandjean, D. Sander, and K. R. Scherer, "FACSGen: A Tool to Synthesize Emotional Facial Expressions through Systematic Manipulation of Facial Action Units," *Journal of Nonverbal Behavior* 35 (2011): 1–16; E. Krumhuber, A. S. Manstead, and A. Kappas, "Temporal Aspects of Facial Displays in Person and Expression Perception: The Effects of Smile Dynamics, Head-Tilt, and Gender," *Journal of Nonverbal Behavior* 31 (2007): 39–56; W. Sato and S. Yoshikawa, "Enhanced Experience of Emotional Arousal in Response to Dynamic Facial Expressions," *Journal of Nonverbal Behavior* 31 (2007): 119–135.

38. C. M. Hurley and M. G. Frank, "Executing Facial Control During Deception Situations," *Journal of Nonverbal Behavior* 35 (2011): 119–131; M. Mendolia, "Explicit Use of Categorical and Dimensional Strategies to Decode Facial Expressions of Emotion," *Journal of Nonverbal Behavior* 31 (2007): 57–75; A. P. Atkinson, J. Tipples, D. M. Burt, and A. W. Young, "Asymmetric Interference Between Sex and Emotion in Face Perception," *Perception and Psychophysics* 67 (2005): 1199–1213.

39. C. A. Braithwaite, "Cultural Uses and Interpretations of Silence." *The Nonverbal Communication Reader: Classic and Contemporary Reading* 2e, edited by L. K. Guerrero, J. DeVito, and M. L. Hecht (Prospect Heights, IL: Waveland, 1999), 163–172.

40. Ekman and Friesen, *Unmasking the Face*.

41. P. M. Cole, "Children's Spontaneous Control of Facial Expression," *Child Development* 57 (1986): 1309–1321.

42. K. Floyd, P. M. Pauley, and C. Hesse, "State and Trait Affectionate Communication Buffer Adults' Stress Reactions," *Communication Monographs* 77 (2010): 618–636; K. Floyd and S. Riforgiate, "Affectionate Communication Received from Spouses Predicts Stress Hormone Levels in Healthy Adults," *Communication Monographs* 75 (2008): 351–368; N. M. Punyanunt-Carter and J. S. Wrench, "Development and Validity Testing of a Measure of Touch Deprivation," *Human Communication* 12 (2009): 67–76; T. Field, "Touch Deprivation and Aggression Against Self Among Adolescents," in *Developmental Psychobiology of Aggression*, edited by D. M. Stoff and E. J. Susman (New York: Cambridge University Press, 2005), 117–140.

43. D. K. Ivy and S. T. Wahl, *The Nonverbal Self: Communication for a Lifetime* (Boston: Pearson, 2009).

44. P. A. Andersen, "Tactile Traditions: Cultural Differences and Similarities in Haptic Communication," in *The Handbook of Touch: Neuroscience, Behavioral, and Health Perspectives*, edited by M. Hertenstein and S. Weiss (New York: Springer, 2011), 351–371.

45. R. DiBiase and J. Gunnoe, "Gender and Culture Differences in Touching Behavior," *Journal of Social Psychology* 144 (2004): 49–62; E. T. Hall, *The Hidden Dimension* (Garden City, NY: Anchor, 1990); E. T. Hall, *Beyond Culture* (New York: Doubleday, 1981); M. S. Remland, T. S. Jones, and H. Brinkman, "Proxemic and Haptic Behavior in Three European Countries," *Journal of Nonverbal Behavior* 15 (1991): 215–231; M. S. Remland, T. S. Jones, and H. Brinkman, "Interpersonal Distance, Body Orientation and Touch: Effect of Culture, Gender, and Age," *Journal of Social Psychology* 135 (1995): 281–295.

46. J. Knight, "The Truth About Lying," *Nature* 428 (2004): 692–694; J. Ruscio, "Exploring Controversies in the Art and Science of Polygraph Testing," *The Skeptical Inquirer* 29 (2005): 34–39.

47. Ivy and Wahl, *The Nonverbal Self*; A. Vrij, "Nonverbal Communication and Deception," in *The Sage Handbook of Nonverbal Communication*, edited by V. Manusov and M. L. Patterson (Thousand Oaks, CA: Sage, 2006), 341–359; P. A. Andersen, *The Complete Idiot's Guide to Body Language* (New York: Alpha, 2004); L. Anolli and R. Ciceri, "The Voice of Deception: Vocal Strategies of Naive and Able Liars," *Journal of Nonverbal Behavior* 21 (1997): 259–284; P. Ekman, W. V. Friesen, and K. R. Scherer, "Body Movement and Voice Pitch in Deceptive Interaction," *Semiotica* 16 (1976): 23–27; P. Ekman, M. O'Sullivan, W. V. Friesen, and K. R. Scherer, "Face, Voice, and Body in Detecting Deceit," *Journal of Nonverbal Behavior* 15 (1991): 125–135; M. O'Sullivan, "Emotional Intelligence and Deception Detection: Why Most People Can't 'Read' Others, but a Few Can," in *Applications of Nonverbal Communication*, edited by R. E. Riggio and R. S. Feldman (Mahwah, NJ: Lawrence Erlbaum, 2005), 215–253.

48. M. Imhof, "Listening to Voices and Judging People," *International Journal of Listening* 24 (2010): 19–33; S. Hughes, S. Farley, and B. Rhodes, "Vocal and Physiological Changes in Response to the Physical Attractiveness of Conversational Partners," *Journal of Nonverbal Behavior* 34 (2010): 155–167; A. Karpf, *The Human Voice: How This Extraordinary Instrument Reveals Essential Clues About Who We Are* (New York: Bloomsbury, 2006); A. Nelson and S. K. Golant, *You Don't Say: Navigating Nonverbal Communication Between the Sexes* (New York: Prentice Hall, 2004); L. K. Wells, *The Articulate Voice: An Introduction to Voice and Diction* 4e (Boston: Allyn & Bacon, 2004); S. Feldstein, F. A. Dohm, and C. L. Crown, "Gender and Speech Rate in the Perception of Competence and Social Attractiveness," *Journal of Social Psychology* 141 (2001): 785–808.

49. F. Roberts, A. L. Francis, and M. Morgan, "The Interaction of Inter-Turn Silence with Prosodic Cues in Listener Perceptions of 'Trouble' in Conversation," *Speech Communication* 48 (2006): 1079–1093; T. DeGroot and S. J. Motowidlo, "Why Visual and Vocal Interview Cues Can Affect Interviewers' Judgments and Predict Job Performance," *Journal of Applied Psychology* 84 (1999): 986–993; N. Christenfeld, "Does It Hurt to Say Um?" *Journal of Nonverbal Behavior* 19 (1995): 171–186.

50. M. Zuckerman and V. Sinicropi, "When Physical and Vocal Attractiveness Differ: Effects on Favorability of Interpersonal Impressions," *Journal of Nonverbal Behavior* 35 (2011): 75–86.

51. M. M. Reda, "What's the Problem with Quiet Students? Anyone? Anyone?" *The Chronicle of Higher Education* (September 10, 2010): A68; M. M. Reda, *Between Speaking and Silence: A Study of Quiet Students* (Albany: SUNY Press, 2010); M. Ephratt, "The Functions of Silence," *Journal of Pragmatics* 40 (2008): 1909–1938; A. Georgakopoulos, "The Role of Silence and Avoidance in Interpersonal Conflict," *Peace and Conflict Studies* 11 (2004): 85–95; M. L. Knapp and A. L. Vangelisti, *Interpersonal Communication and Human Relationships* 5e (Boston: Allyn & Bacon, 2005); A. Jaworski, "The Power of Silence in Communication," in *The Nonverbal Communication Reader: Classic and Contemporary Readings* 2e, edited by L. K. Guerro, J. DeVito, and M. L. Hecht (Prospect Heights, IL: Waveland, 1999), 156–162.

52. S. J. Baker, "The Theory of Silence," *Journal of General Psychology* 53 (1955): 145–167.

53. T. Bringslimark, T. Hartig, and G. Grindal Patil, "Adaptation to Windowlessness: Do Office Workers Compensate for a Lack of Visual Access to the Outdoors?" *Environment & Behavior* 43 (2011): 469–487; F. U. J. Paul, M. K. Mandal, K. Ramachandran, and M. R. Panwar, "Interpersonal Behavior in an Isolated and Confined Environment," *Environment & Behavior* 42 (2010): 707–717; A. Vogler and J. Jorgensen, "Windows to the World, Doors to Space: The Psychology of Space Architecture," *Leonardo* 38 (2005): 390–399; P. Harris and D. Sachau, "Is Cleanliness Next to Godliness? The Role of Housekeeping in Impression Formation," *Environment & Behavior* 37 (2005): 81–99.

54. I. Vilnai-Yavetz, A. Rafaeli, and C. Schneider-Yaacov, "Instrumentality, Aesthetics, and Symbolism of Office Design," *Environment & Behavior* 37 (2005): 533–551; J. Sandberg, "Want to Know Someone's Job Status? Look at Desk Location," *Corpus Christi Caller Times* (March 2, 2003): D4.

55. L. Biemiller, "To College Employees, the Work Environment Is All-Important," *The Chronicle of Higher Education* (July 18, 2008): B12, B14, B17; S. D. Gosling, S. J. Ko, T. Mannarelli, and M. E. Morris, "A Room with a Cue: Personality Judgments Based on Offices and Bedrooms," *Journal of Personality and Social Psychology* 82 (2002): 379–398; A. Lohmann, X. B. Arriaga, and W. Goodfriend, "Close Relationships and Placemaking: Do Objects in a Couple's Home Reflect Couplehood?" *Personal Relationships* 10 (2003): 437–449.

56. J. F. Sallis and J. Kerr, "Physical Activity and the Built Environment," in *The Nonverbal Communication Reader* 3e, edited by L. K. Guerrero and M. L. Hecht (Long Grove, IL: Waveland, 2008), 270–286.

57. P. Monaghan, "Design for Disability Will Become the Norm," *The Chronicle Review* (February 12, 2010): B6–B7; T. R. Vandenbark, "Tending a Wild Garden: Library Web Design for Persons with Disabilities," *Information Technology & Libraries* 29 (2010): 23–29; D. K. White et al., "Are Features of the Neighborhood Environment Associated with Disability in Older Adults?" *Disabilities & Retention* 32 (2010): 639–645.

58. For more information on design for people with disabilities, see G. Pullin, *Design Meets Disability* (Cambridge, MA: MIT Press, 2009).

59. Hall, *The Hidden Dimension*.

60. S. Li and Y. Li, "How Far Is Far Enough? A Measure of Information Privacy in Terms of Interpersonal Distance," *Environment & Behavior* 39 (2007): 317–331; D. Matsumoto, "Culture and Nonverbal Behavior," in *The Sage Handbook of Nonverbal Communication*, edited by V. Manusov and M. L. Patterson (Thousand Oaks, CA: Sage, 2006), 219–235; C. M. J. Beaulieu, "Intercultural Study of Personal Space: A Case Study," *Journal of Applied Social Psychology* 34 (2004): 794–805.

61. L. Van Doorn, "Perception of Time and Space of (Formerly) Homeless People," *Journal of Human Behavior in the Social Environment* 20 (2010): 218–238; Burgoon and Dunbar, "Nonverbal Expressions of Dominance and Power in Human Relationships"; D. R. Carney, J. A. Hall, and L. Smith LeBeau, "Beliefs About the Nonverbal Expression of Social Power," *Journal of Nonverbal Behavior* 29 (2005): 105–123.

62. M. Costa, "Interpersonal Distances in Group Walking," *Journal of Nonverbal Behavior* 34 (2010): 15–26; J. A. Hall, "Women's and Men's Nonverbal Communication: Similarities, Differences, Stereotypes, and Origins," in *The Sage Handbook of Nonverbal Communication*, edited by V. Manusov and M. L. Patterson (Thousand Oaks, CA: Sage, 2006), 201–218.

63. G. Brown and S. L. Robinson, "Reactions to Territorial Infringement," *Organization Science* 22 (2011): 210–224; J. Koen and K. Durrheim, "A Naturalistic Observational Study of Informal Segregation: Seating Patterns in Lectures," *Environment & Behavior* 42 (2010): 448–468; N. Kaya and B. Burgess, "Territoriality: Seat Preferences in Different Types of Classrooms," *Environment & Behavior* 39 (2007): 859–876; S. M. Lyman and M. B. Scott, "Territoriality: A Neglected Sociological Dimension," in *The Nonverbal Communication Reader: Classic and Contemporary Reading* 2e, edited by L. K. Guerro, J. DeVito, and M. L. Hecht (Prospect Heights, IL: Waveland, 1999), 175–183; A. L. S. Buslig, "'Stop' Signs: Regulating Privacy with Environmental Features," in *The Nonverbal Communication Reader: Classic and Contemporary Reading* 2e, edited by L. K. Guerro, J. DeVito, and M. L. Hecht (Prospect Heights, IL: Waveland, 1999), 241–249.

64. Doering and Poeschl, "Nonverbal Cues in Mobile Phone Text Messages: The Effects of Chronemics and Proxemics"; V. Cho and H. Hung, "The Effectiveness of Short Message Service for Communication with Concerns of Privacy Protection and Conflict Avoidance," *Journal of Computer-Mediated Communication* 16 (2011): 250–270; Ivy and Wahl, *The Nonverbal Self*; Knapp and Hall, *Nonverbal Communication in Human Interaction*.

65. Mehrabian, *Nonverbal Communication*.

66. For applications of Mehrabian's immediacy principle, see P. B. O'Sullivan, S. K. Hunt, and L. R. Lippert, "Mediated Immediacy: A Language of Affiliation in a Technological Age," *Journal of Language and Social Psychology* 23 (2004): 464–490; L. Martin and T. P. Mottet, "The Effect of Instructor Nonverbal Immediacy Behaviors and Feedback Sensitivity on Hispanic Students' Affective Learning Outcomes in Ninth-Grade Writing Conferences," *Communication Education* 60 (2011): 1–19; P. L. Witt and J. Kerssen-Griep, "Instructional Feedback I: The Interaction of Facework and Immediacy on Students' Perceptions of Instructor Credibility," *Communication Education* 60 (2011): 75–94; F-Y. F. Wei and Y. K. Wang, "Students' Silent Messages: Can Teacher Verbal and Nonverbal Immediacy Moderate Student Use of Text Messaging in Class?" *Communication Education* 59 (2010): 475–496; P. King and P. Witt, "Teacher Immediacy, Confidence Testing, and the Measurement of Cognitive Learning," *Communication Education* 58 (2009): 110–123; H. S. Park, S. A. Lee, D. Yun, and W. Kim, "The Impact of Instructor Decision Authority and Verbal and Nonverbal Immediacy on Korean Student Satisfaction in the U.S. and South Korea," *Communication Education* 58 (2009): 189–212; A. B. Frymier, M. B. Wanzer, and A. M. Wojtaszczyk, "Assessing Students' Perceptions of Inappropriate and Appropriate Teacher Humor," *Communication Education* 57 (2008): 266–288; P. Schrodt and P. L. Witt, "Students' Attributions of Instructor Credibility as a Function of Students' Expectations of Instructional Technology Use and Nonverbal Immediacy," *Communication Education* 55 (2006): 1–20.

67. Argyle, *Bodily Communication*.

68. P. A. Andersen, *Nonverbal Communication: Forms and Functions* 2e (Long Grove, IL: Waveland, 2008): 168.

69. D. Lakens and M. Stel, "If They Move in Sync, They Must Feel in Sync: Movement Synchrony Leads to Attributions of Rapport and Entitativity," *Social Cognition* 29 (2011): 1–14; J. Wilt, K. Funkhouser, and W. Revelle, "The Dynamic Relationships of Affective Synchrony to Perceptions of Situations," *Journal of Research in Personality* 45 (2011): 309–321; K. McGinty, D. Knox, and M. E. Zusman, "Nonverbal and Verbal Communication in 'Involved' and 'Casual' Relationships Among College Students," *College Student Journal* 37 (2003): 68–71; B. Le Poire, A. Duggan, C. Shepard, and J. Burgoon, "Relational Messages Associated with Nonverbal Involvement, Pleasantness, and Expressiveness in Romantic Couples," *Communication Research Reports* 19 (2002): 195–206.

70. D. R. Carney and L. Smith LeBeau, "Beliefs About the Nonverbal Expression of Social Power," *Journal of Nonverbal Behavior* 29 (2005): 105–123; M. Schmid Mast and J. A. Hall, "Who Is the Boss and Who Is Not? Accuracy of Judging Status," *Journal of Nonverbal Behavior* 28 (2004): 145–165; M. Helweg-Larsen, S. J. Cunningham, A. Carrico, and A. M. Pergram, "To Nod or Not to Nod: An Observational Study of Nonverbal Communication and Status in Female and Male College Students," *Psychology of Women Quarterly* 28 (2004): 358–361; L. Z. Tiedens and A. R. Fragale, "Power Moves: Complementarity in Dominant and Submissive Nonverbal Behavior," *Journal of Personality and Social Psychology* 84 (2003): 558–568; Mehrabian, *Nonverbal Communication*.

## Chapter 5

1. R. Emanuel, J. Adams, K. Baker, E. K. Daufin, C. Ellington, F. Fits, J. Himsel, L. Holladay, and D. Okeowo, "How College Students Spend Their Time Communicating," *International Journal of Listening* 22 (2008): 13–28; also see L. Barker et al., "An Investigation of Proportional Time Spent in Various Communication Activities for College Students," *Journal of Applied Communication Research* 8 (1981): 101–109; also see K. Dindia and B. L. Kennedy, "Communication in Everyday Life: A Descriptive Study Using Mobile Electronic Data Collection," paper presented at the annual conference of the National Communication Association, Chicago (November 2004).

2. For an excellent review of listening research, see M. L. Beall, J. Gill-Rosier, J. Tate, and A. Matten, "State of the Context: Listening in Education," *International Journal of Listening* 22 (2008): 123–132; also see A. D. Wolvin, "Listening Engagement: Intersecting Theoretical Perspectives," in *Listening and Human Communication in the 21st Century*, edited by A. D. Wolvin (Oxford: Wiley-Blackwell, 2010), 7–30.

3. J. Brownell, "Perceptions of Effective Listeners: A Management Study," *Journal of Business Communication* (Fall 1990): 401–415; D. A. Romig, *Side by Side Leadership* (Austin, TX: Bard, 2001).

4. One study found that only 5 percent of colleges and universities offered a course in listening. See K. G. Wacker and K. Hawkins, "Curricula Comparison for Classes in Listening," *International Journal of Listening* 9 (1995): 14–28.

5. For additional support for the importance of listening in interpersonal relationships, see L. Sparks, S. S. Travis, and S. R. Thompson, "Listening for the Communication Signals of Humor, Narratives, and Self-Disclosure in the Family Caregiver Interview," *Health & Social Work* 30.4 (2005): 340–343; S. Wright, "The Beauty of Silence: Deep Listening Is a Key Nursing Skill That Can Be Learned with Practice," *Nursing Standard* 20.50 (2006): 18–20; M. R. Jalongo, "Listening in Early Childhood: An Interdisciplinary Review of the Literature," *International Journal of Listening* 24.1 (2010): 1–18.

6. P. Skaldeman, "Converging or Diverging Views of Self and Other: Judgment of Relationship Quality in Married and Divorced Couples," *Journal of Divorce & Remarriage* 44 (2006): 145–160.

7. For a review of the role of listening in business contexts, see J. Flynn, T. R. Valikoski, and J. Grau, "Listening in the Business Context: Reviewing the State of Research," *International Journal of Listening* 22 (2008): 141–151.

8. For a review of literature documenting the importance of listening in the health professions, see D. L. Roter and J. A. Hall, *Doctors Talking with Patients/Patients Talking with Doctors: Improving Communication in Medical Visits* (Westport, CT: Praeger, 2006); J. Davis, C. R. Thompson, A. Foley, C. D. Bond, and J. DeWitt, "An Examination of Listening Concepts in the Healthcare Context: Differences Among Nurses, Physicians, and Administrators," *International Journal of Listening* 22 (2008): 152–167.

9. C. Jacobs and D. Coghlan, "Sound of Silence: On Listening in Organizational Learning," *Human Relations* 58.1 (2005): 115–138.

10. K. W. Hawkins and B. P. Fullion, "Perceived Communication Skill Needs for Work Groups," *Communication Research Reports* 16 (1999): 167–174.

11. R. Bommelje, J. M. Houston, and R. Smither, "Personality Characteristics of Effective Listeners: A Five Factor Perspective," *International Journal of Listening* 17 (2003): 32–46.

12. M. S. Conaway, "Listening: Learning Tool and Retention Agent," in *Improving Reading and Study Skills*, edited by A. S. Algier and K. W. Algier (San Francisco: Jossey-Bass, 1996), 51–63.

13. For a review of how listening is discussed in public speaking textbooks, see W. C. Adams and E. S. Cox, "The Teaching of Listening as an Integral Part of an Oral Activity: An Examination of Public-Speaking Texts," *International Journal of Listening* 24.2 (2010): 89–105.

14. Adapted from the International Listening Association's definition of *listening*, which may be found on its website <http://www.listen.org>; for a theoretical explanation of the attending listening process, see L. A. Januskik, "Building Listening Theory: The Validation of the Conversational Listening Span," *Communication Studies* 5.2 (June 2007): 139.

15. S. C. Bentley, "Listening in the 21st Century," *International Journal of Listening* 14 (2000): 129–142; also see A. D. Wolvin and C. G. Coakley, "Listening Education in the 21st Century," *International Journal of Listening* 14 (2001): 143–152. For an excellent literature review of definitions and perspectives on defining listening, see S. Bentley, "Benchmarking Listening Behaviors: Is Effective Listening What the Speaker Says It Is?" *International Journal of Listening* 11.1 (2008): 51–68.

16. D. Mount and A. Mattila, "Last Chance to Listen: Listening Behaviors and Their Effect on Call Center Satisfaction," *Journal of Hospitality & Tourism Research* 26.2 (2002): 124–137.

17. A. Mulanx and W. G. Powers, "Listening Fidelity Development and Relationship to Receiver Apprehension and Locus of Control," *International Journal of Listening* 17 (2003): 69–78.

18. D. A. Schwartz, "Review Essay Listening Out of the Box: New Perspectives for the Workplace," *International Journal of Listening* 18 (2004): 47–55.

19. W. L. Randall, S. M. Prior, and M. Skarborn, "How Listeners Shape What Tellers Tell: Patterns of Interaction in Lifestory Interviews and Their Impact on Reminiscence by Elderly Interviewees," *Journal of Aging Studies* 20.4 (2006): 381–396.

20. K. W. Watson, L. L. Barker, and J. B. Weaver, *The Listener Style Inventory* (New Orleans: Spectra, 1995).

21. D. Worthington, G. D. Bodie, and C. Gearhart, "The Listening Styles Profile Revised (LSP-R): A Scale Revision and Validation," paper presented at the Eastern Communication Association, Arlington, VA (2011); G. D. Bodie and D. L. Worthington, "Revisiting the Listening Styles Profile (LSP-16): A Confirmatory Factor Analytic Approach to Scale Validation and Reliability Estimation," *International Journal of Listening* 24.2 (2010): 69–88.

22. D. L. Worthington, "Exploring the Relationship Between Listening Style Preference and Personality," *International Journal of Listening* 17 (2003): 68–87; D. L. Worthington, "Exploring Juror's Listening Processes: The Effect of Listening Style Preference on Juror Decision Making," *International Journal of Listening* 17 (2003): 20–37.

23. M. D. Kirtley and J. M. Honeycutt, "Listening Styles and Their Correspondence with Second Guessing," *Communication Research Reports* 13 (1996): 174–182.

24. G. D. Bodie and W. A. Villaume, "Aspects of Receiving Information: The Relationship Between Listening Preferences, Communication Apprehension, Receiver Apprehension, and Communicator Style," *International Journal of Listening* 17 (2003): 48–67.

25. J. B. Weaver III and M. Kirtley, "Listening Styles and Empathy," *Southern Communication Journal* 2 (1995): 131–141.

26. Worthington, "Exploring the Relationship Between Listening Style Preference and Personality."

27. Worthington, "Exploring Jurors' Listening Processes."

28. S. L. Sargent and J. B. Weaver, "Correlates Between Communication Apprehension and Listening Style Preferences," *Communication Research Reports* 14 (1997): 74–78.

29. M. K. Johnston, J. B. Weaver, K. W. Watson, and L. L. Barker, "Listening Styles: Biological or Psychological Differences?" *International Journal of Listening* 14 (2000): 14–31.

30. See C. Kiewitz, J. B. Weaver III, B. Brosius, and G. Weimann, "Cultural Differences in Listening Style Preferences: A Comparison of Young Adults in Germany, Israel, and the United States," *International Journal of Public Opinion Research* 9 (1997): 233–248; N. Dragon and J. C. Sherblom, "The Influence of Cultural Individualism and Collectivism on U.S. and Post Soviet Listening Styles," *Human Communication* 11 (2008): 177–192.

31. L. L. Barker and K. W. Watson, *Listen Up* (New York: St. Martin's Press, 2000); also see M. Imhof, "Who Are We as We Listen? Individual Listening Profiles in Varying Contexts," *International Journal of Listening* 18 (2004): 36–45.

32. Imhof, "Who Are We as We Listen?"

33. W. Winter, A. J. Ferreira, and N. Bowers, "Decision-Making in Married and Unrelated Couples," *Family Process* 12 (1973): 83–94.

34. R. Montgomery, *Listening Made Easy* (New York: Amacom, 1981); also see O. Hargie, C. Sanders, and D. Dickson, *Social Skills in Interpersonal Communication* (London: Routledge, 1994); O. Hargie, ed., *The Handbook of Communication Skills* (London: Routledge, 1997).

35. R. G. Owens, "Handling Strong Emotions," in *The Handbook of Communication Skills*, edited by O. Hargie (London: Croom Helm/New York University Press, 1986).

36. D. Goleman, *Emotional Intelligence: Why It Can Matter More Than IQ* (New York: Bantam Books, 1995); also see D. Goleman, "Emotional Intelligence: Issues in Paradigm Building," in *The Emotionally Intelligent Workplace*, edited by C. Cherniss and D. Goleman (San Francisco: Jossey-Bass, 2001), 13.

37. For an excellent review of emotional intelligence research, see D. Grewal and P. Salovey, "Feeling Smart: The Science of Emotional Intelligence," *American Scientist* 93 (2005): 330–339. Also see J. Keaton and L. Kelly, "Emotional Intelligence as a Mediator of Family Communication Patterns and Reticence," *Communication Reports* 21.2 (2008): 104–116; R. Pishghadam, "Emotional and Verbal Intelligences in Language Learning," *Iranian Journal of Language Studies* 3.1 (2009): 43–64.

38. Goleman, *Emotional Intelligence*; Grewal and Salovey, "Feeling Smart."

39. J. L. Gonzalez-Balado, ed., *Mother Teresa: In My Own Words* (New York: Gramercy Books, 1997).

40. C. Rousseau, "Ebert Returns to TV with New Show, New Voice," *Austin American-Statesman* (January 22, 2011): E1.

41. R. G. Nichols, "Factors in Listening Comprehension," *Speech Monographs* 15 (1948): 154–163; G. M. Goldhaber and C. H. Weaver, "Listener Comprehension of Compressed Speech When the Difficulty, Rate of Presentation, and Sex of the Listener Are Varied," *Speech Monographs* 35 (1968): 20–25.

42. M. Fitch-Hauser, D. A. Barker, and A. Hughes, "Receiver Apprehension and Listening Comprehension: A Linear or Curvilinear Relationship?" *Southern Communication Journal* 56 (1988): 62–71; P. E. King and R. R. Behnke, "Patterns of State Anxiety in Listening Performance," *Southern Communication Journal* 70.1 (2004): 72–81.

43. Fitch-Hauser et al., "Receiver Apprehension and Listening Comprehension."

44. K. Watson, L. Barker, and J. Weaver, "The Listening Styles Profile (LPP16): Development and Validation of an Instrument to Assess Four Listening Styles," *Journal of International Listening Association* (1995), research cited on *20/20*, ABC television network, September 1998.

45. C. Y. Cheng, "Chinese Philosophy and Contemporary Communication Theory," in *Communication Theory: Eastern and Western Perspectives*, edited by D. L. Kincaid (New York: Academic Press, 1987).

46. T. S. Lebra, *Japanese Patterns of Behavior* (Honolulu: University Press of Hawaii, 1976).

47. A. Yugi (trans. N. Chung), *Ilbon-in ye usikkoo-jo (Japanese Thought Patterns)* (Seoul: Baik Yang. [in Korean], 1984).

48. J. O. Yum, "The Impact of Confucianism on Interpersonal Relationships and Communication Patterns in East Asia," in *Intercultural Communication: A Reader*, edited by L. A. Samovar and R. E. Porter (Belmont, CA: Wadsworth, 2000), 86.

49. Imhof, "Who Are We as We Listen?"

50. A. Carruthers, "Listening, Hearing and Changing," *Business Communication* 5 (2004): 3.

51. K. K. Halone and L. L. Pecchioni, "Relational Listening: A Grounded Theoretical Model," *Communication Reports* 14 (2001): 59–71.

52. I. W. Johnson, C. G. Pearce, T. L. Tuten, and L. Sinclair, "Self-Imposed Silence and Perceived Listening Effectiveness," *Business Communication Quarterly* 66 (2003): 23–45.

53. M. V. Redmond, "The Functions of Empathy (Decentering) in Human Relations," *Human Relations* 42 (1993): 593–606.

54. A. Mehrabian, *Nonverbal Communication* (Chicago: Aldine Atherton, 1970); A. Mehrabian, *Silent Messages* (Belmont, CA: Wadsworth, 1981); also see D. Lapakko, "Three Cheers for Language: A Closer Examination of a Widely Cited Study of Nonverbal Communication," *Communication Education* 46 (1997): 63–67.

55. I. M. Imhof, "Listening to Voices and Judging People," *International Journal of Listening* 24.1 (2010): 19–33.

56. M. Argyle and M. Cook, *Gaze and Mutual Gaze* (Cambridge, UK: Cambridge University Press, 1976).

57. Hargie et al., *Social Skills in Interpersonal Communication;* Hargie, *The Handbook of Communication Skills.*

58. For an excellent review of listening skills and research supporting listening skill development, see J. Brownell, "The Skills of Listening-Centered Communication," in *Listening and Human Communication in the 21st Century,* edited by A. D. Wolvin (Oxford: Wiley-Blackwell, 2010), 141–157.

59. For a review of literature about measuring empathy, see G. D. Bodie, "The Active Empathic Listening Scale (AELS): Conceptualization and Validity Evidence," *Communication Quarterly* (in press).

60. K. J. Anderson and C. Leaper, "Meta-Analyses of Gender Effects on Conversational Interruption: Who, What, When, Where, and How," *Sex Roles* 39 (1998): 225–252.

61. For a review of the literature on gender, listening, and communication, see D. K. Ivy, *GenderSpeak* 5e (Boston: Pearson, 2012).

62. B. R. Burleson, L. K. Hanasono, G. D. Bodie, A. J. Holmstrom, J. D. McCullough, J. J. Rack, and J. Gill Rosier, "Are Gender Differences in Responses to Supportive Communication a Matter of Ability, Motivation, or Both? Reading Patterns of Situation Effects Through the Lens of a Dual-Process Theory," *Communication Quarterly* 59 (2011): 37–60.

63. S. L. Sargent and J. B. Weaver, "Listening Styles," *International Journal of Listening* 17 (2003): 5–18.

64. C. G. Pearce, I. W. Johnson, and R. T. Barker, "Assessment of the Listening Styles Inventory," *Journal of Business & Technical Communication* 17 (2003): 84–113.

65. Sargent and Weaver, "Listening Styles."

66. J. Silverman, "Attentional Styles and the Study of Sex Differences," in *Attention: Contemporary Theory and Analysis,* edited by D. I. Mostofsky (New York: Appleton-Century-Crofts, 1970), 61–79.

67. See R. G. Nichols and L. A. Stevens, "Listening to People," *Harvard Business Review* 35 (September–October 1957): 85–92.

68. K. McComb and F. M. Jablin, "Verbal Correlates of Interviewer Empathic Listening and Employment Interview Outcomes," *Communication Monographs* 51 (1984): 353–371.

69. A. Clark, "Communication Confidence and Listening Competence: An Investigation of the Relationships of Willingness to Communicate, Communication Apprehension, and Receiver Apprehension to Comprehension of Content and Emotional Meaning in Spoken Messages," *Communication Education* 38 (1989): 237–248.

70. Halone and Pecchioni, "Relational Listening."

71. Pearce et al., "Assessment of the Listening Styles Inventory."

72. Pearce et al., "Assessment of the Listening Styles Inventory."

73. G. D. Bodie, "The Nature of Supportive Listening II: The Role of Verbal Person Centeredness and Nonverbal Immediacy," *Western Journal of Communication* (in press).

74. Jacobs and Coghlan, "Sound of Silence."

75. E-A. Doohan, "Listening Behaviors of Married Couples: An Exploration of Nonverbal Presentation to a Relational Insider," *International Journal of Listening* 21 (2007): 24–41.

76. For a classic discussion of empathy and interpretive listening, see J. Stewart, "Interpretive Listening: An Alternative to Empathy," *Communication Education* 32 (1983): 379–391; Bommelje et al., "Personality Characteristics of Effective Listeners"; J. Hakansson and H. Montomery, "Empathy as an Interpersonal Phenomenon," *Journal of Social & Personal Relationships* 20 (2003): 267–284.

77. Goleman, *Emotional Intelligence.*

78. A. De Saint-Exupery, as quoted in Goleman, *Emotional Intelligence.*

79. P. Toller, "Learning to Listen, Learning to Hear: A Training Approach," *Time to Listen to Children: Personal and Professional Communication,* edited by C. Birgit (Florence, KY: Taylor, Frances/Routledge, 1999), 48–61;

T. Drollinger, L. B. Comer, and P. T. Warrington, "Development and Validation of the Active Empathetic Listening Scale," *Psychology & Marketing* 23.2 (2006): 161–180; S. L. Do and D. L. Schallert, "Emotions and Classroom Talk: Toward a Model of the Role of Affect in Students' Experiences of Classroom Discussions," *Journal of Educational Psychology* 96.4 (2004): 619–634.

80. H. J. M. Nouwen, "Listening as Spiritual Hospitality," in *Bread for the Journey* (New York: HarperCollins, 1997).

81. C. R. Rogers, "Empathic: An Unappreciated Way of Being," in *A Way of Being* (Boston: Houghton Mifflin, 1980), 137–163.

82. J. C. McCroskey and M. J. Beatty, "The Communibiological Perspective: Implications for Communication in Instruction," *Communication Education* 49 (2000): 1–6; M. J. Beatty and J. C. McCroskey, "Theory, Scientific Evidence and the Communibiological Paradigm: Reflections on Misguided Criticism," *Communication Education* 49 (2001): 36–44.

83. D. F. Barone, P. S. Hutchings, H. J. Kimmel, H. L. Traub, J. T. Cooper, and C. M. Marshall, "Increasing Empathic Accuracy Through Practice and Feedback in a Clinical Interviewing Course," *Journal of Social and Clinical Psychology* 24 (2005): 156–171.

84. Weaver and Kirtley, "Listening Styles and Empathy."

85. Goleman, *Emotional Intelligence.*

86. W. R. Miller, K. E. Hedrick, and D. R. Orlofsky, "The Helpful Responses Questionnaire: A Procedure for Measuring Therapeutic Empathy," *Journal of Clinical Psychology* 47 (1991): 444–448; A. Paukert, B. Stagner, and K. Hope, "The Assessment of Active Listening Skills in Helpline Volunteers," *Stress, Trauma, and Crisis* 7 (2004): 61–76; D. H. Levitt, "Active Listening and Counselor Self-Efficacy: Emphasis on One Micro-Skill in Beginning Counselor Training," *Clinical Supervisor* 20 (2001): 101–115; V. B. Van Hasselt, M. T. Baker, S. J. Romano, K. M. Schlessinger, M. Zuker, R. Dragone, and A. L. Perera, "Crisis (Hostage) Negotiation Training: A Preliminary Evaluation of Program Efficacy," *Criminal Justice and Behavior* 33 (2006): 56–69; H. Weger Jr., G. R. Castle, and M. C. Emmett, "Active Listening in Peer Interviews: The Influence on Perceptions of Listening Skill," *International Journal of Listening* 24 (2010): 34–49.

87. H. Weger Jr., G. R. Castle, and M. C. Emmett, "Active Listening in Peer Interviews: The Influence on Perceptions of Listening Skill," *International Journal of Listening* 24 (2010): 34–49; also see M. R. Wood, "What Makes for Successful Speaker-Listener Technique? Two Case Studies," *Family Journal* 18.1 (2010): 50–54.

88. Hargie et al., *Social Skills in Interpersonal Communication;* R. Boulton, *People Skills* (New York: 1981). We also acknowledge others who have presented excellent applications of listening and responding skills in interpersonal and group contexts: D. A. Romig and L. J. Romig, *Structured Teamwork* (D Guide) (Austin, TX: Performance Resources, 1990); S. Deep and L. Sussman, *Smart Moves* (Reading, MA: Addison-Wesley, 1990); P. R. Scholtes, *The Team Handbook* (Madison, WI: Joiner Associates, 1988); Hargie, *The Handbook of Communication Skills.*

89. R. Lemieux and M. R. Tighe, "Attachment Styles and the Evaluation of Comforting Responses: A Receiver Perspective," *Communication Research Reports* 21 (2004): 144–153; also see W. Samter, "How Gender and Cognitive Complexity Influence the Provision of Emotional Support: A Study of Indirect Effects," *Communication Reports* 15 (2002): 5–16.

90. Our discussion of appropriate and inappropriate social support responses is taken from B. D. Burleson, "Emotional Support Skill," in *Handbook of Communication and Social Interaction Skills,* edited by O. Greene and B. R. Burleson (Mahwah, NJ: Lawrence Erlbaum, 2003), 566–568.

91. L. B. Comer and T. Drollinger, "Active Empathic Listening and Selling Success: A Conceptual Framework," *Journal of Personal Selling & Sales Management* 19 (1999): 15–29; S. B. Castleberry, C. D. Shepherd, and R. Ridnour, "Effective Interpersonal Listening in the Personal Selling Environment: Conceptualization, Measurement, and Nomological Validity," *Journal of Marketing Theory and Practice* (Winter 1999): 30–38.

92. F. C. B. Hansen, H. Resnick, and J. Galea, "Better Listening: Paraphrasing and Perception Checking—A Study of the Effectiveness

of a Multimedia Skills Training Program," *Journal of Technology in Human Services* 20 (2002): 317–331; D. Ifert Johnson and K. Long, "Evaluating the Effectiveness of Listening Instruction in Introductory Communication Courses," paper presented at the International Communication Association (2008).

## Chapter 6

1. For a discussion of the role of self-awareness as a strategy for enhancing intercultural competence, see R. C. Weigl, "Intercultural Competence Through Cultural Self-Study: A Strategy for Adult Learners," *International Journal of Intercultural Relations* 33 (2009): 346–360.

2. Research documents several culture-based differences in communication, including approaches to leadership, deception, and conflict management styles. See N. Ensari and S. E. Murphy, "Cross-Cultural Variations in Leadership Perceptions and Attribution of Charisma to the Leader," *Organizational Behavior and Human Decision Processes* 92 (2003): 52–66; M. K. Lapinski and T. R. Levine, "Culture and Information Manipulation Theory: The Effects of Self-Construal and Locus of Benefit on Information Manipulation," *Communication Studies* 5 (2000): 55–73; D. Cai and E. L. Fink, "Conflict Style Differences Between Individualists and Collectivists," Communication Monographs 69 (2002): 67–87; MS. Kim and A. S. Ebesu Hubbard, "Intercultural Communication in the Global Village: How to Understand 'The Other,'" *Journal of Intercultural Communication Research* 36.3 (2007): 223–235.

3. C. Darwin, *On the Origin of Species by Means of Natural Selection, or the Preservation of Favoured Races in the Struggle of Life* (London: John Murray, 1859).

4. M. E. Heilman, S. Caleo, and M. L. Halim, "Just the Thought of It! Effects of Anticipating Computer-Mediated Communication on Gender Stereotyping," *Journal of Experimental Social Psychology* 48 (2010): 672–675.

5. J. Gray, *Men Are from Mars, Women Are from Venus* (New York: HarperCollins, 1992).

6. D. K. Ivy, *GenderSpeak: Personal Effectiveness in Gender Communication* 5e (Boston: Pearson, 2012); D. J. Canary and T. R. Emmers Sommer, *Sex and Gender Differences in Personal Relationships* (New York: Guilford, 1997).

7. D. Tannen, *You Just Don't Understand* (New York: William Morrow, 1990).

8. S. D. Farley, A. M. Ashcraft, M. F. Stasson, and R. L. Nusbaum, "Nonverbal Reactions to Conversational Interruption: A Test of Complementarity Theory and the Status/Gender Parallel," *Journal of Nonverbal Behavior* 34.4 (2010): 193–206.

9. A. C. Selbe, *Are You from Another Planet or What?* Workshop presented at the Joint Service Family Readiness Matters Conference, Phoenix, AZ (July 1999).

10. R. B. Rubin, E. M. Perse, and C. A. Barbato, "Conceptualization and Measurement of Interpersonal Communication Motives," *Human Communication Research* 14 (1988): 602–628; D. Tannen, *That's Not What I Meant!* (London: Dent, 1986).

11. T. Mottet, "The Role of Sexual Orientation in Predicting Outcome: Value and Anticipated Communication Behaviors," *Communication Quarterly* 43 (Summer 2000): 223–239; for an excellent review of literature summarizing attitudes toward gay men and lesbians, see J. Soliz, E. Ribarsky, M. M. Harrigan, and S. Tye-Williams, "Perceptions of Communication with Gay and Lesbian Family Members: Predictors of Relational Satisfaction and Implications for Outgroup Attitudes," *Communication Quarterly* 58.1 (2010): 77–95.

12. G. M. Herek, "Heterosexuals' Attitudes Toward Lesbian and Gay Men: Correlates and Gender Differences," *Journal of Sex Research* 25 (1988): 451-477.

13. Herek, "Heterosexuals' Attitudes Toward Lesbian and Gay Men"; M. S. Weinberg and C. J. Williams, *Male Homosexuals: Their Problems and Adaptations* (New York: Free Press, 1974); Mottet, "The Role of Sexual Orientation in Predicting Outcome."

14. J. Soliz, E. Ribarsky, M. M. Harrigan, and S. Tye-Williams, "Perceptions of Communication with Gay and Lesbian Family Members: Predictors of Relational Satisfaction and Implications for Outgroup Attitudes," *Communication Quarterly* 58.1 (2010): 77–95.

15. APAStyle.org, "Removing Bias in Language; Sexuality," March 2006, <www. apastyle.org/sexuality.html>.

16. A. Williams and P. Garrett, "Communication Evaluations Across the Life Span: From Adolescent Storm and Stress to Elder Aches and 'Pains,'" *Journal of Language and Social Psychology* 21 (June 2002): 101–126; also see D. Cai, H. Giles, and K. Noels, "Elderly Perceptions of Communication with Older and Younger Adults in China: Implications for Mental Health," *Journal of Applied Communication Research* 26 (1998): 32–51.

17. J. Montepare, E. Koff, D. Zaitchik, and M. Albert, "The Use of Body Movements and Gestures as Cues to Emotions in Younger and Older Adults," *Journal of Nonverbal Behavior* 23 (1999): 133–152.

18. J. Harwood, E. B. Ryan, H. Giles, and S. Tysoski, "Evaluations of Patronizing Speech and Three Response Styles in a Non-Service-Providing Context," *Journal of Applied Communication Research* 25 (1997): 170–195.

19. T. C. Segrin, "Age Moderates the Relationship Between Social Support and Psychosocial Problems," paper presented at the International Communication Association, San Diego, CA (May 2003).

20. N. Howe and W. Strauss, *Millennials Rising: The Next Great Generation* (New York: Vintage Books, 2000).

21. Howe and Strauss, *Millennials Rising*.

22. K. Meyers and K. Sadaghiani, "Millennials in the Workplace: A Communication Perspective on Millennials' Organizational Relationships and Performance," *Journal of Business & Psychology* 25.2 (2010): 225–238.

23. Our discussion of generational differences and communication is also based on J. Smith, "The Millennials Are Coming," workshop presented at Texas State University, San Marcos, TX (2006).

24. Howe and Strauss, Millennials Rising; H. Karp, C. Fuller, and D. Sirias, *Bridging the Boomer-Xer Gap: Creating Authentic Teams for High Performance at Work* (Palo Alto, CA: Davies-Black, 2002).

25. Information summarized from Howe and Strauss, *Millennials Rising*.

26. *Random House Webster's Unabridged Dictionary* (New York: Random House, 1998), 1590.

27. R. Lewontin, "The Apportionment of Human Diversity," *Evolutionary Biology* 6 (1973): 381–397.

28. S. Saulny, "Black? White? Asian? More Young Americans Choose All of the Above," *New York Times* (January 30, 2011): 1, 20–21.

29. D. Matsumoto and L. Juang, *Culture and Psychology* (Belmont, CA: Wadsworth/Thomson, 2004), 16; also see H. A. Yee, H. H. Fairchild, F. Weizmann, and E. G. Wyatt, "Addressing Psychology's Problems with Race," *American Psychologist* 48 (1994): 1132–1140.

30. B. J. Allen, *Differences Matter: Communicating Social Identity* (Long Grove, IL: Waveland Press, 2004).

31. Allen, *Differences Matter*.

32. Matsumoto and Juang, *Culture and Psychology*, 80–81.

33. S. Roberts, *Who We Are Now: The Changing Face of America in the Twenty-First Century* (New York: Henry Holt, 2004).

34. M. E. Ryan, "Another Way to Teach Migrant Students," *Los Angeles Times* (March 31, 1991): B20, as cited by M.W. Lustig and J. Koester, *Intercultural Competence: Interpersonal Communication across Cultures* (Boston: Allyn & Bacon, 2009), 11.

35. S. Saulny, "Black? White? Asian?"

36. G. Chen and W. J. Starosta, "A Review of the Concept of Intercultural Sensitivity," *Human Communication* 1 (1997): 7.

37. U.S. Census Bureau, <http://www.census.gov/newsroom/releases/archives/population/>.

38. *Newsweek* (July 12, 1999): 51.

39. Robert Bernstein, press release, Public Information Office, U.S. Census Bureau, <http://www.census.gov/Press-Release/www/releases/archives/population/ 010048.html>.

40. "One Nation, One Language?" *U.S. News & World Report* (September 25, 1995): 40, as cited by Lustig and Koester, *Intercultural Competence*, 10.

41. Bernstein, press release.

42. Roberts, *Who We Are Now*, 122; A. Caldwell, "Census: More Than Half of Texans Are Minorities," *Austin American-Statesman* (August 11, 2005): lB.

43. Roberts, *Who We Are Now*, 126.

44. Los Angeles Almanac, <http://www.laalmanac.com/population/po5.htm>, retrieved May 26, 2008.

45. Yankelovich, Inc., 2003, "Beyond the Boomers: Millennials and Generation X," <http://resources.ketchum.com/weblboomers.pdf>, retrieved May 26, 2008.

46. Adapted from *Information Please Almanac* (Boston: Houghton Mifflin, 1990) and World Almanac and Book of Facts (New York: World Almanac, 1991), as cited by Lustig and Koester, *Intercultural Competence*, 11.

47. T. Friedman, *The World Is Flat: A Brief History of the Twenty-First Century* (New York: Farrar, Straus and Giroux, 2005).

48. A. G. Smith, ed., Communication and Culture (New York: Holt, Rinehart and Winston, 1966).

49. E. T. Hall, *Beyond Culture* (Garden City, NY: Doubleday, 1976).

50. For example, see A. V. Matveeve and P. E. Nelson, "Cross Cultural Competence and Multicultural Team Performance: Perceptions of American and Russian Managers," *International Journal of Cross Cultural Management* 4 (2004): 253–270.

51. G. Hofstede, *Culture's Consequences: International Differences in Work Related Values* (Beverly Hills, CA: Sage, 1980); G. Hofstede, *Cultures and Organizations: Software of the Mind* (London: McGraw-Hill, 1991).

52. H. J. Ladegaard, "Global Culture—Myth or Reality? Perceptions of 'National Cultures' in Global Corporation," *Journal of Intercultural Communication Research* 36.2 (2007): 139–163; also see T. R. Levine, H. S. Park, and R. K Kim, "Some Conceptual and Theoretical Challenges for Cross-Cultural Communication Research in the 21st Century," *Journal of Intercultural Communication Research* 36.3 (2007): 205–221.

53. Peter Coy, "The Future of Work," *Business Week* (August 20 and 27, 2007): 43.

54. See J. B. Walther, "Interpersonal Effects in Computer-Mediated Interaction: A Relational Perspective," *Communication Research* 19 (1992): 52–90; J. B. Walther, "Relational Aspects of Computer-Mediated Communication: Experimental and Longitudinal Observations," *Organizational Science* 6 (1995): 186–203; J. B. Walther, J. F. Anderson, and D. Park, "Interpersonal Effects in Computer-Mediated Interaction: A Meta-Analysis of Social and Anti-Social Communication," *Communication Research* 21 (1994): 460–487.

55. Heilman et al., "Just the Thought of It!"

56. For an excellent overview of issues in teaching intercultural communication, see Levine et al., "Some Conceptual and Theoretical Challenges."

57. C. Ward, S. Bochner, and A. Fumham, *The Psychology of Culture Shock* (Hove, UK: Routledge, 2001).

58. C. H. Dodd, *Dynamics of Intercultural Communication* (New York: McGraw-Hill, 1998).

59. Hall, *Beyond Culture*.

60. L. A. Samovar, R. E. Porter, and L. A. Stefani, *Communication Between Cultures* (Belmont, CA: Wadsworth, 1998).

61. Hofstede, Culture's Consequences; G. Hofstede and G. J. Hofstede, *Cultures and Organizations: Software of the Mind* 2e (New York: McGraw-Hill, 2005).

62. S. Ting-Toomey, "Applying Dimensional Values in Understanding Intercultural Communication," *Communication Monographs* 77.2 (2010): 169–180.

63. For research about the effect of individualistic and collectivistic cultural values on communication and conflict management, see R. Kaushal and C. T. Kwantes, "The Role of Culture and Personality in Choice of Conflict Management Strategy," *International Journal of Intercultural Relations* 30 (2006): 579–603.

64. H. C. Triandis, "The Many Dimensions of Culture," *Academy of Management Executive* 18 (2004): 88–93.

65. M. Voronov and J. A. Singer, "The Myth of Individualism-Collectivism: A Critical Review," *Journal of Social Psychology* 142 (2002): 461–480.

66. For an excellent review of Hofstede's work, see J. W. Bing, "Hofstede's Consequences: The Impact of His Work on Consulting and Business Practices," *Academy of Management Executive* 18 (2004): 80–87.

67. Hofstede and Hofstede, *Cultures and Organizations*.

68. W. B. Gudykunst, *Bridging Differences: Effective Intergroup Communication* (Newbury Park, CA: Sage, 1998).

69. Hofstede, *Culture's Consequence*; Hofstede and Hofstede, *Cultures and Organizations*.

70. G. Hofstede, "Cultural Dimensions in Management and Planning," *Asia Pacific Journal of Management* (January 1984): 81–98; Hofstede and Hofstede, *Cultures and Organizations*.

71. For a discussion of a nation's long- and short-term time orientation, see Hofstede and Hofstede, *Cultures and Organizations*, 210–238.

72. Hofstede and Hofstede, *Cultures and Organizations*.

73. See L. Davis, "Domestic Violence," in *Encyclopedia of Social Work*, vol. 1 (Washington, DC: National Association of Social Work, 2008): 780–789; Federal Bureau of Investigation, *Violence Against Women: Estimates from the Redesigned Survey*, August 1995, <http://www.ojp.usdoj.gov>; L. K. Hamberger, D. G. Saunders, and M. Hovey, "The Prevalence of Domestic Violence in Community Practice and Rate of Physician Inquiry," *Family Medicine* 24 (1992): 283–287; Women's Action Coalition, *WAC Stats: The Facts About Women* (New York: New Press, 1993).

74. J. W. Neuliep, "Assessing the Reliability and Validity of the Generalized Ethnocentrism Scale," *Journal of Intercultural Communication Research* 31 (2002): 201–215. For additional research on the role of ethnocentrism in communication, see Y. Lin, A. Rancer, and A. Sunhee Lim, "Ethnocentrism and Intercultural Willingness to Communicate: A Cross-Cultural Comparison Between Korean and American College Students," *Journal of Intercultural Communication Research* 32 (2003): 117–128.

75. See Ensari and Murphy, "Cross-Cultural Variations"; Lapinski and Levine, "Culture and Information Manipulation Theory"; Cai and Fink, "Conflict Style Differences."

76. C. Kluckhohn and S. Murray, 1953, as quoted by J. S. Caputo, H. C. Hazel, and C. McMahon, *Interpersonal Communication* (Boston: Allyn & Bacon, 1994), 304.

77. Y. Kashima, E. S. Kashima, U. Kim, and M. Gelfand, "Describing Social World: How Is a Person, a Group, and a Relationship Described in the East and in the West?" *Journal of Experimental Social Psychology* 42 (2006): 388–396.

78. D. E. Brown, "Human Universals and Their Implications," in *Being Humans: Anthropological Universality and Particularity in Transdisciplinary Perspectives*, edited by N. Roughley (New York: Walter de Gruyter, 2000, 156–174). For an applied discussion of these universals, see S. Pinker, *The Blank Slate: The Modern Denial of Human Nature* (London: Penguin Books, 2002).

79. D. W. Kale, "Ethics in Intercultural Communication," in *Intercultural Communication: A Reader* 6e, edited by L. A. Samovar and R. E. Porter (Belmont, CA: Wadsworth, 1991).

80. L. A. Samovar and R. E. Porter, *Communication Between Cultures* (Stamford, CT: Wadsworth and Thomson Learning, 2001), 29.

81. C. S. Lewis, *The Abolition of Man* (New York: Macmillan, 1944).

82. M. Gladwell, *Blink: The Power of Thinking Without Thinking* (New York: Little, Brown, 2005).

83. S. Kamekar, M. B. Kolsawalla, and T. Mazareth, "Occupational Prestige as a Function of Occupant's Gender," *Journal of Applied Social Psychology* 19 (1988): 681–688.

84. E. Roosevelt, as cited by Lustig and Koester, *Intercultural Competence*.

85. S. Ting-Toomey, "Intercultural Conflict Training: Theory-Practice Approaches and Research Challenges," *Journal of Intercultural Communication Research* 36.3 (2007): 255–271.

86. J. G. DeJaeghere and Y. Cao, "Developing U. S. Teachers' Intercultural Competence: Does Professional Development Matter?" *International Journal of Intercultural Relations* 33 (2009): 437–447.

87. For a discussion of how intercultural competence has been applied to educational context, see P. Bayless, *Assessing the Intercultural Sensitivity of Elementary Teachers in Bilingual Schools in a Texas School District*, doctoral dissertation, University of Minnesota, Minneapolis (2009).

88. M. R. Hammer, M. J. Bennett, and R. Wiseman, "Measuring Intercultural Sensitivity: The Intercultural Development Inventory," *International Journal of Intercultural Relations* 27 (2003): 422.

89. Hammer, et al., "Measuring Intercultural Sensitivity," 421–443.

90. For additional research about the validity of measuring intercultural adaptation, see J. F. Greenholtz, "Does Intercultural Sensitivity Cross Cultures? Validity Issues in Porting Instruments Across Languages and Cultures," *International Journal of Intercultural Relations* 29 (2005): 73–89.

91. R. Vollhardt, "Enhanced External and Culturally Sensitive Attributions After Extended Intercultural Contact," *British Journal of Social Psychology* 49.2 (2010): 363–383.

92. A. N. Miller and J. A. Samp, "Planning Intercultural Interaction: Extending Anxiety Uncertainty Management Theory," *Communication Research Reports* 24.2 (2007): 87–95.

93. W. B. Gudykunst and Y. Kim, *Communicating with Strangers* (New York: Random House, 1984); Gudykunst, *Bridging Differences*.

94. Miller and Samp, "Planning Intercultural Interaction."

95. For a classic discussion of egocentrism and ethnocentrism, see T. W. Adorno, E. Frenkel-Brunswik, D. J. Levinson, and R. N. Sanford, *The Authoritarian Personality* (New York: Harper & Brothers, 1950).

96. Neuliep, "Assessing the Reliability and Validity of the Generalized Ethnocentrism Scale"; Lin et al., "Ethnocentrism and Intercultural Willingness to Communicate."

97. S. DeTurk, "Intercultural Empathy: Myth, Competency, or Possibility for Alliance Building?" *Communication Education* 50 (2001): 374–384.

98. S. Glazer, "Social Support Across Cultures," *International Journal of Intercultural Relations* 30 (2006): 605–622.

99. M. V. Redmond, "The Functions of Empathy (Decentering) in Human Relations," *Human Relations* 42 (1993): 593–606; also see M. V. Redmond, "A Multidimensional Theory and Measure of Social Decentering," *Journal of Research in Personality* 1 (1995): 35–88; for an excellent discussion of the role of emotions in establishing empathy, see D. Goleman, *Emotional Intelligence* (New York: Bantam, 1995).

100. See B. J. Broome, "Building Shared Meaning: Implications of a Relational Approach to Empathy for Teaching Intercultural Communication," *Communication Education* 40 (1991): 235–249. Much of this discussion is based on the treatment of social decentering and empathy in S. A. Beebe, S. J. Beebe, and M. V. Redmond, *Interpersonal Communication: Relating to Others* 6e (Boston: Pearson, 2011).

101. For an excellent discussion of empathy as it relates to intercultural communication, see D. W. Augsburger, *Pastoral Counseling Across Cultures* (Philadelphia: Westminister Press, 1986), 28–30.

102. H. J. M. Nouwen, *Bread for the Journey* (New York: HarperCollins, 1997).

103. See for example: A. Molinsky, "Cross-Cultural Code-Switching: The Psychological Challenges of Adapting Behavior in Foreign Cultural Interactions," *Academy of Management Review* (2007), 622–640.

104. R. H. Farrell, ed., *Off the Record: The Private Papers of Harry S. Truman* (New York: Harper & Row, 1980), 310.

105. S. M. Fowler, "Training Across Cultures: What Intercultural Trainers Bring to Diversity Training," *International Journal of Intercultural Relations* 30 (2006): 401–411.

106. L. J. Carrell, "Diversity in the Communication Curriculum: Impact on Student Empathy," *Communication Education* 46 (1997): 234–244.

107. Ting-Toomey, "Intercultural Conflict Training"; D. F. Barone, P. S. Hutchings, H. J. Kimmel, H. L. Traub, J. T. Cooper, and C. M. Marshall, "Increasing Empathic Accuracy Through Practice and Feedback in a Clinical Interviewing Course," *Journal of Social and Clinical Psychology* 24 (2005): 156–171; J. Hamilton and R. Woodward-Kron, "Developing Cultural Awareness and Intercultural Communication Through Multimedia: A Case Study from Medicine and Health Sciences," *System* 38.4 (2010): 560–568.

## Chapter 7

1. B. D. Grill, "From Telex to Twitter: Relational Communication Skills for a Wireless World," in *Making Connections: Readings in Relational Communication* 5e, edited by K. M. Galvin (New York: Oxford University Press, 2011), 89–96; J. B. Walther and A. Ramirez Jr., "New Technologies and New Directions in Online Relating," in *New Directions in Interpersonal Communication Research*, edited by S. W. Smith and S. R. Wilson (Los Angeles: Sage, 2010), 264–284; E. A. Konijn, S. Utz, M. Tanis, and S. B. Barnes, *Mediated Interpersonal Communication* (New York: Routledge, 2008); S. B. Barnes, *Computer-Mediated Communication: Human-to-Human Communication Across the Internet* (Boston: Pearson, 2003); L. C. Tidwell and J. B. Walther, "Computer-Mediated Communication Effects on Disclosure, Impressions, and Interpersonal Evaluations: Getting to Know One Another a Bit at a Time," *Human Communication Research* 28 (2002): 317–348.

2. K. M. Galvin and C. A. Wilkinson, "The Communication Process: Impersonal and Interpersonal," in *Making Connections: Reading in Relational Communication* 5e, edited by K. M. Galvin (New York: Oxford University Press, 2011) 5–12.

3. E. Berscheid, "Interpersonal Attraction," in *The Handbook of Social Psychology*, edited by G. Lindzey and E. Aronson (New York: Random House, 1985), 413–484, as reported in J. A. Simpson and B. A. Harris, "Interpersonal Attraction," in *Perspectives on Close Relationships*, edited by A. L. Weber and J. H. Harvey (Boston: Allyn & Bacon, 1994), 45–66; W. G. Graziano and J. W. Bruce, "Attraction and the Initiation of Relationships: A Review of the Empirical Literature," in *Handbook of Relationship Initiation*, edited by S. Sprecher, A. Wenzel, and J. Harvey (New York: Psychology Press, 2008), 269–295; S. Sprecher and D. Felmlee, "Insider Perspectives on Attraction," in *Handbook of Relationship Initiation*, edited by S. Sprecher, A. Wenzel, and J. Harvey (New York: Psychology Press, 2008), 297–313.

4. P. Regan, *Close Relationships* (New York: Routledge, 2011); W. Stoebe, "Self-Esteem and Interpersonal Attraction," in *Theory and Practice in Interpersonal Attraction*, edited by S. Duck (London: Academic Press, 1977).

5. J. N. Shelton, E. Thomas, T. V. West, and H. B. Bergsieker, "From Strangers to Friends: The Interpersonal Process Model of Intimacy in Developing Interracial Friendships," *Journal of Social and Personal Relationships* 27 (2010): 71–90; N. J. Shook and R. H. Fazio, "Social Network Integration: A Comparison of Same-Race and Interracial Roommate Relationships," *Group Processes and Intergroup Relations* 14 (2011): 399–406; N. J. Shook and R. H. Fazio, "Interracial Roommate Relationships: An Experimental Field Test of the Contact Hypothesis," *Psychological Science* 19 (2008): 717–723; A. K. Foeman and T. Nance, "From Miscegenation to Multiculturism: Perceptions and Stages of Interracial Relationship Development," in *Making Connections: Reading in Relational Communication* 5e, edited by K. M. Galvin (New York: Oxford University Press, 2011), 159–163.

6. M. P. Orbe and T. M. Harris, *Interracial Communication: Theory into Practice* 2e (Thousand Oaks, CA: Sage, 2008).

7. D. M. Amodio and C. J. Showers, "'Similarity Breeds Liking' Revisited: The Moderating Role of Commitment," *Journal of Social and Personal Relationships* 22 (2005): 817–836.

8. A. Bleske-Recheck, M. W. Remiker, and J. P. Baker, "Similar from the Start: Assortment in Young Adult Dating Couples and Its Link to Relationship Stability over Time," *Individual Differences Research* 7 (2009): 142–158; R. M. Montoya, R. S. Horton, and J. Kirchner, "Is Actual Similarity Necessary for Attraction? A Meta-Analysis of Actual and Perceived Similarity," *Journal of Social and Personal Relationships* 25 (2008): 889–922; B. Fehr, "Friendship Formation," in *Handbook of Relationship Initiation*, edited by S. Sprecher, A. Wenzel, and J. Harvey (New York: Psychology Press, 2008), 29–54; L. K. Guerrero, P. A. Andersen, and W. A. Afifi, *Close Encounters: Communicating in Relationships* 2e (Los Angeles: Sage, 2011); D. Byrne, "An Overview (and Underview) of Research and Theory Within the Attraction Paradigm," in *Understanding Research in Personal Relationships: A Text with Readings*, edited by W. Dragon and S. Duck (Thousand Oaks, CA: Sage, 2005), 14–26; R. Miller and D. Perlman, *Intimate Relationships* 5e (New York: McGraw-Hill, 2008).

9. A. C. High and D. H. Solomon, "Locating Computer-Mediated Social Support Within Online Communication Environments," in *Computer-Mediated Communication in Personal Relationships*, edited by K. B. Wright and L. M. Webb (New York: Peter Lang, 2010), 119–136; A. Kappas and N. C. Kramer (Eds.), *Face-to-Face Communication over the Internet: Emotions in a Web of Culture, Language, and Technology*

(Cambridge, UK: Cambridge University Press, 2011); L. Shedletsky and J. E. Aitken, *Human Communication on the Internet* (Boston: Pearson/Allyn & Bacon, 2003); K. Y. A. McKenna, A. S. Green, and M. E. J. Gleason, "Relationship Formation on the Internet: What's the Big Attraction?" *Journal of Social Issues* 58 (2002): 9–31.

10. M. T. Whitty and J. K. Gavin, "Age/Sex/Location: Uncovering the Social Cues in the Development of On-Line Relationships," *Cyberpsychology and Behavior* 4 (2001): 623–630.

11. D. K. Ivy and S. T. Wahl, *The Nonverbal Self: Communication for a Lifetime* (Boston: Pearson, 2009); L. K. Guerrero and K. Floyd, *Nonverbal Communication in Close Relationships* (Mahwah, NJ: Lawrence Erlbaum, 2006); J. H. Harvey and A. L. Weber, *Odyssey of the Heart: Close Relationships in the 21st Century* 2e (Mahwah, NJ: Lawrence Erlbaum, 2002).

12. M. Boler, "Hypes, Hopes, and Actualities: New Digital Cartesianism and Bodies in Cyberspace," in *The New Media and Cybercultures Anthology*, edited by P. K. Nayar (Malden, MA: Wiley-Blackwell, 2010), 185–208; D. Currier, "Assembling Bodies in Cyberspace: Technologies, Bodies, and Sexual Difference," in *The New Media and Cybercultures Anthology*, 254–267; J. A. McCown, D. Fisher, R. Page, and M. Homant, "Internet Relationships: People Who Meet People," *Cyberpsychology & Behavior* 4 (2001): 593–596; A. Cooper and L. Sportolari, "Romance in Cyberspace: Understanding Online Attraction," *Journal of Sex Education and Therapy* 22 (1997): 7–14; McKenna et al., "Relationship Formation on the Internet."

13. A. Cooper, I. P. McLoughlin, and K. M. Campbell, "Sexuality in Cyberspace: Update for the 21st Century," *Cyberpsychology & Behavior* 32 (2000): 521–536.

14. Guerrero et al., *Close Encounters*, 51–52.

15. S. W. Duck, *Personal Relationships and Personal Constructs: A Study of Friendship Formation* (New York: Wiley, 1973).

16. S. A. Takeuchi, "On the Matching Phenomenon in Courtship: A Probability Matching Theory of Mate Selection," *Marriage and Family Review* 40 (2006): 25–51; G. B. Forbes, L. E. Adams-Curtis, B. Rade, and P. Jaberg, "Body Dissatisfaction in Women and Men: The Role of Gender-Typing and Self-Esteem," *Sex Roles* 44 (2001): 461–484; D. Bar-Tal and L. Saxe, "Perceptions of Similarity and Dissimilarity of Attractive Couples and Individuals," *Journal of Personality and Social Psychology* 33 (1976): 772–781.

17. Fehr, "Friendship Formation"; Regan, *Close Relationships*; Guerrero et al., *Close Relationships*; Ivy and Wahl, *The Nonverbal Self*.

18. M. Prensky, "Digital Natives, Digital Immigrants," *On the Horizon* 9 (2001); *Digital Native*, <www.digitalnative.org/wiki>, retrieved July 6, 2011.

19. M. A. Dourin, "College Students' Text Messaging, Use of Textese, and Literacy Skills," *Journal of Assisted Learning* 27 (2011): 67–75; B. Jim and N. Park, "In-Person Contact Begets Calling and Texting: Interpersonal Motives for Cell Phone Use, Face-to-Face Interaction, and Loneliness," *CyberPsychology, Behavior, & Social Networking* 13 (2010): 611–618; A. Angster, M. Frank, and D. Lester, "An Exploratory Study of Students' Use of Cell Phones, Texting, and Social Networking Sites," *Psychological Reports* 107 (2010): 402–404; A. J. Johnson, M. Haigh, J. Becker, E. A. Craig, and S. Wigley, "College Students' Use of Email to Maintain Long Distance and Geographically Close Relationships: An Examination of Friend, Family, and Romantic Partner Email Correspondence," *Journal of Computer-Mediated Communication* 13 (2008): 381–404; S. Utz, "Media Use in Long-Distance Friendships," *Information, Communication, & Society* 10 (2007): 694–713.

20. K. Shonbeck, "Thoughts on CMC by an E-mailer, IMer, Blog Reader, and Facebooker," in *Making Connections: Readings in Relational Communication* 4e, edited by K. M. Galvin and P. Cooper (Los Angeles: Roxbury, 2006), 372–378.

21. D. Ballard-Reisch, B. Rozzell, L. Heldman, and D. Kamerer, "Microchannels and CMC: Short Paths to Developing, Maintaining, and Dissolving Relationships," in *Computer-Mediated Communication in Personal Relationships*, edited by K. B. Wright and L. M. Webb (New York: Peter Lang, 2010), 56–78; K. Shonbeck, "Communicating in a Connected World," in *Making Connections: Reading in Relational Communication* 5e, edited by K. M. Galvin (New York: Oxford University Press, 2011), 393–400.

22. P. M. Markey and C. N. Markey, "Romantic Ideals, Romantic Obtainment, and Relationship Experiences: The Complementarity of Interpersonal Traits Among Romantic Partners," *Journal of Social and Personal Relationships* 24 (2007): 517–533; Guerrero et al., *Close Encounters*; Miller and Perlman, *Intimate Relationships*.

23. W. Schutz, *FIRO: A Three-Dimensional Theory of Interpersonal Behavior* (New York: Holt, Rinehart and Winston, 1960).

24. H. Fisher, "The First Three Minutes," *O: The Oprah Winfrey Magazine* (November 2009): 140.

25. A. Mehrabian, *Nonverbal Communication* (Chicago: Aldine-Atherton, 1972).

26. M. L. Houser, S. M. Horan, and L. A. Furler, "Dating in the Fast Lane: How Communication Predicts Speed-Dating Success," *Journal of Social and Personal Relationships* 25 (2008): 749–768; P. W. Eastwick and E. J. Finkel, "Speed-Dating: A Powerful and Flexible Paradigm for Studying Romantic Relationship Initiation," in *Handbook of Relationship Initiation*, edited by S. Sprecher, A. Wenzel, and J. Harvey (New York: Psychology Press, 2008), 297–313.

27. P. Collett, *The Book of Tells* (London: Bantam, 2004); J. A. Daly, E. Hogg, D. Sacks, M. Smith, and L. Zimring, "Sex and Relationship Affect Social Self-Grooming," in *The Nonverbal Communication Reader: Classic and Contemporary Readings* 2e, edited by L. K. Guerrero, J. DeVito, and M. L. Hecht (Prospect Heights, IL: Waveland, 1999), 56–61.

28. M. T. Whitty, "Cyber-Flirting: An Examination of Men's and Women's Flirting Behaviour Both Offline and on the Internet," *Behaviour Change* 21 (2004): 115–126. For more information on flirting and conveying attraction, see D. D. Henningsen, M. Braz, and E. Davies, "Why Do We Flirt?" *Journal of Business Communication* 45 (2008): 483–502; L. J. Kray, "To Flirt or Not to Flirt? Sexual Power at the Bargaining Table," *Negotiation Journal* 24 (2008): 483–493; J. Hall, M. Cody, G. Jackson, and J. Flesh, "Beauty and the Flirt: Attractiveness and Approaches to Relationship Initiation," paper presented at the meeting of the International Communication Association, Montreal (May 2008); D. D. Henningsen, "Flirting with Meaning: An Examination of Miscommunication in Flirting Interactions," *Sex Roles* 50 (2004): 481–489; M. T. Whitty and A. N. Carr, "Cyberspace as Potential Space: Considering the Web as a Playground to Cyber-Flirt," *Human Relations* 56 (2003): 869–891.

29. D. Menaker, *A Good Talk: The Story and Skill of Conversation* (New York: Twelve Publishers, 2011); D. Menaker, "How to Break the Ice," *O: The Oprah Winfrey Magazine* (January 2010): 121; D. Pillet-Shore, "Doing Introductions: The Work Involved in Meeting Someone New," *Communication Monographs* 78 (2011): 73–95.

30. E. R. Merkle and R.A. Richardson, "Digital Dating and Virtual Relating: Conceptualizing Computer-Mediated Relationships," *Family Relations* 49 (2000), 190; for research on initial interaction in online relationships, see A. Ramirez Jr. and J. K. Burgoon, "The Effect of Interactivity on Initial Interactions: The Influence of Information Valence and Modality and Information Richness on Computer-Mediated Interaction," *Communication Monographs* 71 (2004): 422–447; J. B. Walther and M. R. Parks, "Cues Filtered Out, Cues Filtered In: Computer-Mediated Communication and Relationships," in *Handbook of Interpersonal Communication* 3e, edited by M. L. Knapp and J. A. Daly (Thousand Oaks, CA: Sage, 2002): 529–563; J. A. McCown, D. Fischer, R. Page, and M. Homant, "Internet Relationships: People Who Meet People," *Cyberpsychology & Behavior* 4 (2001): 593–596; McKenna et al., "Relationship Formation on the Internet."

31. M. Sunnafrank and A. Ramirez, "At First Sight: Persistent Relational Effects of Get-Acquainted Conversations," *Journal of Social and Personal Relationships* 21 (2004): 361–379.

32. C. R. Berger and R. J. Calabrese, "Some Explorations in Initial Interaction and Beyond: Toward a Developmental Theory of Interpersonal Communication," *Human Communication Research* 1 (1975): 99–112; C. R. Berger and J. J. Bradac, *Language and Social Knowledge: Uncertainty in Interpersonal Relations* (Baltimore: Edward Arnold, 1982).

33. For more recent research on relational uncertainty, we refer you to the work of Leanne Knobloch; see L. K. Knobloch and J. A. Theiss,

"Relational Uncertainty and Relationship Talk Within Courtship: A Longitudinal Actor-Partner Interdependence Model," *Communication Monographs* 78 (2011): 3–26; L. K. Knobloch, "Relational Uncertainty and Interpersonal Communication," in *New Directions in Interpersonal Communication Research*, edited by S. W. Smith and S. R. Wilson (Los Angeles: Sage, 2010), 69–93; L. K. Knobloch, "Uncertainty Reduction Theory: Communicating Under Conditions of Ambiguity," in *Engaging Theories in Interpersonal Communication: Multiple Perspectives*, edited by L. A. Baxter and D. O. Braithwaite (Los Angeles: Sage, 2008), 133–144.

34. A. Lenhart, O. Lewis, and L. Rainie, "Teenage Life Online: The Rise of the Instant Message Generation and the Internet's Impact on Friendships and Family Relationships," in: *Making Connections: Reading in Relational Communication* 4e, edited by K. M. Galvin and P. Cooper (Los Angeles: Roxbury, 2006), 355–362; M. White, "On the Internet, Everybody Worries That You're a Dog: The Gender Expectations and Beauty Ideals of Online Personals and Text-Based Chat," in *Readings in Gender Communication*, edited by P. M. Backlund and M. R. Williams (Belmont, CA: Thomson/Wadsworth, 2004), 284–298; McCown, "Internet Relationships"; Whitty, "Cyberspace as Potential Space"; A. N. Joinson and B. Dietz-Uhler, "Explanations for the Perpetration of and Reactions to Deception in a Virtual Community," *Social Science Computer Review* 20 (2002): 275–289.

35. D. Freitas, *Sex and the Soul: Juggling Sexuality, Spirituality, Romance, and Religion on America's College Campuses* (New York: Oxford University Press, 2010).

36. C. L. Kleinke, F. B. Meeker, and R. A. Staneski, "Preference for Opening Lines: Comparing Ratings by Men and Women," *Sex Roles* 15 (1986): 585–600; E. Weber, *How to Pick Up Girls!* (New York: Bantam Books, 1970).

37. C. Senko and V. Fyffe, "An Evolutionary Perspective on Effective vs. Ineffective Pick-up Lines," *Journal of Social Psychology* 150 (2010): 648–667.

38. D. Dickson and O. Hargie, "Questioning," in *The Handbook of Communication Skills* 3e, edited by O. Hargie (London: Routledge, 2006), 121–145.

39. A. L. Vangelisti, M. L. Knapp, and J. A. Daly, "Conversational Narcissism," *Communication Monographs* 57 (1990): 251–274; J. M. Twenge, S. Konrath, J. D. Foster, W. K. Campbell, and B. J. Bushman, "Egos Inflating over Time: A Cross-Temporal Meta-Analysis of the Narcissistic Personality Inventory," *Journal of Personality* 76 (2008): 875–901; J. M. Twenge, *Generation Me: Why Today's Young Americans Are More Confident, Assertive, Entitled—and More Miserable Than Ever Before* (New York: Free Press, 2006); J. M. Twenge and W. K. Campbell, *The Narcissism Epidemic: Living in the Age of Entitlement* (New York: Free Press, 2011).

40. C. Derber, *The Pursuit of Attention: Power and Ego in Everyday Life* (New York: Oxford University Press, 2000).

41. J. Holmes, "Complimenting—A Positive Politeness Strategy," in *Language and Gender: A Reader*, edited by J. Coates (Malden, MA: Blackwell, 1998), 100–120.

42. M. Strobel, *The Compliment Quotient: Boost Your Spirits, Spark Your Relationships, and Uplift the World* (New York: Wise Roads Press, 2011); C. Matheson, *The Art of the Compliment: Using Kind Words with Grace and Style* (New York: Skyhorse Publishing, 2009); D. C. Marigold, J. G. Holmes, and M. Ross, "More Than Words: Compliments from Romantic Partners Foster Security in Low Self-Esteem Individuals," *Journal of Personality and Social Psychology* 92 (2007): 232–248; E. M. Doohan and V. Manusov, "The Communication of Compliments in Romantic Relationships: An Investigation of Relational Satisfaction and Sex Differences and Similarities in Compliment Behavior," *Western Journal of Communication* 68 (2004): 170–194; C. Parisi and P. Wogan, "Compliment Topics and Gender," *Women & Language* 29 (2006): 21–28.

43. M. Beck, "Why It's Harder to Receive Than to Give," *O: The Oprah Winfrey Magazine* (September 2006): 81–83.

44. "The Health Benefits of Strong Relationships," *Harvard Women's Health Watch* 18 (December 2010): 1.

45. Harvey and Weber, *Odyssey of the Heart*, 105–106.

46. S. Jourard, *The Transparent Self* (Princeton, NJ: Van Nostrand, 1971).

47. D. W. Johnson, *Reaching Out: Interpersonal Effectiveness and Self-Actualization* 10e (Boston: Pearson, 2009), 48–49.

48. V. J. Derlega, B. Winstead, A. Mathews, and A. L. Braitman, "Why Does Someone Reveal Highly Personal Information? Attributions For and Against Self-Disclosure in Close Relationships," *Communication Research Reports* 25 (2008): 115–130.

49. V. Cho and H. Hung, "The Effectiveness of Short Message Service for Communication with Concerns of Privacy Protection and Conflict Avoidance," *Journal of Computer-Mediated Communication* 16 (2011): 250–270; J. T. Child and S. Petronio, "Unpacking the Paradoxes of Privacy in CMC Relationships: The Challenges of Blogging and Relational Communication on the Internet," in *Computer-Mediated Communication in Personal Relationships*, edited by K. B. Wright and L. M. Webb (New York: Peter Lang, 2010), 21–40; T. Afifi and K. Steuber, "The Revelation Risk Model (RRM): Factors That Predict the Revelation of Secrets and the Strategies Used to Reveal Them," *Communication Monographs* 76 (2009): 144–176; A. M. Hosek and J. Thompson, "Communication Privacy Management and College Instruction: Exploring the Rules and Boundaries That Frame Instructor Private Disclosures," *Communication Education* 58 (2009); 327–349; S. Petronio and W. T. Durham, "Communication Privacy Management Theory," in *Exploring Theories in Interpersonal Communication*, edited by L. A. Baxter and D. O. Braithwaite (Los Angeles: Sage, 2008), 309–322; S. Petronio, "Translational Research Endeavors and the Practices of Communication Privacy Management," *Journal of Applied Communication Research* 35 (2007): 218–222; S. Petronio, "The Boundaries of Privacy: Praxis of Everyday Life," in *Balancing Secrets of Private Disclosure*, edited by S. Petronio (Mahwah, NJ: Lawrence Erlbaum, 2000), 37–49; L. B. Rosenfeld, "Overview of the Ways Privacy, Secrecy, and Disclosure Are Balanced in Today's Society," in *Balancing Secrets of Private Disclosure*, edited by S. Petronio (Mahwah, NJ: Lawrence Erlbaum, 2000), 3–17.

50. K. B. Carnelley, E. G. Hepper, C. Hicks, and W. Turner, "Perceived Parental Reactions to Coming Out, Attachment, and Romantic Relationship Views," *Attachment and Human Development* 13 (2011): 217–236; M. Vaughan and C. Waehler, "Coming Out Growth: Conceptualizing and Measuring Stress-Related Growth Associated with Coming Out to Others as a Sexual Minority," *Journal of Adult Development* 17 (2010): 94–109; L. Heatherington and J. A. Lavner, "Coming to Terms with Coming Out: Review and Recommendations for Family Systems-Focused Research," *Journal of Family Psychology* 22 (2008): 329–343; M. L. Rasmussen, "The Problem of Coming Out," *Theory into Practice* 43 (2004): 144–151.

51. J. Kim and K. Dindia, "Online Self-Disclosure: A Review of Research," in *Computer-Mediated Communication in Personal Relationships*, edited by K. B. Wright and L. M. Webb (New York: Peter Lang, 2010), 156–180; C. L. Toma and J. T. Hancock, "A New Twist on Love's Labor: Self-Presentation in Online Dating Profiles," in *Computer-Mediated Communication in Personal Relationships*, edited by K. B. Wright and L. M. Webb (New York: Peter Lang, 2010), 41–55; C. M. H. Bane, M. Cornish, N. Erspamer, and L. Kampman, "Self-Disclosure Through Weblogs and Perceptions of Online and 'Real-Life' Friendships Among Female Bloggers," *Cyberpsychology, Behavior, & Social Networking* 13 (2010): 131–139; R. West and L. H. Turner, "Technology and Interpersonal Communication," in *Making Connections: Reading in Relational Communication* 5e, edited by K. M. Galvin (New York: Oxford University Press, 2011), 379–386; S. Young, D. Dutta, and G. Dommety, "Extrapolating Psychological Insights from Facebook Profiles: A Study of Religion and Relationship Status," *CyberPsychology & Behavior* 12 (2009): 347–350; K. Y. A. McKenna, "MySpace or Your Place: Relationship Initiation and Development in the Wired and Wireless World," in *Handbook of Relationship Initiation*, edited by S. Sprecher, A. Wenzel, and J. Harvey (New York: Psychology Press, 2008), 235–247; J. B. Walther, "Social Information Processing Theory: Impressions and Relationship Development Online," in *Exploring Theories in Interpersonal Communication*, edited by L. A. Baxter and D. O. Braithwaite (Los Angeles: Sage, 2008), 391–404.

52. Shonbeck, "Thoughts on CMC by an E-mailer, IMer, Blog Reader, and Facebooker," 377.

53. L. R. Baker and D. L. Oswald, "Shyness and Online Social Networking Services," *Journal of Social and Personal Relationships* 27 (2010): 873–889; W. S. Sanders and P. Amason, "Communication Competence and Apprehension During CMC in Online and Face-to-Face Relationships," in *Computer-Mediated Communication in Personal Relationships*, edited by K. B. Wright and L. M. Webb (New York: Peter Lang, 2010), 79–97.

54. E. Butler, E. McCann, and J. Thomas, "Privacy Setting Awareness on Facebook and Its Effect on User-Posted Content," *Human Communication* 14 (2011): 39–55; B. Debatin, J. P. Lovejoy, A-K. Horn, and B. N. Hughes, "Facebook and Online Privacy: Attitudes, Behaviors, and Unintended Consequences," *Journal of Computer-Mediated Communication* 15 (2009): 83–108; J. P. Mazer, R. E. Murphy, and C. J. Simonds, "I'll See You on 'Facebook': The Effects of Computer-Mediated Teacher Self-Disclosure on Student Motivation, Affective Learning, and Classroom Climate," *Communication Education* 56 (2007): 1–17.

55. V. Brown and E. Vaughn, "The Writing on the (Facebook) Wall: The Use of Social Networking Sites in Hiring Decisions," *Journal of Business and Psychology* 26 (2011): 219–225; R. Stross, "How to Lose Your Job on Your Own Time: Your Employer Can Learn Far Too Much About You on the Internet," *Corpus Christi Caller Times* (January 6, 2008): 1D, 3D.

56. I. Altman and D. Taylor, *Social Penetration: The Development of Relationships* (New York: Holt, Rinehart and Winston, 1973); B. M. Montgomery, "Communication in Close Relationships," in *Perspectives on Close Relationships*, edited by S. Sprecher, A. Wenzel, and J. Harvey (New York: Psychology Press, 2008), 67–87; P. A. Mongeau and M. L. Miller Henningsen, "Stage Theories of Relationship Development: Charting the Course of Interpersonal Communication," in *Exploring Theories in Interpersonal Communication*, edited by L. A. Baxter and D. O. Braithwaite (Los Angeles: Sage, 2008), 363–375.

57. J. Luft, *Group Process: An Introduction to Group Dynamics* (Palo Alto, CA: Mayfield, 1970).

58. P. D. Bolls, "Understanding Emotion from a Superordinate Dimensional Perspective: A Productive Way Forward for Communication Processes and Effects Studies," *Communication Monographs* 77 (2010): 146.

59. M. Lewis, J. M. Haviland-Jones, and L. Feldman Barrett (Eds.), *Handbook of Emotions* 3e (New York: Guilford, 2010); B. R. Burleson, "Understanding the Outcomes of Supportive Communication: A Dual Process Approach," *Journal of Social and Personal Relationships* 26 (2009): 21–38; S. Metts and B. Wood, "Interpersonal Emotional Competence," in *Studies in Applied Interpersonal Communication*, edited by M. T. Motley (Los Angeles: Sage, 2008), 267–285; S. Metts and S. L. Mikucki, "The Emotional Landscape of Romantic Relationship Initiation," in *Handbook of Relationship Initiation*, edited by S. Sprecher, A. Wenzel, and J. Harvey (New York: Psychology Press, 2008), 353–371; A. M. Bippus and S. L. Young, "Owning Your Emotions: Reactions to Expressions of Self- versus Other-Attributed Positive and Negative Emotions," *Journal of Applied Communication Research* 33 (2005): 26–45; C. Scott and K. Kroman Myers, "The Socialization of Emotion: Learning Emotion Management at the Fire Station," *Journal of Applied Communication Research* 33 (2005): 67–92; P. Mehta and M. S. Clark, "Toward Understanding Emotions in Intimate Relationships," in *Perspectives on Close Relationships*, edited by S. Sprecher, A. Wenzel, and J. Harvey (New York: Psychology Press, 2008), 88–109.

60. M-S. Kim and A. S. Ebesu Hubbard, "Intercultural Communication in the Global Village: How to Understand 'The Other,'" *Journal of Intercultural Communication Research* 36 (2007): 223–235; A. Molinsky, "Cross-Cultural Code-Switching: The Psychological Challenges of Adapting Behavior in Foreign Cultural Interactions," *Academy of Management Review* 32 (2007): 622–640; S. Glazer, "Social Support Across Cultures," *International Journal of Intercultural Relations* 30 (2006): 605–622.

61. E. R. McDaniel, "Nonverbal Communication: A Reflection of Cultural Themes," in *Intercultural Communication: A Reader* 8e, edited by L. A. Samovar and R. E. Porter (Belmont, CA: Wadsworth, 1997), 256–265.

62. F. Warren, *PostSecret* (New York: William Morrow, 2005), 2.

63. U. Hess, R. B. Adams Jr., K. Grammer, and R. E. Kleck, "Face Gender and Emotion Expression: Are Angry Women More Like Men?" *Journal of Vision* 9 (2009): 1–8; A. Campbell and S. Muncer, "Intent to Harm or Injure? Gender and the Expression of Anger," *Aggressive Behavior* 34 (2008): 282–293; T. B. Kashdan, A. Mishra, W. E. Breen, and J. J. Froh, "Gender Differences in Gratitude: Examining Appraisals, Narratives, the Willingness to Express Emotions, and Changes in Psychological Needs," *Journal of Personality* 77 (2009): 1–40; R. W. Simon and L. E. Nath, "Gender and Emotion in the United States: Do Men and Women Differ in Self-Reports of Feelings and Expressive Behavior?" *American Journal of Sociology* 109 (2004): 1137–1176.

64. Jourard, *The Transparent Self.*

65. B. B. Burleson, "Introduction to the Special Issue: Psychological Mediators of Sex Differences in Emotional Support," *Communication Reports* 15 (2002); 1–4; W. Pollack, *Real Boys: Rescuing Our Sons from the Myths of Boyhood* (New York: Owl Books, 1999); O. Silverstein and B. Rashbaum, *The Courage to Raise Good Men* (New York: Penguin, 1995).

66. <www.wildxangel.com>; <www.thirdage.com>; <www.onlinedating-magazine.com>, retrieved July 8, 2011.

## Chapter 8

1. W. K. Rawlins, *The Compass of Friendship: Narratives, Identities, and Dialogues* (Los Angeles: Sage, 2009); M. Monsour, *Women and Men as Friends: Relationships Across the Life Span in the 21st Century* (Mahwah, NJ: Lawrence Erlbaum, 2002); M. Paul, *The Friendship Crisis: Finding, Making, and Keeping Friends When You're Not a Kid Anymore* (New York: Rodale Books, 2004); B. Fehr, *Friendship Processes* (Thousand Oaks, CA: Sage, 1996); W. Rawlins, *Friendship Matters: Communication, Dialectics, and the Life Course* (Hawthorne, NY: Aldine de Gruyter, 1992); W. J. Dickens and D. Perlman, "Friendship over the Life-Cycle," in *Personal Relationships 2: Developing Personal Relationships*, edited by S. W. Duck and R. Gilmour (London: Academic Press, 1981).

2. N. Way, *Deep Secrets: Boys' Friendships and the Crisis of Connection* (Cambridge, MA: Harvard University Press, 2011); R. Blieszner, "Close Relationships over Time," as reported in J. A. Simpson and B. A. Harris, "Interpersonal Attraction," in *Perspectives on Close Relationships*, edited by A. L. Weber and J. H. Harvey (Boston: Allyn & Bacon, 1994), 1–18.

3. J. Yager, *Friendshifts: The Power of Friendship and How It Shapes Our Lives* (Stamford, CT: Hannacrois Creek Books, 1999); W. Rawlins, "Being There for Friends," in *Making Connections: Readings in Relational Communication* 4e, edited by K. M. Galvin and P. Cooper (Los Angeles: Roxbury, 2006), 329–332.

4. B. McEwan and L. K. Guerrero, "Freshmen Engagement Through Communication: Predicting Friendship Formation Strategies and Perceived Availability of Network Resources from Communication Skills," *Communication Studies* 61 (2010): 445–463; B. Fehr, "Friendship Formation," in *Handbook of Relationship Initiation*, edited by S. Sprecher, A. Wenzel, and J. Harvey (New York: Psychology Press, 2008), 29–54; G. Foster, "Making Friends: A Nonexperimental Analysis of Social Pair Formation," *Human Relations* 58 (2005): 1443–1465; A. J. Johnson, E. Wittenberg, M. M. Villagran, M. Mazur, and P. Villagran, "Relational Progression as a Dialectic: Examining Turning Points in Communication Among Friends," *Communication Monographs* 70 (2003): 230–249.

5. Work and Family Facts & Statistics, <www.aflcio.org>, retrieved July 5, 2010; M. J. Fay and S. L. Kline, "Coworker Relationships and Informal Communication in High-Intensity Telecommuting," *Journal of Applied Communication Research* 39 (2011): 144–163; P. M. Sias and D. J. Cahill, "From Coworkers to Friends: The Development of Peer Friendships in the Workplace," *Western Journal of Communication* 62 (1998): 273–299; G. A. Fine, "Friendships in the Workplace," in *Making Connections: Readings in Relational Communication* 4e, edited by K. M. Galvin and P. Cooper (Los Angeles: Roxbury, 2006), 270–277.

6. M. Hughes, K. Morrison, and K. J. K. Asada, "What's Love Got to Do with It? Exploring the Impact of Maintenance Rules, Love Attitudes, and Network Support on Friends with Benefits Relationships," *Western Journal of Communication* 69 (2005): 49–66.

7. A. Paik, "'Hookups,' Dating, and Relationship Quality: Does the Type of Sexual Involvement Matter?" *Social Science Research* 39 (2010): 739–753; M. A. Bisson and T. R. Levine, "Negotiating a Friends with Benefits Relationship," *Archives of Sexual Behavior* 38 (2009): 66–73; M. Epstein, J. P. Calzo, A. P. Smiler, and L. M. Ward, "'Anything from Making Out to Having Sex': Men's Negotiations of Hooking Up and Friends with Benefits Scripts," *Journal of Sex Research* 46 (2009): 414–424; A. K. Goodboy and S. A. Myers, "Relational Maintenance Behaviors of Friends with Benefits: Investigating Equity and Relational Characteristics," *Human Communication* 11 (2008): 71–85; J. Puentes, D. Knox, and M. E. Zusman, "Participants in 'Friends with Benefits' Relationships," *College Student Journal* 42 (2008): 176–180; E. L. Paul, A. Wenzel, and J. Harvey, "Hookups: A Facilitator or a Barrier to Relationship Initiation and Intimacy Development?" in *Handbook of Relationship Initiation*, edited by S. Sprecher, A. Wengel, and J. Harvey (New York: Psychology Press, 2008), 375–390; K. McGinty, D. Knox, and M. E. Zusman, "Friends with Benefits: Women Want 'Friends,' Men Want 'Benefits,'" *College Student Journal* 41 (2007): 1128–1131; K. Bogle, *Hooking Up: Sex, Dating, and Relationships on Campus* (New York: New York University Press, 2008); D. Freitas, *Sex and the Soul: Juggling Sexuality, Spirituality, Romance, and Religion on America's College Campuses* (New York: Oxford University Press, 2008); E. M. Eshbaugh and G. Gute, "Hookups and Sexual Regret Among College Women," *Journal of Social Psychology* 148 (2008): 77–89.

8. Hughes et al., "What's Love Got to Do with It?"

9. J. Harwood, *Understanding Communication and Aging* (Los Angeles: Sage, 2007); L. Gee, *Friends: Why Men and Women Are from the Same Planet* (New York: Bloomsbury, 2004); Monsour, *Women and Men as Friends*.

10. "A Woman's Nation Changes Everything," in *The Shriver Report* (Washington, DC: Center for American Progress, 2009), <awomansnation.com>, retrieved October 29, 2009; *Women in America: Indicators of Social and Economic Well-Being*, March 1, 2011, <www.whitehouse.gov>, retrieved March 13, 2011. K. Galvin and C. Bylund, "First Marriage Families: Gender and Communication," in *Women and Men Communicating: Challenges and Changes* 2e, edited by L. P. Arliss and D. J. Borisoff (Prospect Heights, IL: Waveland, 2001), 132–148; V. Satir, "The Rules You Live By," in *Making Connections: Readings in Relational Communication* 4e, edited by K. M. Galvin and P. Cooper (Los Angeles: Roxbury, 2006), 168–174; R. Miller and D. Perlman, *Intimate Relationships* 5e (New York: McGraw-Hill, 2009).

11. *Miami Herald* (July 9, 1982): 12A.

12. L. Schnurnberger, "Happiness Is a Full House," *Parade Magazine* (May 2, 2010): 6–8; L. Libby, "Grandparents Can Get Help in Raising Kids," *Corpus Christi Caller Times* (September 27, 2009): B1; P. Schrodt, J. Soliz, and D. O. Braithwaite, "A Social Relations Model of Everyday Talk and Relational Satisfaction in Stepfamilies," *Communication Monographs* 75 (2008): 190–217; K. Floyd and M. T. Morman, *Widening the Family Circle* (Los Angeles: Sage, 2006); D. O. Braithwaite, P. W. Toller, K. L. Daas, W. T. Durham, and A. C. Jones, "Centered but Not Caught in the Middle: Stepchildren's Perceptions of Dialectical Contradictions in the Communication of Co-Parents," *Journal of Applied Communication Research* 36 (2008): 33–55; R. L. Deal, *The Smart Stepfamily: Seven Steps to a Healthy Family* (New York: Bethany House, 2006).

13. V. Satir, *The New Peoplemaking* (Mountain View, CA: Science & Behavior Books, 1988), 4.

14. P. Schrodt, P. L. Witt, and A. S. Messersmith, "A Meta-Analytical Review of Family Communication Patterns and Their Associations with Information Processing, Behavioral, and Psychosocial Outcomes," *Communication Monographs* 75 (2008): 248–269.

15. Work and Family Facts & Statistics; *Contexts: A Publication of the American Sociological Association* 3, 2004, <www.contextsmagazine.org>.

16. National Association of Colleges and Employers, "Job Outlook 2011," <http://www.jobweb.com>.

17. R. B. Adler and J. M. Elmhorst, *Communication at Work* 10e (New York: McGraw-Hill, 2010); D. O'Hair, G. W. Friedrich, and L. A. Dixon, *Strategic Communication in Business and the Professions* 7e (Boston: Pearson, 2010).

18. M. L. Knapp and A. Vangelisti, "Relationship Stages: A Communication Perspective," in *Making Connections: Readings in Relational Communication* 4e, edited by K. M. Galvin and P. Cooper (Los Angeles: Roxbury, 2006), 132–139; M. L. Knapp and A. L. Vangelisti, *Interpersonal and Human Relationships* 6e (Boston: Pearson, 2008); K. N. Dunleavy and M. Booth-Butterfield, "Idiomatic Communication in the Stages of Coming Together and Falling Apart," *Communication Quarterly* 57 (2009): 416–432; P. A. Mongeau and M. L. Miller Henningsen, "Stage Theories of Relationship Development: Charting the Course of Interpersonal Communication," in *Engaging Theories in Interpersonal Communication: Multiple Perspectives*, edited by L. A. Baxter and D. O. Braithwaite (Los Angeles: Sage, 2008), 363–375; S. A. Welch and R. B. Rubin, "Development of Relationship Stage Measures," *Communication Quarterly* 50 (2002): 24–40; L. K. Guerrero, *Close Encounters: Communication in Relationships* 3e (Thousand Oaks, CA: Sage, 2011).

19. D. Hauani Solomon, K. M. Weber, and K. R. Steuber, "Turbulence in Relational Transitions," in *New Directions in Interpersonal Communication Research*, edited by S. W. Smith and S. R. Wilson (Los Angeles: Sage, 2010), 115–134; R. M. Dailey, A. D. Hampel, and J. B. Roberts, "Relational Maintenance in On-Again/Off-Again Relationships: An Assessment of How Relational Maintenance, Uncertainty, and Commitment Vary by Relationship Type and Status," *Communication Monographs* 77 (2010): 75–101; R. M. Dailey, K. Rossetto, R. A. Pfiester, and C. A. Surra, "A Qualitative Analysis of On-Again/Off-Again Romantic Relationships: 'It's Up and Down, All Around,'" *Journal of Social and Personal Relationships* 26 (2009): 443–466; R. M. Dailey, R. A. Pfiester, B. Jin, G. Beck, and G. Clark, "On-Again/Off-Again Dating Relationships: How Are They Different from Other Dating Relationships?" *Personal Relationships* 16 (2009): 23–47.

20. Knapp and Vangelisti, *Interpersonal Communication and Human Relationships*; Knapp and Vangelisti, "Relationship Stages."

21. S. W. Duck, "A Topography of Relationship Disengagement and Dissolution," in *Personal Relationships 4: Dissolving Relationships*, edited by S. W. Duck (New York: Academic Press, 1982); Guerrero, *Close Encounters*.

22. A. Sutherland, "The Science of Heartbreak," *Women's Health* (April 2010): 70; M. Pelaez, T. Field, M. Diego, O. Deeds, and J. Delgado, "Insecurity, Control, and Disinterest Behaviors Are Related to Breakup Distress in University Students," *College Student Journal* 45 (2010): 333–340; H. Fisher, "Of Lost Love and Old Bones," *The Chronicle Review* (June 6, 2008): B5; D. Davis, P. R. Shaver, and M. L. Vernon, "Physical, Emotional, and Behavioral Reactions to Breaking Up: The Roles of Gender, Age, Emotional Involvement, and Attachment Style," *Personality and Social Psychology Bulletin* 29 (2003): 871–884.

23. Knapp and Vangelisti, *Interpersonal Communication and Human Relationships*; M. L. Knapp and A. L. Vangelisti, "Relational Decline," in *Making Connections: Readings in Relational Communication* 4e, edited by K. M. Galvin and P. Cooper (Los Angeles: Roxbury, 2006), 269–273; W. R. Cupach, "Dialectical Process in the Disengagement of Interpersonal Relationships," in *Making Connections: Readings in Relational Communication* 4e, edited by K. M. Galvin and P. Cooper (Los Angeles: Roxbury, 2006), 274–280.

24. L. Locker Jr., W. D. McIntosh, A. A. Hackney, J. H. Wilson, and K. E. Wiegand, "The Breakup of Romantic Relationships: Situational Predictors of Perception of Recovery," *North American Journal of Psychology* 12 (2010): 565–578; D. Cullingson, *Breaking Up Blues: A Guide to Survival* (New York: Routledge, 2008); K. Matthews, "The Dear John Talk and Other Dreaded Conversations: Eight Ways to Make Them Easier, Kinder, Gentler," *O: The Oprah Winfrey Magazine* (August 2007): 144, 146; L. Sapadin, *Now I Get It! Totally Sensational Advice for Living and Loving* (Parker, CO: Outskirts Press, 2006).

25. T. Levine and S. L. Fitzpatrick, "You Know Why; The Question Is How? Relationships Between Reasons and Methods in Romantic Breakups," paper presented at the meeting of the International Communication Association, New York (May 2005), New York; S. P. Banks, D. M. Altendorf, J. O. Greene, and M. Cody, "An Examination of Relationship Disengagement: Perceptions, Breakup Strategies, and Outcomes," *Western Journal of Speech Communication* 51 (1987): 19–41.

26. D. K. Ivy, *GenderSpeak: Personal Effectiveness in Gender Communication* 5e (Boston: Pearson, 2012).

27. Duck, "A Topography of Relationship Disengagement and Dissolution."

28. P. J. Lannutti and K. A. Cameron, "Beyond the Breakup: Heterosexual and Homosexual Post-Dissolutional Relationships," *Communication Quarterly* 50 (2002): 153–170.

29. K. Koenig Kellas and S. Sato, "'The Worst Part Is, We Don't Even Talk Anymore': Post-Dissolutional Communication in Break Up Stories," in *Making Connections: Readings in Relational Communication* 5e, edited by K. M. Galvin (New York: Oxford University Press, 2011), 297–309; A. N. Lambert and P. C. Hughes, "The Influence of Goodwill, Secure Attachment, and Positively Toned Disengagement Strategy on Reports of Communication Satisfaction in Nonmarital Post-Dissolution Relationships," *Communication Research Reports* 27 (2010): 171–183; J. Koenig Kellas, D. Bean, C. Cunningham, and K. Y. Cheng, "The Ex-Files: Trajectories, Turning Points, and Adjustment in the Development of Post-Dissolutional Relationships," *Journal of Social and Personal Relationships* 25 (2008): 23–50.

30. L. A. Baxter and D. O. Braithwaite, "Relational Dialectics Theory, Applied," in *New Directions in Interpersonal Communication Research*, edited by S. W. Smith and S. R. Wilson (Los Angeles: Sage, 2010), 48–66; L. A. Baxter and D. O. Braithwaite, "Relational Dialectics Theory: Crafting Meaning from Competing Discourses," in *Engaging Theories in Interpersonal Communication*, edited by L. A. Baxter and D. O. Braithwaite (Los Angeles: Sage, 2008), 349–361; L. A. Baxter and B. M. Montgomery, *Relating: Dialogues and Dialectics* (New York: Guilford, 1996); L. A. Baxter and B. M. Montgomery, "Rethinking Communication in Personal Relationships from a Dialectical Perspective," in *Communication and Personal Relationships*, edited by K. Dindia and S. Duck (New York: Wiley, 2000), 31–53; D. Goldsmith, "A Dialectic Perspective on the Expression of Autonomy and Connection in Romantic Relationships," *Western Journal of Speech Communication* 54 (1990): 537–556; R. A. Bell and N. L. Buerkel-Rothfuss, "S(he) Loves Me, S(he) Loves Me Not: Predictors of Relational Information-Seeking in Courtship and Beyond," *Communication Quarterly* 38 (1990): 64–82; R. Nozick, "Love's Bond," in *Gender Basics: Feminist Perspectives on Women and Men*, edited by A. Minas (Belmont, CA: Wadsworth, 1993), 152–159; L. A. Peplau, "Men and Women in Love," in *Gender, Families, and Close Relationships*, edited by D. L. Sollie and L. A. Leslie (Newbury Park, CA: Sage, 1994), 19–49; Galvin and Bylund, "First Marriage Families."

31. E. Sahlstein and T. Dun, "'I Wanted Time to Myself and He Wanted to Be Together All the Time': Constructing Breakups as Managing Autonomy-Connection," *Qualitative Research Reports in Communication* 9 (2008): 37–45.

32. R. L. Duran, L. Kelly, and T. Rotaru, "Mobile Phones in Romantic Relationships and the Dialectic of Autonomy Versus Connection," *Communication Quarterly* 59 (2011): 19–36.

33. C. Prentice, "Relational Dialectics Among In-Laws," *Journal of Family Communication* 9 (2009): 67–89.

34. L. Stafford, S. L. Kline, and J. Dimmick, "Home E-Mail: Relational Maintenance and Gratification Opportunities," *Journal of Broadcasting & Electronic Media* 43 (1999): 659–669.

35. V. S. Millner, "Internet Infidelity: A Case of Intimacy with Detachment," *Family Journal* 16 (2008): 78–82; B. H. Henline, L. K. Lamke, and M. D. Howard, "Exploring Perceptions of Online Infidelity," *Personal Relationships* 14 (2007): 113–128; B. L. Avila Mileham, "Online Infidelity in Internet Chat Rooms: An Ethnographic Exploration," *Computers in Human Behavior* 23 (2007): 11–31; K. M. Hertlein and F. P. Piercy, "Internet Infidelity: A Critical Review of the Literature," *Family Journal* 14 (2006): 366–371.

36. M. Rabbitt, "Is Infidelity Obsolete?" *Women's Health* (July/August 2010): 144.

37. I. Tsapelas, H. E. Fisher, and A. Aron, "Infidelity: When, Where, Why," in *The Dark Side of Close Relationships II*, edited by W. R. Cupach and B. H. Spitzberg (New York: Routledge, 2011), 175–196; E. Nersesian-Solé, "What He's Hiding from You," *Women's Health* (November 2010): 98–100; J. A. Samp and J. L. Monahan, "Alcohol-Influenced Nonverbal Behaviors During Discussions About a Relationship Problem," *Journal of Nonverbal Behavior* 33 (2009): 193–211; F. S. Christopher and S. Sprecher, "Sexuality in Marriage, Dating, and Other Relationships: A Decade Review," in *Speaking of Sexuality: Interdisciplinary Readings*, edited by J. K. Davidson Sr. and N. B. Moore (Los Angeles: Roxbury, 2005): 54–71.

38. M. L. Hans, B. D. Selvidge, K. A. Tinker, and L. M. Webb, "Online Performances of Gender: Blogs, Gender-Bending, and Cybersex as Relational Examples," in *Computer-Mediated Communication in Personal Relationships*, edited by K. B. Wright and L. M. Webb (New York: Peter Lang, 2010), 303.

39. K. Y. A. McKenna, A. S. Green, and P. K. Smith, "Demarginalizing the Sexual Self," *Journal of Sex Research* 38 (2001): 302–316; A. Cooper, I. P. McLoughlin, and K. M. Campbell, "Sexuality in Cyberspace: Update for the 21st Century," *Cyberpsychology & Behavior* 3 (2000): 521–536.

40. N. E. Dunbar and M. Jensen, "Digital Deception in Personal Relationships," in *Computer-Mediated Communication in Personal Relationships*, edited by K. B. Wright and L. M. Webb (New York: Peter Lang, 2010), 324–343; McKenna et al., "Demarginalizing the Sexual Self."

41. T. A. Coffelt, "Is Sexual Communication Challenging Between Mothers and Daughters?" *Journal of Family Communication* 10 (2010): 116–130; P. W. Toller and D. O. Braithwaite, "Grieving Together and Apart: Bereaved Parents' Contradictions of Marital Interaction," *Journal of Applied Communication Research* 37 (2009): 257–277; E. Sahlstein and K. C. Maguire, "Contradictions and Praxis Conceptualized by Wartime Deployment: Wives' Perspectives Revealed Through Relational Dialectics," *Communication Monographs* 76 (2009): 421–442; A. F. Herrmann, "How Did We Get This Far Apart? Disengagement, Relational Dialectics, and Narrative Control," *Qualitative Inquiry* 13 (2007): 989–1007.

42. J. G. Oetzel and S. Ting-Toomey, eds., *The Sage Handbook of Conflict Communication* (Thousand Oaks, CA: Sage, 2006).

43. M. Deutsch, "Cooperation and Competition," in *The Handbook of Conflict Resolution: Theory and Practice*, edited by M. Deutsch, P. T. Coleman, and E. C. Marcus (New York: Jossey-Bass, 2006), 23–42.

44. Deutsch, "Cooperation and Competition."

45. W. W. Wilmot and J. L. Hocker, *Interpersonal Conflict* 8e (New York: McGraw-Hill, 2010).

46. G. R. Miller and M. Steinberg, *Between People: A New Analysis of Interpersonal Communication* (Chicago: Science Research Associates, 1975).

47. S. Ting-Toomey and L. Chung, *Understanding Intercultural Communication* 2e (New York: Oxford University Press, 2011); J. Oetzel and S. Ting-Toomey, eds., *The Sage Handbook of Conflict Communication: Integrating Theory, Research, and Practice* (Los Angeles: Sage, 2006); M. D. Hazen and R. Shi, "Harmony, Conflict, and the Process of Argument in Chinese Societies," in *Intercultural Communication: A Reader* 13e, edited by L. A. Samovar and R. E. Porter (Belmont, CA: Wadsworth, 2011), 445–456; S. E. Quasha and F. Tsukada, "International Marriages in Japan: Cultural Conflict and Harmony," in *Intercultural Communication: A Reader* 13e, edited by L. A. Samovar and R. E. Porter (Belmont, CA: Wadsworth, 2011), 126–143; P. R. Kimmel, "Culture and Conflict," in *The Handbook of Conflict Resolution: Theory and Practice*, edited by M. Deutsch, P. T. Coleman, and E. C. Marcks (New York: Jossey-Bass, 2006), 625–648; P. Pederson, "Multicultural Conflict Resolution," in *The Handbook of Conflict Resolution: Theory and Practice*, edited by M. Deutsch, P. T. Coleman, and E. C. Marcus (New York: Jossey-Bass, 2006), 649–670; D. Tjosvold, K. Leung, and D. W. Johnson, "Cooperative and Competitive Conflict in China," in *The Handbook of Conflict Resolution: Theory and Practice*, edited by M. Deutsch, P. T. Coleman, and E. C. Marcus (New York: Jossey-Bass, 2006), 671–692.

48. M. E. Roloff and K. L. Johnson, "Serial Arguing over the Relational Life Course: Antecedents and Consequences," in *Stability and Change in Relationships* (Cambridge, UK: Cambridge University Press, 2002), 107–128, as cited in M. E. Roloff and R. M. Reznik, "Communication During Serial Arguments," in *Studies in Applied Interpersonal Communication*, edited by M. T. Motley (Thousand Oaks, CA: Sage, 2008), 97.

49. P. T. Coleman, "Intractable Conflict," in *The Handbook of Conflict Resolution: Theory and Practice*, edited by M. Deutsch, P. T. Coleman, and E. C. Marcus (New York: Jossey-Bass, 2006), 533–559; C. Waite

Miller, "Irresolvable Interpersonal Conflicts: Students' Perceptions of Common Topics, Possible Reasons for Persistence, and Communication Patterns," in *Making Connection: Readings in Relational Communication* 5e, edited by K. M. Galvin (New York: Oxford University Press, 2011), 240–247.

50. C. Segrin, A. Hanzal, and T. J. Domschke, "Accuracy and Bias in Newlywed Couples' Perceptions of Conflict Styles and the Association with Marital Satisfaction," *Communication Monographs* 76 (2009): 207–233; J. Benjamin, "Sex + Love: Learn to Fight Right," *Women's Health* (April 2010): 91–93; H. Chen, P. Cohen, S. Kasen, J. G. Johnson, M. Ehrensaft, and K. Gordon, "Predicting Conflict Within Romantic Relationships During the Transition to Adulthood," *Personal Relationships* 13(2006): 411–427; R. Domingue and D. Mollen, "Attachment and Conflict Communication in Adult Romantic Relationships," *Journal of Social and Personal Relationships* 26 (2009): 678–696.

51. P. T. Coleman, "Power and Conflict," in *The Handbook of Conflict Resolution: Theory and Practice*, edited by M. Deutsch, P. T. Coleman, and E. C. Marcus (New York: Jossey-Bass, 2006), 120–143.

52. C. R. Berger, "Social Power and Interpersonal Communication," in *Explorations in Interpersonal Communication*, edited by G. R. Miller (Newbury Park, CA: Sage, 1976).

53. Miller and Perlman, *Intimate Relationships*.

54. F. E. Millar and L. E. Rogers, "Relational Dimensions of Interpersonal Dynamics," in *Interpersonal Process: New Directions in Communication Research*, edited by M. E. Roloff and G. R. Miller (Newbury Park, CA: Sage, 1987), 117–139.

55. M. Schuessler Harper, *Keeping Quiet: Self-Silencing and Its Association with Relational and Individual Functioning Among Adolescent Romantic Couples*, unpublished doctoral dissertation, University of Tennessee, Knoxville, 2004; "Unhealthy for Women Not to Speak Up During Marital Spats," *Harvard Women's Health Watch* (January 2008): 6–7; T. Parker-Pope, "Marital Spats, Taken to Heart," *New York Times*, October 7, 2007, <nytimes.com>.

56. A. Buchanan, "How to Make the Big Ask," *Women's Health* (March 2010): 104–105; E. Tien, "Just Say What You Want, Dammit!" *O: The Oprah Winfrey Magazine* (September 2008): 245–249.

57. A. S. Rancer and T. A. Avtgis, *Argumentative and Aggressive Communication: Theory, Research, and Application* (Thousand Oaks, CA: Sage, 2006); A. S. Rancer, "Argumentativeness, Verbal Aggressiveness, and Persuasion," in *Perspectives on Perswasion, Social Influence, and Compliance-Gaining*, edited by J. S. Seiter and R. H. Gass (Boston: Allyn & Bacon, 2004), 113–131; D. A. Infante, A. S. Rancer, and D. F. Womack, *Building Communication Theory* 4e (Prospect Heights, IL: Waveland, 2003). For more research on verbal aggression, see P. Schrodt and A. N. Finn, "Students' Perceived Understanding: An Alternative Measure and Its Associations with Perceived Teacher Confirmation, Verbal Aggressiveness, and Credibility," *Communication Education* 60 (2011): 231–254; C. M. Anderson and M. Banerjee, "Aggressive Communication and Conflict in Small Groups," in *Arguments, Aggression, and Conflict*, edited by T. Avtgis and A. S. Rancer (New York: Routledge, 2010), 305–317; C. D. Kennedy-Lightsey and S. A. Myers, "College Students' Use of Behavioral Alteration Techniques as a Function of Aggressive Communication," *Communication Education* 58 (2009): 54–73; M. S. McCloskey, R. Lee, M. E. Berman, K. L. Noblett, and E. F. Coccaro, "The Relationship Between Impulsive Verbal Aggression and Intermittent Explosive Disorder," *Aggressive Behavior* 34 (2008): 51–60; J. M. Lang, "Anger Management," *The Chronicle of Higher Education* (October 24, 2008): A39; D. A. Infante and A. S. Rancer, "Argumentativeness and Verbal Aggressiveness: A Review of Recent Theory and Research," *Communication Yearbook* 19 (1996): 319–351; P. Yelsma, "Couples' Affective Orientations and Their Verbal Aggressiveness," *Communication Quarterly* 43 (1995): 100–114.

58. Satir, *The New Peoplemaking*; Wilmot and Hocker, *Interpersonal Conflict*.

59. L. L. Putnam and C. E. Wilson, "Communicative Strategies in Organizational Conflicts: Reliability and Validity of a Measurement Scale," in *Communication Yearbook* 6, edited by M. Burgoon (Beverly Hills, CA: Sage, 1982).

60. D. Cloven and M. E. Roloff, "The Chilling Effect of Aggressive Potential on the Expression of Complaints in Intimate Relationships," *Communication Monographs* 60 (1993): 199–219; M. L. Gunlicks-Stoessel, "Romantic Partners' Coping Strategies and Patterns of Cortisol Reactivity and Recovery in Response to Relationship Conflict," *Journal of Social and Clinical Psychology* 28 (2009): 630–649; J. Oduor-Frimpong, "Semiotic Silence: Its Uses as a Conflict Management Strategy in Intimate Relationships," *Semiotica* 167 (2007): 283–308; M. Hojjat, "Sex Differences and Perceptions of Conflict in Romantic Relationships," *Journal of Social and Personal Relationships* 17 (2000): 598–617; D. J. Canary and S. Lakey, *Strategic Conflict* (New York: Routledge, 2012); B. A. Budjac Corvette, *Conflict Management: A Practical Guide to Developing Negotiation Strategies* (New York: Prentice Hall, 2006); M. Deutsch, P. T. Coleman, and E. C. Marcus, *The Handbook of Conflict Resolution: Theory and Practice* (New York: Jossey-Bass, 2006).

61. M. A. Gross, L. K. Guerrero, and J. K. Alberts, "Perceptions of Conflict Strategies and Communication Competence in Task-Oriented Dyads," *Journal of Applied Communication Research* 32 (2004): 249–270.

62. Deutsch, "Cooperation and Competition"; R. Fisher, W. Ury, and B. Patton, *Getting to Yes: Negotiating Agreement Without Giving In* 2e (New York: Penguin Books, 1991).

63. This information is based on several excellent discussions of conflict management skills. We acknowledge W. R. Cupach, D. J. Canary, and B.H. Spitzberg. *Competence in Interpersonal Conflict* 2e (Long Grove, IL: Waveland, 2009); D. Borisoff and D. A. Victor, *Conflict Management: A Communication Skills Approach* 2e (Boston: Allyn & Bacon, 1999); D. Yankelovich, *The Magic of Dialogue: Transforming Conflict into Cooperation* (New York: Touchstone, 2001); Wilmot and Hocker, *Interpersonal Conflict*; O. Hargie, ed., *The Handbook of Communication Skills* 3e (London: Routledge, 2006); O. Hargie, C. Saunders, and D. Dickson, *Social Skills in Interpersonal Communication* 3e (London: Routledge, 1994); W. A. Donohue, with R. Holt, *Managing Interpersonal Conflict* (Newbury Park, CA: Sage, 1992); D. A. Romig and L. J. Romig, *Structured Teamwork© Guide* (Austin: Performance Resources, 1990); S. Deep and L. Sussman, *Smart Moves* (Reading, MA: Addison-Wesley, 1990); Fisher et al., *Getting to Yes*; M. D. Davis, E. L. Eshelman, and M. McKay, *The Relaxation and Stress Reduction Workbook* (Oakland, CA: New Harbinger, 1982); R. Boulton, *People Skills* (New York: Simon & Schuster, 1979).

64. J. B. Rubin, "Stand Back from the Rope!" *O: The Oprah Winfrey Magazine* (March 2005): 193.

65. B. M. Gayle and R. W. Preiss, "Language Intensity Plus: A Methodological Approach to Validate Emotions in Conflicts," *Communication Reports* 12 (1999): 43–50; Wilmot and Hocker, *Interpersonal Conflict*.

66. E. G. Lindner, "Emotion and Conflict: Why It Is Impossible to Understand How Emotions Affect Conflict and How Conflict Affects Emotions," in *The Handbook of Conflict Resolution: Theory and Practice*, edited by M. Deutsch, P. T. Coleman, and E. C. Marcus (New York: Jossey-Bass, 2006), 268–293; D. Cramer, "Emotional Support, Conflict, Depression, and Relationship Satisfaction in a Romantic Partner," *Journal of Psychology* 137 (2004): 532–542; C. R. Knee, C. Lonsbary, A. Canevello, and H. Patrick, "Self-Determination and Conflict in Romantic Relationships," *Journal of Personality and Social Psychology* 89 (2005): 997–1009; M. Mongrain, "Conflict over Emotional Expression: Implications for Interpersonal Communication," *Personality and Social Psychology Bulletin* 29 (2003): 545–555.

67. A. Ellis, *A New Guide to Rational Living* (North Hollywood, CA: Wilshire Books, 1977).

68. L. C. Lederman, "The Impact of Gender on the Self and Self-Talk," in *Women and Men Communicating: Challenges and Changes* 2e, edited by L. P. Arliss and D. J. Borisoff (Prospect Heights, IL: Waveland, 2001), 78–89; Ellis, *A New Guide to Rational Living*.

69. H. Gardner, as cited in D. Raffel, "Brain to Brain: How to Get Anyone to Agree with You," *O: The Oprah Winfrey Magazine* (May 2005): 201–202.

70. Fisher, *Getting to Yes*.

## Chapter 9

1. For a comprehensive review of group process research, see G. Randsley de Moura, T. Leader, J. Pelletier, and D. Abrams, "Prospects for Group Processes and Intergroup Relations Research: A Review of 70 Years' Progress," *Group Processes & Intergroup Relations* 11 (2008): 575–596.

2. R. K. Mosvick and R. B. Nelson, *We've Got to Start Meeting Like This!* (Glenview, IL: Scott, Foresman, 1987).

3. Mosvick and Nelson, *We've Got to Start Meeting Like This!*

4. D. C. Strubler and K. M. York, "An Exploratory Study of the Team Characteristics Model Using Organizational Teams," *Small Group Research* 38 (2007): 670–695.

5. K. W. Hawkins and B. P. Fillion, "Perceived Communication Skill Needs for Work Groups," *Communication Research Reports* 16 (1999): 167–174; also see S. Burkhalter, J. Gastil, and T. Kelshaw, "A Conceptual Definition and Theoretical Model of Public Deliberation in Small Face-to-Face Groups," *Communication Theory* 12 (2002): 398–422.

6. S. A. Beebe and J. T. Masterson, *Communicating in Small Groups: Principles and Practices* 10e (Boston: Pearson, 2012).

7. N. Katz and G. Koenig, "Sports Teams as a Model for Workplace Teams: Lessons and Liabilities," *Academy of Management Executive* 15 (2001): 56–67; L. G. Snyder, "Teaching Teams About Teamwork: Preparation, Practice, and Performance Review," *Business Communication Quarterly* (2009): 74–79.

8. Our discussion of teams and teamwork is from Beebe and Masterson, *Communicating in Small Groups;* for an excellent review of teamwork theoretical models, see V. Rousseau, C. Aube, and A. Savoie, "Teamwork Behaviors: A Review and an Integration of Frameworks," *Small Group Research* 27 (2006): 540–570.

9. T. D. Fletcher and D. A. Major, "The Effects of Communication Modality on Performance and Self-Ratings of Teamwork Components," *Journal of Computer Mediated Communication* 11 (2006): 557–576.

10. A. G. Sheard and A. P. Kakabadse, "From Loose Groups to Effective Teams: The Nine Key Factors of the Team Landscape," *Journal of Management Development* 21 (2002): 133–151; also see R. A. Meyers and D. R. Seibold, "Making Foundational Assumptions Transparent: Framing the Discussion About Group Communication and Influence," *Human Communication Research* 35 (2009): 286–295.

11. See F. C. Broadbeck and T. Breitermeyer, "Effects of Individual Versus Mixed Individual and Group Experience in Rule Induction on Group Member Learning and Group Performance," *Journal of Experimental Social Psychology* 36 (2002): 621–648.

12. S. B. Shimanoff, *Communication Rules: Theory and Research* (Beverly Hills, CA: Sage, 1980).

13. M. Hoegl, "Goal Setting and Team Performance in Innovative Projects: On the Moderating Role of Teamwork Quality," *Small Group Research* 34 (2003): 3–19; A. W. Woolley, M. E. Gerbasi, C. F. Chabris, S. M. Kosslyn, and J. R. Hackman, "Bringing in the Experts: How Team Composition and Collaborative Planning Jointly Shape Analytic Effectiveness," *Small Group Research* 39 (2008): 352–371; H. Van Mierlo and A. Kleingeld, "Goals, Strategies, and Group Performance: Some Limits of Goal Setting in Groups," *Small Group Research* 41 (2010): 524–555.

14. R. Rico, M. Sanchez-Manzanares, F. Gil, and C. Gibson, "Team Impact Coordination Processes: A Team Knowledge-Based Approach," *Academy of Management Review* 33 (2008): 163–184.

15. Beebe and Masterson, *Communicating in Small Groups.*

16. S. A. Rains and V. Young, "A Meta-Analysis of Research on Formal Computer-Mediated Support Groups: Examining Group Characteristics and Health Outcomes," *Human Communication Research* 35 (2009): 309–336.

17. B. Bell and S. W. J. Kozlowski, "A Typology of Virtual Teams: Implications for Effective Leadership," *Group & Organizational Management* 27 (2002): 14–49; A. Thatcher, "Small Group Decision-Making in Face-to-Face and Computer-Mediated Environments: The Role of Personality," *Behavior & Information Technology* 22 (2003): 203–218; D. R. Lemus, D. R. Seibold, A. J. Flanagin, and M. J. Metzger, "Argument and Decision Making in Computer Mediated Groups," *Journal of Communication* 54 (2004): 302–320; E. V. Hobman, P. Bordia, B. Irmer, and A. Chang, "The Expression of Conflict in Computer-Mediated and Face-to-Face Groups," *Small Group Research* 33 (2002): 439–464; R. Benbunan-Fich, S. R. Hiltz, and M. Turoff, "A Comparative Content Analysis of Face-to-Face vs. Asynchronous Group Decision Making," *Decision Support Systems* 34 (2002): 457–469; D. S. Staples and J. Webster, "Exploring Traditional and Virtual Team Members' 'Best Practices,' " *Small Group Research* 38 (2007): 60–97; S. Z. Schiller and M. Mandviwalla, "Virtual Team Research: An Analysis of Theory Use and a Framework for Theory Appropriation," *Small Group Research* 38 (2007): 12–59; J. T. Polzer, C. B. Crisp, S. L. Jarvenpaa, and J. W. Kim, "Extending the Faultline Model to Geographically Dispersed Teams: How Colocated Subgroups Can Impair Group Functioning," *Academy of Management Journal* 4 (2006): 679–692; also see C. Garon and K. Wegryn, *Managing Without Walls: Maximize Success with Virtual, Global and Cross-Cultural Teams* (Lewisville, TX: MC Press, 2006); T. Brake, *Where in the World Is My Team? Making Success of Your Virtual Global Workplace* (San Francisco: Jossey-Bass, 2008); D. Derosa and R. Lepsinger, *Virtual Team Success: A Practical Guide for Working and Leading from a Distance* (San Francisco: Jossey-Bass, 2010).

18. J. M. Wilson, S. G. Straus, and B. McEvily, "All in Due Time: The Development of Trust in Computer-Mediated and Face-to-Face Teams," *Organizational Behavior and Human Decision Processes* 99 (2006): 16–33.

19. Wilson et al., "All in Due Time."

20. C. E. Timmerman and C. R. Scott, "Virtually Working: Communicative and Structural Predictors of Media Use and Key Outcomes in Virtual Work Teams," *Communication Monographs* 73 (2006): 108–136.

21. For a comprehensive discussion of bona fide groups, see L. L. Putnam, "Rethinking the Nature of Groups: A Bona Fide Group Perspective," in *Small Group Communication Theory and Practice: An Anthology*, edited by R. Y. Hirokawa, R. S. Cathcart, L. A. Samovar, and L. D. Hennman (Los Angeles: Roxbury, 2003).

22. K. D. Benne and P. Sheats, "Functional Roles of Group Members," *Journal of Social Issues* 4 (1948): 41–49; for a good review of role development in groups, see A. P. Hare, "Types of Roles in Small Groups: A Bit of History and a Current Perspective," *Small Group Research* 28 (1994): 433–438; A. J. Salazar, "An Analysis of the Development and Evolution of Roles in the Small Group," *Small Group Research* 27 (1996): 475–503.

23. T. Halfhill, E. Sundstrom, J. Lahner, W. Calderone, and T. M. Nielsen, "Group Personality Composition and Group Effectiveness: An Integrative Review of Empirical Research," *Small Group Research* 36 (2005): 83–105.

24. G. M. Wittenbaum, H. C. Shulman, and M. E. Braz, "Social Ostracism in Task Groups: The Effects of Group Composition," *Small Group Research* 41 (2010): 330–353.

25. R. F. Bales, *Interaction Process Analysis* (Chicago: University of Chicago Press, 1976).

26. Shimanoff, *Communication Rules.*

27. For a discussion of monochronic and polychronic time, see E. T. Hall, *The Silent Language* (New York: Doubleday, 1959).

28. M. J. Waller, M. E. Zellmer-Bruhn, and R. C. Giambatista, "Watching the Clock: Group Pacing Behavior Under Dynamic Deadlines," *Academy of Management Journal* 45 (2002): 1046–1055.

29. Hall, *The Silent Language.*

30. M. Shaw, *Group Dynamics: The Psychology of Small Group Behavior* (New York: McGraw-Hill, 1981), 281.

31. J. I. Hurwitz, A. F. Zander, and B. Hymovitch, "Some Effects of Power on the Relations Among Group Members," in *Group Dynamics: Research and Theory*, edited by D. Cartwright and A. Zander (New York: Harper & Row, 1953), 483–492; D. C. Barnlund and C. Harland, "Propinquity and Prestige as Determinants of Communication Networks," *Sociometry* 26 (1963): 467–479; G. C. Homans, *The Human Group* (New York: Harcourt Brace and World, 1992); H. H. Kelly, "Communication in Experimentally Created Hierarchies," *Human Relations* 4 (1951): 36–56.

32. C. Anderson, J. S. Beer, J. Chatman, S. Srivastava, and S. E. Spataro, "Knowing Your Place: Self-Perceptions of Status in Face-to-Face Groups," *Journal of Personality and Social Psychology* 91 (2006): 1094–1110.

33. M. R. Singer, *Intercultural Communication: A Perceptual Approach* (Englewood Cliffs, NJ: Prentice Hall, 1987), 118.

34. J. R. P. French and B. H. Raven, "The Bases of Social Power," in *Group Dynamics: Research and Theory*, edited by D. Cartwright and A. Zander (New York: Harper & Row, 1953), 607–623.

35. D. Neumann, "Small Group Cohesion and Frequency of Idiom Use," paper presented at the annual meeting of the National Communication Association, Chicago, November 2004.

36. M. R. Barrick, B. H. Bradley, A. L. Kristof-Brown, and A. E. Colbert, "The Moderating Role of Top Management Team Interdependence: Implications for Real Teams and Working Groups," *Academy of Management Journal* 50 (2007): 544–557.

37. Adapted from E. G. Bormann and N. C. Bormann, *Effective Small Group Communication* (Minneapolis: Burgess, 1980), 70–72.

38. C. Y. Yuan, J. Fulk, P. R. Monge, and N. Contractor, "Expertise Directory Development, Shared Task Interdependence, and Strength of Communication Network Ties as Multilevel Predictors of Expertise Exchange in Transactive Memory Work Groups," *Communication Research* 37 (2010): 20–47.

39. N. Katz, D. Lazer, H. Arrow, and N. Contractor, "Network Theory and Small Groups," *Small Group Research* 35 (2004): 307–332.

40. M. Huang, "A Conceptual Framework of the Effects of Positive Affect and Affective Relationships on Group Knowledge Networks," *Small Group Research* 40 (2009): 323–346.

41. Huang, "A Conceptual Framework."

42. S. Wheelan, B. Davidson, and F. Tilin, "Group Development Across Time: Reality or Illusion?" *Small Group Research* 34 (2003): 223–245; S. Furst, M. Reeves, B. Rosen, and R. S. Blackburn, "Managing the Life Cycle of Virtual Teams," *Academy of Management Executive* 18 (2004): 6–22; P. A. Hare, "Theories of Group Development and Categories for Interaction Analysis," *Small Group Research* 41 (2010): 106–140.

43. B. A. Fisher, "Decision Emergence: Phases in Group Decision Making," *Speech Monographs* 37 (1970): 60.

44. For a discussion of primary tension and group phases, see E. Bormann, *Discussion and Group Methods* (New York: Harper & Row, 1975).

45. For an examination of the practical role of conflict in jury deliberations, see M. S. Poole and M. Dobosh, "Exploring Conflict Management Processes in Jury Deliberations Through Interaction Analysis," *Small Group Research* 41 (2010): 408–426.

46. M. A. Von Glinow, D. Shapiro, and J. Brett, "Can We Talk, and Should We? Managing Emotional Conflict in Multicultural Teams," *Academy of Management Review* 29 (2004): 578–592.

47. M. Janssens and J. M. Brett, "Cultural Intelligence in Global Teams: A Fusion Model of Collaboration," *Group & Organization Management* 31 (2006): 124–153.

48. G. Hofstede, *Culture's Consequences: International Differences in Work Related Values* (Beverly Hills, CA: Sage, 1980); G. Hofstede, *Cultures and Organizations: Software of the Mind* (London: McGraw-Hill, 1991).

49. Adapted from J. Mole, *Mind Your Manners: Managing Business Cultures in Europe* (New York: Nicholas Brealey, 1995).

50. S. A. Wheelan and T. Williams, "Mapping Dynamic Interaction Patterns in Work Groups," *Small Group Research* 34 (2003): 433–467; Wheelan et al., "Group Development Across Time."

51. M. S. Poole, "Decision Development in Small Groups: A Multiple Sequence Model of Group Decision Development," *Communication Monographs* 50 (1983): 321–341; also see C. Pavitt and K. Kline Johnson, "Scheidel and Crowell Revisited: A Descriptive Study of Group Proposal Sequencing," *Communication Monographs* 69 (2002): 19–32.

52. Beebe and Masterson, *Communicating in Small Groups*.

## Chapter 10

1. See N. R. F. Maier, "Assets and Liabilities in Group Problem Solving: The Need for an Integrative Function," *Psychological Review* 74 (1967): 239–249; M. Argyle, *Cooperation: The Basis of Sociability* (London: Routledge, 1991); H. A. M. Wilke and R. W. Meertens, *Group Performance* (London: Routledge, 1994).

2. Maier, "Assets and Liabilities in Group Problem Solving"; Argyle, *Cooperation*; Wilke and Meertens, *Group Performance*.

3. R. Y. Hirokawa, "Discussion Procedures and Decision-Making Performance: A Test of a Functional Perspective," *Human Communication Research* 12 (1985): 203–224.

4. R. Y. Hirokawa, "Why Informed Groups Make Faulty Decisions: An Investigation of Possible Interaction-Based Explanations," *Small Group Behavior* 18 (1987): 3–29.

5. R. Y. Hirokawa and K. Rost, "Effective Group Decision-Making in Organizations: Field Test of the Vigilant Interaction Theory," *Management Communication Quarterly* 5 (1992): 267–288; Hirokawa, "Why Informed Groups Make Faulty Decisions"; R. Y. Hirokawa, "Group Communication and Decision-Making Performance: A Continued Test of the Functional Perspective," *Human Communication Research* 14 (1988): 487–515; M. O. Orlitzky and R. Y. Hirokawa, "To Err Is Human, to Correct for It Divine: A Meta-Analysis of Research Testing the Functional Theory of Group Decision-Making Effectiveness," paper presented at the meeting of the National Communication Association, Chicago, November 1997.

6. Hirokawa, "Discussion Procedures and Decision-Making Performance."

7. D. F. Crown, "The Use of Group and Groupcentric Individual Goals for Culturally Heterogeneous and Homogeneous Task Groups: An Assessment of European Work Teams," *Small Group Research* 38 (2007): 489–508.

8. C. E. Larson and F. M. J. LaFasto, *Teamwork: What Must Go Right/ What Can Go Wrong* (Beverly Hills, CA: Sage, 1989); also see D. D. Chrislip and C. E. Larson, *Collaborative Leadership* (San Francisco: Jossey-Bass, 1994); D. A. Romig, *Breakthrough Teamwork: Outstanding Results Using Structured Teamwork* (Chicago: Irwin, 1996); M. A. Marks, J. E. Mathieu, and S. J. Zaccaro, "A Temporally Based Framework and Taxonomy of Team Processes," *Academy of Management Review* 26 (2001): 356–376; N. Katz, "Sports Teams as a Model for Workplace Teams: Lessons and Liabilities," *Academy of Management Executive* 15 (2001): 56–67.

9. Larson and LaFasto, *Teamwork*; Chrislip and Larson, *Collaborative Leadership*; Romig, *Breakthrough Teamwork*.

10. L. A. DeChurch and C. D. Haas, "Examining Team Planning Through an Episodic Lens: Effects of Deliberate, Contingency, and Reactive Planning on Team Effectiveness," *Small Group Research* 39 (2008): 542–568.

11. Larson and LaFasto, *Teamwork*.

12. C. M. J. H. Savelsbergh, B. I. J. M. van der Heijden, and R. F. Poell, "The Development and Empirical Validation of a Multidimensional Measurement Instrument for Team Learning Behaviors," *Small Group Research* 40 (2009): 578–607.

13. T. Reimer, A. Reimer, and V. B. Hinsz, "Naive Groups Can Solve the Hidden-Profile Problem," *Human Communication Research* 36 (2010): 443–467.

14. For a review of research about the importance of sharing information to reach a quality decision or solution, see J. A. Bonito, M. H. DeCamp, and E. K. Ruppel, "The Process of Information Sharing in Small Groups: Application of a Local Model," *Communication Monographs* 75 (2008): 136–157; W. P. van Ginkel and D. van Knippenberg, "Group Information Elaboration and Group Decision Making: The Role of Shared Task Representations," *Organizational Behavior and Human Decision Processes* 105 (2008): 82–97; T. Reimer, S. Kuendig, U. Hoffrage, E. Park, and V. Hinsz, "Effects of Information Environment on Group Discussions and Decisions in the Hidden-Profile Paradigm," *Communication Monographs* 74 (2007): 1–28; W. P. van Ginkel and D. van Knippenberg, "Knowledge About the Distribution of Information and Group Decision Making: When and Why Does It Work?" *Organizational Behavior and Human Decision Processes* 108 (2009): 218–229.

15. O. S. Chernyshenko, A. G. Miner, M. R. Baumann, and J. A. Sniezek, "The Impact of Information Distribution, Ownership, and Discussion on Group Member Judgment: The Differential Cue Weighting Model," *Organizational Behavior and Human Decision Processes* 91 (2003): 12–25.

16. D. R. Seibold and R. A. Meyers, "Group Argument: A Structuration Perspective and Research Program," *Small Group Research* 38 (2007): 312–336.

17. D. D. Henningsen and M. L. M. Henningsen, "Do Groups Know What They Don't Know? Dealing with Missing Information in Decision-Making Groups," *Communication Research* 34 (2007): 507–525.

18. Orlirzky and Hirokawa, "To Err Is Human, to Correct for It Divine."

19. Orlirzky and Hirokawa, "To Err Is Human, to Correct for It Divine"; B. L. Smith, "Interpersonal Behaviors That Damage the Productivity of Creative Problem Solving Groups," *Journal of Creative Behavior* 27 (1993): 171–187.

20. H. Ding and X. Ding, "Project Management, Critical Praxis, and Process-Oriented Approach to Teamwork," *Business Communication Quarterly* 71 (2008); 456–471.

21. A. B. Henley and K. H. Price, "Want a Better Team? Foster a Climate of Fairness," *Academy of Management Executive* 16 (2002): 153–155.

22. J. L. Thompson, "Building Collective Communication Competence in Interdisciplinary Research Teams," *Journal of Applied Communication Research* 37 (2009): 278–297.

23. A. T. Pescosolido, "Group Efficacy over Time on Group Performance and Development," *Small Group Research* 34 (2003): 20–43.

24. J. S. Prichard and M. J. Ashleigh, "The Effects of Team-Skills Training on Transactive Memory and Performance," *Small Group Research* 38 (2007): 696–726; T. L. Rapp and J. E. Mathieu, "Evaluating an Individually Self-Administered Generic Teamwork Skills Training Program Across Time and Levels," *Small Group Communication* 38 (2007): 532–555.

25. See A. B. VanGundy, *Techniques of Structured Problem Solving* (New York: Van Nostrand Reinhold, 1981), 4; Romig, *Breakthrough Teamwork*.

26. S. A. Beebe and J. T. Masterson, *Communicating in Small Groups: Principles and Practices* 10e (Boston: Allyn & Bacon, 2012); Van-Gundy, *Techniques of Structured Problem Solving*.

27. J. K. Brilhart and L. M. Jochem, "Effects of Different Patterns on Outcomes of Problem-Solving Discussion," *Journal of Applied Psychology* 48 (1964): 174–179; W. E. Jurma, "Effects of Leader Structuring Style and Task Orientation Characteristics of Group Members," *Communication Monographs* 49 (1979): 282–295; S. Jarboe, "A Comparison of Input-Output, Process-Output, and Input-Process-Output Models of Small Group Problem-Solving Effectiveness," *Communication Monographs* 55 (1988): 121–142; VanGundy, *Techniques of Structured Problem Solving*.

28. D. M. Berg, "A Descriptive Analysis of the Distribution and Duration of Themes Discussed by Task-Oriented Small Groups," *Speech Monographs* 34 (1967): 172–175; E. G. Bormann and N. C. Bormann, *Effective Small Group Communication* 2e (Minneapolis: Burgess, 1976), 132; M. S. Poole, "Decision Development in Small Groups III: A Multiple Sequence Model of Group Decision Development," *Communication Monographs* 50 (1983): 321–341.

29. For an excellent summary of the literature documenting these problems, see Sunwolf and D. R. Seibold, "The Impact of Formal Procedures on Group Processes, Members, and Task Outcomes," in *The Handbook of Group Communication Theory and Research*, edited by L. Frey (Thousand Oaks, CA: Sage, 1999) 395–431.

30. J. Dewey, *How We Think* (Boston: D.C. Heath, 1910).

31. This explanation of the Journalist's Six Questions method is based on a discussion by J. E. Eitington, *The Winning Trainer* (Houston: Gulf Publishing, 1989), 157.

32. Based on the research of K. Lewin, "Frontiers in Group Dynamics," *Human Relations* 1 (1947): 5–42.

33. M. Gladwell, *Blink: The Power of Thinking Without Thinking* (New York: Little, Brown, 2005).

34. See S. Taggar, "Individual Creativity and Group Ability to Utilize Individual Creative Resources: A Multilevel Model," *Academy of Management Journal* 45 (2002): 315–330; C. E. Johnson and M. A. Hackman, *Creative Communication: Principles and Applications* (Prospect Heights, IL: Waveland, 1995).

35. A. F. Osborn, *Applied Imagination* (New York: Scribner's, 1962).

36. A. L. Delberg, A. H. Van de Ven, and D. H. Gustason, *Group Techniques for Program Planning: A Guide to Nominal Group and Delphi Processes* (Glenview, IL: Scott, Foresman, 1975), 7–16.

37. D. Straker, *Rapid Problem Solving with Post-it Notes* (Tucson: Fisher Books, 1997).

38. Adapted from Beebe and Masterson, *Communicating in Small Groups*.

39. M. A. Roberto, "Strategic Decision-Making Processes: Beyond the Efficiency-Consensus Trade-Off," *Group & Organizational Management* 29 (2004): 625–658.

40. R. Y. Hirokawa, D. S. Gouran, and A. Martz, "Understanding the Sources of Faulty Group Decision Making: A Lesson from the *Challenger* Disaster," *Small Group Behavior* 19 (1988): 411–433.

41. R. K. M. Haurwitz, "Faculty Doubted Bonfire's Stability," *Austin American-Statesman* (December 10, 1999): A1, A2.

42. D. Jehl, "Panel Unanimous: 'Groupthink' Backed Prewar Assumptions, Report Concludes," *New York Times* (July 10, 2004), 1; also see *The 9/11 Commission Report: Final Report of the National Commission on Terrorist Attacks upon the United States* (Washington, DC: National Commission on Terrorist Attacks, 2004).

43. J. F. Veiga, "The Frequency of Self-Limiting Behavior in Groups: A Measure and an Explanation," *Human Relationships* 44 (1991): 877–895.

44. I. L. Janis, *Victims of Groupthink* (Boston: Houghton Mifflin, 1973).

45. C. M. Mason and M. R. Griffin, "Group Task Satisfaction: The Group's Attitude to Its Task and Work Environment," *Group & Organizational Management* 30 (2005): 625–652.

46. M. S. Limon and B. H. La France, "Communication Traits and Leadership Emergence: Examining the Impact of Argumentativeness, Communication Apprehension, and Verbal Aggressiveness in Work Groups," *Southern Communication Journal* 70 (2005): 123–133; also see A. M. L. Raes, U. Glunk, M. G. Heijltjes, and R. A. Roe, "Top Management Team and Middle Managers: Making Sense of Leadership," *Small Group Research* 38 (2007): 360–386.

47. See B. M. Bass, *Stodgill's Handbook of Leadership* (New York: Free Press, 1981).

48. A. Srivastava, K. M. Bartol, and E. A. Locke, "Empowering Leadership in Management Teams: Effects of Knowledge Sharing, Efficacy, and Performance," *Academy of Management Journal* 49 (2006): 1239–1251.

49. G. J. Calanes, "In Their Own Words: An Exploratory Study of Bona Fide Group Leaders," *Small Group Research* 34 (2003): 741–770.

50. P. Balkundi and D. Harrison, "Ties, Leaders, and Time in Teams: Strong Inference About Network Structure's Effects on Team Viability and Performance," *Academy of Management Journal* 49 (2006): 49–68.

51. R. White and R. Lippitt, "Leader Behavior and Member Reaction in Three Social Climates," in *Group Dynamics* 3e, edited by D. Cartwright and A. Zander (New York: Harper & Row, 1968), 319.

52. M. Van Vugt, S. F. Jepson, C. M. Hart, and D. De Cremer, "Autocratic Leadership in Social Dilemmas: A Threat to Group Stability," *Journal of Experimental and Social Psychology* 40 (2004): 1–13.

53. S. Halverson, S. E. Murphy, and R. E. Riggio, "Charismatic Leadership in Crisis Situations: A Laboratory Investigation of Stress and Crisis," *Small Group Research* 35 (2004): 495–514.

54. S. S. K. Lam, X. P. Chen, and J. Schaubroeck, "Participative Decision Making and Employee Performance in Different Cultures: The Moderating Effects of Allocentrism/Idiocentrism and Efficacy," *Academy of Management Journal* 45 (2002): 905–914.

55. D. S. DeRue, C. M. Barnes, and F. P. Morgeson, "Understanding the Motivational Contingencies of Team Leadership," *Small Group Research* 41 (2010): 621–651.

56. D. C. Korten, "Situational Determinants of Leadership Structure," *Journal of Conflict Resolution* 6 (1962): 222–235.

57. P. Hersey, K. Blanchard, and D. Johnson, *Management of Organizational Behavior: Utilizing Human Resources* 9e (Englewood Cliffs, NJ: Prentice–Hall, 2007).

58. R. F. Fiedler, *A Theory of Leadership Effectiveness* (New York: McGraw-Hill, 1967), 144.

59. B. M. Bass and M. J. Avolio, "Transformational Leadership and Organizational Culture," *International Journal of Public Administration* 17 (1994): 541–554; also see F. J. Yammarino and A. J. Dubinsky, "Transformational Leadership Theory: Using Levels of Analysis to Determine Boundary Conditions," *Personnel Psychology* 47 (1994): 787–809.

60. For additional research about the efficacy of transformational leadership, see J. McCann, P. Langford, and R. M. Rawlings, "Testing Behling and McFillen's Syncretical Model of Charismatic Transformational Leadership," *Group & Organization Management* 31 (2006): 237–263;

R. F. Piccolo and J. Colquitt, "Transformational Leadership and Job Behaviors: The Mediating Role of Core Job Characteristics," *Academy of Management Journal* 49 (2006): 327–340; R. S. Rubin, D. C. Muniz, and W. H. Bommer, "Leading from Within: The Effects of Emotion Recognition and Personality on Transformational Leadership Behavior," *Academy of Management Journal* 48 (2005): 845–858; A. Ergeneli, R. Gohar, and Z. Temirbekova, "Transformational Leadership: Its Relationship to Culture Value Dimensions," *International Journal of Intercultural Relations* 31 (2007): 703–724.

61. P. M. Senge, "The Leader's New Role: Building Learning Organizations," *Sloan Management Review* 32 (1990).

62. D. I. Jung and J. J. Sosik, "Transformational Leadership in Work Groups: The Role of Empowerment, Cohesiveness, and Collective Efficacy on Perceived Group Performance," *Small Group Research* 33 (2002): 313–336; also see T. Dvir, D. Eden, B. J. Avolio, and B. Shamir, "Impact of Transformational Leadership on Follower Development and Performance: A Field Experiment," *Academy of Management Journal* 45 (2002): 735–744; C. L. Hoyt and J. Blascovich, "Transformational and Transactional Leadership in Virtual and Physical Environments," *Small Group Research* 34 (2003): 678–715.

63. V. U. Druskar and J. V. Wheeler, "Managing from the Boundary: The Effective Leadership of Self-Managing Work Teams," *Academy of Management Journal* 46 (2003): 435–457.

64. M. Zellmer-Bruhn and C. Gibson, "Multinational Organization Context: Implications for Team Learning and Performance," *Academy of Management Journal* 49 (2006): 501–518.

65. For an excellent discussion of transformational leadership applied to teams, see S. D. Dionne, F. J. Yammarino, L. E. Atwater, and W. D. Spangler, "Transformational Leadership and Team Performance," *Journal of Organizational Change Management* 17 (2004): 177–193.

66. See K. W. Phillips, G. B. Northcraft, and M. A. Neale, "Surface-Level Diversity Collide: The Effects on Dissenting Group Members," *Organizational Behavior and Human Decision Processes* 9 (2006): 143–160; J. R. Larson, "Deep Diversity and Strong Synergy: Modeling the Impact of Variability in Members' Problem-Solving Strategies on Group Problem-Solving Performance," *Small Group Research* 3 (2007): 413–436.

67. R. Rodriguez, "Challenging Demographic Reductionism: A Pilot Study Investigating Diversity in Group Composition," *Small Group Research* 26 (1998): 744–759.

68. Phillips et al., "Surface-Level Diversity Collide."

69. J. A. Raelin, "Don't Bother Putting Leadership into People," *Academy of Management Executive* 18 (2004): 131–135; M. W. McCall, "Leadership Development Through Experience," *Academy of Management Executive* 18 (2004): 127–130; J. Conger, "Developing Leadership Capability: What's Inside the Black Box?" *Academy of Management Executive* 18 (2004): 136–139; D. Vera and M. Crossan, "Strategic Leadership and Organizational Learning," *Academy of Management Review* 29 (2004): 222–239.

70. D. Barry, *Dave Berry Turns 50* (New York: Ballantine, 1998), 182.

71. R. K. Mosvick and R. B. Nelson, *We've Got to Start Meeting Like This!* (Glenview, IL: Scott, Foresman, 1987).

72. Suggestions about organizing meeting agendas are based on M. Doyle and D. Straus, *How to Make Meetings Work* (New York: Playboy Press, 1976); Mosvick and Nelson, *We've Got to Start Meeting Like This!*; G. Lumsden and D. Lumsden, *Communicating in Groups and Teams: Sharing Leadership* (Belmont, CA: Wadsworth, 1993); D. B. Curtis, J. J. Floyd, and J. L. Winsor, *Business and Professional Communication* (New York: HarperCollins, 1992); Romig, *Breakthrough Teamwork*; T. A. Kayser, *Mining Group Gold* (El Segundo, CA: Serif, 1990); J. E. Tropman and G. Clark Morningstar, *Meetings: How to Make Them Work for You* (New York: Van Nostrand Reinhold, 1985): 56; Beebe and Masterson, *Communicating in Small Groups*.

73. J. E. Tropman, *Making Meetings Work* (Thousand Oaks, CA: Sage, 1996).

74. See J. A. Bonito, "A Longitudinal Social Relations Analysis of Participation in Small Groups," *Human Communication Research* 32 (2006): 302–321; M. W. Kramer, P. J. Benoit, M. A. Dixon, and J. Benoit-Bryan, "Group Processes in a Teaching Renewal Retreat: Communication Function and Dialectal Tensions," *Southern Communication Journal* 72 (2007): 145–168; J. A. Bonito, M. H. DeCamp, and E. K. Ruppel, "The Process of Information Sharing in Small Groups: Application of a Local Model," *Communication Monographs* 75 (2008): 136–157.

75. See D. S. Gouran, "Variables Related to Consensus in Group Discussions of Questions of Policy," *Speech Monographs* 36 (1969): 385–391; T. J. Knutsun, "An Experimental Study of the Effects of Orientation Behavior on Small Group Consensus," *Speech Monographs* 39 (1972): 159–165; A. Kline, "Orientation and Group Consensus," *Central States Speech Journal* 23 (1972): 44–47.

76. J. B. Walther and U. Bunz, "The Rules of Virtual Groups: Trust, Liking, and Performance in Computer-Mediated Communication," *Journal of Communication* (December 2005): 828–846.

77. Several suggestions adapted from *Leading Virtual Teams* (Boston: Harvard Business Press, 2010).

78. *Leading Virtual Teams.*

79. D. S. Staples and J. Webster, "Exploring Traditional and Virtual Team Members' 'Best Practices': A Social Cognitive Theory Perspective," *Small Group Research* 38 (2007): 60–97.

80. Mosvick and Nelson, *We've Got to Start Meeting Like This!*

81. S. A. Beebe and J. K. Barge, "Evaluating Group Discussion," in *Small Group Communication: Theory & Practice*, edited by R. Y. Hirokawa, R. S. Cathcart, L. A. Samovar, and L. D. Henman (Los Angeles: Roxbury, 2003).

## Chapter 11

1. G. Bodie, "A Racing Heart, Rattling Knees, and Ruminative Thoughts: Defining, Explaining, and Treating Public Speaking Anxiety," *Communication Education* 59 (2010): 70–105.

2. S. Booth-Butterfield, "Instructional Interventions for Reducing Situational Anxiety and Avoidance," *Communication Education* 37 (1988): 214–223.

3. Survey conducted by R. H. Bruskin and Associates, *Spectra* 9 (December 1973): 4.

4. M. Beatty, J. McCroskey, and A. D. Heisel, "Communication Apprehension as Temperamental Expression: A Communibiological Paradigm," *Communication Monographs* 65 (1998): 197–219.

5. The sample presentation developed in this chapter is adapted from T. Longoria, "Excessive Facebooking: What You Need to Know," *Communication 1310: Student Speeches for Texas State University* (CD). Pearson Learning Solutions, 2010.

6. K. Savitsky and T. Gilovich, "The Illusion of Transparency and the Alleviation of Speech Anxiety," *Journal of Experimental Social Psychology* 39 (2003): 618–625.

7. K. Dwyer and D. Fus, "Perceptions of Communication Competence, Self-Efficacy, and Trait Communication Apprehension: Is There an Impact on Basic Course Success?" *Communication Research Reports* 19 (2002): 29–37.

8. M. Booth-Butterfield, "Stifle or Stimulate? The Effects of Communication Task Structure on Apprehensive and Non-Apprehensive Students," *Communication Education* 35 (1986): 337–348; Charles R. Berger, "Speechlessness: Causal Attributions, Emotional Features, and Social Consequences," *Journal of Language and Social Psychology* 23 (2004): 147–179.

9. J. Ayres, "Speech Preparation Processes and Speech Apprehension," *Communication Education* 45 (July 1996): 228–235.

10. P. Addison, E. Clay, S. Xie, C. R. Sawyer, and R. R. Behnke, "Worry as a Function of Public Speaking State Anxiety Type," *Communication Research Reports* 16 (2003): 125–131.

11. S. C. McCullough, S. G. Russell, R. R. Behnke, C. R. Sawyer, and P. L. Witt, "Anticipatory Public Speaking State Anxiety as a Function of Body Sensations and State of Mind," *Communication Quarterly* 54 (2006): 101–109; P. L. Witt, K. C. Brown, J. B. Roberts, J. Weisel, C. R. Sawyer, and R. R. Behnke, "Somatic Anxiety Patterns Before, During, and After Giving a Public Speech," *Southern Communication Journal* 71 (2006): 87–100.

12. Addison et al., "Worry as a Function of Public Speaking State Anxiety Type."

13. Critics of systematic desensitization argue that there may be a placebo effect: Just thinking that a treatment will reduce apprehension may contribute to reduced apprehension. See D. C. Duff, T. R. Levine, M. J. Beatty, J. Woolbright, and H. S. Park, "Testing Public Anxiety Treatments Against a Credible Placebo Control," *Communication Education* 56 (2007): 72–88.

14. J. Ayres and B. Huett, "An Examination of the Impact of Performance Visualization," *Communication Research Reports 16* (1999): 29–39; J. Ayres and B. Huett, "An Examination of the Long-Term Effect of Performance Visualization," *Communication Research Reports* 17 (2000): 229–236.

15. L. Tracy, "Taming Hostile Audiences," *Vital Speeches of the Day* 71.10 (2005).

16. J. Humphrey, "Taking the Stage: How Women Can Achieve a Leadership Presence," *Vital Speeches of the Day* 67.14 (2001).

17. Data provided by Center for Defense Information, "Chronology of Major Terrorist Attacks Against U.S. Targets," *CDI Terrorism Project*, June 27, 2002, <www.cdi.org/terrorism/chronology-pr.html>; "September 11 Fatalities Make 2001 the Worst Year," *Airwise News*, January 4, 2002, <news.airwise.com/ stories/2002/01/1010177858. html>.

18. Ramin Setoodeh, "My Favorite Mistake" (Interview with Ann Curry), *Newsweek* (June 5, 2011).

19. These criteria for evaluating web resources are adapted from E. Kirk, "Practical Steps in Evaluating Internet Resources," Johns Hopkins University, 2010, <http://guides.library.hhu.edu>. See also M. Tate and J. Alexander, *Web Wisdom: How to Evaluate and Create Information Quality on the Web* (Mahwah, NJ: Lawrence Erlbaum, 1999).

20. G. W. Bush, State of the Union address, January 28, 2008, *Vital Speeches of the Day* 74.3 (March 2008).

21. M. Sanchez, "Diplomatic Immunity Unjustified," in *Winning Orations 1996* (Mankato, MN: Interstate Oratorical Association, 1996), 66.

22. M. Limon and D. Kazoleas, "A Comparison of Exemplar and Statistical Evidence in Reducing Counter-Arguments and Responses to a Message," *Communication Research Reports* 21 (2004): 291–298.

23. D. Lessing, "On Not Winning the Nobel Prize," *Vital Speeches of the Day* 74.2 (2008).

24. J. Davidson, "Managing the Pace with Grace," *Vital Speeches of the Day* 76.6 (2010).

25. S. Horton, "How Hollywood Learned to Stop Worrying and Love the (Ticking) Bomb," *Vital Speeches of the Day* 74.4 (2008).

26. K. Gunderson, "Following Fiscal Footsteps: Can European Tax Trends Work for America?" *Winning Orations 2006* (Mankato, MN: Interstate Oratorical Association, 2006), 28.

27. R. Pausch, "Really Achieving Your Childhood Dreams," lecture given at Carnegie Mellon University, September 18, 2007, <download.srv. cs.cmu.edu/~pausch/>.

28. J. Celoria, "The Counterfeiting of Airline Safety: An Examination of the Dangers of Bogus Airline Parts," *Winning Orations 1997* (Mankato, MN: Interstate Oratorical Association, 1997), 79.

29. J. Sweeney, "Fairness and Economic Equality," *Vital Speeches of the Day* 74.5 (2008).

30. C. Liu, "The Tarahumarans," prepared for Individual Events/Informative Speaking competition, University of Texas, Spring 2011.

31. S. Agha, "The International Landmine Crisis," prepared for the Interstate Oratorical Association competition, Texas State University–San Marcos, Spring 2011.

32. J. Pruitt, "College Credit Card Crisis," *Winning Orations 1996* (Mankato, MN: Interstate Oratorical Association, 1996), 26.

33. R. Brown, "Seven Ways of Looking at a Crisis," *Vital Speeches of the Day* 76.6 (2010).

34. D. Terry, "Sun and Sand Attract Crowds, and Also Trouble," *New York Times* (June 10, 2011).

35. See D. A. Lieberman, *Public Speaking in the Multicultural Environment* 2e (Boston: Allyn & Bacon, 1997).

36. J. T. Masterson and N. Watson, "The Effects of Culture on Preferred Speaking Style," paper presented at the meeting of the Speech Communication Association, (November 1979).

## Chapter 12

1. J. Pearson, J. Child, and D. Kahl Jr., "Preparation Meeting Opportunity: How Do College Students Prepare for Public Speeches?" *Communication Quarterly* 54 (August 2006): 351–366.

2. "Example of providing general statistics before moving to specific illustration," Author: Kerlin Aristilde, © 2006, in "Ignorance and Poverty," *Winning Orations* 2006, © 2006, pp. 33. Used with permission of Interstate Oratorical Association.

3. D. A. Lieberman, *Public Speaking in the Multicultural Environment* 2e (Boston: Allyn & Bacon, 1997), 23.

4. Lieberman, *Public Speaking in the Multicultural Environment*.

5. S. Agha, "The International Landmine Crisis," prepared for the Interstate Oratorical Association competition, Texas State University–San Marcos, Spring 2011.

6. K. Chiu, "Persuasive Speech on Abusing the FBI National Security Letter Program," prepared for Individual Events/Persuasive Speaking competition, University of Texas, Spring 2011.

7. M. Erikson, "See Jane, See Jane's Dilemma," *Winning Orations 1997* (Mankato, MN: Interstate Oratorical Association, 1997), 63.

8. R. Pausch, "Achieving Your Childhood Dreams," lecture given at Carnegie Mellon University, September 18, 2007, <www.cmu.edu/randyslecture/>.

9. S. Hamilton, "Cruise Ship Violence," *Winning Orations 2000* (Mankato, MN: Interstate Oratorical Association, 2000), 95.

10. B. Ruet, "Sudan's Forgotten War," *Winning Orations 2006* (Mankato, MN: Interstate Oratorical Association, 2006), 49.

11. C. O'Brien, Dartmouth College commencement address, June 12, 2011, <www .dartmouth.edu>.

12. B. Obama, "A More Perfect Union," *Vital Speeches of the Day* 74.5 (2008): 194–199.

13. C. Reed, "Decreasing Red Meat in Your Diet," speech delivered at Texas State University–San Marcos, 2005.

14. A. Watson, "Post-Traumatic Stress Disorder: Our Soldiers' Next War," *Winning Orations 2007* (Mankato, MN: Interstate Oratorical Association, 2007), 81.

15. Watson, "Post-Traumatic Stress Disorder."

16. A. Lincoln, "Gettysburg Address," delivered at Gettysburg, PA, November 19, 1863, Douglass Archives of American Public Address, August 19, 1998, <douglass .speech.nwu.edu/linc_b33.htm>.

17. D. MacArthur, "Farewell to the Cadets," address delivered at West Point, May 12, 1962, in *Contemporary American Speeches* 7e, edited by R. L. Johannesen, R. R. Allen, and W. A. Linkugel (Dubuque, IA: Kendall/Hunt, 1992), 393.

18. M. L. King Jr., "I Have a Dream," delivered in Washington, DC, August 28, 1963, in *Contemporary American Speeches*, 369.

19. T. Kirchhefer, "The Deprived," *Winning Orations 2000* (Mankato, MN: Interstate Oratorical Association, 2000), 151.

20. S. Brunner, "Advanced Technology: Solving the DUI Dilemma," *Winning Orations 2007* (Mankato, MN: Interstate Oratorical Association, 2007), 78.

21. The preparation outline on pages 323–324 and the speaking notes that appear on page 325 are adapted from a speech by T. Longoria, "Excessive Facebooking: What You Need to Know," *Communication 1310: Student Speeches for Texas State University* (CD). Pearson Learning Solutions, 2010.

22. Tony decides that the introduction traditionally used by Alcoholics Anonymous and other twelve-step groups falls into the category of "common knowledge," or information so widely known that he does not need to provide an oral citation of a source.

## Chapter 13

1. P. Heinbert, "Relationship of Content and Delivery to General Effectiveness," *Speech Monographs* 30 (1963): 105–107.

2. A. Mehrabian, *Nonverbal Communication* (Hawthorne, NY: Aldine, 1972).

3. J. Detz, "Delivery plus Content Equals Successful Presentation," *Communication World* 15 (1998): 34.

4. Adapted from R. Ailes, *You Are the Message* (New York: Doubleday, 1989), 37–38.

5.  P. Begala, "Flying Solo," PBS, *The Clinton Years: Anecdotes*, 2000, <http://www .pbs.org>.

6.  J. Wareham, "Doing It Off-the-Cuff," *Across the Board* 35 (1998): 49–50.

7.  Wareham, "Doing It Off-the-Cuff," 49–50.

8.  L. White and L. Messer, "An Analysis of Interstate Speeches: Are They Structurally Different?" *National Forensic Journal* 21.2 (2003): 15.

9.  G. Orwell, "Politics and the English Language," in *About Language*, edited by W. H. Roberts and G. Turgeson (Boston: Houghton Mifflin, 1986), 282.

10. M. Klepper, *I'd Rather Die Than Give a Speech* (New York: Carol Publishing Group, 1994), 45.

11. W. Safire, "Faithful, Even in Death," *New York Times Magazine* (April 18, 1999): 72–74. Quotes from Vest's speech are from the text reprinted in this article.

12. B. Moyers, "What Adam Said to Eve," prepared remarks for the annual conference of the Association for Education in Journalism and Mass Communication, Washington, DC, August 8, 2007, <www.pbs.org>.

13. J. F. Kennedy, inaugural address, January 20, 1961, in *Speeches in English*, edited by B. Aly and L. F. Aly (New York: Random House, 1968), 272.

14. J. Carter, address to the Democratic National Convention, July 2004, <www .dems2004.org>.

15. J. McCain, "A Leader We Can Believe In," address delivered June 3, 2008, in Kenner, LA, <www.americanrhetoric.com>.

16. J. Biden, remarks commemorating the fiftieth anniversary of Kennedy's "Moon Shot" Speech, delivered at the John F. Kennedy Library and Museum, Boston, MA, May 25, 2011, <www.whitehouse.gov>.

17. N. Giovanni, convocation address at Virginia Tech, April 17, 2007, <www.vt.edu>.

18. B. Obama, state of the union address, January 25, 2011, *The New York Times* (January 25, 2011), <www.nytimes.com>.

19. S. A. Beebe, "Eye Contact: A Nonverbal Determinant of Speaker Credibility," *Speech Teacher* 23 (1974): 21–25; S. A. Beebe, "Effects of Eye Contact, Posture and Vocal Inflection upon Credibility and Comprehension," *Australian Scan Journal of Nonverbal Communication* 7–8 (1979–1980): 57–70; M. Cobin, "Response to Eye Contact," *Quarterly Journal of Speech* 48 (1963): 415–419.

20. Beebe, "Eye Contact."

21. E. Adler, "Gestures May Give You a Hand with Speaking," *Austin American-Statesman* (November 25, 1998): E6.

22. J. C. McCroskey, V. P. Richmond, A. Sallinen, J. M. Fayer, and R. A. Barraclough, "A Cross-Cultural and Multi-Behavioral Analysis of the Relationship Between Nonverbal Immediacy and Teacher Evaluation," *Communication Education* 44 (1995): 281–290.

23. M. J. Beatty, "Some Effects of Posture on Speaker Credibility," library paper, Central Missouri State University, 1973.

24. R. Schmid, "Study: Posture Able to Communicate Fear," Yahoo! News, November 16, 2004, <news.yahoo.com>.

25. P. Ekman, W. V. Friesen, and S. S. Tomkins, "Facial Affect Scoring Technique: A First Validity Study," *Semiotca* 3 (1971).

26. P. Ekman and W. Friesen, *Unmasking the Face* (Englewood Cliffs, NJ: Prentice Hall, 1975).

27. M. M. Gill, "Accents and Stereotypes: Their Effect on Perceptions of Teachers and Lecture Comprehension," *Journal of Applied Communication Research* 22 (1994): 348–361.

28. E. Bohn and D. Jabusch, "The Effect of Four Methods of Instruction on the Use of Visual Aids in Speeches," *Western Journal of Speech Communication* 46 (1982): 253–265.

29. A. Wilson, "In Defense of Rhetoric," *The Toastmaster* 70.2 (2004): 11.

30. U.S. Bureau of the Census, "Young Adults Living at Home, 1960–2005," Information Please Database, Pearson Education, Inc., September 21, 2006, <www .infoplease.com>.

31. Adapted from D. Cavanaugh, *Preparing Visual Aids for Presentation* (Boston: Allyn & Bacon/Longman, 2001).

32. Detz, "Delivery plus Content Equals Successful Presentation."

33. T. Smith and A. B. Frymier, "Get 'Real': Does Practicing Speeches Before an Audience Improve Performance?" *Communication Quarterly* 54 (2006): 111–125.

34. "Presidential Seal Falls Off Podium as Obama Speaks," *The Washington Times* (October 6, 2010), <www.washingtontimes.com>.

35. J. Masterson, S. Beebe, and N. Watson, *Invitation to Effective Speech Communication* (Glenview, IL: Scott, Foresman, 1989), 4.

## Chapter 14

1.  J. R. Johnson and N. Szczupakiewicz, "The Public Speaking Course: Is It Preparing Students with Work-Related Public Speaking Skills?" *Communication Education* 36 (1987): 131–137.

2.  For an excellent discussion of teaching someone to perform a skill, especially a social skill, see M. Argyle, *The Psychology of Interpersonal Behavior* (London: Penguin, 1990).

3.  For an excellent discussion of strategies for informing others, see K. E. Rowan, "A New Pedagogy for Explanatory Public Speaking: Why Arrangement Should Not Substitute for Invention," *Communication Education 44* (1995): 236–250.

4.  This suggestion is based on an excellent review of the literature found in Rowan, "A New Pedagogy for Explanatory Public Speaking."

5.  M. Groover, "Learning to Communicate: The Importance of Speech Education in Public Schools," in *Winning Orations 1984* (Mankato, MN: Interstate Oratorical Association, 1984), 7.

6.  See, for example, M. Patterson et al., "Effects of Communication Aids and Strategies on Cooperative Teaching," *Journal of Educational Psychology* 84 (1992): 453–461; L. Rehling, "Teaching in a High-Tech Conference Room: Academic Adaptations and Workplace Simulations," *Journal of Business and Technical Communication* 19 (2005): 98–113.

7.  M. Klepper and R. Gunther, *I'd Rather Die than Give a Speech* (New York: Carol Publishing Group, 1995).

8.  Our discussion of using humor is adapted from Klepper and Gunther, *I'd Rather Die Than Give a Speech.*

9.  J. Meyer, "Humor as a Double-Edged Sword: Four Functions of Humor in Communication," *Communication Theory* 10 (2000): 311.

10. Klepper and Gunther, *I'd Rather Die Than Give a Speech.*

11. M. Knowles, *The Adult Learner: A Neglected Species* 3e (Houston: Gulf Publishing, 1990).

12. A. Adair, "Up in the Air: The Trials and Tribulations of Commercial Air Travel," *Communication 1310: Student Speeches for Texas State University-San Marcos* (CD). Pearson Learning, 2010.

## Chapter 15

1.  S. McLaughlin, "The Dirty Truth About Your Kitchen: Using Common Sense to Prevent Food Poisoning," in *Winning Orations 1996* (Mankato, MN: Interstate Oratorical Association, 1996), 73.

2.  A. Maslow, "A Theory of Human Motivation," in *Motivation and Personality* (New York: Harper & Row, 1954), Chapter 5.

3.  See I. L. Janis and S. Feshback, "Effects of Fear Arousing Communications," *Journal of Abnormal and Social Psychology 48* (1953): 78–92; F. A. Powell and G. R. Miller, "Social Approval and Disapproval Cues in Anxiety Arousing Situations," *Speech Monographs 34* (1967): 152–159; K. L. Higbee, "Fifteen Years of Fear Arousal: Research on Threat Appeals, 1953–1968," *Psychological Bulletin 72* (1969): 426–444; P. A. Mongeau, "Another Look at Fear-Arousing Persuasive Appeals," in *Persuasion: Advances Through Meta-Analysis*, edited by M. Allen and R. W. Preiss (Cresskill, NJ: Hampton Press, 1998), 65.

4.  R. Petty and D. Wegener, "The Elaboration Likelihood Model: Current Status and Controversies," in *Dual Process Theories in Social Psychology*, edited by S. Chaiken and Y. Trope (New York: Guilford, 1999), 41–72; see also R. Petty and J. T. Cacioppo, *Communication and Persuasion: Central and Peripheral Routes to Attitude Change* (New York: Springer-Verlag, 1986).

5.  E. McQuarrie and B. Phillips, "Indirect Persuasion in Advertising: How Consumers Process Metaphors Presented in Pictures and Words," *Journal of Advertising* 34.2 (Summer 2005): 7–20.

6.  Aristotle, *Rhetoric*, translated by L. Cooper (New York: Appleton-Century-Crofts, 1960).

7.  For a discussion of the effects of both verbal and nonverbal messages on the persuasiveness of a speech, see N. Jackob et al., "The Effects of Verbal and Nonverbal Elements in Persuasive Communication:

Findings from Two Multi-Method Experiments," *Communications: The European Journal of Communication Research* 36 (2011): 245–271.

8. A. Bogeajis, "The Danger of Child Safety Seats: Why Aren't They Safe?" in *Winning Orations 1996* (Mankato, MN: Interstate Oratorical Association, 1996), 10.

9. N. Barton, "The Death of Reading," in *Winning Orations 2004* (Mankato, MN: Interstate Oratorical Association, 2004), 33–35.

10. S. Groom, "Hope for Foster Care," in *Winning Orations 2004*, 60–62.

11. Adapted from L. Ford and S. Smith, "Memorability and Persuasiveness of Organ Donation Message Strategies," *American Behavioral Scientist* 34 (1991): 695.

12. D. Ehninger, B. Gronbeck, R. McKerrow, and A. Monroe, *Principles and Types of Speech Communication* (Glenview, IL: Scott, Foresman, 1986), 15.

13. The illustrations for the steps of the motivated sequence are adapted from S. Agha, "The International Landmine Crisis," prepared for the Interstate Oratorical Association competition, Texas State University–San Marcos, Spring 2011.

14. D. C. Bryant, "Rhetoric: Its Functions and Its Scope," *Quarterly Journal of Speech* 39 (1953): 26.

15. B. Sosnowchick, "The Cries of American Ailments," in *Winning Orations 2000* (Mankato, MN: Interstate Oratorical Association, 2000), 114.

16. G. Ficca, et al. "Effects of Different Types of Hand Gestures in Persuasive Speech on Receivers' Evaluations," *Language and Cognitive Processes* 24 (2009): 239–266.

17. K. Slone, "Real Men *AND* Women Wear Pink," *Communication 1310: Student Speeches for Texas State University-San Marcos* (CD). Pearson Learning, 2010.

## Appendix A

1. Examples from CareerBuilder.com, as cited by *Reader's Digest* (May 2008): 34.

2. Our discussion of interview questions is based on J. T. Masterson, S. A. Beebe, and N. Watson, *An Invitation to Effective Speech Communication* (Glenview, IL: Scott, Foresman, 1989). We especially acknowledge the contributions of Norm Watson to this discussion.

3. <www.CareerBuilder.com>, retrieved March 21, 2008.

4. This resumé and our suggestions for developing a resumé are based on the 2011 *Texas State University Career Services Manual* (San Marcos, TX: Office of Career Services, 2011).

5. J. L. Winsor, D. B. Curtis, and R. D. Stephens, "National Preferences in Business and Communication Education: A Survey Update," *Journal of the Association for Communication Administration* 3 (1997): 174.

6. D. Dean, "How to Get an On-Site Interview," *Black Collegian*, Second Semester Super Issue (2010): 54.

7. <www.CareerBuilder.com>, retrieved March 21, 2008. Suggestions for managing your online persona were taken from A. Simmons, "How to Click and Clean," *Reader's Digest* (April 2008): 154–159.

8. S. Armour, "Employers: Enough Already with the E-Resumés," *USA Today* (July 15, 1999): B1. Also see K. Hansen, "Your E-Resume's File Format Aligns with Its Delivery Method," <www.quintcareers.com/e-resume_format.html>, accessed March 30, 2011.

9. "Advantages of Web Resumés," April 2, 2005, <http://www.eresumeiq.com/web-resume-advantages.html>.

10. "Advantages of Web Resumés."

11. "Advantages of Web Resumés."

12. "Advantages of Web Resumés."

13. M. Minto, "The Relative Effects of Content and Vocal Delivery During a Simulated Employment Interview," *Communication Research Reports* 13 (1996): 225–238.

14. Adapted from M. S. Hanna and G. Wilson, *Communicating in Business and Professional Settings* (New York: McGraw-Hill, 1991), 263–265.

15. *Texas State University Career Services Manual.*

## Appendix B

1. C. Liu, "The Tarahumarans," prepared for Individual Events/Informative Speaking competition, University of Texas, Spring 2011.

2. K. Akerman, "The Misspoken Epidemic," prepared for Individual Events/Informative Speaking competition, University of Texas, Spring 2011.

# Index